Zimbabw

and Botswar

THE ROUGH GUIDE

There are over seventy Rough Guide titles covering
destinations from Amsterdam to Zimbabwe & Botswana

Forthcoming titles include
Costa Rica • Bali • Hawaii • Mallorca • Rhodes

Rough Guide Reference Series
Classical Music • World Music • Jazz

Rough Guide Phrasebooks
Czech • French • German • Greek • Italian • Spanish

ROUGH GUIDE CREDITS

Text Editor:	Greg Ward
Series Editor:	Mark Ellingham
Editorial:	Martin Dunford, Jonathan Buckley, Samantha Cook, Jo Mead, Alison Cowan, Amanda Tomlin, Annie Shaw, Lemisse al-Hafidh, Catherine McHale
Production:	Susanne Hillen, Andy Hilliard, Alan Spicer, Melissa Flack, Judy Pang, Link Hall, Nicola Williamson
Finance:	John Fisher, Celia Crowley, Simon Carloss
Publicity:	Richard Trillo (UK), Jean-Marie Kelly, Jeff Kaye (US)

Our thanks for this edition to all at the *Rough Guides* for help and support, especially to Greg and Richard, and to Jeanette Clarke and the Clarke family, all at Alexandra Drive, Anne Rorke, Rita Harvey, Fausto Carbone, Iain Jackson, Val van Wyk, Leon and Mags Varley, staff at Fothergill and Chikwenya, *Wild Horizons*, Clive of *Kandahar Safaris*, Landela Lodge, Zindele, *Africa Dawn*, Richard Peek, Caroline Avens at Heinemann, Ilala Lodge, Tongabezi, *Air Zimbabwe* and *Air Ethiopia*.

Special thanks to Annie Holmes, Lucy Phelan, Michael Philips, Alec Campbell, Ian Games, Dave Bristow, Keith Shiri, Ilse Mwanza, Judy Kendall and John Bradshaw for contributions.

And to all the many unmentioned people in Zimbabwe, Botswana, Zambia and Britain, who helped make this book, our deep appreciation.

The publishers and authors have done their best to ensure the accuracy and currency of all the information in *The Rough Guide to Zimbabwe and Botswana*; however, they can accept no responsibility for any loss, injury, or inconvenience sustained by any traveller as a result of information or advice contained in the guide.

This second edition published October 1993 by Rough Guides Ltd, 1 Mercer Street, London WC2H 9QJ. Reprinted twice in 1994 and November 1995.
Distributed by The Penguin Group:

Penguin Books Ltd, 27 Wrights Lane, London W8 5TZ
Penguin Books USA Inc., 375 Hudson Street, New York 10014, USA
Penguin Books Australia Ltd, 487 Maroondah Highway, PO Box 257, Ringwood, Victoria 3134, Australia
Penguin Books Canada Ltd, 10 Alcorn Avenue, Toronto, Ontario, Canada M4V 1E4
Penguin Books (NZ) Ltd, 182–190 Wairau Road, Auckland 10, New Zealand

First edition published in 1990 by Harrap Columbus.

Rough Guides were formerly published as *Real Guides* in the United States and Canada.

Typeset in Linotron Univers and Century Old Style to an original design by Andrew Oliver.
Printed in the UK by Cox & Wyman Ltd, Reading, Berks.

Illustrations in Part One and Part Four by Edward Briant.
All other illustrations and woodcut by Tony Pinchuck.

448p. includes index

A catalogue record for this book is available frorn the British Library.
ISBN 1-85828-041-9

Zimbabwe
and Botswana

THE ROUGH GUIDE

Written and researched by
Barbara McCrea and Tony Pinchuck

THE ROUGH GUIDES

LIST OF MAPS

Zimbabwe and Botswana	vi	Chimanimani area	235
Zimbabwe chapter divisions	31	Chimanimani National Park	236
Harare, The Midlands and Around	54	Botswana chapter divisions	243
Central Harare	60	Gaborone and the Eastern Corridor	257
Greater Harare	68	Gaborone	260
Gweru	87	Tuli Block	274
Kariba and the Middle Zambezi Valley	96	Chobe and the Northeast	279
Kariba	102	Francistown	281
Lake Kariba East	105	The Pans	286
Mana Pools National Park	112	Chobe National Park	292
Bulawayo and the Matobo District	127	Kasane and Kazungula	294
Bulawayo	128	Serondella	297
Naletale and Danangombe	140	Okavango Delta area	301
Matobo National Park	148	Maun and the Matlapaneng Lodges	307
Victoria Falls and Hwange National Park	157	The Okavango Delta	314
Victoria Falls	158	The Kalahari Desert	329
Livingstone	172	Ghanzi	335
Hwange National Park	177	The Shona States	346
Great Zimbabwe and the Lowveld	188	Nineteenth Century	349
Masvingo	191	Land Apportionment	354
Great Zimbabwe	193	Populations in 1800	363
Lake Mutirikwe (Kyle)	201	Pre-Colonisation	365
The Eastern Highlands	209	Southern Africa in 1896	368
Mutare	213	Travelling onwards	395
Nyanga National Park	222		

CONTENTS

Introduction viii

| PART ONE | BASICS | 1 |

Getting There from Europe (3) / Getting There from North America (6) / Getting There from Australasia (8) / Travel in Southern Africa (9) / Safaris (11) / Red Tape and Visas (13) / What to Take (15) / Health & Insurance (16) / Maps, Books & Information (21) / Food and Drink (23) / Photography (25) / Travelling in Deeply Rural Areas (26) / Wildlife & National Parks (27)

| PART TWO | ZIMBABWE | 31 |

Introduction (33) / Languages & Religions (34) / Money & Costs (37) / Getting Around (39) / Accommodation (42) / Communications – Post & Phone Services (44) / The Media: Press, Books, Radio & TV (45) / Opening Hours & Holidays (46) / Music & Drama (47) / Sports & Outdoor Activities (47) / Crafts (49) / Trouble (49) / Directory (50)

■ 1 Harare, The Midlands and Around 53

■ 2 Kariba and the Middle Zambezi Valley 94

■ 3 Bulawayo and the Matobo District 125

■ 4 Victoria Falls and Hwange National Park 155

■ 5 Great Zimbabwe and the Lowveld 187

■ 6 The Eastern Highlands 208

| PART THREE | BOTSWANA | 243 |

Introduction (245) / Languages & Peoples (246) / Money & Costs (248) / Getting Around (249) / Accommodation (251) / Communications – Post & Phone Services (252) / The Media – Press, Radio & TV (252) / Opening Hours & Holidays (253) / Music & Entertainment (253) / Crafts (253) / Trouble (254) / Directory (255)

■ 7 Gaborone and the Eastern Corridor 257

■ 8 Chobe and the Northeast 279

■ 9 The Okavango Delta 301

■ 10 The Kalahari Desert 329

| PART FOUR | CONTEXTS | 343 |

Zimbabwe: An Historical Framework 345
Botswana: An Historical Framework 363
Writing from Zimbabwe 374
Writing from Botswana 381
Zimbabwe's Pop Music 386
Travelling Onwards in the Region 394
Books 408

Index 415

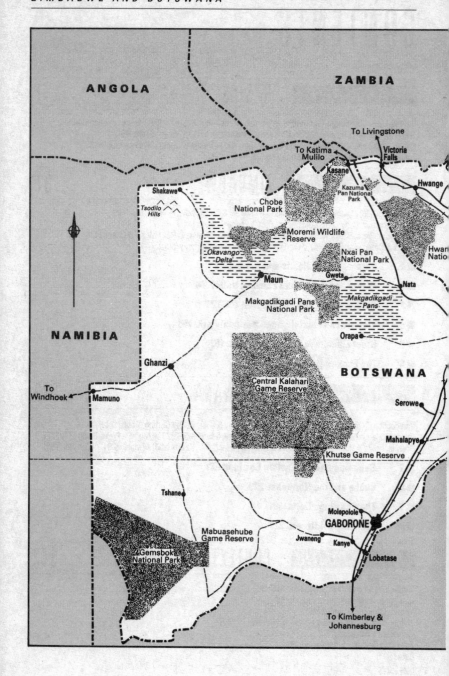

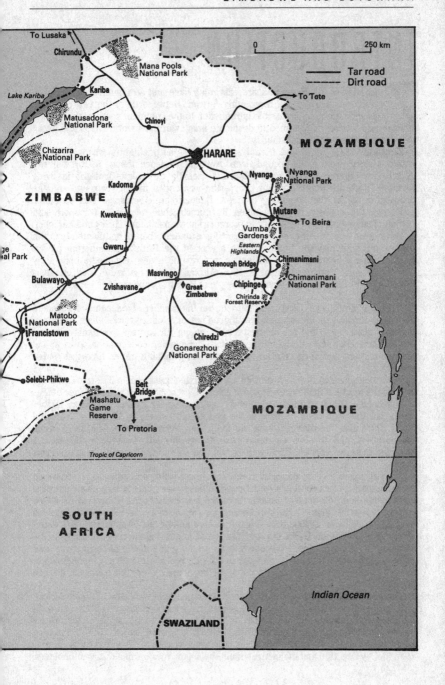

To Lusaka
Chirundu
Mana Pools
National Park
Lake Kariba
Kariba
To Tete
Matusadona
National Park
Chinoyi
MOZAMBIQUE
Chizarira
National Park
HARARE
ZIMBABWE
Kadoma
Nyanga
Nyanga
National Park
Kwekwe
Mutare
Vumba
Gardens
To Beira
Gweru
Eastern
Highlands
Birchenough Bridge
Chimanimani
al Park
Bulawayo
Masvingo
Chipinge
Chimanimani
National Park
Zvishavane
Great
Zimbabwe
Matobo
National Park
Chirinda
Forest Reserve
Francistown
Chiredzi
Selebi-Pikwe
Gonarezhou
National Park
Beit
Bridge
MOZAMBIQUE
Mashatu
Game
Reserve
To Pretoria
Tropic of Capricorn
SOUTH
AFRICA
Indian Ocean
SWAZILAND

0   250 km

————— Tar road
- - - - - Dirt road

INTRODUCTION

Zimbabwe and **Botswana** are easygoing, safe and straightforward places to visit, yet they are still thoroughly African. Between them the two countries provide the most accessible introduction to the continent south of the Sahara, and visitors accustomed to desperate images of third world chaos and decay are struck by their order and stability.

Zimbabwe is a warm and friendly destination – surprisingly, perhaps, given its recent history. Now in its second decade of independence it has, in the last two decades, weathered a **civil war** and more recently the worst **drought** in living memory. Both are thankfully now over – the war ended fifteen years ago and the drought broke at the beginning of 1993. Despite these setbacks, and economic problems, the country has maintained its infrastructure of roads, transport, and communication links; and its people have, remarkably, maintained their good humour.

Botswana boasts Africa's fastest growing economy, based on diamond wealth discovered, with majestic timing, within a year of the British surrendering power. Furthermore, it bears a unique distinction in Africa of having remained a multi-party democracy since its independence in 1966. Although it may lack the good transport links found in Zimbabwe, it nevertheless offers exciting opportunities to get off the beaten track.

Neither country is yet overrun by tourists, but the number of independent travellers coming is certainly on the increase – with good reason. Both countries share a range of beautiful landscapes, and are unquestionably among Africa's top five **game viewing** destinations. Each has utterly unique habitats, outstanding conservation policies, and restrictions on numbers entering game parks – making them first-class safari countries.

While elsewhere in Africa **elephants** are seriously threatened, in Botswana's **Chobe National Park** and Zimbabwe's **Hwange** they are present in a superabundance of tens of thousands. **Black rhinos** are another species almost extinct anywhere further north, but they still hang on here in the broken hill country of **Chizarira National Park**. You'll also find the rest of the **big five** (lions, leopards and buffalo) in respectable numbers, and the two countries possess virtually all of southern Africa's 291 recorded mammal species. Birdwatchers will find six hundred species to get to grips with.

Activity pursuits – kayaking, bush walking, horse riding and canoeing – are a fast-expanding area, often combined with opportunities to see game at very close quarters. For anyone keen on outdoor action, there are few experiences to beat **white-water rafting** below the Victoria Falls, **canoeing** for two or more days down the Zambezi from Mana Falls, or travelling by dug-out *mokoro* among the islands and lilied waterways of the **Okavango Delta**. On land, there is an almost infinite range of things to do, including tracking big game on foot with an armed guide in the national parks, and some superb mountain hiking, with possibilities for real wilderness at Chimanimani in eastern Zimbabwe. If you really want to let go, there's even the option of bungee jumping.

The huge **landscapes** of Zimbabwe and Botswana fulfil with ease all those African clichés of endless blue skies, wide-open space, and vermillion sunsets. Botswana, with the great **Kalahari desert** at its heart, is virtually flat, although peppered with rocky outcrops and the amazing **Tsodilo Hills**. Zimbabwe is more varied, with its **Eastern Highland** of peaks, mountain pools and well-watered valleys. The country is punctuated, too, by beautiful and distinctive granite hills and "rock-gardens" of vast boulders.

Both countries make up for their lack of coastline with some of Africa's great **waterways**: the Zambezi River, Okavango Delta and Lake Kariba.

Although their present national boundaries are recent colonial inventions, human culture in Zimbabwe and Botswana goes back tens of thousands of years. Early inhabitants have left their marks in caves and on rock faces all over the sub-continent. The **rock paintings** at Botswana's Tsodilo Hills moved Laurens van der Post to talk of a "Louvre in the desert", while Zimbabwe has the highest concentration of rock art in the world. Finely realised paintings of animals and people in everyday life, ritual and myth, are scattered about the various granite rock formations, at their best at Matopos Hills. Zimbabwe also has an extensive sequence of stone ruins to explore, from the ancient states that once held domain on this great plateau. The awesome **Great Zimbabwe** is just the best known of several hundred complexes.

But, beyond any doubt, the art in which Zimbabwe most excels today is **music** – a major cultural export in recent years as Western ears have tuned into the high energy guitar pop of bands like the Bhundu Boys, the Real Sounds of Africa and Thomas Mapfumo's Blacks Unlimited. For each of these international stars, there are dozens of talents waiting to be discovered, playing every night in nightclubs, hotels, beer gardens and outdoor venues in Harare, Bulawayo and across the country. Explore and enjoy!

Climate: when to go

Though technically a tropical country, **Zimbabwe** refuses to conform to hot, sticky stereotypes. The highveld climate (Harare and Bulawayo) is as close as possible to perfection, with dry season temperatures similar to those of the Mediterranean, but without the humidity. Few people realise that Harare's highest recorded temperature peak of 35°C (95°F) is below that of London. Altitude is the most important determinant. The low-lying areas off the plateau – Kariba, the Zambezi river valley and Victoria Falls – get considerably hotter than the higher towns, and can be uncomfortably humid in the steaming rainy season.

Botswana weather follows a roughly similar pattern, although much of the country experiences extremes from the semi-desert that sweeps across its surface. Wet season temperatures in the southern Kalahari have exceeded 40°C (104°F), while in the cool months they can drop at night to -5°C (23°F). The climate around the Okavango Delta and Eastern Corridor tends to be less severe, though even here wet season temperatures can soar uncomfortably, and some years the rains flood the roads.

Deciding **when to come** is really a question of what you're after:

• For **game viewing**, the **dry season** (May–Oct) is recommended, as wildlife concentrates around scarce water; it's very cold at night and in the early morning, but warm enough for T-shirts in the middle of the day. Temperatures climb towards September – an optimum "spring" month which combines good wildlife with vegetation coming into flower amidst the dust and browns. October, the hottest month, is the prime time for wildlife when animals are restricted to a few water-holes.

• The arrival of the **rainy season** in November does much to damp temperatures. The rains, which last till March, are a time of lush new growth – a scenically beautiful period. Rain usually comes in the form of afternoon thunderstorms, leaving most of the day clear. There can be several days, or even weeks between falls. The Eastern Highlands receive the highest rainfall, where you may experience a series of cool, wet days.

• **April and May**, the "autumn" months, are perhaps ideal for overall travels – warm and dry with the land still fresh from the rains, though long grass may make game viewing more difficult.

A detailed chart of mean temperatures and rainfall, as well as seasonal variations, can be found over the page.

SOUTHERN TROPICAL SEASONS

- **November to mid-March.** Rainy "summer" season: thunderstorms; hot.
- **Mid-March to mid-May.** Post-rainy "autumn" season: limited rainfall; cooling off.
- **Mid-May to mid-August.** Cool dry "winter" season: virtually no rainfall; cool to moderate but very sunny and clear.
- **Mid-August to November.** Warm dry "spring" season: virtually no rainfall; temperatures rise to peak.

MEAN TEMPERATURES (C) AND RAINFALL (mm)

The first figure is the mean **maximum** temperature; the second the mean **minimum**; and the third the average rainfall per month

	Jan	Feb	Mar	Apr	May	Jun	Jul	Aug	Sep	Oct	Nov	Dec
Harare	26	26	26	26	24	22	22	24	27	29	27	26
(Highveld:1478m)	16	16	16	13	9	7	7	9	12	15	14	16
	188	169	80	43	11	5	0	3	8	32	93	189
Beit Bridge	33	33	32	30	28	25	25	28	30	32	32	33
(Lowveld: 457m)	22	21	20	17	12	8	8	11	15	19	20	21
	70	50	36	24	5	4	1	1	8	21	39	66
Nyanga	21	21	21	20	18	16	16	18	21	23	22	21
(Eastern Highlands: 1878m)	13	13	12	10	8	6	6	7	9	11	12	13
	257	219	135	51	17	16	14	15	13	43	125	215
Francistown	30	30	29	27	25	24	24	26	30	33	32	31
(Eastern Botswana: 1100m)	17	17	16	13	9	5	5	7	12	16	18	18
	106	79	72	19	6	4	0	0	0	23	55	85
Shakawe	30	30	30	30	27	25	27	29	32	34	32	31
(Okavango Delta: 1000m)	20	20	19	16	15	6	5	8	12	16	17	18
	150	160	80	30	2	0	0	0	2	6	50	100

THANKS

More thanks to those readers who wrote to us with information:

Peta Jones, Major Ian Tomes, Julie Griffith, Jeremy Redford, Leda Stott, Nigel Watt, Andrew Kenningham, Sarah Lampert, Anne Philpott, Constance van Lange, Dave Macdonald, Rebecca Over, John Bateman, Nadja Daykers, Peter Moers, Andrea Morris, Carple Kenyon, K. Makepeace, Veronica Mathew, Isolde and Julian Price, Peter Tovey, Judy Gowenlock, Frieda Potemans, Jeff Cave, Bianca De Vivo, Julian Tyacke, Binit Somaia, Val Delue, Gavin Thomson, John Peet, E. Tippett, Michael Adams, Barbara Baron, Neil Sayer, Carry Punter, Margaret Gobby, Heather Alexander, Cate Brown, Debbie Lawlor, Seth Jenkson, Ian Fraser, Marieke Clarke, Michael Newett, Beverley Hogg, Patrick McKenna, Gian Pozzy, James Murdoch, Clara van der Zwan, David Bartell, Luc Francois, Kristopher Walmsley, N. Townsend, D. Netherway, David Towson, Graham Hanson, Mary Holt, Kim Burke, Clare Johnson, Ian Hamnett, Rochelle Bolton, Dr Karel Roskam, Helen Davis, David and Helen Handley, Jeremy Cox, Giles Pearson, Kate Worster, Diana Clement, Jeff Taylor, and Juliet Wilson.

PART ONE
THE
BASICS

GETTING THERE FROM EUROPE

Most people travel to Zimbabwe or Botswana by air. There are direct flights to Harare from Britain and several other European countries, while direct flights to Gaborone operate from London and Paris.

Overland options include journeys via North or East Africa, either driving or travelling by rail or on local buses. Organised trips that show you the sights run on a number of routes, some starting in Britain.

NONSTOP FLIGHTS FROM BRITAIN

Air Zimbabwe flies nonstop from Gatwick to **Harare** three times a week, plus once a week via Frankfurt. **British Airways** has three flights weekly from Heathrow. These two cover the distance in ten hours – the fastest currently available. Both airlines officially quote low-season prices of around £750 and high-season at around £1300.

In reality, few people purchase tickets at officially quoted prices, booking instead through agents which offer hefty discounts. It is usually possible to buy flights on both the above airlines from around £500 in low season.

British Airways – twice a week to **Gaborone** – provides the only nonstop direct flights from the UK to Botswana.

All the European airlines listed in the next section offer flights from London with fairly brief changeovers in their countries of origin.

FLIGHTS VIA EUROPE

The growing popularity of Zimbabwe means there's a choice of easy flights from London via Europe. Convenient transfers, relatively short journey times and discounted prices make these definitely worth considering.

The best option is the weekly *Air France* routing via Paris which costs £500 throughout the year. *Lufthansa* (twice a week via Frankfurt), *KLM* (twice a week via Amsterdam) and *Air Portugal* (once a week via Lisbon) also offer good deals through their agents.

The only cheap flight to Botswana from Europe (or virtually anywhere else) is the weekly one on *Air France* from Paris. A flight from London connects with it and the entire routing from Britain works out at under £600 in low season and about £100 more in peak.

FLIGHTS VIA CENTRAL EUROPE AND AFRICA

Other airlines which fly to Harare are *Zambia Airways, Aeroflot* (twice a month via Moscow), *Balkan Bulgarian Airlines* (twice weekly via Sofia and Lagos/Cairo), *Ethiopian Airlines* (twice a week via Addis) and *Kenya Airlines.*

With cheap flights now available on major European airlines none of these can be recommended as a first choice unless they drastically drop their fares.

All will fly you from London to their national base where you will need to change planes for the second leg to Harare, but the waiting times are invariably long.

Of the five, *Ethiopian Airlines* unquestionably rates as the best. It's certainly a decently run airline but the length of the trip to Harare (18hr or more) must act as a serious deterrent.

FLYING SEASONS

Approximate flight seasons to Zimbabwe and Botswana. These will vary slightly from one airline to the next.

Low April–May
Shoulder Feb–March, June & Oct–Nov
High Dec–Jan and July–Sept

AIRLINES

LONDON ADDRESSES

Air France (*AF*), Colet Court, 100 Hammersmith Rd, London W6 (☎081/742 6600).

Air Zimbabwe (*UM*), Colette House, 52–55 Piccadilly, London W1V SAA (☎071/491 0009).

Balkan Bulgarian Airlines (*LZ*), 322 Regent St, London W1 (☎071/637 7637).

British Airways (*BA*), 75 Regent St, London W1 (☎081/759 5511).

Ethiopian Airlines (*ET*), 4th Floor, 166 Piccadilly, London W1 (☎071/491 9119).

Kenya Airways (*KQ*), 16 Conduit St, London W1 (☎071/409 0277).

Lufthansa (*LH*), 10 Old Bond St, London W1 4EN (☎071/408 0442).

Qantas Airways (*QF*), Arundel Great Court, 180–182 Strand, London WC2 (☎0345 /747767).

TAP Air Portugal (*TP*), 19 Regent St, London SW1 (☎071/839 1031).

Zambia Airways (*QZ*), 163 Piccadilly, London W1 (☎071/491 7521).

DISCOUNTED FLIGHT AGENTS IN BRITAIN AND IRELAND

Africa Travel Shop, 4 Medway Court, Leigh St, London WC1H 9QX (☎071/387 1211)

Airbreak Leisure, South Quay Plaza 2, 183 Marsh Wall, London E14 9SH (☎071/712 0303). Flights from Manchester and Gatwick.

Campus Travel, 52 Grosvenor Gardens, London SW1 (☎071/730 8111); 541 Bristol Rd, Selly Oak, Birmingham (☎021/414 1848); 39 Queen's Rd, Clifton, Bristol (☎0272/292494); 3 Emmanuel St, Cambridge (☎0223/324283); 53 Forest Rd, Edinburgh (☎031/225 6111); 13 High St, Oxford (☎0865/242067); also in YHA shops and on university campuses all over Britain.

Council Travel, 28a Poland St, London W1 (☎071/437 7767). General student discount agent.

Cruxton Travel, Cruxton House, Harrovian Business Village, 1 Hobbs Bessborough Rd, Harrow, Middlesex HA1 3EX (☎081/863 4522). Agents for *Ethiopian Airlines*.

Skylink, 10–16 Rathbone St, London W1P 1AH (☎071/396 9911). Agents for *KLM*.

South Coast Student Travel, 61 Ditchling Rd, Brighton BN1 4SD (☎0273/570 226). Plenty to offer non-students as well, and good associate agents in Bangkok.

STA Travel, 117 Euston Rd, London NW1 2SX (☎071/465 0486); 74 Old Brompton Rd, London SW7 (☎071/937 9962); 25 Queen's Rd, Bristol; 38 Sidney St, Cambridge (☎0223/66966); 88 Vicar Lane, Leeds; 75 Deansgate, Manchester (☎061/834 0668); 36 George St, Oxford; and offices at the universities of Birmingham, Kent, London (all colleges) and Loughborough.

Trade Wings, Morley House, Room 18, 5th Floor, 320 Regent St, London W1R 5AG (☎071/631 1840). Agents for *Balkan Bulgarian Airlines*.

Trailfinders, 42–48 Earls Court Rd, London W8 (☎071/938 3366); 194 Kensington High St, London W8 (☎071/938 3939); 58 Deansgate, Manchester M8 (☎061/839 6969).

Travel Bug, 597 Cheetham Hill Rd, Manchester M8 (☎061/721 4000).

Travel Cuts, 295a Regent St, London W1 (☎071/255 2082).

Unique Travel, Dudley House, 2nd Floor, 169 Piccadilly W1 (☎071/495 4848). The main *Aeroflot* outlet.

USIT, Aston Quay, O'Connell Bridge, Dublin 2 (☎01/778117) & 13b College St, Belfast BT1 6ET (☎0232/324073). Ireland's main outlet for discounted, youth and student fares.

INCLUSIVE HOLIDAYS

There are quite a number of tour operators and travel agents that specialise in travel to southern Africa. You can buy off-the-peg packages or ask them to organise a tailor-made one for you. It's not always cheaper to make arrangements on arrival, especially if you're planning to stay in safari lodges or hotels – which have to charge sales tax inside Zimbabwe, but not if you pay outside the country. Packages start at around £1800 all-in (flights, accommodation, tours) for two weeks. Alternatively, you might consider making reservations for only some parts of your holiday, particularly the more popular activities and places that may get overbooked. Canoeing

---

SOUTHERN AFRICA SPECIALISTS IN THE UK

Abercrombie and Kent Ltd, Sloane Square House, Holbein Place, London SW1 (☎071/730 9600). Large upmarket operator with comprehensive and professional programmes in both Zimbabwe and Botswana.

Africa Travel Shop, 4 Medway Court, Leigh St, London WC1H 9QX (☎071/387 1211). Experienced and knowledgeable Africa specialists with a wide range of interesting options.

Art of Travel, 268 Lavender Hill, London SW11 1LJ (☎071/738 2038). Highly flexible specialist agent, who book trips to suit any budget – and for all or just part of a trip – through tried and tested local operators.

Grenadier Travel, 36 East Stockwell St, Colchester CO1 1ST (☎0206/549585). Small but expert. Genuine knowledge of the countries with

an affection for the region based on several years' residence. Highly personalised with great attention to detail.

Okavango Tours and Safaris, 28 Bisham Gardens, London N6 6DD (☎081/341 9442). Based in Botswana, this company can meet most of your requirements for both countries.

Wild Africa Safaris, Highgate House, 214 High St, Guildford, Surrey GU1 3JB (☎0483/5744939). Mix and match tailor-made safaris taking in all Zimbabwe's major sights and activities.

Worldwide Journeys and Expeditions, 8 Comeragh Rd, London W14 9HP (☎071/381 8638). Tailor-made travel programmes by this company with an excellent track record and outstanding first-hand knowledge of both Zimbabwe and Botswana.

---

trips, white-water rafting and such frequently visited destinations as the Mana Pools and the Okavango Delta fall into this category. Most of the agents below can offer partial pre-booking.

OVERLAND OPTIONS

Road conditions in Africa are best described as inconsistent. Major tarred routes are frequently good, although in some countries, where maintenance tends to be poor, they can get badly potholed. Some roads – usually those leading off the main arteries – are seasonal and will be out of commission during heavy rains. There's also a reputation for erratic opening and closing of borders which is hard to shift. Although the 1980s saw some significant improvements, conflicts and coups do occasionally erupt and it's wise to keep up with the news.

There are some interesting possibilities if you want to work your way down gradually through the continent. The **longer routes** start in north-

west Africa, from where you make your way over the Sahara, loop around the west of the continent and cross to the east **via Zaire**. A less ambitious option would be to start in **Kenya** and then to head through **Tanzania**, **Malawi** and **Zambia**, to eventually arrive in Zimbabwe or Botswana. The once popular **Nile route**, through Egypt and Sudan, and into Uganda and Kenya, is currently off limits; the Sudanese civil war effectively barred the route from 1984 onwards.

ORGANISED OVERLAND TRIPS

Several overland operators run **trans-Africa routes** starting in Britain, working down through West Africa, across to Nairobi and down to Harare or even beyond. These take up to 22 weeks and cost in the region of £2000. On the more modest five- to six-week trips, for example from Nairobi to Harare, Harare to Cape Town or Harare to Namibia and back you can expect to pay around £800.

BRITISH OVERLAND OPERATORS

Dragoman Ltd, Camp Green, Renton Rd, Debenham, Suffolk IP13 9AG (☎0728/861133).

Encounter Overland, 267 Old Brompton Rd, London SW5 9JA (☎071/370 6845).

Exodus Overland, 9 Weir Rd, London SW12 0LT (☎081/675 7996).

Explore Worldwide, 1 Frederick St, Aldershot, Hants GU11 1LQ (☎0252/319448).

Guerba Expeditions, 101 Eden Vale Rd, Westbury, Wiltshire BA13 3YB (☎0373/826689).

Tracks, *World Tracks Ltd*, 12 Abingdon Rd, London W8 6AF (☎071/937 3028, ☎071/937 3029 or ☎071/937 3030).

GETTING THERE FROM NORTH AMERICA

There are no direct flights to Zimbabwe or Botswana from North America. The best buys to Southern Africa vary frequently and dramatically. Until recently travellers from the US and Canada flew to London or one of the other European destinations connected to Zimbabwe, and continued from there.

The recent lifting of sanctions against South Africa, however, has reopened the more convenient option of flying from the US to South Africa and then taking another plane on to adjacent Zimbabwe or Botswana, which are just a brief flight away (See "Travel in Southern Africa", p.9, for details). At the time of writing *South African Airways* was the sole carrier operating between the two countries, with four flights a week from New York to Johannesburg and one a week from Miami to Cape Town.

The cheapest standard return is the Apex fare, valid for stays of three weeks to three months and payable a month in advance. Prices are around $2000, varying with the season. Low season is January to May; high is June to August and December to mid-January.

South African Airways has in the past offered fares of $1000 on round flights when booked with package holidays. Enquire whether any such deals are currently on offer.

Air traffic between South Africa and North America is bound to increase during the 1990s, and competition is likely to bring a choice of discounted fares.

PACKAGES

Most North Americans coming to Zimbabwe and Botswana do so on packages which emphasise safaris. Many take in these countries as part of a larger African trip, often including both East and Southern Africa.

On the whole the packages offered to Americans are more upmarket than some available through British bookers, so it may be worth checking out what's available on both sides of the Atlantic. British agencies are listed on p.5. If you want an activity holiday, treks, white-water rafting and game-tracking can all be arranged as part of your package. Prices excluding flights start at around $2000 for two weeks.

NORTH AMERICAN AIRLINE AND DISCOUNT AGENT ADDRESSES

In addition to the agents listed below the Southern Africa specialists can provide up-to-date information on current best deals on flights.

Discount Club of America, 61–63 Woodhaven Blvd, Rego Park, NY 11374 (☎718/335 9612).

Moment's Notice, 425 Madison Ave, New York, NY 10017 (☎212/486 0503).

STA Travel, 48 East 11th St, New York, NY 10003 (☎212/477 7166); 166 Geary St, Suite 702, San Francisco, CA 94108 (☎415/391 8407).

South African Airways, 900 Third Ave, New York, NY 10022-4771 (☎212/418 3701).

Travel International, Ives Building, 114 Forrest Ave, Suite 205, Narbeth, PA 19072 (☎1-800/221 81390 or ☎215/668 2182).

UniTravel, Box 12485, St Louis, MO 63132 (☎314/569 2501 or ☎1-800/325 2222).

NORTH AMERICAN SOUTHERN AFRICA SPECIALISTS

Abercrombie and Kent Ltd, 1420 Kensington Rd, Oak Brook, IL 60521 (☎708/954 2944 or ☎1-800/323 7308). Large upmarket operator with comprehensive and professional programmes in both Zimbabwe and Botswana.

Africa Adventure Company, 1620 S Federal Highway, Suite 900, Pompano Beach, FL 33062 (☎305/781 3933). One of the best agencies in the business, and well regarded inside Zimbabwe, it offers over 100 programmes to Africa with thousands of safari options. President, Mark Nolting, has extensive first-hand experience of Africa.

Africa Travel Centre, 499 Ernston Rd, Parlin, NJ08859. PO Box 815 (☎908/721 2929 or ☎1-800/631 5650; Fax 908/721 2344; Telex 219955UR). Also at 23830 Highway 99#112, Edmonds, WA98026 (☎206/672-3697; Fax 206/672 9678). Sister company to the long-established London-based *Africa Travel Shop*.

Desert & Delta Safaris, 16179 E Whittier Blvd, Whittier, CA 90603 (☎213/947 5100 or ☎213/943 378718). Owners of two of Botswana's leading

Okavango Delta camps, they can also arrange a complete southern Africa itinerary.

Journeys, 1536 NW 23rd Ave, Portland, OR 97210 (☎503/226 7200); also at *Powell's Travel Store*, Pioneer Courthouse Square, Portland, OR (☎503/226 4849). Organise both individual safaris as well as group tours at select departure dates. Focus for groups is on participation camping, trekking and backroad adventures in Zimbabwe and Botswana. To receive their quarterly newsletter, *The African Traveler*, send $10 annual subscription to address above to cover postage.

Tamsin & Cook, PO Box 8, Franklin Lakes, NJ 07417 (☎201/337 6151). In-depth knowledge of Zimbabwe based on thirty years' residence. Wide choice of custom safaris for two or more. Emphasis on variety including walking, night drives and game-viewing from water. Can arrange safaris with several of the country's top professional guides, as well as bird-watching with Kenneth Newman, leading authority on the region's avifauna.

NORTH AMERICAN TRANS-AFRICA OPERATORS

UNITED STATES

Force 10 Expeditions, PO Box 8548, Waukegan, IL 60079 8548 (☎312/336 2070 or ☎1-800/922 1491).

Adventure Center, 1311 63rd St, Emeryville CA 91608 (☎510/654 1879 or ☎1-800/227 8747).

Himalayan Travel Inc, PO Box 481, Greenwich, Connecticut 06836 (☎203/622 6777 or ☎ 1-800/225 2380) or at the *Safari Center*, 3201N Sepulveda Blvd, Manhattan Beach, CA 90266 (☎310/546 4411 or ☎1-800/223 6046).

CANADA

Blyth and Co, 68 Scollard St, Toronto, Ontario M5R 1GR (☎416/964 2569 or ☎1-800/387 1387).

Goway Travel Ltd, 2300 Yonge St, Box 2331, Toronto, Ontario M4P 1E4 (☎416/322 1034) & 402 W Pender St, Vancouver V6B 1T9 (☎604/687 4004).

Westcan Treks, 8412 109th St, Edmonton T6G 1EZ (☎403/439 9118).

World Expeditions, 78 George St, Ottawa, Ontario K1N 5W1 (☎613/230 8676).

TRANS-AFRICA OVERLAND

The more adventurous and those with a bit of time to kill can opt for several weeks travelling from North Africa to Harare or beyond. A number of operators have well-organised group trips of varying length on the continent. One of the most common routes takes you from Nairobi to Harare over five or six weeks. Other trips on the market include a round trip from Harare through Botswana and Namibia (4 weeks) and Harare to Cape Town (5 weeks).

GETTING THERE FROM AUSTRALASIA

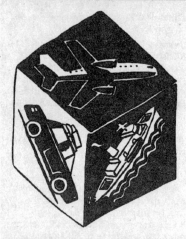

The direct weekly route from Sydney to Harare via Perth is shared between *Air Zimbabwe* and *Qantas*. Book early, it's highly popular; cheapest on Apex, which is valid for up to three months with no seasonal fare variation. Australasian branches of *STA Travel* have student fares on this route.

Qantas and *Air Zimbabwe* also offer the attractive round-trip option of breaking return journeys from Australia to London (or vice versa) in Harare at no additional cost. These fares are cheapest between April and June, a superb time of year in Zimbabwe. There are no direct flights to Gaborone from Australia; it's best to fly via Harare.

For the more adventurous with plenty of time overlanding is a real possibility, perhaps as part of a round-the-world trip. On such tickets sections like the one between Johannesburg and Harare are excluded, and travellers must either buy extra flights or complete the sector by some other means – a good opportunity for some overland travel using public transport.

For something more organised, there's also the possibilty of joining one of the Africa overland trips that work their way down the continent (See *Getting There from Europe* for details).

PACKAGES

Packages are an expensive way of organising your trip if you're planning to stay any length of time. On the other hand, for trips of two to three weeks they can save you a lot of hassle, and ensure you really get to see the highlights that interest you.

AUSTRALASIAN AIRLINES AND AGENTS

Air New Zealand, Air New Zealand House, Queen St, Auckland (☎09/797 515).

British Airways, 64 Castlereagh St, Sydney (☎02/258 3300); Dilworth Bldg, Queen and Customs St, Auckland (☎09/367 7500).

Qantas, Qantas International Centre, International Square, Sydney (☎02/236 3636).

STA, 222–224 Faraday St, Carlton, Melbourne 3053 (☎03/347 4711); 1a Lee St, Railway Square, Sydney 2000 (☎02/519 9866); 10 High St, Auckland (☎09/309 9723).

TRANS-AFRICA OPERATORS

AUSTRALIA

Dragoman, *Access Travel*, 58 Pitt St, Sydney 2000 (☎02/241 1128).

Encounter, *Sundowners Travel Centre*, 108 Albion St, Sydney (☎02/281 4066).

Exodus, *Adventure World*, 8th Floor, 37 York St, Sydney, NSW 2000 (☎02/290 3222).

Tracks can be booked through *African Wildlife Safaris* (see below).

NEW ZEALAND

Encounter, *Sun Travel*, Market Rd, Auckland (☎09/523 3521).

Exodus and **Tracks**, *Adventure World*, 101 Great South Rd, Remuera, PO Box 74008, Auckland (☎09/524 5118).

SOUTHERN AFRICA SPECIALISTS AND AGENTS

AUSTRALIA

Abercrombie and Kent, 90 Bridport St, Albert Park, Melbourne 3206 (☎03/699 9766). Large international operator with comprehensive and professional programmes in both Zimbabwe and Botswana. Upmarket.

Africa Travel Centre, Level 12, 456 Kent St, Sydney, NSW 2000 (☎02/267 3084). Experienced and knowledgeable Africa specialists with a wide range of interesting options. Sister

company to the long-established London-based *Africa Travel Shop.*

African Wildlife Safaris, ACN 006 516 285, 1st Floor, 259 Coventry St, South Melbourne VIC 3205 (☎03/696 2899 or free on ☎008/333 022). A range of packages and safaris all over Africa with activities such as walking and canoeing in Zimbabwe. Agents in Adelaide, Brisbane, Perth and Sydney. Phone the Free Call number for details.

NEW ZEALAND

Africa Travel Centre, 21 Remuera Rd, PO Box 9365, Newmarket, Auckland 3, (☎09/520 2000).

From the same stable as the Australian company listed above.

TRAVEL IN SOUTHERN AFRICA

The forthcoming decade will see the huge region of southern Africa become increasingly integrated as a tourist destination. Namibian independence, developments in South Africa, reforms in Zambia, and changes in Mozambique, and the well-oiled transport connections will facilitate the whole process.

More international flights touch down in **Johannesburg** than any other southern African city, and many visitors now head straight there and take in Zimbabwe and Botswana as part of a larger Southern Africa package. Johannesburg is connected with **Harare** by daily flights and coaches (via Bulawayo), and a weekly direct train. To get to **Bulawayo** from Johannesburg, there are direct flights, a weekly train that trundles through Botswana, and minibus services. There are also flights between Harare and **Durban**.

Weekly trains and daily flights go from Jo'burg to **Gaborone**, with regular services to Victoria Falls and Maun (for Okavango).

In addition to the scheduled transport services, there are a number of companies operating Southern Africa **overland trips** and **mobile safaris**, which can be a covenient and

During the 1980s the African National Congress (ANC) explicitly discouraged tourist visits to South Africa, and many African countries forbade entry to anyone with a South African stamp in their passport. Nelson Mandela has since called for the lifting of person-to-person sanctions and has made it respectable for visitors to go to South Africa. Some people still refuse to visit, but the truth is that tourism is lifting off. For the conscience-stricken, the issue now is what you do when you get there rather than whether you should go.

organised way of reaching less accessible parts. Many of those which operate in restricted localised areas are listed in their relevant section in this book.

OVERLAND THROUGH AFRICA

For overland travellers coming down Africa there are several trodden paths to the south.

From **MALAWI**, the quickest route through **MOZAMBIQUE** brings you into Zimbabwe's northeastern corner, a few hours from Harare. This is a dangerous route, running through territory harassed by Mozambican Renamo (MNR)

	CONNECTIONS WITH JOHANNESBURG		
From	**Flights**	**Trains**	**Coaches**
Harare	1 or 2 daily *	Sunday	Daily except Thurs & Sun**
Bulawayo	Daily	Thursday	Daily except Thurs & Sun**
Victoria Falls	Mon & Thurs direct Daily via Bulawayo & Harare	–	–
Kariba	Tues & Sat	–	–
Gaborone	Daily	Friday	–
Francistown	2 per week	Thursday	–
Kasane	2 per week	–	–
Maun	2 per week (direct) Daily via Gaborone	–	–

*   There is a direct flight from Harare to Durban each Sunday.
**   Informal minibus services regularly leave from Harare and Bulawayo for South Africa.
      Scheduled minibuses also run from Bulawayo to Johannesburg twice per week.

rebels, but people do bag rides with the trucks which run the route in convoy. Under the Portuguese this was known as the "Tete Hell Run" and the "enemy" were Frelimo guerillas. Although Frelimo now run the country, the dangers from anti-government Renamo bandits make this road much the same as ever. The other option from Malawi is much longer, going through Zambia to Livingstone and into Zimbabwe at Victoria Falls, or into Botswana at Kazungula.

From **MOZAMBIQUE** you can fly from Maputo (twice weekly) or Beira (three times weekly) to Harare. The road from Mutare to Beira is now safe, and minibuses go from the border post on the Mozambique side to the coast.

From **ZAMBIA**, it's straightforward enough to hitch to the Victoria Falls or take a daily coach from Lusaka to Harare. A train connects Dar-es-Salaam in Tanzania to Kapiri Mposhi in central Zambia, where it's necessary to change. Another service from a nearby, but separate, station goes via Lusaka to Livingstone, from where buses and taxis ply the route to the Zimbabwe border. Victoria Falls town is a short walk across the bridge. There's also a regular coach service between Lusaka and Francistown in Botswana.

Zimbabwe and Botswana are both also directly connected by air to the independent enclave kingdoms of **LESOTHO** and **SWAZILAND** – both effectively within South Africa.

SOUTH AFRICAN MOBILE SAFARIS COVERING ZIMBABWE AND BOTSWANA

Afro Ventures Safaris, PO Box 2339, Randburg (☎011/789 1078, ☎879 1079 or ☎787 7590). Overland safaris in Botswana, Zimbabwe and South Africa graded according to difficulty. Can be joined in Victoria Falls, Maun or Johannesburg.

Karibu Safari, PO Box 35196, Northway 4065, Durban; 50 Acutt Ave, Rosehill, Durban (☎031/

839 774). Truckback overland camping trips through Zimbabwe, Botswana, Malawi, Namibia and South Africa with an upmarket alternative of lodge-based safaris.

Wilderness Safaris, PO Box 651171, Benmore 2010 (☎011/884 1458 or ☎ 884 4633). Also at 180 Helen Rd, Strathaven, Sandton.

OTHER AFRICAN CONNECTIONS

Harare is well connected to a number of destinations in Africa, making multi-stop travel easy.

Air Zimbabwe flies between Harare and the following cities: five times weekly to Gaborone; three times weekly to Lilongwe and Lusaka; twice weekly to Francistown and Nairobi; and once weekly to Dar-es-Salaam, Maputo and Mauritius.

If you plan to head on to further African travels, many national airlines of these countries operate additional flights. Nairobi is probably the most useful hub to head for. You can also fly Harare to Addis Ababa non-stop for *Ethiopian*

> For further details about the countries listed in this section, see Travelling Onwards In The Region (p.394 in *Contexts*).

Airlines' excellent connections across the continent. Alternatively, for West Africa, you can fly direct to Lagos (*Balkan Bulgarian Airlines*) and Accra (*Ghana Airways*).

Gaborone has fewer connections: three times weekly to Lesotho and Victoria Falls; twice weekly to Harare, Lusaka, Nairobi and Bulawayo; and once weekly to Dar-es-Salaam, Lilongwe and Swaziland.

SAFARIS

Everyone wants to see big game on their African trip. Prepare to put away your watch and your preconceptions and relax. Even if you don't encounter the lioness with cubs that someone else saw half an hour ago, you're bound to be repeatedly rewarded with the unexpected: a bat-eared fox resting in the grass, a dung beetle determinedly rolling a ball of elephant droppings or a large grey mongoose stalking through the grass.

Spotting game takes skill and experience. It's easier than you'd think to mistake a rhino for a large boulder, or to miss leo in the tall lion-coloured grass – African game is after all designed with camouflage in mind. Having someone knowledgeable to point things out makes it that much easier to have a good time.

Zimbabwe scores high as a wildlife destination precisely because it is eminently well endowed with first-class **game guides**. Although it's a pity not to take advantage of this resource, it's still possible to do it yourself more cheaply.

Safari operators are listed under their area in the guide. The main safari regions in Zimbabwe are **Kariba**, the **Middle** and **Lower Zambezi** and **Mana Pools** (Chapter Two); **Hwange** and **Victoria Falls** (Chapter Four) and **Gonarezhou** (Chapter Five). In Botswana the chief areas are

Chobe (Chapter Eight) and the **Okavango Delta** (Chapter Nine).

DOING IT YOURSELF

The most basic way to see game is to hitch or drive into the national parks and stay in national parks accommodation – or to camp.

For anyone on a tight budget it may be the only chance of getting into a national park and you won't be tied down by a fixed itinerary. In Zimbabwe, National Parks accommodation – geared mainly for locals – is extremely cheap. And if you're carrying a tent, you can take advantage of the excellent campsites for next to nothing.

Hitching cuts down your options of viable destinations and unless you're steel-nerved, intrepid and have endless time, it really isn't worth attempting anywhere more ambitious than **Hwange National Park**'s Main Camp. You could do a lot worse. Main Camp is one of the best places to catch sight of a wide spectrum of game in a small area. From here you can catch minibuses or more personalised game drives into the park.

The minibuses are unquestionably a second-rate option. Drivers on such trips are essentially there to get you around the park, and can't be relied on to be as well informed as a qualified guide.

ORGANISED SAFARIS

MOBILE SAFARIS

The least expensive of the package deals, **mobile safaris** offer the chance to get off the beaten track with a professional. You'll camp rather than stay in luxury lodges or fixed bush camps, but that doesn't mean you'll be excessively uncomfortable. While some mobile safaris do expect clients to share chores, many others are fully serviced. In the top-of-the-range versions, you'll sleep under canvas on camp beds, be woken in the morning with tea and you'll arrive back at camp to cooked meals.

Most mobile safaris set out from one of the main centres and set up tents in the national parks campsites. **Prices** start at US$100 per person per day.

BUSH CAMPS AND SAFARI LODGES

Traditional-style safaris based in **bush camps** are still immensely popular. Zimbabwe's best camps and lodges are located either in national parks or in adjacent game-rich concessions.

Guests at the more exclusive places usually number between twelve and sixteen, giving an intimate atmosphere with the chance to talk to guides during meals. Some of the larger lodges resemble hotels and lack this personal feel.

Animals are often free to wander through the grounds, and you'll get a very direct experience of the wild. It's not uncommon for guests to peer through a window at a bush camp to see antelope grazing a few feet away or even a languid lion padding by. Many safari lodges have their own water holes, where you can watch animals drinking from the safety of your room or the bar.

Accommodation is under canvas or in more permanent thatched structures. Chalets frequently have en-suite toilets and bush showers (a hoisted bucket of hot water with a shower nozzle attached) behind reed screens but open to the sky. One of the great thrills of the bush is taking a shower under the southern sky as an elephant strolls by.

Food is usually good and plentiful. On a typical day at a camp or lodge you're woken at dawn for tea or coffee followed by guided game viewing: a drive, walk or trip on the water depending on where you are. Outings are restricted to no more than seven people, which means personalised attention. Mid-morning you return for breakfast. After that there's the chance to spend until

lunch on a viewing platform or in a hide (blind) just quietly watching the passing scene. Late afternoon game-viewing is a repeat of early morning but culminating with sundowners as the light fades.

Prices, from US$150 per person per day, are fully inclusive of accommodation, food and game activities.

SAFARI FARMS

Some **farms** in Zimbabwe have now been turned over to **game-ranching**, and offer the chance for cheaper safaris. This is a new concept for the region, and has yet to prove itself as a viable alternative to the real thing. However, the farms are spread throughout the country (some adjacent to national parks and others near towns), and so provide the chance for easy outings from centres such as Harare or Bulawayo. There's also considerable variation in the cross-section of game you'll see from one farm to the next – often just herbivores.

If you really can't afford a safari in or around the national parks, or you're pushed for time, it's certainly worth considering one of these. You can expect the same personalised treatment you'd get at a bush camp.

Zimbabwe Safari Farms (24 Downie Ave, Belgravia, Harare; ☎733573; Fax 35585) acts a central booking agency for about fifty of these ranches. Independent ones must be booked directly or through a travel agent.

Prices range between US$60 and US$200 (per person all-inclusive).

ACTIVITY AND SPECIALIST SAFARIS

Safaris – in Zimbabwe at least – aren't just about sitting in landrovers and looking at animals. If you're moderately fit and active and game drives sound too sedentary, there are walking, canoeing, horse-riding and even elephant-back safaris. **Walking safaris** take groups of up to six people headed by a tracker and a licensed guide. Trips are supported by a backup vehicle which carries all supplies as well as your personal effects. All you carry is your own camera, binoculars and anything else you may feel you need for half a day's walking.

Supported trips are based at a tented camp where you eat and from which you take morning and afternoon walks. You will see fewer animals than you would from a vehicle but what you do see is more intensely experienced.

Part of the excitement of this kind of trip is in the actual tracking of the animal you're trying to see. There's a real sense of achievement when you finally catch sight of that rhino after a three-hour trek. But no less important is the insight you gain into the bush from your guide who will point out the minutiae of insect, bird and plant life, which seems part of the backdrop until you realise how integral it is to the whole system.

Canoeing safaris vary from those where participants muck in and help cater to those where it's all laid on. All go down either the **Upper Zambezi** above Victoria Falls or the **Lower Zambezi** beyond Lake Kariba. Game-viewing from a canoe is one of the nicest ways to see animals. Some canoe trips include sections of walking.

White-water kayaking on the Upper Zambezi above the Victoria Falls has the added frisson of negotiating rapids at intervals between paddling down the river through the Zambezi National Park.

Horse Safaris leave from Victoria Falls and are open to experienced riders who can go on several day excursions or novices who are restricted to shorter stints. There's nothing like

riding close to a herd of buffalo, who allow horses far closer than they ever would lone humans.

With 640 recorded **bird** species Zimbabwe has a lot to offer bird-watchers. All licensed guides know a lot about the subject but a particularly good bet would be a specialist **bird safari**, as run by *Peter Ginn Birding Safaris* (PO Box 44, Marondera; ☎179 4543; Fax 179 3340). Also highly recommended, especially for beginners, are *Rhodes Nyanga Safaris* (P Bag 2056, Nyanga; ☎129 377).

Trains are the focus of another type of safari. Chugging up from Bulawayo to Victoria Falls, **steam safaris** recreate the romance of rail travel in the days of Empire. Part of the trip takes you through the Hwange National Park and there's a stop on the way with the option of spending the night at *Hwange Safari Lodge*.

And for something completely different you can even go riding **elephants** in Botswana. Since starting in the early 1990s it has become an incredibly popular pursuit and gets booked out. The elephants aren't wild African beasts, having all been born in captivity, and are used to human company. Prices vary depending on the activity and region.

RED TAPE AND VISAS

Neither Zimbabwe nor Botswana requires that citizens of Commonwealth or EC countries, Scandinavia or US obtain visas before coming into the country. South Africans

need only a valid passport to enter Botswana; they no longer need to apply in advance for a Zimbabwe visa, which can be issued at the port of entry for US$25.

For both countries, all travellers need a passport valid for at least six months, an air ticket home (one flying to your place of origin from another African country will usually do) or enough money to get a ticket home, and sufficient funds to cover your costs in the country. These requirements are taken seriously, though there is no statutory daily minimum you are expected to spend.

BORDER FORMALITIES

For stays of up to six months, most passport holders can enter **Zimbabwe** with few formalities, although three months is the usual length granted on your entry stamp. **Botswana** issues one-month entry permits initially, and visitors are strictly allowed to stay no longer than three months in any year.

DIPLOMATIC MISSIONS ABROAD

ZIMBABWE

Belgium, 21–22 Avenue de Arts, B-1040 Brussels (☎02/230 8551, ☎02/230 8535, or ☎02/230 8567).

Botswana, 1st Floor, IGI Building, PO Box 1232, Gaborone (☎4495, ☎4496, or ☎4497).

Canada, 112 Kent St, Place de Ville Tower "B", Ottawa, Ontario KIP 5PT (☎613/237 4388 or ☎613/237 4389).

France, 5 rue de Tilsitt, Paris 75008, Paris (☎1/763 48 31).

Germany, Victoriastrasse 28, 5300 Bonn2, Bonn (☎0228/35 6071 or ☎0228/35 6072).

Kenya, 6th Floor, ICDC Building, PO Box 30806, Nairobi (☎721071, ☎721073, or ☎721076).

Malawi, 7th Floor, Gemini House, PO Box 30187, Lilongwe 3 (☎733 458, ☎733 997, or ☎733 988).

Mozambique, Caiza Postal 743, Maputo (☎744201).

Nigeria, 6 Kasumu Ekemonde St, Victoria Island, PO Box 50247, Ikoyi, Lagos (☎619328).

South Africa, Bank of Lisbon Building, Sauer St, Johannesburg (☎838 2156).

Sweden, Oxtoget 5, 10390 Stockholm (☎304355).

Switzerland, 250 route de Lausanne, Chemin du Rivage, 1292 Chambesy, Geneva (☎022/32 04 34 or ☎022/32 10 19).

Tanzania, Plot 439 Maliki Rd, Upanda West, PO Box 20762, Dar-es-Salaam (☎30455 or ☎32595).

UK, 429 The Strand, London WC2 (☎071/836 7755).

USA, 2851 McGill Terrace NW, Washington DC 20008 (☎202/332 7100); 19 East 47th St, New York, NY 10017 (☎212/980 9511).

Zambia, 4th Floor, Ulenda House, PO Box 33491, Lusaka (☎219025 or ☎219026).

BOTSWANA

UK, 6 Stratford Place, London W1 (☎071/499 0031).

US, Suite 404, 103 East 37th St, New York, NY 10016 (☎212/889 2277).

Zimbabwe, Southern Life Building, Jason Moyo Ave, Harare (☎729551, ☎729552, or ☎729553).

Don't overstay in Botswana, even by one day, without **renewing** your visa. Extending your permission to stay can quite easily be done through one of the local Department of Immigration offices; be warned that if you fail to do so they get very heavy about it. When dealing with Botswana officials, your best tactic is to keep your cool even if it all seems intolerably bureaucratic. If you lose your temper they're almost certain to make life even more difficult for you.

If you're a **journalist** coming to Zimbabwe – particularly if you're just going on holiday – consider stating an alternative occupation on your entry form. Anyone even vaguely connected with the media is generally given a 24-hour visa, and must then get accreditation at the Ministry of Home Affairs. However, if you are on a press assignment, it's probably best to say so, otherwise you could get into a tight corner if found out later.

CURRENCY DECLARATIONS

In both Zimbabwe and Botswana, **currency** must be declared on entry and exit, but there are no restrictions on how much you bring in. In Zimbabwe, your currency declaration form will be checked carefully – don't lose it and if you do, report it to the police. Botswana has more lax exchange control regulations and tends to be more laid-back about currency forms. For more details see "Money and Costs" in the Practicalities sections for each country.

ARRIVING OVERLAND

If travelling overland, make sure things are timed so you don't end up stranded at a closed border post. Most of **Zimbabwe**'s border posts with Zambia, Botswana and South Africa open from 6am to 6pm, seven days a week, apart from Beit Bridge, which opens until 8pm. **Botswana**'s borders have more erratic opening hours, as detailed below.

BOTSWANA BORDER OPENINGS

Zimbabwe
Kazungula Rd Mon–Fri 6am–6pm
Kasane/Victonia Falls Sat & Sun
8am–noon
Mpandamatenga Mon–Fri 8am–5pm
Ramokwebana 6am–6pm

Namibia
Mamuno 8am–4pm
Ngoma Bridge 8am–4pm
Shakawe 8am–4pm

South Africa
Baines Drift 8am–4pm
Bokspits* 8am–4pm
Bray* 8am–4pm
Martin's Drift 8am –6pm
McCarthysrus * 8am–4pm
Parr's Halt 8am–4pm
Pioneer Gate 7am–8pm
Pitsane * 7.30am–4.30pm
Platjanbridge 8am–4pm
Pont Drift 8am to 4pm

Ramatlhabama 7am–8pm
Ramotswa 8am–4pm
Sikwane 6am–7pm
Tlokweng 7am–8pm
Werda* 8am–4pm
Zanzibar 8am–4pm

Zambia
Kazungula Ferry 6am–6pm

* Borders closed when Molopo River in flood makes crossing impassable.

WHAT TO TAKE

You can get most necessary items in Zimbabwe and Botswana, although you shouldn't expect a lot of variety or sophistication, nor, in the remote rural areas, more than the barest of essentials. Locally manufactured products, however, such as shoes and clothes, are easy to come by and usually quite cheap.

As far as food is concerned, unless you're on a macrobiotic diet, you'll have no problem finding a good selection, particularly in the major towns.

On the general goods front, there are occasional shortages of odd items in Zimbabwe, although the situation has improved with the recent imposition of the Structural Adjustment Plan and the liberalising of import regulations. Zimbabweans have, in any case, become extremely creative at "making a plan".

Botswana's import policies are even less strict, and you'll find many more specialised goods there that can't be bought in Zimbabwe. These items are almost invariably South African imports, and Zimbabweans frequently cross the border specifically to buy South African luxuries in Botswana.

HIGH-TECH GOODS

Foreign exchange restrictions in Zimbabwe mean that imported goods are often hard to come by and very expensive. This applies to all types of electronic goods and spares for Western toys. Things such as **torch bulbs** and **batteries** are worth taking with you, as locally made batteries are poor quality and long-life ones are unobtainable. Take all the **film** you need, and any hardware such as **binoculars** – indispensible for game-viewing – as you won't be able to buy it on arrival.

PERSONAL ITEMS

Most essential **drugs** are available in both countries, but if you're on any medication take your own supplies. You'll also be able to get most **toiletries** you need, though Zimbabwean razor blades leave a lot to be desired.

Disposable nappies and anti-mosquito tablets (the blue ones for use with electronic vaporisers) are unavailable in Zimbabwe. However there are plentiful supplies of mosquito coils.

CLOTHES

You can generally get away with a few **light clothes** in Zimbabwe and Botswana. But don't be fooled by average temperature figures. The weather is capricious and even in mid-summer night temperatures can plummet in some places.

From the end of August to October, take light cotton clothes, a long-sleeved T-shirt and a sweater or jacket. The same goes for the period from November to March, though in this **rainy season** it's just as well to include a light plastic mac or hooded jacket. A light woollen jumper is a good idea, even in summer, if you're visiting the cooler Eastern Highlands, or planning on early morning game drives. Modest-looking tracksuits are good game-viewing gear too, allowing you to peel off as the day warms, and practical for camping all year round.

From August to May, shorts or a light skirt are well worth having. **Sunglasses** are recommended all year round. **Hats** or caps are indispensable if you're spending a lot of time outdoors, for example canoeing or walking. A length of light cotton cloth, available from fabric shops in Zimbabwe, is extremely useful as a wrap to ward off the fierce summer sun, and it doubles as a makeshift towel.

Lightweight, quick-drying **walking boots** or shoes are a must if you're planning any energetic activities. Leave behind waterproof, heavy-duty leather hiking boots: while they may be excellent for European hikes, they weigh far too much and you'll just sweat in them. For less ambitious walks and scrambles, tennis or running shoes are ideal.

For **game-viewing** you'll need dark or neutral-coloured clothes. Plain green or khaki gear available from army surplus shops is perfect. White might look stylish but it's not a good idea; in white clothes you stand out like a beacon to the animals you're discreetly trying to watch. And don't take camouflage clothes of any kind; they're illegal for civilians.

Finally, it's worth being forewarned about the southern African idiosyncrasy of "**smart-casual wear**", demanded by many Western-style hotels after 6pm — cocktail time in other words. Exactly what they mean by it is somewhat ad hoc and most of it applies to men. Shorts are out, as are jeans. Trainer shoes are usually acceptable but sandals aren't. If you take a pair of slacks, closed shoes and a smartish shirt with a collar (short sleeves are okay) you should pass. Smart-casual doesn't appear to apply to women, unless you're looking really scruffy.

HEALTH AND INSURANCE

You can put aside most of the health fears that may be justified in some parts of Africa. Bad hospitals and even worse "tropical" diseases aren't typical of Botswana and Zimbabwe. As in the rest of Africa, HIV is rampant, but there's little chance of catching it other than through unprotected sex.

The sunny, dry climate and unpolluted air suits most people and Zimbabwe's temperate central plateau — where Harare and most other major towns are situated — is exceptionally healthy, with a complete absence of malaria. There are generally high standards of hygiene and safe **drinking water** in all tourist areas.

INOCULATIONS

Although no **inoculations** are compulsory if you arrive from the West, it's wise to make sure that your **polio** and **tetanus** jabs are up to date. **Yellow fever** vaccination certificates are necessary if you've come from a country where the disease is endemic, such as Kenya or Tanzania.

Cholera vaccination is unpleasant, pretty ineffective and not recommended unless you are going to be working for a period in terribly deprived areas. Some authorities recommend a course of **typhoid** shots, which for similar reasons is something to think twice about. Despite their terrible reputation, typhoid fever and cholera are both eminently curable and few, if any, visitors to southern Africa ever catch them.

INOCULATION AND HEALTH ADVICE

BRITAIN

British Airways Medical Department, 75 Regent St, London W1 (☎071/439 9584. For advice on other *BA* clinics around the country ☎071/831 5333).

Hospital for Tropical Diseases Clinic, 1st Floor, Queen's House, 180–182 Tottenham Court Rd, London (☎071/637 9899). Advice as well as all the jabs you need. The clinic can also provide the items you may need to stay healthy on your travels, including malaria prevention tablets and mosquito nets.

Hospital for Tropical Diseases Healthline (☎0839/337733). Up-to-the-minute advice on how to stay healthy in the tropics. Personal advice won't be given but the computer-operated system

dishes out detailed health information about Zimbabwe (code 61) and Botswana (code 73). Calls are charged at 48p per minute peak rate.

MASTA (*Medical Advisory Services for Travellers Abroad*), Bureau of Hygiene and Tropical Diseases, Keppel St, London WC1E 7HT. A commercial service providing detailed "health briefs" for all countries. Student discounts.

Thomas Cook Vaccination Centre, 45 Berkeley Square, London W1 (☎071/499 4000). A long-established and fast travel agency centre.

Trailfinders Immunisation Centre, 194 Kensington High St, London W8 7RG (☎071/938 3999). Inoculation service operated by the respected and knowledgeable travel agency.

UNITED STATES

Center for Disease Control (☎404/39 3311). Supply *Health Information for International Travel* – an informative booklet giving details on jabs and general health advice.

A **gamma-globulin** shot gives some protection against hepatitis A for a short visit and may be worthwhile. It's greatly preferable to the disease itself, which is caught from contaminated water or food. A new vaccine is currently being developed – your doctor should be able to advise you. Hepatitis B vaccine is only essential for anyone involved in health work. It's spread by the transfer of blood products, usually dirty needles, so most travellers need not worry about it.

Many **naturopaths** and **homeopaths** counsel quite differently on the subject of immunisation. For an overview, read the summer 1984 issue of *The Homeopath*. If you normally take homeopathic remedies and know enough about them, *Ainsworth's*, 38 New Cavendish Street, London W1 (☎071 935 5330) does a first-aid wallet of 24 vials of remedies which you make up as you like.

GETTING THE JABS

If you decide to have an armful of jabs, start organising them six weeks before departure. A first-time cholera inoculation needs at least two weeks between the two injections of the course. If you're going to another African country first and need the yellow fever jab, remember that a yellow fever certificate only becomes valid ten days after you've had the shot.

In Britain several organisations provide jabs and up-to-the-minute advice. In North America, ask your doctor for the necessary injections.

STAYING HEALTHY

The best way to stay healthy is to keep your resistance up by eating a **healthy regular diet** and by avoiding **stress** – sometimes more easily said than done. The following tips should help you to stay well on your travels and help you over the illness if you succumb.

MEDICAL AIR RESCUE SERVICE

Even if your worst nightmare comes true and you catch malaria in Zimbabwe's bush or you fall victim to some other medical misfortune, don't panic. Zimbabwe's **Medical Air Rescue Service**, 3 Elcombe Ave, Belgravia, Harare (☎734 513, ☎734 514, or ☎734 515; Fax 735 517), can rapidly fly you from anywhere in the country to a hospital. Most safari operators subscribe to the service, which is available to all their clients. Make sure your operator is part of the scheme. If not, or if you're an independent traveller, you can still be covered. Rates start at US$8 per week.

WATER – AND STOMACH UPSETS

Only in extremely remote places do you need to **boil** your water or use **water purification** tablets. **Stomach upsets** from food are equally rare. You'll only find salad and ice – the danger items in some other countries – in hotels and smarter restaurants. Both are perfectly safe and not to be missed. As anywhere, though, **wash** fruit and vegetables as thoroughly as possible, and don't overindulge on fruit – no matter how tempting – when you first arrive.

If you do get a stomach bug, the best cure is lots of water and rest. Papayas, the flesh as well as the pips, are a good tonic to offset the runs.

Avoid jumping for **antibiotics** at the first sign of illness; keep them as a last resort – they don't work on viruses and annihilate your "gut flora", most of which you want to keep, making you more susceptible next time round. Most upsets will resolve themselves by adopting a sensible fat-free diet for a couple of days, but if they do persist unabated or are accompanied by other unusual symptoms then see a doctor as soon as possible.

AIDS AND SEXUALLY TRANSMITTED DISEASES

Horror stories of rusty syringes and HIV-infected blood transfusions are not relevant to Zimbabwe or Botswana. Disposable needles are routinely used and the Zimbabwean health authorities have screened all donated blood for AIDS for several years. Zimbabwe was the third country in the world to do so – after the United States and Germany, and some months ahead of Britain.

So there's no special risk from medical treatment in Zimbabwe. If travelling overland, though, and you want to play safe, take your own needle and transfusion kit (from *SAFA*, 59 Hill Street, Liverpool L8 5SA, or *Thomas Cook*'s in London).

Your biggest chance of getting AIDS is through unprotected sex. AIDS, as well as various venereal diseases, is widespread in southern Africa.

Some estimates put HIV incidence at a staggering 20 percent of Zimbabwe's population. The chance of catching the virus through sexual contact is very real. Follow the usual precautions regarding safer sex: abstain – or use a condom.

BILHARZIA

One ailment which you need to take seriously in both countries is **bilharzia**, carried in all Zimbabwe's waterways outside the Eastern Highlands. Bilharzia (schistosomiasis) is spread by a tiny, water-borne parasite. These worm-like flukes leave their water snail hosts and burrow into human skin to multiply in the bloodstream. They work their way to the walls of the intestine or bladder where they begin to lay eggs.

Avoid swimming in dams and rivers where possible. If you're canoeing or can't avoid the water, have a test when you return home. White water is no guarantee of safety; although the snails favour sheltered areas, the flukes can be swept downstream. Returning to Britain, you can get referred by your GP to the Hospital for Tropical Diseases Clinic (see address on p.17). The chances are you'll have avoided bilharzia even if you swam in the Zambezi, but it's best to be sure.

Symptoms may be no more than a feeling of lassitude and ill health. Once infection is established, abdominal pain and blood in the urine and stool are common. Fortunately it's easily and effectively treated these days with praziquantel, although the drug can make you feel ill for a few days. No vaccine is available and none foreseen.

HEAT AND DUST

The **sun** could be the most dangerous thing you encounter. A hat and sunglasses are recommended. Ordinary sun screens and lotions can be bought in pharmacies in Zimbabwe and Botswana, though you should buy the **total block** or **high-protection** variety before you leave. Tanning should be a very gradual process.

MEDICAL KIT

Don't let your fears run away with you and lumber yourself with a heavy kit. You can buy medicines over the counter in pharmacies in both countries. If you need specialised drugs bring your own supply, but any first-aid items can be easily replaced. A very basic kit should include scissors, fine tweezers for removing thorns or glass, sticking plasters, one wide and one narrow bandage, lint, cotton wool, pins, aspirins and an antiseptic cream such as *Bacitracin*. *Nelson's* natural calendular ointment is invaluable as a healing agent for any stings, rashes, cuts, sores or cracked skin. A bottle of eyedrops is wonderfully soothing if you're travelling on dusty roads in Botswana. Some people also like to include a course of broad-spectrum antibiotics.

If you're not used to dealing with continuous heat over long periods of time, take care to avoid heat exhaustion. Be aware that you may be overheating, and if you start feeling ill – headaches or nausea – get to a cool shady place. Make sure you're getting enough water and that your salt levels aren't depleting.

Botswana is particularly **dusty** – take this on board if you're asthmatic or allergic to dust. If you're just flying in to the Delta and staying near the water, you shouldn't have any problems.

TEETH AND EYES

Have a thorough **dental check-up** before leaving home. You'll find dentists in the main towns in Zimbabwe and Botswana, although they're few and far between in Botswana. Treatment, also, is expensive. In Zimbabwe, dentists are listed after doctors at the beginning of each town in the telephone directory. In Botswana, they're in the pink pages right at the front of the phone book.

If you wear **glasses** or **contact lenses** bring a spare pair with you, along with all the cleaning gear you need.

SNAKES, INSECTS AND OTHER UNDESIRABLES

Zimbabwe and Botswana both feature all sorts of potential bites, stings and rashes – which rarely, if ever, materialise.

Snakes are common, but hardly ever seen as they get out of the way quickly. Puff adders are the most dangerous because they lie in paths and don't move, but they're not commonly seen by travellers. The best advice if you get bitten is to remember what the snake looked like (kill it if you can, for identification) and get to a clinic or hospital. Most bites are not fatal and the worst thing is to panic: desperate measures with razor blades and tourniquets risk doing more harm than good.

Tick-bite fever is occasionally contracted from walking in the bush, particularly in March and April when the grass is long and wet. The offending ticks are minute and you're unlikely to spot them. Symptoms appear a week later – swollen glands and severe aching of the bones, backache and fever. Since it is a self-limiting disease, it will run its course in three or four days. Ticks you may find on yourself are not dangerous, just repulsive at first. Make sure you pull out the head as well as the body (it's not painful). A good way of removing small ones is to smear vaseline or grease over them, making them release their hold.

Scorpions and **spiders** abound but are hardly ever seen unless you turn over logs and stones. If you're collecting wood for a camp fire, knock or shake it before picking it up. Contrary to popular myth, scorpion stings and spider bites are painful but almost never fatal. Most are harmless and should be left alone. A simple precaution when camping is to shake out your shoes and clothes in the morning before you get dressed.

Rabies exists in both countries. Be wary of strange animals and go to a clinic if bitten. It can be treated effectively with a course of injections.

HOSPITALS

Hospitals in Zimbabwe are fairly well equipped and attempt to maintain high standards. In remoter parts, the clinics are usually adequate although there are shortages of some drugs. Botswana has a few prestigious new hospitals.

Private clinics are often a better option for visitors and you're likely to get more personal treatment. Costs are nowhere as prohibitive as in the US and if you're insured they should certainly pose no problem.

In emergencies, or for extremely serious conditions, patients from both countries are sometimes flown to Johannesburg where the full range of up-to-date treatment is available.

INSURANCE

All British banks and most travel agents will sell you a variety of travel insurance policies, covering both loss or theft of possessions and health treatment costs. Taking out a policy of some kind is highly advisable; and if you're a regular traveller, the cheapest way to do so is take a one-year policy to cover all trips made within a 12-month period.

In Britain, travel insurance bought through branches of **STA Travel** (see p.4) or **Endsleigh** (☎071/589 6783) is one of the cheapest available. Around £30 for a fortnight or £40 for a month will cover you against all sorts of calamities including lost bags, cancelled flights and hospital charges.

Columbus Travel Insurance (☎071/375 0011; Fax 071/375 0022) offer a similar service at slightly lower rates. The premium for several months of travel is high but it's probably money well spent. *Columbus* (who should not be confused with *Columbus Insurance Services*) have one of the best packages around at £20 per month for basic cover for up to one year.

US travellers should check their current policy. You may find that you are already covered for medical expenses or other losses while abroad. If you do need to buy insurance or want to be covered against specific risks try one of these companies:

Access America International, 600 Third Ave, New York, NY 10163 (☎212/949 5960 or on ☎1-800/284 8300).

Travel Guard, 110 Centrepoint Drive, Steven Point, WI 54480 (☎715/345 0505 or ☎1-800/826 1300).

MALARIA

Malaria, caused by a parasite carried in the saliva of Anopheles **mosquitos**, is endemic in tropical Africa: many Africans have it in their bloodstream and get occasional bouts of fever. It has a variable **incubation period** of a few days to several weeks, so you can become ill long after being bitten. If you go down with it, you'll know: the fever, shivering and headaches are like severe flu and come in waves, usually beginning in the early evening. Malaria is not infectious but it can be dangerous and even fatal if not treated quickly.

Protection against malaria is absolutely essential. Although much of Zimbabwe and Botswana, including most of the main towns, is free of malarial mosquitos, you have to keep taking the tablets to maintain your resistance for when you're bitten by a carrier mosquito, in a low-lying game park for example.

TABLETS
Doctors can advise on which kind of **preventive tablets** to take – generally the latest anti-resistant creation – and you can buy most without a prescription at a pharmacy before you leave. It's important to keep a routine and cover the period before and after your trip with doses. Take enough pills with you to cover your entire stay, as the types of tablet sold in Botswana and Zimbabwe are different.

NETS, OILS AND COILS
Sleep under a **mosquito net** when possible – they're not expensive to buy locally – and burn **mosquito coils** (which you can buy everywhere) for a peaceful, if noxious, night. Whenever the mosquitos are particularly bad – and that's not often – cover your exposed parts with something strong. So-called "*Neat Deet*" (the insecticide diethyltoluamide) works well. It is available by post from *MASTA* (see "Getting The Jabs"). Other locally produced repellents such as *Peaceful Sleep* are widely available. Citronella oil is a help too, but hardly smells better.

Electric mosquito-destroyers which you fit with a pad every night are less pungent than mosquito coils, but more expensive in use – and you need electricity. Mosquito "buzzers" are useless.

Female Anopheles mosquitos – the aggressors – prefer to bite in the evening.

IF YOU FALL ILL
If you contract malaria, you'll need to take a **cure**. Don't compare yourself with local people who may have considerable immunity. The priority, if you think you might be getting a fever, is treatment. Delay is potentially risky.

First, confirm your **diagnosis** by getting to a doctor and having a blood test to identify the strain. If this isn't possible take two quinine tablets (600mg) twice daily for five days and then three *Fansidar* tablets. This should clear up any strain of malaria. If you don't have quinine tablets (you'd probably need to have obtained them abroad) then take ordinary chloroquine tablets at the rate of 10mg per kilo body weight up to a maximum of 600mg (usually four tablets) immediately, then half as much (usually two tablets) eight hours later. Assuming you feel an improvement, take this second dose again on the second and third days. If you notice no improvement after the initial dose, try again to see a doctor or take three *Fansidar* tablets if you have them; your malaria is chloroquine-resistant. The *Fansidar* should clear it up within a few hours.

HEALTH PUBLICATIONS

British Department of Health Booklet

T4:The Travellers Guide to Health

Place your order by phone free of charge anytime (☎0800/ 555 777).

Books

Dr Richard Dawood (ed), *Traveller's Health* (OUP/ Viking Penguin). A compendious volume of ills to afflict your travels. Good writing and advice.

MAPS, BOOKS AND INFORMATION

The Zimbabwe Tourist Organisation (ZTO) is well organised and you can sometimes pick up basic maps and information on hotels and organised tours. If there's an office in you country, it's worth paying a visit just to browse around and whet your appetite. Elsewhere, contact the nearest Zimbabwe diplomatic mission (see Red Tape) or office of Air Zimbabwe.

Information about Botswana is more difficult to find but the High Commissions are worth a try.

ZIMBABWE

Really good **maps of Zimbabwe** are rare outside the country and it's most useful to go for a map of the whole southern Africa region. The classic travellers' maps for Africa are produced by *Michelin*. The #955 *Africa Central and Southern* is an excellent map showing road conditions, fuel and supply points and other salient

details with loads of information on Zimbabwe, even at the scale of 40km to 1cm.

The **Zimbabwe Tourist Office** has produced quite a good free map which covers Zimbabwe only, accurate on main routes but weak on minor roads. The *Automobile Association of Zimbabwe* map is better, with detailed coverage of even very minor roads – good if you want to venture off the beaten track. Beware of outdated maps such as the *Shell* one, which you see in plentiful supply in service stations; the map itself is very good but it is confusing in that it shows all the old, pre-Independence names.

Zimbabwe is well covered by detailed ordnance survey (OS) maps, which are indispensible for walking in any of the national parks. They're available from the Surveyor General's Office, Electra House, Samora Machel Avenue, Harare (☎794545). The office also has a wealth of maps covering everything that can be mapped, from rainfall patterns to geology and land use; it's fascinating just to browse around.

The **Parks Department** provides useful fact sheets, available in Harare, which cover facilities and attractions in most of the national parks. And finally, local information is available from town publicity associations. These are often very helpful, with up-to-date hotel and camping information, brochures and some usefully detailed (if often very old) regional maps.

BOTSWANA

The *Michelin* #955 (see Zimbabwe) is again the best general map. Botswana itself isn't as well documented as Zimbabwe, although there are several adequate maps. The best is the *Botswana Minimap* produced by *Okavango Tours and*

Safaris (28 Bisham Gardens, London N6 6DD; ☎081/341 9442), which has a map of the whole country and up-to-date detailed plans of all the major tourist areas.

In Botswana you can get a free *Shell* map from most tourist information offices. It's similar to the *Minimap*, though bigger and less accurate. *B&T Directories* (PO Box 1549, Gaborone; ☎37 1444) has produced a set of two maps – containing one of the whole country and plans of the

main towns. It costs a few pula and is most easily available from Gaborone bookshops. The most detailed map of Botswana is the 1:1,000,000 sheet, which comes in two parts, available from the Director, Department of Surveys and Lands, Private Bag 0037, Gaborone.

For pamphlets about attractions in Botswana, get in touch with one of the country's diplomatic missions (see p.14). They have some well-produced material.

SPECIALIST BOOK AND MAP SUPPLIERS

For general background information about the history, geography, literature and natural history of Botswana and Zimbabwe, two British bookshops lead the way:

Africa Centre Bookshop, 38 King St, Covent Garden, London WC2 (☎071/836 1973). A unique resource centre, library and excellent bookshop – also a place to meet Batswana and Zimbabweans informally (bar and restaurant open daily, live bands, discos).

Dillons, 82 Gower St, London WC1 6EQ (☎071/636 1577). Substantial southern Africa shelves in the Africa section and a fine selection of fauna and flora field guides to the region in the natural history section.

For **maps**, the best specialist outlets in Britain and North America include:

London *Daunt Books*, 83 Marylebone High St, W1 (☎071/224 2295); *National Map Centre*, 22–24 Caxton St, SW1 (☎071/222 4945); *Stanfords*, 12–14 Long Acre, WC2 (☎071/836 1321); *The Travellers' Bookshop*, 25 Cecil Court, WC2 (☎071/836 9132).

Chicago *Rand McNally*, 444 North Michigan Ave, IL 60611 (☎312/321 1751).

New York *The Complete Traveller Bookstore*, 199 Madison Ave, NY 10016 (☎212/685 9007); *Rand McNally*, 150 East 52nd St, NY 10022 (☎212/758 7488); *Traveller's Bookstore*, 22 West 52nd St, NY 10019 (☎212/664 0995).

San Francisco *The Complete Traveler Bookstore*, 3207 Filmore St, CA 92123; *Rand McNally*, 595 Market St, CA 94105 (☎415/777 3131).

Seattle *Elliot Bay Book Company*, 101 South Main St, WA 98104 (☎206/624 6600).

Montréal *Ulysses Travel Bookshop*, 4176 St-Denis (☎514/289 0993).

Toronto *Open Air Books and Maps*, 25 Toronto St, M5R 2C1 (☎416/363 0719); *Ulysses Travel Bookshop*, 101 Yorkville.

Vancouver *World Wide Books and Maps*, 1247 Granville St.

FOOD AND DRINK

Food in Zimbabwe and Botswana is an unfortunate mish-mash of traditional staples and English colonial diet – a very bland combination indeed. Standard dishes are either downmarket maize porridge and stew or more upmarket meat and two veg. Fortunately the meat is very good and cheap – steaks are not to be missed – and you'll find a range of international food in all the larger towns, which breaks the monotony of ubiquitous burgers, chips, pizzas and fried chicken takeaways, or more expensive sit-down cuisine. And there are those mainstays of white southern Africa: *braaivleis* (barbecue) and *biltong* (dried meat).

You'll find all the usual drinks, but beer in various guises is the commonest. Zimbabwe produces its own drinkable wines and also spirits, while Botswana imports better-quality liquor.

EATING IN ZIMBABWE

The traditional diet in Zimbabwe tends to be a variation on local produce: maize and beef. The local staple is *sadza* and relish, *sadza* being a stiff maize porridge slowly cooked for some time. Relish can be any kind of stew, sometimes based on vegetables but most commonly *nyama* (meat). The meat is unspecified – it can be goat, mutton, beef or chicken – but usually unpalatably plain.

If you stay at hotels and stick to the city centre, you're unlikely to sample any of this. You'll need to go to one of the many cheap eating houses around the bus or train stations which, besides *sadza*, serve deep-fried doughy concoctions, chips, filling buns and an unending supply of *Coca-Cola*. *Sadza* is usually steaming and freshly cooked. One **vegetarian** option at these places, which often sell a few groceries as well, is to buy a tin of baked beans and have that with *sadza*, instead of meat.

White bread – big sandwich loaves of it – is the other staple. Brown bread is available only in the big centres and not always in hotels. The national preference is definitely for white loaves, which are also cheaper. You may see queues for bread in the early morning at city shopping centres. Don't be put off, it's only for white bread; you can always buy brown or "fancy loaves" without queuing.

STREET FOOD AND BREAKFAST

Street food, sold around bus stations, varies according to season, but you'll find boiled or roasted corn on the cob, peanuts, some varieties of beans, hard-boiled eggs and lots of fruit. Out of working class areas and into the middle class-dominated city centres, there's a noticeable absence of street food. Instead, you find western-style cafés, restaurants and burger joints.

Food in hotels, restaurants and snack bars is solidly British-based – old familiars such as tomato sauce, pickles, baked beans, peanut butter, marmalade, cornflakes and a marmitey spread called *Vegex*. Terrific value English breakfasts are always on offer at the large hotels, suitable for vegetarians too. You can stuff yourself with fruit and fruit juice, cereal, eggs, bacon, sausages (and even steak sometimes), cheese, toast, scones and jam.

BUFFETS AND BARBECUES

If you skip breakfast and want a big lunch, the larger hotels do buffets of equally good value, with huge spreads of salad, cold cuts and puddings. Although they may appear at first sight to be expensive, you'll probably eat enough to last you the rest of the day. Among all this, you'll still find enough to eat if you're a vegetarian, and some places will give you a discount if you're not eating meat.

Barbecues – *braaivleis* – are an integral part of the social scene in southern Africa. The centre of attraction is a slab of steak to gorge on and *boerewors*, a delicious spicy sausage of Afrikaans origin. A pot of *sadza* may well be on offer as an accompaniment at these occasions. Every camping site in the country will have a place to cook outdoors and "*braai*" your meat.

The other meat speciality to try is **biltong** – sun-dried, salted meat cut into strips. It can be made from beef or, much tastier, from game, and is available from most butchers, or from supermarkets. *Biltong* is an invaluable camping food, but you can't always get it during the summer months when the sun is too hot for proper curing of the meat. **Game** meat – including crocodile tail, shoulder of impala, and warthog – is on offer at some of the expensive hotels.

FISH

Fish and **seafood** is second-rate in Zimbabwe, as you might expect from a landlocked country, but in the Eastern Highlands there's excellent trout and at Lake Kariba, bream. You won't find tinned fish or much fresh fish in supermarkets, but instead large packets of **kapenta** – tiny dried fish from Kariba. *Kapenta* has a strong taste and is eaten mainly by low-income families, but it's also served as a tasty snack at the Kariba hotels.

FRUIT AND VEGETABLES

Although Zimbabwe has no distinctive cuisine, the range of **fruit** and **vegetables** is special. Interesting vegetables to try include members of the marrow variety – gem squash, butternut and pumpkin. Avocados are plentiful, cheap and delicious.

Recommended fruits include guavas, paw-paws (papaya), lady-finger bananas and mangos. At markets you'll also see unfamiliar wild fruit, often delicious – but ask to sample before buying.

EATING IN BOTSWANA

Botswana, like its neighbour, has no great national dishes. Meat is cheap and plentiful and the range of foodstuffs is superior to that in Zimbabwe – although it's all imported from South Africa.

Botswana lacks good fruit and vegetables as it's too dry and sandy for most things to grow. In the big towns you'll find adequate imported fruit and vegetables in supermarkets, but nothing in rural areas. Rural desert-dwellers get their vitamins and minerals from a vast array of wild food. Some drought-resistant crops are cultivated too. Sadly, fewer and fewer people have the kind of knowledge necessary to gather wild food and the combination of overgrazing and drought has decimated the vegetation. Moreover, there's a social stigma attached to eating roots – considered food for only the poorest of the poor.

Sorghum porridge, **mabele**, eaten with some kind of relish, has always been the staple food in Botswana, but it has now been largely replaced by white maize meal. Made into a stiff porridge, maize porridge is often called by the Afrikaans name *mielie-pap*, not *sadza*, as in Zimbabwe. Maize doesn't grow well in much of Botswana, but packets of meal are available cheaply in shops throughout the country. In dry areas people grow drought-resistant melons and beans, millet, gourds and groundnuts (peanuts). What you will find by the tubfull at markets is *madila*, a thickened form of sour milk drunk on its own or as a relish.

DRINKING

Alcohol – mainly **beer** – is cheap and consumed in large quantities in both Zimbabwe and Botswana. Beer comes as lager, pilsener or chibuku. In Zimbabwe, all that distinguishes the lagers is brand name: *Castle*, *Lion*, *Black Label*, or the more expensive *Zambezi*. Beer is always ordered by name brand, as loyalty is strong. Lager is served ice-cold; you won't find warm British bitter.

It takes a bit of courage to drink **chibuku** – a thick mixture more like porridge than lager, served in large containers. It's not available in hotels or bars, but only in working-class beer halls and beer gardens. Finely atmospheric focal points of social life as they are, the beer halls are not, however, recommended for women alone.

The ceremonial brewing and drinking of beer is an integral part of African life, for occasions ranging from marking a rite of passage to getting a new job. Even beer drunk at urban gardens is drunk ritualistically as the bucket-sized mugs are passed from one person to the next, or momentarily set down while people talk or exchange greetings. Night-time drinking happens in small shebeens in the high-density areas. You'd need to be invited to one of these, firstly to find it, and secondly to feel at all comfortable once you're in.

Zimbabwe produces its own **wine** – the only kind that is available there. Although it has improved over the years, it can't compete internationally and is mostly just plonk – though for all that often very drinkable. Unfortunately wines are inconsistent, which makes recommendations a bit hazardous, but at a few pounds, a bottle of the most expensive can't go too far wrong.

Locally produced cognac and whiskey tend to be rough and best drunk with a mixer. Imported spirits are extremely expensive, and frequently unobtainable in Zimbabwe, so gifts of duty-free liquor go down exceptionally well.

SOFT DRINKS

Non-alcoholic drinks come down to extremely cheap minerals – including *Coca-Cola* and also one of Zimbabwe's best products, *Mazoe* orange and lime squashes, which retain the gorgeous flavour of the fruit – not sickly sweet or chemical ridden. Zimbabwe has several varieties of bottled water – both still and sparkling – mostly from springs in the Eastern Highlands.

One iced soft drink speciality in both countries is the **rock shandy**, a mix of lemonade, soda water and Angostura bitters with ice and a slice of lemon. In Zimbabwe, Malawi shandies are a slightly sweeter alternative which replaces the lemonade with ginger beer. If you're offered a "Zambezi cocktail", refuse politely unless you want water – a little local joke.

Botswana produces none of its own booze besides beer; South African wines are widely sold. Spirits and liqueurs, as well as a range of natural fruit juices are also products of its southern neighbour. One non-alcoholic traditional drink available in shops is *mageu*, made from both grain and fruit.

CAMPING FOODS

Zimbabwe has a very limited range of **lightweight food**. If you're doing some serious hiking you'll probably manage on local goods, but it's worth considering bringing the odd packet with you. Locally, maize meal is extremely cheap and you can make either a thin porridge in the morning, or clods of *sadza* as part of a main meal. Other lightweight food includes dried milk, *Pronutro* breakfast food (a nutritionally balanced, and not unpalatable, concoction developed in South Africa), crispbread, *biltong*, dried milk, packeted soup, groundnuts and dried slices of mango. Cheese is always available, as are tinned meat and beans, suitable fruit and vegetables, brown rice and pretty awful pasta.

Botswana has lots of (South African) imports on offer. Soya mince in various guises, on sale under the name of *Toppers*, makes an excellent fallback, and there's always a good choice of tins, snacks and processed cheese triangles, all of which keep well. With rye bread, good crisp bread, tomato purée, pickled fish or tuna, dried fruit and just about anything else you could conceivably need, you're in no danger of facing starvation.

If you're four-wheel driving and camping, fresh produce which keeps includes potatoes, cabbages, onions, carrots, oranges and lemons. Buy oil and vinegar in screw-top containers, rather than tops which can pop off from the pressure and bumping around. Dust gets in everywhere, so packet food such as dried milk or sugar should be decanted into screw-top containers. Keep a day or two's worth of food at hand in a separate, easy-to-reach box, and leave the rest in a food trunk.

PHOTOGRAPHY

Zimbabwe and Botswana are immensely photogenic and with any kind of camera, you can get beautiful pictures. What kind of camera you take depends on how much weight you're prepared to carry, how much like a tourist you want to look, and whether you want to photograph animals.

Small, compact cameras are great because you can keep them unobtrusively in your pocket and whip them out for a quick shot. But they're hopeless for wildlife – a nearby lion will end up a furry speck in savannah. Compacts can also be potentially dangerous – tales abound of tourists with little cameras sneaking up too close for comfort to big game and ending up in very sticky predicaments.

If you take your photography seriously, you'll probably want a single-lens reflex camera (SLR) and two or three lenses – a heavy and cumbersome option. For decent wildlife photography you definitely need a **telephoto lens**. A 300-mm lens is a good all-rounder; any bigger and you'll need a tripod. The smallest you could get away with for animals is 200mm, while 400mm is the best for birds. All long lenses need fast film, or you'll find you're restricted to the largest apertures, and hence the narrowest depth of focus. If you simply want good snaps from your SLR, think about one well-chosen zoom lens.

PROTECTION

The biggest problem in Botswana is **dust**, which will penetrate straight into a normal camera case or cloth bag. Cameras need to be inside sealed plastic bags, or in some dustproof container, and got out only for the business of taking pictures. You'll need to carry a blower-brush to blow dust off lenses.

Another problem – in both countries – is the heat. Never leave your camera or films lying in the sun. The film in a camera left exposed on a car seat, for instance, will be completely ruined. Keep rolls of film cool in the middle of your clothes or sleeping bag.

LIGHT READINGS

You really have to rely on a judicious combination of the camera's light readings and your own common sense. The contrast between light and shade can be huge, so expose for the subject and not the general scene. This can mean setting your camera to manual, approaching the subject to get a reading and then using that. With a zoom you can zoom in for a reading and then return. Some of the new multi-mode cameras will do much of this for you.

If you're photographing a black person, especially in strong light, use more exposure than usual, otherwise they'll be underexposed; the light and your eyes (which are more sophisticated than any camera) can deceive you.

Early morning and late afternoon are the best times for photography. At midday, with the sun overhead, the light is flat and everything is lost in glare.

FILM

Film is expensive in Botswana and can be both expensive and in short supply in Zimbabwe, so bring all you'll need. It's best, though bulky and more expensive, to have rolls of twenty, so you don't get stuck with the same film for too long. And don't let anyone tell you it's unnecessary to have fast film because the sun is so bright in Africa. Even if you opt for a compact with a fast lens (i.e. one that's very light-sensitive) you'll need at least some 400 ASA film if you want to take pictures at dawn and dusk and in heavy cloud or forest. With long lenses on an SLR, fast film is essential. Also bring spare batteries as these can be impossible to replace.

Processing is undoubtedly best left until you return home. If you're away for a long time, send films back or store them in someone's fridge, rather than keep them in warm conditions.

SUBJECTS AND PEOPLE

As for subjects, **animal photography** is a question of patience and resisting taking endless pictures of nothing happening. If you can't get close enough, don't waste your film. While taking photos, try keeping both eyes open and, in a vehicle, always turn off your engine.

You should always ask before taking **photographs of people**, or of for example a dwelling decorated with colourful paintings. Some kind of interaction and exchange is customarily implied; people often ask for a copy of the photograph and you'll end up with several names and addresses and a list of promises. In Botswana, desert-dwellers and Herero women appreciate and indeed expect a couple of pula; it's no good trying to bargain them down.

On the issue of **sensitivity**, don't take photographs of anything that could be construed as strategic. This includes any kind of military or police building, prisons, airports, bridges, dignitaries and anyone in uniform, as well as in refugee camps such as Dukwe (see Chapter Eight).

TRAVELLING IN DEEPLY RURAL AREAS

Out in the wilds, you will need to tune into local sensitivities – and avoid some obvious pitfalls. You'll undoubtedly commit some unwitting faux pas but people are tolerant if they can see you're making an effort and are commonly too polite anyway to point out the error of your ways. Always remember that you are the stranger.

BEHAVIOUR

You should always ask before helping yourself to borehole or tap water in rural areas – travellers are never refused. And if you come across a breakdown on a remote road, the form is to stop and offer assistance – yours may be the first vehicle in a week.

Women are expected to be modest, so wearing shorts, or short skirts, away from tourist areas is not a good idea. Nor is the display of affection in public. Gobbling your food and/or failing to share it with others present is not acceptable.

If you're travelling alone, people may find it very odd that you do so by choice, as being alone is regarded as a great affliction by many rural people. There's also common surprise and deep regret and condolences if you're the right age but haven't had any children.

GETTING INFORMATION

If you want reliable information, the way you frame questions is vitally important. People generally dislike disappointing a visitor, so when you ask "is it far?" you will invariably hear "oh no, not far at all." So, if you don't wan't to go astray, don't ask leading questions. It's better to ask "how long does it take you on foot/by bicycle?" By the same token, don't ask distances. The need to know specific numbers of kilometres or miles is rarely uppermost in people's minds in Africa.

Lastly, when asking about road conditions in remote parts of Botswana or Zambia ask "how long ago has a car/bicycle passed here?", and not "is this road passable?" It may be passable for cattle and people but not for cars.

CAMPING IN THE BUSH

Camping in the bush throughout Botswana, you will find people to be unsuspicious and easy about you setting up camp in the middle of nowhere, although it is always polite to ask permission from the local chief if you're near a settlement.

In Zimbabwe, the situation is somewhat different. Land distribution patterns haven't yet changed significantly from colonial days. Generally the best land is fenced off in the hands of private farmers and the rest is called "communal land", (formerly "tribal trust lands") with large numbers of peasant farmers.

Little more than a decade ago, rural people in the communal lands were in the midst of bitter and bloody conflict. The only whites in these areas at the time were those connected with the army, the government or missions. Today, while there are aid workers about, you still don't find people holidaying in the communal lands and there's certainly nothing in the way of camping sites or tourist facilities.

This is not to say that Zimbabwe's communal lands are off limits: you could have a fascinating and rewarding time in rural areas, where you'll find people terrifically friendly. You could ask for lodgings in a village hut, or stay in former district commissioner's or government official's accommodation in some of the bigger settlements. But do make yourself known to the district administrator so as to avoid arousing any concern or suspicion at your unusual behaviour. Men, in particular, should be aware of the danger of being picked up as South African spies, especially in areas bordering that country.

WILDLIFE AND NATIONAL PARKS

With its progressive conservation policy and a budget to match – the biggest on the continent outside South Africa – Zimbabwe is rich in wildlife. You'll see herds of animals here that are heading for extinction elsewhere on the continent. Although they're the victims of waves of attacks by poachers, you can still find both varieties of rhino – sadly in shrinking numbers – and Zimbabwe's parks are literally trampled by elephants – a great conservation success. All the other herbivores you could want are also there: giraffes, zebras, buffaloes, hippos and many species of antelope (buck). Also represented is the whole range of African predators.

Conservation in Botswana is more *laissez faire*, but it seems to have worked effectively thus far and you'll see many of the same animals as in Zimbabwe, including Africa's largest elephant herds – 67,000 strong – and several species not found across the border.

WILDLIFE

Between them, Zimbabwe and Botswana have among the world's finest and most diverse surviving cross-sections of **mammals**. If they exist in southern Africa, these two countries are the likeliest places you'll see them. Of the 291 species recorded south of the Zambezi, most occur in Zimbabwe. Botswana, with its predominantly Kalahari sands habitat, contains a smaller and more specialised population – though a still impressive 140 species.

Large parts of the region remain untamed and you'll still find wildlife wandering beyond the unfenced confines of the national parks, though mostly only in rural areas. At Kariba, however, the **elephants** sometimes come into town to make a meal of trees growing in gardens, and around smaller towns, especially in the Zambezi and southern lowvelds, it's not uncommon to spot game – usually the odd antelope.

Antelope are the commonest species and the prolific impala are likely to become a very familiar sight. Other common herbivores that you're bound to come across if you spend any time at all in the national parks include zebra, giraffe, hippo and buffalo. Species mostly restricted to Botswana include gemsbok, sitatunga and red lechwe.

Wherever you find grazers and browsers, **predators** aren't far behind. The big cats are there as well as smaller and lesser-known felines such as the caracal and black-footed cat, but are only found far from human habitation. Night brings out a different cast and any operator taking game drives will have a spotlight to reveal hyenas, springhares and – if you're lucky – porcupines, pangolins and leopards.

For specific advice on **safaris** in Zimbabwe and Botswana, see pp.11–13.

SMALLER CREATURES

In the smaller range, **spiders** and **scorpions** will do their best to get away from you, while the butterflies are all you could hope for. **Lizards** are common, often beautifully coloured and completely harmless, as are the prehistoric-looking chameleons, which are found absolutely everywhere, even in suburban gardens. And don't be disturbed if you see small gravity-defying reptiles running across the ceiling, they're insect-eating geckos (whose adhesive toes allow the acrobatics) and should be encouraged.

BIRD LIFE

With their diverse habitats, Botswana and Zimbabwe are home to a marvellous range of **birds** – a great attraction to ornithologists from all over. From the exquisite, hovering sunbirds on the miniature side to huge land-bound ostriches, there are over 600 species in Zimbabwe alone, many of which, together with mammals, insects and reptiles, are detailed in their relevant habitats throughout this book.

ZIMBABWE'S PARKS

Zimbabwe's National Parks, administered by the Department of National Parks and Wildlife Management, are sanctuaries free of human settlement, except of course for tourist lodges and campsites. Of the eleven National Parks, seven are primarily game reserves, the remainder being areas of outstanding natural beauty.

The game parks are: **Gonarezhou**, **Chizarira**, **Kazuma Pan**, **Mana Pools**, **Matusadona**, **Hwange** and **Zambezi**. Other areas have been designated as of unique cultural or scenic importance; they are: **Chimanimani** (montane vegetation), **Matobo** (granite rock formations and rock art), **Nyanga** (scenery and grasslands) and **Victoria Falls** (the Falls themselves).

Game reserves are unfenced and animals are free to come and go, but they rarely venture into areas of human habitation. Reserves frequently abut on hunting areas, which tend to prevent animals wandering into rural farmland. In any case, animals tend to shy away from land occupied by people and domestic stock.

If you're **camping out** in a National Park, there's little to fear from animals so long as you take a common-sense attitude. Safety hints are given on p.114. Rogue elephants and man-eating lions aren't serious dangers you need to worry about. Wildlife shies away from people and accidents invariably result from reckless human behaviour that threatens animals – rather than vice versa.

Entrance fees for the game reserves, paid at the reception office when you arrive, are standardised (and payable in local currency) at about US$1 per day for adults and half that for under-sixteens; one-week unlimited entrance is approximately US$2 for adults. For long stays, the Department of National Parks will quote an annual rate giving unlimited entrance for each park. Unless you've pre-booked **accommodation**, that too can be arranged, if available, at reception on arrival, as can camping (US$2 per tent per night).

The parks and reserves are all open to private visits. With one or two notable and very exclusive exceptions, there is virtually no private accommodation within the national parks, but accommodation and facilities provided by the Department of National Parks are excellent by any standard – and very cheap.

Apart from Hwange – the most accessible of the game parks and serviced by reasonably priced game-viewing minibuses – the reserves are negotiable only in private cars or by going on organised safaris or game drives. Transport options for each park are outlined in the relevant chapters.

BOTSWANA'S PARKS

Botswana's National Parks are far wilder than Zimbabwe's – and far less well maintained. There are few facilities laid on for self-caterers – a handful of campsites with makeshift showers and cold running water – but most of these are in a poor state. These public campsites, however, are not to be confused with what are called camps, or sometimes lodges. These camps, the only organised accommodation in the parks, are expensive

and very comfortable with laid-on game drives and activities – all very much in line with Botswana's policy of "low-density high-cost" tourism.

This upmarket approach led the government to impose **hefty park entrance fees** in 1989 to discourage self-catering travellers (South Africans in particular), who bring their own supplies from outside the country and spend little or nothing during their visit. The wisdom of the policy is hotly debated in Botswana but as long as it stands it means daily entrance fees of P50 per person in most parks or P30 if you're staying in one of the lodges or on a licensed safari. There are additional fees for vehicles (foreign reg, P10 per day/ Botswana reg, P2 per day) and for camping (self-catering P20 per person per night/ through a licensed operator P10). Entrance and camping fees for children are half price, and all charges for Botswana residents and citizens are a fraction of the cost.

This means that if you want to make your own way, camping in the National Parks, it will cost a minimum of P70 per day per person. On the upside, because Botswana's small population (just over a million) is concentrated along its eastern flank, most of the country is very wild. A massive 35 percent of the country is unfenced wilderness, roamed by game. Outside the National Parks, therefore, you'll still see wildlife, and while you won't get into the heart of Botswana's two prime game areas – **Moremi Wildlife Reserve** in the Okavango Delta and **Chobe Game Reserve** – without paying, you can still have a terrific time around the edges. With a 4WD vehicle and good supplies of food and water you could camp rough and have an unparalleled wilderness adventure. How and where to do this is covered in chapters Eight, Nine and Ten.

PART TWO

ZIMBABWE

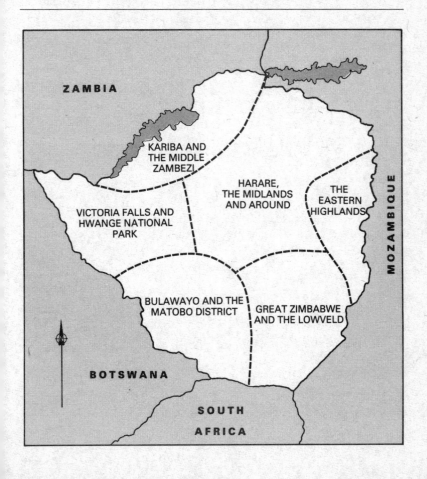

ZAMBIA

KARIBA AND
THE MIDDLE
ZAMBEZI

HARARE,
THE MIDLANDS
AND AROUND

THE
EASTERN
HIGHLANDS

VICTORIA FALLS AND
HWANGE NATIONAL
PARK

BULAWAYO AND THE
MATOBO DISTRICT

GREAT ZIMBABWE
AND THE LOWVELD

MOZAMBIQUE

BOTSWANA

SOUTH

AFRICA

Introduction

In its second decade of independence, Zimbabwe is waking to the potential of tourism. Its natural assets – abundant wildlife and beautiful scenery – are now supplemented by a growing tourism infrastructure. Whether you're after a classic African safari or something more piquant – white-water rafting, canoeing or tracking African wildlife with a professional guide – you won't find a better choice anywhere on the continent. Which is not to say the country is overrun by visitors. You'll still find solitude and wild places, preserved by scrupulous policies of restricting numbers in national parks. If you're travelling independently, you'll find Zimbabwe an easy and rewarding country.

Considering that Zimbabwe was locked in a civil war just over a decade ago, the neat, well-kept feeling of the country and the openness of its people are remarkable. Inevitably certain post-Independence economic problems remain, and imports of luxury items are often in short supply, though local produce is both easy to come by and inexpensive. Furthermore, despite the dearth of vehicles and spares – Zimbabwe's roads resemble a museum of old cars – there are well-maintained roads and a reliable, inexpensive transport network of buses, trains, coaches and planes. It's no exaggeration to say that Zimbabwe provides one of the friendliest African experiences.

Which is not to suggest that the country will key with images of "unchanging Africa". For while Zimbabwe's beautiful wilderness and game areas feel thoroughly African, in other respects the marks of **colonialism** are deeply etched. Even in remote rural areas traditional costume has all but disappeared and the city suburbs retain those British niceties of milk, postal and newspaper deliveries. Things are changing, though, and in town most hotels have replaced tinkling pianos with the energetic guitars of Zimbabwe pop.

For a small nation, Zimbabwe has a generous share of **traditional cultural sights**, from the **rock art** of long-gone hunter-gatherers to the ruined stone palaces of past Shona rulers – most notably **Great Zimbabwe** itself. And on a contemporary level, if you look beyond the airport art of the curio shops, you'll find one of the most vibrant movements in modern African **sculpture**.

The drastic water shortages experienced during the **drought** of the early 90s are thankfully now a thing of the past, although the country's lakes and dams will take some years to recover.

■ Physical make-up

Physically, Zimbabwe is divided by the central **highveld** plateau, which is covered by massive granite outcrops called **kopjes**. Because of its malaria-free, moderate climate and prime lands, the highveld became the white-dominated political and economic hub of Rhodesia. Rising from the plateau 350km along the Mozambique border are the **Eastern Highlands**, peaking at 2400m in the narrow belt of the **Nyanga and Chimanimani Mountains**. The colonial carve-up of Rhodesia has left the country's richest farms and all the large towns and cities above 1200m, on the highveld.

To the north and south, the plateau falls away through the intermediate **middleveld plateaus**, lying between 600 and 1200m, to the **lowveld** regions. A further 600m below the northern lowveld is a narrow strip in the **Zambezi Valley** and a broader tract to the south, between the **Limpopo and Save rivers**. These two lowveld sections share a similar climate and vegetation, quite distinct from that of the highveld – lower rainfall and hotter. On Zimbabwe's dry western flank, the tree **savannah** of the **Hwange area** drifts across the border to merge with the Kalahari sands of Botswana.

■ Where to go

Obviously, your own personal interests – and time – will dictate where you travel. If you just have a couple of weeks to spare, then the major attractions must include **Lake Kariba**, with its boating and game-viewing; **Hwange National Park**, the country's largest game reserve; the **Victoria Falls**; and the stone ruins at **Great Zimbabwe**. All are easily accessible on local transport, or you can make life easy with cheap flight packages or airtours that drop you down at hotels and take you to the sights.

Away from these brochure-highlights, Zimbabwe has miles of untramelled country to offer: some easily reached and some remote. For **hikers**, the 350-km strip of the **Eastern Highlands** provides dramatic and varied countryside in the shadow of Zimbabwe's highest peak, 2592m **Mount Nyangani**. The **Matobo Hills**, near Bulawayo, in the south, combine limitless walks through beautiful **granite hills** with one of the world's highest concentrations of ancient **rock paintings**. The finest national parks for face-to-face **game-viewing** are **Mana Pools** and **Chizarira** in the north.

In the cities, lively sounds blasting out from street corners and small shops immediately confirm Zimbabwe's reputation for **music**. At nightclubs you'll certainly have a chance to hear some of the big names that form the country's number one cultural export. Music aside, the **cities** are enjoyable simply to stroll about, taking in markets, parks, beer gardens, street life and local style.

Languages and Religions

Nearly seventy percent of Zimbabweans are mother-tongue Shona-speakers, spread across most of the country and beyond its borders, while Ndebele is the first language of fifteen percent, living around Bulawayo and the Matabeleland area of the southwest. Both are official languages, as is English – the most widely used language in Zimbabwe.

English is the language of the media, shop and street signs. You will need nothing else to book a room, eat out, make travel arrangements or ask directions – there's hardly anywhere in the country where you won't find someone who speaks it and particularly in the cities people speak it excellently.

Even between blacks, you'll hear English spoken – sometimes simply as a lingua franca, but also as a status symbol, especially among the middle class. In the city streets you may also hear a style of banter that lurches back and forth between English and Shona or Ndebele.

Although attempts to speak Ndebele or Shona as a means of communication may be more or less redundant, however, don't be put off trying – a symbolic attempt to greet people in their mother tongue is much appreciated, although also an invitation for you to be jokingly tested to the limits of your ability. Just mastering the greetings will open up channels of communication and assure friendly responses.

Ndebele

As a young language derived from Zulu within the last 170 years, **Ndebele** is fairly homogenous and closely related to its ancestral roots. When Mzilikazi (founder of the Ndebele) fled north from Zululand in the 1820s he forged a new state from his core of followers and Sotho, Pedi, Tswana and other elements that he collected on his way. Ndebele and Zulu are mutually understandable – about 95 percent of the languages remains common. Zulu is one of South Africa's most widely spoken languages.

Shona

Shona is a relatively ancient language which has had many centuries on the plateau to diversify into six main dialects, which are divided into over thirty minor ones. Of the major dialects, **Zezuru**, spoken in central Zimbabwe, has assumed the status of a prestige form because it's spoken in Harare and on the radio.

As a magnet for people from all over the country, Harare has become a linguistic melting pot, where a new Shona form, known as "Town Shona" or "ChiHarare", has begun to develop. Characteristics include borrowings from English and an informality, particularly in the disappearance of pronoun forms to denote respect.

Chilapalapa

Finally, it's worth mentioning **Chilapalapa**, a pidgin English/Ndebele that evolved so whites could give orders to their black workers. It has no proper grammar – all verbs exist only in the imperative form – and has now become a very unfashionable symbol of exploitation. It is nevertheless still used by some white households, and on farms.

■ Religion

Despite unfounded pre-Independence fears that "Marxist ZANU" would ban religion and abolish Christmas, Zimbabwe remains a predominantly Christian country – with a strong undercurrent of traditional religion. Spirit mediums are consulted to make contact with the ancestors, who are still important.

Probably because it incorporated indigenous beliefs, **Catholicism** is the biggest church with nearly a million adherents.

There's also a plethora of **African churches**, like the 300,000-strong **Zimbabwe Assemblies of God** denomination, which became independent in 1960 and now spreads throughout central Africa. Others, like the **Vapostori** sects, arose spontaneously in Zimbabwe and have their own

SHONA AND NDEBELE WORDS AND PHRASES

GREETINGS AND RESPONSES

Greetings are very important in both Shona and Ndebele society. They can also get quite complicated. The following greetings will be appropriate for most situations you'll encounter, and are the ones to use when you first meet someone or pass them on the road. Other greetings exist for use between people who know each other. When you approach someone's homestead or yard it's polite to wait outside until you're invited in.

	SHONA	NDEBELE
A: Hello (s)	Mhoro	Sawubona
Hello (pl)	Mhoroi	Salibonani
B: Hello (reply)	Ehoi	Yebo
A: How are you?	Makadii/Makadini	Unjani (s) Linjani (pl)
B: Fine, and you?	Tiripo makadiiwo	Sikhona, unjani wena
A: Fine	Tiripo	Sikhona
Good morning	Mangwanani	Livuke njani
Good afternoon	Masikati	Litshonile
Good evening	Manheru	Litshone njani
Thank you	Ndatenda/Masvita	Siyabonga kakulu
Come in/forward	Tiswikevo!	Ekuhle!

AFTER GREETING

What's your name?	Munonzi ani?	Ubani ibizo lakho?
My name is Tony	Zita rangu ndi Tony	
I am Tony	Ndini Tony	Elami igama ngingu (pron:nyingu) Tony
Pleased to meet you	Ndinofara ku-ku-ziva-i	Ngiya thaba ukukwazi
Where are you from?	Munobva kupi?	Uvelaphi?
I'm from Britain/	Ndinobva kuBritain/	Ngivela e Bilithani/
US/Germany	kuAmerica/kuGermany	Melika/Jelimana

SAYING GOODBYE

Stay well (Person leaving)	Chisarai	U/Lisale kuhle
Go well (Person staying)	Fambai zvakanaka	Uhambe kuhle(s) Nihambe kuhle(pl)
See you	Tichaonana	Sizalibona njalo

TRAVEL

Where is the bus stop?	Chiteshi chiri kupi?	Singaphi isiteshi samabhasi
When does the bus leave?	Bhazi richaenda rihni?	Izawuhamba nini ibhasi
When will the bus come?	Bhazi richauya rihni?	
Is there a bus to Bulawayo today?	Nhasi pane bhazi ririkuenda kuBulawayo here?	Kunebhasi leya KaBulawayo lamuhla?
Does this bus go to Harare?	Bhazi iri rinoenda kuHarare here?	Lebhasi iyaya yini e-Harare
Where's the road to Binga?	Mugwagwa unoenda kuBinga uri kupi?	Uphi umgwaco loya e-Binga
Road	Mugwagwa	Mugwaco
Car	Motokari	Imoto
Train	Chitima	Isitimela
Station/bus stop	Chiteshi	Isiteshi
Go on foot	Ku-enda netsoka	Hamba ngonya wo

SHOPPING

Where's the market?	Musika uri kupi?	Ikuphi imakethe
Have you got . . .?	Mune . . . here?	Une. . . yini?
I'd like . . . please	Ndipei/wo	Ngicela
How much is it?	Imarii?	Yimalini?

BASICS AND SIGNS

	SHONA	NDEBELE		SHONA	NDEBELE
Yes	Ehe	Yebo	When?	. . . rihni?	. . . nini?
No	Aiwa	Hayi	Where?	. . . kupi?	. . . ngaphi?
Thank you	Tatenda/	Siyabonga	Now	Zvino	Khathesi
	masviita		Today	Nhasi	Lamuhla
after a meal	Taguta		Tomorrow	Mangwana	Kusasa
Please	Ndapota		Yesterday	Nezuro	Izolo
Good/nice!	Zvakanaka!	Kuhle	DANGER	NGOZI	INGOZI
Sorry	Ndine urombo	Ncesi	MEN	VARUME	AMADODA
			WOMEN	VAKADZI	ABAFAZI

FOOD

Fruit	Michero	Izithelo	Vegetables		
Banana/s	Bhanana/	Ama-	Potatoes	Mbatatisi	Amagwili
	mabhanana		Tomatoes	Matomasi	Utamatisi
Orange	Ranjisi	Ama-orintshi	Leaves/greens	Muriwo	Umbhido
Peanuts	Nzungu	Ama-zambane			
Guava	Gwavha	Ama-gwava	**Meat**	**Nyama**	**Inyama**
			Meat of . . .	Nyama ye . . .	Inyama ye . . .
Grains			chicken	huku	nkukhu
Stiff	Sadza	Sadza	beef	mombe	nkomo
porridge			goat	mbudzi	mbuzi
Maize	Chibage	Umbila	pork	nguruve	ngulube
Drinks			**Miscellaneous**		
Tea	Tii	Itiye	Bread	Chingwa	Sinkhwa
Coffee	Kofi	Ikofi	Salt	Munyu	Uswayi
Water	Mvura	Amanzi	Sugar	Shuga	Ushukela
Milk	Mukaka	Uchago	Honey	Uchi	Uju
Beer	Doro/hwahwa	Utshwala	Butter	Bhata	Ibatha
Fruit squash	Mazoe	Mazoe	Fish	Hove	Inhlanzi
			Eggs	Mazai	Amaqanda

Classes in Shona and Zulu (very close to Ndebele) are run regularly in the UK at the *Africa Centre* 38 King Street, London WC2 (☎071/836 1973).
Harald Vieth's **Shona phrasebook** *Have a nice trip in Zimbabwe: a colloquial guide to Shona*, published by Mambo press in Zimbabwe, is a useful start. Unfortunately no similar book exists for Ndebele.

PLACE NAMES

After Independence, many place names were changed. Some changes like Salisbury to Harare were substantial. Others were more subtle – orthographic adjustments and corrections of colonial mispronunciation. This can be confusing as some diehards still insist on using the old names. These are the important ones you're likely to encounter:

NEW NAME	OLD NAME	NEW NAME	OLD NAME	NEW NAME	OLD NAME
Chimanimani	Melsetter	Harare	Salisbury	Mazowe	Mazoe
Chinoyi	Sinoia	Hwange	Wankie	Mutare	Umtali
Chipinge	Chipinga	Kadoma	Gatooma	Mvurwi	Umvukwee
Chivu	Enkeldoorn	Kwe Kwe	Que Que	Nyanga	Inyanga
Dete	Dett	Marondera	Marandellas	Shurugwi	Selukwe
Guruve	Sipolilo	Masvingo	Fort Victoria	Somabhula	Somabula
Gweru	Gwelo	Matobo	Matopos	Zvishavane	Shabani

Many **street names**, too, have been changed. The most important are detailed where relevant in the text.

practices and martyrs. The Mazowe Vapostori believe that their founder, Shoniwa, died and was resurrected as John of the Wilderness. You could well come across the characteristic services of these sects, held outdoors in remote places.

There are also small **Hindu**, **Muslim** and **Jewish** communities, based almost exclusively in the urban centres.

Money and Costs

Zimbabwe's currency is Zimbabwe dollars (Z$ or ZWD), often styled *bucks*. Notes come in 2, 5, 10 and 20 dollar denominations and there are coins of 1, 5, 10, 20 and 50 cents and Z$1. At the time of writing the rate is around Z$6 = US$1, and Z$9 = £1.

■ Banks and Exchange

Changing money can be a tedious business, frequently involving long queues in banks. Some have foreign exchange counters to help speed up the process. The most convenient of all are the bank branches inside some of the expensive hotels, like those in the *Zimbabwe Sun* chain, whose rates are the same as in town banks. There's rarely any queue, but you're normally asked for a room number.

Usual **bank opening hours** are Monday–Friday 8am–3pm, with Wednesday early closing at 1pm and Saturday at 11am. Out of hours, you can sometimes change money at the hotel cashier's desks – particularly in larger establishments. But don't count on it, if you're not staying there.

Exchange Control Regulations

Zimbabwe has strict **exchange control regulations**, but you can bring in as much foreign currency as you wish, in cash or

travellers' cheques. Everything must be declared on arrival, when you'll be given a **currency declaration form** which you need to have stamped each time you change money and hand in when you leave the country. It may or may not be scrutinised.

Because of the heavy restrictions on Zimbabweans taking money out the country, you'll find people prepared to make favourable **exchange deals**. It's pretty risky, requires considerable trust and is generally only done by people who know each other. You may also be approached to change Zimbabwe dollars for travellers' cheques or cash at somewhere around twice the bank rate. If you decide to do so, make sure you can account for it on your currency declaration form, or that you have a good story. Whether to succumb is a matter of conscience in a country trying to preserve its resources, and also a question of nerve – currency-fiddling is taken seriously.

One attempt to rein in the black market is the insistence that tourists pay **hotel bills in foreign currency**.

■ Costs

As a general rule, all kinds of **imported goods** – and locally manufactured goods based on imported raw materials – are very expensive, especially so for local people whose wages are low. Zimbabwe can also be fairly expensive if you

---

A NOTE ON CURRENCY AND PRICES

Zimbabwe's currency has fluctuated wildly over the past five years. In just two years after 1990 it lost nearly two-thirds of its value against sterling and the US dollar. Meanwhile Z$ prices have rocketed, making any attempt to give prices in local currency pointless. This has not, however, made the country much more expensive for foreign visitors. Despite the instability of the Z$, most prices, when translated into hard currency have remained surprisingly constant. Many tourist facilities such as hotels and safaris now officially quote prices in US$, although other services such as car hire and transport are still officially quoted in Z$. In this book, for the sake of consistency, **all** Zimbabwean prices are quoted in a US dollar equivalent. (See also *Hotel and Safari Rates*, p.38, for an explanantion of Zimbabwe's three-tier pricing structure for hotels.)

want to go on **safaris**, white-water rafting or **rent a car**. **Food and drink**, on the other hand, are cheap, particularly farm produce, and even better value if you buy at markets.

By staying in more economical hotels, using *National Parks'* accommodation, eating a large breakfast every day at one of the hotels and a couple of smaller meals and using local transport you could get by on **US$20–30 per day**. If you are camping or staying in the cheapest accommodation, eating in local places, and using local transport, you could cut that by about 30 percent. For around **US$35–65 per day** you could live it up, staying in medium-range hotels, taking the odd flight or travelling by express coach or train and eating three meals a day at restaurants. If you're staying in five-star international hotels or private game lodges you can expect to pay anything upwards of **US$150** per day.

Transport is inexpensive. If you use local buses rather than tourist facilities you can cover large distances for a few dollars. Express coaches and first or second class train travel are more expensive but still extremely reasonable. (Most trips, such as Harare to Bulawayo, or Bulawayo to Victoria Falls, cost under **US$10** by coach or train). **Car rental**, on the other hand, starts at around US$45 a day (unlimited distance) – plus petrol.

Accommodation is generally cheaper for two or more sharing. In **larger towns**, cheap doubles in hotels go for US$15–35. You'll get a taste of luxury (newspapers, swimming pool and breakfasts thrown in) for around US$35-65 at the mid-range hotels.

Some small towns have only a single hotel, which may be beyond reach on a very tight budget but there's usually a **campsite** or disused **caravan park**. **Camping** or dormitory accommodation in **hostels** costs out at around US$5 per person.

Many game and recreation areas have excellent value **National Parks accommodation** for under US$10 per person for fully equipped self-contained lodges with one or two double bedrooms. Some parks, including the popular Hwange National Park also have two-person chalets (shared cooking, washing and toilets) for even less.

Food is cheap if you eat where the locals do and combine it with self-catering. You can easily eat a filling meal of *sadza* and chicken or meat for a couple of dollars. A simple meal at one of the smarter restaurants need not cost much more than US$5 a head, while for US$15–20 you can get a three or four course blow-out. Good **street snacks** like corn on the cob (*chibage*) can be had for under a dollar. A couple of these can make a reasonable lunch. Beer and minerals such as *Coca-Cola* are the standard drinks – both plentiful and considerably cheaper than in Britain or the US.

HOTEL AND SAFARI RATES

All Zimbabwe's hotels and safari lodges are obliged to demand payment from foreign visitors in hard currency. You can pay either with travellers' cheques, foreign bank notes or by credit card. **Do not** change money into Z$ to make payments – it is no longer possible to simply show a bureau de change or bank receipt proving that you've legitimately changed sufficient money.

To further complicate matters, most hotels and safari operators also charge a higher rate (usually quoted in US$) to visitors. They are **not** obliged to and one or two hotels steadfastly adhere to a single rate (quoted in Z$). Even if you pay no more than a Zimbabwean, you do still have to pay it in forex.

Most (but not all) hotels and safari lodges and operators, in fact, have three charge bands: a local one for Zimbabeans, a higher regional one for residents of neighbouring countries including South Africa and (steepest of the lot) a non-residents' one for everyone else.

There is no standardised ratio for the three rates, but as a rough rule Southern Africans pay thirty percent less than visitors from outside the region. Like other non-residents they have to settle up in forex – rands and pula are fine.

SALES TAX – SAVE MONEY, BOOK AHEAD

Zimbabwe charges **sales tax** of around ten percent on many goods and services, including most tourist activities. The levy is already included in prices so you won't be aware of it most of the time. However, you can save the tax by **booking before you leave home** if you know you're going on safari, or staying in hotels or lodges. At the time of writing just about everything paid for abroad is exempt from sales tax.

(See *Sleeping* on pp.42–44 for further accommodation details, including the hotel price codes used throughout this book.)

Getting Around

As elsewhere in Africa, patience is critical for getting around on public transport. Leave yourself plenty of time for journeys and be prepared for long waits if you take local buses or hitch. Trains are a bit erratic, sometimes arriving spot on time, sometimes hours late. Luxury coaches and air travel are pretty reliable.

▨ Buses and Coaches

In the absence of a national bus system, the country is covered by a complex network of private, local bus companies, which are cheap and crowded. These **private line buses** run short routes as well as long hauls and while they're sometimes dilapidated, and irregular, they're also fun to travel in, even when they occasionally break down. Passengers are friendly and display remarkable stoicism on wearing journeys. There are also some new-style "articulated" buses, which are faster and less congested. If you've more money to spare, you can pay for more comfort on the **express coaches,** which operate along a few major routes.

Long distance local buses

Catching **local buses** (still referred to by whites as *African buses*) can be confusing. They're not geared to tourism, so clear information is thin on the ground. Several companies often ply the same route with no central co-ordination, and often you'll receive conflicting information about bus times. Ask around to build up a plausible picture of departure times.

The safest rule, however – certainly in smaller towns – is to **arrive early** at the bus station. Buses often leave at 6am and, although the 6am bus may be delayed for want of passengers until after 7am, it may also leave before schedule if there's heavy demand. Between the main cities an early start is less crucial as buses depart throughout the day.

Most centres have a **main bus station** – invariably adjoining the market. Cities have several: one for town services, one for the surrounding area, and another for long-distance routes. In most areas the long-distance bus station is referred to as the *musika*, which means market (or in Bulawayo the *renkini*). The one for town or the immediate region is usually called the *terminus*. In rural areas the **bus stop**

may be under a prominent tree with a hand-painted sign tacked onto the trunk.

Long-distance buses stop along the way. You can buy boiled eggs, cooked maize and beans, roasted peanuts, buns or local fruit through the window. Carry plenty of coins – change can be a problem. You can also get off to buy minerals, but it's advisable to carry an empty bottle to exchange against the deposit or the shopkeeper may be reluctant to let you take your drink away. Take a full water bottle – you'll need the liquid. Several hours' consumption of syrupy, tooth-stripping drinks can get a bit much.

A lot of travelling goes on at the **weekend**, especially towards the end of a month and around public holidays, most notably Christmas. Buses get jam-packed, so try to plan your journeys to avoid these times.

On all buses, most people are scrupulously honest, but it pays to watch your **baggage**. Especially during busy periods, *tsotsis* (crooks) prey on travellers, either picking pockets or stealing baggage from the roof-rack. Wherever possible travel light and take your luggage onto the bus, where you can keep an eye on it. Hefty packs are a distinct disadvantage in any case. There are no luggage racks inside and you may end up with your luggage on your lap if the bus is full, besides having to struggle past dozens of people.

Express coaches

Express coaches run between main centres, stopping at important towns along the way. They are the most comfortable, reliable and fastest form of public transport – and cost about the same as second class rail travel.

The expresses have a totally different ambience to the local services. Efficiently run, they keep to an accurate timetable with scheduled stops for hotel teas; many pick up from one of the tourist hotels – easier to get to than local bus stations which are always some way from the centre. Between them, *Ajay* and *Express* run services Harare–Mutare, Harare–Bulawayo, Bulawayo–Victoria Falls and further afield to Francistown in Botswana. It's usually possible to get a seat, though booking ahead is advisable (especially for an international run).

Town buses

Municipal bus services operate in both high- and low-density suburbs in the larger towns:

Harare, Bulawayo, Mutare, and Masvingo. In the first two, though, buses are often full and infrequent, so expect to queue for a long time for a bus during rush hours. Public transport is a real problem in the cities and in Harare you'll see people still waiting to get home at 9pm. If you travel during the late morning or early afternoon things are considerably better. You pay the driver when you get on. Fares are cheap.

■ Trains

You'd have to be a jaded old cynic to pass up the opportunity to take the **steam train to Victoria Falls**, one of those Great Railway Journeys of the World. The two other routes, **Harare–Bulawayo** and **Harare–Mutare**, though no longer steam, also have a lot going for them.

Rail travel is a comfortable and laid-back way of getting around, particularly for couples cornering a *coupe* (small private compartment). As a couple, you need to go under the same name to fulfil notions of married respectability. On your own, you share a four- or six-berth (depending on which class you travel) single-sex compartment.

There's a **night service** on each of the three routes above, plus a day train between Harare and Bulawayo, which isn't recommended. Travelling overnight, your seat becomes a bunk, hence throwing in a night's accommodation for the fare. If you're keeping costs down, the berths are comfortable enough in a sleeping bag. But inexpensive **bedding** is well worth it for a night of freshly ironed sheets with plump feather pillows and thick woollen blankets. Someone comes round once the train is moving to make up your bed. **Dinner** – meat and three veg style – and **drinks** are served on the Victoria Falls train. Don't expect linen tablecloths and silver service. It's all a bit cursory, but can be fun if you're not expecting too much. Take some snacks in case you're delayed in arriving as they don't do breakfast.

Reservations

To ensure a *coupe* you need to **book in advance**. The Bulawayo-Victoria Falls service is US$8 first class, US$5 second. Names and compartment numbers are posted up at the station an hour or two beforehand so you know where to board the train. First class has bigger compartments with wider and fewer beds and is much quieter. Second class is thoroughly acceptable, but can get a bit raucous, either from the level of partying, or the number of babies. Economy (third) class is best avoided; you sit upright all night with nowhere to stretch out.

Buying tickets for trains can be as confusing as for local buses. You have to queue twice; first to reserve your place and then again at the ticket office to pay the fare. If you want bedding on the train, buy your bedding voucher at the same time – it's a little cheaper and saves you the hassle of finding elusive ticket inspectors on the train.

■ Flights

Air Zimbabwe has efficient, regular and cheap flights between the main towns and to the big four tourist centres – Victoria Falls, Hwange, Kariba and Great Zimbabwe. If you travel on **standby** at the weekend, there are substantial reductions.

The regular single fare between Harare and Bulawayo is roughly US$45. For US$120 you can get a return ticket from **Harare to Victoria Falls** which allows you to stop off at Hwange and Kariba at no extra cost and for however long you like. To visit the Great Zimbabwe ruins, a return

---

STEAM TRAINS

It's hard not to regard as eccentric a package that lists as attractions: supper in a dining car stabled at a steam depot, sleeping in a coach in the grounds of a railway museum, and travelling along the world's third longest stretch of straight track.

If, however, old locos steam you up, *Rail Safaris* offer the option of two weeks railing along Zimbabwe's tracks, passing nights among rolling stock in shunting yards and days making your acquaintance with Garratt locomotives. They also operate the more conventional six-day *Zambezi*

Special steam safari – aimed more at romatics than steamheads. Prices start at US$550 per person for the full Bulawayo-Vic Falls return trip. It's twenty or forty percent cheaper if you only go one way depending on which direction you choose.

In Zimbabwe you can book through *Rail Safaris*, 2c Prospect Ave, Raylton, Bulawayo (Fax and ☎75575). **In Britain** contact: *Leisurail*, PO Box 113, Peterborough PE1 1LE (☎0733/51780; Fax 892601).

fare from **Harare to Masvingo** costs around US$50.

Flights are **bookable in advance** in the UK at *Air Zimbabwe*'s London office (☎071/491 0009). The main office in Harare is at Third St/ Speke Ave (☎794481).

■ Taxis and ETs

Taxis and ETs (emergency taxis) run in most towns. **Taxis** are usually (but not exclusively) *Renault 4s* and will pick up any number of people for a single metered fare. They're moderately priced and are certainly worth using to get to nightspots outside city centres.

All official taxis are metered and there's little point in asking for an estimate before you leave — the drivers tend to make up a random underestimate. Few rides, however, should cost more than US$8 and most short trips in town will be closer to US$3. Illegal unlicensed taxis operate openly in spite of frequent fines, which they afford through higher fares. Licensed taxis are cheaper, but aren't always easy to find. The confusion is increased by the unlicensed taxis' practice of operating under remarkably similar names and logos to their legal counterparts. Amongst others in Harare you'll find *Rixi Taxis* (licensed) and *Trixi Taxis* (unlicensed).

ETs are larger, usually *Peugeot 404s*, and charge a fixed fare for a fixed route, usually leaving from a bus station. They set out only when they're bursting with passengers, which can mean an uncomfortable wait while people are gathered to shoehorn inside. They are quite difficult to use, because they're usually full and their routes require prior knowledge — but they are worth figuring out if you're staying in Harare or any of the big towns for a while.

■ Driving and Car Rental

Zimbabwe has **low traffic** and a well-maintained **tarred road network** covering most of the country. This combination makes for very pleasant driving. In a week — albeit a rather full one — you could hit most of the highlights, and in a fortnight you could do a full circuit of the country. Distances between towns aren't great: Harare to Bulawayo or Kariba takes about five hours, for example, and it's three or four hours from the capital to the Eastern Highlands.

There's a snag however. Vehicle and spares **shortages**, due to lack of foreign currency, are a major problem. New cars are virtually

unobtainable and second-hand ones enormously expensive. Vehicles often lie crippled from the lack of spares. This makes **car rental** expensive, with *Hertz*, *Avis* and *Echo* — the only operators with national networks — all running dwindling fleets of ageing vehicles. In Harare *Truck and Car Hire*, *Afric-Car Hire*, *Fleet Budget Car Rentals*, *Impexo Rent-a-Car* and *Mike Harris Car Sales* also rent cars. In Bulawayo there's *Transit Car & Truck Hire*. The locally based operators are worth looking up, because some of their deals are better than the big three.

If you know exactly when you'll want a car, it's also worth thinking about organising **rental in your home country** (see details of the package operators in *Basics*) before you leave — it can work out cheaper. Booking ahead, either from abroad or in Zimbabwe, is wise too at times of heavy demand.

Wherever you book, look through the **small print** before taking a vehicle. The collision damage waiver is usually invalid if you go into certain areas — such as 10km or more beyond **Hwange's Main Camp**, where several cars have suffered damage through bad road conditions. The same is true of renting cars at Kariba to go to **Mana Pools**. People do take the cars over Mana's rough roads but if anything goes wrong, the responsibility and expense are yours.

Driving

Driving in this British ex-colony is on the left. Foreign driving **licences** are valid for up to 90 days, indefinitely if they're from the following countries: Botswana, Malawi, Namibia, South Africa, Swaziland or Zambia. **Petrol** is easily available.

A **word of warning**. Because cars are often in poor condition, lights and brakes don't always work well. People tend also to drink and drive as a matter of course. So, always drive defensively and never rely on the good sense of other motorists.

■ Hitching

Hitching is easy. People aren't afraid to pick up hitchers and they will often go out of their way to be helpful.

There are two types of hitching: either with middle-class people, where payment is not in question, or with people who pick up hitchers to help pay for the journey. **"Paying rides"** may well be obvious, because you'll be with fellow

CAR RENTAL DEALS

	Echo	Avis	Hertz	Mike Harris	Truck & Car	Afric-Car Hire	Impexo	Fleet	Transit
	Nationwide offices (see listings for each town for addresses)								
Harare	✔	✔	✔	✔	✔	✔	✔		✔
Bulawayo	✔	✔	✔					✔	
Victoria Falls		✔	✔						
Mutare	✔		✔						
Kariba		✔	✔						
Masvingo			✔						
Hwange			✔						
Chiredzi			✔						

passengers in the back of a pick-up for instance, or not so obvious if it's just you in an ordinary car. In the latter case enquire if you can make a contribution. Payments never exceed the equivalent of local bus fares, so it's always affordable.

Leaving Bulawayo and Harare, it's easiest to catch a bus or taxi to the outskirts and wait on the main road.

■ Cycling

Zimbabwe is great for **cycling** if you have the stamina. Roads are generally in good shape and tarred, and in cities bikes are ideal as there are cycle tracks everywhere alongside the streets. The distances between towns are long, but there are small settlements en route where you can stop at a rural store for a rest and a drink. Zimbabwe's stable inland climate means strong wind isn't a problem, but cycling is nicest during the dry, cool months. Bicycles can easily be transported on top of local buses or on trains if you need a break.

The big drawback however is that bicycle **spares** are not readily available, even in Harare. If you've brought a **mountain bike** with you, you definitely will not be able to get replacement parts. Maintenance apart, though, mountain bikes have major advantages if you want to venture off the tar, giving you a really wide measure of freedom and sparing punctures and spoke breakages.

Buying a bike in Zimbabwe is an option, but they tend to be expensive and of the sturdy and reliable variety – hard on the thighs. And remember, before you sell it at the end of your stay, that you can't take the money out of the country. **Bike rental** is possible at Victoria Falls, in Bulawayo and Harare, where you can rent mountain bikes from an operator that also takes cycling tours around the city.

Accommodation

Finding places to stay in Zimbabwe should rarely pose problems. There's a wide variety of good accommodation across a broad price range – from US$5 for a two-person chalet in one of the national parks to US$100 per person and more for sheer luxury in Harare's international hotels and safari lodges. And if you're on the lowest of budgets you can rely on campsites throughout the country.

■ Hotels

There are few very cheap **hotels** in Zimbabwe but, considering the generally high (and frequently luxurious) standards, most are quite reasonably priced.

The cheapest hotels are to be found in the large towns. In Harare, Bulawayo and Mutare you'll find basic doubles from US$15 and up.

Smaller centres usually have a single hotel with doubles from US$30. In tourist areas like Victoria Falls, Kariba and Nyanga expect to pay US$35 upwards. All the main tourist centres also have hotels of international standard – which can be fun now and then, but are obviously far removed from the daily reality of Zimbabwe.

All but the cheapest hotels are invariably clean, with freshly ironed linen. The worst are noisy watering holes doubling up as brothels; warnings are given where relevant in the guide.

■ National Parks Accommodation

The **National Parks accommodation** lodges, cottages and chalets are some of Zimbabwe's real bargains. Set in the loveliest spots in the parks, they offer outstanding self-catering deals, in one- or two-bedroomed units, at very low rates. All come with basic furniture, fridges, pots and pans, blankets, linen and towels and are serviced daily.

Most basic are the **chalets**, starting at US$5 for one double bedroom and providing outside cooking and communal washing facilities. Self-contained **cottages** with kitchen and bathroom start from under US$8. The **lodges**, from US$10, have everything, including crocks and cutlery.

Across the country during school holidays and at weekends near the cities, *National Parks'* places get pretty full and advance **booking** is essential. It's not a bad idea to reserve at other times too, especially for more popular places like Hwange and Mana Pools. You can book up to six months ahead – not as excessive as it sounds as some places are in such demand that accommodation is allocated by ballot.

Don't be put off, however, if you haven't reserved. You may be lucky if you just turn up. Outside the school holiday periods (see *Opening*

BOOKING FOR NATIONAL PARKS ACCOMMODATION

IN PERSON

Harare: *Department of National Parks and Wildlife Management*, National Botanical Gardens (☎706077), open Mon–Fri 7.45am to 4.15pm. To get there take Borrowdale Rd out of central Harare, turn left into Sandringham Ave, then take the first left into the Gardens.

Bulawayo: *Department of National Parks and Wildlife Management*, 140a Fife St (☎63646).

BY POST

Department of National Parks and Wildlife Management, Central Booking Office, PO Box 8151, Causeway, Harare; PO Box 2283, Bulawayo.

Hours and Holidays, pp.46–47), the majority of places have space during the week and at weekends. You can always phone to check on the position if you're in the vicinity.

■ Private self-catering

Cottages, along similar lines to National Parks' lodges, are rented out privately in several areas from around US$20 and up per night, depending on the number of beds. These are listed in the travel section under their appropriate areas.

■ Bush Camps and Safari Lodges

The ultimate place to stay in Zimbabwe is in a **bush camp**. Set in the remotest parts of the country you'll spend nights where African wildlife roams. You pay (from US$150 to several times that) not for conventional luxury but for the privilege of being in one of the world's great wilderness areas – and for the personal expertise of a professional guide constantly on hand.

Accommodation is very variable as is location. You'll find stilted "tree-houses", walk-in tents, thatched chalets, old farmhouses, stone lodges and houseboats.

■ Safari Farms and Country Lodges

Since the beginning of the 1990s a large number of farms have restyled themselves as country lodges. The emphasis is on intimacy and personalised service. You're made to feel a guest in someone's home (which indeed most of them are). They're all over the country, some near towns and others near game-viewing areas.

Those near towns provide a rural alternative to staying in the impersonal upmarket city hotels. The remoter ones are run as safari farms, set in their own game estates. The animals you'll see may include predators and antelope, but will usually represent only a small selection of Zimbabwean game. Most safari farms are no replacement for the real thing , but do provide a less demanding way of retreating to the country. Prices range from US$60 to US$200. See *Safaris* p.12 for booking details.

■ Bed and Breakfasts

Another new departure for Zimbabwe is the **Bed and Breakfast**. There aren't many at the moment, but it's worth enquiring if you want decent accommodation that bridges the gap between crash pads and hotels. B&Bs in Zimbabwe are closer to the British model than the American, with accommodation normally consisting of a room in someone's home. Breakfast is included in the price, which is usually about US$20 for a double.

■ Youth Hostels and crash pads

Harare and Bulawayo each has a youth hostel geared to travellers. Crash pads, of varying standards, but run along roughly similar lines, are a more viable option as the youth hostels fill up fast.

New crash pads are constantly springing up – mainly in the urban centres with a particularly high concentration in Harare. Prices in dorms start at US$5 per person. The worst ones are terrible fleapits, but some of the better ones offer an outstanding service to budget travellers, laying on meals and transport. Double rooms, where available, go for around US$15.

■ Camping

If you don't want to rely on hotels as a fallback then **camping** is a reliable option. The white Rhodesian passion for outdoor life has left campsites in all but the remotest parts. In towns, too, a tent will prove a big money-saver.

On the whole, **campsites** are outstandingly maintained. They provide good cooking and washing facilities, and there's usually an attendant, which greatly reduces the chances of theft. On the minus side, summer heat can make sleeping under nylon a bit of a sweat and in the national parks it's hardly any dearer to stay in a chalet. Taking a tent means you'll never be stuck for somewhere to stay, but it's worth trying to anticipate how much you'll actually use it.

As to camping supplies, a **portable stove** is useful, though there are usually plentiful supplies of firewood and fireplaces. If you want the convenience of instant heat take a cooker, but avoid gas if possible – canisters that fit *Camping Gaz* appliances are manufactured in Zimbabwe but they can be hard to come by. If you've brought your gas stove regardless, your best bet for replacement canisters is *Fereday and Sons* (see Harare Listings). Meths and petrol are more easily available fuels, and, if you can afford it, one of the compact climbers' petrol stoves is a good bet.

Communication – Post and Phone Services

Zimbabwe is pretty good for communications, both by phone – which now features direct dial – and by an albeit rather slow mail service.

■ Mail

The **postal service** retains a British colonial flavour, with familiar-looking signs in post offices instructing you how to use services and pack parcels. On the whole, mail services are reliable, if slow – though letters do sometimes fail to arrive. If you are sending anything of value, it's wise to register it.

Airmail letters to Europe don't cost much and take about a week to arrive on average. Aerogrammes are available and are even cheaper, and save the hassle of carrying a pad. All post offices (their addresses are given under listings for the main towns and cities) offer **poste restante** facilities.

INTERNATIONAL PHONE CODES

Phoning Zimbabwe from outside the country

Country code: **263**

Zimbabwe's internal trunk codes begin with 1. Drop this digit (just after the country code) when phoning from abroad.

International calls from Zimbabwe

International access code: **110**

Country codes:	Country codes:
Australia 61 (+6 to 8 hrs)	Ireland 353 (-1 to 2 hrs)
Britain 44 (-1 to 2 hrs)	New Zealand 64 (+10 hrs)
Canada 1 (-6 to 10 hrs)	US 1 (-6 to 10 hrs)

Southern Africa regional calls from Zimbabwe

When phoning within the region the international access code is replaced by a regional one.

Regional access code: **119**

Country codes:	Country codes:
Botswana 267	Namibia 264
Malawi 265	South Africa 27
Mozambique 258	Zambia 260

■ Phone

Zimbabwe's ever-improving **phone system** does sometimes get a little overloaded, but it'll usually work given enough persistence. International connections are much quicker and easier than local calls, with clearer lines overseas than to places close by. Internal lines worsen during the **rainy season**.

By far the easiest ways to make calls is to dial '0' to use the **free operator service** to connect you, though you will have to wait. It is possible, however, to **direct dial** most places within Zimbabwe and outside. There are plenty of **public call boxes** in the cities – most of them modern, user-friendly Scandinavian instruments – though you can expect to queue for public phones, especially in Harare and Bulawayo.

The Media: Press, Books, Radio and TV

Considering Zimbabwe's economic climate, the country has a healthy range of papers, magazines and books available. And with Africa's best music scene, the local radio can be a major attraction.

■ The Press

You'll see a fair quantity of **magazines and newspapers** on sale at bookshops and on city-centre street corners. Most newspapers and periodicals are in English, although you'll also find Shona and Ndebele publications.

There are two **national dailies**: *The Herald* based in Harare and *The Chronicle* in Bulawayo. Along with several other publications, they fall under the Zimbabwe Mass Media Trust, an organisation formed in 1981 to foster a press more sympathetic to government policies, but not under direct government control. Both tend towards dull worthiness, but they have occasional sparks of independence. *The Chronicle* had its hour of glory during the "Willowgate" car corruption scandal of 1988. The editor stood up to the Minister of Defence, and pursued some valiant investigative reporting, causing the Minister's eventual resignation. The editor has since been "promoted".

On **Sundays** you can pick up *The Sunday Mail* in Harare and *The Sunday News* in Bulawayo. On Fridays the *Financial Gazette* comes out, providing a staunch capitalist alternative to the mainstream press and an international supplement that gives the best world news coverage of any.

For the best news coverage in Southern Africa pick up the South African liberal *Weekly Mail*, which comes out on Fridays. In addition to excellent regional coverage you get the bonus of Britain's *Guardian Weekly*, thrown in as a regular free supplement.

Outside Harare and Bulawayo you might also check out the **local weeklies**. These tend to be quaintly parochial: reading the letters pages feels almost voyeuristic. In the Eastern Highlands look for *The Manica Post* and in Kwe Kwe the *Midlands Observer*.

Of the **monthly magazines**, the popular *Parade* achieves a delicate mix of feature articles, sport, politics and gossip, while the resilient *Moto* is definitely worth a read. A critical and very readable journal of analysis and opinion, *Moto* was founded in 1959 by *Mambo Press* (a Catholic publishing house), and reflected African views through the Sixties until its 1974 banning. It resumed publication in 1980, failed due to lack of money in 1981 and bounced back in 1982, fighting on contemporary issues like land reform.

■ Book publishing and bookshops

Zimbabwe's flourishing **publishing industry** produces fiction, poetry, drama, folk tales and children's literature. *Zimbabwe Publishing House* and *Baobab* concentrate on high-quality literature, while *Pacesetters* and *Drumbeat* produce fast-paced light reading.

There's also a wealth of well-produced and very readable school texts for all levels that provide excellent introductory material on history, geography and other aspects of Zimbabwe and a comprehensive array of reference material on flora, fauna, culture and geography. (See the

BBC WORLD SERVICE AND VOA

If you want to keep in touch with world news, the **BBC World Service** gives wider coverage than local broadcasts, and there are also excellent programmes in its Africa Service. Principal BBC wavelengths (times are GMT) are as follows:

12.095 (5–7.30am) 21.71 MHz and 17.79 MHz (9am–3.15pm), 15.07 MHz (7am–9.15pm) and 6.195 (8–10.45pm). The BBC's Harare address is PO Box 3655.

You can also receive **Voice of America** transmissions between 3 and 6.10am and from 4 to 9.30pm.

Contexts pieces on "Recent English Writing from Zimbabwe" and "Books".)

Bookshops can be found all over the country, the largest chain being *Kingstons*. Don't expect a wide range of western books, as foreign exchange restricts the number imported and they work out very expensive. Foreign paperbacks, when they don't consist of remaindered job lots, retail at around twice their cover price. Bring novels with you to swap or give away, and take the opportunity to sample the excellent and reasonably priced locally published books. The *Grass Roots Book Shops* and *Mambo Press* in Harare are worth visiting for wide selections of African literature.

■ Radio and TV

Zimbabwe has four radio stations and a TV channel, plus TV2 in Harare. **Radio 1** is the "English Service", a mixture of classical music and talk. **Radio 2** – "the music lovers' station" – broadcasts in Shona and Ndebele and plays local and South African jive. **Radio 3** is the hit-parade oriented "English Music Station", serving a mixed menu of local jive, "Europop", funk, rap, reggae, rock and so on. **Radio 4** is largely educational. Radios 1 and 3 are in stereo.

Although there are some locally produced **television** programmes it's cheaper for ZBC (Zimbabwe Broadcasting Corporation) to import, hence the large quantity of American and British padding. Broadcasts are in colour though most TVs still black and white.

Music TV is growing but it's difficult to predict programmes. Regulars are *Mvenge-mvenge* (Thurs night TV1, Wed night TV2) and *Sounds on Saturday*. Mvengemvenge is the better of the two – local and South African music videos in the main. *Sounds on Saturday* features mainly American and European pop along with the odd local, South African or reggae video. Look out also for *Our Africa*, which often features West African music, and *Teen Scene*, for local videos.

Opening Hours and Holidays

Most things start early in Zimbabwe, and shops are no exception, opening at 8am, and closing at 5pm on weekdays and at noon or 1pm on Saturdays. You can usually expect shops to close between 1 and 2pm for lunch during the week, in small places, although

PUBLIC HOLIDAYS

January 1 *New Year's Day*
Easter *Good Friday to Easter Monday*
April 18 *Independence Day*
May 1 *Worker's Day*
May 25 *Africa Day*
August 11 *Heroes Day*
August 12 *Armed Forces Day*
December 25/26 *Xmas/Boxing Day*

School Holidays (approximate)
Early December – Mid-January
Mid-April – Mid-May
Early-August – Mid-September

this isn't cast in stone. **A few large city centre supermarkets have late opening hours, while small suburban grocers and cafés selling basics also stay open after 5pm.**

Post offices open at 8.30am, and close at 4.30pm Monday to Friday and at 11am on Saturdays. **Banks** have their own irregular rhythm, opening at 8am Monday to Saturday and closing at 3pm except Wednesday (1pm closing) and Saturday (11.30am closing).

Music and Drama

For live music listings, scan the entertainments pages of the press (see Media above) and look for roughly printed posters wrapped around lamposts and on walls. Every weekend brings a choice of bands competing for punters. Details on specific venues are included through the guide. A personal selection of names to look out for is given in the *Contexts* **piece on Zimbabwean music.**

There's no awe of megastars in Zimbabwe. Musicians work hard for a living, and have to play often. **Harare** is the best place to see and hear them. The biggest events come at **month-ends**, when the names, like Thomas Mapfumo, the Bhundu Boys or Oliver Mtukudzi hold *pungwes* – a word derived from all-night rallies held by guerillas during the war – till the early hours.

Music and performance from Zimbabwe's **oral tradition** is less well known outside the country. A few collections of **folk tales and** **praise poetry** have been published in translation, but the tradition lives on and develops most effectively through **drama**. Find out about productions by affiliates of the Association of Community Theatres as well as those by the University theatre group in Harare and independent groups such as Amakhosi in Bulawayo. Most publishers have a drama list, which includes play scripts from Zimbabwe.

■ Records

Records (vinyl) are far cheaper than the equivalent outside the country and are usually good quality due to small pressing runs. Pre-recorded cassettes are another story and best avoided if possible. Blank cassettes are prohibitively expensive when they're available.

There are two record companies, *Gramma Records* and the *Zimbabwe Music Corporation (ZMC)*. The fact that they pay no advances and low royalties to their groups enables them to take chances with recordings, which ensures that a large number of groups get onto vinyl, only to disappear if they show no instant profit. Several of the records recommended in the *Contexts* section on music may well prove to be unavailable – the negative flip side of small runs – and re-issues are sporadic. Combing the smaller **record shops** often produces a rare gem, so don't give up on finding the original 7" single of "Take Cover" – try downtown.

Downtown, in fact, is always the place for 7" singles, old and new. The big record stores have binfuls of LPs and 12" singles, but usually only the current top 20 singles. The best places for records, not surprisingly, are Harare and Bulawayo – the top shops are listed under these cities in the travel section.

Sports and Outdoor Activities

White Rhodesians had a formidable taste for sports and the great outdoors. Although many whites left after Independence the tradition has continued and even expanded. Outstanding public sports facilities exist all over the country and other more exciting offerings, taking in the wild, are now becoming more common. On the spectator front, soccer is a national obsession, as are cricket and horse-racing.

■ Participatory sports

Every town of any size has at least one public **swimming pool** – wonderful outdoor Olympic-sized places. If you usually use goggles or earplugs, bring them along because you can't buy them inside the country. Bathing is also an option in **mountain pools**, particularly in the Eastern Highlands, which are bilharzia-free.

Tennis courts are plentiful too; if you're a keen player planning on a long stay, be sure to bring a racket. For the odd casual game, you'll find little-used courts at many of the National Parks – and equipment for rental. Many of the National Parks also have small artificial lakes stocked with fish.

Fishing is permitted with a licence obtainable from the park's reception, who'll also rent rowing boats where available. There's more exciting fishing at parks and resorts along the Zambezi and at Lake Kariba. The most exciting catches include trout and bream, but the ultimate fishy adversary is the fighting tiger fish. You can buy tackle in the big cities or rental at resorts, but if you need anything fancy, again, bring it along.

Finally, if **golf** is your game, bring along your clubs – every town in Zimbabwe has at least one golf course.

■ Spectator sports

Like most African countries, Zimbabwe's national sport is **soccer**, which draws crowds of between 30,000 and 45,000 for big matches. The game is played in both rural and urban areas, but the competitive league structure is confined to the towns and cities. The **season** runs from February to November.

From provincial level, amateur teams seek promotion to the first division **Super League** involving fourteen or so teams. Apart from the league there are four major club **competions**: the *Chibuku Trophy*, the *BAT Rosebowl*, the *Natbrew Cup* and the *Rothmans Shield*. For most of the past decade *Dynamos* have dominated Zimbabwe's club soccer; among other **teams** worth looking out for are *Highlanders*, *Zimbabwe Saints*, *CAPS United* and *Black Rhinos* (the army team).

Horse-racing ranks as one of Zimbabwe's most popular spectator sports. Cutting across all race and class divisions the annual tote turnover tops Z$36 million – a huge figure for a small developing country. A number of events take place at the country's two main venues: Ascot in Bulawayo and Borrowdale Park in Harare. The principal racing **season** is May to July.

As far as international competition goes, **cricket** is Zimbabwe's most successful sport. Every year two international sides come for month-long tours. Most have been beaten by the home team in limited-overs matches, although Zimbabwe has only won about half of its first-class competitions. At **national level** the premier events are the *Rothmans National League* and the *Logan Cup*. Matches are played on a limited-overs basis on Sundays. Because of the longer daylight hours, cricket in Zimbabwe is a summer game.

■ Outdoor activities

The post-Independence revival of Zimbabwean tourism has brought some exciting outdoor options that combine adventure activities with Zimbabwe's natural attractions; details of individual attractions are given in the relevant chapters throughout this book.

Two Zambezi adventures must share the top spot as the most thrilling experiences available. For the ultimate one-day adrenaline surge **white-water rafting** (see Chapter Three) on the rapids below the Victoria Falls can't be beaten, and it's become a big attraction of the Falls in its own right, while the other involves three or more days **canoeing** (see Chapter Two) down the Zambezi through some of Zimbabwe's wildest and best game country.

Another exciting way to see **game** is from horseback, and a couple of operators offer the option of **riding** into big game country (see Chapter Three). For some less demanding riding, you can rent horses very cheaply in some of the national parks, although – obviously enough – only at ones with no big cats.

Hiking safaris, (see Chapter Three), too are an exciting way to touch the wild in a way that just isn't possible from the confines of a vehicle. There's a choice of going out with a licensed guide with everything laid on, which doesn't come cheap but is always good value, or self-catering outings with national park game scouts, which is far cheaper.

And for less organised activities like **hiking** and **climbing** you'll find miles and miles of eminently walkable wilderness all over Zimbabwe, where you can do it yourself.

Crafts

In spite of the shortages of certain high-tech goods, there's a lot worth buying in Zimbabwe – and not just tourist souvenirs.

Zimbabwe produces its own fine **cotton** and you can get a good range of commercially made clothes and fabrics. Local prints, with vibrant designs and bold colours, are well worth looking at; they make useful multi-purpose wraps and easily transported souvenirs. A number of local artists also work with cottons to produce a distinctive and refined Zimbabwean school of **batik**, that appears on sale both as lengths of fabric or made-up into garments – surprisingly cheap for handmade goods. Look for this type of stuff at the craft shops in Harare or visit the artists at home.

Much of the **carving** you'll come across, both in wood and stone, is of the repetitive "laughing hippo" school – not really worth buying when there's so much more creative work about. There are some real artists working in softwoods, and **Zimbabwe's stone carvers** represent a significant international art movement.

In 1983 the London **Sunday Telegraph**'s art critic wrote that "it is extraordinary to think that of the ten leading sculptor-carvers in the world, perhaps five come from one single African tribe (ie the Shona)". His **top three** were Sylvester Mubayi, Joseph Ndandarika and Nicholas Mukomberanwa. You can see their work and, if you have the means, you can buy it and stunning sculpture by other big names, from Harare's commercial **galleries**. If you have an eye for it, you can pick up cheap (but potentially valuable) work by unknowns at the **National Gallery shops** in Harare and Bulawayo, or from the sculptors' community at **Tengenenge**.

You can also buy good-quality **crafts** all over the country, at curio shops, at some of the markets in larger centres or from roadside stalls. Items to look for include distinctive **baskets**, which vary from region to region.

In Bulawayo and around Victoria Falls, look out for **Batonga crafts**, often antique family heirlooms that won't be around for much longer, and pipes and hardwood stools. Many of the repetitive items – walking sticks, grass hats, and full-colour wooden chickens and guinea fowls from Zambia and the six-foot-high wooden giraffes – retain considerable vibrancy and are worth sorting through for the one that stands out from the crowd.

Easy-to-carry souvenirs include a range of Zimbabwe **T-shirts** decorated with above-average designs and beautiful polished, egg-shaped **stones**. And of course there's a host of rigorously commercial and tacky tourist bits and pieces from the ghastly stuffed specimens to the copper clock in the shape of Zimbabwe that you always wanted in your front room.

Trouble

Violent crime is thankfully rare in Zimbabwe. However, in a country of great extremes of wealth and poverty, it would be a miracle if there wasn't some theft. That visitors should take all the usual precautions is therefore advisable.

■ Crime

If you're robbed in Zimbabwe you're unlikely to be aware of it while it's happening. Pickpockets are quite common, though by taking a few simple precautions and being aware you can minimise the risk.

Be particularly mindful when in and around bus stations and markets – places where there are large numbers of people milling around. Keep tabs on what's going on around you. And carry your valuables where you can keep an eye on them – in crowded places, keep your bag or rucksack in front of you, rather than on your back, at least where nimble fingers can't dip into your goods without you noticing. You also should avoid leaving valuables in vehicles – another major target for thieves.

■ Drugs

Drug consumption in Zimbabwe has not reached the baroque proportions of the West ,and all you're likely to come across is *dagga* or *mbanje* (cannabis in dried leaf form), which grows quite happily in Zimbabwe and can occasionally be seen alongside footpaths or at bus stops. Growing it is a criminal offence and seldom a week passes without press coverage of yet another mbanje queen going to jail. Nevertheless marijuana-smoking is widespread and if you're reasonably discreet you should encounter no problems.

■ Sexual attitudes and harassment

Despite a liberation struggle that saw women fighting and dying alongside men, gender distinctions still run deep in Zimbabwe. Even in urban areas African women are still expected to show due respect to men, though more extreme practices seem likely to dwindle as more women take up paid employment. Attitudes to black women are quite restrictive and there have been clamp-downs on single women out at night in Harare, including mass arrests and trumped-up accusations of prostitution. Tourists are unlikely to experience any of this, although women on their own are considered fair game by men.

Context is important, however, and if you want to avoid **harassment** you'll have to avoid certain places: cheaper hotels, bars and jive joints. Even if you're obviously with a male companion, many **drunks** at nightspots will fail to be put off. The alternative is to go out anyway but to let the suggestions pass – if you're a white woman the danger of sexual assault is minimal. There have been reports of single women being hassled on trains by drunks but fortunately there are separate compartments for males and females and they can be locked from the inside. Away from drunks women can walk quite freely without fear of catcalls or being pestered.

"Rhodies" (white Zimbabweans who hang on to colonial attitudes), on the other hand, are staunchly sexist in an old-fashioned way. They'll open doors for women, buy them drinks and chat them up, but few will force their attentions if they're clearly unwelcome.

■ Gay life

Homosexuality is illegal and official statements deny that it exists among blacks, while white society is very macho and homophobic. There are, of course, gay men and women in Zimbabwe, but no representative organisations. Cruising goes on, primarily in the two main cities and one or two tourist resorts. Keep a low profile.

■ The police

Most Zimbabwean **police** are friendly and polite and you're unlikely to have much contact with them unless you're robbed. If you do have any dealings then a respectful response is likely to pay off. Police resources are limited – they don't even have vehicles in some places – so don't place too much hope on seeing your goods again.

It's worth weighing up the value and likelihood of getting your stuff back against the hassle of filling in forms and answering questions, which is often done with great thoroughness by policemen genuinely keen to help. For **insurance** purposes or replacement of **travellers' cheques** and **passports** you'll have no choice. Be sure to get a copy of the police report stating what you've lost or had stolen, to give to embassies, insurers or travellers' cheque companies.

Directory

AIRPORT TAX of US$20 is payable on leaving Zimbabwe. It can be paid in Zimbabwe dollars to the equivalent value – a good way to use up notes you can't export. You can buy the necessary stamp, which you should stick to your plane ticket, at banks or the airport bureau de change just before checking in.

CONTRACEPTIVES Condoms are available from pharmacies, as are contraceptive pills – on prescription – but to ensure the continued use of your particular type bring your own supplies.

ELECTRICITY is 220 volts, so British appliances can be used without any problem, apart from the fact that both round and square pin sockets are used, so you may have to change your plug or get an adaptor.

EMERGENCIES Police, fire and ambulance ☎99. Doctors are listed in the telephone directory at the front of each town or city section.

TAMPONS are available from supermarkets and general stores. If you do get caught out in a small village that's run out you'll always be able to get panty pads.

TIME is GMT+2hrs. Daylight is roughly 6am to 6pm, slightly extended in mid-summer.

TIPS are rarely added to bills and are obviously appreciated. About ten percent or loose change, depending on the bill, should do.

TOILETS Public ones aren't that common, although you will find some in the big cities, rarely with any paper. Those around the tea rooms and restaurants of department stores are always quite salubrious and do have toilet rolls. In rural areas you'll come across long-drop toilets – holes you squat over – and the ingenious Blair toilets invented in Zimbabwe.

TOPLESS BATHING is completely unacceptable in Zimbabwe – in fact it's an arrestable offence.

WORK Unless you line up a job or voluntary work before leaving for Zimbabwe, you have very little chance of getting employment. Particular skills are sometimes in demand, but you're unlikely to be granted a work permit while hundreds of thousands of Zimbabweans remain unemployed.

CHAPTER ONE

HARARE, THE MIDLANDS AND AROUND

ike most African capitals, after only a century of existence, Harare lacks an identifiable soul that might give it personality. That doesn't mean the city is devoid of charm. It's an unthreatening centre to spend time in and can be a great place to simply stroll around, bask in the languid warmth and enjoy the contradictions of a post-colonial city. British sobriety is collaged with the louder glass towers of the past decade and a very un-English tropical feel. It is at once the unrivalled metropolitan centre of Zimbabwe while at the same time exuding the parochial respectability of an English provincial capital. If you're passing through from wilder parts, you should draw some pleasure from its quiet, easygoing cityscape of flowering trees and tracts of red earth running between streets and exuberant gardens.

In the absence of compelling sights demanding your attention, there are a number of small but entertaining ways to pass a few easy hours – or even days. Harare has several **museums**, including a first-class collection of local **sculpture**, good **craft shops** and some pleasant outdoor cafés. If you're enraptured by Zimbabwean **music**, you'll find a scene of encouraging vitality here.

Sites in the **suburbs**, or a little way beyond, include the **rock paintings** at Dombashawa, set in typical Zimbabwean granite country, **Lake Chivero (Lake McIlwaine)**, the **Botanical Gardens** and **Mukuvisi Woodlands**; all these provide space when you want to get out of the city for a few hours. Given half a day's travelling you can plunge further afield into the wild country of the **Mavuradonna range** in the north, or push into the mellower purlieus of the provincial **Midlands**.

Harare is also an easy, secure, respectable place in which to make **travel arrangements** for more exciting parts. As a base or springboard for countrywide travels, the capital is, as you'd expect, very well connected, with excellent tarred roads radiating out to most places you're likely to want to go. Kariba and Bulawayo are five hours away in opposite directions **by road**, while Nyanga in the Eastern Highlands and Great Zimbabwe to the south are a mere three hours distant. Although there is no direct link by road to Victoria Falls and Hwange (you have to go via Bulawayo), you can reach them from Kariba, taking the ferry westwards along the lake. **By train**, you can head east to Mutare, or south to Bulawayo (and thence to Victoria Falls). Inevitably, too, Harare is also the centre of all domestic and international **flights**.

ACCOMMODATION PRICE CODES

Every hotel and accommodation option listed in this chapter has been given a **price code** in US$ to indicate the cost of a single night's lodging.

For a full explanation, see p.43.

    ① under US$8   ② US$8–14   ③ US$15–29   ④ US$30–59

        ⑤ US$60–89   ⑥ US$90–149   ⑦ US$150+

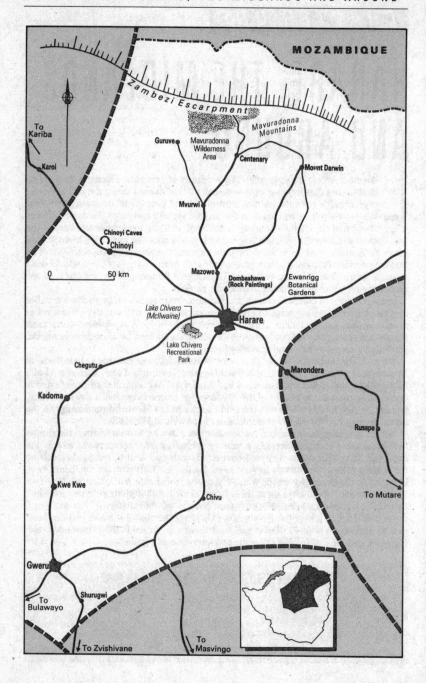

HARARE

If you arrive in **HARARE** expecting the exotica, decay and vibrancy so familiar elsewhere in Africa, you're bound to be disappointed. The city is predominantly sedate and clean with its share of familiar urban symbols – fast-food restaurants, western clothes shops and the same old petrol stations. As the new nation's show-piece it has attracted resources denied elsewhere, and in many ways stands apart from the rest of the country. Gleaming glass towers of the 1980s proclaim post-Independence prosperity in striking contrast with the lacklustre, 1960s slabs that give the place its provincial feel. The pace is unhurried and the centre pleasant and undemanding to stroll around.

There is an unquestionably African city alongside, however, and colonial planning still divides rich and poor. The influx of white immigrants over the last 90 years and the presence of a ready black workforce provided a development blueprint for Harare as an affluent town with elegant suburbs and hidden **working class districts**. Walk through the downmarket, downtown **Kopje** and **Robert Mugabe Road** quarters and you'll discover a bustling area of ageing buildings and shops selling bric-a-brac and essentials. Mingling with the street clamour, the beat of local music thumps out from a hundred shop counter record players. A couple of kilometres further on you hit **Mbare** – a "high-density suburb", with its huge market spreading out, and also the country's biggest bus station, hub of the public transport network.

Some history

Many whites were outraged when Zimbabwe's capital was renamed **Harare** after Independence in 1980. But history was just completing a cycle. Long before Rhodes' pioneers pitched up, armed with intent to rename the area **Fort Salisbury** (after the British prime minister), the region was the domain of **Chief Neharawa** of Seki. The white government called one of the African areas Harare – from Harawa – but to generations of blacks through the colonial years that was the name of the capital itself. In **September 1890**, the Union Jack was hoisted on the site of present African Unity Square, and the British South Africa Company (BSAC) marched in and took over.

Salisbury was intended as a base for working the **goldfields** of the Zambezi Valley, which speculators believed matched the ore-rich veins of South Africa. This was wishful thinking, yet the unlikely marshland became the country's main urban centre as settlers were enticed by the promise of large farms and substantial mining claims. The town took its earliest shape from the traders who haphazardly set up shop at the foot of the Kopje; in 1891 Captain Thomas Ross was brought in by the Company to impose some town planning on this dangerously organic tendency. The result was the collision of two street grids: Ross incorporated the existing plots below the Kopje and created a rectangular grid parallel to Pioneer Street, ensuring that future development would be constrained by a second grid of martial regularity, aligned due north.

During the 1890s Salisbury's commercial centre shifted east from the Kopje to the district around present-day **African Unity Square**. At the same time **racial segregation** crept in. The first "location" for black workers was a dismal affair, a kilometre south of Kopje, with a white superintendent and a nine o'clock curfew. Not surprisingly, few blacks were attracted. It was only after the suppression of the First Chimurenga (liberation war) in 1896, and the imposition of **taxes** to force blacks to work in town, that the workers' housing shortage became serious. In 1907, a new location was built across the Mukuvisi River in a choice spot near the town cemetery, abattoir and sewage disposal works.

Salisbury was officially recognised as a city in 1923, when it became the seat of colonial government. But the real boost came after World War II, when it was made **capital** of the newly formed **Federation of Southern Rhodesia, Northern Rhodesia and Nyasaland**. The city expanded with new enterprises and industry. By the time the

Federation broke up in 1963, the industrial base was firmly established. Following **UDI** in 1965, construction slowed down, and reached a standstill by the time the Smith regime capitulated. The pace picked up dramatically after **Independence** – especially during the 1980s – with an energy to make up for the stagnant years of sanctions. New buildings shot up around the centre with Yugloslav, Korean and Chinese construction agencies all involved in prestige projects in Zimbabwe's first decade of independence. Despite growing debt problems, prestige buildings have continued to go up in the 1990s.

Arrival, orientation and transport

Central Harare is compact, walkable and, because of its regular street plan, hard to get lost in. Although greater Harare is a sprawl of suburbs, there's little need to venture out of town unless you're planning a long stay.

Arrival

By **air** you arrive at **Harare Airport**, southeast of the city, which has a **bureau de change** open for all international flights. From the airport, when planes are arriving, there's an hourly *Air Zimbabwe* bus, which takes about 20 minutes and drops off at the terminal next to *Meikles Hotel* in central Harare. Metered taxis (the meters do work!) are thick on the ground and worth it if there are two of you.

By **train** you arrive at the southern end of the city centre. Most central places are walkable, but if you need a taxi there's a rank outside the station in Kenneth Kaunda Avenue. Failing that try the one at *Meikles Hotel* four blocks up in Third Street.

Buses and coaches are more complicated. **Luxury coaches** run by *AJAY Motorways* drop off passengers at the *Monomotapa Hotel*, while *Express Motorways* arrive at the Rezende Street terminus – both in the centre. All **long distance local buses** terminate at **Mbare bus station**, but many pass through the centre on the way; from Mbare, catch an urban bus or taxi.

> Important note: the stretch of **Chancellor Avenue**, leading north off North Avenue, past the **President's Residence**, is off limits from 6pm to 6am. A barrier operated by armed troops is usually lowered between these hours. This restriction is to be taken very seriously – several motorists have been shot dead for venturing down this no-go street during prohibited hours, even on occasion with the boom raised. If the President's cavalcade is passing, you're required by law to stop and pull over.

Orientation

Harare splits up quite neatly into functional districts. The **main commercial area**, with smart shops, banks and restaurants, is largely confined to the section west of Fourth Street, around **African Unity Square** and up to the **Harare Gardens**. **First Street** is an attractive pedestrian mall where you can sit at outdoor cafés and survey the passing scene. The distinctively curving *Monomotapa Hotel*, scraping more sky than most, makes an effective landmark. **Jason Moyo Avenue**, between Second and Fourth streets, is a tourist strip, with the Publicity Association information offices, the Zimbabwe Tourist Development Corporation, *Sun Hotels*, *National Parks* booking office, and travel agents and the *Air Zimbabwe* terminal around the corner in Third Street.

The greatest density of **hotels** is to be found along **the Avenues** – the chunk northeast of the Harare Gardens (usually referred to simply as "the gardens") between Second Street and Enterprise Road. These streets are quiet and lined with jacaranda

STREET NAME CHANGES			

The following Harare streets were renamed in 1990; you may still come across the old names from time to time.

North Ave	Josiah Tongogara Ave	*Salisbury Drive*	Harare Drive
Gordon Ave	George Silundika Ave	*Salisbury Way*	Harare Way
Stanley Ave	Jason Moyo Ave	*Salisbury St*	Harare St
Rhodes Ave	Herbert Chitepo Ave	*Queensway North/*	Airport Rd
Manica Rd West/	Robert Mugabe Rd	*Queensway Rd*	
Manica Rd		*Montagu Ave*	Josiah Chinamano Rd
Gaul Ave	Bishop Gaul Ave	*Hatfield Rd/Prince*	Seke Rd
Kings Crescent	Julius Nyerere Ave	*Edward Dam Rd*	
Sinoia St	Chinhoyi St	*Mazoe St*	Mazowe St
Victoria St	Mbuya Nehanda St	*Mazoe Rd*	Mazowe Rd
Moffat St	Leopold Takawira St	*Umtali Rd*	Mutare Rd
Pioneer St	Kaguvi St	*Mtoko Rd*	Mutoko Rd
Widdecombe Rd	Chiremba Rd	*Harare Rd North*	Harare Rd
Harare/Beatrice Rd	Masvingo Rd	*Forbes Ave*	Robson Manyika Ave
Sir James	Rekayi Tangwena Ave	*Beatrice Rd/Watt Rd/*	Simon Mazorodze
McDonald Rd		*Chandler Way*	Way

and flamboyant trees. This is where you'll find the oldest colonial-style town houses, with their colonnaded verandahs and shady gardens.

On the other side of the centre, in the **Kopje area**, the roads suddenly skew off-centre and you're in a different city. From here zip over the Kopje itself and you're in Harare's **high-density suburbs**, hidden from view – and conscience – by the hill.

Transport

Most places of interest can be reached on **foot** and Harare's wide streets and established cycle tracks make it an ideal city for cycling (See "Listings", p.79, for bike rental). For access to the suburbs there are taxis, buses and emergency taxis. Taxis are by far the easiest option in a city with crowded and poor public transport. Taxis are metered – around the centre fares are affordable, but expect to pay from US$5 upwards for a ride into the suburbs. **Buses** and **emergency taxis** (ETs) are cheap but overflowing. If you use the buses, always try to catch them at the terminus, where they fill up and don't stop again until people get off much later on. As a rule, most routes have an hourly service.

Five main bus **termini** serve the suburbs:
• Bank/Mbuya Nehanda streets
• Speke Avenue/Chinhoyi Street
• South Avenue/Angwa Street
• Fourth Street/Robert Mugabe Road
• Rezende Street

Like buses, **ETs** (usually old Peugeot estate cars) follow fixed routes and take a number of passengers. They charge a cheap flat rate for any distance, but it takes a while to work out routes – worthwhile only if you're planning a long stay. **Hitching** is also possible – you'll see many people thumbing to and from work, usually paying for a lift in privately owned cars.

Guided tours are run by *UTC*, which offers a city tour twice daily plus less regular trips to places in the suburbs and out of town; for details and bookings, contact their desk at *Meikles Hotel* or their head office at 4 Park Street.

SECURITY

Although muggings are on the increase, Harare is no more dangerous than most cities, even at night. Theft is a major problem, however, and vigilance pays. Watch out particularly for **pickpockets** in crowded places: the bus stations and the market are favourite hunting grounds for nimble-fingered criminals. If you have a car, always lock it, and don't leave valuables inside – car break-ins are common. Beware particularly of the gardens and the area around the National Gallery at night. This vicinity is also favoured by kids with bogus sponsorship forms seeking donations. Check out their credentials.

Accommodation

Finding a bed in Harare is no longer easy. The international four- and five-star hotels are expensive, and the middle bracket places fill up fast. Most of the medium budget rooms are good value though, clean, well serviced and generally in easy walking distance of the centre, though some are a taxi ride away in the suburbs. Most have swimming pools and all can be booked ahead.

At the bottom of the range, cheap hotels can be a slightly seedy option, some doubling up as brothels. Better than these hotels, if you're on a tight budget, are the backpackers' crashpads springing up to cater for the influx of budget travellers. Most are old houses near the centre, with bedrooms converted into small dorms with cooking facilities provided. Some have gardens and swimming pools. At the other end of the scale, a number of tourists opt to avoid staying at the plush city centre hotels, and head out instead to the game ranches and country hotels just outside the capital which offer all-inclusive rates.

Camping and Backpacker Crashpads

Backpackers ConXshon, 932 Delport Rd, Airport (☎5074115). The best of the crashpads and definitely worth the slightly higher price. Camping is available and there are double rooms as well as a women-only dorm. It's near the airport with a swimming pool and garden and offers free and regular transport in and out of town, (pick up point *Lido Café*, Union Ave) as well as to the airport and railway station. You can self-cater or eat their reasonably priced evening meal. ①–②.

Backpackers Rest, corner Livingstone St/Third St. En suite double rooms with neither linen nor cooking facilities. Dorm space available. ①.

Coronation Park Campsite, 6km east of the centre on the Mutare Road. The campsite is cheap but distant. (Hitch or take the Greendale bus from Rezende Street; taxi fare will eat up any money saved by camping). It's a pleasant enough place, good washrooms, a public phone, and is near shops. ①.

E Khaya Lodge, 77/79 Greengrove Drive, Greendale (☎44230 or ☎44294). Clean shared accommodation in a converted nursery school with one double room, and a hospitable atmosphere. The main drawback is that it's out of town. The owners can provide lifts into town for a fee. ①.

Fala Fala Lodge, 161 Union Ave (☎796606). Old house with dorms. Outside courtyard rooms often buzzing with traders from west and east Africa – pretty ropey. ①.

Harare Youth Hostel, 6 Josiah Chinamano Ave (☎796436). An unenthralling hostel which is often full. Bunks are in dorms and you can cook. Doors open only 5–10pm, and you're thrown out in the morning. On a more positive note, it's centrally located and a good place to meet other travellers. ①.

Kopje Lodge, 38 Fort Rd (☎790637). Recently renovated building close to the main post office, with private rooms, dorms, and very cheap roof space. Also kitchen and laundry facilities, as well as home-baked bread and pizzas. ①–②.

Msafiri Guest House, 130 Samora Machel Ave. A clean and friendly place, opposite the Holiday Inn, convenient for the taxi rank and breakfasts there. Double rooms, or four sharing and use of the kitchen. ①.

Paw Paw Lodge, 262 Herbert Chitepo Ave (☎724014). A bit tatty, but offering the usual backpacker facilities in a central location. ①.

Sable Lodge, 95a Selous Ave (☎72601). The most popular of the central city crashpads in colonial-styled house with a swimming pool, kitchen, shared rooms and plenty of overlanders. Some double rooms are also available. ①–②.

Cheap hotels

Earlside Hotel, Fifth St/Selous Ave (☎721101). The elegant colonial facade with a swimming pool hides a tatty interior with shared facilities, though it is good value nevertheless. There is also a backpackers' dorm in the hotel, but valuables are not safe. Good, cheap dinners. ①–②.

Elizabeth Hotel, Julius Nyerere Way/Robert Mugabe Rd (☎708591). A regular venue for live music and haunt of pickpockets, though the rooms are clean. Not recommended for women travellers. ③.

Executive Hotel, Fourth St/Samora Machel Ave (☎792803). Also central, this converted block of flats has large rooms, all with bath and is good value. ③.

Feathers Hotel, Sherwood Drive, Mabelreign (☎28472). Out in the suburbs, but clean enough. ③.

Federal Hotel, 9 Harare St (☎706118). Close to Mbare and gives a good taste of African Harare. ③.

Kentucky Airport Hotel, 27 St Patrick's Road, Hatfield (☎50109). Convenient for the airport, with free transport, but a fair distance from the centre. ③.

Mushandire Pamwe Hotel, Nyandoro Rd, Highfield (☎64355, ☎64356, or ☎64357). Cheap rooms are offset by the taxi fare into central Harare from this former African township. But if you want music, you're on the doorstep of one of the capital's main music venues, with nightly gigs. ③.

Number 10 B&B, 10 Cleveland Ave, Milton Park (☎721696). A comfortable house not far from the centre with a couple of spotless rooms. The house is serviced and meals can be cooked for you. Book in advance. Recommended. ③.

Queens Hotel, Robert Mugabe Rd/Kaguvi St (☎738977). Live music here every weekend, and pretty frenetic. Watch out for pickpockets. Not recommended for women travellers, though rooms are clean with a cup of hot tea and two sugars, provided first thing. ③.

Red Fox Hotel, Stewart Rd opposite Honey Dew Farm (☎45466). Pretty clean and decent hotel in an incongruous mock-Tudor style. ③.

Russell Hotel, 116 Baines Ave (☎791894). Plenty of acceptable rooms, but tends to get full, especially during polytechnic exams in October and November. ③.

Selous Hotel, Selous Ave/Sixth St (☎727940, ☎727948, or ☎727949). All rooms with bath. ③.

Suraj Hotel, 16 Luck St (☎704398). The cheapest of the cheap, but not recommended, particularly for women travelling alone. The somewhat basic rooms share run-down baths and the place is a bit of a dive. ②.

Middle range

There are several medium range places along the Avenues – many quieter than the cheap central city hotels. This range also includes some low key hotels further out in the suburbs which are only worth considering if you have your own transport, or if the central hotels are full. Most have restaurants and bars attached.

Ambassador Hotel, Union Ave, PO Box 872 (☎708121 or ☎708126). Central and smart, with radio, TV and phone in each room. ④.

Astor Jabulani Hotel, 190 Herbert Chitepo Ave (☎721664). Standing on the opposite side of the gardens to the *Monomotapa* (see below), this is definitely the less prestigious of the two. Perfectly adequate, if characterless, rooms. ④.

Bronte Hotel, 132 Baines Ave (☎796631 or ☎796634). In a gracious colonial building with big gardens – most rooms with bath for only a little more than the above. Highly recommended. ④.

Cresta Lodge, Samora Machel Ave/Robert Mugabe Rd, Coronation Park (726401/5). Six kilometres from the city, offering international standards at a cheaper rate. All rooms are ensuite with colour TV, videos etc. Transport can be provided to and from the city centre and airport. ⑤.

Cresta Oasis Motel, 124 Baker Ave (☎704217). Top of the range – all rooms with bath and TV, morning newspaper delivered, and a swimming pool. ⑤.

Courteney Hotel, Selous Ave/Eighth St (☎706411). All rooms with bath, located in the quiet Avenues. ④.

George Hotel, King George Road, Avondale (☎36677). Nicest of the suburban hotels, close to town and in a very good area, near shops. ⑤.

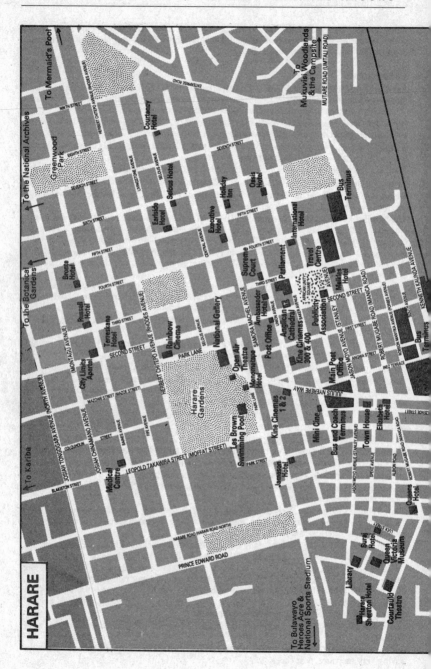

HARARE

To Mermaid's Pool

To the National Archives

To the Botanical Gardens

To Kariba

ENTERPRISE ROAD

To Mukuvisi Woodlands & the Campsite

MUTARE ROAD (UMTALI ROAD)

NINTH STREET

HERBERT CHITEPO AVENUE (RHODES AVENUE)

Greenwood Park

Courtney Hotel

EIGHTH STREET

SEVENTH STREET

SEVENTH STREET

LIVINGSTONE AVENUE

SELOUS AVENUE

Selous Hotel

Oasis Hotel

SIXTH STREET

Earlside Hotel

Holiday Inn

FIFTH STREET

Executive Hotel

CENTRAL AVENUE

International Hotel

Bus Terminus

FIFTH STREET

Bronte Hotel

FOURTH STREET

Supreme Court

FOURTH STREET

Parliament

THIRD STREET

Travel Centre

KENNETH KAUNDA AVENUE

SEVENTH STREET

Russell Hotel

Terreskane Hotel

THIRD STREET

(MONTAGU AVENUE)

SECOND STREET

AFRICAN UNITY

Meikles Hotel

SAMORA MACHEL AVENUE

Ambassador Hotel

SECOND STREET

City Limits Apartel

SELOUS AVENUE

National Gallery

Rainbow Cinema

UNION AVENUE

BAKER AVENUE

Publicity Association

Anglican Cathedral

PARK LANE

Post Office

Kine Cinemas 300 & 400

FIRST STREET

JASON MOYO AVENUE (STANLEY AVENUE)

Bus Terminus

HERBERT CHITEPO AVENUE (RHODES AVENUE)

Open Air Theatre

Monomatapa Hotel

ROBERT MUGABE ROAD (MANICA ROAD)

NELSON MANDELA AVENUE (FORBES AVENUE)

SINOIA STREET

Main Post Office

MAZOWE STREET (MAZOE STREET)

Harare Gardens

Les Brown Swimming Pool

PARK LANE

Kine Cinemas 1 & 2

Mini Cine

Bus and Coach Terminus

Tower House

JULIUS NYERERE WAY

JASON MOYO AVENUE (STANLEY AVENUE)

Elizabeth Hotel

ZIMBRE STREET

(NORTH AVENUE)

JOSIAH TONGOGARA AVENUE

JOSIAH CHINAMANO AVENUE

COLQUHOUN

BAINES AVENUE

FIFE AVENUE

PARK STREET

Jameson Hotel

ANGWA STREET

INEZ TERRACE

KAGUVI STREET

ALBION ROAD

ROBERT MUGABE ROAD (MANICA ROAD)

BLAKISTON STREET

Medical Centre

LEOPOLD TAKAWIRA STREET (MOFFAT STREET)

PARK STREET

Queens Hotel

HARARE ROAD (HARARI ROAD NORTH)

PRINCE EDWARD ROAD

Surf Hotel

FEMBE ROAD

Queen Victoria Museum

To Bulawayo Heroes Acre & National Sports Stadium

Library

Harare Sheraton Hotel

Courtauld Theatre

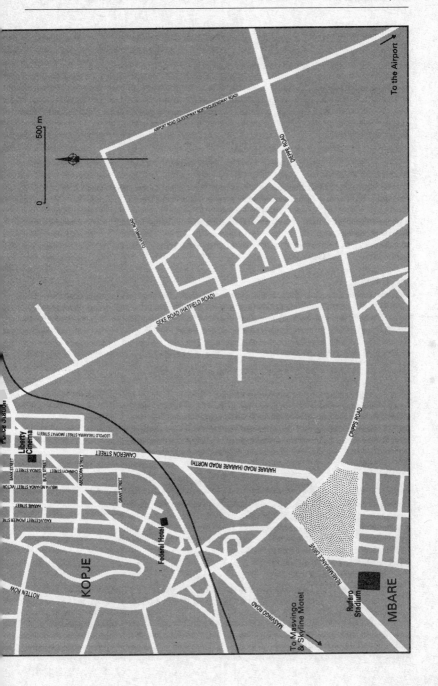

To the Airport

500 m

AIRPORT ROAD (QUEENSWAY) NORTH/QUEENSWAY ROAD

DIEPPE ROAD

OLD FARREL ROAD

SEKE ROAD (HATFIELD ROAD)

DIEPPE ROAD

Police Station

Liberty Cinema

LEOPOLD TAKAWIRA STREET (MOFFAT STREET)

BANK STREET

ANGWA STREET

SPEKE AVENUE

CAMERON STREET

CHINHOYI STREET

JULIUS NYERERE WAY (KINGSWAY)

UNION AVENUE

MBUYA NEHANDA STREET (VICTORIA STREET)

MERCURY STREET

HARARE STREET

HARARE ROAD (HARARE ROAD NORTH)

KAGUVI STREET (PIONEER STREET)

GRANT STREET

ROTTEN ROW

KOPJE

Federal Hotel

MASVINGO ROAD

To Masvingo & Skyline Motel

REMEMBRANCE DRIVE

Rufaro Stadium

MBARE

International Hotel, Baker Ave/Fourth St (☎700332). Position on the main route to one of the bus stations means that some rooms can be noisy. ④.

Terreskane Hotel, Fife Ave/Second St (☎707031, ☎707032, ☎707033 or ☎707034). A bit of a drinking spot – lively, but not the place for a quiet night. ④.

International hotels

Harare's multi-star outfits match their counterparts throughout the world – and considering this, are relatively low-priced, though still firmly in the expense account bracket.

Cresta Jameson Hotel, Samora Machel Ave/Park St (☎794641). Conveniently central with everything you'd expect in this price range. ⑥.

Harare Holiday Inn, Samora Machel Ave/Fifth Street (☎795611). Most casual of the hotels in this bracket, with a nice pool. ⑥.

Harare Sheraton, Pennefather Ave (☎729771 or ☎796678). Part of the international chain – inside, you could be anywhere. Zimbabwe's ultimate prestige place to stay. ⑦.

Meikles Hotel, Third St/Jason Moyo Ave (☎707721). Located opposite African Unity Square, you can't get more central than this, right opposite the main tourist offices and the *Air Zimbabwe* bus drop-off point. ⑥.

Monomotapa, 54 Park Lane (☎704501). On the edge of the Harare Gardens, with the best views in town – ask for the top floors. ⑦.

Out of town

Landela Lodge, P.O. Box 66293, Kopje, Harare (☎702634). Wonderful farmhouse, near Ruwa, 35 mins from the airport with lush gardens and superb food, for the safari set. Highly recommended and a great option if international hotels pall. Sightseeing trips into town can be arranged and you will be met at the airport. Drop-ins not possible. All-inclusive price of US$100 per person per night, plus US$30 for return transfers.

Mwanga Lodge, Bally Vaughan Game Park, Safari Promotions (☎729025). Luxury lodge on a game farm, 44km north of Harare. No drop-ins, but day trips can be arranged from Harare. There are lions and elephants on the farm. US$135 per person per night.

Pamuzinda Safari Lodge, Box 2833, Harare (☎707411). A lodge on a game farm, ideal for jetsetters with no time for Hwange, or a recommended treat for your first or last night in Zimbabwe. About 80km (one hour's drive) from Harare on the Bulawayo road, prior bookings only and transfers from the *Cresta Jameson Hotel*. US$110 per person.

Zindele Safaris, Private Bag 232A, Harare (☎721696). A very pleasant guest farm, located 69km from Harare on the Mazowe Road, which places an emphasis on walking and relaxing. US$80 per person.

FARM STAYS AND B&Bs

Many white Zimbabweans on superbly located farms are providing farm stays, some on game ranches, others on working farms. If you choose to cool out in the "bush", you'll be assured of great hospitality, lashings of food and an ambivalent taste of comfortable pre-Independence lifestyle. Others, in town, are moving towards providing British-style B&B. Two Harare-based agencies can arrange bookings.

Bed'n'Breakfast, 161 Second Street Ext, Harare (☎724331 or ☎724332). Homestay and farmstay bookings.

Safari Farms, PO Box 592, Harare (☎733573). Booking for several game farms accessible from Harare as well as country-wide. It covers a range of prices, some farms have lovely cottages at very reasonable prices, while others in prime game areas are much more upmarket. You can write away for their list of farms and prices. Great for weekends away, either for pure lazing, or taking advantage of activities like walking, fishing and horse riding.

The City Centre: Architecture and Parks

You can read Harare's history in its skyline. Post-Independence confidence is reflected in individualistic 1980s towers, clad in coats of many colours, looking down on the post World War II buff-coloured boxes. The heavy liberation struggle years are on record, too, in the absence of buildings from the 1970s – guns came before bricks.

One notable exception to the lack of 1970s buildings is the distinctive slender curve of the **Monomotapa Hotel** (on the edge of the Harare Gardens), one of the few modern buildings to make reference to the meandering walls of Great Zimbabwe – and the country's ancient architectural tradition.

The **National Gallery of Zimbabwe** (for the museum's collections see overpage) is in spitting distance from the *Monomotapa* (frequently referred to as "Monos") in Park Lane. Completed in 1957, the gallery is an example of the International Style developed by twentieth-century European and American architects and so named because they thought it was universally appropriate – a symbol of international modernity.

The **Judges' Chambers** of the **Supreme Court of Zimbabwe** occupy the corner of Third Street and Union Avenue. The 1927 building was originally conceived as the headquarters of Rhodes' British South Africa Company (BSAC), which governed the country in its infancy. When construction began in 1895 on the nearby **Parliament Buildings**, on the corner of Baker Avenue and Third Street, it was going to be a hotel. But the First Chimurenga brought building to a standstill as troops putting down the rebellion were billeted in the unfinished shell. When the developers went bust in 1898 the BSAC took it over to use as a post office, but soon after the newly formed Legislative Assembly was installed. As the first session sat in 1899, the builders were still at work. For **guided tours** or seats in the **visitors gallery** during debates, apply to The Chief Information Officer, Parliament of Zimbabwe, PO Box 8055, Causeway, Harare (☎700181 or ☎729722). There are plans for a new Parliament on the Kopje.

Harare's **Anglican Cathedral**, on Baker Avenue and Second Street, took a mere fifty years to complete after inception in 1913. The designer, Sir Herbert Baker, was South Africa's leading architect; he was responsible for the Union Buildings in Pretoria and worked on the design of New Delhi with Lutyens, the master of imperial architecture. Baker wanted the Harare cathedral to have a cylindrical bell tower as a reference to the conical tower at Great Zimbabwe – a rare acknowledgement of indigenous forms – but this eccentric idea was, sadly, overruled. The sombre interior is relieved by the cartoon-like murals of the stations of the cross. The columns, carved from solid granite are starkly impressive. If you're lucky you may hear Shona women at choir practice, using traditional percussion. Try to look in on a Shona Eucharist for some beautiful vernacular hymns.

The **Town House** in Julius Nyerere Way (between Speke and Jason Moyo Ave) is the seat of Harare's municipal government. It was built in 1933 in an eclectic classical style with somewhat incompatible Florentine and Art Deco features. Like Parliament, it can be visited by appointment (☎706536).

Stroll down **Robert Mugabe Road** for some of Harare's less studiedly monumental – and more rewarding – **historic buildings**. Most of these are found towards Fourth Street, but there are also a handful on the way to the Civic Centre in Rotten Row. Among these are the 1902 **Vasan's Footwear**, originally an outfitters, with a typical turn-of-century pavement canopy supported on slender columns, and **Queen's Hotel**, dating from 1900, but largely refurbished in 1930. Nearby, bunched together in **Rotten Row**, are the **Courtauld Theatre**, the **Central Library** and the **Queen Victoria Museum**, with giant concrete snail, pangolin, praying mantis and chameleon standing guard outside.

A short walk away is the country's most controversial post-Independence building. The **Sheraton Hotel** and **Harare International Conference Centre** is a shimmering gilt glass slab of monumentally enlarged cigarette-pack proportions. Going inside is to step off the streets of third world Harare and to enter a brassy Midas-world where everything that can be is gold, from the gold-tinted windows, gold light fittings and gold finished furniture down to the guests' gold watches and medallions. The building is the work of the Yugoslavian *Energoprojekt* company, who brought in their own building teams and materials to produce this futuristic zone of theatrical totalitarianism. Rumour has it that the government wanted Zimbabweans to work on the project and, when they persisted in this demand in mid-construction, *Energoprojekt* deserted, taking their drawings with them and leaving local architects to work it all out. They must have succeeded.

Parks and gardens

In central Harare you're never more than ten minutes from green space. It is partly the size of the place and partly the generous climate combined with the heritage of British parks. **African Unity Square**, between Parliament and *Meikle's Hotel*, is a pleasant, fountain-decked piazza frequented by relaxed *Herald* readers and jazzed up by flower sellers. Its former name, Cecil Square, was changed in 1988 to celebrate unification of Zimbabwe's two main parties, though the Publicity Association blurb still curiously describes it as "a memorial to the early pioneers".

The largest and loveliest of the city's public spaces, the **Harare Gardens** are well manicured and well used. On afternoons schoolkids loll about doing homework and on weekends wedding parties parade around – the women in white chiffons and shiny red fancy dress, the men charcoal-suited. People stroll the thoroughfare, which cuts through it from Park Lane to Herbert Chitepo Avenue and it's a good place to take a break and watch Harare. In the park behind the *Monomotapa* is the Olympic-sized Les Brown public **swimming pool**, open throughout the year and with lawns for sunbathing. On Sundays, around late morning/lunchtime, a big market brings a bit of bustle to the gardens, and makes a pleasant place to go craft hunting.

The main attraction of **Greenwood Park**, between Seventh and Eighth streets and Herbert Chitepo and Josiah Chinamano avenues, is the children's playground with miniature railway and boating pool (Sat 2–5.30pm; Sun 10am–1pm & 2–5pm).

And finally, fronting up to the northern suburbs, the **National Botanic Gardens** (open sunrise to sunset) are Zimbabwe's answer to Britain's Kew: a place where you can immerse yourself in fantasy African vegetation, neatly divided into ecological zones. There's a fine collection of the continent's **trees**, including most of Zimbabwe's 750 species, while large areas are closely cropped **parkland** ideal for picnicking or lazy afternoons. The gardens are about 30 minutes on foot from the centre. Go north up Fifth Street, which becomes Sandringham Drive; the main entrance is on the right. You can also catch any bus down Second Avenue and get off at Downie Avenue, where there's another entrance.

Harare's Galleries and Museums

Harare's galleries are a major attraction. If you have only a day in the city, make sure to take at least a brief look at the **National Gallery**, with its superb array of modern sculpture and traditional African art. Given more time, it's worth checking out some of the **commercial galleries** too, many of which deal exclusively in the soapstone works of Zimbabwe's now internationally renowned sculptors. The capital's museums are less rewarding, though the **National Archive** features some interesting historical material.

The National Gallery of Zimbabwe

Baker Ave/Third St. Tues–Sun 9am–12.30pm & 2–5pm. Nominal entrance fee.

Opened in 1957, Zimbabwe's National Gallery houses a major collection of African art, drawn from throughout the continent. But, from the outset, it has also promoted local talent and has served as an institution for all races. An initial interest in painting was soon surpassed when the curators became aware of **stone sculptures** by Joram Mariga. In the 1960s a workshop was founded, with stone being brought in from Nyanga and given to the employees, and Zimbabwe's formidable movement in sculpture was thus established. Initially, under the directorship of Frank McEwan, it produced works geared towards European expectations, but in recent years the emphasis has become truly national, while the movement has gained world recognition.

Stone Sculptures

Modern stone sculpture gets a good showing in the **permanent indoor collection** and in a well-populated **sculpture garden**, inhabited by mythological creatures and beast-humans frozen in mid-transformation. **Bernard Matemera**, master of this species-conversion, has a number of distinctively distorted works scattered about. Amongst other big names, the **Takawira brothers** drag exquisitely refined busts from rough hewn stone that remains part of the work.

The walls, hung with mostly unexceptional **paintings** and **drawings**, pale against the boldly confident stone works that hold the floor. But from time to time the gallery holds **special exhibitions** with more interesting international works. And the annual **Nedlaw competition**, which draws entries from up and down the country, is always worth taking in.

African Art

Upstairs, the real treasure house of the museum is formed by the permanent **collection of African art**. Oddly, the east and west of the continent dominate, though richly patterned domestic objects from Zimbabwe feature at the end of the collection. The works from the more northerly Côte d'Ivoire, Mali, Ghana and Central African Republic are more representational and less utilitarian than the Zimbabwean offerings of headrests, stools, beadwork and weapons. Throughout Africa there's no traditional concept of art for its own sake. These artefacts were social and religious objects in everyday use and carry their creators' belief in a universally present life force in all things. The carver was frequently a highly respected and feared figure who channelled the power of the spirits into works which seem to contain pent-up energy.

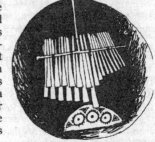

Among numerous highlights, look out for the large wooden carving of the mythical **porgaga** bird from Burkina Faso. With huge bill and distended belly symbolising fertility, it adorns shrines where girls are taught womanly matters and go through the ritual passage of genital mutilation. The spherical face of the **akua'ba** doll from Ghana represents the Ashanti ideal of beauty; these dolls were carried by the pregnant women for perfect children. The Malian **chi wara** eland headress is used in ceremonial re-enactments of the birth of agriculture; Bambara legend has it that the antelope taught humans grain cultivation. It's worn to portray the animal's magical relationship to fertility.

The Museum Shop

More than just a heritage display case, the National Gallery is also a market-place for arts and crafts, with the gallery shop extending the same hands-on approach of the collections. In addition to the expected books and publications, you will be able to buy a range of local arts and crafts. While much of it is mediocre, there's more **sculpture** in the shop than the gallery's own collection and you can pick up something good by an unknown name very reasonably – or pay thousands for works by the well-established figures.

There's also a good selection of **local crafts** at affordable prices (in spite of the often hefty mark-up): baskets from the Binga district, gudza dolls, gourds, jewellery and hand-dyed and printed fabrics and garments.

Commercial Galleries

Harare has a clutch of good private galleries dealing mainly in sculpture. The enthusiast can browse around works by Zimbabwe's established names.

Sculpture: Central Harare

Matombo Gallery, 114 Leopold Takawira St (Mon–Fri 8am–6pm; Sat 8am–1pm). Good centrally located gallery.

Stone Dynamics Sculpture Gallery, 56 Samora Machel Ave (Mon–Fri 8am–5.30pm; Sat 8.30am–1pm). A select batch of big name works. The gallery emphasises work by the "second-generation artists" – the newcomers developing on the work of 1960s veterans.

Vukutiwa Gallery, Blakiston St/Harvey Brown Ave (daily 9am–6pm) is a twenty-minute walk from the centre. The crowded sculpture garden is arranged around the swimming pool of a once-grand house and among the less special clutter you'll find works by Zimbabwe's best.

Sculpture: in the Suburbs

Nyati Gallery, Spitzkop Rd, 20km peg Bulawayo Road. Founded by the renowned sculptor David Mutasa, this sculpture garden, where you can watch sculptors at work, is a fair distance out, but worthwhile particularly if you're out Lake Chivero (Lake McIlwaine) way.

The Gallery – Shona Sculpture, "Doon Estate", 1 Harrow Road (daily 6.30am–4.30pm). Attached to *Chapungu Village* near Coronation Park campsite, it's the nicest of the city's galleries, with sculpture spread around the large grounds and some select works indoors. There's a tea garden, traditional dancing at the weekend, and you can stroll around and watch the resident sculptors at work. There are often good, and cheapish, pieces by unknown local artists.

Other Media

A couple of further venues are good for seeing examples of local talent in other media.

Gallery Delta, "Robert Paul's Old House", 110 Livingstone Ave/Ninth St. Worthwhile exhibitions of graphics, textiles, weavings and ceramics.

John Boyne Gallery, Speke Ave/Inez Terrace. Free display space for up-and-coming artists. The standard of work is uneven but there's often interesting stuff.

The National Archives

Weekdays 7.45am–4.30pm, Sat 8am–noon. Free.

The **National Archives** in Borrowdale Road/Churchill Avenue is an important resource for researchers – and the staff are strict about access to the closed shelves – but much of the collection remains open to the public, and worthwhile.

The **Beit Gallery**, on the first floor, is perhaps the best and most accessible collection – a rich reserve of historic books, documents, newspapers, stamps and paintings relating to Zimbabwe's history. Books dating back to the mid-sixteenth century include original African travelogues by Portuguese adventurers, with scientific and ethnographic coverage that read like science fiction; one antique colour plate shows a fantastic hippo baring jagged carnivorous fangs. The **newspaper display**, on the same floor, traces Zimbabwe's history in press reports, through federation, UDI and post-Independence – interesting not just for the history, but the way events were reported at different times. Climb the spiral stairs from here and you'll reach the **stamp collection**, including some from turn-of-century Cape Colony, overprinted with the British South Africa Company's initials. True to British form, a postal service was one of the first things organised in the new territory.

The downstairs **lobby** often has lively **public exhibitions**. A recent one showed Rhodesian and Zimbabwean political T-shirts and posters from both sides. A classic poster uses a publicity pic of Ian Smith as a target practice and turns it on its head with the caption: *Wanted for Murder*. During the bush war, when tourism was almost dead and the whole world against the government, T-shirts were printed with the slogan *Rhodesia is Super* and a cheery, plump elephant logo. The same logo is used today, with a companion elephant added to break the Rhodesian one's isolation – and, of course, the country has been renamed.

The **reading room** and **illustrations room**, also on the ground floor, are very browsable, and the former's glass wall, revealing an ornamental pond, must make it one of the most pleasant anywhere. All the printed matter on Zimbabwe you're ever likely to want can be dredged up from the public archives, or you can just immerse yourself in the large ready reference section. Dress warmly in winter – there's no heating and it gets surprisingly cold.

Victoria Museum

Mon–Sat 9am–5pm. Nominal entrance fee.

Knocked into a cocked hat by the excellent National Museum in Bulawayo, the capital's more modest historical museum gives a digestible chance to whizz through Zimbabwe's basics before heading out. But if you're soon moving on to Bulawayo don't waste your time here.

Amidst the motley collection of didactic bric-a-brac – fresh water aquaria, a history of life, the world and everything – just one exceptionally well-displayed gallery stands out. This is the **habitat exhibition** in the **natural sciences gallery**, a sure-draw for any wildlife enthusiast en route to the game parks. More than just museum pieces, this series of displays recreates Zimbabwe's variety of landscapes so realistically that you're left wondering how they got the granite kopje inside (adorned with appropriate flora and fauna). The other habitat displays are equally good – and more informative than a dozen books.

From far earlier times, there's a reconstruction of a fast moving **dinosaur** – half bird, half lizard and warm blooded. In one place in the Zambezi Valley over twenty of these small predators were found in a group. The **oldest fossils** discovered were found near Bulawayo – primitive plants 2700 million years old.

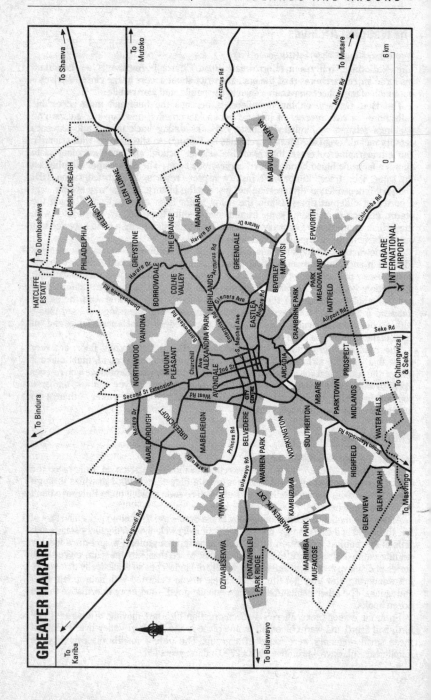

GREATER HARARE

Mbare

If Harare has a heart, **Mbare** must be it: a quarter that should on no account be missed. Once away from the orderly centre, Harare becomes an African city and Mbare is the liveliest part of the city, still close to the centre (3km), and with streams of people walking down the road and hanging about the run-down blocks of flats. Poverty is all around, though you're unlikely to see anything desperate. Begging is, however, on the increase.

Called Harare Township during the colonial days, Mbare's new name comes from the a chief who once held court on the kopje. The quarter is the decades-old **trading area** for Africans bringing their produce in from the country, and it remains so today, hosting the country's biggest **market** – known as the *musika* – at the nexus of all road transport. Leave by bus from here for the rural areas or the provincial towns and you'll be part of a vast crowd of travellers, especially at weekends and holidays.

The Market

In 1981, following Independence, the City Council developed the trading area by adopting the idea of communal markets being successfully developed at the time in China, and laid on washing facilities and covered stalls. The enormous complex of the *musika* nowadays has endless different sections, selling produce, clothes, crafts, live poultry, traditional medicines and the unrecognisable. This is also your chance to try *chibuku* at one of the **beer halls** or some **street food**. The **fresh produce** area is a banquet of primary-coloured fruits and vegetables – mounds of the stuff for bulk buyers or smaller carefully arranged piles if you just want a salad's worth. Expect to be appoached by a market porter who will trail after you, usually with a wheelbarrow, carrying your purchases for a tip.

In another part of the *musika*, **second-hand gear** ranges from piles of clothes on the pavement, to old plastic bottles and bags. In this litter-free country nothing is thrown away, everything is recyclable and almost anything broken can be cobbled together again. Invention is boundless – one stall sells buckled spectacle frames and broken sunshades. Look out, too, for the sandals made from worn down tyres with cross-over straps. It's a standing joke in Harare that if you get something ripped off, the second-hand market at Mbare is the first place to look.

Herbal medicines are sold at several stalls and you can track down traditional healers (*n'angas*) who work in the area. The stalls are a mishmash of skins and seed pods, things in bottles, bunches of dried plants, and prized items like cowrie shells and gemsbok tails. The government has passed a bill strengthening the position of *n'angas*. An association was formed in 1981 and there's now some co-operation between modern and traditional practices. Some spirit medium *n'angas* are concerned only with the cause of the illness, while others just treat the physical symptoms.

Mbare is also one of the best places around for **souvenirs** and all kinds of odd and easy-to-carry gifts. A lot of the **handiwork** on sale is for local consumption, most of it functional and not aimed at tourists, although increasing numbers are coming here. **Baskets** and **carved work** are common. Look out for hand-lathed objects like the snuff-boxes wrought from exotic woods, which are very popular with African women to whom smoking is traditionally prohibited. Hand-beaten copper and brass **bracelets** are good buys. The women, particularly, are open to **bargaining**, but they're tough dealers.

Not far from the market is the **Canon Paterson Art Centre**, where you can watch **stone sculptors** working. Their stuff is sold at a small shop crammed full of elephants, Zimbabwe birds and the like. The stone itself is much more beautiful than most of the pieces, but small sculptures are inexpensive and easy enough to transport.

Getting to Mbare

There's constant **transport** to Mbare. **Buses** leave from the city terminus on Angwa Street/South Avenue. You can get **emergency taxis** just opposite. **Taxis** are probably the easiest. **Walking** is possible, but will take a while: continue along Rotten Row or Cameron Street and ask for the *musika*.

The Suburbs

The once exclusively white areas of the capital are worth visiting if only as a monument to the British – or perhaps more truly American – suburban dream. But most travellers only pass through these elegant garden suburbs when en route to a handful of other sights.

Heroes' Acre

Heroes' Acre should top any list of out-of-the-centre attractions. Although you may not share the aesthetic, this shrine of the liberation struggle is undeniably imposing. It's a mixture of abstract monumental architecture, sculptures and friezes in an Afro-Korean version of socialist realism. From the un-African result it's easy to see that the Koreans dominated the design team.

One of the soldiers guarding the place will **guide** you up the monumental black **staircase**, give you a run-down on the entombed heroes and provide a commentary on the two friezes. The hefty granite slabs scale to a crescendo at the **eternal flame**, echoed in the flag raised by the triumphant figures of the foreground **monument to the unknown soldier**. (The eternal flame is actually an electric light switched on nightly.) On the lower first tier, burnished slabs bear down on the **graves of heroes** of the revolution while another series of unmarked stones waits eerily for tomorrow's luminaries.

Back on the ground, two didactic **friezes** in bronze relief flank the monument. The first traces **oppression**: vicious BSAP cops (the Rhodesian police force continued to bear the name of the British South Africa Police right up until Independence) and dogs savage youngsters and a mother and child, while the outraged parents organise opposition, eventually sending their children across the border for military training. The second frieze depicts the **armed struggle** with large dashes of heroism culminating in a triumphant, Leninesque, Robert Mugabe declaiming to the masses.

Permits for Heroes' Acre, issued while you wait, are required from the Ministry of Information, Enquiries and Public Relations Office at Linquenda House, Baker Street. The site is 5km from the centre, just off the Bulawayo road: catch any Bulawayo bus, or the Warren Park bus from a block past the *Jameson Hotel* on Samora Machel Avenue for the 15-minute ride. If you take a taxi, ask the driver to wait, or find your own way back.

On the way, near Heroes' Acre, you'll see an impressive new **stadium** – Chinese-built to Olympic proportions. There's a story, hopefully apocryphal, that the running track falls short by one metre. Huge political rallies and celebrations are held here, with mega-screens projecting images of the president for all to see.

Mukuvisi Woodlands

Tucked away in Harare's southern suburbs the msasa wooded **nature reserve of Mukuvisi** is stocked with antelope, zebra, wildebeest, elephants and rhino. Even before the enclosure was erected in 1980 there were resident populations of duiker, steenbok, hares and guinea fowl. Luckily for the wildlife, City Council attempts to put up a housing estate here were quashed when concerned residents appealed to the High Court.

The antelope roam free; fiercer denizens are penned off. Orphaned elephant calves, hand-reared at the woodlands, are a popular attraction, and easily seen at the 3.30pm feeding time. For intrepid urban adventuring, join one of the two-hour **foot safaris** that leave on Saturdays at 2.30pm and Sundays at 8.30am. You can get refreshments from the kiosk, open on weekends. The remaining 168 hectares, the majority of the woodlands, is open to all for walking and is thoroughly pleasant (though there have been odd reports of muggings). Over 230 **bird species** have been recorded: lucky ornithologists may spot the ground-nesting nightjars or some of the wildfowl. Most of the region's trees grow here in the last patch of indigenous woodland inside the city limits.

Chapungu Village

Despite the promise of an "insight into the cultural and traditional life of Zimbabwe", you'd be lucky to feel the pulse of Africa at **Chapungu** – a commercially run sculpture garden and cultural centre. In fairness, the nineteenth-century **Shona huts** are well constructed and the weekend dance and music performance (Sat 3pm; Sun 11am and 3pm) reputedly worth seeing. But given the fairly high entrance fee, the place is no big deal. The real highlight is the huge **sculpture garden** with well-known artists chiselling away, although the claim that it's Africa's biggest is an exaggeration; the one at Tengenenge in northern Zimbabwe is of staggering extent.

Chapungu is 8km east of town, near the Coronation Park campsite, just off the Mutare Road.

Borrowdale Park

There is **horse racing** at **Borrowdale Park**, 7km northeast of the centre, most weekends. Cutting across social classes, a day at the races is an enjoyable way of getting under the skin of local life, and one with food, drink and gambling on hand. If you just want to bet, try one of the seven off-course totes in town.

The Borrowdale **bus** picks up in Second Street on its way to the track.

Epworth Balancing Rocks

The **balancing rocks** at **Epworth**, just outside the eastern city limits and about 12km from the centre, don't hold huge attraction if you're planning to visit the Matopos district (where such phenomena abound). The main attraction of the place is the sheer concentration of rock formations in a small area. There's nothing unusual about the stones themselves – you'll see similar along roadsides all over Zimbabwe – but *en masse* they feel there as if by design. Young boys from the nearby settlement are persistent with offers to guide you and demands for cash, but you are free to clamber about the rocks and the visit costs only a few cents.

The **local community** here grew up on mission land as a squatter camp for war refugees. You'll notice how dissimilar it is from the rest of the country's planned suburbs, with its shanty-town look and some of the worst living conditions. In the early 1980s a cholera epidemic was hushed up, but the government has since worked hard to improve the people's lot with a successful programme of *Blair pit* latrine building and the installation of protected wells.

Catch the fairly frequent Epworth **bus** in town at the Fourth Street/Jason Moyo Avenue terminus. By **car**, take the Mutare Road turning right into Chiremba Road just outside the centre.

Eating and Drinking

There's no shortage of places to eat in central Harare, but don't expect anything too imaginative or beautifully presented. You can have *sadza* and *nyama* with the *povo* for next to nothing, or for something more familiar use the transatlantic-style snack bars. Alternatively, pay a bit more and you can choose from steak houses, Italian, Indian or Greek restaurants.

Budget bites

Around the station and Kopje endless joints sell cheap and filling **sadza meals**, rice with relish, and fried bread chunks. More centrally you'll get similar fare at the *OK Bazaars'* first floor snack bar, *Toff's Take-aways* in Rezende Street or *Baker's Inn,* First Street (next to *Chicken Inn*). Street food is noticeably absent in the centre, but at Mbare Market you'll find roasted *chibage*, boiled eggs and stalls for sadza and relish.

Coffee bars

The **coffee bars** serve reasonably priced sandwiches and snacks. With outdoor seating, for your contemplation of the passing scene, the best are the *Brazita* and *Le Paris* in the Parkade Shopping Centre and the *Wise Donkey* in the First Street mall, open from breakfast till shop closing. Harare's closest imitation of a continental coffee bar is the *Europa*, near the *Monomotapa Hotel*, in Samora Machel Avenue, open at night as well as for breakfast. Another trendy venue is the *Sandrock Café*, near the cinemas on Julius Nyerere Way, which has foreign newspapers and pavement seating. The best place for cappuccino, pastries and pizza is in the suburbs at the *Italian Bakery*, Avondale Shopping Centre, 144 King George Road (6am–11.30pm). *Scoop*, in the same centre, does great Italian ice cream.

Buffets and self-service

For lunch you can have a hotel buffet or sit outdoors at one of the snack bars. *Sherrol's in the Park* in Harare Gardens is pleasant for light meals under shady trees; they have freshly squeezed orange juice and various vegetarian options. *Europa* serves fry-ups, sandwiches and pasta. And you can get burgers, pizzas and pie and chips at the hotels, department stores and fast-food places. *Meikles Hotel* has a good outdoor restaurant on the ground floor, as does *Barbour's Terrace Restaurant* in First Street on the third floor. Of the two parts to *Barbour's*, the outside is cheaper and less formal. If you want to pig out at lunchtime, the *Holiday Inn* and the *Monomotapa* do substantial poolside buffets with a great selection of salads – a good choice for vegetarians.

Breakfast

Full **English breakfasts** to set you up for the day are the rule at most hotels. The *Monomotapa,* the *Sheraton,* the *Holiday Inn* (quite the best), and the *Cresta Jameson* do buffet breakfasts which give the opportunity to binge for a fixed fee.

Restaurants

Meals run from a couple of US dollars and up at most of Harare's restaurants. Standards are reasonable, but don't expect anything out of the ordinary.

Zimbabwean

National Handicraft Centre, Chinhoyi St/Grant St (☎721815). More a café than a restaurant, and open daytime only, this is a good place to try Zimbabwean staple food.

Ramambo Lodge, 1st floor, BB House, Samora Machel Ave/Leopold Takawira St (☎792029). This "safari camp restaurant" is the place to try game dishes you'll never taste elsewhere. The menu includes Zimbabwean fish as well as vegetarian specialities. There is marimba music at lunchtimes and traditional dancing in the evening. Recommended.

Greek
Demis, Speke Ave/Leopold Takawira St (☎723308). Starters here can make a full meal. A favourite with locals.
Aphrodite Taverna, Strathaven Shopping Centre (☎355000). Out of the centre location makes for a quiet atmosphere. Casual and very reasonably priced.

Italian
Guidos, Montagu Shopping Centre, Josiah Chinamano Ave (☎723349). Popular and inexpensive pizzeria near the Youth Hostel. Expect to wait for a table.
Garibaldi's, Baker Avenue between First and Second St (☎724387). Excellent Italian restaurant, with panache and real Italian food.
Pino's, 73 Union St (☎792303). Specialises in seafood.
Spagos Restaurant, *Russell Hotel* (☎790565). Recommended for good Italian pasta, as well as other un-Italian dishes. It's worth booking as it gets full.
Sherrol's in the Park, Harare Gardens (☎725535). Nice location, more especially during the day when the patio is open.

Chinese
Bamboo Inn, 81–83 Robert Mugabe Rd (☎705457). Best Chinese restaurant in town.
Manchurian, Second St Extension, Avondale (☎36166). Excellent Mongolian barbecue, the chef cooks your choice of vegetables and meat on a large central grill, inexpensive.
Mandarin, 1st floor, Ivory House, Robert Mugabe Road (☎726227). Good Chinese food, reasonably priced.

Portuguese
Coimbra, 61 Selous Ave (☎725467). Their speciality – spicy piri-piri chicken – is one good reason to eat here.

Indian
Bombay Duck, 7 Central Ave (☎721487). Big tasty helpings of rather un-Indian curries.
Sitar Restaurant, 39a Newlands Shopping Centre, Enterprise Road (☎729132). More authentic than the *Bombay Duck*, but inconveniently located in the suburbs.

Formal
Alexander's, 7 Livingstone Ave (☎700340). Possibly the best – and most expensive – restaurant in town.
L'Escargot, *Courtenay Hotel* (☎706411). One time winner of Harare's best restaurant award offering an a la carte menu.
Harvest Garden, *Sheraton Hotel*. "Africa night" every Thursday, serving African food from around the continent accompanied by a traditional band and dancing. Very expensive.

Vegetarian
The **Indian** and **Italian restaurants** above also have vegetarian dishes. Or you can hang the expense and feast to repletion at the pricey *Harvest Garden*'s buffet (see above) for a good salad selection , or at the *Holiday Inn*'s lunchtime buffet. *Ramambo Lodge*, (see above) has a couple of appetising vegetarian dishes despite its game orientation.
Homegrown Restaurant, Speke Ave/Leopold Takawira St (☎703545). Appetising choice of meals and excellent fruit juices, as well as juicy steaks.

Second Flight Up, First St. Excellent self-service salads and at least one vegetarian option daily. Daytime only.

Tacos Mexican Restaurant, Lintas House, 46 Union Ave (☎700377). Vegetarians should do fine on beans and avocadoes here.

Bars

Bars are invariably attached to **hotels**. At the cheaper ones things tend to be more **raucous**, particularly as the evening wears on – but this is where you're likely to find music (see below) and company if you want it. The *Terreskane* in the Avenues is a recommended outdoor place as is the garden at the *Earlside*. For more **sedate** – and often a little sedative – imbibing, the upmarket hotels with their "smart-casual" after-dark dress code are the obvious choice.

Music, Theatre and Films

Music vies with drinking to be Zimbabwe's unofficial national sport – and there's no shortage of jive joints in Harare. You'll find **live gigs** virtually every night, but while the pop-jaded west looks to Africa for inspiration, many Zimbabweans prefer American funk. Night clubs and discos spinning British and American discs cater to different social cliques all over town. Nevertheless local rock music is easy to find.

Besides rock, there are one or two venues for **classical music**. Watch the press for visiting international orchestras and performing groups. Countries eager to make a cultural mark on the developing world often lay on performances and there's sometimes the chance to take in exceptional stuff. There's also a nascent **drama** scene and you can sometimes see interesting performances. And if all else fails, there's always the **cinema**.

Rock Music and Clubs

Every weekend brings a choice of bands competing for punters. Zimbabwean musicians (see the *Contexts* piece for background and recommendations) work hard for a living, play frequently and often don't even own their instruments.

The biggest events are at the end of each month – right after payday. This is the time when you'll catch the big names well known in Britain like the **Bhundu Boys** and **Thomas Mapfumo**. Till the early hours they hold *pungwes* – a word derived from the all-night rallies organised by guerillas during the war. The best way to find a gig is to look at the posters wrapped around poles or tree trunks, or pasted up around town. The *Herald* also advertises major gigs and has a listing of nightclubs. These include some decidedly un-African night spots frequented by young whites, or first world-oriented blacks.

Central

Archipelago, Linquenda House, Baker Ave. A cocktail bar and dancing place, mostly white.

Harpers, *Holiday Inn*, Samora Machel Ave/Fifth St. Best jazz in town on Thursday evenings.

Job's Nite Spot, 15 Wonder Shopping Centre, Julius Nyerere Way. Separate drinking and dancing.

Manhattan Cocktail Bar, *Monomotapa Hotel,* 54 Park Lane. Live music most nights, often with an American or British flavour, but look out for the local brand of jazz with its traditional Shona rhythms.

Marilyn's, 99 Robert Mugabe Rd. You'll see the shortest skirts in town here, predominately a club for whites of all ages, with pop and jazz on different nights and plenty of picking up.

Playboy Night Club, 40 Union Ave. This club's mid-Atlantic flavour makes it popular with local groovers.

Queens, Federal and Elizabeth Hotels (see Accommodation for addresses). Hectic weekend venues, all very similar, but reliable spots for local bands. As big names often play at *Queens* or the *Liz*, these should be your first port of call if Zimbabwean pop is what you're after. Be on your guard for pickpockets and prostitutes. Muggings also occur frequently.

Samantha's, Avondale Shopping Centre. A fashionable hang-out for Harare youth.

Sandro's, 50 Union Ave, corner Julius Nyerere Way. Pretentious haunt of government officials and journalists, with cabaret shows and restaurants.

Solos, corner Jason Moyo/Harare streets. The city's swankiest club, in a converted synagogue with mirrored dance floor and waiter service. A wide variety of sounds, no sexual harassment and easy atmosphere. Recommended.

Away from the Centre

Most of the following venues are outdoor places where people go drinking and dancing on Saturday and Sunday afternoons and evenings.

The Skyline Motel, 19km peg, Masvingo Road. You'll need your own wheels to get here, or splash out for a taxi – worth it if someone good is playing. Reckoned by some to be the best music venue in Southern Africa, it's a favourite of the Real Sounds, and you'll find consistently excellent bands playing in the garden at weekends. Go in the evening and bop to the setting sun, while your steak sizzles. No need to take your own meat, buy it there and *braai* it yourself.

Club Hideout 99, 36 Cedrella Ave, Lochinvar, Southerton. A major outdoor venue for big name bands, with three bars and a big tent covering the whole place during the rainy season.

Sanganayi Inn, Kirkman Rd (Dzivaresekwa turn-off). Orchestra Mangalepa, billed as the *rumba kings from Zaire*, are resident throughout the week; occasional guest artists.

Spillway Restaurant, Lake Chivero (Lake McIlwaine). A good weekend venue with lakeside jams in the afternoons.

Seven Miles Motel, Masvingo Road. Bands strike up every Saturday from 4pm till late.

The Red Lantern, Mutare Road, Msasa. Near the *Nitestar* drive-in cinema; also recommended.

The Rose and Crown, Hatfield. Pay less than town centre to see the same bands, although the taxi fare is steep if you're on your own.

The High-density Suburbs

You're in for a different experience in the **high-density suburbs**, where admission is less exclusive than in the centre or in the out-of-reach outer areas – though you may also feel a bit more of an outsider. For the undeterred, though not recommended for single women, there's often live music at **Club Saratoga**, Jabavu Drive, Highfields; **Machipisa Nightclub**, Nyandoro Road; and **Mushandire Pamwe Hotel**, Nyandoro Road – all within 100 metres of each other, and all a rave.

Daytime Concerts

Daytime concerts, staged occasionally in one of the stadiums or gardens, tend to be fun, family-oriented affairs. There's sometimes something going on in the Harare Gardens. Bigger concerts with imported stars or local big names, and festive occasions (bands play on Independence Day) take place in the National or Rufaro Stadiums. Also look out for daytime events at all the out of town venues.

Films

Action-packed American **films** are favoured by Zimbabwean cinema audiences. But only a limited selection of these and other popular movies make the circuit. Check the *Herald* for what's on. The **central cinemas** are the *Rainbow* in Park Lane, the *Mini Cine* in Baker Avenue, the four *Kine* cinemas in Union Avenue, and the *Liberty Theatre* in Cameron Street, which specialises in kung-fu, violence and mayhem. *Alliance Francaise*, 328 Herbert Chitepo Avenue (☎720777), sometimes has seasons of French films.

Theatre

The most regular **theatre** consists of missable musicals and sitting room dramas at the large auditorium at the *Reps Theatre*, down Second Street Extension. The small auditorium has more interesting productions from time to time. More adventurous productions of **African plays** like Soyinka's *Opera Wonyosi* have been staged in the courtyard at *Delta Gallery*.

Booking for many events may be arranged through the *Spotlight*, Theatre Booking Office, Chancellor House, 69 Samora Machel Ave (Mon–Fri 8am–noon & 1–4pm; ☎724754).

Shopping

There's little exotic about the actual experience of shopping in central Harare: shopping malls, department stores and supermarkets give the place a humdrum, old-fashioned feel. Nevertheless it's an excellent place to buy crafts and a few distinctly Zimbabwean items. **Crafts** worth buying include wall hangings and fabrics, inventive handmade wire toys and African printed fabrics. A growing network of informal African commercial links has meant the influx of traders from around the continent bringing West African **carvings** and Ethiopian silver **jewellery**. You can pick up wonderful items of **clothing** such as locally printed T-shirts with designs by leading Zimbabwean artists, extremely cheap and lively canvas shoes, and desert boots.

Stone sculptures by internationally acclaimed Shona carvers make more expensive and more substantial souvenirs – or investments. Locally produced records and cassette tapes cost far less than British pressings of Zimbabwean pop. The centre of the city is good for **curios, crafts and records**, and the more colourful **Kopje** area for African fabrics. The most interesting place to buy souvenirs and produce, however, is **Mbare Market** (see p.69), while, if you're keen on **sculpture crafts**, see the *Galleries* section on pp.65–66.

Food

Grocers are liberally distributed throughout Harare and **food shopping** is easy. Try the big **supermarkets**, *OK* or *TM*, or one of the **delicatessens** in the Avenues selling slightly more exciting foods. The Fife Avenue shopping centre is recommended, as is the **greengrocer** in the central Parkade Shopping Centre – comparatively expensive but dependable for good fruit and vegetables.

In the suburbs and around the central bus terminus you'll find modest markets where women sell fruit and vegetables by the handful-sized pile, wrapped in newspaper. If you're mobile, try *Honeydew* farm shop just off Mutare Road (turn off at the *Red Fox Hotel* sign); the shop has a wide selection of produce, including bean sprouts, honey, jams and other home-made goodies. And, best of all, Mbare market should be experienced.

Crafts and fabrics

Harare has a surfeit of **souvenir shops** but as the quality of **curios** varies very greatly, it's worth a fair bit of looking around. There are several curio shops around First Street if you aren't too particular and just want to take something back. You're also likely to be pestered by people in the street selling small stone carvings – a laughing hippo or elephant – cheaper than the official curio outlets. Shops selling better **quality arts and**

crafts are thinner on the ground and listed below. For Java prints and colourful printed cottons, walk along South Street near the station. Check out *Dayal's* or *Adam Brothers*, cave-like and packed with prints from Zimbabwe, Zambia and Malawi. *Adam Brothers* also have a more spacious shop in Kenneth Kaunda Avenue. *Plaza Oriental*, Robert Mugabe Road (toward *Queens Hotel*) is the best shop for Java prints with a terrific selection, well displayed on the walls. If you're in Zimbabwe for a while, consider using one of the African tailors who could make up whatever you wanted from local fabrics for a modest fee – find one through the fabric shops or enquire from one of the men you'll see sewing at old treadle machines on the street. Bright pumps *(tackies)*, sneakers and desert boots are available very cheaply at any of the Bata shoe shops, the main chain of shoe shops throughout Zimbabwe.

Danhiko Project, 123 Mutare Rd. The colourful and distinctive Danhiko products (prints, dyed cloths, bags, clothes and wooden carvings) sold at the better craft shops can be bought well below shop prices, directly from the project on the eastern side of town opposite the *Nitestar* Drive-In, though you'll need your own transport or take a taxi to get there.

Dendera Gallery, Second St/Robert Mugabe Rd. The most upmarket and stylish of the craft shops with a superb collection of domestic and ritual artefacts, musical intruments, textiles and baskets. It's not cheap, but is the place to go if you are looking for something old. It also sells the exceptional amber and Ethiopian silver jewellery, under the *Rayne* label. *Rayne* also use old, clear glass trading beads in their beautiful necklaces and earrings.

Jairos Jiri, Park Lane Building, Julius Nyerere Way. One of the countrywide chain selling fine crafts by disabled craft workers, close to the *Monomatapa Hotel* and National Gallery. Worth browsing, though the Bulawayo shop is better stocked.

Limited Editions, Africa House, 100 Jason Moyo St. Sells good quality clothing, jewellery, prints and traditional arts and crafts. It's conveniently opposite *Air Zimbabwe* and next door to *Grass Roots* bookshop between Third and Fourth Streets.

Little Cave, 103 Kaguvi St. Good for T-shirts, verdite carvings, pottery, basketware and a range of ethnic crafts.

Mbare Market (see p.69). The biggest selection of curios, and a vast array of stalls in the indoor crafts section where you're guaranteed to find something unusual. Check out the crafts in the building on the corner of the large open market.

National Gallery Shop, Park Lane. An enormous sculpture selection, as well as basketry, fabrics and a representative sample of Zimbabwean craft.

National Handicraft Centre, Grant/Chinoyi Sts. Excellent crafts as well as a restaurant serving traditional food to make your walk down to the Kopje district worthwhile.

Trading Company, First Street between Samora Machel and Union Ave. Top of the list if you're after clothes. They sell safari clothing and leather accessories as well as a full range of locally printed T-shirts, sweat shirts and fabrics, with a selection of crafts thrown in.

Zimba Co-op, Parkade Arcade, Samora Machel Ave. A good bet for traditional crafts, wire toys, basketry and hand-dyed cloth.

Music and traditional instruments

Harare is second to Bulawayo for record stores, though there are some promising places nonetheless. Also worth a look are some of the record bars in the big department stores, plus the many small record shops and pavement vendors in the Charter Road area. Some sell **traditional instruments** too, as do the National Gallery shop, *Jairos Jiri* opposite, *Zimba Craft Co-op* and *Dendera Gallery*.

Pop Shop, First St. The selection here is pretty much up with Bulawayo standards. A good last stop to stock up on discs before leaving.

Spinalong, Hungwe House, George Silundika Ave. Great selection of West African sounds, as well as Zimbabwean.

Music, 86 Rezende St. Mostly second-hand LPs.

EMBASSIES AND HIGH COMMISSIONS

Angola Doncaster House, Speke Ave/Angwa St ☎790675.

Australia Karigamombe Centre, 4th Floor, 53 Samora Machel Ave ☎794591.

Austria Room 216, New Shell House, 30 Samora Machel Ave ☎702921.

Belgium Tanganyika House, 23 Third St/Union Ave ☎793306.

Botswana 22 Phillips Ave, Belgravia ☎729551.

Bulgaria 15 Maasdorp Ave, Milton Park ☎730509 or ☎730504.

Canada 45 Baines Ave ☎733881.

Denmark UDC Centre, Union Ave/First St ☎790398 or ☎790399.

Ethiopia 14 Lanark Rd, Belgravia ☎725822 or ☎725823.

France Ranelagh Rd, Highlands ☎49096 or ☎49098.

Germany 14 Samora Machel Ave ☎302272.

Greece 8 Deary Ave, Belgravia ☎723747.

Ghana 1 Downie Ave, Belgravia ☎738652 or ☎738653.

Hungary 2 Rivonia Drive, Mount Pleasant ☎884705.

India 12 Natal Rd, Belgravia ☎795955 or ☎795956.

Italy 7 Bartholomew Close, Greendale ☎47279 or ☎48199.

Japan Commercial Union House, Baker Ave ☎727500 or ☎727769.

Kenya 95 Park Lane ☎790847.

Malawi Malawi House, 42 Harare St ☎705611.

Mozambique 152 Herbert Chitepo Ave ☎790837.

Namibia visas from Zambia High Commission.

Netherlands 47 Enterprise Rd , Highlands ☎731428.

New Zealand 57 Jason Moyo Ave, Batanai Gardens ☎728681.

Portugal 10 Samora Machel Ave ☎725107 or ☎722291.

Russia 70 Fife Ave ☎720358.

South Africa Trade Mission, Temple Bar House, Baker Ave ☎707901. Slow for visas.

Spain 16 Phillips Ave, Belgravia ☎304118 or ☎304119.

Sweden Pegasus House, Samora Machel Ave ☎790651.

Switzerland 9 Lanark Rd, Belgravia ☎703997.

Tanzania 23 Baines Ave ☎721870.

United Kingdom Stanley House, Jason Moyo Ave/First St ☎793781 or ☎793789.

USA 172 Herbert Chitepo Ave ☎794521.

Zambia, Zambia Hse, Union Ave☎ 302272.

Listings

Airlines *Air Zimbabwe*, City Air Terminal, Third St/Speke Ave (☎794481); *British Airways*, First Floor, Batanai Gardens, First St/Jason Moyo Ave (☎794616); *Qantas*, 5th Floor Karigamombe Centre, 54 Union Ave (☎703494); *Ethiopian Airlines*, CABS Centre, Jason Moyo Ave (☎790705); *Zambia Airways*, Pearl Assurance Building, First St (☎793235); *Air Malawi*, Throgmorton House, Samora Machel Ave/Julius Nyerere Way (☎706497); *Kenya Airways*, 1st Floor, Batanai Gardens, 1st St/Jason Moyo Ave (☎792181); *Balkan Airlines*, Trustee House, 55 Samora Machel Ave (☎729213); *Air India*, Batanai Gardens, 57 Jason Moyo Ave/First St (☎700318); Air Tanzania, Lintas House, Union Ave (☎706444); *TAP Air Portugal*, Prudential House, Speke Ave/Angwa St (☎706231); *UTA*, 95 Jason Moyo Ave (☎703868); *KLM Royal Dutch Airlines*, Harvest House, Baker Ave (☎705430); *Lufthansa German Airlines*, Mercury House, 24 George Silundika Ave (☎707606). *South African Airways*, 2nd Floor, Takura House, 69–71 Union Avenue (☎738922/738923). **Flight information & airport** (☎737011). *Air Zimbabwe* also has a reservations office conveniently at the airport.

Alternative therapies *Acupuncture* Jenny Sanders (☎47931), *Homoeopathy* Adel Smith (☎42181) or David Stobbs (☎33149), *Osteopathy* Trevor Howard (☎705373).

American Express is represented by *Manica Travel Services*, 2nd Floor, Travel Centre, Jason Moyo Ave (☎703421/7) and *Halmac Travel*, Wetherby House, 55A Baker Ave (☎725673/5).

Automobile Association, Fanum House, Samora Machel Ave (between First and Angwa Sts, ☎707021).

Banks are open weekdays 8.30am–2pm, except Wednesday (8.30am–midnight) and Saturday (8.30–11am). There are branches scattered all over town. Head offices: *Zimbank*, First St/Speke Ave; *Barclays*, First St/Jason Moyo Ave; *Standard Chartered*, Second St/Baker Ave; *Grindlays*, Baker Ave (between First and Second St).

Bike rental *Bushtrackers,* 24 Downie Ave, Belgravia (☎ 733573; Fax 35585). Mountain bikes for day rent around Harare, or for extended trips around Zimbabwe, from US$8 per day. Refundable cash deposit Z$200.00. Bicycle tours may be run by this company, situated off Second St, beyond the Royal Harare Golf Course.

Bookshops *Grassroots*, Jason Moyo Ave (between Third and Fourth St) has a selection of books covering social and political issues. The *Mambo Press Bookshop*, Mutual House, Speke Ave, is also good on history and politics, though with more emphasis on religious books. *Kingstons'* two bookshops, on Jason Moyo Ave/Second St and in the Parkade Shopping Centre, are the biggest in Harare and have a wide selection of periodicals.

Book exchange *Treasure Trove* 26 Second St, opposite the Information Bureau. *Booklovers Paradise*, 48 Angwa St, between Union Ave and Julius Nyerere Way.

Bus companies *Zupco*, Mbare Terminus (☎702121) goes to Zambia. Local bus enquiries for all destinations are best made in person at Mbare Terminus where several different companies operate services. See also *Coach Companies*, below.

Camping equipment A selection of basic stuff including locally made gas canisters to fit Camping Gaz equipment can usually be found at *Fereday and Sons*, 72 Robert Mugabe Rd. Equipment hire at *Rooney's Hire Service*, Shop 1, St Barbara House, Baker Ave/Leopold Takawira St (☎706340).

Car rental is cheapest from *Mike Harris Car Sales*, Leopold Takawira St/Jason Moyo Ave (☎705734/705508, ext 01/7), but they don't have the national network of the big three. For one-way rent the best is *Avis*, 5 Samora Machel Ave (☎720351) or after hours at the Airport (☎50121). There's little to choose between the rest: *Hertz*, Meikles Hotel Desk, Third St/Jason Moyo Ave (☎792791/2/3); *Echo Europcar*, 19 Samora Machel Ave (☎702221); and *Truck and Car Hire*, PO Box 1315 (☎700443). *Impexo*, 7 Charter Rd (☎705763/705767/8) hire standard vehicles as well as a few 4WD's, but book before you arrive as 4WD's are exceedingly thin on the ground. Hertz for instance has its 4WD's permanently leased to the government.

Car repairs and spares garages down Kaguvi St. Note that spares are virtually unavailable and extremely expensive.

Coach companies *Express Motorways*, Julius Nyerere Parkade, Rezende St/Baker Ave (☎720392). Services for Bulawayo and Mutare depart from the Rezende St terminal. *Express* also has information about services to Malawi. *Ajay Motorways*, 2nd Floor, Travel Centre, Jason Moyo Ave (☎703421). *Ajay* services for Bulawayo depart from *Monomatapa Hotel*.

Doctors are listed in the front of the Harare telephone directory.

Emergencies Police, fire and ambulance ☎99.

Hospitals and private clinics *Parirenyatwa Hospital*, Mazowe St/Josiah Tongogara Ave (☎726121). There's a **fever ward** at *Wilkens Hospital*, Drummond Chaplin St (entrance in Josiah Tongogara Ave). For a **private consultation** there are several doctors at the *Avenues Clinic*, Baines Ave/Mazowe St (☎732055) or *Medical Chambers*, Leopold Takawira St/Burns Ave.

Left luggage at the station "cloak room" costs a few cents per day per item.

Libraries The **Harare City Library** (weekdays 9am–5.30pm, Sat 9am–1pm) has a reasonable reference section with a lot on Zimbabwe. The **British Council Library**, Jason Moyo Ave/Park St (Tues–Fri 9am–5.30pm, Sat 9am–1pm) is also free, with a dazzling array of British periodicals and week-old (or more) newspapers in its reading room.

Maps The Surveyor General's Office, Electra House, Samora Machel Ave (near the *Jameson Hotel*), PO Box 8099, Causeway (☎794545). For the best maps available of Zimbabwe, covering more or less anything you're likely to need including hiking maps.

Passport photos For emergency one hour service try the studio in Fredor House, Speke St (☎793572) or the one in the Parkade Shopping Centre, 5 Samora Machel Ave. They're expensive, so bring photos with you if you're applying for visas. There are no do-it-yourself booths.

Pharmacies are open during normal shopping hours apart from *QV Day and Night Pharmacy* (8am–8pm daily) on Union Ave/Angwa St (☎722678).

Post office The main one is on Inez Terrace/Jason Moyo Ave; another is in Union Ave, opposite the Parkade. Mon–Fri 8.30am–4pm; Sat 8.30–11am.

Samaritans (☎722000; 24hr).

Swimming pool The Les Brown Pool is an Olympic-sized affair off Park Lane, opposite *Monomotapa Hotel*. Mid-May to mid-Aug open daily 11am–4pm; rest of the year open daily 10am–6.25pm.

Taxis can be called: *Creamline* (☎703333); *A1* (☎706996); *Rixi* (☎707707); *Avondale* (☎35883); Harare Minicabs (☎50867); Pfumo Minicabs (☎67530). There are also a number of ranks: outside the station in Kenneth Kaunda Ave; the east side of Cecil Square; near the Civic Centre in Kaguvi St and others peppered around the centre, especially at the big hotels.

Telephone booths are scattered about the centre, usually functional and well used – expect a very long wait. The nicest place to queue is outside the four booths in the First St mall. There are phones in *Meikles Hotel* foyer and outside the *Monomotapa Hotel*. For international calls use the phones on the first floor of the main post office and have plenty of Z$1 coins to feed continuously into the greedy machines.

Telephone directory enquiries. Local ☎92. Trunk ☎91. Dial ☎0 for operator to make trunk calls.

Thomas Cook Pearl Assurance House, First St (☎728961).

Tourist information Staff at the *Publicity Association* on the Second St side of African Unity Square usually seem reluctant to part with information, but you can sometimes get answers to specific questions; they sell a good map of Harare and publish a free monthly events containing an adequate map. The *Zimbabwe Tourist Development Corporation* in Jason Moyo Ave/Fourth St has information on Zimbabwe in general and is altogether more friendly.

Travel agents are all over the place. The biggest is *Manica Travel*, 2nd Floor, Travel Centre, Jason Moyo Ave (☎703421 or ☎703427).

AROUND HARARE

If you're spending some time in Harare a number of nearby destinations make pleasant breaks, although they aren't really worth a special excursion if you're pressed for time and plan only a brief stay in the capital. **Lake Chivero** is a popular weekend outing for Hararians and there's a string of low-key wildlife distractions along the way. **Ewanrigg Botanical Gardens**, too, are a pleasant place to spend a few hours. If the Matopos Hills (Chapter 3), with their typically Zimbabwean rock kopjes, aren't on your itinerary, then it's worth a trip to **Dombashawa** north of Harare to see the inspiring granite formations and rock paintings.

Lake Chivero

The damming of the Hunyani River in 1952, to provide year-round water for Salisbury's growing population, opened up an accessible "Recreation Park" around the artificial lake. Though very much a resort for Harare weekend trippers, **Lake Chivero**, 32 km southwest of Harare (and known until the early 1990s as **Lake McIlwaine**), is pretty enough – *msasa*-clad hills encircling wide stretches of water and the lure of game-viewing in the National Park on the southern side.

The northern side, which is generally a place for just a day out, is more developed and commercialised, but to the south there are National Parks **chalets** for a cheap and restful weekend.

On the way: birds, snakes and lions

Tourist blurbs always promote the Lion and Cheetah Park, Larvon Bird Gardens and the Snake Park – all on the way to Chivero – as essential Harare excursions. **Larvon Bird Gardens** (Mon–Wed & Fri 11am–5pm, Sat & Sun 9am–5pm; closed Thurs) is the one with most allure, housing 400 species of local and exotic birds in reasonably spacious conditions. By car, turn right at the sign, 17km out of Harare on the Bulawayo road.

A few kilometres past the birds is the **Snake Park** (daily 8.30am–5pm) where you can look at a representative sample of Zimbabwe's snakes coiled behind glass-fronted cages. Further down the same road, the **Lion and Cheetah Park**, while it's little more than a zoo, affords real close-ups of the big cats lounging around the entrance waiting to be fed. A recent shock-horror press story featured someone who crept into the enclosure at night; all that was found the next day was a driving licence and car keys. A follow-up report revealed the victim was a fundamentalist Christian who committed suicide trying to emulate the Roman martyrs.

Without a car the only way to see the park (unless you're similarly obsessed) is on the daily *UTC* tour, with departure at 9.30am from *Meikles*. *UTC* also does a daily afternoon tour of the Lion and Cheetah Park, combined with Lake Chivero game park.

Northern Chivero – water sports, tea and scones

The north–south divide is pretty strong at Chivero. Southern shore wilderness purists curl up their lips at the thought of the developed north side, while north coast enthusiasts descend en masse for *braais* and boating.

Two roads make for the **northern side**. The first, 16km from the city, leads to the peaceful upper reaches of the lake, good for picnics. The shore itself is 10km from the main road. The next sign is for the northern shore, 13km further on, which takes you to **Admiral's Cabin**, the **Hunyani Hills Hotel** and the **Sailing Club**. You can hire canoes at *Admiral's Cabin* (and at the *Ancient Mariner*) but there's little else to recommend it. Weekends draw hordes of radio-blasting picnickers who come here simply for a booze-up.

The *Hunyani Hills Hotel* (☎162-2236; ③) is much nicer; you can have **tea** in the garden, survey the lake and stroll along the shore to get a view of the dam wall. For this, go to the gate of the sailing club, and ignoring the No Entry sign, walk on past the club house to follow the path along the wooded lake shore until you see the wall. It's about 45 minutes there and back. The hotel itself is 28km from Harare on the Bulawayo Road. At Turnpike Garage turn left and continue 2km to the lakeshore and hotel.

The **lake water** is always beautiful in the sunlight but bilharzia and the odd crocodile make it off-limits for swimming. If the urge to cool off becomes irresistible, however, there's a **swimming pool** at *Admiral's Cabin*.

Getting there and spending the night

Getting to Chivero from Harare is easy enough. From the *Jameson Hotel* on Samora Machel Ave **buses** go to several destinations on the Bulawayo Road which can drop you at the northern shore turn-off or at a point out of town you could hitch from. A daily bus also leaves Mbare at about 9am bound for **fishing spots on the northern side**; it takes an hour and then returns to the terminus, but may be difficult to track down. Alternatively, hitching should be pretty straightforward, especially at the weekend.

The Southern Shore and Game Park

Open dawn to dusk.

With the rather wonderful exception of **rhino**, there's no **big game** in Lake Chivero park. But there's plenty of antelope, giraffe, zebra and smaller mammals to compensate, and a wide variety of water birds – as well as species favouring the *msasa* woodland. The lake provides a good opportunity to spot smaller denizens, too, like butterflies, insects, reptiles and amphibians. Look out for the tiny white and pink tree frogs clinging onto branches. The prettiest time for a visit is September, when the *msasas* confoundingly unfurl their autumn-coloured spring leaves in preparation for the rains.

The park is fairly small and covered well by a network of game drives. You'll invariably see zebra and antelope in open grassy areas, and giraffe browsing in more wooded spaces. Accompanied **horse riding** is an excellent way to get around the park if you don't have a car, and it can get you really close to the rhinos. Book at the Parks Office for a ride, either first thing in the morning or at 3pm.

Bushman's Point

Bushman's Point in the east is the only area where **walking** is permitted but you need a car to get there. This thickly wooded waterside area is alive with foraging *dassies* – rock rabbits. On a rock face overlooking the shoreline path are some faded **rock paintings**. Look for the line of thirteen identical kneeling figures at the bottom of the face – perhaps a dance chorus. Also low down are three figures with sticks, standing, sitting and recumbent, which overlie some striped forms.

Crocodile Rock

The other rock painting sites in the park are to be found at **Crocodile Rock**, for which you'll need transport and to take a *Parks* guide with you. They are well worth seeing, though – two large crocs, one painted belly up, make a unique panel with nine hunters to the left of them executed in great detail – and the rock is the most attractive of the park's several designated **picnic sites**. It is the haunt of herons and pied kingfishers, rather than crocodiles, and has a marvellous view over the lake.

Transport and accommodation

There's **no public transport** to the National Park but **hitching or busing** to the turn-off is much the same as for the northern side: just get off at the signpost after crossing the Hunyani River and you'll find the Park entrance 6km from the main road. The best bet is to wait at the signpost for a lift right into the park. Alternatively, *UTC* does an **afternoon trip** to the Lion Park and Game Park and, if you want to stay, it may be possible to arrange to be picked up a couple of days later.

Chivero is incredibly popular and accommodation fills up quickly at weekends and school holidays, but at other times you'll usually find a place. **Book** through the *National Parks Central Booking Office* for the chalets (☎706077; ①–②). Of these, *Kingfisher Lodge* has the best view of the lake.

Ewanrigg Botanical Gardens

Small admission fee.

Set in commercial farmlands, **Ewanrigg Botanical Gardens** are just half an hour's drive northeast of the city – and a lovely place to spend the day. They are most famous for **cycads** and **aloes** – red-hot-poker-like succulents whose flowers span the spectrum from yellow to a brilliant red – but there's also a herbarium and a water garden. During the week you can have a walk in solitude. At weekends the place fills up with trippers out for a lunchtime *braai* using the fireplaces and picnic spots provided. The most impressive time to visit is mid-winter, when the aloes are in flower. It's rather dusty and dried out in August and September before the pre-rains flowering.

For the traditional-style **herb garden**, head through the aloes and up steep steps colonnaded by thickly planted young trees. Down on the other side you'll find the **water garden**. Bear left through an open grassy area, planted with trees and massive bamboos, to get back to the entrance gate.

Take the Shamva **bus** from Mbare and ask to be put down at the Ewanrigg turn-off; the gate is about 1km down the dirt road. Or, **by car**, drive out on the Enterprise Road, taking the Shamva fork about 15km from the city centre; Ewanrigg is signposted.

Chinamora Rock Paintings

There's a multitude of painted caves in the communal lands around Harare. The two best known sites are at **Dombashawa** and **Ngomakurira**, in the Chinamora Communal Lands north of the city limits. Dombashawa is well visited and you're unlikely to be alone. Ngomakurira, 10km further on is a lonelier and altogether more arresting spot.

Transport to either site is straightforward. For both you should take the Bindura **bus** that goes via Dombabshawa from Mbare bus station. For Dombashawa get off at its turn-off and for Ngomakurira continue on to the Sasa Road stop. Buses are frequent and leave central Harare along Chancellor Avenue and past Borrowdale race track. You could try catching one en route, or hitch from Chancellor; the route out of town is interesting in itself, passing by the mansions, pools and flourishing gardens of Harare's plushest suburbs.

By **car or hitching** take the Borrowdale/Dombashawa road. For Dombashawa turn right at the sign 30km from Harare. The car park for the cave is just under a kilometre further and the cave is a twenty-minute walk along a clear path up the hillside.

Dombashawa

The attraction of **DOMBASHAWA** lies in the enormous whaleback rocks of the site, which you can clamber over to gain vantage points – each allowing you to slip back in time as you survey the valleys. The paintings themselves are, by comparison, disappointing, having fallen victim to fire, smoke, vandalism, graffiti and cleaning. Don't base your judgement of the form on what you see here.

But the largest collection of paintings spreads out on the inner walls of the **main cave**. Buffaloes, zebras, elephants, kudus and rhinos keep human figures company. One of the most interesting groups, in a cleft 20m left of the main cave, has an indistinct elephant harassed by hunters. Slightly further, but off to the right, are some human and semi-human figures, believed to be associated with rainmaking ceremonies. Around the area, several other clefts and small areas of rock are also daubed with the (now pale and delicate) pictures of animals and people.

A small **interpretation centre**, next to the parking lot at the foot of the hill, gives an interesting overview of the art, with astonishing facts about the age of some of these ancient works.

Ngomakurira

To reach **NGOMAKURIRA**, carry on along the main road for just under 12km past the Dombashawa turnoff. Turn right at the signposted Sasa Road, and there's parking about 1km from the main road. For the **walk up to the site**, it's worth considering any offers from local kids to guide you as it's not that easy to find the way. A large isolated tree on the left at the foot of Ngomakurira's massive dome makes a shady parking place and a useful landmark; walk from it along a path between maize fields to the base of the hill, then take one of the paths which lead up to a wooded valley watered by a clear stream and rock pools. The stream leads to the bottom of a sheer cliff on which are the numerous faint but beautiful paintings.

The Site

Some say that Ngomakurira – *the place where the spirits beat the drums* – takes its name from the echoes one hears in this perfect amphitheatre. It's a powerful and otherworldly place, abundant with elegant paintings which decorate the bottom of the dayglo-orange-stained cliff. In that enclosed space its sweep and height are enormously magnified. When you sit on the back of the granite hump opposite, you can hear your own words perfectly, and mockingly, reproduced by the ancestors.

The paintings here include four huge **elephants**, rated amongst the best of their type by Peter Garlake, Zimbabwe's leading rock art expert. There is no shortage of other fine renderings, either, with some fascinating scenes of **human groups**. One shows a man, arms raised in terror, being clubbed by another. It was scenes like these that led some anthropologists to impose an interpretation of ritual regicide (king-killing) on examples of Southern African stone age art. One conclusion was that such motifs could not have been produced by hunter-gatherers like the **San** (see Chapter Ten, "The Kalahari Desert").

Current theories disagree, pointing out that the lifestyles depicted in the paintings are very similar to those of San groups like the !Kung. And the regicide theory sounds, in any case, somewhat sensational. There is no evidence of such acts having been carried out anywhere in the country.

THE MIDLANDS

For its tourist image, the **Midlands** proclaims itself *the heart of Zimbabwe* – and each of its towns claims to distil the country's essence. **Gweru**, the only place that can make any real claims as an urban centre, declares itself the *big heart of Zimbabwe*, while diminutive **Kwekwe** asserts it's *the industrial heart of Zimbabwe*. In all fairness, there's some truth in these claims. The Midlands are rich in gold, asbestos, nickel and chrome, and the region is the base for the country's important textile and steel industries.

For visitors, much of the Midlands is eminently missable, but its towns aren't totally devoid of charm. To really get to know Zimbabwe, it's worth spending a night in at least one Midlands town – all are pretty, very quiet and, if you're in no hurry, they make likely stopovers for a north–south journey. (The real tourist highlights of the Midlands – the wonderful stone ruins at Danangombe and Naletale – are actually covered in Chapter Four with Khami, as they are sited mid-way between Gweru and Bulawayo.)

Two main arteries cut through this heartland, each splaying out from Harare. The **road and railway line to Bulawayo** takes in the larger towns of Gweru, Kwekwe and Kadoma, while the **Masvingo route** whips through the Chivu and the old mining town of Mvuma.

The Bulawayo Road: Chegutu, Kadoma and Kwekwe

The towns on the Harare–Bulawayo road see few, if any tourists, but were well visited by **elephant hunters** in the past. The Portuguese set up an ivory trading post in the eighteenth century near Chegutu. They soon went, but the hunters stayed; in fact, so many people came up to Chegutu from Bulawayo in the second half of the last century that the route became known as Hunters Road.

Chegutu and Kadoma

First stop down the line towards Bulawayo is the tiny farming settlement of
CHEGUTU. The local hotel burnt down in 1989, leaving a village quiet even by
Midlands standards.

KADOMA is larger, with its very smart *Ranch Motel,* Bulawayo Road (☎2321,
☎2322, ☎2323, or ☎2324; ⑥) where the intercity coaches break for tea or a meal.
Beyond that, it's a typical colonial railway town, by-passed by the main road, with well-
preserved buildings a short hop from the station. Everything worth seeing is in fact
conveniently near the station. What bustle there is happens around the nearby
Cameron Square, planted with palms, gum trees and jacarandas. Fronting the square
is the *Grand Hotel,* its elegant facade recalling the gold-rush days when it hosted dancing girls, hunters and prospectors. Little more than a knocking-shop these days, it's
best admired from the outside. The place to survey the passing scene is the *Blue Jay
Café* also on the square.

If you're tempted to stay in Kadoma, head to *Speck's Hotel,* Union Street (☎Kadoma
3302; ③) also colonial-styled, but saved from the fate of the *Grand.*

Kwekwe

The Harare–Bulawayo road passes the scarred, mine-dumped outskirts of **KWEKWE**,
where a colossal rifle aimed at the dumps announces "Kwekwe Shooting Club".
Kwekwe represents the Midlands of hunched office blocks, with its downtown district
an aspiring city centre lacking the means. Walk a hundred metres and you're in the
suburbs among downmarket shops. Older, more photogenic buildings are concentrated
a block up, in Second Street.

Mining

Kwekwe was built on **gold**, growing up as a mining settlement for the rich surrounding
reefs, and its one tourist attraction is the **National Museum of Goldmining** (daily
8am–5pm). This is a treat if you enjoy antique machinery – suction pumps, engines and
rock crushers – otherwise it's not over-inspiring, except for the amazing **paper house**.
This, almost a century old and made of wire-reinforced papier mâché, was Zimbabwe's
first prefabricated building. It has stood since 1894, when it was shipped out from
England as a residence for the general manager of Kwekwe's *Globe and Phoenix Mine.*

Like most of Zimbabwe's mines, the *Globe and Phoenix* operated on **ancient
diggings**, which had been run using manual implements, or fires lit against rocks to
make them crack. Gold already had a thousand-year history here and trade in the
precious metal was one of the ways the ruling classes consolidated their power. In the
sixteenth century it had brought the first **European interference** in the region, with
the arrival of Portuguese; their attempts at conquest and control flopped, but not before
they'd brought in Spanish experts to develop the ancient workings.

In the late nineteenth century, after the defeat of Lobengula, **British** El Dorado-
seekers flooded into the district. The gold rush never came to much but, by the 1930s,
one in every thirty whites was a small-scale prospector. Today, a few big mines pull in
the bucks, and there are still some determined prospectors. In the northeast, Shona
women continue to pan the Mazowe and Luenha rivers with homemade wooden trays
and transport their finds in porcupine quills.

Practicalities

In so small a place, it's a surprise to find no less than four **hotels**. Of the cheaper
options, the *Sebakwe Machipisa Hotel* (☎2198; ③) just off the main road beyond Fifth

Street, is a little more salubrious with en suite rooms, than the *Phoenix Hotel* (☎3748; ②) – a run-down jive dive. More comfortable and reasonably priced, the smart *Shamwari Hotel*, First Street (☎2387; ③) is the best central place to stay. Prices are only slightly higher at the *Golden Mile Motel* (☎3711; ④), 2km out on the Bulawayo road, where *Ajay* and *Express* coaches set down and pick up. It has the advantage of a swimming pool.

The cheap campsite has a macabre position next to the cemetery; look for the signs in First Street.

Gweru

GWERU was established in the 1890s as a staging post between Bulawayo and Harare. Today it is mainly a goods marshalling centre, linked by rail to South Africa, Mozambique and Zimbabwe's major towns. As a stop-off between Bulawayo and Harare, it's no tourist magnet but an agreeable place nonetheless. With wide streets and some lovely colonial architecture blooming among the ubiquitous 1960s stubs, the town seems to bask in a permanent Sunday afternoon feel: the Midlands capital living like a suburb in search of a city.

Of the "tourist attractions" the town struggles hard to find, the unfortunately named Boggie's Clock Tower deserves some kind of booby prize. "Erected by Mrs Jeannie Boggie in memory of her husband Major Boggie", it stands at the junction of Main Street and Robert Mugabe Way (formerly Livingstone Avenue), the two major axes.

The 1898 Stock Exchange Building, a little further along Main Street, deserves at least a quick look. It's a splendid example of colonial architecture, the oldest building of consequence in the city, constructed after the defeat of the First Chimurenga – a reflection of business confidence.

The Midlands Museum in Lobengula Ave (9am–5pm) might also while away some time, with its impressive display of firepower from both world wars – guns, aircraft, grenades, you name it. But there's little of note from the liberation struggle and the displays aren't very informative. An aircraft museum is being built here to house over sixty planes – one of the finest displays in southern Africa. The siting is appropriate as Gweru's Thornhill airbase is the country's largest. The town is also the home of the Zimbabwe Military Academy, which trains officer cadets and junior officers.

Although well away from the main game parks, Gweru does have its Antelope Park (small entry fee), some 8km out of town on the road going past the industrial estate. It's pretty quiet, but you will see antelope, zebras, giraffes and other herbivores as well as a dozen or so (caged) lions in the centre.

Practicalities

Ajay and *Express* coaches stop at the *Fairmile Motel* and the Kudzenai terminus for local buses, by the town market, behind the *Midlands Hotel*. The station is located at the end of Tenth Street. There are taxi ranks at the *Midlands Hotel* and the bus terminus.

Of the six hotels that graced the town by 1895 only three remain, catering for travelling salesmen during the week and empty on weekends. Cheapest is the *Chitukuko Hotel*, Third Street/Moffat Ave (☎2861; ④). Right in the centre, the *Midlands Hotel*, Main Street (☎708121; ⑦), an impressive colonial building with an arcaded facade that conceals a smart if characterless interior, is definitely more upmarket. Slightly less expensive is the *Fairmile Motel*, 1.6km south of the city on the Bulawayo Road (☎4144; ⑥), an airy place with a swimming pool. The coaches to and from Harare make their

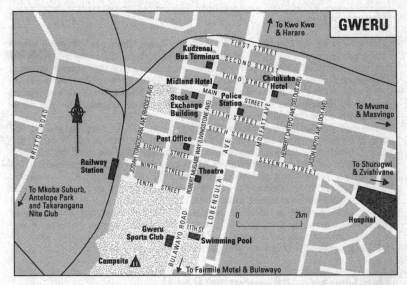

Gweru stop here. The **campsite** is at the Gweru Sports Club, along Robert Mugabe Way, (which becomes the Bulawayo road). Conveniently adjacent is the public **swimming pool.**

After dark, the *Dandaro Bar* at the *Midlands Hotel* is the centre's hottest **nightspot,** playing disco and reggae, and second-rate live music on weekends. What the place lacks in glitter and sophistication, it makes up for with sheer energy. **Away from the centre,** taxi down to the *Takarangana Nite Club* in Mkoba High Density Suburb; there's a better resident band and nightly disco. The council **beer hall,** in the same shopping centre, is where Harare bands play. Back in the centre, the *Embassy Cinema* in Fifth Street (off Robert Mugabe Way) shows mainly popular American films, but you might be lucky and coincide with one of the occasional performances at the *Gweru Theatre.*

Thinking about **food,** the hotels are the only places for big meals. There are **snack bars** strung down Main Street. Try the *Chicken Hut,* open late, for good, cheap chicken curry and rice, or the *Polar Milk Bar,* a little further on. In Fifth Street you can get sit-down pancakes, doughnuts and omelettes at the mainly white-patronised *Dutch Oven* or the similar place next door with a predominantly black clientele. **Nearest the campsite,** in Robert Mugabe Way, *Granny's Restaurant* serves reasonably priced snacks and larger meals.

Listings
American Express c/o *Manica Travel Services,* Zesa House, Sixth St (☎3316).
Automobile Association, Fanum House, Lobengula Ave/Sixth St (☎4251).
Doctors and dentists are listed at the beginning of the Gweru section of volume one of the telephone directory.
Emergencies Police, fire and ambulance: ☎99.
Hospital General Hospital, Shurugwi Rd (☎51301).
Swimming pool, Robert Mugabe Way/Eleventh St, is the best thing in town. (Tues–Fri 10am–2pm & 3–6pm; Sat & Sun 10am–12.30pm & 2.30–6pm; closed May–Sept).

Shurugwi

SHURUGWI nestles in a hollow in the Sebakwe Range. The name – from the Shona *Churugwe*, "pig pen" – refers to the surrounding topography. Shurugwi is actually the handsomest of the Midlands towns, a neglected and forgotten place somehow out of time. Its aptly named *Grand Hotel* has closed down; there are no eating places and not a single bar in town – a unique distinction in Zimbabwe. Shurugwi's gentle decay offers great photo opportunities – streets lined with fading pastel buildings and red corrugated iron roofs against a luminous sky.

The **campsite** looks unused and a family has taken over the huts. But you can still camp in pleasant surroundings – reached about 2km down Ferny Creek Road. For the nearest **hotel**, turn off just before town and continue 2km downhill; as its name suggests, the *Chitukuko Pleasure Garden* (③) is primarily a boozing establishment, but you can get hefty meals and cheap, seldom used **double rooms**. For ordinary **supplies**, there is no shortage of **shops** in the tiny centre, and a branch of the *Standard Chartered Bank* is open usual hours.

Shurugwi is sometimes called "the highlands of the Midlands". In reality it's hardly higher than Gweru, but it is hilly and there are lovely **walks** through woods and waterfalls just south of town on the road to Zvishavane. As for **entertainment**, the store opposite the train station (goods only) has some antique pinball machines.

The Harare–Masvingo Road

On the three-hour stretch from Harare to Masvingo, the only reason to stop is for drinks at the two main towns. **CHIVHU** used to be known by the Afrikaans name *Enkeldoorn* (lone thorn), after the particularly fine *acacia robusta* found growing at the site. It was first settled by **Afrikaners** in 1896 who were attracted by its similarity to the Boer heartland of the Orange Free State in South Africa. Cecil Rhodes actively encouraged Afrikaners to settle in Zimbabwe and it's not uncommon to this day to hear Afrikaans spoken throughout the Midlands. Right up to the UDI years, the town was jokingly referred to as the "Independent Republic of Enkeldoorn", and became legendary for its bar in which anti-Smith comment was punished with incarceration in the bar's jail.

One popular stop for drinks or a meal is *Denise's Kitchen*, 16km after Chivhu at the 156km peg, on a ranch with zebra and kudu which come for morsels from your table. 51km further through the grasslands, the mining town of **MVUMA**, like Shurugwi, has photogenic qualities, though on a considerably less grand scale. It enjoyed a gold boom from 1914 until 1925 when the local Falcon Mine closed, and nothing has changed since then. It's worth a quick stop-over to check out the old-style stores in the two main streets but, regrettably, there's nowhere to stay. The name *Mvuma* comes from the local river – "place of the magical singing" – believed in legend to be the site of a pool from which drumming, singing and the lowing of cattle could be heard.

Northeast: Tengenenge and Mavuradonna

Four roads radiate **north from Harare**, terminating at small towns on the edge of the Zambezi escarpment where it drops away to the remote, arid areas on the Mozambique border. The towns here have always been outposts, vulnerable to guerilla attack and suffering severely during the bush war which had its origins in the region. Long before the Independence struggle, the spiritual inspiration for the **First Chimurenga** was conjured here and two famous early liberation heroes, Mbuya Nehanda and Mapondera (see box overleaf), operated locally.

The most travelled road in this region leads west to Kariba; apart from farmers and peasants, few people travel the others. One you might want to follow heads off through the citrus farms of Mazowe to Mvurwi and Guruve, nearest town to the marvellous **sculpture community at Tengenenge**. On the way, 160 km from Harare at **Raffingora**, is Danga Farm, ideal for a couple of nights to sample farm life and take excursions to rock paintings or Tengenenge. Further attractions lie north beyond Mvurwi, on the edge of the Zambezi lowlands, where the middleveld plateau rises in the upward swoop of the **Mavuradonna mountains**, Zimbabwe's newest discovered **hiking area**, easiest approached from the village of Centenary. For this, the two beautiful **raffia palm reserves**, or **Hippo Pools**, off the road to **Mount Darwin** further east, however, you'll need your own transport.

Tengenenge

If Harare has awakened your interest in Zimbabwean sculpture, don't miss **TENGENENGE**. This artists' community just south of the Zambezi Escarpment in the rolling grassy hills of the Great Dyke requires some motivation to reach, but it's an extraordinary place and well worth the effort. The roads are poor and it's difficult to find (see overpage), but you'll know you're nearly there when you come across sentinel sculptures lining the way.

The Sculpture Revolution

So prolific is the output of Africa's largest artists' community that acres of land around Tengenenge seem to have been planted with sculptural works – primitive, crude, representational or grotesque, and in overwhelming quantities. Sculptures perch on walls, window-sills and above the doors of derelict buildings; others stand on wooden plinths driven into the ground or lie tossed aside in the grass. You can walk around the village looking at the carvings and chat to sculptors chipping away at new works. Almost everything is for sale and if you're looking for a quality bargain by an unknown, this is definitely the place.

Tengenenge is one of the great formative influences in Zimbabwe's sculpture revolution. When **Tom Blomefield** took over the farm here after World War II, he began by ploughing with oxen until he discovered **chrome** on his lands, which earned him enough money in two years to make bricks to build drying sheds and to employ someone to manage his tobacco production. Then came UDI, sanctions and the collapse of the tobacco industry. Blomefield decided to chuck it all in and become an artist. But with an entire black labour force to consider, he thought of absorbing their labour in arts and crafts groups.

Miraculously, around this time, huge deposits of **serpentine** (the beautifully mottled stone in yellowish to almost black shades of green) were discovered on the farm. Blomefield was joined by **Lemon Moses**, a Malawian sculptor, and gradually the place began to attract people from all over. During the bush war this area was one of the hottest but Tengenenge was left alone. Blomefield believes this was because he always showed due respect to the local chief and respected the **ancestral spirits**, frequently arousing the ire of the local church, which was doing its best to suppress them.

Workers at Tengenenge come from Angola, Malawi, Zambia and as far away as Tanzania, and each brings a distinctive tradition which has breathed diversity into the

Zimbabwe sculpture movement. Each culture has its own cosmology of **gods, ancestors and spirits** that influence humans in different ways and make all sorts of demands. The Shona supergod **Mwari** is a disinterested figure approached through the ancestors, while **Kalunga**, god of the Angolan Mbunda people, is very personal. The Malawian **Chewa** and **Yao** cultures express religion through very formal ritual dances using masks, and highly **stylised mask-like sculptures** are one hallmark of their work. Local **Shona** sculptors, too, frequently draw on folklore. Cautionary tales and transformations of people into beasts are common subjects.

There are now over a hundred artists associated with the farm, some of them affiliates producing at home and using Tengenenge's distribution channels, but many resident and stipended if their talent is insufficiently recognised by the commercial art world to make ends meet. Several of Zimbabwe's big names are products of this community, and artists like **Bernard Matemera** still live here. Matemera was the winner of the 1986 Delhi sculpture triennial, produced a ten-ton stone sculpture for the non-aligned conference in Titograd and has several pieces in the National Gallery in Harare. Others, like **Henry Munyaradzi**, have exhibited in Europe, America and Australia.

Access

By car turn off onto Gurungwe Road (12km before Guruve at the 35.5km peg). Once on the road, follow the Tengenenge signs all the way. The one exception is at a farmhouse, where there's no sign – turn right here. From the Guruve Road turnoff, the first 10km or so is tarred followed by about 5km of poor gravel track.

To get to Tengenenge by **public transport**, take a bus from Mbare to MVURWI and change there for **GURUVE**. From here, walking is the only way to do the remaining 20km to Tengenenge; if you get stuck overnight, Guruve's one **hotel** has cheap doubles. It's well worth buying the 1:250,000 *Mhangura Map* (SE-36-1), available from the Surveyor-General's office in Harare to locate Tengenenge (grid reference TS 7951).

Raffingora – Danga Farm

One of the few places to stay in the northeast promises a real taste of colonial farm days. The owners of Danga Farm – a comfortable lodge on a tobacco farm – can arrange for transfers from Harare (under 2 hours drive) and deposit you at Kariba if you're doing a circuit. It's a great place for horse riding, walking and swimming and trips can be arranged to see the sculptors at Tengenenge. While there's no big game on the farm, you'll be able to go bird spotting and see smaller mammals. Book through Kythe Weld-Forester, PO Box 8, Raffingora (☎0-2830; ⑦).

The Mavuradonna Range

Quite unknown, even by most Zimbabweans, the **Mavuradonna Wilderness Area** is the country's newest conservation region: uncultivated and mountainous, it was a no-go area for many years during the bush war. Although largely hunted out, it remains a beautiful and deserted part of the country, and one which is due to be restocked with game.

It lies about 20km north of Tengenenge on the **Zambezi Escarpment**. From Tengenenge you should make for CENTENARY, 50km north of which the **Alfa Trail**, the only mapped road into the area, heads into the mountains. There is a **campsite** with A-frame shelters and rustic open-air showers, close to the main road. Walks from the campsite include one to a waterfall with impressive views down the escarpment.

The project scheme for the area attempts to break away from colonial-style game management of taking local land and excluding the people who lived around it. In an about-turn, poachers will probably be employed as trackers and game scouts. Funds

MAPONDERA – ZIMBABWE'S ROBIN HOOD

An inspirational outlaw-hero, **Mapondera** was an early **freedom fighter**, whose stamping ground was the Zambezi Valley, near the Mavuradonnas. In the late nineteenth century, he would slip eel-like across the river, between British and Portuguese territory, avoiding the armies of both.

An independent warrior-ruler, descended from a Rozvi royal family, he put up a firm **resistance to colonial rule** and rejected the hut tax. In 1894 Mapondera and a band of followers fled from a settler force sent to arrest them. They emerged from their refuge to raid administrative offices, ambush tax collectors and burn shops they felt were exploiting the peasants.

To the government he was nothing more than a bloody murderer, but the Zimbabwean and Mozambican peasants who fed and sheltered him passed a different judgement. For several years he and his army held out against the white invaders. In 1901, with an army numbering nearly 1000 he attacked their settlement at **Mount Darwin**, notorious as a place of fighting during the Second Chimurenga, and nearly wiped it out. But in the end, it was a stalemate.

Mapondera continued his campaign for several more years under increasing pressure from the multiplying tentacles of colonial control. As white influence on both sides of the Zambezi closed in, his operational zone became restricted. Hunted by Portuguese and British, unable to get food or grow crops, and exhausted by nearly a decade on the run, he returned to his home at Mount Nyota, resigned to defeat. He sent a final message to his people saying that the old order was now finished and offering words for the new: *I leave my children here. They will look up for themselves.*

Soon afterwards he was arrested, tried and sentenced to a hefty seven years. He found confinement unbearable, went on hunger strike, and starved himself to death. The Mugabe government has honoured him as a folk hero by naming a building in Harare after him.

from the park will be channelled back into the local district council to improve facilities and so hopefully discourage poaching. Of the game that remains, a couple of herds of elephants walk the riverbanks, while leopards and lions have been seen as well as various antelopes, monkeys and baboons.

Exploring the area on horseback is one of the best ways to see the Mavuradonna. *O'Connor Carew Safaris* run 3–5 day camping and riding safaris, with transfers from Harare. Book through P/Bag 296A, Harare (☎795258; Fax 726911).

The Palm Reserve

In the adjacent Tingwa State Land is the **Palm Reserve**, one of the small concentrations of **raffia palms** in Zimbabwe. These incredible trees, with the longest leaves in the world, live only twenty or thirty years, producing the most exquisite waxy amber cones – like compact gleaming pine cones. Growing on the confluence of crystal-clear streams, no-one is quite sure how these isolated pockets of palms came to be where they are. One theory is that they were brought with trading Portuguese, and have clearly found an environment very much to their liking.

Hippo Pools

Of the few established attractions in the north, **HIPPO POOLS CAMP** on the banks of the Mazowe River deserves a mention: a pleasant weekend place with hutted accommodation, river walks and some game. The Camp, with chalets and a campsite, is a commercial operation in the Umfurudzi Safari area which is administered by *National Parks*. Situated in beautiful broken granite country, it's highly recommended as a break from Harare and a worthwhile stopoff if you're touring the northern circuit around

Mount Darwin and Centenary. There's thankfully no hunting, but you can fish, canoe (under supervision and steering well clear of hippo) and walk along the Mazowe River. There's a fair amount of game, with the big five making rare appearances.

Getting to Hippo Pools requires your own transport. The camp is 160km from Harare past Shamva on the Mount Darwin Road. Turn off at Madziwa Mine and from there follow the road due east for 25km. There are a limited number of chalets, so book ahead (Hippo Pools Camp, PO Box 90 Shamva ☎3302). Fridge and utensils are provided at the camp, but take your own food and linen. It's also possible and cheaper, to take your own tent and camp.

travel details

Harare is unsurprisingly the nexus of travel, with excellent, and lightly trafficked tarred **roads** to Mutare, Masvingo, Bulawayo and Kariba. Hwange and Victoria Falls, though, are reached by road from Bulawayo, not Harare. There are overnight **rail** services to Bulawayo and Mutare with comfortable sleepers, and a daytime service to Bulawayo only, if you want to see some of the scenery inbetween. Harare has one international rail connection per week, a 24-hour journey to Johannesburg. Bulawayo and the Midlands are well served by **luxury coach** twice a day, while coaches go to Mutare five times a week and to Masvingo only at the weekend. **Local buses** from Mbare will take you almost anywhere, starting at undefined times early each day. They are slow and crowded. **Domestic flights** are excellent value with countrywide connections daily, though none to Mutare which only has a military airport. They are sometimes prone to delays, but regional and international flights leave punctually.

Trains
From Harare to:
Bulawayo via Kwekwe, Shangani (for Danangombe and Naletale Ruins) and Gweru (2 daily 8am/9pm; 10/8hr).
Mutare (daily 9.30pm, 8hr 30min).
Johannesburg (Sun 7am; 24 hr).

Coaches
From Harare to:
Kwekwe / Gweru / Bulawayo (Mon, Wed, Fri, Sat 7.45am/ Tues, Thur, Sat, Sun 1pm – Express Motorways) (Tues, Thurs, Sun 8am/ Mon,Wed, Sat 11am – Ajay Motorways; both services 3/4/ 6hr).
Marondera / Rusape /Mutare (daily exc Tues, Thurs 7.45am; 4hr). Express Motorways.

Bulawayo / Francistown / Gaborone (Thurs, Sun 6am; 6/9/16hr). Express Motorways.
Masvingo & Great Zimbabwe (Fri, Sat 2pm; 4hr). Express Motorways.
Johannesburg (5 weekly, except Thur & Sun 6pm; 22 hr). All via Bulawayo & Beit Bridge border on Express Motorways.

Buses
From Harare to:
Bulawayo (at least 5 daily, 5am on; 7hr).
Mutare (daily).
Chirundu/Lusaka (daily, 6.45 am ; 7/12 hr Zupco Buses).
Kariba (daily; 7hr).
Karoi / Siabuwa (daily).
Masvingo for Great Zimbabwe (daily; 4hr).
Nyanga (daily; 5 hr).

Flights
From Harare to:
Bulawayo (2 daily; 40mins).
Kariba, Hwange National Park, Victoria Falls (daily, to connect with international arrivals. 1 direct flight per day to Vic Falls in addition, without stops at Kariba and Hwange).
Masvingo (daily; 30min).
Johannesburg (1–2 per day, 90 min) One month excursion fare is best value on return tickets. Minimum stay 10 days. Fares are the same on either SAA or Air Zimbabwe, the only carriers on this route, with interchangeable flights. To dip into South Africa, as part of a Zimbabwe circuit, there is a good value Circular fare (which may need some persistence to establish with Air Zimbabwe) which allows you to depart from Victoria Falls to Johannesburg and return directly to Harare.

Durban (Sun direct; 2hr)
Gaborone (2 weekly; 90min).

Air Zimbabwe has direct connections, at least once a week, to several African destinations – Maputo, Lilongwe, Addis Ababa, Mauritius, Manzini, Dar-es-Salaam, Windhoek, and Nairobi. Other African airlines with flights to Harare include *Air Ghana, Zambia Airways, Air Botswana, Kenya Airways, Ethiopian Airlines, Air Tanzania* and *Air Malawi* (see *Basics* p.3).

TELEPHONE AREA CODES	
Chegutu 153	**Kwekwe** 155
Guruve 158	**Mazowe** 175
Gweru 154	**Mount Darwin** 176
Harare 14	**Mvurwi** 177
Kadoma 168	**Shurugwi** 152

CHAPTER TWO

KARIBA AND THE MIDDLE ZAMBEZI VALLEY

Zimbabwe's northern border is formed by the **Zambezi River**, which is dammed at Kariba to form the vast artificial **Lake Kariba**. The river traverses some of the wildest and hottest parts of the country, with **Mana Pools National Park**, below the dam, the **wildlife** centrepiece: a place where you'll see animals without the slightest effort, and where walking in a group – the big attraction – is permitted, provided you are used to the bush and observe safety procedures.

The **lake** itself has a strange quality – hardly surprising given that a whole valley was drowned to create it, and a people, the Batonga, moved out. From the shallows, dead treetops poke out, while camel-hump formations dominate the lakeshore, sprouting grotesque baobabs and dessicated mopane woodland. Amid the creeks and islands, however, lies the rewarding **Matusadona National Park**, and on the escarpment is **Chizarira National Park**, an important refuge for black rhino.

Independent access to these wildlife areas is, unfortunately, neither easy nor cheap, and this is a part of the country where it is generally worth joining an organised expedition. Many of these tours (see pp.121–123 for details of operators) are adventurous and fairly intrepid options. If you want a taste of African expedition life, with the reassurance of an experienced guide or leader, it's hard to beat the excitement of a **canoeing trip** down the Zambezi, taking in Mana Pools en route, or a **backpacking safari** in one of the three national parks, ensuring equally close encounters with big game.

Kariba Town, five hours by road from Harare and well connected by air, is the hub of Zambezi tourism, promoted as a fabulous riviera but perhaps a little defeated by its own hype. While the blues of mountain and lake are very beautiful, there's nothing much to do here without a boat and fishing gear. Kariba is often the first stop for visitors doing the "milk run" – Kariba, Hwange National Park and Victoria Falls. If you're **circuiting the country**, the **Kariba ferry** conveniently connects the northeast of Zimbabwe to its west.

Travelling on overland, one of Zimbabwe's longest hauls by bus runs through the dusty and remote **back routes south of the lake**. Starting at Harare, the bus veers west at **Karoi** into some of the country's least developed communal lands, scattered with stilt-perched lookout huts, maize fields and sandy villages. The trip takes an overnight breather in the sprawling settlement of **Siabuwa**, where a second bus takes passengers the rest of the way to Bulawayo and close to **Binga**, the thoroughly untouristed centre of Lake Kariba's west. It was to this harsh and infertile territory that the **Batonga** people – today perhaps the poorest group in the country – were moved after they were uprooted by the construction of the Kariba dam.

THE ROAD FROM HARARE

The towns diminish steadily in size as you head northwest from Harare towards Kariba. None particularly merits a night's stop, though all have at least one hotel should the need arise. Tobacco and maize farms line the route to the escarpment, with a scenic highlight as you cross the **Great Dyke**, a massive topographic spine which bisects the highveld plateau, and is the source of many springs and streams.

The road is an easy one to hitch on Saturday mornings and daily **buses** to each of the towns or right to Kariba leave Mbare bus station in Harare. If you're wondering what's in the small sacks people wave at you from the roadside, they contain worms for bream fishing at Kariba.

Chinoyi Caves

CHINOYI, 115km from Harare, is a farming and mining centre and still a white stronghold. The petrol stations are all most people see of it, though it has claims to fame, with its much vaunted caves, and a place in history as the spot where the Second Chimurenga began, on 28 April 1966, with the killing of seven ZANLA guerillas in a confrontation with Rhodesian forces. The date is celebrated as the annual Chimurenga Day, and a memorial to the *Gallant Chinoyi Seven* has been erected in the town.

The Caves

Chinoyi Caves make an interesting break on an otherwise dull journey to Kariba. Enclosed by a recreational park 8km north of the town, they're open dawn to dusk.

The labyrinth of the Caves centres on the legendary **Sleeping Pool**, whose waters appear strikingly deep and vivid blue as you approach down the passage. However, the none too fragrant odour does its best to deflate the dreamy atmosphere promised by the name. The best time to see the pool is at noon, when light pours from a natural skylight onto the still surface. If you don't find caves claustrophobic, descend into **Dark Cave**, nearby, which has steps and electric lighting until you get to the viewing platform at the end of the tunnel. There's a good view from here of the Sleeping Pool, overhung by stalactites in shades of blue that vary with the time of day. Numerous passages and galleries lead off from the Dark Cave for more serious exploration.

Archaeologists have found ancient traces of troglodyte occupation in these subterranean dolomite caves. In the 1830s the Nguni are supposed to have used them as a place of execution, and later in the century **Chief Chinoyi** used them as a refuge from Ndebele raiders.

If you want to stay at Chinoyi Caves, there's a **campsite** within the recreational park and the comfortable *Caves Motel* (☎2340; ③) at the turn-off to it. The other option, similarly priced, is the *Orange Grove Motel*, Independence Way (☎2785; ③), which also has a caravan park.

ACCOMMODATION PRICE CODES

Every hotel and accommodation option listed in this chapter has been given a **price code** in US$ to indicate the cost of a single night's lodging.

For a full explanation, see p.43.

    ① under US$8   ② US$8–14   ③ US$15–29   ④ US$30–59

        ⑤ US$60–89   ⑥ US$90–149   ⑦ US$150+

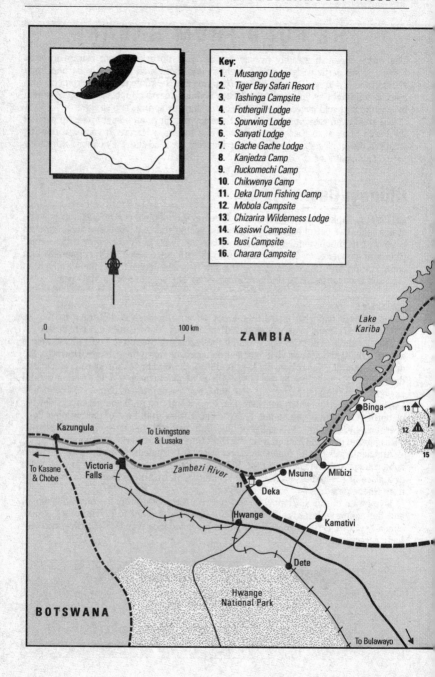

Key:
1. Musango Lodge
2. Tiger Bay Safari Resort
3. Tashinga Campsite
4. Fothergill Lodge
5. Spurwing Lodge
6. Sanyati Lodge
7. Gache Gache Lodge
8. Kanjedza Camp
9. Ruckomechi Camp
10. Chikwenya Camp
11. Deka Drum Fishing Camp
12. Mobola Campsite
13. Chizarira Wilderness Lodge
14. Kasiswi Campsite
15. Busi Campsite
16. Charara Campsite

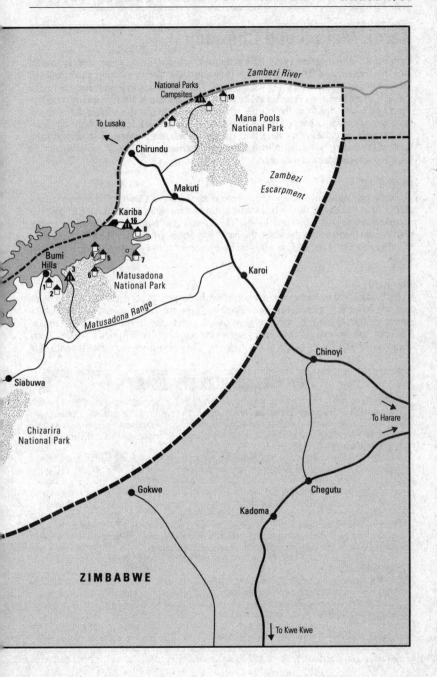

Zambezi River

National Parks
Campsites

9

Mana Pools
National Park

To Lusaka

Chirundu

Zambezi
Escarpment

Makuti

Kariba
16
8

Bumi
Hills
5
3
6
7
1
2

Matusadona
National Park

Karoi

Matusadona Range

Chinoyi

Siabuwa

To Harare

Chizarira
National Park

Gokwe

Chegutu

Kadoma

ZIMBABWE

To Kwe Kwe

Karoi, Makuti and Chirundu

Under a Rhodesian government land settlement scheme, many white farmers moved into the area around **KAROI** between 1945 and 1950. Tobacco-curing sheds and tall brick chimneys stand on each of these farms. The two **hotels** in town reflect the racial divide – white farmers assemble at the newer, smarter *Karoi Hotel* (Karoi ☎317; ④) a couple of kilometres from the centre, while blacks gather at the original hotel downtown, now primarily a bar and pretty run down. If you're stuck in Karoi, there's a pleasant campsite overlooking the dam. Security here is minimal, however. Karoi marks the start of the bizarrely named **Nicolle Hostes Highway** – 400km of gruelling dirt to Matusadona, Chizarira and Binga.

Makuti

En route to Kariba or Mana, everyone stops for drinks at *Cloud's End Hotel* (Makuti ☎526; ③) in **MAKUTI**, the high point with stupendous views before the road begins to tumble down into the Zambezi Valley. The *Cloud's End* bar is a real hunter's grotto, with buffalo leering from the walls; the hotel also organises safaris. The village consists of little more than the hotel, and it is the last place for petrol and supplies before Mana Pools.

Chirundu

CHIRUNDU, 63km further on, is equally small, despite its border status as the point that you cross the Zambezi River into Zambia. There are **daily buses** from Mbare bus station in Harare, and the twice-weekly *Giraffe* coach runs right through to Lusaka. You can get **rooms** at the inexpensive but comfortable *Chirundu Valley Hotel* (Chirundu ☎618; ③) or **camp** along the river. They also have some family rooms for

---

THE MUTAPAS

The Zambezi valley has been inhabited since the first **hunter-gatherers** lived there, and Bantu-speaking **Iron Age farmers** have navigated the river for centuries. Numerous Iron Age sites are scattered along the Zambezi, including the **Ingombe Ilede** burial site near Chirundu which showed that external trade had reached this far up the Zambezi by the sixth century AD.

Later, **Muslim merchants** traded up the river for gold and ivory: romantic notions persisted of the Zambezi being one of the gateways to the biblical Ophir. At the Zambezi's Indian Ocean delta, in 1497, the Portuguese adventurer, Vasco da Gama, supposedly found Arab dhows laden with gold dust. Hot on his heels other **Portuguese** fortune-seekers arrived in large numbers, spending four centuries on the lower Zambezi in search of riches. Although the Portuguese didn't penetrate much further than Chirundu, below the lake, in the sixteenth century, this was considerably further inland than any European had previously advanced in Africa and, from their reports, we know something about the Mutapa State of the Zambezi Escarpment.

The Mutapas

The **Mutapas** were originally Shona-speakers, who had drifted north from Great Zimbabwe sometime during its disintegration (final collapse came around 1450), and had conquered the Tavara – another Shona group. The Mutapa state is only the most famous of several small Shona kingdoms around the northeast at this time. For the Portuguese, however, the Mutapa king, who they knew as the Monomotapa, was a magnificent figure of untold wealth who ruled over an enormous empire. The empire was a myth, but the Mutapas did control the important Zambezi trade route.

four to seven people which are even cheaper. Don't be put off by the hotel's array of parked trucks and trailers lining up for the border crossing – through reception are lawns, and a swimming pool which hosts thirsty elephants and buffalo from time to time. The steaks here are also excellent. A one-kilometre walk from the hotel to the top of the hill gives magnificent views of the Zambezi with game on the banks, but keep a wary lookout for elephants en route, especially in the late afternoon. Since the hotel is primarily run for fishermen, it's possible to hire boats from the hotel and get onto the water.

KARIBA, ZAMBEZI CANOEING AND MANA POOLS

Kariba offers a remarkable choice of activities. For those who want a few day's lazing by the pool, the **town-resort** has all the facilities: a boon, since the lake (except for its deepest, central reaches) is frustratingly out of bounds for swimming due to crocodiles and bilharzia. With more adventurous pursuits in mind, there are a host of **wildlife safari** options, including the **Matusadona National Park**, with its massive dry season herds of buffalo and elephant and dazzling array of lakeshore animals and birds. And there's the chance of gliding down **the Zambezi by canoe**, headed for Mana (four days) or beyond.

The Zambezi, downstream from Kariba, creates a hunting enclave which spreads across 10,000 square kilometres to the Mozambique border, consisting of Charara, Sapi, Chewore, Dande and Doma Safari areas. In the centre of all this is **Mana Pools**, a unique wildlife sanctuary, where, because of the open terrain, the National Park authorities allow walking without guides and weapons are prohibited.

According to tradition, the Mutapas had their own Adam and Eve: **Nebedza** and his sister **Nehanda**. Nehanda is Zimbabwe's archetypal mother-earth heroine, closely associated with the land, which is the fundamental element of religious, social and material life. The land is the source of food, but it is also the home of the ancestors.

The Chimurengas
Portuguese incursion into the interior marked the beginnings of colonial brutality and bloodletting in the north. Perhaps for this reason the **spiritual inspiration** behind both of the past century's **Chimurengas** came from here. In both liberation struggles, Nehanda rematerialised as a powerful figure, urging the people to liberate the country from the white invaders. On both occasions she spoke through mediums, who themselves took on her persona and became known by the respectful title Mbuya (grandmother) Nehanda.

In the First Chimurenga, a Nehanda medium from Mazowe, **Charwe**, encouraged people to avoid all dealings with whites. As far as the authorities were concerned, Charwe was a witch and rabble-rouser and she was arrested. Photographs taken just before her execution in Salisbury, in 1898, show her dignified and self-possessed. She's said to have gone to her death singing and dancing, confident that her spirit would return for final victory.

The spirit of Nehanda re-emerged in the **Second Chimurenga** winning the people's support for the guerillas. When mediums of important spirits such as Nehanda gave their approval to efforts to win back the land, many peasants were persuaded to join the struggle. In 1972 ZANLA guerillas secretly took the medium over the border to their base at Chifombo in Mozambique to rally the fighters.

Kariba Town

Engineers faced with the problem of building a road from the escarpment down the hill-ridden way to **KARIBA**, turned to the ancient paths worn by **elephants** who knew the easiest descent. The road built on that elephant track twists around massive bush-clad hills to the lakeside. As you near the water look out for elephants crossing the road or tugging at trees.

Orientation

The precise location of Kariba Town is perplexing, as there's nothing much on the main road besides a *Shell* garage. Every few kilometres, however, a small turn-off disappears through the trees to one of the lakeside resorts. Stretched over twelve kilometres, each of the **hotels** and **campsites** has its own hill-cupped bay, cut off from the next by the rising and falling landscape.

There are two commercial and residential centres – **Kariba Heights**, perched 600m above the lake, and **Mahombekombe** township on the shore. Before Independence, the Heights was the white residential area, with its palpably cooler temperatures and lofty views. Set slightly back from the commercial fishing harbour and creeping up Sugar Loaf hill, Mahombekombe was built to house construction workers and continues to be the main residential area for fishermen and people working in the tourist industry. It has the nearest shops and post office to the resorts and it's where the **buses** pull in. Some distance away, near the airport, **Nyamhunga** was built in the 1970s to increase housing for Africans.

Arrival

If you arrive by air, the *UTC* minibus which meets all flights will drop you off at any hotel, or at the harbour if you're connecting to Fothergill Island or one of the resorts further afield. For two people, taking a taxi is cheaper than the bus. There is no *Air Zimbabwe* bus as at the bigger airports.

Local buses from Harare stop at Mahombekombe **bus terminus**, from where it's a 3-km walk to the *MOTH* campsite and chalets or *Tamarind Lodges* (see below). However, some buses go on as far as the *Swift Depot*, which is much closer.

Getting around

Without a car, you can reckon on doing a lot of walking. A **bus** from the *Swift Transport Depot* goes to Mahombekombe, Heights and Nyamhunga about every half-hour, and **hitching** along the main road is easy, but the myriad branches usually mean a walk at least part of the way. **On foot**, rather than climbing up to the main road, you can cut distances drastically by following any of the well-worn paths directly along the shorefront. During the dry season, keep an eye open for elephants which sometimes wander about Kariba's hills and shoreline.

Taxis (☎2453 or ☎2454) are based at *Caribbea Bay; UTC* also runs between resorts. Car hire is another way of traversing the distances. *Hertz* (☎2662) has offices at the *Cutty Sark*, *Caribbea Bay* and *Lake View Inn*, while *Echo* (☎2227) has an office at Andora Harbour.

Accommodation

Kariba **hotels** are popular weekend destinations for people from Harare, especially during the winter when Kariba is much warmer than the capital. All have pools, shady gardens and are mostly air-conditioned to beat the humidity. There is also camping for the budget-minded.

Camping and self-catering

Caribbea Bay Resort, PO Box 120, Kariba (☎2454). This has **campsites** close to its hotel and casino complex, over on the other side of Mahombekombe. ①.

MOTH Holiday Resort, c/o The Warden, PO Box 67, Kariba (☎2809). The *MOTH* comprises a series of pleasant, shady campsites, as well as cheap self-catering rooms and chalets, but don't count on getting a room if you haven't booked. You can camp at *Lions Club*, next door, for the same price, picking up the key at *MOTH*. The only advantage, though, is the hall if it rains. Both complexes share the *Lion's Club* swimming pool. From either resort, a 15-min shortcut up the hill to your right (facing the lake) takes you to *Lakeview Inn* for food and drink; the Mahombekombe shops are some 3km away. ①.

Mopani Bay Campsite, Kariba Town Council, Box 130, Kariba (☎2485). Far from the action, Mopani's sole advantage is the small store and swimming pool. ①.

Nyanyana Camp. If you're self-sufficient and want to be in the wild, this National Parks' camp, 28km from Kariba in Charara Safari Area, is perfect; campsites are next to the lake and there are elephants around. Located 5km off the Makuti road; nearest supplies at Kariba. ①.

Tamarind Lodges, PO Box 1, Kariba (☎2697). The nicest of the self-catering options, these newish stone and thatch lodges are between the *Cutty Sark Hotel* and *Kariba Breezes Marina*. Although there is no pool, lodgers can use the one at the *Cutty Sark*, and also eat there if you're not into using the braai facilities at *Tamarind*. Lodges sleep either 4 or 6 people, and you're required to pay a fairly substantial deposit when you book in. ②–③.

Hotels

Although the hotels around Kariba do not have street addresses, each is clearly sign-posted off the main road.

Caribbea Bay Resort, (☎2454). Has a casino, is the most expensive of the resorts and is popular with Harare's golden youth. ⑥.

Cutty Sark, (☎2321 or ☎2322). Second choice after *Kariba Breezes* (below), with unrenovated rooms slightly cheaper. Although rates for Zimbabwean residents are exactly the same at both hotels, *Breezes* charges less for non-residents. ④.

Most High Hotel, Kariba Heights (☎2964 or ☎2965). The cheapest of the central resorts but a long way from the water. Christian-run, complete with piped religious music. ③.

Kariba Breezes Hotel, (☎2433). Relaxed and especially recommended. Boat rental from the hotel with a driver goes for US$25 per day for 5 people. ④.

Lakeview Inn, (☎2411 or ☎2413). Peaceful and elegant, offering great vistas. The most expensive after *Caribbea Bay*. ⑥.

Zambezi Valley Hotel, Nyamhunga near the airport (☎2926). A good place for live music at weekends and for meeting black Zimbabweans. You listen to music in the beer garden and there are trees on the stage. ③.

Around the town

Nobody really comes to Kariba for the town. It's often too hot to do anything other than lie around, have an iced something or other, and maybe rouse yourself to go on a cruise. If you can beat the torpor, then take in the **Santa Barbara church**, built in memory of the workers who died during the construction of the dam, and have a look at the **dam wall** itself.

The Dam

Many animals, and not a few people, died in the **creation of Lake Kariba**, so that hydroelectric power could be harnessed to feed industry in Zambia and Zimbabwe. The dam was, at the time, the largest in the world, and its size and strength remains awesome. Its arching form is like a vast, Roman load-bearing arch turned on its side; the convex shape absorbs the pressure and the base straining to spring apart is solidly checked by the ancient gorge walls.

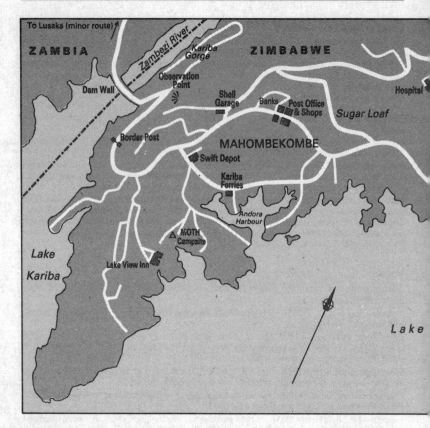

The Batonga, who suffered most of all, by being shoved off their ancestral riverside lands into the harsh interior, were convinced that the wrathful river god **Nyaminyami** would destroy the dam project. In July 1957, the first confirmation of their belief was delivered, as a once-in-10,000-years storm saw the Zambezi burst through the coffer dam to destroy months of work. Later, the angry god whipped up a tempest, which swept away the Zimbabwe–Zambia road bridge, and soon afterwards turned his attention to the suspension footbridge, which went the same way. When the rains stopped, Nyaminyami sent unusually murderous temperatures: workers died from heatstroke and the tools had to be carried in buckets of water. Eighteen men also perished when they fell into wet concrete during construction. The wall was, of course, eventually completed, but to some Batonga the battle isn't over – and, well, there are nervous reports of cracks.

The lake's biggest crisis to date has been the drought of the 1980s and early 1990s, which saw water levels sink below the level necessary to supply the country's hydro-electricity needs. Zimbabwe experienced frequent power cuts and in the end was obliged to buy in electricity from South Africa. A good rainy season in 1993 saw water levels start to rise again, but it will take several consecutive good seasons to fill the lake.

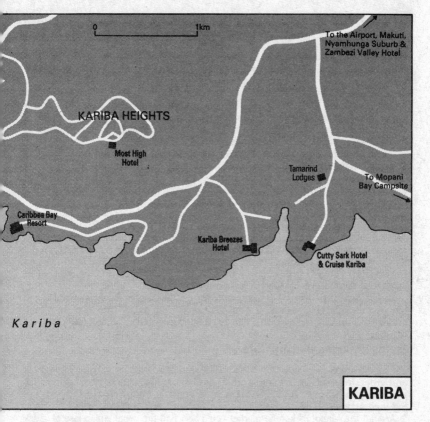

KARIBA

Observation Point

A couple of kilometres walk from the *Lakeview Inn* or *MOTH Campsite* takes you to the wall, from where it's a long uphill trudge to the elevated **Observation Point**. From this vantage point, you can see the wall in its entirety – 128m high and 579m wide at its base, with the pent-up Zambezi, when in flood, leaping through the gates to the gorge below. **To walk on the wall**, you have to cross the border into Zambia. For a quick visit you just report in with your passport – no long forms or currency declarations involved. There are **refreshments** and a **craft shop** at the Observation Point; the best buys are intricately carved Nyaminyami (the fish-headed god with snake's tail) walking sticks, and the small wooden latticed **lampshades** which cast a nice stripey light. The Kariba **publicity bureau** is here too.

Santa Barbara

The dam's main construction contracts went to an Italian company, and hence the chapel in Kariba Heights commemorating those who died is dedicated to an Italian saint. The chapel is a poignant place, built in a circular form to represent the coffer dam, with a trellised front open to the elements. The church's adaptation to the climate is perhaps the most interesting thing about the building, but it's not honestly worth much effort to get to, except on Sunday mornings, when traditional singing, of mostly black congregations, floats out. Evening services are at 6pm.

Getting on the water

Sundowner cruises are a Kariba institution. This is, after all, primarily a drinking person's retreat. On a launch, you can enjoy gorgeous sunsets, beer in hand, after the day's heat has subsided. *UTC* and *Cruise Kariba* (☎2697) both offer 4.30pm departures. You can book and get driven to the harbour from the *Cutty Sark*, *Lake View Inn* or *Caribbea Bay* hotels. *Cruise Kariba* also does a **siesta cruise** at 2pm which returns to shore in time to catch the Harare flight. The siesta cruise includes time for a **swim in the lake** – stopping in a croc-and-bilharzia-free area.

If you fancy spending more than a couple of hours on the water, **full day cruises** to Fothergill Island are available from *Cruise Kariba* and *Lake Safaris* (☎2474). The advantage of a full-day cruise, which includes a stop for lunch, is that you go far enough afield to spot big game. *Cruise Kariba* leaves the *Cutty Sark* at 9am while *Lake Safaris* departs from Andora harbour at 9.30am returning around 4pm.

If money's no object, hire a **luxury cruiser** or houseboat for a few days on the lake. Boats go with drivers and take six to ten people on board, and provide all cutlery, crockery and linen. Cruisers are restricted to the Kariba basin, which includes the area around Spurwing and Fothergill islands. Enquire at *Kariba Breezes Marina* (PO Box 15, Kariba; ☎2475) or *Anchorage Marina* (PO Box 61, Kariba; ☎254). The *DDF* (District Development Fund) (PO Box 2694, Kariba; ☎2392) has boats for hire by the hour or longer and ships local people and cargo over the whole lake.

Buffalo Safaris (PO Box 113, Kariba; ☎2827 or ☎2645) offer houseboat and canoe hire, Kariba sightseeing as well as game drives and bush walks. They also run recommended trips to Matusadona (see p.109) and canoeing down the Zambezi (see p.110).

Eating, drinking and nightlife

For campers, self-catering is the cheap option, with basic supplies of **fruit, vegetables and groceries** available from the market and shops in Mahombekombe. Look out for locally grown bananas. A similar selection is available from *Emerald Butchery and Supermarket* in the Heights. A small shop at *Caribbea Bay* provides essentials.

Around the Mahombekombe market you'll also find the usual cheap fare of sadza and relish. For snacks, refreshments and menued meals try the **hotels**. With the best views across the lake to the Matusadona Range, the *Lakeview Inn* terrace is worth visiting for a drink or for their gargantuan breakfasts. For the peckish, a plate of the local speciality, crunchy fried *kapenta* (tiny fish) makes a delicious stopgap. More expensively, try a serving of crocodile tail; it's a surprisingly light and delicate meat.

Drinking takes place at the hotels or the **beer hall** in Mahombekombe. The *Zambezi Valley Hotel* has its own resident band, the **Generator Sounds**, and towards the end of each month, Zimbabwe's musical crowd-pullers occasionally appear at Mahombekombe town council stadium.

Matusadona National Park

Open all year. Small entry fee by road, free by boat.

It is the **Matusadona Mountains** that form a backdrop to all those picturesque shots of Kariba sunsets, with drowned treetops in the foreground. The National Park, with all the big game, borders the southern lakeshore and rolls over the Zambezi escarpment into wild, largely inaccessible hills and valleys. The lakeshore with its inlets, gorges, bays and islands is the most easily reached area of the park, and certainly where the

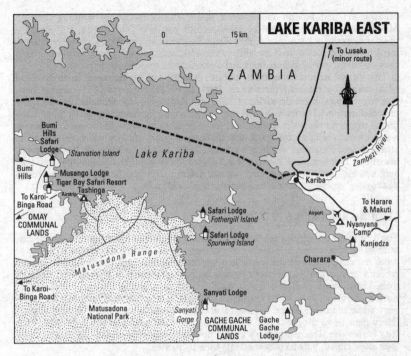

LAKE KARIBA EAST

0   15 km

ZAMBIA

To Lusaka
(minor route)

Bumi
Hills
Safari
Lodge   Starvation Island   *Lake Kariba*   Zambezi River

Bumi
Hills   Musango Lodge
Tiger Bay Safari Resort
Tashinga
Airstrip   Kariba

To Karoi-
Binga Road   To Harare
& Makuti

OMAY
COMMUNAL
LANDS   Airport   Nyanyana
Camp

Safari Lodge
Fothergill Island   Kanjedza

Safari Lodge
Spurwing Island

M a t u s a d o n a   R a n g e   Charara

To Karoi-
Binga Road   Sanyati Lodge

Matusadona
National Park   Sanyati
Gorge   GACHE GACHE
COMMUNAL
LANDS   Gache
Gache
Lodge

game concentrates during the dry season. Most visitors, largely white Zimbabweans
with their own fishing or houseboats, camp at **the national parks campsites** at
Tashinga or **Sanyati**. Tashinga is the very appealing main Parks campsite and headquarters, bigger than Sanyati and with an airstrip. Both camps have tents for hire,
though Tashinga is better stocked. There are no shops or fuel supplies, so bring all you
need.

There are also three fabulous national parks camps along the shore which are for
the exclusive use of one party each (up to 12 people) for a minimum of a week's stay, at
Ume, **Muuyu** and **Mbalabala.** To book, write to the Central Booking Office,
Department of National Parks, PO Box 8151, Causeway, Harare (☎706077), or better
still, go to their office at the Botanical Gardens.

If you're driving, only the dry season is recommended to attempt the 468-km gut-
shaking journey from Harare, and you'll need 4WD or a high-clearance vehicle. Access
to the park is via the gravel road from Karoi to Binga. Approximately 150km west of
Karoi, a signposted turnoff leads into the park through the
Chifudze gate. With your own vehicle, you could easily and
rewardingly combine a trip to Matusadona with Chizarira.

Without a landrover or boat, the only real solution to
experience Matusadona is to splurge on one of the excellent **safari camps** bordering the National Park to see the
massive dry season herds of **buffalo** and **elephant** and a
dazzling array of other lakeshore animals and birds. A
couple of safari companies based at Kariba organise **camping**, **walking**, **canoeing** and **photographic safaris** in

Matusadona and around the Eastern basin. The attraction of **walking** through Matusadona lies in following the rivers, which run into Lake Kariba, and attract a greater diversity of game inland, than along the shoreline. Antelope such as the magnificent black sable with their exquisitely masked faces and extremely long and gently curving horns, as well as bushbuck and duiker, prefer wooded inland areas.

There's an extremely outside chance though, for backpackers to make it to Matusadona by catching the weekly *DDF* **ferry** (☎2349 or ☎2392) running from Kariba's Andora Harbour to Bumi Hills via Tashinga – an arduous, exposed and crowded journey. The ferry returns the following day. Unless you're doing it just to be on the water, it's not really worth going for just one night, so take adequate supplies for a week's stay. Without transport or a fishing rod your activities will be restricted to lazing around the camp, watching birds and beasts wandering through. If you're easily bored this isn't the place for you. If a National Parks scout is available they can take you walking, but they may well be out dealing with poachers or shooting crop-destroying "problem animals" in adjacent communal lands.

Wildlife and fishing

You'll certainly see **elephants** drinking and frolicking in the water, and, if you're lucky, swimming. Most animals, including surprisingly enough lion, can swim well. Elephants swim using their trunks as snorkels. One remarkable – and photographed – story records an epic thirty-hour swim by two young bull elephants who crossed the lake from Matusadona, and passed Spurwing to land on a beach between two hotels at Kariba. Altruistic, even when exhausted, the one in front inflated his lungs for buoyancy while the other placed his front feet on the leader's back and did the paddling. Every hour or so they swapped over and finally made it, trunks and legs white from long immersion. The conclusion was that they were following ancient migration routes long since cut off, but still patterned into their memories.

THE LAKE ECOLOGY

Matusadona and **Chete Safari Area** received some of the 5000 animals saved, in 1959, from the flooding Zambezi Valley. There are pitiful stories of animals moving to higher and higher ground as the waters rose and being besieged on shrinking islands with diminishing food supplies. Starvation Island had one of the biggest concentrations of stranded animals. Many thousands died and much of the money for the project (one of the earliest wildlife mass appeals) arrived too late. But **Operation Noah**, mounted by conservationist Rupert Fothergill, fought hard against the inevitable. Not only big game, but also the less obvious snakes and tortoises were bundled off to the mainland. Charles Nicholls' book *Operation Noah* recounts the story.

Nearly 5200 square kilometres of wilderness died with the valley. Desolate trees, still poking branches from the water thirty years on, bear vivid testimony to the destruction. But all is not gloom and doom – a **new ecology** has replaced the old in a turn of events that shows the resilience of the natural world. Fish eagles and darter colonies nest in the branches and the decaying wood feeds underwater life. Buffalo and elephants graze on green swards of lakeside **torpedo grass** (*Panicum repens*), which miraculously saved the day for the young lake slowly being choked by notorious Kariba weed. In this crisis, weed-eating grasshoppers were introduced and arsenic-based poisons considered to clear the floating strangler which blocked all navigation in the west. Mysteriously, it began to die off on its own, piling up on newly barren shores and creating a mulch in which torpedo grass rapidly seeded.

Torpedo grass is able to survive long periods underwater, yet it also thrives when water levels sink during the dry season or droughts. The grass is gradually exposed to provide

Fishing attracts many at Matusadona, particularly for the fierce **tigerfish** you'll undoubtedly see mounted in hotel bars – glassy-eyed and open-mouthed to display their razor teeth. Prime fishing months are September and October when Kariba hosts an international tiger contest. The big thing about tigerfish is their fighting ability – they make determined rushes followed by an impressive leap from the water to shake the hook. **Sanyati Gorge**, a narrow tear in the map on the eastern boundary of the park, is a creek navigable for about 12km and has a reputation for having loads of tigerfish just waiting for combat.

Fish Eagles

You'll see **fish eagles** sitting sentinel in riverine forest all over the Zambezi, and guarding their territory from Kariba's half-submerged trees. They're definitely among the most spectacular water birds, and always a thrill to see – especially swooping from the heights on an underwater fish. But according to recent reports they're facing extinction as the result of DDT, which is still not banned in Zimbabwe and is used extensively both in tsetse and malarial control and as a crop spray. Its main effect is on the birds' reproductive processes, causing eggshells to dry out in the heat or become thin and too weak to support the brooding parent.

Other birds in danger are the peregrine falcon, herons and cormorant, the black sparrowhawk and the rare fishing owl. All these birds are at the top of their food chains, so DDT accumulates heavily in their bodies and is passed to their offspring in increasingly intolerable concentrations.

Bush Camps

The most comfortable way to see Lake Kariba and the Matusadona wildlife is in one of the **bush camps** on the fringes of the park. These are stylish, thatched places with swimming pools and, unlike the Kariba resorts, they are able to boast superb

lush grazing for wildlife forced down to the lake when inland grazing and water becomes exhausted. Once the rains begin the animals disperse into the interior and the grass is covered again by the rising water. This movement to the water echoes an old pre-lake pattern, when game came down to the Zambezi riverine forest as it still does at Mana.

Aquatic life is rich. Apart from tiger fish, people catch bream, pink lady, chessa, barbel, mudsucker, eel, bottle nose and huge vundu. Freshwater sponges and tiny jellyfish are some of the less familiar species. The Zambezi was habitat to the same fish as are now found in Kariba, with the exception of the tiny sardine-like **kapenta**, introduced for **commercial fishing** from Lake Tanganyika in the 1960s. At night you'll see myriad lights on the lake from *kapenta* rigs attracting the fish into deep water nets. You can walk around and see the *kapenta* drying on racks in Mahombekombe; it's cheap and sold in big plastic bags throughout the country as an accompaniment to sadza.

Trawling is a tough job – contract-based, wet, uncomfortable and dangerous. Fishermen working for commercial companies have a more reliable income, though it's still low. The **gill-net fishermen**, however, freelancers after the big fish, live along the shoreline and are plagued by completely unpredictable catches. Some waters are fished out and the strict allocation of fishing territory prevents them moving elsewhere, with poaching in richer waters an unfortunate consequence. The **fishing villages** are rather deserted, despondent places – wives and families generally live inland, coaxing crops out of barren soil. The catch is dried and salted, and sold in communal areas surrounding the lake, or else sold fresh to commercial boats making the rounds of the camps. In 1984, one of the biggest companies was offering as little as nine cents a fish. To address the problems of distribution, low prices and fishing rights, a number of **fishing co-operatives** have been formed, some successfully increasing profits for their members.

game-watching, walking and cruising or canoeing. There is daily **transport** to all camps, by air or boat. Two of the major resorts, *Spurwing* and *Fothergill*, are still usually mapped as adjacent islands – though they have become peninsulas joined to the Matusadona mainland since the level of the lake dropped, due to persistent drought throughout the 1980s and early 1990s.

Luxury lodges and Camps

All the lodges below operate full-board tariffs, and are pricey, with the exception of the recommended *Nyamasowa Camp*. The rates given are per person per day, but you pay extra for boat transfers to and from Kariba town at approximately US$80 return, US$180 by light aircraft. Game activities, comprising drives, power boat outings, canoe hire and conducted walks are generally included.

Bumi Hills Safari Lodge, *Zimbabwe Sun Hotels*, Central Reservations, Travel Centre, Jason Moyo Ave, Harare (☎736644). *Bumi*, 50km uplake from Kariba, is a beautiful place with excellent guides, but is more like a chic hotel (40 beds) than a bush camp. Its open layout with narrow arched entrances prevents buffalo strolling into the bedroom wing – although they do occasionally come up at night and munch the lawn outside, around the swimming pool. From US$235 per person per day. Linked to *Bumi* is *Water Wilderness*, where guests can safari for a night or two on a houseboat amid lots of game, for an inclusive US$254 per day.

Fothergill Island Safari Lodge, Private Bag 2081, Kariba (☎2253). Very sociable and friendly, with up to 40 guests and several guides and drivers on hand for game drives and cruises. It's also possible to be left at a game viewing platform or take yourself canoeing up creeks and inlets. Fothergill Island is where Operation Noah began and there's plenty of game about. Children are allowed at the camp and an electrified fence around the thatched chalets plus bright lights ensure sleepwalkers are safe. It has a pool, good food and stylish ethnic decor. Kariba boat **transfer** US$80 return. US$180 per day.

Gache Gache Lodge, PO Box 293, Kopje, Harare (☎702634). Overlooks the Gache Gache River on the shores of Kariba with walks, game drives (including night drives), canoeing and excursions by motorboat. Accommodation is in thatched, ensuite chalets. US$195 per day.

Musango Lodge, PO Box UA 306, Union Ave, Harare (☎796821). Situated on a small island near the Ume River between Bumi Hills and Tashinga in the Matusadona National Park. Accommodation is in six luxury tents under thatch. Run by two young professional guides who can take game walks and drives (including night drives) in the Park. Transfers to the camp are by light aircraft to Bumi Hills and then a 15-min boat trip to camp, US$130 per person return. Canoeing and boating are on offer in the all-inclusive rate of US$210.

Nyamasowa Camp, *Kushanya Africa Safaris*, 109 Coronation Ave, Greendale, Harare (☎/Fax 707675). Reservations in the UK via *Wildlife Enterprises* (☎/Fax 0788/890076). Set in the Kuburi Wilderness Area, which borders the Zambezi River in the north and Lake Kariba in the south and west, and is significant as the first conservation area in which the Department of National Parks has leased part of its estate to a non-governmental organisation – the Wildlife Society of Zimbabwe. *Nyamasowa* is the cheapest, by far, of all the Kariba safari camps; in fact it's the best-value safari camp in Zimbabwe. Accommodation is in five large insect-proof twin-bedded tents, under a thatched roof. Guests can view game on foot or from vehicles, accompanied by licensed guides. Among canoeing and hiking trips offered is the combined one day/one night Chikombe/Chimwa Trail, which costs US$200 per person. Basic rates are US$55 per person per night.

Sanyati Lodge, PO Box 4047, Harare (☎703000). One of Zimbabwe's top lodges, at the mouth of the Sanyati Gorge. Thoroughly luxurious and relaxing with brilliant food. Guests (max 12) sit en famille under cool thatch, on a stoney hillside overlooking the lake. The lodge has hosted the likes of Prince Philip and doesn't allow kids. US$250 per day.

Spurwing Island, Private Bag 101, Kariba (☎2466). A casual and friendly place 40 minutes by boat from Kariba. It's the least expensive with strong local loyalty – many white Zimbabweans take advantage of the good fishing and come by boat with their families. Accommodation is in chalets, cabins or tents and it has great views of the Matusadona mountains. The activities include game viewing by boat and canoeing, and there is a swimming pool next to the thatched bar for lazing about. Kariba boat transfer US$50 return. US$160–180 per day.

Tiger Bay Safari Resort, PO Box 102, Kariba (☎2569). Primarily a luxury fishing resort up the Ume River with 12 comfortable thatched chalets and game viewing by boat or landrover, with an option of canoe rental.

Chris Worden – Kanjedza, PO Box 221, Kariba (☎2321). Three walk-in luxury safari tents under lovely trees in the Kuburi Wilderness Area, a 20-minute drive from Kariba airport, overlooking the Ruwisa River. It's purely a walking camp (no game drives) with plenty of tracking of unusual species like roan and sable, though there is not a tremendous amount of big game. Chris stood in for Clint Eastwood during the elephant-hunting sequences in the film *White Hunter Black Heart* which was filmed in Kariba and Hwange. US$225 per person per day.

Matusadona canoeing and walking safaris

Buffalo Safaris Zambezi Canoeing and Lake Wilderness Safaris, PO Box 113, Kariba (☎2645 or ☎2827). Hans van der Heiden, an ex-game ranger and hunter who is now a professional guide, organises very good canoeing safaris from Kariba to Chirundu, Mana Pools or Kanyemba. He also has houseboats along the Matusadona National Park's shoreline, used as safari bases for walking trips, fishing and lakeside game viewing by canoe.

Chris Worden Safaris, PO Box 221, Kariba (☎2321). One of Zimbabwe's best professional hunter-guides (see above) runs highly recommended personalised photographic safaris in Matusadona.

Kariba to Kanyemba: Canoeing the Zambezi

Gliding for a few days down the Zambezi through stunning wilderness areas is one of Zimbabwe's great travel experiences: spend the money and steel your nerves. Depending on the depth of your pocket and your adrenalin reserves, you can take on the whole course from **Kariba to Kanyemba** in nine days or do a portion of the river in three or four. Once on a trip, you'll never come across other canoes – only one small party per day is allowed on each stretch of water – so you feel it's all just for you. In two-person canoes, moving with the current, paddling isn't too strenuous – but it can be very hot from November to February, and in August and September strong winds can make it tough going.

Being in a silent vessel is a great way to approach game. You can get right up to watering elephants and skim past grazing buffalo, heads raising quizzically as you pass by. Herds of antelope splash through the shallows from one sandbank to the next and, if you're lucky, you'll see lions on the bank shading under an acacia or mahogany. The water itself is exquisite, changing colour and texture during the day. And of course there are those sunsets.

You don't need to have had previous canoeing experience, although obviously it helps – you may feel rather vulnerable setting off on this massive river having just signed an indemnity form. Take a hat, sunglasses, loads of sunscreen and a *kikoi* for your legs – the sun reflected off the water is fierce. The **pace** is leisurely – there are frequent stops for campfire meals, walks on the banks and swimming in shallow places safe from crocodiles. **Camping** is usually on sandy islands where there is less game, though you're still sure to be treated to sounds of an African night as you lie under your mosquito net close to the fire – lions and hyenas calling, something being chased in the grass, baboons shrieking in alarm and hippos stomping around. In a very rare incident in 1992, a tourist was attacked by a lion which had crossed from the mainland, with Zambezi water levels exceptionally low from the drought.

CANOE SAFARI OPTIONS

The operators listed below use experienced and licensed, but unarmed, **canoe guides**, who are allowed to take you on the water but only 50m inland. This can be a bit frustrating on days when you don't have to paddle more than 25km and have quite long rest periods on the river bank. But at Mana Pools, they are allowed to take you right into the park; most have a good knowledge of birdlife, flora and fauna and carry reference books on the trip. It's well worth booking your trip ahead of time as they fill up. The variations in prices between different companies is usually to do with the level of participation in setting up camp, the quality of food and service and amount of alcohol provided. Residents of Southern Africa and Zimbabwe pay less than the non-resident prices quoted below.

Buffalo Safaris, PO Box 113, Kariba (☎2645). Good year-round trips along the Zambezi; less expensive than *Shearwater*. *Buffalo* also run trips on Lake Kariba and in Matusadona. One of the few companies to employ black guides. Prices range upwards from US$370 per person.

You'll certainly see all the **hippos and crocodiles** you ever wanted to. Crocodiles are obviously very shy creatures, slithering off the bank as you approach, while hippos tend to duck under the water. To avoid hippos you should steer very close to the bank and shallows when passing – they always make for the deep water. One or two territorial old bulls can make fearsome displays on occasion, but the canoe leaders know the channels where they lurk and warn you beforehand that Mad Max or Harry has to be negotiated. Despite the potential dangers, these canoeing trips have an excellent safety record.

Canoeing options

Safaris begin at **Kariba**, **Chirundu** or **Mana**. From Kariba, you paddle through the steep gorge below the dam wall into the wide country of the Middle Valley floodplains. It takes three days to Chirundu and five or six to Mana, an obvious goal. The longest trip begins at Kariba and ends at Kanyemba, nine days later, most of it through completely wild country.

Several companies (see box above) run canoeing safaris, with the four days/three nights **Chirundu to Mana** trip being the most popular, and costing around US$580. A great deal of the trips runs through channels, past sandbanks and islands, with the Zambian escarpment mountains flanking the river all the way. Unless it's the rainy season when the park is closed, this trip includes a night at Mana and some walking. Occasionally optimistic types stay on and hitch out. During the rainy season you camp on the border of the park and usually have a picnic at the main camping site before driving through Mana and back to Kariba or Harare.

Mana to Kanyemba (US$800) is even more exciting, with the added thrill of coping with whirlpools in the precipitous **Mpata Gorge**. Ironstone cliffs with baobabs growing from them replace savannah, creating a magnificent entrance to the chasm. You exit by way of "the gate", a triangular-shaped granite outcrop where the river widens again. Towards Kanyemba, as the hills disappear, huts and farmlands claim the river banks, a transition from a magical, elemental realm to the more worldly. Many of the people here are **VaDema** – the only hunter-gatherers left in Zimbabwe – removed from their land in the Chewore Safari Area, and now tilling instead of hunting. A family defect gave rise to the incorrect nickname, *the three-toed people*.

Perhaps the least interesting section is **Kariba to Chirundu** – you can expect less game and it's a pity to get so close to the real wilderness of Mana without touching it. Nevertheless it's convenient if you're already at Kariba, and the gorge is spectacular.

Chipembere Safaris, PO Box 9, Kariba (☎2946). Throughout the year, the Chirundu to Mana run departs every Sunday, returning Wednesday. The cheapest deal in this section, at US$400 per person. This company also organises walking safaris in Mana Pools.

Frontiers Lower Zambezi Canoeing, PO Box 5920, Harare (☎720527; Fax 722872). Excellent luxury trips, but along the Zambian side. Transfers from Kariba or Lusaka. No trips Dec 15–March 15.

Goliath Safaris, PO Box CH294 Chisipite, Harare (☎Arcturus 30623). Three nights starts at US$600; year-round. *Goliath* may by now have a licensed hunter/guide, and the food is good. Their higher prices ensure some luxury in the bush.

Shearwater, 5th Floor, Karigamombe Centre, Harare (☎735712). From three nights for US$420 per person right up to US$1450 for the ten-day Kariba to Kanyemba trip. One trip has the option of two nights at *Ruckomechi Luxury Camp*. The season runs from March to mid-Jan only.

Zambezi Whitewater Adventures, PO Box 66293, Kopje, Harare (☎702634). One-, two- and three-day safaris. Reliably recommended.

Transfers are arranged from **Kariba or Harare** to starting points at **Chirundu** and **Mana** and back out again at the end of the trip, but this isn't included in the cost of the safari. The best option of all is to arrange your own party of at least six friends to do the trip. Lastly, choose your paddling partner carefully: it helps to go with someone you don't have full freedom to shout at!

Mana Pools National Park

Open May–Oct. Closed during the rainy season (Nov–April). Small entrance fee.

At **MANA POOLS** the Zambezi meanders through a wide valley, repeatedly splaying out into islands, channels and sandbanks, and with escarpments rising dramatically on either side. Looking across to Zambia, the land appears as an alluring quilt of blue mountains descending into another tract of wilderness – the Luangwa Valley. On the Zimbabwe side, alluvial river terraces, reaching inland for several kilometres, flank the 50km river frontage of the **National Park**.

Along these banks are the pools which give Mana its name – depressions filled with water in abandoned river channels. **Chine** and **Long Pool** hold water throughout the year, and attract large animal concentrations in the dry season. Magnificent trees grow on the fertile terraces. The enduring image of Mana is of thorn trees, *Acacia albida*, which create parklike expanses on the river bank, before giving way to dense stands of dark green mahogany, figs, sausage trees, rain trees, tamarinds and tawny *vetivaria* grass. Away from the water, the valley floor is a harsh environment, especially in the dry season. Spikey *jesse* bush deters any thoughts of walking: mopanes are stark and lifeless, while baobabs punctuate the greys and browns. Several baobabs, in fact, remain tenaciously in the middle of the park's main road, which splits to accommodate them.

The great attraction of Mana, though, is the **wildlife** – and, specifically, the possibilities of close contact, as due to its open terrain, you're allowed to **explore on foot**, as long as you are not alone. Which doesn't mean there's nothing to worry about. Lions roar nightly around the riverbank campsite and elephants, stepping carefully over guy ropes, think nothing of investigating tents and cars if they smell fresh fruit, or fancy the seed pods beneath the tree you've chosen. After dark, hyenas and honey badgers prowl about, and anything edible, even shoes, will be chewed up. There are still a few black rhino away from the river, in thick bush, and heavily armed poachers after them.

Many in the safari business believe that it is irresponsible to allow tourists to walk in the vicinity of dangerous game. There have been some fatalities and heart-stopping incidents over the years because of tourists' lack of bush experience – mainly through people wanting to get too close to animals for the sake of a good photograph. If you want to stay alive, you must follow certain fundamental bush rules (see p.114); if you do so, the whole place is enormously thrilling and rewarding. Unless you've walked in the bush before, it's much safer to explore the Mana area on an organised walk.

Mana Pools has been declared a **world heritage site** by UNESCO, and the number of visitors to the park is strictly controlled. There are no striped *combis* here to wheel the dust – nor other ugly products of tourism: a situation that, ironically, makes it impossible to reach without a car (or canoe). Without your own vehicle, there are only two ways to see the park, either on a canoe safari which takes in Mana, or to fly into one of the two luxury bush camps – *Chikwenya* or *Ruckomechi*. There is no cheap way to do it; intrepid **hitchers** have made it, but there are no local supplies, it is illegal to hitch, and there's no guarantee of getting a lift out again. If you're determined, weekends are best, when Harare's golden youth zoom up to the river for the weekend. Car hire companies do not allow their vehicles to go to Mana because of the rough roads.

If you have your own car, you'll probably be camping – National Parks' have several campsites, but the two lodges are so popular that they're allocated on a lottery system.

Getting there

By car, the 400km from Harare to Mana takes six hours on the Chirundu to Lusaka road. This is tarred to the park turn-off at the foot of the escarpment. You need to get an **entry permit** by 3.30pm from Marongora, a Parks outpost on top of the escarpment, before winding 80km into the valley and across the dry river bed country to **Nyamepi Camp**. The road is exceedingly rough but you don't need 4WD.

Accommodation

Mana's campsites and lodges are all on the river, where you'll be serenaded by hippos and other sounds of the night. There are just two **lodges**, which are allocated on a draw system. Booking for them at the main parks office in Harare opens six months before the time you want to go – a fair indication of popularity. Lodges sleep eight and go for the usual modest parks' cost.

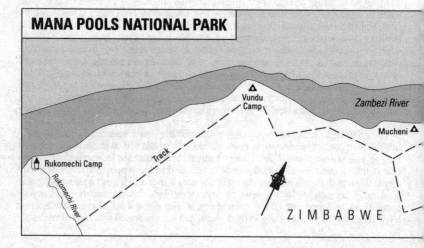

MANA POOLS NATIONAL PARK

Vundu Camp

Zambezi River

Mucheni

Rukomechi Camp

Track

Rukomechi River

ZIMBABWE

Most people stay at the **campsites**, which also need prior booking, though you can usually get in at **Nyamepi** by the park headquarters. This is a large site and gets a bit crowded at peak times; buffalo graze around the office, against which rhino skulls are stacked serving as gory reminders of the relentless poaching of black rhino in the area. Secluded, and further off, **Mucheni**, has four campsites: **Nkupe** and **Old Tree Lodge** have one each, while **Vundu**, 13km upstream, has some basic huts for one party plus hot and cold water, which the other exclusive sites lack.

One reasonably priced option, and certainly an adventurous one, is to explore Mana with *Chipembere Safaris* (PO Box 9, Kariba; ☎2946). A fully licensed professional guide runs a **back-packing trail** on the Zambezi flood plain in the wilderness area east of the main camp sites, where game viewing is maximised by camping in the vicinity of the places where animals come to drink. The charge is US$400 per person if you're self-catering, and US$525 with full catering. The *Chitake Spring Wilderness Safari* is run over four days at full moon between May and October. The Chitake Spring is within Mana Pools National Park, 50km from the river, at the foothills of the escarpment. As the only source of water for a vast area, it attracts large herds of animals and lots of predators.

The two **luxury camps** in the area – *Chikwenya* and *Ruckomechi* – fly their guests in from Kariba in very small planes, though some clients reach *Ruckomechi* by road and boat. They provide the ultimate in safari experience in Zimbabwe, set upon the river, and have professional guides to show you the abundance of birds and animals – with prices to match.

Chikwenya, (*Acacia Hotels*, George Hotel, King George Rd, Avondale, Harare; ☎707438 or ☎707439). Situated in its own small concession on the eastern boundary of Mana, *Chikwenya* is the smaller of the two luxury camps, having capacity for a maximum of twelve guests. Guests are picked up from their thatched chalets after dusk and have an armed escort – elephant and lion regularly walk right through camp. Meals are under a marvellous canopy of riverine trees and you can look at the stars from the ensuite shower and toilet which are open to the sky. Activities are game drives, river cruising on a pontoon, early-morning escorted walks and late-morning sitting in game hides perusing the changing wildlife displays. Undoubtedly one of Zimbabwe's top five bush camps. Closed Nov – April. Transfer US$180 return. Rates from US$225 per day.

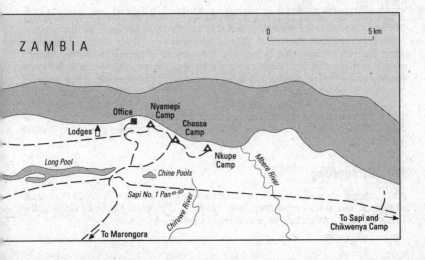

SAFETY CONSIDERATIONS

In order to enjoy the **walking** at Mana without feeling paralysed by fear, you need to know some basics. Meeting a lion on foot feels very different from staring at one from a safari vehicle. Most animals, though, aren't out to get you and will only cause problems if surprised, scared or threatened, any of which you *can* do unwittingly. To forestall disaster (accidents are exceptionally rare), follow this eight-point survivor's guide to tramping the bush.

1. **Keep a safe distance**, especially from large animals like rhino, buffalo and elephant.
2. **Don't run if you come across a lion**: stand still, keep quiet, then back off slowly. Running triggers their impulse to chase. Remember too, as you fill your viewfinder, both lions and hyenas may defend their kills if you come near them.
3. **Stay well clear of cow elephant herds** with calves. Get downwind and detour or let them pass.
4. **Don't cut off an animal's retreat.** Hippos on land usually make for the river, land mammals for dense bush or woodland.
5. **Keep a keen lookout** at all times and don't enter thick bush or grass where your visibility is severely reduced.
6. **Leave** white clothes at home, they're a loud announcement of your presence to the animals you're trying to see.
7. **Bilharzia** isn't common on this stretch of the river but **crocodiles** are. Watch out when you draw water.
8. **Fresh fruit**, especially oranges, courts disaster (elephants have a remarkable sense of smell). Leave it behind.

You're sure to be regaled with some **horror stories** about Mana. Often it's the same bush-myth recycled: the man who had his face ripped off by a hyena, or the hunter who retreated from a buffalo up a tree and had the soles of his dangling feet licked away (through shoes and all!) by the vindictive beast's abrasive tongue, or the person who got trapped all night in the campsite loo by a herd of elephants. A few people have been injured or lost their lives at Mana over the years, but when the orchestra of the night begins, remember you're safe in your tent, but not if you sleep out in the open. **Hyenas** come to the campsites nightly finding even such unlikely items as shoes, tin trunks of food and unwashed pots and pans very attractive.

Ruckomechi Camp, (*Shearwater Adventures*, PO Box 3961, Harare; ☎7355712; fax 735716). Located in an enormous stand of acacia and mahogany on the western reaches of the Mana Pools flood plain, *Ruckomechi* is a bigger and more luxurious camp than Chikwenya, able to welcome a maximum of twenty guests. Its features include a wider choice of game viewing activities, a more extensive area for game spotting and a greater number of guides. A three-night canoe trip departing from the camp can be added onto your stay for an additional US$590. Besides ensuite chalets, the camp boasts a marvellous roofless bathroom on the high river bank, with one side completely open to the water. Transfers by air from Kariba US$160 return or by boat from Chirundu US$80. Closed Dec, Jan & Feb. Daily all-inclusive rates from US$240 per person.

Wildlife spotting

Mana experiences similar **seasonal game movements** to Kariba. Soon after the rains, when food and water in the deep bush begins to dry out, the animals move to the Zambezi to find enough food to carry them through the dry season.

By October, Mana provides a spectacle of wildlife concentrated at the pools and river. **Elephant** are so common you become quite blasé about seeing them, while **buffalo** congregate in herds up to two thousand strong. **Impala, waterbuck** and **zebra** are everywhere and **numerous predators** stalk in their wake. Nearly everyone sees **lions; cheetahs** are rare, but around in small numbers, as are packs of **wild dogs** and secretive **leopards**. Animals you won't see include giraffe, wildebeest and white rhino.

Nyala antelope, found only at Mana and Gonarezhou Area, are a special sight not to be confused with **kudu** or hefty **eland** browsing off the mahoganies.

Dawn is the best chance for seeing **hippos** on land, before they move into the water. Creatures of habit, they use well-worn paths up the bank where they graze at night, crunching up long grey sausage tree pods. They also have similar underwater paths on the riverbed. The crescent-shaped seedpods of the *Acacia albida* are gourmet delicacies for **elephant** and **buffalo**; each tree bears several hundred pounds of them, which elephants shake to get down or vacuum clean from the ground underneath. The trees have a reverse foliage cycle, their leaves developing during the dry season to nourish and shade animals on the river bank, and falling once the rains begin and the animals move to fresher grazing.

The **birdlife** at Mana will leave you gasping. Brilliant **scarlet carmine bee-eaters** nest in colonies on the river bank, **fish eagles** stand sentinel on treetops, while solitary **goliath herons** wade through the shallows searching for fish and frogs. You'll see the brilliant flashes of **kingfishers** and numerous **geese** and **storks**. Away from the river, look for **hornbills, eagles, kites** and Zambezi chickens – a long-standing local name for **guineafowl** – especially the less common crested ones. Over 350 species have been recorded.

What's most appealing of all, perhaps, is not having to go on long game drives to see animals. Besides campsite action you can go to the permanent **Long Pool** near Nyamepi or the rarely dry **Chine Pool** – both good places to spend a couple of hours watching creatures coming to drink. Hippo and croc spotting at Long Pool is always fun even when nothing much else turns up. Chine Pool, 1km south of Mana River Drive, straddles the river terraces and valley hinterland, attracting animals such as sable and nyala antelope, and black rhinos, which don't come to terrace woodlands very often.

THE WESTERN LAKE AND CHIZARIRA NATIONAL PARK

Western Kariba is much less developed than the east side of the lake, and all that most people experience of it is a view from the cross-lake ferry. However, doing Kariba **overland** – on the faint road to the south of the lake marked *uninhabited* on some maps – is worthwhile if you can organise a sturdy vehicle or take your chances on local buses veering off the main Harare–Chirundu road at Karoi. Beware that the road is sandy, skiddy and impassable during heavy rains.

In fact, the area is not uninhabited, but to the west of Karoi the commercial, largely white-owned farms fade out into an area of desert – where the post-Kariba **Batonga** were dumped. Their communal lands stretch out to **Binga**, the regional administrative centre. Long stretches are just bush with the odd tree thrown across the track by elephants; schools form the nuclei of dotted settlements announced by home-made bus stop signs tacked onto baobab trees.

You won't find tourists in the villages (there's nowhere to stay anyway), except for the odd person foraging for Batonga crafts or perhaps hoping to photograph the old women, bones through noses and minus front teeth, smoking long *mbanje* (marijuana) pipes.

THE BATONGA

The Batonga are some of Zimbabwe's poorest rural people, still living mostly outside the influences of the modern nation. Cut off for centuries in the Gwembe section of the Zambezi valley, up-river from Portuguese trading stations, they maintained a subsistence lifestyle until the building of the **Kariba dam**. In 1959, when the last lorry – piled high with evicted villagers and their belongings – was on the point of departure from the doomed valley, a small green bush was tied to the vehicle's tailboard to trail along behind. Villagers explained this was to allow their ancestral guardian spirit to ride until they reached their new home: it was essential that this spirit remained on the ground during the journey for it to settle comfortably into its new surroundings and maintain a relationship with the ancestors.

The **removal of the Batonga** created considerable anguish abroad (not to mention among the people themselves). Anthropologists rushed to amass details of Batonga society before everything changed. Some interesting theories about their **origins** still question whether they ever migrated to their present area in southern Africa, as other Bantu people are supposed to have done. Unique among Bantu-speakers, the Batonga have no migration myth, so the puzzle arises: have they forgotten their history, or have they been in the Gwembe valley since much more ancient times? Anthropologists have suggested that they were indigenous hunter-gatherers who adopted the language stock and farming methods of Bantu immigrants, but not enough research has been done to be sure. Certainly, **Tonga** is a very old language, apparently a proto-form of Shona, though they may both derive from an earlier Bantu tongue, Shona having undergone more profound changes over the last millennium.

Little of this heritage seems to have found its way back to enrich **the Batonga today**. The people no longer engage in beadwork because they can't afford to buy the imported beads. Indeed, many have sold off their beaded, family heirlooms, as well as some very beautiful stools and carved hut doors, in order to raise money for the next meal. There's no evidence of traditional dress either, and the cosmetic practice of knocking out women's front teeth has (perhaps mercifully) died out. You may see the occasional old woman with a bone through her nose, but it's just as likely to be a stalk of grass. **Baskets** are certainly still being made either for domestic use or for co-operatives which distribute them through the mainstream curio centres.

Those few who bother to take this road do so to see **Chizarira National Park**, the least visited but arguably most beautiful and isolated of all Zimbabwe's game reserves, and a major sanctuary for black rhinoceros. The best way to see the park is to walk it with a safari company such as *Backpacker's Africa*, who are based at Victoria Falls and organise walking safaris with excellent professional hunter-guides. It is not the most rewarding park to see game if you're in your own vehicle as the thick bush hides the animals and you're extremely unlikely to see rhino unless you track them on foot. If camping and walking doesn't appeal, there is a new luxury lodge perched on a hill just outside the national park. The only other tourist development hinges on small **fishing resorts** like Binga, and, on a slightly larger scale, **Mlibizi** – the Kariba ferry terminus.

The Kariba Ferry

The **Kariba ferry** is by far the easiest way to journey the length of the lake, saving the circuitous 1250-km route you have to follow to drive to Victoria Falls via Bulawayo on tarred roads. But while the voyage has an *African Queen* romance to it, through wild country all the way, the experience rather depends on who you're sitting next to and how active the boozers are: people often rave it up for the entire 22-hour journey.

After this checklist of loss, at least the layout of villages and **architectural techniques** remain much as they've always been. The thatching is an untidy affair, not groomed into flawless sections like Ndebele huts. The small huts on stilts are for chickens or children, with ladders removed at night to keep the precious charges safe from attack by wild animals. Huts on stilts in the fields are baboon watchtowers, occupied all day long before the harvest. These days, high-status building materials like cement and corrugated iron are used if someone has the money.

The Batonga live over the border in Zambia, too, both in the Zambezi valley and on the plateau (before the existence of political frontiers, valley people crossed the river in dug-outs). But studies of the language and culture have concentrated on the plateau Batonga, who have always been broadly integrated with the rest of the country. In contrast, the isolation of the Gwembe valley inhabitants has earned them the label "backward" among urban Zimbabweans. An obvious target for **aid money**, they attract attention from organisations like the *Save the Children Fund*, who have concentrated on improving **sanitation and water supplies** to communities with some of the worst child mortality rates in the country. Landrovers shuttle between villages transporting pipes and machinery for other projects like collective grain winnowing. And the government's desire to see universal primary **education** has seeded schools in many settlements. People no longer have to walk for days to get to a secondary school. One worker at Bumi Hills, remembering his schooling, recounted walking three days at the start and end of each term, accompanied by his older brother armed with axe and spear to fend off wild animals.

But nothing can compensate the Batonga for the forced substitution of a viable – even flourishing – farming and fishing economy on the Zambezi, for the poor soils and uncertain rainfall of the interior. Evicted overnight from familiar, well-watered ancient lands, the Batonga have floundered ever since in their new and alien home.

An ironic postscipt to the story of the Batonga is the **trendiness** they've accumulated. Perhaps it's their *mbanje*-smoking (women from long calabash pipes, men from shorter clay ones) that's created a special niche for these people in colonial cosmology. You come across tales of young middle-class whites who became strange and went to live among the "Tonkies". Often this seems to be a symbolic fall from grace into liberalism or socialism. Usually the person who "went native" is alive and well and living in a city somewhere.

Tickets for the trip cost $US55 for a reclining seat, with meals, tea and coffee all included. Cars cost $US40 to load up, payable in forex. Residents pay less. The ferry is often booked up months in advance and you need to pay half the cost to secure your booking two weeks before the sailing date. After this time, seats are sold off, so keep on enquiring if you're told it's full. Without a car, your chances of getting on are better. On board, there's an outside sun deck and a shaded lounge. It's well worth bringing **binoculars** to spot animals en route, otherwise you'll have to be content with frustrating specks on the shoreline.

Departure dates vary. During peak months and school holidays (Jan, April, May, July, Aug, Sept & Dec) ferries sail frequently but in February, March, June and October there are only a couple a month and none at all in November. In the busy months, the ferry leaves Kariba every Tuesday and Friday for Mlibizi, returning to Kariba on Wednesday and Saturday, while in low season the ferry leaves Kariba on Friday, returning the next day. Details, sailing schedules and booking from *Kariba Ferries (Pvt) Ltd.*, PO Box 578, Harare (☎65476; Fax 67660), or call the local office in Kariba on ☎2475.

If you're **hitching**, once across the lake you should be able to line up a lift with a driver while on the ferry. Alternatively, there are organised but pricey **landcruiser transfers.** *Zimbabwe Rendezvous* (PO Box BE267, Belvedere, Harare; Fax ☎22836) will pick up four or more passengers from the ferry terminal for a trip to Hwange) or Victoria Falls; they also collect at these places for the return to Mlibizi. Book ahead.

South of the Lake: Wild Country

The land south of Lake Kariba is among Zimbabwe's poorest and most remote. Travelling about the region, unless on an organised tour or with your own vehicle, you are dependent on a very few local buses – somewhat erratically scheduled and none too comfortable. **Hitching** in this region would be very chancey – traffic is very sparse and about your only hope would be to find an aid vehicle prepared to take you. Carry food and plenty of water, and expect long delays.

It's best not to get off except at villages as wild animals abound in this region. A familiar sight along the roadsides are aid-built pumps where locals fill buckets, and *blair toilets*, built behind huts in every village. These are an ingenious Zimbabwean design, solving the problem of flies and smell which plague the traditional long-drops; painted black inside and spiral-shaped with a chimney airvent, they trap flies escaping to the only source of light – the gauze-covered airvent, which also allows air to circulate.

Siabuwa

SIABUWA is the halfway staging post on the 400-km trip from Karoi to Binga – the largest settlement en route and the place where buses begin and terminate. Eaten out by goats, it's a large congregation of huts, schools, a garage and a basic store or two. The shop verandahs are handy to sleep on if you're waiting overnight for public transport. A daily **bus** sets off in the early hours of the morning for Bulawayo via Binga on what must be the longest haul in the country; people sleep at the stop to ensure catching it, as the drivers leave when they get up.

Siacobvu and Bumi Hills

Almost as long is the journey from Bumi Hills via **SIACOBVU** to Harare, which is covered by bus a few times a week. Siacobvu, a tiny place on the escarpment overlooking the Ume River, is one of the deprived locations designated as a "growth point" by the government. The rather snazzy library – a fine example of low-cost development architecture which was designed by a prestigious Harare architect – is becoming better used, while the done-up District Council offices have wall charts showing the local **cooperatives**, which include school uniform and basket-making as well as a bakery.

Not far from Siacobvu, in the Omay Communal Lands is **BUMI HILLS**. Besides its luxurious hilltop **hotel** (see p.108), Bumi Hills has administrative offices, a store and police station. Scandinavian aid workers have set up a non-profit craft shop down at the harbour, where local products are sold to hotel guests and to people stopping in off houseboats.

Binga

The Kariba ferry sails past **BINGA** without stopping, so if you are planning to visit this village, with its Chizarira Mountain view, you will have to come overland. Which is all the better, if you're prepared for the isolation, for this is both an interesting and scenic (as yet) un-resort, spreading over a couple of hills and along the lakeshore. Like Kariba, it has no real centre, so without a car you'll find yourself doing long, sandy trudges to get around.

If you're interested in travelling around the remote villages and getting a taste of Batonga life, a local teacher and archaeologist leads cultural tours on donkey back.

PARKS VERSUS PEOPLE

As elsewhere in Zimbabwe, there's extreme tension between villagers and the National Parks over **wildlife** – a conflict which has deep roots.

Game parks were set up from the 1930s to maintain game populations that had been decimated by hunting and habitat removal for commercial farming. White rhinos had been completely exterminated and diaries of early settlers reveal obscene hunting excesses – twenty-five giraffe in an afternoon was nothing. To create the parks, however, people were moved out and banned from subsistence hunting. Long-established balances had enabled people to coexist with wild animals for thousands of years, yet, suddenly, wildlife had become a luxury for the rich. Colonial legislation stated that wildlife in communal (black) areas was state property, while on private (white) farms, it was not.

Shortly after Independence a host of new conservation measures were introduced but the problem of human versus animal interests remains unresolved and **poaching** is still heavy in all the national parks. One major way forward is the Campfire Project (Communal Areas Management for Indigenous Resources) which has a philosophy of sustainable rural development to enable rural communities to manage, and benefit directly from indigenous wildlife and other resources. Getting a community interested in the Campfire programme rests on changing the belief that the State owns the wildlife, to the belief that the wildlife is owned by the community who lives with it.

The first Campfire Project to be set up was the **Nyaminyami Wildlife Trust** in the Omay Communal Lands, adjoining Matusadona National Park. Wild animals tend to be viewed either as food or as a crop menace by peasant farmers, who resent wildlife getting so much land, while they're forced to keep livestock numbers low to prevent encroachment on game areas. As hunting is forbidden, *National Parks* are frequently called out to shoot "problem animals" which are endangering either people's lives or crops in the fields – rather too often in the view of some parks officials. From this arrangement, the people get the meat and *Parks* services the skins and tusks (elephants are frequently the culprits and victims). The other difficulty is that the number of claims for crop compensation, paid in cash, tends to exceed the budget and may be open to abuse.

The Campfire Project is also trying to make people aware that although they want to acquire cattle, it's in their interests to limit numbers as wildlife is potentially more lucrative. In the Omay Communal Lands the number of goats is roughly equal to the number of impala, but the meat value alone of the impala far exceeds that of goat, and the hunting of impala brings in considerable revenue.

On the hunting front, to provide local people with the incentive not to poach, Chizarira and the neighbouring hunting area of Chirisa pioneered a scheme in 1980 called **Operation Windfall**, to channel revenue from game back to the communal lands. When elephants are culled, the meat, hides and tusks are handed over to neighbouring rural councils and the proceeds used to build schools and clinics.

The Town

Binga was created as an **administrative centre** for Batonga resettlement, though, ironically, despite the dam's creation for hydroelectric power, electricity has only recently arrived, and the water supplies, piped uphill, don't always work.

Missionaries, however, are well ensconced, and a **hospital** and **foreign aid worker village**, **secondary school** and surprisingly well-stocked **supermarket**, near the main **bus stop**, form an ensemble of public buildings. The **school** is interesting, with an impressive library open to the community, and innovative experiments in farming are under way. On the riverbank, the Batonga used to cultivate millet, which doesn't thrive inland, so agriculturalists are trying poor soil crops like **manioc**, with the hard work done by schoolchildren in exchange for remission of their school fees.

Pupils come from both Batonga and Ndebele communities. Teachers notice big differences in the children's responses to authority. The Ndebele, who come from a highly organised culture, accept what they are told, without demur, whereas the Batonga, whose social system of virtually autonomous homesteads is much looser, question everything.

The Rest Camp and Hot Springs

Binga has a few lakeside villas – holiday homes for the affluent from Bulawayo – which the locals refer to as "The Palaces". Down at the lakeside, too, 5km downhill from the administrative centre and bus terminus, is the former District Commissioner's residence, now the **Binga Rest Camp** (☎244; ③).

This is the only accommodation in the area and has a **swimming pool**, filled by a nearby **hot spring**. The springs are distinctly reviving after the long journey here, and the hotel gardens with their exotic trees provide a wonderful respite from the dust. Prices are very modest for **rooms** and only a few dollars more for self-contained **chalets**. **Camping** is also possible. **Meals** and **snacks** are available; it appears that more people frequent the lively **bar** than ever stay here. The *Rest Camp* also has the centre's only commercial **filling station**, plus a shop. For lifts into town (you won't want to walk) approach people at the garage.

Between town and hotel, another **hot spring** is the local bathing and washing place – *Surf* bubbles scud along the surface. These *Chibwatatata* springs were originally meeting places where rituals were performed. Some of the mystique lingers on; rumour has it that a *n'anga* heals and performs miracles there, though no one seems to know whether he's alive or dead.

Batonga craft

The Binga area is the most promising place to track down the much sought-after Batonga handicrafts. A major cooperative at Kariangwe, about 60km south of Binga, collects baskets from all over the region for resale and they're available from the craft shop in Binga. There are also several roadside sellers dotted along the road from Hwange towards Chizarira. Prices are so low that bargaining is not on.

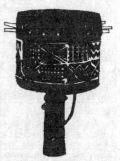

The best items are the wide-mouthed **winnowing baskets** with plaited square bottoms, tricoloured v-patterned **beadwork** and the **carved stools** you see people sitting on under the trees. The Batonga are people who really know about travelling and roadside waits, and they make wonderful, portable stools with carrying handles. You won't be able to stash one of the free-standing Batonga drums in your baggage, but they're worth seeing (or even playing) all the same. Traditionally decorated with beautiful, archetypal zigzag motifs, they are now, sadly, a disappearing art.

Village Visits

One of the most rewarding ways to experience traditional rural Zimbabwe is to take a day trip to one of the remote Tonga homesteads with Dr Peta Jones, an archaeologist and anthropologist living in Binga. You'll either walk along paths (for a maximum of two hours) or go by donkey to a homestead for a meal which would normally be served to the family's own friends or visitors. Secondary school graduates from Tonga villages in the area are on tap to act as interpreters. The organisers stress that people should dress modestly, so as not to make their hosts feel disadvantaged, and if you feel philanthropic not to hand out money directly to people, but make a donation instead to an educational fund. The day includes a visit to the community craft centre where you can buy baskets and the like. Charges for a day out are very reasonable, and bookings should be made at least two weeks in advance to Enzo Rossi, Private Bag 5705, Binga (☎313).

Getting around the region

Public transport is minimal with wildly erratic bus timetables – keep asking around to get a reasonable idea of what's going on – but buses can get you to Bulawayo, Hwange National Park and Victoria Falls without too much difficulty. Two daily services connect Bulawayo and Siabuwa via Binga – one in each direction. For Victoria Falls (all day trip) change at Dete Cross; for Hwange National Park (4hr) get off at Safari Cross. For Harare, sleep at the Siabuwa bus stop and catch the next morning's bus via Karoi. There are no buses between Binga and lakeside Mlibizi (see below), as the Mlibizi ferry terminus is 15km off the main road; once on the main road however, you could pick up a bus.

With your own car, Binga is more accessible with a recently completed tarred road all the way from Hwange (188km). Hitching is not easy as traffic is sparse; start out early in the morning and take the bus if nothing else has materialised. Getting onto and around the lake itself is a little easier now with boat hire available from Enzo Rossi, Private Bag 5705, Binga (☎313).

The Western fishing resorts: Mlibizi and Deka

Since game has been shot out at this southwest end of the lake, fishing is the main draw. To catch the Kariba ferry you'll have to overnight at **MLIBIZI** to make the 9am departure. The fairly luxurious **Mlibizi Zambezi Resort** (PO Box 2335, Bulawayo; ☎78060 or ☎78064; ④) here has Spanish-styled self-contained **chalets** as well as camping, or try the **Mlibizi Safari and Holiday Camp** (PO Box 298, Hwange; ③), which is cheaper but further from the ferry terminal.

On the confluence of the Zambezi and Deka rivers, 50km from Hwange, the **Deka Drum Fishing Resort** (PO Box 2, Hwange; ☎50524; ① & ③) is a more modest and a wonderfully old-fashioned place – cheap, with **camping** and **chalets**, a swimming pool and bar. It's not worth a special trip unless it's fishing you're after, but it's definitely worth stopping over if you're in the region. It is also one of the few places selling petrol in the area and you can call in for a drink or lunch on the verandah. A rural store nearby sells basic foods if you're camping.

Chizarira National Park

Open year round. Small entrance fee.

Very few travellers make it to **Chizarira**, Zimbabwe's most remote National Park. Isolated and undeveloped, it is a spectacular region, a kingdom on top of the steep Zambezi escarpment well watered by rivers cutting sheer gorges through the mountains and full of natural springs. Besides black rhinoceros, the usual Zambezi valley game is to be seen, including elephant, buffalo, zebra, kudu, reedbuck, waterbuck, bushbuck, eland, grysbok, impala and tsessebe. It's not a great place for lion, though you will hear them and are more likely to see them in the south. There have been some exceptional daytime sightings of leopard, less shy here than in other parks because tourists are few and far between. But when people talk about the park, it's the scenic beauty that invariably makes them wax lyrical.

This becomes understandable as soon as you approach the park. From a long way off the jagged mountains of Chizarira are visible, dominated by **Tundazi** – home, local legend has it, to an immense and powerful serpent. Once you've arrived, the views across to Lake Kariba, 40km north, are equally magnificent. The Chizarira **mountains** give you a clue to the nature of the place. Their name derives from a Tonga word meaning to close off or create a barrier – defining the craggy edge of their baobab-wooded world, the Gwembe Valley. The escarpment's roof is another world altogether, of slender trees spaced out across grasslands and well-watered scrub savannah. The **river gorges**, such as Mucheni and Lwizilukulu, are really exciting, with their thick vegetation cascading down places too steep for any vehicle. This doesn't stop the **elephants**, however; you'll notice their paths, less than a metre wide, cutting into slopes held together by the determined roots of stunted trees. On the escarpment in the north are plateaux of typical highveld Brachystegia woodland and mopane scrub and woodland as you move southwards. The southern boundary is marked by the Busi River which is flanked by plains of characteristic Mana Pools *Acacia albida* trees.

Access and walking

You won't have much company at Chizarira: it's just too far for most people, when other parks are far more accessible. Most of those visitors who do come drive from Victoria Falls or Hwange, an eight-hour journey mostly on dirt roads. While 4WD isn't essential for the north, except during the rains, it is necessary for the south where you have to cross sandy rivers to reach Busi camp. The nearest **petrol and supplies** are 90km away at Binga so bring all you need. From Harare, Chizarira is 300km of dirt road, once you turn off at Karoi, with Siabuwa the only place en route for petrol.

Guests fly in to *Chizarira Wilderness Lodge*, the only tourist place. The lodge has eight thatched stone chalets shaded by a grove of Mountain Acacia dramatically overlooking the Zambezi Valley. It's just outside the park, half an hour's drive from the park headquarters, and is managed by a fully licensed professional guide who can take walks into the park, and do game drives. Book through *Zambezi Wilderness Safaris* (Box 18, Victoria Falls; ☎4637; Fax 4417).

If you want to do more walking and tracking, contact *Backpackers Africa*, who camp right in the park and unlike most other operators go into the south. *Backpackers'* walking safaris in Chizarira are perhaps the ultimate adventure safari in Zimbabwe, with almost every trip managing to see black rhino. The safaris are fully backed up – a 4WD carries two camp attendants who put up the tents, make the fires, prepare all the food and heat the water for your portable washbasins and bush showers. You don't have to carry anything besides your binoculars and camera. Nor is the walking uncomfortable – you're not pushed excessively and you rest up during the heat in the middle of the day. If this sounds too cushy, *Backpackers* does offer safaris where you carry everything yourself and rough it.

An African tracker walks with the armed guide and you spend a good deal of time identifying and following game tracks. It's a fascinating experience, estimating how far ahead the elephants are by feeling the warmth of their dung (it's mainly grass after all), or how old the remains of a lion kill are, and noticing the insects and birds you miss when driving. Expect to pay US$160 in low season (Nov–May) per day all-in, and US$195 the rest of the year. While you can do a walking trip just to Chizarira, *Backpackers* offers a twelve-day *Rhino Trail* once a month which takes in the Zambezi National Park, Hwange, Kazuma Pan as well as Chizarira. Bookings for *Backpackers Africa* can be made through *Shearwater Adventures* (PO Box 125, Victoria Falls; ☎4471 or ☎4472; Fax 4341).

If you're visiting the park under your own steam, you can ask an armed national parks game scout to take you walking. They will take groups out for a small fee. Unlike Mana Pools, however, you can't wander off on your own.

The overland safari company *Afroventures* (PO Box 125, Victoria Falls; ☎4471), spends a night or two at Chizarira en route to Kariba from Victoria Falls, but they only go to the northern section. *Afroventures* sometimes hires a professional guide to take walks in Chizarira, or uses a Parks game scout to accompany a group.

National Parks Camps

Park headquarters are at Manzituba, 22km up the escarpment from the Binga–Siabuwa road. There are no chalets or lodges here but there are three **camping sites** nearby, the most developed of which is at Kasiswi on the Lusilukulu River, 6km from the park HQ, which has thatched shelters on stilts. Two spectacular sites overlooking the Mucheni Gorge have no facilities. Only one party at a time is allowed in each; booking is through National Parks' Central Reservations office in Harare and the costs are reasonable as usual for the Parks.

Mabolo Bush Camp on the Mucheni river, below the Manzituba spring, 6km from the camp HQ, has running water, a flush toilet and shower. If you prefer flood plains and lowveld vegetation go 35km over very rough roads to **Busi Bush Camp**, which has thatched sleeping shelters, but no running water. You have to dig water from the river bed and boil it. It's a marvellous site under *Acacia albidas* with herds of impala wandering around and a night chorus of hyenas and lions.

The wildlife – and poachers

Chizarira is your best chance of seeing a passing species – black or hook-lipped **rhinos** browse around thick bush and wooded gulleys in the northern part of the park. Zimbabwe has the world's last viable breeding herd of **black rhinos** and nothing seems able to halt their steady extermination. Twenty years ago there were 40,000 black rhinos in Africa. In early 1992 it was estimated that there were fewer than 3000 on the continent, of which 2000 were in Zimbabwe. However in November 1992 a count throughout Zimbabwe found only 250 black rhinos living in the wild. Experts predict that Zimbabwe's last rhino will be finished off in the next few years. Despite the international ban on the trade in rhino horn, it is, even today, widely available in markets in Hong Kong and Taiwan at a cost of up to US$900 per pound. The market for knife handles in the Yemen and apothecarial ingredients in the Far East continues to propel their unrelenting slaughter.

In 1985, the Zimbabwean government began shooting poachers on sight and capturing and **translocating** rhinos to safer parks, but this strategy hasn't worked. **Poachers** move quickly on foot, cutting out only the horn before ferrying back to their camps in Zambia. In an area of dense bush, they often escape undetected. The poachers themselves are not the ones to cream off vast amounts of money, but are offered enough by middlemen to make it worth risking their lives. Many are unemployed Zambians. Zimbabwe's next step in the early 1990s was a massive **dehorning programme.** Since then, sadly, dehorned rhinos have been killed simply for their stumps.

Zimbabwe has longed blamed Zambian poachers, backed by international rings, for killing rhino, but there is evidence of **high-level government involvement** in the trade. An MP was jailed in early 1993 for five years for possession of two horns. The deaths in suspicious circumstances of two army officers who were looking into top-level military involvement in rhino, as well as elephant poaching, have led to calls from *Amnesty International* for a government investigation.

TELEPHONE AREA CODES		
Binga 115	**Kariba** 161	**Mazowe** 175
Bulawayo 19	**Karoi** 164	**Mount Darwin** 176
Chirundu 163-7*	**Makuti** 163	**Sanyati** 168-7*

A hyphen indicates a second dialling tone.

travel details

Buses
The length of these routes, and Zambezi Valley road conditions, compound the usual vagueness of local bus times. On the Karoi–Binga road buses break down more than is usual elsewhere and the drivers often set off when they wake up. Many of the buses start somewhere else and what's happened en route is a mystery. Ask around. The best advice is to be there as early as the locals.

From Kariba to Harare 2 daily first thing (8hr).

Chirundu to Harare daily noon (8hr).

Chirundu to Lusaka daily 2pm (7hr).

Binga to Bulawayo 1 daily 5.30–8.30am (8hr), via **Hwange** (2hr 30min).

Binga to Hwange via **Deka** approx 3 per week: unreliable due to bad road.

Binga to Hwange 4 weekly.

Siabuwa to Binga 1 daily between 2.30pm and 5.30pm (3hr).

Siabuwa to Harare via **Karoi**, 1 daily between 1am and 2am (all day to Harare).

Karoi to Siabuwa 1 daily (from Harare).

Coaches
Various coach companies take on the Harare–Kariba route from time to time, then stop because of unprofitability. Check with local hotels in Kariba or the Publicity Association in Harare for the latest. At present *B&C* are plying the route, stopping at Makuti, Karoi and Chinoyi. Coaches are faster, more comfortable and more expensive than buses.

From Kariba to Harare dep Carribbea Bay Tues & Thurs 7.45am, Sun 1pm (journey time 6hr) .

Ferries
The timetable of the private *Sealion* ferries varies seasonally; ring Harare ☎65476 or Kariba ☎2475. The government ferries, run by the District Development Fund (DDF), also run to a flexible timetable; enquiries on Binga ☎323 and Kariba ☎2349.

Here's a rough outline:

From Kariba to:

Mlibizi approx weekly at peak; enquire *Kariba Ferries.*

Binga approx fortnightly; enquire DDF.

Matusadona and **Fothergill** approx weekly; enquire DDF.

Flights
From Kariba to:

Harare daily 4.50pm (55min).

Victoria Falls daily 11.05am (1hr 50min) via **Hwange National Park** (55min).

Bulawayo 2 per week.

Johannesburg 2 per week.

CHAPTER THREE

BULAWAYO AND THE MATOBO DISTRICT

Set apart by language and history from the rest of the country, **Bulawayo** is often bypassed by travellers. Which is a pity, for Zimbabwe's second city is unquestionably more interesting than its capital: whereas Harare uses Western symbolism to make its mark as an international capital, Bulawayo's character comes from a history of going its own way and developing its own style. Although Bulawayo's citizens have long considered their city to have suffered unjust neglect at the expense of Harare, the upside is that there has been little demolition or hasty redevelopment, and the wide, regularly gridded streets remain studded with gracious colonial-era buildings. Overall, in fact, the city has something of a sepia-toned feel, compounded by rather conservative dress and ageing cars – a slow, laid-back ambience that makes it a thoroughly pleasant place to stroll about and explore.

Perhaps the best reason to visit the city is for the nearby **Matopos Hills** and **Matobo National Park**. Although such granite outcrops can be found all over the country, the Dali-esque compositions of lichen-streaked balancing rocks and grassy valleys are at their best at Matopos. The world's highest concentration of prehistoric **rock paintings** is found here, too, and you can spend days climbing kopjes and discovering painted caves and rock shelters – human history in the area goes back over 100,000 years. Much later, the **Torwa** and **Rozwi** states had court centres in the Bulawayo region, the remains of which lie scattered in the countryside. None competes with Great Zimbabwe in size but the local style is exemplified by the beautifully laid walls at **Khami**, 22km from Bulawayo.

Since colonial times, Bulawayo has served as a **transport hub** between the African hinterland and the continent's southern tip. It is the jumping off point for Hwange and Victoria Falls and onward journeys to Zambia, Botswana, and South Africa, as well as being well poised for eastward travel to Great Zimbabwe and the Highlands.

BULAWAYO AND AROUND

Arriving in **BULAWAYO** is like jumping back fifty years. More like the set of an old movie than a modern African city, the town stood in for late-1950s Johannesburg in the shooting of *A World Apart*, the film about South African anti-apartheid activist, Ruth First. The South African connection actually goes deeper than film maker's licence. In the nineteenth century, Bulawayo was the capital of the **Ndebele state** and the majority language, Sindebele, is very close to the original Zulu. The local *Smanje Manje* **music** has crossover elements of Shona and South African township pop.

Tourist **attractions** in town are limited, but what there is can fill a day or two. In Centenary Park, the **Museum of Natural History** is the finest in central Africa. The **art gallery** has some excellent Ndebele craft work and the **Mzilikazi Art and Craft Centre** is good for a few hours, set as it is in the oldest and most interesting high-density suburb. On the fringes of the city, the **Tshabalala Animal Sanctuary** – which is completely wild – offers walking or horse riding, plus the chance to see antelope, while, further out, **Chipangali Wildlife Orphanage** obliges with big cats and elephants.

Beyond the city itself, the best day trip (though it deserves longer) is to the Matopos Hills, which could easily be combined with a visit to the unexpected artistic hive of **Cyrene Mission**. Half a day will take you to the **Khami ruins**, while other stone ruin sites lie, less accessibly, off the Harare road. Lastly, in the little-visited far southwest of the country, the **Tuli Circle** fauna and flora enclave is worthy of serious investigation by determined enthusiasts.

Bulawayo

The name **BULAWAYO** means, in Ndebele, "Place of Slaughter", a reference, it is thought, to the fierce succession battles that took place in the late nineteenth century. These culminated in the accession of one of the key figures of pre-colonial Zimbabwean history, **King Lobengula** in 1870. His reign, peppered with heavy doses of heroism, lying, betrayal and death, reads like mythology or grand opera: an era which came to a close in 1894, with Lobengula's death, and Ndebele collapse before the relentless northwards advance of the **British South Africa Company**. For the events, see "The Historical Framework" on p.351.

Although Bulawayo kept its name, the new **colonial town** was re-sited along a classic British grid. Almost immediately it was at the centre of a mining rush: within two months four hundred gold prospectors had acquired licences and within ten years the population had reached six thousand. Quick to see an opportunity, the *Standard Bank of South Africa* set up its first branch in a tent, guarded day and night by the Matabeleland Mounted Police. In 1898, as the proposed Cape to Cairo **railway** reached Bulawayo, the town developed into an important clearing house for goods from the colonies further north, and became the country's main communications centre.

Resistance to the white invasion, however, hadn't ended in 1894. While the first *Chimurenga* marked the last great survival struggle of the old societies, colonial rule brought new forms of protest. Bulawayo – because of its strong industrial base in engineering, metal founding, manufacturing, garment making, printing, packaging and food production – was at the forefront of the development of worker organisations. The first African **trade union**, the Rhodesian Industrial and Commercial Workers Union, was formed here in 1927; African railway workers staged a successful strike in 1945; and the country's first general strike began here in 1948. **Joshua Nkomo**, general secretary of the railway workers' union and president of the TUC, later emerged in the 1950s as leader of the Bulawayo-based **African National Congress**.

Nkomo's strong regional following in Matabeleland led inevitably to much bad feeling when he was cold-shouldered by the government after **Independence**. The **dissident years** that followed – in which rebels and their village supporters were brutally repressed by government forces – posed a great threat to the government and fuelled white fears that tribal warfare might sound the death knell of the new Zimbabwe. The

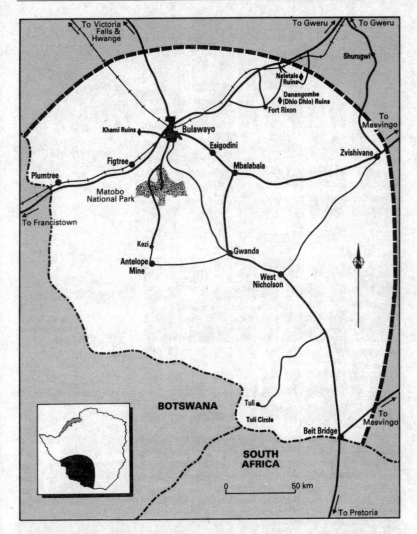

grievances of the early Eighties, however, turned out not to be beyond negotiated settlement.

With the May 1988 **Unity Accord**, dissidents left the bush and laid down their arms. Joshua Nkomo is now one of President Mugabe's two vice-presidents and the formerly jailed Zipra leader Dumisa Dabengwa is home affairs minister. A second national university has been built in Bulawayo to equalise some of the disparity between developments in the capital and neglected Bulawayo. Horrific evidence, though, of the extent of the killings, particularly by the notorious Fifth Brigade in the early Eighties, keeps emerging – the 1992 drought revealed skeletons down dried-out mineshafts – and there have been calls for the report of a full inquiry held into the atrocities to be published.

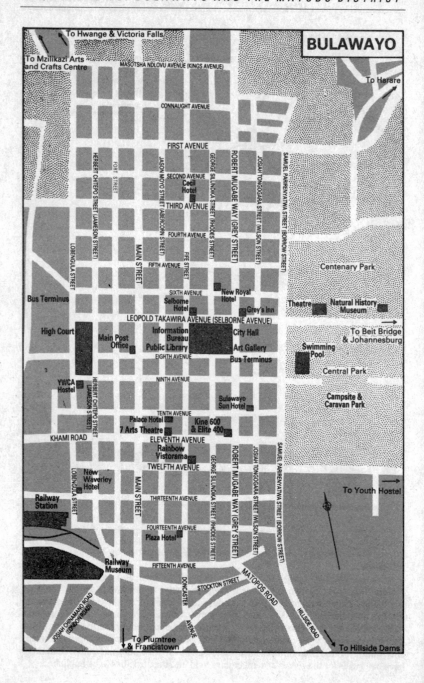

BULAWAYO

To Hwange & Victoria Falls

To Mzilikazi Arts
and Crafts Centre

MASOTSHA NDLOVU AVENUE (KINGS AVENUE)

To Harare

CONNAUGHT AVENUE

FIRST AVENUE

SECOND AVENUE

Cecil
Hotel

THIRD AVENUE

FOURTH AVENUE

FIFTH AVENUE

FORT STREET

JASON MOYO STREET (ABERCORN STREET)

MAIN STREET

FIFE STREET

HERBERT CHITEPO STREET (JAMESON STREET)

LOBENGULA STREET

GEORGE SILUNDIKA STREET

ROBERT MUGABE WAY (GREY STREET)

JOSIAH TONGOGARA STREET (WILSON STREET)

SAMUEL PARIRENYATWA STREET (BORROW STREET)

Centenary Park

SIXTH AVENUE

New Royal
Hotel

Selborne
Hotel

Grey's Inn

Bus Terminus

Theatre

Natural History
Museum

LEOPOLD TAKAWIRA AVENUE (SELBORNE AVENUE)

High Court

Main Post
Office

Information
Bureau
Public Library

City Hall

Art Gallery

Bus Terminus

To Beit Bridge
& Johannesburg

Swimming
Pool

EIGHTH AVENUE

Central Park

NINTH AVENUE

YWCA
Hostel

Campsite &
Caravan Park

HERBERT CHITEPO STREET (JAMESON STREET)

Bulawayo
Sun Hotel

TENTH AVENUE

Palace Hotel

7 Arts Theatre

Kine 600
& Elite 400

KHAMI ROAD

ELEVENTH AVENUE

Rainbow
Vistorama

TWELFTH AVENUE

New
Waverley
Hotel

LOBENGULA STREET

MAIN STREET

THIRTEENTH AVENUE

GEORGE SILUNDIKA STREET (RHODES STREET)

ROBERT MUGABE WAY (GREY STREET)

JOSIAH TONGOGARA STREET (WILSON STREET)

SAMUEL PARIRENYATWA STREET (BORROW STREET)

Railway
Station

To Youth Hostel

FOURTEENTH AVENUE

Plaza Hotel

Railway
Museum

FIFTEENTH AVENUE

DONCASTER AVENUE

STOCKTON STREET

MATOPOS ROAD

HILLSIDE ROAD

JOSIAH CHINAMANO ROAD (LONDON ROAD)

To Plumtree
& Francistown

To Hillside Dams

Orientation, transport and accommodation

The centre of Bulawayo is marked by **City Hall**, right outside which runs **Eighth Avenue**, the town's principal axis. This leads on to the main public buildings and culminates in the **High Court** – a colossal building with a copper dome mounted high on a three-storey plinth. In earlier times a statue of Cecil Rhodes stood dead in the middle of Eighth Avenue and Main Street, framed by the powerfully symbolic high court; after Independence the statue was literally pulled from its pedestal, to be kicked and beaten by bystanders. It has now found a new home behind the Natural History Museum.

Along **Leopold Takawira Way**, which parallels Eighth Avenue, a long stretch of **parkland** shelters the campsite. On the opposite side of town, off Lobengula Street, is the **railway station**. The stretch from here down Lobengula Street to the **bus terminus** is the centre's main **African quarter**, where bicycles weave through the traffic, small colonnaded shops sell cloth, blankets and cooking pots, and local music bellows from record bars. West of Lobengula Street lie the **industrial sites** and **high-density areas**.

Peaceful **suburbs** surround central Bulawayo, the wealthiest being in the hillier east, where granite outcrops grace the large gardens, and the poorest in the west, where maize and the odd stubby pawpaw and mango trees grow fitfully in the dusty backyards of one- or two-roomed dwellings. The oldest and most interesting houses lie just south of the city centre in what was the earliest white residential area – inventively called **Suburbs**. Here, colonial-style homes with wrap-around verandahs front onto jacaranda-lined streets.

Points of arrival

However you arrive, getting into central Bulawayo should present few problems. An *Air Zimbabwe* bus meets all flights at the **airport** (☎26491 or ☎26492), 22km north of town on Robert Mugabe Way, and deposits passengers at the central *Bulawayo Sun Hotel*.

The *Sun* also serves as the depot for *Ajay Motorways* **coach services** to and from Harare, Hwange and Victoria Falls. Most **long-distance buses**, however, arrive at Renkini bus terminus in Sixth Avenue Extension, opposite the Mzilikazi Police Station and a little off the main drag. From there, assorted **buses** head into town – though you may prefer to avoid the hassle and take a taxi. A few long-distance buses arrive at the more central terminus, on Lobengula Street/Sixth Avenue, nearer the downtown district. Bulawayo's **railway station**, at the end of Lobengula Street, is a short hop by taxi from the centre.

Getting around

Central Bulawayo is easy to get around on **foot**, and though the wide streets make the distance from one side of town to the other feel endless, most places around town can be reached in under half an hour. For **bike hire**, try the *Youth for Christ Centre*, 117 George Silundika Street/Twelfth Avenue (☎63656) or *Transit Car & Truck Hire*, Robert Mugabe Way/Twelfth Avenue (☎76495 or ☎76496).

Taxis are cheap for short trips. **Buses** are more practicable for destinations further afield such as the Townsend Road Youth Hostel, the Hillside Dams, or for reaching a spot out of town from which to hitch to the Matopos.

Bulawayo has two urban **bus stations**. The **City Hall terminus**, on Eighth Avenue between Fife Street and Robert Mugabe Way, serves all but the western suburbs. Services are fairly frequent and there's a patchily accurate timetable. Buses to the low-income suburbs run from **Lobengula Street terminus** on Sixth Avenue. These are invariably crowded and sadly inadequate, and you'll see people still waiting to get home two hours after the shops have closed.

Accommodation

Bulawayo's hotels accommodate all but the emptiest of pockets, and most are conveniently central and clean. Backpacker crash pads, similar to those in Harare, are sure to spring up, along with homestays and B&B's. The excellent Publicity Association in City Hall will have the latest information. At the other end of the scale, small safari operators have blossomed, and it's certainly an option to stay out of town on a game farm at an all-inclusive rate, rather than a city hotel. Several alternatives have recently opened up in the Matopos if you plan to head straight out of town. City hotels tend to fill up during the Trade Fair at the end of April, so book ahead at that time.

LOW-BUDGET OPTIONS

Municipal Campsite, off Jason Moyo Ave, opposite the museum. Adjoining the park, this immaculate site is shaded by jacarandas and palms and has the advantage of being a stone's throw from Josiah Tongogara Street swimming pool. There's 24-hour supervision and you can leave your luggage in the guard's hut during the day. Take a taxi at night – muggings are on the increase. ①.

Youth Hostel, Townsend Rd/Third St (☎76488). An old colonial house, with two 8-bedded rooms and a kitchen for self-catering. Inconveniently located, out in the suburbs, but close to shops. From the City Hall take either of two buses: the Waterford bus runs down 12th Ave and will drop you outside the hostel; alternatively, catch the hospital bus and get off at the *Bulawayo Inn* (still known around town as the *Holiday Inn*) and walk from there. ①.

YWCA hostel, 35 Ninth Avenue/Lobengula St (☎60185). The YWCA caters for both sexes, though in term-time it is usually filled with scholars and students from out of town. Pricier than the cheap hotels for double and single rooms in male and female wings, but you can get a good deal on full board. ①.

CHEAP HOTELS

Berkeley Place, 71 Josiah Tongogara St between Sixth Ave and Leopold Takawira Way (☎67701). Cheap and clean boarding house with shared bathrooms. The lack of liquor licence ensures a quiet night. ②.

Cecil Hotel, Fife St/Third Ave (☎60295). A bit more comfort than usual in this price bracket; breakfast thrown in, and a TV and radio in the room. A private bath is a little extra. ③.

Manor Hotel, Lobengula St/Eighth Ave (☎61001). Backs conveniently onto the bus terminal, but has a poor reputation for safety. ①.

Palace Hotel, Jason Moyo St, between Tenth and Eleventh aves (☎64294). A few bucks more and pretty noisy, but marginally more salubrious though not recommended for women alone. The beer garden is a popular venue for visiting bands. ②.

Plaza Hotel, Fourteenth Ave, between Jason Moyo and Fife streets. Clean rooms in a slightly decaying building; ask for one with a balcony. Public bar raucous. Okay for women travelling together. ③.

Waverley Hotel, 133–134 Lobengula St/Thirteenth Ave (☎60033). The cheapest hotel you're likely to find in Zimbabwe, with a good share of prostitution and drunkenness. Near to the station, it's an exuberant place with a local band playing every evening. Definitely not recommended for women travelling alone. ②.

STREET NAME CHANGES

The following Bulawayo streets were renamed in 1990.

Selborne Ave	Leopold Takawira Ave	*Rhodes St*	George Silundika St
Johannesburg Rd	Gwanda Rd	*Wilson St*	Josiah Tongogara St
Grey St/	Robert Mugabe Way	*Borrow St*	Samuel Parirenyatwa St
Birchenough Rd/	" " "	*Kings Ave*	Masotsha Ndlovu St
Queens Rd	" " "	*Mafeking Rd*	Plumtree Rd
Jameson St	Herbert Chitepo Rd	*London Rd*	Josiah Chinamano Rd
Abercorn St	Jason Moyo St	*Salisbury Rd*	Harare Rd

MID-RANGE HOTELS

Eland Grey's Inn, Robert Mugabe Way/Jason Moyo Ave (☎60121). Reliable, though unexciting. It has the advantage of a swimming pool. ③.

Eland Royal, George Silundika St/Sixth Ave (☎ 65764). Similar to Grey's Inn, though a little pricier, with all rooms en suite. ③.

Selborne Hotel, Leopold Takawira Ave (☎65741). Smack in the centre and opposite the City Hall, this is popular (and often full) but has a fair bit of style and is as pleasant a place to stay as any of the more expensive hotels. ③.

Hilltop Motel, Gwanda Rd (☎72493). 6km out of town, and so suitable only with your own car, but pleasant enough. ③.

Hotel Rio, Old Esigodini Rd (☎41384). 11km out of town, heading out east along Twelfth Ave, but a good bet with your own transport. The bar is noisy at weekends. ③.

UPMARKET

Banff Lodge Hotel, Banff Rd/Leander Ave (☎43176). More a suburban guest house than a hotel, this colonial house near Hillside Dams is the cheapest in this bracket and has a restaurant. ③.

Bulawayo Sun Hotel, Josiah Tongogara St/Tenth Ave (☎601101). Central Bulawayo's smartest hotel, though characterless. ⑥.

Bulawayo Inn, Ascot Centre/Milnerton Drive (☎72464) has the advantage of a swimming pool and is recommended for families. ⑥.

Cresta Churchill, Matopos Rd/Moffat Ave (☎41016) is the best of the upmarket options, though further out and the most expensive. ⑦.

LUXURY ACCOMMODATION

Induna Lodge, 16 Fortunes Gate Rd, Matseumhlope (☎45684). Comfortable suburban house for the safari set. Tours organised by the professional guide owner. From US$80 per person, full board.

Nesbitt Castle, 6 Percy Ave, Hillside (☎427726). Luxurious suites, mainly for businessmen, in a castle built by an eccentric former mayor of Bulawayo. The most expensive place in town, at US $135 per person, full board.

OUT OF TOWN RANCHES

Bembezi Safaris, c/o The Private Secretary, 112a Josiah Tongogara St (☎75406). Stone and thatch cottages overlooking a lake with good bird watching, 80km north of Bulawayo. From US$100 per person per night.

Londa Mela Lodge, PO Box 130, Queens Park, Bulawayo (Turk Mine ☎00831). Thatched chalets half an hour's drive from Bulawayo airport on a private game ranch which offers walking and horse riding. Accommodation from US$170 per person per night. *Londa Mela* also organise excellent mobile safaris around Matabeleland and countrywide, from US$250 for four people per day all-in.

N'tabasinduna Trails, PO Box 7, Bulawayo (☎26110). Luxury bush camp, with all the trimmings, on a farm 15km out of Bulawayo. Run by the very friendly Parsons family who organise tours to the Matopos and historical sites, including Naletale and Danangombe. US$100 per person per night. Self-catering at a reduced rate possible for Southern Africa residents.

The Museums

After Harare, Bulawayo is the best place in the country to catch up with local high culture and get general background information on Zimbabwe as a whole. Between the **museums**, the **Public Library** and the **Art Gallery** you can provide yourself with a one-day crash course in Zimbabwean Studies.

One thing you should not expect, however, is for your cultural experience to include anything that even remotely verges on the avant-garde. A rather daring male-nude metal sculpture by one of the Mzilikazi Centre's students was removed from its position in front of a prestigious tower block recently after complaints at its indecency. The matter caused such consternation that a minister from Harare had to come down to sort it out.

Museum of Natural History

Daily 9am–5pm, except Christmas and Good Friday. Nominal entrance fee.

If you see nothing else, don't miss the **Museum of Natural History**, the highlight of the city's cultural offerings. Imaginative exhibits not only cover the usual natural history topics of wildlife and botany, but also extend into ethnography, geology and history. The strength of the collection is that it concentrates exclusively on Zimbabwe, without spreading itself too thinly by attempting to cover life, the universe and everything.

The **wildlife gallery** gives excellent background to Zimbabwe's fauna – superb preparation if you're planning to go off to Hwange. The extensive **ornithological collection**, with endless stuffed birds crammed like battery hens into boxes, is a little off-putting, but the dioramas of **indigenous mammals** are excellent and include the second largest mounted elephant in the world, which very nearly reaches the ceiling of its ground-floor home.

Surprisingly interesting displays of gold, emeralds and the other minerals found in Zimbabwe are on show in the **geological section**, which is partly designed to simulate a mine shaft. The adjoining outdoor display of mining antiques demonstrates how the industry operated in the nineteenth and early twentieth centuries.

The **ethnographic collection**, which includes some superb carved wooden stools and headrests, gives some kind of yardstick for assessing modern curios. But for social and historical coverage, the **Hall of Man** is the best thing in the building. It gives amazingly comprehensive insights into all aspects of the region's **history**, from ancient prehistory to the twentieth century. Human activity is handled in terms of social practices – hunting, mining, art, healing, war and trade – before culminating in the **Hall of Chiefs**, devoted to Mzilikazi, Lobengula and stacks of Rhodes memorabilia.

Railway Museum

Tues, Wed & Fri 9.30am–noon & 2–4pm. Sun 2–5pm. Nominal entrance fee.

Although near the station, Bulawayo's **Railway Museum** is confusingly signposted and perhaps not worth the difficulty of finding. Created by and for railway enthusiasts, its collection of steam-age artefacts is badly let down by an absence of interpretive or background information. Tantalising displays – the coach of some long-past railway chaplain; items from royal visits of several decades ago; turn-of-the-century letters from Secretary of State for the Colonies Joseph Chamberlain endorsing the extension of the Bechuanaland Railway to Lake Tanganyika – leave you frustrated and mystified.

If you're a steam fan, of course, you'll find the visit rewarding just for the chance to stroll around pristine engines, like the Tenth Class locomotive no. 98, with its 4-8-2 wheel arrangement, or the service coach no. 0831. And, without any doubt, **Rhodes' private coach** is a treat – a really lavish construction, used on many trips after 1895, including that which carried his body from the Cape on a 2500-km trip to Bulawayo.

If you're keen on railway history, and are going to the Victoria Falls, the Zambian Railway Museum in Livingstone is more informative.

The Art Gallery

Sun & Tues–Fri 10am–5pm; Sat 10am–1pm. Nominal entrance fee.

On Robert Mugabe Way, behind the City Hall, the Art Gallery is definitely worth a visit. It's pretty small – just one hangar-like room subdivided into a few exhibitions – but what's there is well displayed. Of particular interest are the **cultural artefacts from Matabeleland** – baskets, sitting mats and other woven products not well represented in the Harare gallery. The work of **local painters** is displayed, too, and there's usually a **visiting exhibition**. The gallery plans to relocate to a splendid old colonial house at the junction of Leopold Takawira Avenue and Main Street, when funds permit.

Open spaces

The urban planners have made a concerted effort to keep Bulawayo's commercial district separate from the rest of the city. In consequence a "moat" of open space – which comprises a golf course, race track, show grounds and school playing fields – surrounds the middle of town. The parks in the central zone form part of this cordon, while the Hillside Dams, out in the suburbs, are a much more appealing area of natural granite and indigenous trees. Best of all, though further out, is the Tshabalala Sanctuary.

The town parks

The shade of **Centenary Park**, ten minutes' walk down Leopold Takawira Avenue, is welcoming after traversing Bulawayo's wide streets. Although not the most inspiring park, it is especially good for kids. On the museum side of the park are a large **aviary** and pens with small **buck**, a **miniature railway** which goes round a lake, the usual swings-and-roundabout **playground**, and a place under the trees for tea and ice-creams. All very Sunday afternoonish.

Central Park, almost a continuation of Centenary Park, is separated only by Leopold Takawira Avenue as it runs into Suburbs. For picnics or roaming it's much the nicer space, with more trees, flowers and lawns and a large illuminated fountain which hasn't worked since the onset of drought some years ago. Best of all, it includes the **Samuel Parirenyatwa Street Swimming Pool** (Sept–May 10am–2pm & 3–6pm), on the town side of the park, with its stylish 1930s changing booths, and lawns and palm trees for lazing about in the sun.

Hillside Dams

There is a small nature reserve surrounding **Hillside Dams**, located some 6km out from the centre. Drought has dried out the dams, but it's a peaceful place for a stroll nevertheless – from down by the lower dam indigenous trees and granite boulders line the way to the upper. To get to Hillside Dams, you take the Hillside Road **bus** from the City Hall terminus as far as Cecil Avenue and walk the remaining (signposted) two kilometres.

Chipangali Wildlife Orphanage

Daily except Mon. Nominal entrance fee.

The **Chipangali Wildlife Orphanage** is not a lot different from a zoo – except that the animals are sick, abandoned or orphaned. You can see the big cats head-on here, as well as antelope, bush pig and warthog.

A favourite place for family weekend outings, Chipangali is a fairly easy 23km hitch out of town on the Gwanda Road. It's also possible to spend the night (①), to hear the lions roar. Three companies, *UTC*, *Black Rhino Safari* and *Africa Dawn* run trips there – current prices can be obtained from the Bulawayo Publicity Association.

Tshabalala Sanctuary

Daily 6am–6pm. Nominal entrance fee.

The main appeal of the small **Tshabalala Sanctuary** is that it offers an opportunity to walk or ride a horse to spot giraffe, kudu, zebra, impala, wildebeest, tsessebe and many species of birds, free from the fear of stumbling into big cats, elephants or rhino. It's a modest place, set in flat thornbush country, 8km from the city centre on the way to the Matopos. If you don't have the energy to rent a bike (see p.129) and cycle, take the roughly hourly Matopos Road **bus** from the City Hall terminus to **Retreat**, and walk or hitch the last couple of kilometres to the entrance.

Markets and shops

Most of the **shops** in Bulawayo which you might need are within five minutes' walk of the City Hall. However, you can get a better view of local life if you make for **Mzilikazi** suburb and its lively beer halls, markets and the Mzilikazi and Home Industries Craft Workshops.

Central crafts shops

Art Gallery, Robert Mugabe Way. Some fine **baskets, sculptures** and **wood carvings. Tonga stools** from the Binga area are much cheaper here than at the Victoria Falls curio outlets.

Chitrin Wholesalers, Jason Moyo St/Sixth Ave. Four-metre and upwards lengths of central African prints.

Designers' Collective, Fife St opposite Haddons. Good collection of T-shirts and cards.

Jairos Jiri, next to the *Art Gallery*. One of the best of this chain found in the main towns, selling products by disabled craft-workers, cards and a wide selection of local handmade goods. There's a large selection of **Matabeleland baskets**, local **pottery**, the usual unexceptional soapstone carvings and some good **Ndebele beadwork**, notably dolls. There is no pressure to buy, so browse as long as you like.

Central food and groceries

Probably the best places to pick up **fresh fruit and vegetables** in Central Bulawayo are the shops along Eighth Avenue, between Robert Mugabe Way and George Silundika Street, opposite the bus terminus.

Haddon and Sly, Fife St/Eighth Ave. An old-fashioned department store with a good ground-floor supermarket.

Haefeli's, Fife St/Tenth Ave. Good for cakes and biscuits.

TM Hypermarket, near the railway station. Wide selection of groceries; late closing.

Record shops

There's no better place in Zimbabwe to buy and browse for records than Bulawayo. The two best stores are both in Jason Moyo Street, though exploring the small **downtown record bars** around Lobengula Street and Sixth Avenue makes for a more atmospheric outing.

Clintons, Clinton House, 88c Jason Moyo St (☎60264). The finest stock of South African jive north of the Limpopo River.

Music, Jason Moyo St (☎66895 or ☎71607). On the corner of Fort St, and offering the country's best selection of Zimbabwean pop.

Lobengula Street and Makokoba market

Around the **Lobengula Street** bus terminal, several street vendors are cheap for fruit and vegetable shopping. For the city's main – and best – market, however, you'll need to take either a bus or Emergency Taxi out to the suburb of **Makokoba**. This is definitely worthwhile, bringing you into contact with stalls selling local delicacies like **dried mopane worms** (sold by the cupful), plus **herbal medicines** and a good selection of **baskets and beads** not intended for tourists.

Mzilikazi Art and Craft Centre

Mon–Fri 8.30am–12.30pm & 2–4pm.

Mzilikazi is a thoroughly established township, with kids playing in the street, freshly swept yards and a strong sense of community. The **Art and Craft Centre** here, set up in the Sixties by the City Council, is near Mpilo Hospital. It is known for its **ceramics**

and the sales are used to subsidise an art school and the training of others to work with clay. In the centre's shop, you can stand around and watch potters at work, laughing, chatting and listening to the radio while, without seeming even to watch what they're doing, pots emerge below their fingers. The stuff is pretty standardised and as close to mass-produced as hands can make it, but there are some nice, modern, ethnic designs. It's cheaper to buy works here than at any of the outlets in town, and in the seconds shop you can pick up stuff very cheaply.

Besides potters, you can watch sculptors working in stone. Painting and drawing classes are held here and there's a small permanent collection of students' work. Across the way at the **Bulawayo Home Industries Centre** they sell **batiks** and **handspun angora pullovers** and **mats**. A new departure is **sisal basketry** – copied from Kenya's best-selling *vyondo*. Workers, drawn from social welfare lists, are paid a piece rate.

The easiest way to get to Mzilikazi is to **walk** down the Old Falls Road as it veers from the northwest corner of the city from Kings Avenue, though there's a more interesting short cut (which takes around 30min) through the township itself, along Third Avenue extension. The less energetic can take the **Mpilo bus** from the Lobengula Street terminus or the less frequent service from the terminus at the City Hall.

Eating and drinking

There's no shortage of sadza spots and greasy takeaways around the station and in the lively area at the bottom of Lobengula Street, near the bus terminus – but these are only open in the daytime. Hotel buffets and snack bars are good for lunch, while steak houses are excellent value in the evening. Formal restaurants tend to cater for a white clientele with night-time dinner/dancing.

Sadza, takeaways and snacks

Bon Journee, 105 Robert Mugabe Way. A bit of a hangout for western Europeans, with grills and good coffee. Excellent piri-piri chicken. Open evenings.

Downings Bakery, Leopold Takawira Ave. Good bread and pies, opposite the City Hall.

Eskimo Hut at the entrance to Showgrounds. Very popular for drive-in icecreams and takeaways.

The Grass Hut, 188 Fife St. Cheap for steak rolls and sandwiches, though you may find the darkness of the place more oppressive than atmospheric. It's also open early for egg breakfasts and is a popular meeting place.

Oriental Takeaway, Eighth Ave. Vegetable burgers, curries and spring rolls.

Pizzaghetti, Eleventh Ave between Robert Mugabe Way and George Silundika St. One of the few takeaways open evenings; chicken and chips as well as good pizza.

The Pantry, 57e Fifteenth Ave. Good traditional fare.

Tuckers, 107 Main St/Eleventh Ave. Salad and cheese takeaways, as well as the usual standards.

YWCA, Ninth Ave/Lobengula St. The cheapest and cleanest place for sadza and traditional accompaniments, dishing up lunch (12.30–3pm), mainly for the resident students but open to outsiders who don't mind the institutional flavour.

Tearooms and hotel buffets

Most of Bulawayo's hotels do substantial (and expensive) **buffet lunches**, with loads of salads and many have outdoor terraces where you can sip a cold beer – the *Homestead* at the *Bulawayo Sun*, and the *Selborne* in Leopold Takawira Avenue, are particularly recommended. If you're into drinking at lunchtime and – no necessary connection – meeting black Zimbabweans, the palm-treed **beer garden** at the *Palace Hotel* is a relaxing place and also serves meat dishes and chips. The *Central Bar*, near the City Hall, is also worth a look.

Haddon and Sly, Fife St/Eighth Ave. During the day this tearoom is a good bet. The second-floor restaurant continues to be supported by out-of-town farmers who appreciate its British-style teas and lunches.

Meikles, Leopold Takawira Ave/Jason Moyo St. An appealing old-style tearoom, in a similar vein to *Haddon's*.

Restaurants

Buffalo Bill's, next to the *Selborne* in Leopold Takawira Ave. Mainly steak – though vegetarians can get baked potatoes, salad and mediocre pizzas.

Capri Restaurant, George Silundika St/Eleventh Ave. More of a nightclub than a restaurant, but it does serve some Portuguese dishes.

Cattleman Restaurant, Josiah Tongogara St/Tenth Ave. Excellent charcoal-grilled steaks and a table of salads, opposite the *Sun Hotel*.

Golden Spur, Robert Mugabe Way (between Eighth and Ninth Avenues). One of the most popular steakhouses in Bulawayo. Vegetarians steer clear.

La Gondola, Robert Mugabe Way/Tenth Ave. Dinner/dancing Italian restaurant

Granada Restaurant, Fife St/Ninth Ave. More like a club than a restaurant, this place is popular with young whites.

Maison Nic, Main St/Fourth Ave. Wins the best restaurant prize year after year for its French cuisine and fish specialities although it's scarcely French. Cheaper than *Les Saisons*.

Matabeleland Safari Grill, Robert Mugabe Way. Specialises in game dishes and Zimbabwean fish.

The Peking, near the *Palace Hotel* in Jason Moyo St. Reasonable and recommended Chinese food.

Les Saisons, Josiah Tongogara St between Sixth Ave and Leopold Takawira Ave. The best of the formal restaurants. An imaginative selection of great vegetarian dishes.

Beer gardens

Beer gardens are a must if you want to get to grips with how Zimbabweans live across the divide, in the high-density areas. And they're fun – people will always chat to you, after they've stared a while. Essentially day time places, serving *chibuku*, braaied meat and sadza, they're open from 10.30am to 8pm.

One of the easiest beer gardens to find in the city is the *Madlodlo Beer Garden*, situated on the Mzilikazi side of the Renkini bus station. It's a pretty typical example, with lots of wooden benches under trees and a predominantly male clientele queuing up to buy mega-sized pots of beer to be shared and passed around. Other good areas for hunting out beer gardens include Luveve Street and around Mzilikazi suburb (see previous page).

Music

You'd be really unlucky not to find **live music** in Bulawayo on any weekend – and there's invariably something good at the end of the month. Crowd-pulling gigs are advertised in the *Chronicle* and on posters stuck up around town; hotels are the most common venues, though big concerts do occasionally take place at the White City Stadium. Here in Matabeleland you should look out for **Smanje Manje** music with its strong South African influence. When it came across the border in the late 1960s, it caused a revolution in Zimbabwean pop by displacing the dominant rhumba rhythms from Zaire.

Disco and funk is the scene at most regular **discos** and **clubs**.

TRADITIONAL MUSIC: KWANONGOMA COLLEGE

The colonialists regarded the **traditional music** they came across in Africa with disdain. It failed to conform to western ideas of harmony and they dismissed it without seeing the complex structures and rules that lay underneath. The music became marginalised and the use of many instruments died out.

One of the most important to survive has been the **mbira**, an instrument found at archaeological sites throughout the country and, in various designs with different names, across Africa. The mbira is commonly called a "thumb-piano" – basically a sound box or gourd, held in both hands, on top of which tongues (or keys) of metal are plucked. The instrument is used in ceremonies to call on the ancestors who speak through a medium.

Bulawayo's **Kwanongoma College**, established in the early 1960s, was central to the revival of the mbira, and its students are at the forefront of promoting traditional music: Dumisaini Maraire took it to the US. The **college workshop** trains students to make and revive lost instruments. One of their big successes is their reconstruction of the **marimba**, a type of xylophone, which died out with colonial intervention and forced migrations.

You may just be lucky enough while in Bulawayo to catch one of the city's highly accomplished traditional groups in performance. Look out, in particular, for the Kwanangoma Marimba Ensemble.

Hotels

Bulawayo Sun Hotel, Josiah Tongogara St/Tenth Ave (☎601101). Live jazz every evening from sundowner time on at the *Alabama*. Smart-casual dress required.

Cecil Hotel, Fife St/Third Ave (☎60295). Nightly disco playing mid-Atlantic pop and some local stuff.

Eland Royal Hotel, George Silundika/Sixth Ave (☎65764). Local bands in the garden on Saturday afternoons.

Waverley Hotel, 133–134 Lobengula St/Thirteenth Ave (☎60033). Raucous venue opposite the train station, hosting end of month gigs in the beer garden and local bands most evenings. Entrance is free unless a visiting big name is playing.

Clubs

Clubs tend to play American disco and funk and are not the places to find Zimbabwean music. Watch out for "the girls" at the end of the evening, who are great to dance with, but may insist on accompanying you home. Half of Zimbabwe's prostitutes are HIV positive.

Talk of the Town, in the Monte Carlo Centre, Fife Street/Twelfth Ave. One of Zimbabwe's hottest clubs, with a mix of house, jive and reggae.

Silver Fox, Robert Mugabe Way/Tenth Ave. Local music and disco.

Film, theatre and classical music

Bulawayo's few **cinemas** are cheap and comfortable, and show mainly middle-of-the-road British and American films. The two *Kines* in Robert Mugabe Way, the *7-Arts Theatre* in Jason Moyo Street and the *Rainbow Vistarama*, George Silundika Street, are central and near each other, while the *Nitestar Drive-In* off the Harare Road is excellent value. The *Alliance Francaise* (☎62797 after 5pm) shows subtitled French films on the first and second Tuesday of each month.

As for drama, the **theatre** in Leopold Takawira Avenue occasionally hosts interesting visiting productions, and you might catch some good **classical music**. The large and small city halls are usual venues for concerts and shows. Check the *Chronicle* for entertainment listings.

Listings

Automobile Association Fanum House, corner of Leopold Takawira Ave and Josiah Tongogara St (☎ 70063). Very friendly and helpful.

Airport 22km from town along Robert Mugabe Way (☎26491 or ☎26492).

Air Zimbabwe office Trager House, Jason Moyo St (☎72051).

Air Zimbabwe buses pick up and deposit their passengers at the *Bulawayo Sun*, Tenth Ave/Samuel Parirenyatwa St.

American Express agents *Manica Travel*, Federal Centre, Tenth Ave (☎ 62521).

Banks The most central is the *Standard* in Fife St (Mon, Tues, Thurs & Fri 8.30am–2pm, Wed 8.30am–noon, Sat 8.30–11am).

Bookshops *Philpott and Collins* in Jason Moyo St have a good selection of books published in Zimbabwe and a remaindered table with some decent paperbacks. *Kingstons* on Jason Moyo St are also recommended. Book exchange at *Basement Book Mart*, 81 Jason Moyo St

Camping equipment *Eezee Kamping*, 99 George Silundika St/Tenth Ave. Good for fishing equipment, but nothing sophisticated.

Car rental *Avis*, Robert Mugabe Way/Tenth Ave (☎68571 or ☎61306); *Hertz*, George Silundika St/Fourteenth Ave (☎ 74701 or ☎61402); both also have offices at the airport. *Echo*, 9a Africa House, Fife St (☎67925 or ☎74157). *Transit Car Hire*, corner Twelfth/Robert Mugabe Ave (☎76495 or ☎76496) are the cheapest.

Doctors and dentists are listed in the front of the Bulawayo section of the telephone directory.

Hospital Central Hospital, St Lukes Way (☎72111) is the easiest to get to.

Immigration Department ☎ 72101.

Information Bureau, City Hall Buildings, Fife St (☎60867). Extremely helpful. Closes 4.30pm.

Libraries Not many people seem aware of the marvellous resource at the **Bulawayo Public Library** in City Hall (Mon–Fri 9am–4pm). For background information on any aspect of Zimbabwe, there are few better places in the country than this historic book collection; until quite recently it was a legal deposit library, which meant that all books and newspapers published in the country were sent there. The librarians are exceptionally helpful, and will guide you to any obscure subject which may interest you. In addition, the **National Free Library**, Leopold Takawira Ave just past the Museum of Natural History and Centenary Park, has reading rooms and a special section on local history.

Maps Best place for general maps is the Information Bureau, see above.

Pharmacies 86 Robert Mugabe Way (☎69781) open Mon–Sat after the shops have closed till 8pm and Sundays/holidays 9am–8pm. *Dae-Nite Pharmacy*, Eighth Ave/Robert Mugabe Way (☎66242); Mon–Fri 8am–6pm, Sat 8am–1pm & 5–7pm, Sun & hols 9am–noon & 5–7pm.

Post office Principal office for telephones and telegrams, etc, is at Main St/Eighth Ave (Mon–Fri 8.30am–5pm, Sat 8.30–11am).

Railway enquiries ☎322411. Reservations ☎322310. It's usually best to ask in person.

Shop hours Mon–Fri 8am–5pm, Sat 8am–12.30pm. Some cafés stay open after shop hours for the sale of bread and milk.

Travel agency There's no shortage of travel agents, but if in doubt one of the biggest is *Sunshine Tours*, Old Mutual Arcade, Eighth Ave/Jason Moyo Ave (☎67791). *Budget Tours*, Fife St/Tenth Ave (☎76645), make reservations for buses to Joburg, while *Manica Travel*, Tenth Ave/Fort St (☎62521) book for *Ajay* and *Express* coach services.

Tour operators *UTC* George Silundika St/Fourteenth Ave (☎61402) run tours to Matopos and Khami Ruins and Chipangali. *Black Rhino Safaris* (☎41662) offer the same as well as camping safaris to the main parks, including Chizarira. *Africa Dawn* (☎46696 or ☎75575) organise similar trips with excellent mobile safaris to Hwange, and recommended walks to Matobo cave paintings. Another option is *Ntaba Trails* (☎26011) who do all the Bulawayo excursions.

Swimming pool Samuel Parirenyatwa St Baths (Sept–May, 10am–2pm & 3–6pm).

Taxis ☎60666,☎61933, ☎72454, ☎60154, and ☎60704.

The Torwa centres: Khami, and Naletale and Danangombe ruins

Some of Zimbabwe's best **stone ruins** stand within striking distance of Bulawayo. All of them are dwarfed in size by Great Zimbabwe (see Chapter Five), but, built later in the Torwa period, they are in many ways more sophisticated, and reflect a development of the state's masonry traditions.

The largest site – and the closest to Bulawayo – is the Torwa capital **Khami**, just outside the city limits. Further out, off the Gweru road in Midlands farming country, lie **Danangombe**, a subsequent Torwa headquarters, and the tiny **Naletale**, perhaps the finest expression of the style.

The Torwa state and architecture

From the tenth to mid-nineteenth centuries, southwestern Zimbabwe enjoyed a political continuity nearly without precedent in Africa. By the twelfth century, offshoot states of **Great Zimbabwe** had walled capitals in the area and were living alongside people of the local **"Leopard's Kopje"** culture, an urban society under a wealthy ruling class. Cattle and gold were the bedrock of Leopard's Kopje wealth, and the elite were often buried with objects covered in the precious metal. They were able to organise teams of labour to produce stone platforms on hillsides, on which their houses were built.

The relationship between the two cultures is unclear, but it is known that by the time Great Zimbabwe collapsed in the fifteenth century, the southwest had been pulled together into a single state. This **Torwa State** was a progressive development of its Great Zimbabwe predecessor in the southeast. Although less extensive, it was more efficient, introducing improvements in architecture, pottery and urban layout, and changes in the economy.

Combining Zimbabwe masonry skills with the Leopard's Kopje stone platform tradition, the Torwa produced beautifully decorated **court complexes**. The old hill platforms were enlarged and turned into huge stages by the accomplished use of retaining walls and the decorative possibilities of stone-walling.

Khami

The largest concentration of stonewall terracing at **KHAMI** (KAME) surrounds the ruler's personal hill complex above the Kame River. Like his Great Zimbabwe counterpart, the ruler (or *mambo*) lived in great privacy, with his hill-perched court surrounded by the zimbabwes of the ruling class. A secret passage went under the platforms to his palace, its top forming the pavement of the courtyard.

As you ascend the stairs to the **upper platform** you can see remains of the posts that held up the daga roof. Elephant tusks lined the passage. On the lowest step, a secret room was uncovered during excavations in 1947. Royal regalia had been hidden there at some time, perhaps when Khami was set alight during the invasion around 1680, when the Rozvi ("destroyers") of the Changamire dynasty swooped down from the Zambezi and conquered the Torwa. The spears and axes of copper and iron, ivory carvings and drinking pots with the *mambo*'s traditional red and black pattern are in the Natural History Museum in Bulawayo.

Several stone platforms **south of the hill complex** probably belonged to acolytes – wives or courtiers – of the *mambo*. The walks around this part of the site can be steep, but worthwhile, revealing such details as a **tsoro-game** carved in stone. The board, of which there are several examples at Khami, has four rows of holes, with usually around

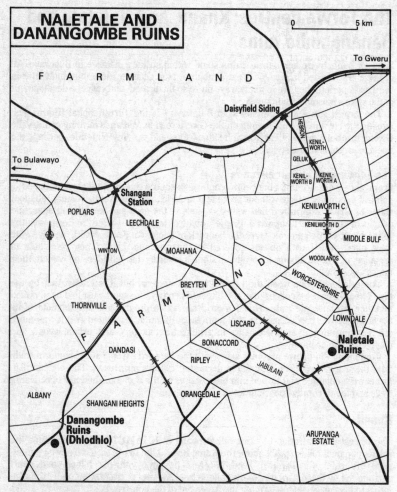

NALETALE AND DANANGOMBE RUINS

0   5 km

To Gweru

FARMLAND

Daisyfield Siding

HEBRON

KENIL-WORTH

To Bulawayo ←

GELUK

KENIL-WORTH B   KENIL-WORTH A

Shangani Station

POPLARS

LEECHDALE

KENILWORTH C

KENILWORTH D

MIDDLE BULF

WINTON

MOAHANA

WOODLANDS

WORCESTERSHIRE

BREYTEN

F A R M L A N D

THORNVILLE

LISCARD

LOWNDALE

DANDASI

BONACCORD

RIPLEY

JABULANI

Naletale Ruins

ALBANY

ORANGEDALE

SHANGANI HEIGHTS

Danangombe Ruins (Dhlodhlo)

ARUPANGA ESTATE

fourteen holes per row. Like a cross between backgammon, chess and chinese checkers, *tsoro* is still played today throughout central Africa, under a variety of names. The speed of play achieved by participants, involving remarkable mental arithmetic feats, can be quite bewildering.

On the **east side of the hill**, to the north and west of the stone structures, are the remains of **huts** belonging to the ordinary people who occupied most of the site. These commoners didn't build their homes on platforms, so the mud walls have by now all but collapsed and consequently there's a lot less to see.

Among the finds interpreted in the small **museum** – worth visiting before you explore the site – are some which date back 100,000 years, providing evidence of a human presence at the site long before Khami was built. A useful pamphlet, *A Trail Guide to the Khami National Monument*, is on sale at the museum.

Getting there

Khami stands on a minor road 22km to the west of Bulawayo. The only buses along the route, impractical for visiting the ruins, are those serving nearby Khami Prison; Khami train station is no nearer the ruins than Bulawayo; and hitching would be very much hit or miss. Without a car, the best bet is to take one of the reasonably priced excursions run by *Africa Dawn* or *Black Rhino Safaris*. If you are going to drive, cycle or hitch, follow Eleventh Avenue (near Bulawayo train station) out of town through the industrial area. There's nowhere nearby to stay, but there are lovely picnic spots overlooking Khami dam.

Danangombe and Naletale

Danangombe and **Naletale**, both of them set in isolated ranching country roughly an hour and a half's drive from Bulawayo off the Harare Road, are equally rewarding sites, but harder to reach than Khami. The turn-offs to both ruins are about two-thirds of the way to Gweru (see p.86–87)and approached via two southbound dirt roads which converge just west of Shangani Station: the more westerly one heads to Danangombe, the other to Naletale. It is possible to drive from one to the other though Naletale is about 45km east of Danangombe on a poorly signposted road that veers wildly north and south, making the trip considerably longer than the direct distance between the two sites.

You'll need your own car to get to either site unless you take your bike on a train or bus and cycle the twenty-odd kilometres along dirt track to Danangombe from Shangani. All Harare-bound buses and trains stop at Shangani, a simple farming settlement with nowhere to stay.

If you don't have access to your own transport, and/or if you feel like spending a couple of days in the area, the best option is to contact *Jabulani Safaris* (Shangani ☎0-1431) who can offer a reasonable all-in daily rate and who will pick you up at Shangani, if you're without a car. Their game farm, *Bon Accord*, abuts the ruins, and is a great place to spend a weekend, with plenty of walks and the opportunity to view game on foot.

If you're visiting these ruins simply as a stopoff en route to Harare and want to sample just one of the sites, then Naletale is the more direct to reach. The southbound dirt track that branches off the main Harare Road, just east of Daisyfield siding is slightly quicker than the road from Shangani.

Naletale

The most interesting of all the zimbabwes, **NALETALE** stands at the top of a natural granite dome. As you gaze onto the wooded valley, it's difficult to imagine a better prospect, with trees growing between the long-deserted walls and *daga* hut fragments. The site is small in size – you could do a circuit of the whole place in fifteen minutes – but it's easy to while away half a day wandering about.

From close up the **walls** don't look terribly special but step back from the northwest section, the best preserved, and take in the patterning. Better still, lie down, prop your head on one of the pillow-sized rocks scattered about, and just gaze. The tapestried wall is, without doubt, the pinnacle of the Zimbabwe-Khami masonry tradition, the only one standing that includes all five types of patterning: chevron, chequer, herring-

MISSIONARIES IN ZIMBABWE

Missionary support was a major source of strength to **Rhodes** in his advance into central Africa. However, many missionaries believed that neither their teaching nor white settlement could be effective until the power of the Matabele was broken. **Lobengula**, in particular, scorned missionary teachings, which he felt consisted mainly of passing the buck for human misdeeds to Christ. He observed that the doctrine was what one might expect from whites because "whenever they did anything wrong they always wanted to throw the blame onto others".

The early missionary lessons literally fell on deaf ears. At the site of the **Jesuit Mission** next to Old Bulawayo you can see the graves of two missionaries murdered in the 1896 Chimurenga, along with their one and only convert who was deaf and dumb. **African converts** were particularly vulnerable to attack during the uprising and Bernard Mizeki, one of the first African proselytes, was killed. But once the uprising was defeated, the way was prepared for the full introduction of Christianity, which is now the predominant religion in Zimbabwe. Inside two years, the *American Brethren of Christ* had established one of the first fully fledged missions in the Matopos hills, while by 1909 there were more black than white Anglicans in Rhodesia.

Subsequently, the church began to concentrate on developing schools, clinics and hospitals – often attached to the old missions. Mission schools have educated many of Zimbabwe's leading figures, Robert Mugabe among them, and in the latter years of white rule they became increasingly involved in politics. During the 1950s a number of church leaders were outspoken against right-wing trends, and many guerilla fighters received mission support during the struggle for independence. At this time, gross atrocities were committed against missionaries, blamed by the Smith government on guerillas, but claimed by nationalists to be the work of government forces committing outrages for propaganda purposes.

bone, cord and ironstone. The outer wall, originally topped by small towers with monoliths, enclosed a large raised platform which was surrounded by a number of courtyards and other smaller platforms. When Donald Randall McIver, the first professional archaeologist to investigate Great Zimbabwe, dug here, he found elephant tusks embedded in the remains of one of the huts.

A path leads up to the site itself from a picnic site and parking place at the bottom of the hill. It's possible to **camp** there, but you should ask for permission from the attendant, who lives in a house on the right of the car park turn-off (and will show you round if you want).

Danangombe (Dhlo Dhlo)

DANANGOMBE, better known by its old name **Dhlo Dhlo**, is equally enjoyable to explore, clambering about the ruins and sitting high up on rocks in the shade to look out over the rolling countryside.

The site became the capital of the Torwa state after Khami was razed to the ground during a combined attack by a dissident Torwa leader and the Portuguese forces of Sismundo Dias Bayao. Later, in their eagerness to pilfer the riches of Danangombe, European treasure hunters managed to destroy many of the buildings by treating them as gold-mining stakes. Unworked gold and jewellery were systematically removed. Early digs found a silver chalice, a bell and medallions of sixteenth-century Portuguese origin. The walls that remain reveal beautiful decorative motifs similar to those at Khami.

As at Naletale, you may be able to camp at the site, but the resident attendant makes it clear that it is only as a favour at his discretion. There's no water or shop nearby.

Cyrene Mission

CYRENE MISSION, 40km from Bulawayo on the northern edge of Matobo National Park, is worth a visit for anyone interested in African art. Named after Simon of Cyrene, the African who helped carry Christ's cross, it was founded in 1939 by one **Canon Paterson**, a Scottish reformed atheist who'd studied art in England – and who later founded the Art Centre in Harare.

From the beginning the aim of the mission was to teach self-sufficiency. Pupils were instructed in farming, building and carpentry in order to construct, furnish and decorate their own homes. Art was also compulsory and students were given the chance to experiment. Paterson was firmly against imposing the western artistic tradition on students and no reproductions were put up on walls. Instead, kids were given a sheet of paper and told to draw, and the buildings are now decorated with their work.

The simple, thatched **Chapel** is decorated with murals and carved furniture which blend African and Christian mythology in a number of scenes from Ndebele history. The paintings are in a naive style, African-influenced but not wholly African. Some of the more symbolic stutter towards lifelessness but they are at their best when depicting stories using familiar local imagery. The *Good Samaritan* spread, for example, is inspired by local rural life, with its *daga* (dried mud) huts and the earthy colours of the Matabeleland countryside. Another success is the *Parable of the Talents*, which blends stylised huts, rocks, trees, plants and people into a whirling abstract composition.

To get to the mission **from Bulawayo**, hitch or take the Figtree or Plumtree **bus** from Renkini terminus and walk the remaining 2km from the main road. **From the Matopos**, it's 12km from the northern gate, past the arboretum and one of the camp-sites in the recreational park; the mission is on a minor detour back to the main Bulawayo road, so hitching is not recommended from this side.

South to Beit Bridge

There are few reasons for travelling along this hot desolate road from Bulawayo to the South African border. Southern Matabeleland, dry at the best of times, saw the worst excesses of the drought in the 1990s. Nevertheless, the area holds several game farms and private hunting and safari areas, focused around the small town of West Nicholson. In one of the most remote parts of the region, the old pioneer-town of **Tuli**, with its adjoining botanical reserves, is worth the trek if you're exploring Matabeleland in a rugged vehicle. The best stopping-off place, if you're heading straight for the border, is **GWANDA**, where the recently refurbished *Hardy's Hotel* offers reasonably priced doubles and good meals.

Beit Bridge

The town of **BEIT BRIDGE** gets sickeningly hot in summer as cars queue for Zimbabwean customs to toothcomb through their baggage. The authorities seem mainly concerned with their own citizens trying to smuggle out more than their allowance of currency to buy consumer goods in South Africa. Nobody would choose to spend the night here, but if you have no choice, a couple of reputable places down the main road leading to the border are *Beit Bridge Hotel* (Beit Bridge ☎ 214 or ☎ 413; ③) and the nicer *Peter's Motel* (Beit Bridge ☎ 309 or ☎ 321; ③). There are no particularly cheap hotels, and neither is there a campsite, though you could try asking for a patch of ground at the police station.

Tuli Circle

TULI CIRCLE, an odd little salient west of the Shashi River, should by rights be in Botswana – the Shashi defines the border most of the way along here. This was, however, the first gateway into Rhodesia, and provided a fort, hospital and supply post for pioneers eyeing the interior. After the defeat of the Ndebele, it was eclipsed by Bulawayo and has since dwindled into a trading post serving the local communal lands.

The pioneer presence is marked by a cemetery, a memorial and a flag marking the site of the fort. There are three **botanical reserves** and a **safari area** in this small enclave. Few maps give any indication that it's worth visiting, but it's recommended if you have a 4WD and plenty of time in Zimbabwe – the palm-lined sandy Shashi startling amid the unpromisingly parched southwest.

Elephants favour the area, and you can expect periodic good game sightings, the circle biting into the best private game reserve in neighbouring Botswana. There are no fences and the animals migrate across the border freely, something visitors are strongly advised against.

Access

To get to Tuli, avoid the road running parallel to the Limpopo, which is used by the understandably twitchy military to patrol the border with South Africa. Take the turn-off near GWANDA instead. It's rugged 4WD country, so you should allow as much as ten hours for the drive from Bulawayo. A daily **bus** goes from Bulawayo via Tuli to Beit Bridge and vice versa but serves the communal areas, not the botanical reserves.

THE MATOPOS

A place of incredible power and beauty, the **Matopos Range** is the most compelling reason to explore the Bulawayo area. Here, among the smooth granites of whale-backed hills and crenellated castle kopjes, the descendants of Zimbabwe's earliest **hunter-gatherer** inhabitants painted elegant images on the walls of overhangs and in weather-scooped caves. These paintings remain to be seen today in the **Matobo National Park** – alongside some of the best hiking in the country. Although now officially known as the Matobo Hills, you'll invariably hear the colonial pronunciation "Matopos" used, and see both versions in print.

The hills themselves have the appearance of volcanic eruptions, though they are in fact geologically extremely ancient, having lain covered for thousands of millennia by softer material. The covering has been gradually worn down to the present-day ground level, exposing the previously buried hills – an impressive illustration of just how hard these rocks are.

Matobo National Park

Many people visit this park, some 50km from Bulawayo, for a day's jaunt, but it's well worth spending a couple of days here in the park itself, or at one of the new luxury lodges on the perimeter. The landscape itself is staggering, there's miles of walking and the world's highest concentration of ancient rock paintings, leopards and black eagles.

The park is punctuated with artificial, though very beautiful dams. The easiest to reach from Bulawayo is **Maleme Dam**, which has Parks lodges, camping, horse riding, tennis and some short walks to nearby painted caves. Most day-trippers head here for a picnic stopping off en route at **World's View** – topped by the grave of Cecil

Rhodes – the remote **Toghwe Wilderness Area** with campsites at **Toghwana** and **Mtsheleli Dams**, and two of Zimbabwe's finest **painted caves** is another day trip.

Lastly, the **Game Park in the Whovi Wilderness area**, although modest compared to Zimbabwe's great game areas, and accessible only by car, provides a wonderful granite backdrop to views of its grazing and browsing herds and regular sightings of rhino.

Accommodation

National Park's **accommodation** is available at Maleme Dam but gets pretty full in peak season, though during the week and outside school holidays a lodge is easy enough to come by. Maleme Dam rest camp is the only place with roofed accommodation, but it is possible to camp at several different sites in the park.

There are no **hotels** in the park itself, but there is one cheap accommodation option just outside its boundaries. The *Inungu Guest House* (②), next to *Fryer's Store* 10km from Maleme Dam, can be booked through *Sunshine Tours* (☎67791). It's not marked on the *Tourist Map of Rhodes Matopos National Park* – available from the Surveyor General's office in Harare – but you can locate it at grid reference 559331. From Maleme follow the main road to World's View, for 3.5km and take the second turning to the left (after the Pomongwe cave turn-off); where the road branches, after about 6km, bear left and the guest house and shop are on your right one kilometre further.

The nearest garages are back at Bulawayo, and it's best to bring everything you'll need while you're here from the city. *Fryer's Store* itself is the nearest place to the park where you can top up supplies, though there is also a shop selling basics at Maleme Rest Camp.

Matopos Private Lodges and Camps

In the last few years, several exclusive camps and lodges have opened up in dramatic settings just outside the park.

Amalinda Camp, *Londa Mela Safaris*, PO Box 130, Queens Park, Bulawayo (Turk Mine ☎0-00831). One of Zimbabwe's top camps with prices to match. Safari tents under thatch nestle amongst boulders with the dining area under a granite overhang. Closest of the camps to the game park where walks can be arranged to track rhino. US$140 per person per night.

Matopos Hills Lodge, *Touch the Wild*, P/Bag 6, Hillside, Bulawayo (☎41225). Close to Maleme and part of an exclusive chain of camps which includes others in Hwange. US$240 per person per night.

Shumba Shaba Lodge, *Zindele Safaris*, PO Box 1744, Bulawayo (☎64128). The least expensive of the lodges and much the smallest, with quite the most spectacular views. Stylish chalets perch on a huge granite whaleback known as Red Lion. Ideal for walking and highly recommended for a recuperative few days. Transfers from Bulawayo cost US$30. From US$90 per person per night.

Malalangwe, *Impi Safaris*, PO Box 1325, Bulawayo (☎74693). Luxurious, small camp on a magnificent game farm on the western edge of the Matopos range, one hour from Bulawayo at Marula, with a good share of animals, rock paintings, archaeological remains and fine walks. Environmental awareness is high on the agenda and while the all-in rate is more than *Shumba Shaba*, it remains good value. US$140 per person per night.

Seeing the Park

The best way to see the park is by car, or to take one of the recommended tours offered by Bulawayo-based companies. There's no public transport to the park, but if you're prepared to walk, there are fairly regular local **buses** from Bulawayo to Kezi, stopping at the edge of the National Park. Ask to be dropped off at the road leading to Maleme Dam: from here it's about a 12-kilometre walk to Maleme, taking you past the Nswatugi cave rock painting and site museum. **Cycling** the 50km from Bulawayo is fine, but heavy going in summer, and it's certainly not possible to cycle there and back

THE MWARI CULT IN MATOPOS

As the Great Zimbabwe state in the east of the country disintegrated, its Shona-speaking inhabitants dispersed, looking for new homes. Some, known as the **Torwa**, went west and eventually arrived in the **Matopos** region, establishing themselves around the fifteenth century as the ruling class of the district, with a headquarters at Khami. Imitating their predecessors at Great Zimbabwe, the Torwa built up a large centralised state, over which they ruled until the arrival in the 1680s of the **Rozvi**, another Shona-speaking group from the Mutapa state in the northeast. The Rozvi conquered and took control of the Torwa state, but without destroying it.

It was under the Rozvi that the **cult of Mwari**, the supreme creator, became dominant. Mwari wasn't the exclusive focus of all religious life, and wasn't a personal god: the ancestral spirits still held sway in the lives of ordinary people, while Mwari, as the deity of politics, dealt with matters of state. Most important of these was the bringing of rain – the basis of all economic life.

The Rozvi *mambo*, or king, had the power to intercede with Mwari, and when custom was broken, the god would administer punishments in the form of sickness or natural disasters. On these occasions the *mambo* would consult Mwari and become possessed by the *mhondoro*, the original ancestor, a cross between Adam and god, whose spirit had entered a lion. A Mwari priesthood mediated between the possessed king and the people, interpreting the leonine growls of the possessed ruler, passing judgement and punishments, and restoring the natural order.

At the turn of the nineteenth century the religious headquarters of the Rozvi state was in the Matopos and the political capital at Danangombe. The state was in the throes of a political revolution and a **power struggle** that had been developing between the Mwari priesthood and the secular *mambo* came to a head. According to oral tradition the *mambo*

in one day. One less strenuous option is to take your bike on the bus and save it for getting around the park. If you're **hitching**, get the Matopos Road bus from Lobengula Street terminus to Retreat (the last stop) before thumbing. Weekends are not difficult, but during the week the road is extremely quiet.

Tours

One of the best ways of seeing the hills, expecially if you do only have a day in hand, is to take a tour with *UTC*, *Black Rhino* or *Africa Dawn*, who do half or full-day tours with knowledgeable guides. If you take one of *Africa Dawn*'s trips, they may be prepared to drop you at Maleme and pick you up a few (specified) days later. They also do fantastic day-long walks to the remote Inanke Cave (see p.153) and three day camping trips through the park.

White heritage and black nationalism

While giving the appearance of being one of old Africa's unchanging places, the **Matobo National Park**, is really a colonial invention, and the story of its creation is fraught with politics and competing black and white ideologies.

From the early days after the defeat of the first Chimurenga, the white Matopos settlers were worried about a supposed threat to their heritage posed by the presence of blacks on the quasi-sacred site of Rhodes' grave. Later, with the consolidation of racial segregation, concerted attempts were made to shove the black peasant farmers elsewhere. However, even as the whites were developing their theories that Africans were hopeless farmers who were destroying the wild game and upsetting the balance of nature, African ideologies arose in parallel, mirroring white claims to the land. By the 1940s, when attempts to shift Africans hotted up, there was a growing conscious-

became fed up with the god's interference. When the king heard Mwari's voice coming from the top of his favourite wife's hut, "using a flintlock gun acquired from the Portuguese", he fired at the roof, whereupon the voice moved into the hut and the *mambo* razed the building to the ground. The voice kept on speaking from trees, grass and rocks, and when the *mambo* continued to harass it, the voice finally in a "wrathful tone" told the *mambo* that because he had chased Mwari away, in his place would come "men wearing skins".

The skin-clad men came in the form of **Nguni raiders** – waves of them, wearing animal hides. These warriors were by-products of battles taking place in South Africa, where Zulu conquests of the early nineteenth century pushed northwards a series of ruthless refugee armies, which raged through the Rozvi state. When the first blood-thirsty forces under **Zwangendaba** swept through, the *mambo* fled to the Matopos and in despair threw himself off a kopje. Zwangendaba's invasion broke down what remained of the already divided Rozvi state; by the time Mzilikazi's **Ndebele** arrived, the softening-up process was complete and Rozvi country was quickly conquered. The Ndebele forged the tattered fragments into a new, well-controlled and centralised state, occupying present-day southwest Zimbabwe.

The **priesthood** of the Mwari cult retreated to the caves of the Matopos, where Mzilikazi, eager to be on good terms with the local god – a wise move considering the *mambo's* fate – sent regular offerings to the shrines. In more recent years, the cult survived even the colonialists. During the 1946 drought many white farmers paid for rain dances to be held in National Park caves; while, acknowledging the still-potent force of the cult, ZAPU leader **Joshua Nkomo** held regular rallies during the liberation struggle at **Njelele**, one of the biggest rain shrines in the Matopos. It is taboo for outsiders to visit these shrine caves. In the late 1980s, the *Herald* reported local outrage at a *n'anga*, who had been taking guided tours of Njelele.

ness of the hills as a holy place of Ndebele tradition (see box overpage), and white accusations of black land mismanagement were countered by the blacks' claims to have been effectively farming the region for centuries before white settlers arrived.

For over a decade, Africans successfully opposed removal, both through the courts and by passive resistance campaigns, but, by 1962, a scheme was approved to clear part of the Matopos to create a national park. Residents were deported south to the Khumalo and east to the Gulati Tribal Trust Lands. African resentment was manifest in the destruction of fences, the lighting of veld fires and petrol-bombing of the park office. The furore was closely linked with burgeoning **nationalist politics**: the young Robert Mugabe even threatened to dig up Rhodes' grave and send the body to England. Through the 1960s fence-cutting and resistance continued. **ZIPRA guerillas**, who arrived in the 1970s, took refuge in the perfect hideouts offered by the hills, gaining the support of local people who believed that the park would be returned to them after the war.

It was perhaps the failure of this to materialise that prompted **dissidents** to return to the Matopos Hills in the early 1980s. Although it's still difficult to gauge, they appear to have had the support of frustrated peasants who felt betrayed by the government. The notorious Korean-trained **Fifth Brigade** was sent in and, unable to get the cooperation of local people, vented their frustration with extreme measures.

Following the **Unity Accord** and amnesty, the Matopos are now quiet again and tourists have returned, though the new government has declined to give back the National Park to its former residents – to deregulate an area nominated for world heritage status would damage its international reputation. The farmlands are now a wilderness and the cultural life that once thrived here is gone, while the **rain shrines** inside the park are deserted. Ironically, it's outside the confines of the heritage-preserving National Park, in the adjoining communal lands, that spiritual shrines like Njelele are still flourishing.

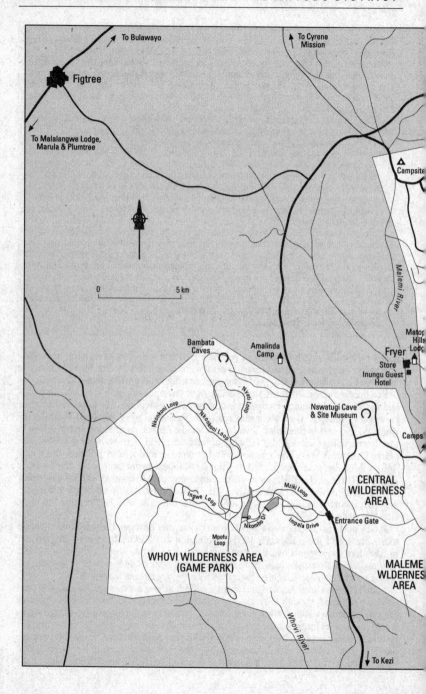

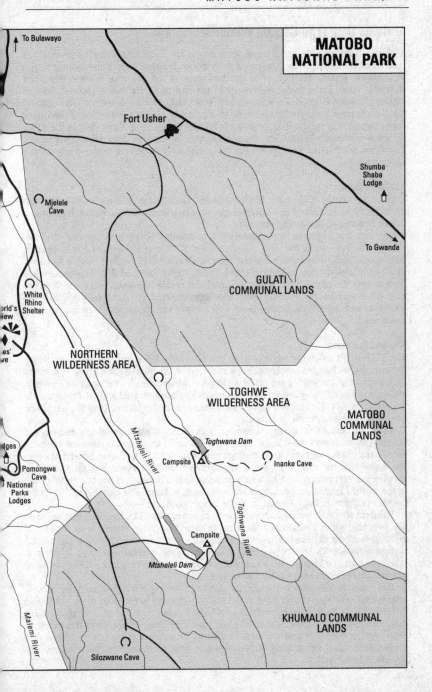

To Bulawayo

MATOBO NATIONAL PARK

Fort Usher

Shumba
Shaba
Lodge

Mjelele
Cave

To Gwanda

White
Rhino
Shelter

orld's
iew

GULATI
COMMUNAL LANDS

es'
e

NORTHERN
WILDERNESS AREA

TOGHWE
WILDERNESS AREA

MATOBO
COMMUNAL
LANDS

Mtsheleli River

Toghwana Dam

dges

Campsite

Inanke Cave

Pomongwe
Cave

National
Parks
Lodges

Toghwana River

Campsite

Mtsheleli Dam

Malemi River

KHUMALO COMMUNAL
LANDS

Silozwane Cave

Maleme Dam (The Central Wilderness Area)

Maleme Dam, with its parks accommodation, is the usual first stop on a good tarred road from Bulawayo. The popular route by car to Maleme from Bulawayo takes you past **White Rhino Shelter**, with the best rock art in the rare outline style, and **World's View**, the colonial equivalent of the liberation struggle's Heroes' Acre in Harare. Maleme is good for walking, or just scrambling over boulders. One exciting short walk goes over vertiginous hills to the barely visible paintings in **Pomongwe cave**, though the outstanding prehistoric images of Nswatugi Cave 7km in the other direction are much better. The remote Toghwe Wilderness Area with campsites at Toghwana and Mtsheleli dams is a full day's walk from Maleme if you're exploring the park on foot.

Maleme Dam

Right at the centre of the park, **Maleme Dam** provides a good base for day trips into the other parts. It is also a good place to get your bearings – and an idea of the terrain – before heading off into the wilder east.

You can stay in **parks accommodation** or **camp** – barely cheaper than the one-roomed chalets – along the dam, but if possible, it's worth forking out a little extra to stay in one of the two **luxury lodges**, *Fish Eagle* and *Black Eagle* if they're available. The best places to stay in Matabeleland, these lodges, perched like their namesakes high among the rocks, treat you to a superb panorama when you wake. Book ahead through the *Bulawayo National Parks Booking Agency*, 140a Fife Street (☎63646 and ☎63647), and keep your lodge door shut to prevent monkeys investigating your groceries.

Around the Dam

There's enough around the dam to keep you busy for a week, and the best ways to see the area are on foot or horseback. Book at the office the night before if you want to try **riding**. Most of the guides are sensitive to your riding ability – you won't be forced to walk if you can canter – and you'll go cross-country through veld and bush too high to negotiate on foot. If committed, you can organise to go for longer than the usual one and a half hours, to get further afield.

You'll see animals, however, on most outings. Herds of **sable antelope, impala** and **zebra** graze in valleys outside the confines of the park; **kudu** and **bushbuck** are to be seen in the grass; and there's no shortage of **baboons and monkeys**. Around Maleme you'll also hear the whistling calls of **klipspringer** antelope which leap up rock faces. Dassies are everywhere and high on unreachable boulders you'll see the nests of one of the world's largest concentration of **black eagles**. **Leopards** also adore this rocky, cave-riddled terrain but, as usual, you'd be lucky to see one.

The dam area offers **walks** appropriate to all energy levels. A half-hour ramble takes you over the hill to **Pomongwe Cave** or, to avoid the climb, stroll the two-and-a-half kilometres along the road. The cross-kopje route is the more interesting but not for vertigo sufferers; its start is signposted and the route waymarked. Steep in parts, it takes you over the hilltop, with a magnificent view and a descent into a thickly wooded granite amphitheatre with a giant cave at one end.

The **cave** is impressive though its paintings have been annihilated by a well-intentioned smearing of glycerine in the 1920s, supposed to preserve them – it seems unbelievable to have oiled the whole cave before experimenting on a small part. Yet this is an important archaeological site and digs have uncovered tens of thousands of Stone Age implements and artefacts as well as Iron Age pottery. It's estimated that people lived here for at least 50,000 years. A **site museum**, to house uncovered objects, is being built.

MATOPOS ROCK ART

The best of the **Matopos rock paintings** compare favourably with Stone Age art anywhere in the world. Yet the handful that are reproduced represent only a small fraction of the hundreds that exist in these hills – all of them within a relatively small radius and some reachable without a car.

Over the last century, anthropologists, archaeologists and historians have speculated as to the meanings of the paintings. Many **theories** were simple projections of what they knew about sites elsewhere in the world – or the imposition of their own, private assumptions. One eminent archaeologist, basing his conclusions on art deep in caves in Spain, suggested that both arose from the symbolic use of sympathetic magic – the depiction of a dead animal would ensure a successful hunt. Others have concluded that the paintings depict aspects of daily life – menus of animals and plants in the area. Newer ideas reject such interpretations. Zimbabwean rock art is unlikely to be an expression of sympathetic magic, which is unknown in any African hunting society; nor is it simply a menu – the remains of animals found at sites don't correlate with the pictures. Researchers now believe the images were concerned with the way people thought about human existence and actions, depicted through animal icons or metaphors.

The problem with attempting to interpret the paintings by means of an understanding of the people who painted them, though, is that no one knows exactly who they were, beyond the idea that they were **Stone Age hunter-gatherer** predecessors of today's Zimbabweans – possibly San ("Bushmen"), hunter-gatherers who roamed all over Southern Africa until quite recently. It seems likely that the paintings were executed between twenty thousand and two thousand years ago.

Many of the paintings have **religious themes**, which share features with the San focus on the ritual dance. This is used to take people into a **trance state** in which a potency or vital force called *n/um* is released. During trance, the experience of feeling stretched out is often described and some trancers have visions of light or movement. These elongated figures appear in rock art and the visions described correlate with the paintings.

As the picture of **hunter-gatherer cosmology** is built up, it may become possible to develop a more sophisticated interpretation of the paintings. Some tentative connections suggest that kudu are a symbol of potency, elephants are associated with rain and baboons with legends in which they taught human beings to dance and sing.

For more information on the subject the best book by far is Peter Garlake's *The Painted Caves* (see "Books" in *Contexts*).

Nswatugi Cave

Some of the best rock paintings of the area adorn the walls of nearby **Nswatugi Cave**. This is *the* place to visit if you've time for only one site. The animals are beautifully realised, full of life and movement, and will knock on the head any ideas about rock art being crude or primitive. You only need look at the superb giraffe series or the delicate kudu to realise these result from an intimate knowledge and years of keen observation of the subject. An informative **site interpretation display**, overseen by an attendant, provides useful background. Nswatugi was one of the shrines in which people used to dance for rain before they were removed from the area in 1962.

To get to the cave, **drive** or **walk** the 7km of road from the parks lodges past the dam. It's easy going on foot. **By horse**, you ride through grasslands surrounded by towering kopjes and through a shallow reedy swamp.

World's View

North from Maleme Dam lodges, a 10-km hike takes you to **World's View** – known to the Ndebele as *Malindidzimu*, Place of Benevolent Spirits – and **Rhodes' Grave**. With its 360-degree panorama this bald hill is an imposing burial site and a fine goal for a hike.

Rhodes' Grave

As requested in his will, **Rhodes' Grave** has been cut into the rock and a simple brass plaque placed over it. Six years before his death Rhodes had gone riding in these hills and found this grandiose spot. When he died in Cape Town in 1902, his body was taken by train to Bulawayo (presumably on ice). Nearly two weeks later, the cortege of coaches, carriages, carts, horses, bicycles and pedestrians left the city for Rhodes' hut on the Matopos farm, stopping overnight before continuing to the top. The old colonialist was then given a traditional salute by assembled Ndebele chiefs (making Rhodes the only commoner to be granted the honour), who asked for shots not to be let off by the firing party, because it would disturb the resident spirits. An **interpretation display** at the foot of the hill has a collection of old photographs covering Rhodes' life.

Shangani Patrol

Contrasting with this quiet resting place and erected at Rhodes' request on the same hilltop, the **Allan Wilson Memorial** commemorates the so-called **Shangani Patrol**. This odd stone confection, penetrating the skyline, is visible for miles. That this colonial monument still stands after Independence is an interesting reflection on the government's regard for white opinion. The facts are these. After Bulawayo fell to the British South Africa Company in 1893, Wilson was part of a hot-pursuit team running to ground the fleeing Lobengula. His patrol went ahead of the main column but, just as they were approaching the king, the Shangani River flooded separating them from reinforcements. On December 4, the entire party of 34 was wiped out by the Ndebele, who suffered over one hundred casualties in the day-long battle. The men were first buried where they fell, then transferred to Great Zimbabwe, and finally brought to the present position in 1904, when the memorial was erected. The heroic reliefs that wrap around the plinth depict the members of the party in a colonial equivalent of socialist realism.

Lizards and curios

The most intriguing and unusual spectacle on offer at World's View, though, is the **lizard-feeding**. Three times daily an attendant repeats his self-appointed task. At first the idea seems hopeless, as he holds out a small ball of *sadza* and calls to the dumb rocks. But gradually a multi-coloured collection of lizards gathers, emerging in incredible numbers from beneath boulders, flying across Rhodes' tomb and clambering over their feeder to attack the meal in a wild scrum. Egging them on, he holds out the ball and shouts "jump" to the frenzied reptiles. Take a camera.

Nearby, on the road to White Rhino Shelter, you will see the only **curio stall** authorised in the National Park. Look for the **Matopos baskets**, typical of the area, and strange little carved baboons with furry tails and gleaming red eyes.

White Rhino Shelter

For some extremely fine **outline paintings**, continue 2km northwards past the World's View turn-off to **White Rhino Shelter**. The paintings are in a small overhang along a clearly marked footpath off the Circular Drive.

The series of wildebeest painted here in different postures has been used to refute the idea that rock art is about magic for a successful hunt. Why would someone interested in the animal purely as meat take the trouble to make subtle distinctions in posture, goes the argument, when one position would be as good as another? Line paintings are quite rare in Zimbabwe and seem to have been executed for only a short experimental period. Some of the most beautiful of all Stone Age paintings were done in this style, in outline only, before being superseded by more elaborate, polychrome works. The outline rhinos of the shelter are to the right, and there's also a black rhino head. The polychrome figures of humans and animals, including a lion, are from a later period (probably executed within the last 1000 years).

Matopos Game Park (Whovi Wilderness Area)

The **Matopos Game Park**, which is open daily from dawn to dusk and charges a small admission fee, has to be one of the easiest places in Zimbabwe to see rhino. Many of the animals in the park have been reintroduced, but it's National Parks policy only to replace animals in areas which their species has previously inhabited. **White rhinos** were brought back after a lengthy absence on the strength of very accurate rock paintings at White Rhino Shelter, which show not some generalised animal but clearly distinguish it from its hook-lipped ("black") relative. Giraffe, zebra and a variety of antelope can be seen, though no elephants or lions. You'll need your own car to get into the park or otherwise you can take one of the many organised day tours which include it.

Toghwe Wilderness Area

Completely undeveloped, bar a couple of campsites, the **Toghwe Wilderness Area** offers adventurous hiking. With a single road brushing along its western flank, connecting **Mtsheleli** and **Toghwana Dams** to the main road, walking is the only way to penetrate it. The outstanding focus, **Inanke Cave** with its excellent paintings, makes a challenging expedition from Toghwana Dam, while **Silozwane Cave**, just outside the park, but more accessible from Mtsheleli Dam, is also impressively decorated.

Hitching from Maleme to the Toghwe dams is a long shot and you should be prepared to **hike**. About 18km to Mtsheleli or Toghwana Dam, it's a pleasant walk along a deserted road that twists around granite outcrops, descending and rising from valleys. There are **campsites** at both dams, where drinking water should be boiled.

Silozwane Cave

Of the two notable **rock art sites** in the area, **Silozwane**, 11km from Mtsheleli Dam in the Khumalo Communal Land, is the easier to reach. From the Cave road, take a left fork just before you get to the school and continue for about 2km along a decrepit track which virtually collapses into the river in places. From the car park, the route heads through forest and up the side of a steep dwala (smooth granite hill).

There's a strange atmosphere as you climb the bald rockfaces, escaping the workaday existence below. You hear village sounds, donkeys braying, people talking and cow bells tinkling distantly on the edge of the unearthly silence. **Silozwane Cave** is a surprise on this smooth rock-sea – a sudden scooped-out cavity. A few steps closer, and you make out a series of huge human figures emerging from the grey granulated wall.

At first these appear to be just a reddish blur smeared along the lower part of the wall, but closer approach reveals a richly detailed surface of image over image in a multitude of sizes and styles. Human figures are bold and clear, and noticeably plentiful. To the right of centre, some two-metre long serpent-like antelope-headed creatures seem to be being ridden by humans, fish and animals, while to the left one especially comical giraffe with a cartoon head looks crude next to the better observed one nearby. The closer you get, the easier it is to pick out animals, humans and abstract shapes from the swirling jumble of figures – painted, faded, peeling and overpainted.

Inanke Cave

Surpassing Silozwane, the paintings at **Inanke Cave**, a 7-km trek from Toghwana Dam, mark the highest expression of local prehistoric art. The cave is teasingly tricky to find but marked at regular intervals by painted arrows and small cairns. Should you lose your way, don't try short cuts. Do your best to retrace your steps – it's easy to become disoriented in the hills and after a while the endless valleys and ranges start to look alike. The walk itself is fabulous, along a wooded stream in a valley with an enormous granite cliff on one side, where black eagles nest, over hills and through open grassland dotted with kopjes. En route you'll pass two small overhangs with paintings, as well as a well-preserved iron-smelting furnace. The final ascent to the cave, up bare rock, is very steep but the richness and complexity of the paintings is sufficient reward. Ten minutes' climb further takes you to the bald summit, with its tremendous views in all directions.

travel details

Trains
These are the details given in timetables. Don't expect trains to run on time, but travel is very inexpensive.

From Bulawayo
To Harare 8am and 8pm daily (8 and 10hr) via **Gweru**, **Kwekwe** and **Midlands towns**.

To Victoria Falls 7pm nightly (12hr 30min).

To Gaborone 11.25am daily (19hr), via **Francistown** (7hr), and with **47 other stops** on the way.

To Johannesburg Thurs 10.30am (25hr 30min), via **Francistown** (4hr 30min) and larger villages.

Coaches
The most reliable form of surface transport. The drivers turn punctuality into an art-form, beating the train.

From Bulawayo
To Harare *Ajay Motorways* Mon, Wed, Fri, Sat, Sun 8am & Tues midday (6hr); *Express Motorways* Tues, Thurs, Sat 7.45am, Mon, Fri 1pm, Sun 4pm (6hr).

To Victoria Falls *Ajay Motorways* Mon, Wed, Fri 7am (6hr 15min), via **Hwange Safari Lodge** and **Hwange** town.

To Francistown *Express Motorways* Thurs & Sun at noon (around 5hr, but depends on how long it takes to clear border formalities).

To Johannesburg *Express Motorways* daily except Thurs & Sun 00.45am (16hr). Book at travel agents or *Express* Harare (☎720392). Minibuses

go at least twice a week, leaving at 7.30am and arriving in the evening. The price (US$70 o.w.) is the same as *Express*, but the journey is quicker and during the day. Book at *Budget Tours*, Fife St/Tenth Ave (☎76445).

Buses
You'll find buses to most places you'll be going. This is an attempt to make some sense of the confusing information about the main places. Arrive early to get a place and pay on the bus.

From Bulawayo, Renkini Terminus
To Harare 5 or more daily 5–11am (7hr+).

To Masvingo 2/3 daily 6–8.30am (5hr); *Hwange Express* Mon, Wed 1.30pm & Tues 11.30am (3hr 30min–4hr 30min).

To Kezi for the **Matopos** daily.

To Beit Bridge daily.

To Tuli daily.

To Binga via **Kamativi** and **Hwange** daily.

To Plumtree daily.

From Bulawayo, Lobengula Street Terminus
To Great Zimbabwe turn-off Mon–Sat 1.30pm (5hr 30min) via **Masvingo**.

Flights
From Bulawayo
To Harare 3 daily (50min).

To Victoria Falls daily except Tues, Sat (50min).

To Gaborone Wed (1hr 10min).

To Johannesburg daily except Tues, Sat (1hr 30min).

TELEPHONE AREA CODES

Beit Bridge 186   **Bulawayo** 19   **Plumtree** 180

Shangani 150   **Turk Mine** 185

Matopos 183-8* (*at a date to be advised; at present most numbers are on the Bulawayo exchange. *Hyphen indicates a second dialling tone*).

Direct dialling does not always work; it costs the same to dial 0 for the operator and ask to be connected.

CHAPTER FOUR

VICTORIA FALLS AND HWANGE NATIONAL PARK

T he **Victoria Falls** are one of Africa's most enduring and famous images, and for some visitors they constitute the full extent of a visit to Zimbabwe. They are at their most impressive in **April** and **May** when the river is in full spate, though the dense spray can sometimes obscure the views. They are clearest, though less spectacular, in **September** and **October**, at the end of the dry season.

Victoria Falls Town exists solely to serve the tourism needs of the big splash, with a fair sprinkling of upmarket hotels. The place is by no means out of reach for budget travellers, though the supply of cheap **accommodation** and camping possibilities in and around town has recently come under pressure from backpackers and overland-truckloads of visitors.

Safari lodges and bush camps near the Falls and in the Hwange region, although far from cheap, promise truly exciting experiences of the bush; and the personalised expert attention you'll get make them worth saving up for. Furthermore, if you do have money to spare, a host of high quality **adventure activities** might well tempt an extended stay. The biggest thrills must be white-water rafting on the rapids below the Falls, or to spend several days kayaking through rapids on the stretch above, but game trails in the nearby reserves – either on foot or on horseback – are equally exciting options.

The **northwest corner** of Zimbabwe also has impressive **wildlife reserves**, and a visit to the Falls combines conveniently with some of the region's finest game-viewing. The **Zambezi National Park**, famed for its herds of beautiful sable antelope, is nearby, and from Victoria Falls you can take walking safaris (the only way in) to the game-rich grasslands of **Kazuma Pan**, to the south on the Botswana border. However, Zimbabwe's wildlife showpiece is the extensive **Hwange National Park**, just 100km south of Victoria Falls by road, and connected by daily flights. The most accessible of the country's wildlife parks, Hwange has easy game-viewing, low-cost accommodation, and a luxury game lodge and smaller exclusive bush camps for real safari style.

The Falls are also shared with Zambia – the Zambezi River defines the Zambia–Zimbabwe border – and a short distance from Botswana and Namibia. This makes Victoria Falls Town a good base for onwards travel and an obvious point of entry for overlanders working their way down from the north. From Zimbabwe you can make a hassle-free day sortie into **Zambia**, crossing the Victoria Falls Bridge to look at the gorge from a different angle, or venturing 10 kilometres further into the country to visit the regional centre of **Livingstone**. Heading west into **Botswana** you can base yourself at **Kasane** on the Chobe River for a couple of days of game-viewing in the fabulous elephant country of **Chobe National Park**. And from here it's a straightforward northward detour into **Namibia**, provided you have your own transport. The basics on these trips are all included in this chapter; for more details on travel to Zambia or Namibia, see "Onwards" in the *Contexts* section.

VICTORIA FALLS

The energy and power of over a mile's width of the **Zambezi River** thundering 100 metres down a sheer chasm is a pretty compelling sight, and combined with the clouds of sunlit spray and rainbows, reason enough to spend a day or two gazing at **Victoria Falls**. But the banks of the river, before it takes the plunge, are enticing, too – a wonderful place to contemplate the **palm-dotted islands** and the water, which changes from sheeny pink at dawn to metallic blue at dusk. And, for closer views, you can get on the water with one of the **cruises**.

The **rainforest** fed by the spray of the Falls, with its ilala palms, white river sand, fiery sunsets and more-or-less constant humidity makes for a lush, darkest Africa landscape, found nowhere else in Zimbabwe. Immediately surrounding the Falls is the **Victoria Falls National Park** where you can see antelope, warthog and vervet monkeys amid the spray.

Just a few kilometres upstream, the **Zambezi National Park** extends for forty forested kilometres along the river, with dry bush and grassland further inland. Stalked by a wide range of Zimbabwe's wildlife, this is one of the many diversions that make it possible to spend days around the Victoria Falls.

At the centre of all this lies **the town** itself, unashamedly geared towards serving the tourists. It provides a springboard for the Falls themselves, but is now expanding into a host of diversions, many of the highest quality, to keep visitors here – and spending.

The Town

VICTORIA FALLS TOWN is a surprisingly sleepy place. By the standards of other international tourist spots it is distinctly – and refreshingly – undeveloped, despite experiencing a belated tourist boom. Each of its scattered hotels exists as a self-contained resort, from which guests venture out to stroll down to the water, visit the curio shops and snake park, or to take part in the standard excursions – a flight or a cruise.

Set amid the flat, hot bush of Matabeleland, the town is actually one of the oldest in Zimbabwe, having become a centre for intrepid traders, travellers and hunters through the second half of the nineteenth century. By the 1890s a store and a hotel complete with roulette wheel had been built, though the town was temporarily abandoned following an outbreak of malaria and blackwater fever and the settlement moved to higher ground away from the river, at Livingstone, across the newly completed railway bridge. The town on the Zimbabwean side of the river only really came back into its own in the late 1960s, when hotels, banks and, most important, an airport were built.

The 1990s has seen Victoria Falls take a huge leap towards becoming the tourism capital of Zimbabwe. Backpackers have begun arriving in increasing numbers, putting some pressure on budget accommodation, and the growing number of activities on offer are attracting more and more visitors who want adventure as well as contemplation. At the end of 1991 the airport was upgraded to international standards – for the benefit of

---

ACCOMMODATION PRICE CODES

Every hotel and accommodation option listed in this chapter has been given a **price code** in US$ to indicate the cost of a single night's lodging.

For a full explanation, see p.43.

① under US$8   ② US$8–14   ③ US$15–29   ④ US$30–59
⑤ US$60–89   ⑥ US$90–149   ⑦ US$150+

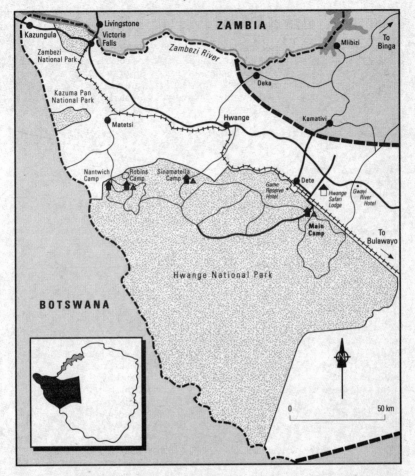

visiting leaders coming "on retreat" at the conclusion of the Commonwealth Heads of Government Meeting (known locally as CHOGM).

With the rapid influx of tourists the town continues to expand. New facilities have sprung up in the fertile entrepreneurial grounds around the Falls. Most controversial of these is the hefty *Elephant Hills Hotel*, which has doubled the total bed capacity of the resort at a single stroke.

Getting there, arrival and orientation

The slowest, but arguably pleasantest, way to cover the distance to the Falls is on the **Bulawayo–Falls train**. It's a twelve-hour overnight affair, leaving Bulawayo daily at 7pm. There are sometimes inexplicably long delays and stops at the tiniest of junctions but the journey is worth the time to view some of Zimbabwe's best wildlife areas from the comfort of a self-contained compartment.

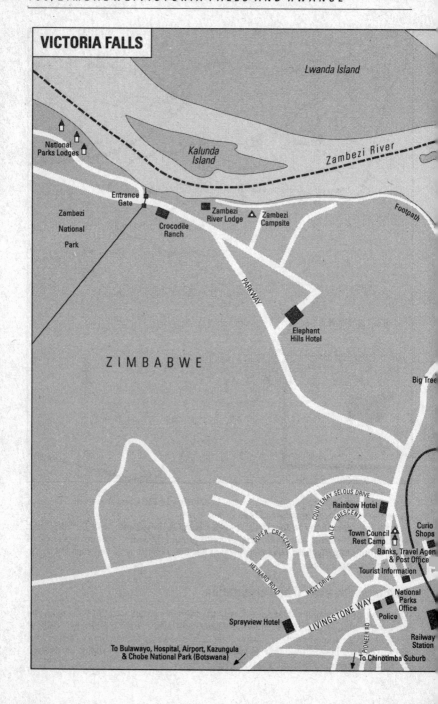

VICTORIA FALLS

Lwanda Island

National Parks Lodges

Kalunda Island

Zambezi River

Footpath

Entrance Gate

Zambezi National Park

Crocodile Ranch

Zambezi River Lodge

Zambezi Campsite

PARKWAY

Elephant Hills Hotel

Z I M B A B W E

Big Tree

COURTENAY SELOUS DRIVE

DALE CRESCENT

Rainbow Hotel

Curio Shops

SOPER CRESCENT

Town Council Rest Camp

Banks, Travel Agen & Post Office

Tourist Information

HEYNARD ROAD

WEST DRIVE

National Parks Office

LIVINGSTONE WAY

Police

PIONEER RD

Sprayview Hotel

To Bulawayo, Hospital, Airport, Kazungula & Chobe National Park (Botswana)

Railway Station

To Chinotimba Suburb

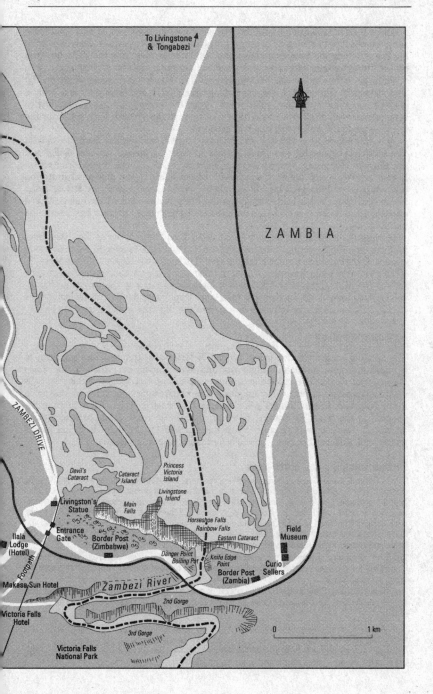

To Livingstone
& Tongabezi

ZAMBIA

ZAMBEZI DRIVE

Devil's
Cataract

Cataract
Island

Princess
Victoria
Island

Livingstone
Island

Livingston's
Statue

Main
Falls

Horseshoe Falls
Rainbow Falls

Field
Museum

Entrance
Gate

Border Post
(Zimbabwe)

Eastern Cataract

Ilala
Lodge
(Hotel)

Danger Point
Boiling Pot

Knife Edge
Point

Curio
Sellers

Footpath

Border Post
(Zambia)

Makasa Sun Hotel

Zambezi River

Victoria Falls
Hotel

2nd Gorge

0   1 km

Victoria Falls
National Park

3rd Gorge

At dawn on the following day of the trip, you travel through remote bush, and there are good chances of seeing such **game** as antelope, zebra, or perhaps even one of the big five watching the train as it chugs past. On its return leg from the Falls, the train passes through some of this area at dusk, an equally prime time for viewing game.

Victoria Falls station itself is magnificent – an Edwardian concoction shaded by flame-flowered flamboyants, sweet-smelling frangipanis and syringas, and with a platform boasting pond and palm trees. From the ceremonial exit (High British Empire), you can stroll down a colonnade of trees to the *Victoria Falls Hotel*; for the town's main street, walk north along the platform.

The *Ajay* **coach** from Hwange and Bulawayo arrives and departs from the *Makasa Sun Hotel*, just beyond the *Victoria Falls Hotel*, as do the **airbuses** that meet all flights at the **airport** (20km out of town on the Bulawayo road). **Local buses** drop off on Livingstone Way near the *Sprayview Hotel*, before going to the hidden **Chinotimba township** down Pioneer Road. All the shops you're likely to need are strung along Livingstone Way, which leads straight to the **Falls National Park** entrance. Almost everything closes for lunch and the town is dead by 4.30pm, so do your business in the morning.

Cycling is the most flexible way to get around, and several places offer bike hire. You can take them overnight to the Zambezi National Park lodges or pedal across to Zambia. **Car rental** can also be arranged (see "Listings" on p.169 for both services).

The **Victoria Falls Rambler** – a set of trailers pulled by a tractor – makes circuits around the main sights. For US$5, which includes entrance to the Crocodile Ranch, you can hop on and off (once only at each stop) throughout the day. Stops include the Ranch, *Rainbow Hotel*, the Publicity Association, the Big Tree and of course the Falls.

Accommodation

The range of accommodation in and around Victoria Falls stretches from **medium to upmarket hotels** down to **budget options** like camping or chalets at the *Town Council Rest Camp*. The growth area, however, is in **safari lodges** within the Falls environs providing a pricey but unquestionably interesting alternative to staying in town. **National Parks lodges** offer a budget alternative if you want to cater for yourself in the bush. Be warned however, that the increasing numbers of visitors arriving in the country's premier resort mean a bed for the night is by no means guaranteed. Advance booking, especially for budget places, is essential.

Budget: camping and crash pads

Town Council Rest Camp, Livingstone Way/Parkway, PO Box 41, Victoria Falls (☎210). The cheapest accommodation with a roof over your head is in segregated men's and women's mini hostels – cramped, but good for meeting other travellers. Moving up a bracket, the triple-bedded, and slightly run-down chalets are still extremely cheap; all the basics are provided, including pots, pans, a small fridge and firewood for braaing outside. Washing facilities are in shared blocks, with hot showers and baths. There are also two-bedroomed en-suite cottages, which won't break the bank, and a large, sandy campsite. ①–②.

Zambezi campsite, alongside the river on Parkway, next to *A'Zambezi Lodge*. While not as convenient for the town centre, it is recommended as the nicer of the two campsites with splendid views of the water. ①.

Zambezi National Park Lodges, 6km outside of town along Parkway. These self-catering park lodges are the best budget place to stay, and accordingly are heavily booked. See p.170 for further details. ①.

Medium-priced Hotels

Vic Falls offers no rock bottom hotels, but the ones in this price range all provide high standards, en-suite bedrooms and swimming pools.

A'Zambezi River Lodge, 5km out of town along Parkway (☎4561). This riverside lodge is a pleasant escape, built in a semicircle, with rooms facing the river. It claims to have the largest thatched roof in the world. Located right next to the Zambezi National Park; warthogs, monkeys and occasionally other animals roam about the grounds. A **courtesy bus** service operates for residents without their own transport so it's easy to get to and from the centre. ④.

Rainbow Hotel, Parkway/Courtney Selous Crescent, PO Box 150 (☎4585). Reasonably central, built in a Spanish style with the attraction of a bar *in* the swimming pool. ④.

Sprayview Hotel, Livingstone Way/Renard Rd, PO Box 70 (☎4344). Cheapest of the Vic Falls hotels, but none the less pleasant for that. About 20min walk from the centre, it serves great steaks and has a pleasantly nostalgic atmosphere. For families it has the advantage of a daytime creche. Recommended. ③.

Upmarket Hotels

In prime locations, the upmarket establishments, bar *Elephant Hills*, are within 10 minutes' easy walk of the Falls.

Elephant Hills, 3km out of town just off Parkway, halfway along the road to the Zambezi National Park (PO Box 8221, Harare). Hideously obtrusive, with piped muzak throughout, this is unquestionably the most controversial new development at the Falls. ⑦.

Ilala Lodge, in the centre, on Livingstone Way, PO Box 18 (☎4203). Rooms look out onto manicured lawns that recede into indigenous forest, from which small game emerges in the mornings and late afternoons. Retains an intimate feel by limiting guest numbers. Highly recommended. ⑥.

Makasa Sun Hotel, Parkway/Mallet Drive, PO Box 4275 (☎4275). On the main drag, with a casino that belies this otherwise characterless slab. ⑥.

Victoria Falls Hotel, Mallet Drive (opposite the railway station), PO Box 10 (☎4203). The place to splurge, it positively oozes bygone elegance (see box overpage). ⑦.

Luxury Safari Lodges

For visitors wanting to combine game-viewing with seeing the Falls, a number of upmarket lodges outside its immediate environs offer luxury in the bush, with game drives, walks or, in some cases, cruises thrown into the all-inclusive price. Although some may seem far out of town, by Zimbabwean standards they aren't, and all are packaged as adjuncts to a Falls visit. Transfers to and from Victoria Falls or the airport are provided. (For more details about their regions see The Upper Zambezi on p.170).

Imbabala Safari Camp, 72km from town on Kazungula road. Bookings through *Wild Horizons*, Parkway, PO Box 159, Victoria Falls (☎4219 or ☎4349; Telex: 51685). On the Zambezi flood plain, near the Botswana border; you can see the meeting point of four countries (Zimbabwe, Botswana, Namibia and Zambia) from lawns which slope down to the water. Accommodation is in A-frame, en-suite chalets, catering to a maximum of 18 guests. Lie on your bed and watch the reflected sun set on the river. Excellent guides, good game-viewing and outstanding opportunities for birdwatching, with species present that don't occur elsewhere in Zimbabwe. Around US$235 per person.

Masuwe Lodge, 7km from Victoria Falls to the Masuwe turnoff along the main airport road and then several kilometres along a private dirt track. Bookings through *African Adventures*, PO Box 293, Kopje, Harare (☎Harare 702634; Fax: 702546; Telex: 26198 ZW). The nearest of the lodges to town. Set in its own concession, it offers promising prospects for game-viewing. A broad range of habitats means birdwatching is rewarding with common sightings of birds of prey. Large walk-in tents (consciously recreating an *Out of Africa* ambience) sit on stilted wooden decks providing panoramas onto surrounding valleys. The lounge/dining room jetties out over a valley providing dramatic views. US$195 per person.

Tongabezi, Zambia. Bookings through Private Bag 31, Livingstone, Zambia (Livingstone ☎323235 or ☎323296; Fax 323224; Telex 24043 ZA). The most deliciously luxurious of the lodges, on the Zambian side and geared more to style than game-viewing. Some gorgeous rooms provide the thrill of sleeping in a four-poster bed on a deck overlooking the Zambezi. In the dark you may see one of the night apes, or other nightlife, that clamber up the lianas that hang down from the tall trees of the riverine forest. Other accomodation is under canvas and there's also a thrilling island camp in the middle of the Zambezi. US$150–190 per person.

Westwood Game Lodge, near Imbabala on the Kazungula road. Bookings through *Westwood Game Lodge*, PO Box 132, Victoria Falls (☎4614 or ☎4571; Telex 51664 SAFTVL). 1hr drive from Victoria Falls, on the western border of the Zambezi National Park. An excellent option for game-viewing with outings into the adjacent Zambezi National Park as well as fine game country on the lodge's own 120,000 acres with a chance of seeing leopard, lion, elephant, buffalo and a large cross-section of antelope. Accommodation is in stone and thatch chalets with en-suite showers. With a maximum of six guests, the emphasis is on intimacy. US$180 per person.

Eating, drinking and nightlife

The **hotel** dining rooms and terraces are more than a match for the couple of restaurants in town. A leisurely patio **breakfast** at the *Victoria Falls Hotel* or *Makasa Sun* (7–10am: eat as much as you want for a fixed amount) will set you up for the rest of the day. All the hotels offer *à la carte* menus with something affordable for lunch, as well as midday and evening braais. Supper under the fairy-lit trees at the *Falls Hotel* consists of piles of braaied meat, salads and puddings.

Most eating joints **in town** cater primarily for locals and backpackers rather than hotel-confined tourists. *Wimpy* in Parkway, with the usual menu, fails to undercut hotel toasted sandwich prices. A couple of yards down Parkway, at the back of *Soper's Centre*, a café does cheap **take-aways**. More good central take-aways are available at the *Boiling Pot*. The *Gorge Restaurant* next door doesn't rate, though the nearby *Explorers' Bar* is recommended for its food, beer and videos.

Carnivores can have a feast at the *Town Council Rest Camp*. Buy a piece of **meat** from the attendant and *braai* it yourself on the fire. The *Sprayview Hotel*'s more elegantly presented meals are equally good value; their Acapulco Steak is highly recommended.

Ilala Lodge has the best menu for **vegetarians**; otherwise you'll be forced to eat toasted sandwiches and salads at the hotels and snack bars.

Nightlife

At the hotels there's often a video or **film** and always **beer and** braaivleis. The **casino** at the *Makasa Sun* is another after-dark possibility.

At the *Victoria Falls Hotel* a **marimba band** plays untraditional music below the terrace outside, and there's the much vaunted *Africa Spectacular* (nightly, 7–8pm). The

---

THE VICTORIA FALLS HOTEL

The **Victoria Falls** is Zimbabwe's grandest hotel – and must be seen even if you can't afford (or can't find a room) to stay.

The first tourists to the Falls had to eat and sleep in the train at the station. In 1905, just after the railway arrived, work began on the construction of a wood and corrugated iron hotel, close to the terminus. That shack has come a long way, with the avenue of scented trees from the station creating merely a build-up to the hotel's colonial legacy of architectural style and impeccable service.

Guests, largely foreign tourists, enjoy rich-*bwana* fantasies here, waited on by discreet and highly efficient black staff in starched white uniforms and gloves. The terrace opens onto views of the low greeny-grey hills of Zambia rising behind the filter of spray. It's all part of the careful setting – the site was chosen for its view of the second gorge and the daring railway bridge.

The short walk from the hotel to the Falls was too much for Edwardian tourists, so a trolley took them down to the Falls. A number of old snaps in Bulawayo's Railway Museum show well-dressed ladies and gents being pushed by black "trolley boys". The tracks were pulled up some time ago but the remaining path is still a thoroughfare, the trolleymen replaced by **hustlers** hawking curios at odd spots along the route.

masks and dancing are impressive and the stilt-dancing particularly worth seeing. There's a brief explanation of each performance, which puts them in some kind of context. There's also traditional dancing at the craft village, which is more convenient if you're staying at the rest camp.

Victoria Falls National Park

When Livingstone arrived at the **VICTORIA FALLS**, and presumptuously named them after his queen, they already had an apt designation – **Mosi oa Tunya** – "The Smoke That Thunders". This name had been given to the waters by the **Makololo**, who, like Livingstone, were newcomers to the region. Following the early eighteenth-century Zulu expansion (in what is today South Africa's Natal province), a refugee fragment had fled north, finally coming to rest around the Falls. They became the Makololo and held domain here briefly during the nineteenth century, ruling over the local tribes.

Stone Age tools uncovered in the area record that humans were living around the Falls for two million years before that. The Zambian side has a dig showing finds at different depths corresponding to different epochs, and the museum in Livingstone has a fine collection of stone tools found at the dig.

The Smoke That Thunders – Viewing the Falls

Daily 6am-6pm. Small entrance fee.

Few geological faults can evoke such anticipation as The Smoke That Thunders: the moment you arrive in Victoria Falls Town, and you hear the roar and see the smokey mist rising half a kilometre skywards, you'll be drawn down the main street to the **National Park** entrance. A walk from here through the rainforest will take at least an hour. At full moon you can see the faint lunar rainbow.

The best times to visit are around opening and closing times – when the light is at its best, and fellow tourists relatively sparse. Take waterproof protection (or pick it up at the entrance) for your camera and other susceptible possessions – you may get wet.

The Chasm, Devil's Cataract – and David Livingstone

You can walk all along the **side of the chasm** opposite the park entrance, through the woods with their sudden spray showers – though beware that some of the most vertiginous drops are unfenced, with just the occasional thorn bush as a barrier. In the **dry season**, when the Falls are lowest, you'll probably escape a wetting, but once the rains have swelled the Zambezi, you'll get the full force of the spray; wear a swimming costume or raincoat. The wettest viewpoints are those directly opposite the Main Falls, in the areas unprotected by trees.

The first view that you get, at the western end of the the chasm, is known as **Devil's Cataract**. Turning left from here takes you to a statue of **Livingstone**, beyond which the river path leads off upstream. It's hard to avoid Livingstone in this neck of the woods. His commanding effigy, overlooking Devil's Cataract, portrays the qualities expected from famous explorers – will and determination. More critical accounts record that he was pig-headed, selfish and sanctimonious. Nevertheless, anti-slavery campaigning was part of his reason for exploring the Zambezi – his aim being to find a west–east route to end the human traffic in the region.

Livingstone's reverential account that "on sights as beautiful as this Angels in their flight must have gazed" has become one of the clichés of the Victoria Falls: a phrase that's even been deconstructed and reassembled to package the daily air tours – *The Flight of the Angels* – that flit above the chasm. To Livingstone, however, there was a real element of revelation in his vision of Mosi oa Tunya – and he backed his own religious emotion by writing about how local chieftains used two of the islands right on the lip of the Falls as "sacred spots for worshipping the deity".

Other Falls and Danger Point

Wander through the rainforest beyond Devil's Cataract and you will see the **other falls** that roar down the mile-wide fissure: **Main**, **Horseshoe**, **Rainbow** and the **Eastern Cataract**. A highlight is **Danger Point**, at the east end, where your walk on the Zimbabwean side finishes with a dizzy promontory near the Victoria Falls Bridge. From the rocks here you can look down into the frightening depths of the abyss, and also get great views of the eastern half of the Falls and of the **Boiling Pot**, a seething whirlpool where two branches of the river collide. It can be wet and slippery at the viewpoint with deluges of spray; during the flood season you won't see much, but when the river is low it's mesmerising.

Rainforest Wildlife

The rainforest is eminently explorable and there's plenty of **wildlife** about. Baboons, monkeys, waterbuck, warthog and banded mongooses (sic) roam around, while the over-400 species of birds include: Livingstone's Lourie with its bright leaf-green breast and crimson flight feathers; the comical trumpeter hornbill; the paradise flycatcher; the nectar-feeding sunbird; as well as more common bulbuls, warblers, barbets and shrikes.

Butterflies are numerous, blowing through the mist between rainbows and shiny grass. During the rainy season the undergrowth acquires a special luxuriance with large blood lilies, scarlet among the mosses and ferns. Wild yellow gladioli grow in patches of open grassland. Palms, ebonies, figs, mahoganies and waterberries thrive in the rich, moist soil.

Activities

It's easy to while away a few hours around the Falls strolling, sightseeing and buying crafts. More institutionalised activities include flights over the chasm, sunset booze cruises on the river and game drives in the Zambezi National Park.

Crafts, crocs and curios

The curio shops around the **Falls Craft Village**, behind the Post Office and banks, are ganged together in a single conglomeration which spills over down Parkway. The first stall was opened in 1903 by the earliest white settler, Percy Clarke, and in 1910 one Jack Soper opened a shop next door with a crocodile pool to attract customers. *Soper's Curios* is still there and so is a pool (a new and larger one) with large crocs snoozing in the slimy water. The stuffed lion in the window with fierce teeth and glassy eyes is part of the range of great-white-hunter goods.

Some of the best **craft works** are available at the *Jairos Jiri* shop (closed Sun) in the Falls Craft complex; they include Batonga baskets from the Zambezi Valley, attractive spoons made from local wood, and carved giraffes with delicate long necks – the best of them eight or nine feet high. For an eclectic mix of antiques and airport art, *Studio Africana* is worth a look. Some things aren't actually for sale – like the carved, wooden **ape god** from Zaire, with a head made from a smoked gorilla skull – but if you want something old this is the place. In a sort of **indoor market** nearby, local women compete with each other to sell **crochet ware, baskets, carvings and bracelets** – cheaper and with considerably more buzz than the curio shops but not half as easy to browse.

THE HIPPO'S TALE

A San folktale relates how the first hippo begged the Great Bureaucrat's permission to live in the water, which it loved more than the earth, the sun, the moon or the stars. Application rejected: such a big mouth with such teeth would soon devour all the fish. Again the hippo begged, promising to eat nothing in the water, and to emerge at night to graze on the grass and plants of the earth. Again, permission denied. Finally it agreed to emerge daily and scatter its dung, so all creatures could examine them for fishbones.

The **Falls Craft Village** proper (Mon–Sat 8.30am–4.30pm, Sun 9am–1pm), is set to one side of the curio shops, and seems designed to prop up out-of-date touristic images of Africa – a mishmash collection of nineteenth-century huts from all over the country. More interesting, if a little startling, is bumping into one of the two **fortune-telling** *n'angas* huddled in the darkness of one of the exhibit huts. For a few dollars they'll lay it all out for you. Though they work out of context here, *n'angas* are widely used in Zimbabwe, by town and country dwellers, as healers and interpreters of the workings of the ever-present ancestors. They have a deep knowledge of illness and both herbal and ritualistic ways of dealing with it. Since Independence, the government has actively encouraged their profession.

River walks for free

If you can't afford any of the organised trips, go on your own up the river towards the national park. A 10-km **walk** starts outside the park fence just beyond Livingstone's statue along a 4-km riverside path to the *A'Zambezi River Lodge*, then 6km back along the road. You'll probably be alone – most people don't venture upstream beyond the first rapids. This excursion can be conveniently combined with a visit to the *Crocodile Ranch* and the *A'Zambezi*.

Be wary of **hippos** leaving the river at dusk for their bankside browse. They return to the water first thing next day. Watch out then too, and avoid blocking their route to the water. During the day they emerge occasionally to scatter their dung on land with a vigorous tail movement, but all you're likely to see of them are noses and ears above water far upriver from people. Be alert as well to the fact that other **wildlife** sometimes ventures onto the path.

Walk upriver to see the **riverine forest** and the changes in current as it gets smoother and quieter. If it's blistering, just walk a kilometre or so to the **Big Tree** and come back along Zambezi Drive and Parkway, which brings you to the doorstep of the campsite. The Big Tree, a large baobab, is no crowd puller, but it has historical interest. Early pioneers camped here and it became a traditional gathering place for crossing the river to the Old Drift Settlement and later to Livingstone.

The Snake Park

The **Snake Park**, close by the Crafts Village, can be diverting for the odd hour or two. The snake attendant has a great line in ghoulish information – where snakes like to hide, how likely they are to bite you, how long you'll live if they do – concluded with graphic descriptions of agonising death. And if you've always wondered how those lifelike animals in museums are created, go to the **taxidermy workshop** where they have mounts on display in various stages of completion and people who'll happily tell you some of the secrets of their morbidly fascinating work. Their shop explores the depths of bad taste for all pockets: a copper ashtray plinthed on an impala leg goes for a few pounds, while there's a lion skin rug (with snarling head) for those with more money than subtlety.

Crocodile Ranch

Spencers Creek Crocodile Ranch (8am–12.30pm & 2–4.30pm), 7km up Parkway just past the *A'Zambezi*, is the place to see loads of the much-maligned reptiles. The ranch serves the dual purpose of restocking the badly depleted river and rearing **crocodiles** for their skin; every year they collect about 2500 eggs, a proportion of which are hatched, reared and returned (some as healthy three-year-olds). The crocodile has an important **ecological role** in balancing the fish population, eating the predators which prey on the marketable fish like bream.

UTC run **daily excursions** to the ranch at 10.30am and 3pm for Z$12, or you could cycle there down Parkway. There's a pleasant tea kiosk at the ranch, and an interesting little museum.

Cruising down the river

The most famous of local outings is the *Sundowner* "booze cruise" run by *UTC* three times each day. Drinks used to be free – with riotous results. Now you buy your own and there's a stiff fine for jumping in or attempting to swim home. The last (early evening) departure is the best time to be on the river, with the darkening forest backlit by a molten sky. Though the launch doesn't berth en route, it does pause for photographs, and you're bound to see hippos and perhaps elephants on the banks and islands. The morning and afternoon cruises stop at Kandahar Island for tea where monkeys try to take your biscuits off you.

Depart from the jetty next to the *A'Zambezi River Lodge* at 10.15am, 2.15pm and 5pm (in winter; the latest leaves at 5.15pm in summer). **Tickets** are sold by *UTC*, who pick up from the central hotels 30 minutes before departure. Drinks are still included for a supplement on the more exclusive *Ilala* – which carries no more than ten passengers.

Flight of the Angels and Microlight Flights

When you soar above the spray in a **light aircraft** the extent of the gorge is dramatically made clear. The *Flight of the Angels* lasts 15 minutes and the price includes transport to the airport; a longer, 75-minute option includes a game flight. Book at *UTC* or one of the travel agents in town. The flights enable you to see what the Falls actually are and to appreciate their immensity. **Microlight flights**, from Livingstone airport, can be booked at *Sobek* in Victoria Falls.

Game Drives

UTC's **game drives** in the nearby game reserve are more down-to-earth. The Zambezi National Park (see section following for a full treatment) runs along the southern bank of the Zambezi towards Botswana. You can see elephant, buffalo, lion, zebra and many different species of antelope – worth it for whistle-stoppers, but not if Hwange's on your itinerary. *UTC* pick up from central hotels at 6.30am and 3pm daily. Book through them.

Adventure

Victoria Falls has become a major centre for outward bound activities. **White-water rafting** established itself in the 1980s as an attraction to rival the Falls themselves. It has since been joined by **kayaking, horseback game-viewing, bungee-jumping** and **walking safaris.**

White-water rafting

Riding the rapids, through some of the world's wildest white water below the Falls, is one of the best things you can do in Zimbabwe and enthusiasts come here expressly for it. Certainly it's a sustained adrenalin surge: once you've walked down to the gorge and cast off there's no backtracking.

The inflatables are guided by trained oarsmen, who take you through the rapids, which are punctuated by stretches of calm waters. White-water runs are graded 1–6 in difficulty. This stretch of the Zambezi rates a 5, the Falls themselves a 6 (unrunnable). You don't have to do anything other than cling on and shift your weight when instructed. People routinely fall off, but injuries are thankfully rare. The experience is actually far less frightening than it sounds – being splashed with water in the heat is very pleasant and Rambo-types may even be disappointed. It's worth noting, though, that the steep walk out of the gorge at the end of the day is strenuous.

The "high-water" trips go from July 1 to August 15 and the "low-water" runs, when, naturally, the rapids are fiercest, from mid-August to sometime in December or January, depending on river levels.

You should book beforehand to ensure getting on; weekends are invariably fully reserved by Zimbabweans. The **Zimbabwe side** is ridden by *Shearwater, Frontiers* and *Mosi oa Tunya* (same price). On the **Zambian side**, the US company *Sobek* starts in March when conditions are suitable. No rafting is done in May and June. The price for one day is in the region of US$90.

Besides scrambling down to it and walking, rafting is the only way you'll get into the 100m deep **Batoka Gorge**, which had never been navigated until *Sobek* achieved it in 1981. Apart from day trips, *Sobek* run week-long **marathon excursions** right the way through the gorge to the mouth of the **Matetsi River**, near Deka – special but expensive trips, which only operate in August, September and October. A third of the way through, you come to the **Moemba Falls**, which are exceptionally beautiful even if they're nothing on the scale of the big ones. They're also very rarely visited; few people even know of their existence. There are no marked roads in the vicinity, just 4WD tracks.

Frontiers offers the standard one-day trip between July and January as well as the choice of an overnight trip into the gorge. Between August and mid-December there's also the chance of the two-night excursion into the Batoka Passage.

White-water kayaking

The latest and one of the most interesting additions to the repertoire of watery attractions is kayaking on the Upper Zambezi. Under the supervision of licensed guides, the emphasis on seeing and feeling the wild distinguishes it from the more immediate surge offered by rafting.

Trips include walking on islands, and looking at flora and fauna as well as paddling. And, of course, there's the intermittent frisson of riding those churning rapids. Craft are solid and well-balanced klepper canoes – so don't worry about the constant duckings novices might experience in faster but less stable eskimo-style kayaks. And should you end up in the Zambezi, you'll be soaked but safe – guides and assistants are on hand to haul you out if you capsize. Under the guidance of these trained professionals you can be assured that safety is primary and also that you'll get first class commentary on local natural history.

One popular trip takes two and a half days. The first afternoon offers a long game drive through the Zambezi National Park to get to the first night's camp. Each night is spent under canvas in two-person tents; camps are prepared ahead with meals cooked by camp staff. During the day, your belongings are carried by vehicle to the next evening's stop while you travel light on the river.

On a typical day you'll paddle along extensive stretches between rapids with the chance of seeing the national park's wildlife from the water. Elephants are plentiful along this stretch and for birders there's the chance of getting close to the local waterfowl as you float by.

Kandahar Safaris runs both **white-water canoeing** and **canoe adventure** safaris between April and October inclusive. White-water trips last anything from half a day (too rushed) up to three days, with prices from US$85. The three-day Kazungula to Victoria Falls trip runs only from April to the end of June and costs about US$500. *Kandahar's* adventure safaris are equally divided between walking and canoeing, with prices starting at just under US$200 for one day and US$600 for four.

Frontiers' white-water trips are similar to *Kandahar's*, with the advantage that they run an extended season from April to the end of November.

Horse safaris

A prime way to see game is from **horseback**. The *Zambezi Horse Trails* outings give a rare chance to see the bush, with informed commentary. Two-hour rides start at the outskirts of town and follow the river to end up at the national park boundary – rather tame-sounding, perhaps, but we saw a huge herd of buffalo just outside town and plenty of antelope, warthogs and birds. During the dry season, lions and elephants come right to the outskirts. The most impressive thing about the trip is the prodigious information that spills from the guide – she's illuminating, not just about mammals and birds, but also the insects and vegetation.

The **rides** include refreshments, and leave at 6.30am, 12.30pm and 4pm from the stables at Courtenay Selous Crescent/Parkway. Full-day rides last from 9.30am until 4pm and include lunch, and in addition, for experienced riders, an overnight outing is available.

Zambezi Horse Trails is the sole operator running equine safaris at Victoria Falls. Prices start at around US$35 for half-day rides, which are open to novices. For the experienced, the choice ranges from full-day rides to four-night fully backed up safaris, and the prices from US$125 to just under US$1000. Bookings can be made through *Shearwater*.

Game trails

Foot safaris are a lot more interesting than driving around in search of game. Though you'll actually see fewer animals than on a drive, because you cover less ground, what you do see is more intensely witnessed. There's nothing like hearing branches cracking next to you and glimpsing the horns of a buffalo as it turns tail and crashes into the thicket.

Guides are reassuringly armed and the stringent standards necessary to obtain a licence in Zimbabwe ensure they're able not only to halt a charging elephant, but also know everything you ever wanted to know about the bush. Before you set out, there's an interesting safety talk about what to do if you meet a lion or encounter enraged buffalo, elephant or rhino. In reality you probably won't have such encounters, but the thought certainly keeps you on your toes. All walks include meals or refreshments in beautiful spots on the river bank.

Backpacker's Africa (book through *Shearwater)* have the most exciting choice of foot safaris anywhere in Zimbabwe including trips and activities offered by no one else. Apart from their standard backed-up safaris, where a vehicle carries the luggage while

you walk unencumbered, they run intrepid excursions (by prior arrangement) for outward bound types who want to carry all their own stuff. The advantage of this of course is that you can go deep into places vehicles can't reach. They take substantial foot safaris (backed up) into the dramatic broken country of rarely visited **Chizarira National Park** – great fun and highly recommended. Most ambitious is their 12-day **Rhino Safari**, which sets

ADVENTURE BOOKINGS

Victoria Falls

Dabula Safaris
Parkway, PO Box 210 (☎4453; Fax 4453; Telex 51687 ABERCROM).

Frontiers
Victoria Falls Centre, Parkway (next to Wimpy), PO Box 35 (☎4267 or ☎4268; Fax 4225; Telex 51649).

Kalambeza Safaris
PO Box 121 (☎4644; Telex 51668 ZW).

Shearwater Adventures
Shop 6 Victoria Falls Centre (off Parkway), PO Box 125 (☎4471 or ☎4472; Fax 4341; Telex 51662 SOS ZW).

Safari Travel Agency
Avis Garage, Livingstone Way, PO Box 185 (☎4571 or ☎4426; Telex 51664 SAF TVF).

United Touring Company (UTC)
Zimbank Building, Livingstone Way (☎4267 or ☎4268).

Livingstone

Sobek Expeditions
Katombara Rd, PO Box 60957, Livingstone, Zambia (☎321432; Fax 323542; Telex 24018).

Harare

Safari Par Excellence Trustee House
55 Samora Machel Ave, PO Box 5920 (☎720527, ☎700911 or ☎700912; Fax 722872; Telex 22171 SFLINK).

Shearwater Adventures
5th Floor, Karigamombe Centre, Samora Machel Ave, PO Box 3961 (☎735712; Fax 735716; Telex 26391 SWATER ZW).

South Africa

Safari Par Excellence
3rd Floor, 328 Kent Ave, Randburg 2194, South Africa (Johannesburg ☎787 9500 or ☎787 9956; Fax 787 9757).

USA

Sobek Expeditions USA
Angels Camp, CA 95222 (☎736 2661).

out in search of these threatened ungulates in Chizarira, but also takes in Kazuma Pan and Zambezi National Park as well as the **Shakwankie Wilderness Area** of Hwange National Park. They are the only operators allowed into this untrodden section of the game reserve, and the trip provides the chance to join a select club in seeing a region of water seeps, which are the only year-round source of natural water in this vast game reserve and consequently a great attraction to Hwange's wildlife.

Kalambeza Safaris have standard **packages**, from morning walks in the Zambezi National Park to three-day safaris in Kazuma Pan (see p.185). They'll usually take a minimum of two people and pick you up wherever you're staying. Prices for both operators start at around US$75 for a half-day walk, rising to US$200 per day for longer fully inclusive safaris.

Listings

Air Zimbabwe (☎4136) have offices in the main administrative block, Livingstone Way, opposite the *Makasa Sun*.

Air Botswana is close to *Air Zimbabwe* in Livingstone Way.

Airport (☎4250 or ☎4552).

Banks in same block as *Air Zimbabwe* in Livingstone Way. Open Mon, Tues, Thurs & Fri 8.30am–12.30pm; Wed 8.30–11am; Sat 8–11am. If you arrive in the afternoon when banks are closed, try changing money at one of the hotels.

Bicycle rental at *Avis* garage, Livingstone Way adjacent to the *Makasa Sun Hotel*; closer to the campsite at *Michael's* in Parkway; outside the *Victoria Falls Hotel*; at the *Sprayview Hotel* or at *Randdik Enterprises*, 309 Parkway.

Border Post open daily 6am–6pm.

Car rental *Avis*, Livingstone Way, adjacent to the *Makasa Sun Hotel* (☎4532) and *Hertz*, across the road (☎4267 or ☎4268).

Coach *Ajay* to Hwange and Bulawayo (Bulawayo ☎62521).

Doctor Town Council Surgery, West Drive off Parkway (☎4319). Mon–Fri 7.30am–4pm.

Emergencies (☎99).

Hospital Pioneer Rd (☎4692 or ☎4693).

National Parks information Bulawayo end of Livingstone Way (☎426520), can arrange Zambezi National Park accommodation.

Police Livingstone Way (☎4206 or ☎4401).

Post office in same complex as *Air Zimbabwe*.

Tourist Information Centre Parkway/Livingstone Way (☎4202).

THE UPPER ZAMBEZI

Few travellers come to Victoria Falls with the express intention of spotting **wildlife**, although astonished visitors were, a couple of years back, treated to the spectacle of a dead hippo plunging down the thundering smoke and into the abyss. Freak incidents aside, the area around the Falls does provide some extremely fine opportunities to see animals in lush riverine surroundings. In fact, from the Falls you can arrange some of Zimbabwe's best outings into the wild.

The nearby **Zambezi National Park** is the most accessible area of the Upper Zambezi, with the possibility of getting in on your own, so long as you have your own transport. For the intrepid the National Parks **fishing camps** on the Zambezi offer a thrilling and lonely taste of the wild – only advisable if you have steel nerves and excellent bush knowledge. Yet further upriver, however, toward the **Botswana border** your only way in is by spending a night at one of the luxury safari lodges set in inspiring riverine country.

Zambezi National Park

Daily 6am–6.30pm. Weekly entrance fee.

Six kilometres upstream from the Falls begins the **ZAMBEZI NATIONAL PARK**. You can ride rented bikes to lodges at the park's edge, but not into the park itself. Take Parkway, which becomes a narrow strip road with bush all around; pass the deserted *Elephant Hills Hotel* and, at the point when the *A'Zambezi* appears on your right you're nearly there.

The park is best known for its large herds of **sable antelope**. Elephants and rhinos are gratifyingly common and kudu, impala, waterbuck, zebra, lion, leopard and hyena are all about for the conscientious spotter. **With a car**, there are lovely riverside **picnic sites** where you can recline in palmy shade and contemplate the flow. The odd fruits under the palm trees that look like cricket balls or exotic animal droppings are the remains of the **mulala fruits**, much prized by elephants. They eat them whole, digesting the succulent outer fruit and depositing the inner seed in a ready-made grow-bag. Remarkably, the old seasonal elephant migration routes are marked by effectively dispersed cross-country lines of mulala palms. In the riverine woods you'll also find ebony trees, figs and *Acacia albida*.

There are two main **roads** through the park, the most popular being the Zambezi Drive which continues past the lodges along the river. The other option is to take the turn-off 6km south of town on the Bulawayo Road to join the Chamabonda Drive, which follows the course of the Masui River.

The National Park Lodges

Facing the Zambezi, the Park's wonderful self-catering **lodges** are laid out for **maximum isolation** – with riverine forest separating each – so you really do feel alone. In the swathes cleared between lodge and river you'll spot buck, monkeys, warthogs and plenty of birds. Occasionally **elephants** stray into the lodge gardens and in the dry season they sometimes swim across from the mainland to the islands of Lwanda and Kalunda opposite the lodges, midway between Zimbabwe and Zambia.

The lodges (book ahead, as usual, through the Harare office) are officially only available from 2pm but if they were vacant the night before you can move in earlier. You can also try your luck if you're already in town at the National Parks office in Livingstone Way. Bring all your food from the Falls or eat at the *A'Zambezi*.

There are **walks** along the river in front of the lodges. Keep your eyes peeled for smaller animals: **turtles** bask on the banks and splash waterwards for safety and you can even see baby **crocodiles** on tree branches that stroke the water's surface. Beware any bigger specimens, and the occasional elephant that wanders through.

Birds are also prolific: cormorants, darters and kingfishers perch on half-submerged dead trees waiting for the right fish to swim by. Hadedas wander about on the grassy margins. The name of these large grey birds is inspired by their raucous call, a familiar Zambezi sound.

Fishing Camps

The National Park **fishing camps**, further up the river off the Zambezi River Game Drive, are in wilder locations than the lodges. You don't have to go fishing to enjoy the magnificence of the undisturbed bush and river but you need tough nerves to enjoy sleeping virtually in the open. While it's a thoroughly recommended experience, however, you do need your own transport to get there.

Of the camps, Kandahar (a few kilometres upstream from *A'Zambezi Lodge*) is open throughout the year. Further upstream, Sansimba (30km) and Mpala Jena (17km) are open during the dry season only (May–Oct). Facilities are basic: concrete shelters, cold showers, flush toilet and drinking taps. There are *braai* places, and you can buy limited firewood at reception, but take your own cooking gear. They all need to be booked in advance at the Central Booking Office in Harare.

The Safari Lodges

Two of the country's best bush camps are in the region of the Upper Zambezi near Kazungula. Both **Imbabala Safari Camp** and **Westwood Safari Lodge** offer en-suite thatched accommodation, game drives, boating, fishing and canoeing (see p.161). The Zambezi flood plain around Kazungula offers birding enthusiasts the chance of sightings they'll get nowhere else in Zimbabwe. The region consists of beautifully shaded riverine forest and flood plain. At Imbabala there've been lion kills on the lawns in front of the lodges and herds of waterbuck have in the past made their resting place there.

OVER THE BORDER

The Victoria Falls mark the meeting place of three of Zimbabwe's neighbours. **Botswana**'s main cross-border attraction is Chobe Game Reserve, easily reached by road at Kasane – which is also the gateway to the Caprivi Strip, the onward corridor to **Namibia** and Botswana's **Western Okavango Delta**. And **Zambia**, just a few hundred metres across the Zambezi, is easy to visit for the day or even a couple of hours. For more details on **onward travel** to Zambia and Namibia, see *Contexts*, p.394.

Into Zambia

You can get a special one-day pass without undue formality to cross to the **Zambian side of the Falls**. The distance is easily walkable but expect the trip to take a couple of hours on foot if you include the lengthy queues to clear Customs and Immigration on both sides.

Zambia, formerly Northern Rhodesia, had a special place in the demonology of the last generation of Rhodesians and continued into the 1990s to exert a morbid fascination in some circles south of the border. The supposed breakdown of civilisation after Independence in 1964 was considered living proof of the need for eternal white rule. Kenneth Kaunda, president until 1991, was branded by many Rhodesians and South Africans as a Marxist bent on destroying Christian values.

While, in retrospect, Kaunda led his country down the dead-end road of one-party corruption and mismanagement, he appears to have retained more personal integrity than most other African leaders. Kaunda was a devout Christian, if a misguided one, who tried to synthesise Christianity and Socialism into an authentically African philosophy that he dubbed "Humanism".

That Kaunda left Zambia in a shambles is indisputable. But some credit is due to him for the gracious – and for Africa virtually unprecedented – way in which he peacefully accepted the people's judgement and stood down after being defeated in democratic elections by Frederick Chiluba.

The Zambian Falls

Once in Zambia, head for **Knife Edge Point** which is, without doubt, the most awesome view of the Falls. You reach it on a path which winds down to a slippery, spray-dashed footbridge and onto an island of high ground where the water roars deafeningly around you. You can also descend to the very bottom of the **Boiling Pot** gorge and watch from a safe distance as the powerful river surges into a terrific whirlpool.

These oblique, rather than head-on, views from Zambia are very different from those from the Zimbabwean side and the gorges are displayed with much more clarity.

The "tourist show" on this side of the Falls, however, is more tattered: no well-kept national park to grace the scene, just a half-broken, sad memorial plinth to the Northern Rhodesian war dead. The **Field Museum**, built around a small archaeological dig, has prehistoric hand tools and elementary wall displays of information about local finds.

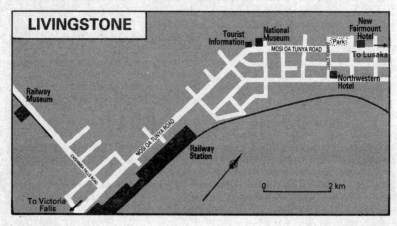

Next door, the **Craft Village** – its stallholders desperate to sell – offers much run-of-the-mill stuff, but also some items that are quite different from Zimbabwean craftwork. There's excellent **basketry** and colourfully decorated **wooden guinea fowls**. If you're bartering, clothes, and particularly T-shirts, are much sought after.

Near the boat club, from which the Zambian sundowner cruises leave, there's the **Mosi oa Tunya Gamepark**. As parks go, this is rather pitiful and really doesn't merit a visit unless you're not going to any of the far better reserves nearby.

Livingstone

For a peek at **Zambia proper**, make a sortie into **Livingstone**, 11km on from the Zambian side of the Falls. Now run-down, this former Falls capital remains a more convincing urban centre than its upstart successor in Zimbabwe. Its main attraction is the National Museum, which displays a host of beautiful artefacts from all over Africa.

Mosi oa Tunya Road runs all the way from the border, slicing through Livingstone's centre. About halfway, you pass the **Maramba Cultural Centre**. The weekend **traditional dancing** here, from 3pm until 5pm, draws tourists and locals. There are also performances on Fridays between June and October, and it works out cheaper than the "Africa Spectacular" at the *Victoria Falls Hotel*.

Once you cross the Maramba River, you meet Livingstone's industrial suburbs trailing into the countryside. You're close to the **centre** of town when you can hear shouts from the sidewalks offering packets of kwacha for dollars. You'll have many approaches – people openly play the blackmarket.

The National Museum

Daily 9am–4.30pm (except Christmas and New Year). Nominal entrance fee.

The **National Museum** is a peculiar place, containing some of the most interesting ethnological items in the region, yet with little explanation – stimulating and mystifying by turn. Helpful Zambian visitors, however, might offer illumination. For this is the country's main museum and is highly popular, attracting Zambians from all over. Among its many and various collections are displays of weaponry, hunting equipment, reconstructed villages and the cape, trunk, thermometer and surgical instruments of David Livingstone.

The collection of **religious fetishes** is fascinating and ghoulish. There's a very fine range of **Tonga artefacts** from the Gwembe Valley, collected before it was flooded to create Kariba, including headrests, stools and a finely decorated waist-high drum used to send long-distance messages at night.

On the ground floor, one of the most interesting exhibits is the **Broken Hill Man of Kabwe** – a copy of the 110,000-year-old Neanderthal skull found in 1921. Our Neanderthal precursors disappeared from the fossil record some 40,000 years ago. The original skull was stolen by the British and the Zambians are still trying to get it back. In return, the British want David Livingstone's case and instruments. Negotiations continue.

In the same part of the museum as the Livingstone memorabilia are some revealing **old photographs**. Don't miss the picture of four Arab traders examining an African slave. The hopeless look on the manacled man's face is tangibly painful, while the arrogance of those around has to be seen to be believed. Nearer the present, the story of Zambia's **path to Independence** is told through press cuttings and photos.

The Railway Museum

Daily 10am–5.30pm. Nominal entrance fee.

The turning to the **Railway Museum** is clearly signposted on your left as you approach the centre of town. Opened in 1987, it aims to educate Zambians about the importance of the railways. A yard full of decrepit coaches and engines lets everyone indulge childhood fantasies; clamber up and fiddle with the knobs or walk down the corridors of decaying carriages.

Inside, rooms full of antique rail souvenirs evoke the old days: wood and brass morse code machines and gleaming brass signal lamps. Exhibits also give accounts of the development of railways in Europe and Africa along with loads of photos.

Into Botswana: Chobe

Botswana's **Chobe National Park** is Africa's top **elephant sanctuary**, with a population estimated at as many as 50,000. Touching Botswana's river-bounded northern frontier, the parts near Zimbabwe consist of beautiful flood plain with abundant birds and the continent's southernmost population of **red lechwe** antelope.

The only reliable way to get to Botswana (and a pricey one at around $US30 one-way) is on the daily *UTC* **bus** plying the Falls–Chobe route. This will drop off at any of the hotels or lodges in KASANE, just outside the game reserve. *UTC* also does an expensive one-day **excursion** to Chobe – or two days for the well-heeled with an overnight at the exclusive *Chobe Game Lodge*. The big hotels offer transfers for clients and frequently return empty. Drivers are sometimes prepared to carry passengers for a small fee.

For more details on this region, see Chapter Eight.

HWANGE NATIONAL PARK

Once regarded as a vast wasteland, useless for farming, **HWANGE NATIONAL PARK** is now Zimbabwe's premier wildlife showcase. During August, September and October, the **game-watching** can be truly spectacular: the park has a shifting population of around 40,000 elephants, and a huge variety of animals and birds. And the great advantage of Hwange is that it is accessible, whether on a tour or doing it your own way using the park's budget accommodation. A number of privately run game lodges and bush camps let you get into remoter parts of the park and surrounds you wouldn't reach under your own steam.

It's only fair to point out, however, that you need to have luck on your side if you're dead set on seeing the big cats, or action as exciting as a lion kill. Frustratingly, you may repeatedly hear about the wonderful things seen by others the day before, or the bounding cheetah and the lion cubs you just missed. If you visit during the **rains**, you may not even clock an elephant. There's the story of a foreign tourist who complained that he had spent a whole day in the park and seen nothing except a pair of tortoises; the game ranger replied that he was actually very lucky as they're not often seen in pairs. Don't be too big-game oriented – take your binoculars and a good field guide, and relax.

GAME–VIEWING AT HWANGE

Hwange's highest concentrations of game are during the **dry season** (May–Oct) when animals congregate around the pans. Once the rains come and there's surface water they disperse all over the park, while long grass after the start of the rains tends to screen the animals from view.

If you plan to do some serious game-viewing, it is well worth getting hold of some **field guides** (see "Books", p.411, for recommendations).

• **Binoculars** are a must for scanning the horizon when you're out viewing. Don't try consciously to spot animals – many are well disguised. Instead, watch for any movement or something which strikes you as a bit out of place. Driving really slowly also pays off, particularly if you stop often. You can sometimes see more in a stationary hour alongside a pan than in a day's frantic driving.

• **Viewing platforms** at the major pans frequently provide the best chance to see something. High off the ground they give good, unobscured panoramas of the surroundings. All animals have to drink at some time.

• **Time of Day** Early morning is the best animal-watching time, when you'll see some of the nocturnals slinking off and others feeding before they hide away in the shade. Dusk is almost as good and certainly the best time to see elephants drinking. The usual pattern for safari operators is three game drives a day: dawn, mid-morning and dusk. An appetite-whetting chart at Main Camp reception shows exactly what you'll see when and each beast's cycle: lions for example, usually drink early, rest in the heat and hunt in the late afternoon.

• **Temperatures** Because it's on the edge of the Kalahari, temperatures in Hwange are extreme, particularly just before the rains and during the summer dry season when it can soar to the high 30°s (C) during the day. Nights, however, are always cool and in the dry season can drop below freezing. Whatever the season, always take a sweater on game drives, especially in the early morning, and in the dry season an anorak won't come amiss.

History

Spreading across 14,620 square kilometres of dry bush country, Hwange was formerly peopled by **San** hunter-gatherers able to survive with little water: the region covers the easternmost edge of the Kalahari, with little surface water, but plenty underground supporting ample vegetation. The National Park was created in 1929 largely because the land was hopeless for agriculture, and borehole water pumped into over sixty pans began attracting large numbers of animals. It's to these pans, several of which are around Main Camp, that visitors also are drawn.

Before adventurers and hunters arrived, parts of Hwange formed a royal **Ndebele hunting reserve**. Dete Vlei, where *Hwange Safari Lodge* is now sited, was later a favourite elephant-hunting ground for **Frederick Selous**, most famous of Zimbabwe's Victorian adventurers. Two hunting areas still adjoin the park, where the rich pay thousands to bag trophies.

Orientation

The public section of Hwange merely skims the eastern edge of the reserve. The bulk of the park, bordering Botswana, is trackless, harsh and off limits. Hwange's thornbush, savannah, mopane and teak forests aren't as spectacular as the landscapes of the great East African parks – there are no huge mountains, craters or vast plains – but the bush savannah has its own striking beauty, the tracks are considerably less worn and you'll be able to see the same game without thousands of tourists dogging your heels.

A number of **luxury bush camps** operate in exclusive concessions inside the park or in the bordering forest lands and safari areas, which all share Hwange's wildlife. All meet their clients at Hwange National Park Airport. You can also arrange to be picked up at *Hwange Safari Lodge*.

If you're keen on a **hotel-based holiday** then other options are to stay at *Hwange Safari Lodge*, the *Game Reserve Hotel* in Dete or *Gwayi River Lodge*, on the Bulawayo to Victoria Falls road, from which game drives into the national park can be arranged.

The next best thing to having your own vehicle – and more adventurous than staying in a hotel or bush camp – is to join one of the **mobile safaris** which take you around Hwange and spend nights inside the park's boundaries.

Getting to Hwange

Despite being outside the reserve boundaries, for independent travellers *Hwange Safari Lodge* effectively acts as the travel terminal for the park. On the main road into Hwange, it's 12km from Main Camp. Beside the obvious attractions of its exceedingly pretty setting, with a swimming pool, lawns that fade off into the bush and its own private water holes which attract wildlife, you're assured of **transport into the park** from here.

If you just want to **get to Main Camp**, the principal gateway to the park itself (see p.181), then hop on the *UTC* game drive, or hitch. There is also a *Hertz* office at the lodge, where you can **hire cars** for a half day or more, if available; you can't, however, drive them through the park to Sinamatella or Robins camps, and they're only for use around Main Camp where the roads are good.

By car

With your own vehicle there's a choice of entering the national park via Natwich or Sinamatella camps in the northwest or Main Camp in the northeast. The first two are reached by means of gravel roads of variable quality. Main Camp remains the most straightforward route in, being the only camp reachable by tar.

If you drive **from Bulawayo, GWAYI RIVER**, the halfway stop between Bulawayo and Victoria Falls, consists of little more than a **hotel**. The *Gwayi River Hotel* at km peg 247 (PO Box 9, Dete; ☎3400; ④) is an old-style country hotel with a charm of its own, having expanded and modernised in the wake of Zimbabwe's 1990s mini-boom in tourism. *Shamwari Safaris* has a professional guide who runs reasonably priced **game drives** into Hwange National Park (enquire at the hotel). *Ajay* makes a stop here for tea before pulling into *Hwange Safari Lodge* and the final leg to Hwange town and the Falls.

The hotel is the centre for the **Gwayi River Valley** – a district of enormous cattle ranches, many of which are now being turned into **game farms.** After decades of shooting predators and struggling to raise cattle, against the odds in terrain that is ideal wildlife country, a number of farmers have seen the wisdom of doing away with domestic stock and encouraging wild animals in the hope of attracting tourists. Some of these farms are close to Hwange and with trips into the park provide a cheaper alternative to staying in a bush camp (see Hwange Accommodation).

Those more distant from the reserve trade on other attractions, such as **birdwatching or walking safaris.** *Mzola Wilderness Trails*, operated by *Nemba Safaris*, PO Box 4, Gwayi (☎Lupane 035 33; Telex 51635 NEMBA ZW), is one of the best such operations. Based on a private ranch, the three-day trails operate along flood plain and in the wilderness regions between the Mzola, Shangani and Karna rivers. Bird life is rich and there are good animal populations. An armed professional guide sets out each morning with groups of up to six people, ending each day at a different camp. Nights are spent in comfortable tree houses and all equipment is provided. *Nemba* also offers two-stop packages combining *Mzola Wilderness Trails* with stays at their sister camp in the Linkwasha area, deep in Hwange National Park (see Hwange Accommodation).

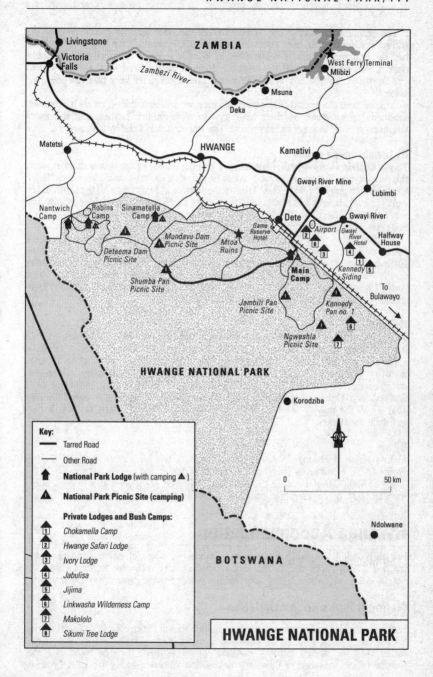

ZAMBIA

Livingstone
Victoria Falls
Zambezi River
West Ferry Terminal
Mlibizi
Msuna
Deka
Matetsi
HWANGE
Kamativi
Gwayi River Mine
Lubimbi
Nantwich Camp
Robins Camp
Sinamatella Camp
Dete
Gwayi River
Halfway House
Deteema Dam Picnic Site
Mundavu Dam Picnic Site
Mtoa Ruins
Game Reserve Hotel
Airport
Gwayi River Hotel
Shumba Pan Picnic Site
Main Camp
Kennedy Siding
To Bulawayo
Jambili Pan Picnic Site
Kennedy Pan no. 1
Ngweshla Picnic Site

HWANGE NATIONAL PARK

Korodziba

0   50 km

Ndolwane

BOTSWANA

Key:

Tarred Road

Other Road

National Park Lodge (with camping ▲)

National Park Picnic Site (camping)

Private Lodges and Bush Camps:
1 Chokamella Camp
2 Hwange Safari Lodge
3 Ivory Lodge
4 Jabulisa
5 Jijima
6 Linkwasha Wilderness Camp
7 Makololo
8 Sikumi Tree Lodge

HWANGE NATIONAL PARK

The penultimate port of call is **HWANGE**, the only sizeable place en route – a stifling **coalmining town** of absolutely no interest. Named after a local Rozvi chief, it had the undignified colonial misspelling of Wankie – which it shared with the game park. If you need to **spend the night** in Hwange Town, head for the *Baobab Hotel* (☎323; ③) on top of a hill on the Bulawayo side of town; it's very pleasant and good value.

Around here the grazed-out communal lands are arid and stoney, rivers become dry sandbeds, goats stand on their hind legs to nibble thorn bushes, and the gaunt longhorned cattle look precarious assets. The last stretch is lined by teak forests.

By thumb, coach or bus

To get to Main Camp, whether **hitching** or coming on one of the **buses** that run along the Bulawayo to Victoria Falls road, ask to be put off at the crossroads known as "Safari Cross" which goes to Gwayi River Mine to the north and Main Camp to the south. If you can't get a lift straight into Main Camp then make for *Hwange Safari Lodge*, exactly half-way between Safari Cross and Main Camp. Even better, is to take the Bulawayo–Victoria Falls **coaches** run by *Ajay Motorways*, which conveniently drop off at the lodge.

An alternative route into Hwange National Park, though a far less certain one if you're without a car, is to go via **Sinamatella Camp**, west of Main Camp, from Hwange town. You can try **hitching** to Sinamatella from the turn-off just before town on the Bulawayo side. *Ajay* will drop you off here but traffic is sparse along the 45-km road. If you don't get any lifts, it's easy enough to spend the night at the *Baobab Hotel* outside town or to carry on to the Falls or Bulawayo.

By train

Taking the **train** to the park's nearest station at Dete is a poor idea. From Victoria Falls it's timetabled to arrive at Dete at 11.13pm – and from Bulawayo it's even worse, at 1.26am. In any case the precision suggested by these times can't be relied on. If you're intent on this approach, the *Game Reserve Hotel* (☎366), 300m from the station, has cheap rooms, but you're advised to phone to tell them you're coming, otherwise you'll find it closed. Once the park's only hotel, it's now run-down and the favoured drinking spot for all the railway workers. With prior warning, *Hwange Safari Lodge* will meet guests at the station.

By air

Flights arrive at Hwange National Park Airport, a few kilometres north of *Hwange Safari Lodge*. **Minibuses** operated by *UTC* meet planes and convey passengers to the lodge or Main Camp. Because the service is well used, it's a good idea to book ahead from any *UTC* office. The safari camps all meet clients arriving at the airport.

Hwange Accommodation

For the mobile Hwange is a dream to travel around on a budget, either camping or staying in National Parks chalets. Without a vehicle you're restricted to Main Camp, the hotels on the outskirts or luxury safari lodges, which provide game drives and transfers.

National Parks accommodation

Hwange provides budget accommodation in its National Parks chalets and self-catering lodges (see *Basics*, p.43, for an explanation of facilities) – built for the local market rather than for foreign tourists. Booking for all of these through National Parks' Central Offices in Harare or Bulawayo makes life a lot easier once you arrive; if you just turn up you may have to vacate your lodge each morning until they reallocate accommodation. Any vacant lodges are let from 4pm onwards. Camping is also permitted at the picnic sites, which are fenced in – but you must have a tent.

Camps
Further details on each camp are given on pages 181–185.

Main Camp. Situated in the most visited eastern section of the game reserve it has lodges, chalets, cottages and camping. You can cater for yourself using communal electric cooking facilities. Lodges and chalets have electric lights and fridges in each living unit. A bar and restaurant add a touch of comfort and a store sells basic items. Good value if you can get a booking. ①–②.

Nantwich Camp, 11km from Robins, (below), to which visitors must report before continuing. Accommodation is in lodges. ①–②.

Robins Camp. In the northwest section of the national park, Robins is the second of the three major Hwange camps, reached along a dirt track off the main Hwange to Victoria Falls. It's 48km to the turnoff and a further 70km to the camp itself. It can also be reached from Main Camp. Lodges, chalets, camping and an exclusive camp. There are no restaurant or bar facilities, although there is a store. Game-viewing roads in the vicinity are closed Nov–April (inclusive). ①–②.

Sinamatella Camp. To the west of Robins, but accessible from Hwange town. Take the turnoff (just south of the town on the main Bulawayo–Hwange road), which soon becomes a dirt track and passes *Mbala Lodge* before continuing the 45km to Sinamatella. The situation on a plateau gives wonderful vistas of the plains below. Similar facilities to Main Camp, including restaurant and bar. ①–②.

Exclusive Camps
All in the Robins-Sinamatella region, each of Hwange's exclusive camps is bookable by groups of up to twelve which have the entire camp to themselves. **Bumbusi Camp,** 24km northwest of Sinamatella, has four twin Å-frame chalets and a cottage. Cooking and washing/toilet facilities are communal. **Deka Camp,** near Robins, has two family units, a sitting room, a dining room and a kitchen. **Lukosi Camp,** which like Bumbusi is 24km northwest of Sinamatella, has similar facilities to its neighbour but is only open November to April outside the hunting season.

The Picnic Sites
Areas have been fenced off for picnickers at the following pans: **Deteema, Jambili** (near Main Camp), **Kennedy 1, Mandavu** (Sinamatella-Robins vicinity), **Shumba** (midway between Main Camp and Sinamatella), and **Ngweshla.** They have outdoor *braai* facilities and toilets, handbasins and running water. You can camp overnight, provided you have a tent – wildlife can, and does on occasion, leap over the chicken wire fencing in the enclosure.

Hotels
Somewhat less thrilling than being in the bush among the animals, the hotels provide for those who want to leave the call of the wild after dark and return to the comforts of bars, telephones and TV. In truth, only *Hwange Safari Lodge* is expressly geared toward a game-oriented stay, or offers any luxury.

Game Reserve Hotel, PO Box 32, Dete (☎Dete 366). The cheapest hotel around the national park, with a seedy reputation. You can arrange ahead to be picked up from the train, and *UTC* will pick you up for game-viewing trips into the national park. ②.

Hwange Safari Lodge, PO Box 5792, Dete (☎ Dete 331). Located outside the park boundaries with all the comfort you'd expect from a luxury three star establishment with en-suite rooms and drinks by the swimming pool. Game drives are provided and you can watch elephants frolic in the lodge's own drinking hole. Ultimately disappointing, though, if you're after a raw experience of the wild. Both the lodge itself and *UTC* run game drives that start here and pull in at Main Camp; the lodge does game trails on foot when they have a guide available. The lodge charges an entrance fee to non-residents, but it could be worth having access to a poolside drink if you've arrived from a long, hot trek. There's also a viewing platform, which overlooks a pan where you'll usually see some game. ⑦.

Luxury Bush Camps

Upmarket bush camps offering all-inclusive packages are located either inside the park boundaries, in private concessions, or on private land adjoing the national park. Often in exclusive regions, they have the added attraction of expert guidance once you're there. All employ professional guides and offer expertly directed game drives. If you stay at one of the camps in the vicinity of Main Camp or near the airport, you will see other visitors, cars and minibuses; choosing a camp further afield ensures a feeling of exclusivity. Closed to casual visitors, they should be booked ahead. Visitors are met at Hwange airport.

Chokamella Camp, 35km from Hwange airport due west of Main Camp entrance. Book through *Safari Farms*, PO Box 592, Harare (☎733573; Fax 706607; Telex 22084 CFU ZW). A compact camp with 20 beds. Day and night drives are available and the camp has its own exclusive access directly into Hwange. US$160 per person.

The Hide, booked through 7 Lonsdale, King George Rd, PO Box 5615, Harare (☎707438 or ☎707438; Fax 723230; Telex 26503 DUGLDZW). One the eastern border of Hwange, one of the select few camps actually inside the park boundaries, near the Kennedy Pans area. Twice daily, guests are taken walking or by vehicle with a licensed guide. Especially adapted game-viewing hides, each overlooking a waterhole, make it ideal for photographers. Accommodation in safari-style tents with en-suite facilities, limited to 16 guests. From US$250 per person.

Ivory Lodge, near Main Camp (PO Box 55, Dete; ☎3402). Book through *Ivory Safaris*, PO Box 9127, Hillside, Bulawayo (☎61709; Telex:33133). One of the most imaginatively conceived of all the lodges around Hwange. On the edge of the Zingweni Vlei, *Ivory* breaks with the usual style of tended lawns and has instead left intact as much as possible of the indigenous bush. The disadvantage is that there are no long views across flattened countryside, but this is more than compensated for by the feeling of being in the wild. Accommodation is in 10 thatched tree houses, each with its own shower and toilet. US$200 per person.

Jabulisa, PO Box 19, Gwayi (☎118 2101 or ☎118 2306; Telex 51612 DEN ZW). Built around an old farmhouse high on a ridge overlooking both the Sikumi Vlei and Gwayi River Valley. *Jabulisa* is one of the few lodges that permits children. Guests can arrange to be met at Hwange Airport, or *Gwayi River Hotel* if arriving on the *Ajay* bus. If you're arriving by car you can also be met at the hotel by lodge staff. There are seven thatched en-suite bungalows with twin beds. US$200 per person.

Jijima, overlooking Jijima Vlei on a private estate bordering the national park. Book through *Wild Horizons*, PO Box 159, Victoria Falls (☎4219 or ☎4349; Telex 51685). *Jijima* is owned and operated by a family of two generations of professional guides. If you want to hear ripping yarns about close shaves with lions then this could be just the place. Jijima uses the Kennedy Pan – *the* place for lions and less crowded than the Main Camp area – for game-viewing. Accommodation is in safari tents under thatched canopies and the number of guests is limited to 16. US$235 per person.

Kanondo Tree Camp, booked through *Touch the Wild*, Pvt Bag 5779, Dete (☎273; Telex 51604 ZW TTW). Just 20min by vehicle from Hwange airport, the camp is set among a stand of camelthorn acacias on a private concession next to the game reserve. Six en-suite twin-bedded tree houses are grouped around a central area. Each has its own view of the waterhole which is regularly visited by special herd of elephants that is protected in perpetuity by a presidential decree. US$240 per person.

Linkwasha Wilderness Camp, *Nemba*, PO Box 4, Gwayi (☎Lupane 0353 3; Telex 51635 NEMBA ZW). Takes its name from the area in which it stands – four hours drive through game country from the airport. Linkwasha Camp is one of the few private bush camps inside Hwange National Park itself. Apart from visiting *Linkwasha* or *Makololo*, there's no other way of seeing this astonishingly beautiful section of Hwange. Vast open plains punctuated with Ilala palms and waterholes, which attract profuse game and bird life, form a landscape that resembles the plains of East Africa more than any other area you're likely to see in Zimbabwe. Probably the most thrilling camp in Zimbabwe, it has played host to the likes of Gerald Durrell. There are no fences here and wildlife is free to roam through the camp at will. Accommodation for a maximum of 14 guests is provided in safari tents under thatch, with en-suite facilities. The dining area is in the shade of a massive leadwood tree. On full moon nights guests can spend the night viewing game from a hide next to a water hole. US$270 per person.

Makololo Camp, booked through *Touch the Wild*, Pvt Bag 5779, Dete (☎273; Telex 51604 ZW TTW). Set under palm trees on the banks of Makolo Pan, this is one of the oldest of the Hwange safari lodges. In the same exquisite vicinity as *Nemba*, with a maximum capacity of 24 guests it doesn't quite match the intimacy of its neighbour, but nevertheless offers a rare experience of a little-visited region of Zimbabwe's number one game reserve. Accommodation is in large tents and there are showers and flush toilets. US$240 per person.

Sable Valley Lodge booked through *Touch the Wild*, Pvt Bag 5779, Dete (☎273; Telex 51604 ZW TTW). Set in the teak woodlands of Sable Valley estate, a 250 sq km private area adjacent to Hwange, the lodge is just 20 minutes' drive from the airport. Because the estate has seen no hunting or culling for over two decades wildlife tends to be less skittish than elsewhere in the region. Manicured lawns add to the sense of luxury and the whole complex is surrounded by an electrified fence to keep animals out at night. Eleven en-suite thatched bungalows accommodate a maximum of 22 people. US$240 per person.

Sikumi Tree Lodge, booked through *Touch the Wild*, Pvt Bag 5779, Dete (☎273; Telex 51604 ZW TTW). In the Sikumi Forest, not far from *Hwange Safari Lodge* and a few minutes drive from the airport. Guided walks in the forest are among the activities offered. One of the handful of lodges permitting children. Accommodation is in tree houses – huts on stilts built among the trees rather than attached to them – with en-suite facilities. US$240 per person.

Sotani Lodge, booked through *Sotani Wilderness Safaris*, PO Box 902, Bulawayo (☎67326; Fax 77113). On the southern end of Hwange National Park adjacent to the Ngamo Forest. Guests are collected from Victoria Falls or Hwange or you can drive there. Walking trails are offered as well as drives into the Kennedy section of the national park. Particularly suited to keen photographers, there are a number of comfortable hides built at several waterholes. Just four luxury thatched chalets ensure intimacy. No price available.

Main Camp and Around

For most people the gateway into Hwange is **MAIN CAMP**. Touring the Park by car you'll start or finish here and without your own transport it's about as far as you'll get. But you don't need to venture much further to get an eyeful of game. The immediate surroundings of the camp have the park's highest concentrations: the **Ten-Mile Drive** between Main Camp and Nyamandlovu Pan regularly shows off all the animals one could hope for. Lions sometimes lie on the road in the evening – the fact that it's tarred doesn't seem to deter them – and elephants often water at **Nyamandlovu Pan** and nearby **Dom Pan**. Even if the lions evade you you're bound to see giraffe, zebra, wildebeest, waterbuck, sable, impala, kudu and buffalo.

Main Camp is situated on Kalahari sand, shaded by aptly named *Acacia giraffae*, arching over the bar and restaurant. Walks, campsites and onward **bookings for other Hwange camps** can all be arranged through Main Camp.

The Main Camp **store** stocks supplies of fresh milk, bread, meat and various tinned food – but no fresh fruit or vegetables. The camp **restaurant** is open for breakfast and also serves steaks and one or two vegetarian dishes: despite its monopoly it's reasonably priced. Main Camp's **bar**, next door, is well known locally as a watering hole, and the barman, a great talker, is bent on consolidating his already formidable repertoire of cocktails.

Main Camp is surrounded by teak **forests** that gradually merge into Kalahari woodlands of thorn trees, mixed scrub and grassy clearings. Assuming you're up in the morning, go for a stroll around the clearings to look for antelope. There are certainly always hundreds of **impala** about. Come to Hwange in the rainy season and you're sure to see their young, just

CREATURES OF THE NIGHT

Night animals occupy special places in African mythology. One, which you'll hear at night from Main Camp and may well see on a night walk, is the **hyena** – said to be the consort of witches. Their special status is due to the females' false scrotum and erectile clitoris giving rise to the belief that they're hermaphrodites.

Hyena's powerful jaws and teeth can crunch up the hardest of bones or hides. Even sharp-beaked vultures have to hold back until the hyenas arrive to tear open something with a tough hide like an elephant. Hyena's don't only scavenge, however; they're capable of hunting down animals as large as a wildebeest or zebra. The eerily drawn out *whoo-op* is their usual call, while the famous giggling laugh is usually heard only when they are burrowing into a kill. The commonest are spotted hyenas, but the rare and shy **brown hyena** – found only in southern Africa's arid terrain – are around too.

Pangolins, primitive scaley anteaters, are seldom seen, except stuffed in museums. Nevertheless, at Hwange you may observe them creeping around at night in their search for ants. Holding an important role in local tradition, they're often presented to chiefs or spirit mediums. When Mugabe came into office, scores of pangolins were brought into Harare for him. The intriguing thing about pangolins is their tongues – as long as the head and body combined, enabling them to lick up ants from deep holes. The heavy scales are a protective armour – especially useful when they curl into a fir cone-like ball, which, having alarmed them, is all that most people ever see.

delivered and utterly appealing. Many animals give birth at the onset of the rains when the new grass springs up, but impala can prolong gestation by up to two months if the rains are late or inadequate. If you walk to the edge of the Main Camp offices, you may also spot **giraffe**, heads above the trees, and you're bound to see **zebra** and **wildebeest** on the plains; these two species always graze in company.

Into the Park: Tours, Game Drives and Walks

Getting beyond Main Camp – which is situated at one of the park gates – is pretty easy, and not too expensive. Hitching (and cycling) are prohibited in the park, but you may well meet people at Main Camp who have a car and are willing to take you along.

The hassle-free way to see game is to hop on the *UTC* **tourbus** as it calls in at Main Camp. The *UTC* outing can be frustratingly uninformative, but their drivers are old hands at finding animals.

Game drives, operated by *Hwange Safari Lodge*, are more than twice as expensive, but you pay for the knowledge of eagle-eyed guides, who know their stuff. These tours are also more intimate than the *UTC* offerings – not more than eight people in an open landrover – and the scouts are in radio contact with each other and alert their colleagues to anything exciting. They're able to answer questions on any aspect of wildlife and local ecology and will often make detours off the tar into parts that are further afield.

National Park **escorted walks** (set fee for groups of up to six) are worthwhile, too – and a good way to get out and break the monotony of hanging around Main Camp waiting for transport. Because of their popularity, they are frequently rationed to one outing per person. The guides often do the 2-km walk to the hide at Sedina Pan, where you sit a while and watch. Few cars ever come here, so it's wonderfully quiet. At the time of a full moon, the Parks also do unmissable **night game-viewing**, when you'll have the chance to see some of the more rarely viewed nocturnal species.

An exciting option is to join one of the **mobile safaris** which make use of National Parks campsites and take you to places you'd see no other way. The great thing is that you stay inside the park at night when most other visitors have returned to their hotels or lodges. One of the best such operators is *Africa Dawn Safaris*, PO Box HG 632,

Highlands, Harare (☎707138 or ☎735614; Fax 735615; Telex 26108 CPR ENT ZW) or PO Box 128, Bulawayo (☎46696). Their professional guide has a special knowledge of Hwange stretching back two decades – he was based there as a warden and helped build the fence around the park. Their luxury fully-serviced safaris are US$165 per person per day (inclusive). They also run budget versions for less than half this price, on which guests muck in with cooking and other preparations.

Sinamatella and nearby

Open all year.

SINAMATELLA is smaller than Main Camp and sited in hillier terrain, high up on a granite summit with views over a deep valley favoured by huge herds of buffalo. While it doesn't have the same concentration of game as Main Camp, the surroundings are prettier – it must be one of the most spectacular views anywhere – and there's a network of roads passing through tall mopane forests. A popular local viewing spot and campsite is **Mandavu Dam**, haunt of hippos and crocodiles. There are no *UTC* drives but you can go on **walks** with Parks' guides.

Access and Camps

Most visitors with a car (there's no public transport) get to Sinamatella by driving through the park from Main Camp; day-tripping, you're required to leave by 2pm to make sure you have ample time to complete the journey back before dusk. A tough vehicle is advisable during the rains. Lukosi is only open from May to October, outside the hunting season. There are natural springs near Bumbusi, which attract game, especially in the dry season. An underground hide has been constructed at one of them for close-up photography.

Nantwich, Robins and Deka

Closed Nov–March.

These three northwestern camps – the smallest and most secluded camps in Hwange – are out of reach unless you have a car. Specific details of the **accommodation** facilities are given on p.179.

LIONS AND WILD DOGS

Despite their fame as fearsome hunters **lions**' ambushes are successful only one time in four and most antelope can outrun them. You sometimes see pitifully thin lions unable to get it together, and much of the time they scavenge or resort to targets as unlikely as porcupines. A good kick from a fleeing zebra or giraffe is enough to break a jaw, which usually leads to starvation. Cattle are easy prey and lions frequently wander out of the national park onto adjoining farms where owners have the right to shoot them. One farmer on the Sikumi side of Hwange is a notorious lion-killer, taking dozens every year. There's nothing anyone can do to stop him. **Robins** is reputedly *the* place for lions.

The most successful hunters at Hwange are **wild dogs**, and you may see a pack trotting along in the evening out on a hunt. Capable of sustained high speeds over long distances, wild dogs lunge at their prey *en masse*, tearing it to pieces – a gruesome finish, but perhaps no slower than the suffocating muzzle-bite of a lion. The whole pack participates in looking after the **pups**, bringing back food – and regurgitating it – for them. For many years dogs were shot on sight; they had gained an unfair reputation as wanton sheep- and cattle-killers and, up to 1975 nearly 4000 were destroyed in *vermin control* operations. But populations now in all the parks are slowly starting to pick up.

ELEPHANTS

With the densest population in Africa, you'd be very unlucky not to see elephants in Hwange. During the rains, however, they can be elusive, disappearing to fresh vegetation in remote zones of the park.

Hwange's elephants are in fact a **conservation over-success** story. By the time the park was created, hunting had reduced the number of elephants to less than a thousand and their extermination was on the cards. But by the 1970s, the elephant count had bounced back dramatically to 20,000 – an over-population which led to habitat destruction. **Culling programmes**, a euphemism for controlling elephants by wiping out whole families, targeting the breeding females and youngsters, were started and continue today, along with a controlled level of trophy-hunting. The park can only properly support around 12,000 elephants, although there are still far more than that even today.

The question of elephant management is more than merely a moral dilemma (shootings are arguably as traumatic for the animals as they would be for defenceless human families) but also leads into arcane **ecological puzzles** in which new factors are continually emerging. While animal over-populations are usually the result of old migration routes being cut off, forcing the creatures into new, unnatural reserves, the consequent foliage destruction caused by crowded herds also puts new life into the soil: experiments carried out at Hwange have shown that four times as many camel acacia seeds sprouted after being eaten and dunged by elephants than a control sample which was left on the ground. Dung beetles, of which Zimbabwe is blessed with a multitude of varieties, gratefully tackle the football-sized elephant droppings, breaking them into pellets and pulling them into their burrows where the seeds later germinate. Elephants also dig up dried-out water holes, providing moisture for other animals. Equally convincing facts can be wheeled out to show how destructive elephants are, with their massive appetites.

More mysteriously, there's evidence of a new natural adaptation to unnatural pressures – **tuskless cow elephants** – which present less attractive targets for poachers. This may change feeding habits, and even breeding cycles, as an elephant uses its tusks (and is either right- or left-tusked), to dig for essential minerals and strip tree bark.

Elephants are the most engaging of animals to watch, perhaps because their interactions have so many human parallels. One of the most entertaining sights is a herd drinking and frolicking at a water hole. They completely abandon themselves, rolling and splashing, or submerging so you can only see the tip of a trunk. Like people, they lead complex, inter-dependent, **social lives**, growing from helpless infancy, through self-conscious adolescence, to adulthood. Babies are born, after a twenty-two month gestation, with other cows in close attendance. Calves suckle for two to three years, from the two breasts between the mother's front legs.

The basic family unit is a group of related females, tightly protecting their babies and young and led by a venerable **matriarch**. These are the animals most likely to bluff a charge – though occasionally vehicles and even people get tusked. Bush mythology has it that elephants become embarrassed and ashamed after killing a human, covering the body with sticks and grass. Elephants certainly pay much attention to the disposal of their own **dead relatives**, often dispersing the bones and spending time near the remains. Old animals die in their eighties when their last set of teeth wears out and they can no longer feed.

Seen in the flesh, elephants seem even bigger than you imagine – you'll need little persuasion from those flapping ears of warning to back off if you're too close – but they're also surprisingly graceful, silent animals on their padded, carefully placed feet. In a matter of moments, a large herd can merge into the trees and disappear, their presence betrayed only by the noisy cracking of branches as they strip trees and uproot saplings – at a rate of 170kg per day in the case of adults.

Nantwich and Robins

NANTWICH and **ROBINS** camps are within 11km of each other, in the northwest of the Park – closer to Victoria Falls than Hwange. People either drive from Main Camp during the dry season (you must leave by noon) or gain access along a gravel road 48km south of Victoria Falls on the Bulawayo road. From that turn-off it's 70km to Robins. En route you'll pass the track to Pandamatenga, just over the border in Botswana.

Deka

DEKA exclusive camp requires 4WD for access. The Deka and Gwayi rivers rise on the watershed here to flow north into the Zambezi, softening the landscape a little. The river courses on the southern side of the watershed once flowed into Botswana. All that remains of them today are long expanses of grassland where game can be spotted.

Kazuma Pan National Park

KAZUMA PAN, south of the Falls on the Botswana border, was first opened to the public in 1987 and you can still only visit with a licensed guide. There's no accommodation here – it remains strictly a wilderness area.

The landscape in the 315 square kilometre park is unique in Zimbabwe but similar to the great pans in Botswana – miles of treeless, open grassland rich in game. The depression is surrounded by dense teak forests and well watered with streams and rock pools.

Backpackers Africa and *Kalambeza* will pick you up at the Falls for three-day **expeditions** to the Pan. You'll see rare species such as roan antelope, gemsbok, tsessebe, cheetah, black rhino, bat-eared fox and wild dogs as well as lions, elephants and buffalos. About the only animals you won't see here are hippopotamuses and black rhinos. The *Rhino Trail* expeditions operated by *Backpackers* tack Kazuma onto Hwange, Chizarira and the Zambezi National Park if you want a longer trip.

When the **pans fill** – as they do every few years – you'll see an extraordinary variety of **waterbirds**. Montagu's harriers are frequent visitors and the rare wattled crane actually breeds in the park.

One of Kazuma's curiosities is a small variety of **fish** – as yet unidentified – which remains dormant during dry years and becomes active when it's wet. How this species survives prolonged drought is a mystery.

travel details

Train
Victoria Falls to Bulawayo and to another 27 stops on the way. 1 daily 5.30pm (14hr) via **Dete** (6hr).

Buses
From Victoria Falls to Bulawayo 1 or more daily 6am (9hr).
From Hwange to Binga Mon, Wed, Thurs, Sat 9–9.30am.
From Dete Cross to Binga Mon, Wed, Thurs, Sat 7am.
From Main Camp to Victoria Falls Daily around 5.30am.

Coach
From Victoria Falls:
To Bulawayo Mon, Thurs 7am, Sun 8am; via Hwange town and **Hwange Safari Lodge** (1hr 15min, 2hr 30min, 6hr 15min). *Ajay.*
To Kasane daily 7.30am (1hr 30min). *UTC.*

Flights
From Victoria Falls:
To Bulawayo Mon, Wed, Thurs, Fri 1–1.25pm, Sun 3.30pm (50min).
To Harare daily 5.10pm except Tues noon (1hr).
To Hwange National Park daily 2.50pm

(35min). A *UTC* bus meets the flight and conveys passengers to the lodges and Main Camp.

To Johannesburg Mon, Thurs direct (1hr 50min). Daily via Bulawayo or Harare.

To Kariba daily 2.50pm (1hr 50min)

To Maun Wed, Fri, Sun 1.20pm (1hr).

From Hwange National Park:

To Harare daily 3.45pm (2hr 10min) via **Kariba** (55min).

To Victoria Falls daily 1pm (35min).

TELEPHONE AREA CODES	
Victoria Falls 113	**Hwange** 181
Dete 118	

CHAPTER FIVE

GREAT ZIMBABWE AND THE LOWVELD

Pyramids apart, **Great Zimbabwe** is Africa's biggest stone monument, and for the century of colonialism it was a potent political weapon. The monument's authorship was long claimed for "the white races" by diehard settlers, and for Africans by most archaeologists – and by the site's Shona inheritors. The archaeology has, therefore, been as much about excavating a detritus of disinformation as about digging under the walls. Nevertheless, the ruins themselves are thrilling and unfathomable, deserving of a day or two in anyone's trip. And their site, moreover, is right beside **Lake Mutirikwe** (Kyle), one of the country's largest and most pleasant recreation parks, with a small but well-stocked **game reserve** attached.

Masvingo, the main town of the lowveld region, is quite an important route centre – connected with Bulawayo to the west, Harare to the north, and Chimanimani and the Eastern Highlands to the east. In itself, it has little to detain you, though if you are driving from Harare it's well worth a stop at the captivating **Serima Mission** – home to Zimbabwe's most inspiring modern carvings.

Wildlife used to be the big incentive for anyone to head **south of Masvingo** and Great Zimbabwe, beyond the sugar boom-town of **Chiredzi** to **Gonarezhou National Park** on the Mozambique border. Gonarezhou is now open to the public after being closed for several years with armed forces fighting off poachers and MNR bandits spilling from the chaos of Mozambique. Years of drought too, have devastated the area, but once it recovers Gonarezhou will deservedly draw its share of wildlife enthusiasts again.

Masvingo

Most people just pass through **MASVINGO** – "Rhodesia's" first white settlement – on their way to the ruins and Lake Mutirikwe. There's not much to keep you in this humdrum town, three hours by car from either Harare or Bulawayo, unless you happen to arrive as nightfall approaches. But if you are travelling under your own steam, you'll find it a solid enough base, and a useful place to stock up with supplies before camping at the ruins or Lake Mutirikwe.

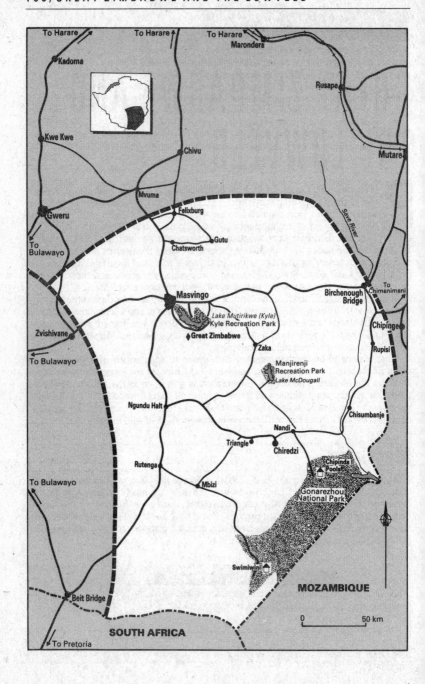

Fort Victoria: the white settlers

Masvingo was established in 1890 by pioneers trekking north, beyond the parched lowveld, to the cooler middleveld plateau. The settlers pitched and fortified their camp and named the spot **Fort Victoria** to link it with the global sisterhood of lakes, falls, towns, pubs and hotels named after the unamused queen. After some days of festivities – reportedly resembling an English village fair – the main force headed off, leaving the earthwork fort under heavily armed protection. When they realised there was little convenient water about, a new and stronger brick fort was built along the Mucheke River, a few kilometres away. One of its watchtowers, perforated with vertical gun-slits, still stands on Masvingo's main street, a reminder of frontier days.

Fort Victoria was the portal to Southern Rhodesia for northward trekking fortune-hunters, and Mashonaland's gold centre: the town's early inhabitants had ambitious hopes of a big strike. In an ironic twist, however, the **Matabele War** of 1893 crushed these local aspirations. After an Ndebele raiding party entered Fort Victoria and killed a number of local Shona tributaries, a force was recruited to invade Bulawayo – a convenient excuse, as it turned out, to lay claim to the richer goldfields of Matabeleland. The destruction of Lobengula's kraal in Bulawayo subsequently served a great propaganda scoop in recruiting immigrants from the south. Enticed by the gold – not to mention the spoils of Ndebele farms and cattle – the whites had few reasons to return to Fort Victoria, condemning it to the small-time provincial status that it has stuck to ever since.

Arriving and accommodation

Local buses from Bulawayo and Harare will drop you off in town before terminating in Mucheke suburb's *musika*, where you can catch a thrice-daily bus to Great Zimbabwe or to other, country-wide destinations. **Taxis** are your best bet to get from the town centre to **Mucheke**. The weekend **coach service** from Harare conveniently deposits you at the centrally located *Chevron Hotel*.

Flights from Harare (four weekly) arrive at the small airport 20 minutes' drive from the centre of Masvingo. Pre-arrange with *UTC* in Harare or *Zimtours* for a transfer to town – there's no airport bus.

Hotels

Masvingo's **hotels** are few and not particularly cheap. The *Chevron* (☎2054 or ☎2055; ④) opposite the publicity bureau on the ruins road is the most central place to stay, with a reasonable pool. Its terrace, facing onto the road, is popular with beer-swilling locals. In Mucheke, the hilltop *Masvingo A1 Hotel* (☎2917; ③)has the best bar in this otherwise dozey town. Both hotels are about 2km from Mucheke bus terminus.

The *Flamboyant Motel* (☎2005; ④), 2km from the centre on the Beitbridge Road at the turn-off to Great Zimbabwe, also has a pool.

If you just want to use one of the hotels for **swimming**, there is a fee for non-guests at the *Chevron* or *Flamboyant*; the public pool on the publicity map is closed at present.

Campsites and backpacking

The **municipal campsite**, 2km out of town on the Mutare road, is a vast and incredibly clean place, usually with a handful of campers corralled into one corner. The presence of a remarkably conscientious attendant means you can leave your packs while you look around town, and the site is convenient for getting a lift on to Mutirikwe's north bank and game park.

At least one backpackers' lodge has opened up, similar to those found in the main centres, offering cheap shared accommodation. To find a room, ask for Mrs Pat Clements at Motor Sales Agencies opposite *OK Bazaars*, or ring Barry or Pat on ☎63282 or ☎62646.

The Town

In the typical style of colonial town planning, the railway line (goods only) slices Masvingo in two: the more salubrious avenues and commercial centre lie to the north, with Mucheke high-density suburb hidden on the wrong side of the tracks.

In the **commercial centre** the focus is provided by **Mucheke Market**. Though this doesn't stand out from its counterparts elsewhere in the country, it has lots of small stores, kiosks and the festive blare of local music. People lounge about waiting for long-distance buses on a grassy island between the shops and beer halls along Charumbira and Makuva streets.

The most interesting place by far, however, and unique in Zimbabwe, is **Ecological Designs**, an appropriate technology centre on Industria Road, parallel to the main road to Harare. The staff are incredibly enthusiastic and will show you round. The place operates both commercially, producing better-known items like solar water heaters and rural equipment, and also as a consultancy. Less glamorous work includes advice on income-generating projects in the communal lands.

It's worth a visit just to see the forecourt's fascinating junkyard-sculpture park of inventive machinery. Intriguing bits of equipment you'll find lying about include the **stabilised soil brick vibrator**, a device that makes bricks using local earth combined with as little as five percent cement. The bricks are unfired – vital in many areas where wood is the basic fuel and deforestation a big problem. The centre also has a solar oven and – you've guessed it – a solar *braai*.

Outside town: the Italian Chapel

You can almost feel the homesickness of the Italian POWs who built the **Chapel of St Francis** during the 1940s in memory of 71 of their fellows who died in captivity in Rhodesia. The interior of the simple, corrugated-iron roofed building, breathes Italy, every surface, walls and ceiling, covered with **paintings**.

One elaborately worked shrine has nostalgic scenes of St Francis in Italian fields and the Virgin in an arcaded Tuscan courtyard. But the real stars of the show are the meticulously painted **mock mosaics**, which you'd swear are real until you get closer. It's an easy stopoff on the way to Kyle game park, 5km from town, a short walk from the main road, situated next to an army base. Hitch, or catch any **bus** going along the Birchenough Bridge road going beyond the Copota Mission turn-off.

Food, drink and entertainment

Whether you want a full-scale **meal** or a snack, you're best off picking one of the **hotels**. Among the alternatives are a sprinkling of grease parlours down Fitzgerald Avenue, while *What's Cooking* in Hofmeyr Street is a good sit-down option, popular with locals and dishing up **cheap eats** like sadza and relish, and toasted sandwiches. For a more sedate atmosphere, *Meikles* department store in Robert Mugabe Street has a tea-room. The *Rising Sun*, opposite *Richards Hardware*, is recommended for snacks, while the *Breadbasket* opposite *OK Bazaars* is good for bread and pies. Away from the centre in **Mucheke**, you'll find the usual street food around the bus terminus and a selection of cheap restaurants.

For provisions, the grocers along Robert Mugabe Street have **fresh produce**, or, with more choice, check out Mucheke Market, alongside the bus terminus. You could also stock up at one of the big supermarkets: *OK Bazaars* in Josiah Tongogara Street or *TM*, Hughes Street/Leopold Takawira Avenue.

Other **shopping** tends to be equally functional. Locally made **handicrafts** are available at the stalls just past the publicity bureau, but there's nothing much to lumber your-

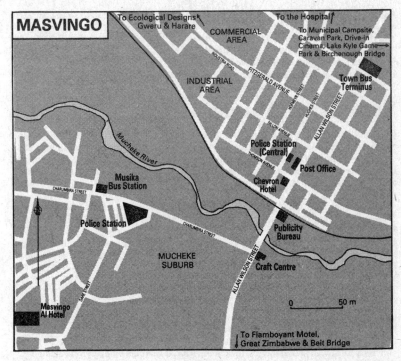

self with unless you like crochet work or anonymous soapstone carving. There are better baskets – and lovely wooden aeroplanes – for sale on the roadside near the ruins.

The main town **bar** and **nightlife** venue is the *Omar Khayyam* on Hellet Street: those bands that come to town play here. The *Mokorokoto Masvingo Bar* at the *A1 Hotel* in Mucheke is another possibility. You might also check what's on at the **theatre**, which hosts good visiting productions from time to time. Otherwise the **drive-in cinema** or drinking at the hotels wraps up Masvingo after dark.

Listings

Banks *Barclays, Standard Chartered* and *Zimbank*, all down Robert Mugabe (formerly Allan Wilson) St, are open Mon, Tues, Thurs & Fri 8am–12.30pm; Wed 8.30am–noon; and Sat 8–11am.

Books and stationery are sold at several shops, but the national chain, *Kingstons* have marginally the best selection, including occasional copies of the South African anti-apartheid newspapers, the *Weekly Mail* and *New Nation*.

Car rental *Hertz* agency is *Travelworld*, Founders House, Robert Mugabe St (☎2131).

Doctors surgery ☎2424 (after hours ☎2420).

Hospital Hay Robertson St (☎2112).

Pharmacy *Masvingo Pharmacy*, Kubatana Centre, Hughes St (☎3884; after hours ☎4136).

Phones are outside the courthouse in Leopold Takawira (formerly Dillon) Ave.

Police Hughes St (☎2222).

Post office Robert Mugabe St/Leopold Takawira Ave. Mon–Fri 8.30am–1pm & 2–4pm; Sat 8–11.30am.

Publicity Association Robert Mugabe St – just across the railway line; (☎2643). Good for maps and leaflets on Great Zimbabwe.

Taxis The best place to hail a taxi is around Mucheke Bus Terminus; otherwise phone ☎3304.

Zimtours Publicity Association Building, Robert Mugabe St (☎4054), opposite the *Chevron* hotel. Recommended local tours as well as safari bookings countrywide.

UTC Book through *Travelworld*, Founders House, Robert Mugabe St (☎2131).

North: Serima Mission

Central Mashonaland may seem an unlikely place for a medieval church, but the **SERIMA MISSION**, 20km from the Masvingo-Mvuma road, does a more than competent impersonation. One of the most striking buildings in Zimbabwe, it was constructed after the last war completely in the spirit of Europe's Middle Ages – both in concept and realisation, the work involving members of the local community in a lengthy process.

The mission was founded by Swiss priest-architect Father John Groeber in 1948. The carved doors, beams and altar were all produced by pupils at the mission school between 1956 and 1959. The art training at Serima was intended to further Christian beliefs. West and Central African carved masks were used as models for the students, and among former pupils of the school is Zimbabwe's leading stone sculptor, Nicholas Mukomberanwa.

The Church

You step inside the church into a pure space that feels carved from the solid shafts of light patterning the walls from clerestory windows. Gloriously carved totem-like, timber columns, sculpted into African angels, rise ten metres from floor to ceiling, and at the centre a crucifix is similarly carved. The materials are all pared back: simple concrete, furnished with benches, makes the superb carvings on every wall stand out.

If you can't make it to Serima have a look at the photographic display at the National Gallery in Harare: the building *is* remarkable.

Access

Serima is tricky to get to and poorly signposted. Without your own transport the best bet is to get the bus that passes through Serima four times weekly on its way from Harare to Gutu; alternatively, there are frequent buses between Chatsworth and Masvingo.

If you are driving, make for Chatsworth and keep going, turning left at the first dirt road after the river; it's more or less straight down this road, but keep asking directions as you go. Or, much easier, take the Felixburg turn-off from the main Harare/Masvingo road; the mission is signposted from this dirt track. This is the best place to try **hitching** from, but expect to wait.

Great Zimbabwe

Open dawn to dusk, small entry fee.

On a continent more used to impermanent buildings of mud, wood and grass, **GREAT ZIMBABWE** is almost miraculous. For nearly a thousand years, ever since it was built, this mysterious city has exercised the imaginations of those who held it, and right up until the nineteenth century it inspired hundreds of other Shona stone palaces in a unitary sphere of influence from the desert lands of the west to the Indian ocean in the east. The first Europeans who saw it, took it both as evidence of the rumoured riches of

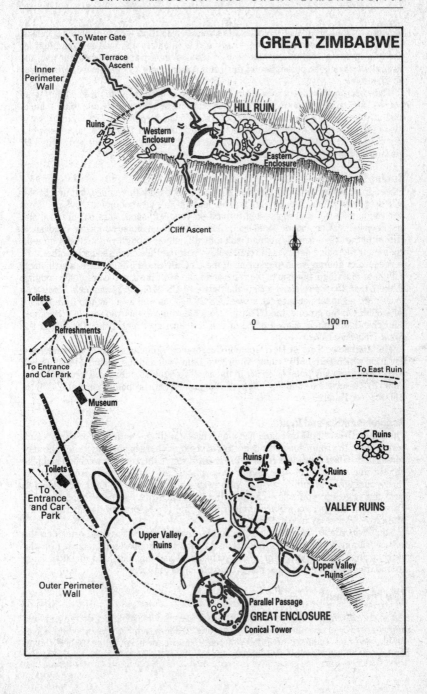

GREAT ZIMBABWE

To Water Gate

Terrace Ascent

Inner Perimeter Wall

Ruins

Western Enclosure

HILL RUIN

Eastern Enclosure

Cliff Ascent

0   100 m

Toilets

Refreshments

To Entrance and Car Park

To East Ruin

Museum

Ruins

Ruins

Ruins

Toilets

To Entrance and Car Park

VALLEY RUINS

Upper Valley Ruins

Upper Valley Ruins

Outer Perimeter Wall

Parallel Passage

GREAT ENCLOSURE

Conical Tower

the country and proof that tentacles of classical civilisation – Phoenicians, Egyptians, Gulf Arabs: they weren't sure who – had been here before and built in stone. And for nearly a hundred years, from the time of Rhodes' incursion to the present day, the struggle for symbolic possession of this central monument has shadowed the struggle for liberation.

The word *zimbabwe* is derived from Shona phrases used freely to mean either "stone houses" or "venerated houses"; which may have amounted to the same thing – buildings in stone being statements about permanence and power. The Great Zimbabwe is the best-known of the country's several hundred zimbabwes. It was the stone heart of a city of as many as 10,000 people, and the home of its ruler, who lived surrounded by his family, court and tributary rulers.

Getting there

Buses from Masvingo to Morgenster Mission (supposedly three daily, but unreliable) will drop you off at the turn-off, a kilometre from the monument. **By car** from Masvingo, take the well-signposted turn-off on your left, about 4km out of town, and just keep going. Cars can be hired from *Hertz* in Masvingo, but arrange this in advance. **Hitching** the 26km from Masvingo isn't difficult, either, though you may end up waiting for a while; stand opposite the craft sellers, past the Publicity Association office.

A speedier alternative is to take one of the *UTC* **air tours** from Harare, which offers a flight to Masvingo, bus trip to the ruins and Lake Mutirikwe, and comfortable lodging at the *Great Zimbabwe Hotel* for an all-in price of US$176. *Air Zimbabwe*'s *Flame Lily* tours offer a similar package for around US$20 less, as well as a day trip from Harare for US$92. On the ground, the *UTC* trips from Masvingo to the ruins are best arranged beforehand with their Harare office; if you just turn up, contact their branch at the *Great Zimbabwe Hotel*.

The Zimbabwe Tourist Development Corporation (Zimtours) offers recommended day trips which take in the ruins, Mutirikwe Dam Wall and the National Park. They'll collect you from any hotel or chalet in the area. To book an outing call in at Zimtours, Publicity Association Building, Robert Mugabe Street, or beforehand at ZTDC in Bulawayo or Harare.

Accommodation and food

The whole Great Zimbabwe area has a nonchalant setting – no fences or gates – and, surprisingly, the ruins don't attract hordes of visitors. There is only one **hotel**, the very comfortable *Great Zimbabwe Hotel* (☎2274; ⓪). If you're there over a weekend and plan on staying more than one night, you might ask about their special rates. Disappointingly, the ruins – a short walk away – aren't visible. To get a view – and to have the stones to yourself – **camp** at the bush-encircled **campsite** beneath them. There's also cheaper roofed accommodation at the two resorts on the shore of Lake Mutirikwe, 7km away (see p.200).

The *Great Zim* is the only place for **food** – toasted sandwiches and drinks on the terrace with more substantial meals inside. Monkeys materialise continuously from the overhanging trees to pounce on sugar sachets and anything else that might be lying around. But these are mundane matters next to Great Zimbabwe.

The Monument

For maximum impact, the **best visiting times** are early morning before the heat and tourists arrive, or evening, after they've gone. Walking among the brooding, silent rubble, you may even see how the Victorians could have been led on their flights of fantasy about lost, classical civilisations. At dawn, from the highest point, the rising sun drenches the expanse of bush and lake in a pink wash. Later in the day, you can escape the heat in the **museum**.

Unless you're driven by more than mere enthusiasm, you won't be able to see every detail of the ruins. There's an incredible quantity of walling, but it's mostly based on simple repeated elements. After a few hours you'll find you acquire a sort of architectural "vocabulary" and everything begins to seem, if no less alien, then part of a coherent vision.

Orientation

On first approach you can hardly discern more than the castellate form of the ruins' hilltop section. This is one of three main complexes of **walls**, spread with abandon across the lifting and dipping contours, covering several square kilometres. If the bush has invaded over the centuries, it was never intended thus: Great Zimbabwe wasn't built to be hidden, nor for defence. It was a loud declaration of power and wealth by the rulers of the first state in this part of Africa.

The **hill complex** is probably the earliest part of the city, and an extraordinary *tour de force* of organic architecture. Its builders, rather than try to force its shapes onto the landscape, melded their masonry with existing boulders, harmonising nature and technology in the most beguiling way. The **Great Enclosure**, which you'll most likely come to first, down below to the south, has entered the record books as sub-Saharan Africa's greatest stone monument. It is also Zimbabwe's most photographed building: the massive tower and narrow, snaking parallel passage instantly recognisable from publicity pictures.

After the other areas, the **Valley Enclosure** offers variations, but little that's new. More dispersed structures repeat many features on a smaller scale. It's likely that the area between this and the hill was at one time a dense maze of *daga* and wooden buildings for the mass of the population, the enclosed stone constructions erected by wealthier citizens accessible via a series of grand entrances. If it's a humbler part to look over now, it's still worth rambling about through the jumble of collapsed walls in the grassy, thorn- and aloe-dotted countryside.

The Great Enclosure

The pinnacle of Rozvi architecture (see box), the **Great Enclosure** sits at the foot of the hill. Originally a **royal palace** and a powerful symbol of the community, it provided privacy to the state's rulers; at the peak of their power, the enclosure is thought to have housed the king, his mother and his senior wives. Following Great Zimbawe's collapse, the building was occupied by the Mugabe dynasty, who headed a minor nineteenth-century tribal grouping. Like the other complexes, its walls are a mixture of fourteenth- to nineteenth-century traditional work, with some (at times inaccurate) modern reconstruction.

Whatever the **conical tower** signified to its builders, it provided ample scope for the imaginations of those who followed. Clearly, it can be seen as a phallic symbol, and some interpreters have suggested, further, that the **stairs** represent femininity, and the

THE "LANGUAGE" OF ROZVI PLANNING

The architecture of Great Zimbabwe is a unique innovation of this part of Africa. Under its spreading cultural influence hundreds of other zimbabwes were built across Central Africa from Botswana to Mozambique. **Khami**, near Bulawayo, took up the architectural principles and developed the style, which became the means for any self-respecting ruling class to gain recognition and publicise itself.

The **walls** meander with a disturbing licence, confounding all western architectural expectations. Their function was mainly symbolic; they twist and turn at will and were never intended to carry roofs. It was these walls that separated commoners from nobility, and you can still see the remains of monumental entrances that gave access to the ruling class homesteads.

One of the reasons it's assumed that Great Zimbabwe wasn't a fortification is that there's no evidence of any doors in the **entrances**. The north entrance of the Great Enclosure, in particular, rewards a good long look. The problem of finishing off a wall without an abrupt and jarring halt is brilliantly resolved, by curving the wall back in on itself. The **stairs** that take you up into the elevated world of the ruler are, meanwhile, fully incorporated as sensuously curving courses, incorporated into the wall's depth – all pure sculpture! Around and about – usually at entrances and particularly on the wall facing the cliff ascent of the hill complex – you'll notice **stone pillars**. It's likely they were topped by symbolic totems, which told you which family lived inside – a kind of street address. The zimbabwe birds were probably the totem of the royal family.

Although the walls are monumental in scale, the architectural **"language"** used is an adaptation of traditional Shona domestic themes; the circular pole and daga hut was the fundamental element of the Shona homestead, just as it remains today in the rural areas. In the ruling class sector, stone walls adjoined daga huts to form an enclosed family living unit. The complexes are organised around the principle of **privacy**: important homes were located at the centre, and walls radiated out to provide secluded courtyards. As they do today, each of the **homesteads** consisted of several huts arranged in a swept, open courtyard – a useful firebreak, and clear space in which intruders, snakes and rodents could be spotted.

Each room had a function. At the heart of the home lay the **kitchen** building, with the hearth at its centre. Each group of huts had stepped platforms, still present in traditional Shona homes, to display a woman's **household pots**. The pots are highly valued vessels and the platforms celebrate the household, marriage and woman's centrality in the family. Close to the kitchen was the main **sleeping** unit, where married couples spent the night together, but in polygamous households the husband would rotate himself about the huts of his several wives. Adolescents slept in sexually segregated dormitories, where visitors would stay if there was no separate guest quarters.

The homestead also included places for **food storage and livestock**. The granary took the form of a hut, but had a metre-high raised floor as protection against damp, insects and rodents; all surfaces were thoroughly plastered to preserve the precious food supply. There was a chicken coop (often on stilts), and a kraal for cattle or goats, although prized animals were sometimes kept inside the main sleeping hut in a special partition.

One of the most important spaces was the **dare** (meeting place), where important family questions or community issues were discussed. Frequently beneath the shade of a tree, it was located near the homestead. During the Second Chimurenga the official title of the supreme military council and government-in-waiting, *Dare re-Chimurenga*, incorporated this ancient notion.

chevron patterns on some of the walls, fertility. But, whether symbolic male organ, hefty symbolic grain store, or prototype safe – all of which are theories that have been considered – the romantics were convinced that it contained hidden treasure, until archaeologists delved beneath in the 1920s and found . . . nothing. It is in fact solid all the way up. The bulging cone, which in form is remarkably similar to the pillar tombs of the East African coast, marks the highest accomplishment of Rozvi masonry skills, and was one of their last constructions. The top of the pillar, now decapitated, was once decorated with three zigzagging lines. Look on the east side of the outer wall for the best remaining example of these.

Leading out of the tower enclosure, a **parallel passage** stretches seventy metres to the north entrance. It gives a good idea of the value of privacy to the Rozvi rulers, screening their domestic arrangements from even the privileged few invited inside. You can walk to the tower enclosure for example, or even to the central area, and still not see where the main huts were. Look, too, at the improvements in Rozvi masonry skills as they gained experience – the inner wall was built at least a century earlier than the smoother, more accurately laid, outer leaf. These mortarless wall faces, standing several times human height, are magnificent: this society had no wheels and no writing.

The Hill Enclosure

The oldest inhabited part of Great Zimbabwe, the **Hill Enclosure**, was for some time known as the "acropolis", a kind of Hellenic compulsion having gripped some of the early observers. It's perhaps even more intriguing than the Great Enclosure, with its slender entrances and passages working their way around enormous balancing boulders. It's also harder work to get to, requiring a steep ascent of one of several stepped routes: this deters a fair proportion of the visitors who ramble about the tower below. But the rewards – at the least, a peaceful view over the kopjes, vleis and beyond to Lake Mutirikwe – are well worth sweating over the climb.

This hill was the site of the earliest settlement of simple **daga and pole huts**, built sometime around the eleventh century. The increasing wealth of the growing state later made the building of stone walls possible. Like the Great Enclosure, the Hill Complex was originally a **royal palace**. It seems likely, however, that it later became the seat of a Rozvi **spirit medium** – the religious counterpart to the secular king's court, some 80 metres below in the Great Enclosure.

The older, hill site would naturally have had closer contact with the Rozvi **ancestors** who once dwelt there, than the newer and more temporal great enclosure. A flight of **curved steps** leads to a space sealed off with a huge rock, probably the domain of spirit mediums who communed with the ancestors here and participated in healing ceremonies. It feels a powerful place and it's wonderful to investigate the crevices, openings and warren of passages that sometimes bring you unnervingly close to sheer drops.

The Museum

Like all great archaeological sites, the ruins of Great Zimbabwe have been diligently pillaged over the years and bits and pieces have turned up all over the world. The modest, but nevertheless fascinating, collection that remains is housed at the small **museum** near the entrance to the site.

Most notable among the exhibits are the seven and a half **soapstone birds** – the inspiration behind the ubiquitous Zimbabwean symbol, and much copied by modern airport artists. Mystery surrounds the significance of these strange, composite creatures, which have been identified as badly executed fish eagles by ornithologists, though archaeologists doubt they signify birds at all, suggesting, rather, that they are mythological.

THE STRUGGLE FOR GREAT ZIMBABWE

For nearly four centuries, European knowledge of Great Zimbabwe was based entirely on hearsay. One of the earliest accounts came from the Portuguese, **Gaspar Veloso**, who wrote of "a fortress of the King of Monomotapa, which he is making of stone without mortar". Almost a hundred years later a fellow countryman, **Brother Joas dos Boas**, had elaborated this modest account into a fantasy of biblical dimensions. He wrote that "these houses were in olden times the trading depots of the Queen of Sheba, and that from these depots they used to bring her much gold".

It was the gold that brought a glint to the eyes of European adventurers in the nineteenth-century scramble for Africa. **Adam Render**, a German hunter, was the first white to cast eyes on Great Zimbabwe, in 1871, later showing them to **Carl Mauch**, a compatriot geologist, who, hungry for fame, took the credit for "discovering" the monument. Clearly no stranger to embroidering the truth, Mauch went on to explain that "the fortress on the hill was a copy of King Solomon's Temple".

But it was in the 1890s that these overblown musings took on a serious significance that ran parallel to the ruthless **colonisation** that was beginning in Rhodesia. Great Zimbabwe stood like a beacon that couldn't be ignored. Adventurers were eager to believe that it was the remains of a long-gone and wealthy civilisation centred in Mashonaland, and that there were precious relics and gold for the taking. At the same time none of the Victorian entrepreneurs or politicians, who were poising themselves to exploit Mashonaland's wealth, wanted to believe that the black people they planned to subjugate were capable of a complex social system. To think otherwise would make nonsense of the supposed civilising mission with which they wrapped the colonial ideology.

It was to resolve this glaring contradiction that the so-called **"Mystery of Zimbabwe"** evolved. The hard-headed Rhodes was the first to see the political importance of the issue, and in 1893 he employed an amateur antiquarian, **Theodore Bent**, to excavate the stones. After all his digging and delving, Bent was disgusted to find that "everything was native". This, however, didn't stop him concluding that an "ancient Mediterranean race" was responsible for the buildings. He nominated, as candidates, "the mythical Pelasgi who inhabited the shores of Greece", Britons, Phoenicians, Arabs, Romans, Persians, Egyptians or "Hebrews" – anyone, in fact, but Africans.

In 1905, **David Randall-McIver** became the first professional archaeologist to investigate Great Zimbabwe. He concluded that the buildings were unmistakably African and of medieval date – and that there wasn't a shred of evidence for European or Oriental involvement. White outrage at this distasteful news was voiced by the journalist R.N. Hall who lambasted McIver's lack of first-hand knowledge of local Africans, asserting that no "authority" believed in "McIver's hazarded hypothesis of 'the natural and unaided evolution of the negroid'". The battle lines were clearly drawn – the professionals standing their ground and building on the findings of McIver, while the white community and white politicians searched more and more frantically for some scrap of ammunition to shoot down the indigenous origin hypothesis.

As the **liberation struggle** escalated, the battle to reclaim the ruins as African heritage intensified. By the time of UDI in 1965 there was scarcely any doubt at the *National Historical Monuments Commission* that Great Zimbabwe was the work of a powerful indigenous culture that once dominated the region. Responding to the discomforting onslaught of scientific findings, Colonel Hartley, MP for Victoria Province, rose in Parliament in 1969 to denounce the Commission, whose portrayal of the "ruins as only being of Bantu origin", he felt should be "corrected".

Iron tools such as hoes may seem pretty ordinary items nowadays, but the ones on display here were extremely valuable possessions, and very expensive to make, in labour and organisation. A hoe was like a car – a tribute item of conspicuous royal wealth – and just one was valuable enough to seal a marriage. Other metal tools like

The following year, **censorship** prevented official publications – guidebooks, museum displays, school textbooks, radio programmes, newspapers and films – from stating unequivocally that Great Zimbabwe was an African creation. Yet while explanations like the Queen of Sheba fantasy implied BC origins, **radiocarbon dating** revealed that the state flourished after 1000 AD. The curator at the ruins commented that not since Nazi Germany had archaeology been so brazenly censored, and for most Rhodesian archaeologists it was the last straw. **Peter Garlake**, the leading expert on Great Zimbabwe, left Rhodesia. Throughout the 1970s the Rhodesian Front regime and its white supporters were left free to wallow in dreamland theories, without fear of informed contradiction.

Current thinking

Garlake returned home in 1981, following Independence, to continue his work, and with censorship set aside, serious research into Great Zimbabwe resumed. Controversy certainly continues among researchers, but it's about detail rather than substance. It's generally agreed now that **Shona-speakers** conceived and built Great Zimbabwe themselves, in response to local conditions.

One theory asserts that the **Zimbabwe state** was transformed from an undistinguished village to a regional power by its pivotal position near the head of the Save river, which placed it perfectly to control the thirteenth-century **gold trade** between Matabeleland and Sofala on the coast. Taxes increased the economic and political power of its ruling class, enabling it to employ craftsmen like stone-carvers, goldsmiths and stonemasons. The rulers found themselves able to finance public works – the great walls – which enhanced their prestige and helped to cement the growing state that was evolving.

Peter Garlake, however, emphasises the primacy of cattle in the growth of the Zimbabwe state, playing down trade as the kingpin of its economy. Garlake's scenario is less titillating than the idea of a trans-African gold trade focused on Great Zimbabwe, but it has a simple, compelling elegance. He points out that Great Zimbabwe, like a number of other similar centres, is positioned at the interface of the highveld and the lowveld, and he argues that the Great Zimbabwe state evolved to cope with a complex **herding system** that grazed huge areas of land. In the hot wet season cattle fed on the fresh grass of the highveld; in the winter they were herded to the better-watered lowveld when the risk of sleeping sickness was at its lowest. This method required a centralised state that was powerful enough to control a vast territory. The simplest way to co-ordinate cattle-movement was as a single herd – the king's property, with animals granted to subjects for private use – moved en masse and protected by armies of men. Organised companies of men could also defend large territories and form a labour force to build walls.

The strength of Garlake's interpretation is that it corresponds to the way powerful cattle-owning states, like the Ndebele, were organised in recent times. Trade could simply have been a sideline, completely consistent with imported goods discovered at Great Zimbabwe. And in the end what made Zimbabwe great – **centralisation** – was what destroyed it. Although Great Zimbabwe revolutionised the state, it failed to develop solutions to the problems of overpopulation that resulted. By the mid-fifteenth century, the lands around the capital had lost their fertility, game was hunted out, firewood was in short supply, and people began to drift away.

Although Great Zimbabwe collapsed, its culture continued. Some Rozvi migrants went west, and took their wall-building know-how with them, merging with the Leopard's Kopje platform-makers of the west at Khami, near Bulawayo (see p.139).

gongs, strikers and spears were also royal regalia, and the quantity discovered in the royal hoard shows the extent of the gulf between rich and poor at Great Zimbabwe. While the king had stacks of symbolic, but functionally useless, metal objects, an ordinary peasant would own just one or two utilitarian items.

Other displays include useful background. One gives a graphic history of the hill from the displacement of its original hunter-gatherer inhabitants by Iron Age people 1700 years ago up to the building of the stone walls. Another exhibit shows how the stone blocks were manufactured using fire to detach them from rock faces.

A small collection of **oriental goods** provides evidence of of Great Zimbabwe's trading links. From the twelfth century onwards, the Rozvis were indirectly in contact with the coast, the Islamic world and even China. Finds include Indian beads, crockery from China and Persia, and odds and ends brought via Swahili traders.

Further information

For a comprehensive explanation of the ins and outs of Great Zimbabwe, the best body of work has been produced by **Peter Garlake**. His findings are well summarised in his authoritative booklet *Great Zimbabwe Described and Explained*, which seems to discuss every bit of stonework and provides a useful bibliography for enthusiasts.

Garlake has also produced another brief booklet, *Life at Great Zimbabwe*, which is in many ways the most accessible publication about the place. With pen and ink illustrations providing an impression of how the city might have been, the discussion succeeds in bringing the ruins alive. It's short enough, and sufficiently easy reading, to consume during a break in the shade at the kiosk.

See "Books" in the *Contexts* section for further details.

Lake Kyle Recreation Park

LAKE KYLE RECREATION PARK*, 35 kilometres from Masvingo, is an obvious resort to pair with Great Zimbabwe, just 6km from the south bank of Lake Mutirikwe: a peaceful, undemanding place, with promising, if somewhat low-key wildlife. Coming from Masvingo, you have a choice of roads – going via Great Zimbabwe to the south bank, or heading direct to the game park on the northern shores.

Zimbabwe's second largest lake – artificial like almost all the rest – Mutirikwe has a varied shoreline: rocky beaches, wooded backdrops and sheer cliffs. Its small islands are secure refuge to a booming bird population and the compact game park on the north bank hosts the country's biggest cross-section of antelope species, as well as a thriving herd of white rhinos – all free from predators. However, the "lake" itself was sadly little more than a muddy pool in 1992 after several years of drought, and it will take some years of good rains to bring the water back to former levels.

The lake is not merely recreational – its *raison d'être* is to irrigate Hippo Valley and Triangle, the mammoth sugar estates to the south. When the lake dried up and rains failed, the sugar plantations withered, causing shortages of sugar, food riots and leaving Zimbabwe with no other choice than to import sugar, at great expense.

South Bank Resorts

Southern Lake Mutirikwe is a collection of campsites and resorts: a mini Kariba without the heat, where people used to come to boat, fish and water-ski before the drought.

You can see Mutirikwe from the hills at Great Zimbabwe. That's the advantage of the less attractive south bank: it's near enough to walk from the ruins and easy enough to hitch. The closest and most beautiful place to base yourself is the *National Parks*

*Until the 1990s the lake as well as the recreation park were both called "Kyle". The waters themselves have now been renamed "Mutirikwe", but the two names are still used virtually interchangeably.

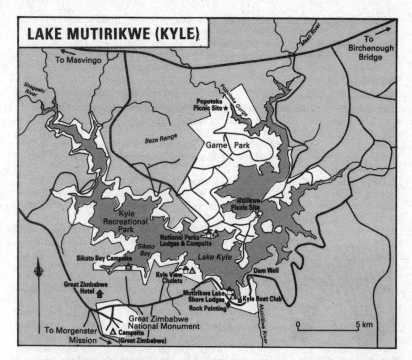

campsite at **SIKATO BAY**, 6km from the ruins on a good dirt road. Because the road to Sikato doesn't lead anywhere else, the car-less are likely to end up walking. There are washing facilities, and each lot has its own *braai* stand, concrete table and water tap. The **resort chalets** a few kilometres east of Sikato, are geared for family holidays – spacious and inexpensive, with the option of camping. Choose between *Kyle View Resort Chalets* (Private Bag 9055, Masvingo; ☎223822; ②), 6km from the ruins, just off the main road, and *Mutirikwe Lake Shore Lodges* (PO Box 518, Masvingo; ☎292421; ②), 2km on. Each has a restaurant, stores with basic supplies, pool and bar. For drinking of another kind make for the beer hall across the main road from *Kyle View Resort*; if you can't see it you'll definitely hear it. It's lively and a good place to meet local people – so long as you're not an unaccompanied woman.

If you're staying at *Kyle View* you can sometimes get a **boat ride** across to the game park on the north. *Mutirikwe* also has a cruiser, that may drop you off. Otherwise it's a long haul around the lake by road – some 65km via Masvingo, slightly longer on the circular drive.

The North Bank and Game Park

Mutirikwe's North Bank is much less developed. The **campsite and lodges** are set high above the water, with enchanting views – better than the resorts at the vanishing lakeside to the south. *National Parks* **lodges** go for the usual low prices, booked in advance at Parks booking offices in Harare or Bulawayo or last minute at Mutirikwe itself (☎2913). *Elephant Lodge*, at the summit of the hill, has the most commanding lake vista; and there are splendidly positioned **campsites**. Bring all supplies from Masvingo and fill up with petrol – there are no shops or garages nearby. Besides National Parks' accommodation, there is also one **hotel**, the pleasant family-run *Glenlivet Hotel* (PO Box 146, Masvingo; ☎272719; ③). Situated on Murray MacDougall Drive, it is only accessible if you're driving.

The Game Park

7am–6pm. Small entry fee.

Kyle Game Park has no big cats and few other predators, and most of its animals have been introduced. But while it's no Hwange or Mana Pools, nor is it tame. You can walk all along the lakeside, in relative security, just outside the park boundary, and, inside, you'll get a full viewfinder of a whole range of herbivores – including buffalo, warthog, white rhino, giraffe, zebra, and an astonishing variety of antelope – as well as numbers of hippos.

The terrain ranges from grassland to wooded clumps and rocky outcrops. Some of the kopjes in the southeast are adorned with **rock paintings**, though none is especially notable. The easiest to reach are the ones signposted above Kyle Boat Club, a couple of kilometres past the *Mutirikwe Lodges.*

For a real treat, take a 90-minute **guided horse ride** through the park. No experience is required, but if you're proficient, you can get permission from the warden for serious riding. At any pace, though, you can get to within a whisker of the quarry; there are fantastic quantities of game right off the road.

Part of Zimbabwe's very active **anti-poaching** campaign involves relocating **rhinos** to reserves in the country's heart, well away from the borders. It was once believed that poachers were all outsiders who sneaked over the border, chopped the horn and zipped back. Sadly, in 1989, two rhinos were killed in Kyle Reserve, probably by people posing as tourists. Don't be alarmed if the wardens ask to search your car.

With a car you can meander around the park's 64-kilometre network of dirt track, though you should beware that the roneo-ed **maps** available at the office are hopelessly inaccurate and unreadable. The most reliable source of information is the *Tourist Map of Lake Kyle and Great Zimbabwe*, but the office often runs out of this; if possible, plan ahead and try to buy one from the Surveyor General's Office in Harare. The Masvingo Publicity Association blurb also has an adequate map.

There are two **picnic sites** with *braai* facilities and toilets – **Mtilikwe**, on the point, and the more remote, **Popoteke** on the river. The approach to the latter is often sentinelled by zebra along the road: they relish its wooded surroundings. You can't camp at these sites, but, as the Rest Camp is inside the park boundary fence, you can drive there for an evening picnic; be discreet though – it's not strictly allowed.

Without transport you can still get around. The official **walking area** is **Mshagashe Arm**, a small peninsula around the huts and campsite. The walks aren't in the game park proper, but you can get to the lakeside and see **hippos**. Stroll down to the water, sit quietly on the rocks and you may be lucky enough to get a close view through binoculars. Be cautious – it's easy to regard these amusing snorters as some kind of oversized aquatic pigs, but they kill more people than any other mammal in Africa. Generally they mind their own business but, if threatened, they can attack viciously. The real danger is getting between them and their element – water. Be vigilant during their landing period after sunset, and especially at dawn, when they're plodding sleepily back to the lake or river.

Heading south: the Lowveld Plateau

At present the lowveld is scarcely visited. **Gonarezhou National Park** has long been out of bounds because of MNR activity and poaching, and with the drought there's been insufficient reason to head for this hot part of the country. But changes in Mozambique and a hopeful, though unpredictable recovery of game stocks and vegetation should mean that the reserve will once again become one of Zimbabwe's big three game-viewing destinations – alongside Hwange and Mana Pools. The central area remains totally wild and undeveloped, the elephant are fierce and apart from one or two safari camps, it's a park which remains inaccessible without your own rugged vehicle.

Chiredzi

CHIREDZI is a creation of the 1960s, established as a centre for the fast-growing lowveld region, and still building today. It's neatly laid out and pretty, with baobab-specked hills. But there's nothing to do and the town's only interest for travellers is as a stopoff for Gonarezhou. You'll find the basics in the centre: **banks**, **post office** and **shops**, but what life exists is in the black side of town around the bus station. Turn down Msasa Drive and left into Lion Drive, about a kilometre from the centre. Here you'll find cheap **eats**, and **taxis** and **buses** for Harare, Bulawayo, Masvingo and Mutare.

If you find yourself stranded and in need of a **hotel**, the business-oriented *Planter's Inn*, Marula Drive (☎2281 or ☎2230; ④), a couple of minutes' walk from the main street, is the only option. They also do toasted snacks, drinks and teas on a very pleasant shaded terrace. If you're mobile, make for the much nicer *Tambuti Lodge Hotel* (☎2575; ④), 10km east of Chiredzi on the road to Nandi and the turn-off to Gonarezhou. It's set on the banks of the thickly wooded Chiredzi River, with the advantages of a beautiful setting, birds galore, and a pool beneath shady acacias.

MACDOUGALLS' SUGAR

Murray MacDougall first encountered sugar cane in Demarara, British Guyana, where he had arrived, aged fourteen, after running away to sea from Britain on an Argentine cattle boat. After World War I he fetched up in Rhodesia, where he was granted a vast tract of dry lowveld. Here he began by grazing cattle, under a registered brand – a triangle – bought from a bankrupt rancher, but his fortunes collapsed in 1924 and he turned to agriculture. Despite official scorn, he was determined to prove that, properly irrigated, the country's parched southeast could be productive.

He spent the next seven obsessive years boring 420 metres through granite to bring the waters of the Mutirikwe River onto his land, and in 1931, at last, managed to grow wheat, cotton, fruit and tobacco. However, large flocks of quelea birds and swarms of locusts feasted on his crops and, on the point of despair, MacDougall recalled his Demarara days. He applied to import sugar plants. The unhelpful government gave him permission to bring three pieces of cane from the Natal sugar estates in South Africa. MacDougall brought his three sticks, and a whole lot more, in bundles hidden beneath his car. The experiment was an unqualified success and the **Triangle Sugar Estates** company was formed in 1939 – just in time to profit from World War II.

Only then did the government take notice and begin work on the lowveld's comprehensive **irrigation scheme**. Although the land is dry much of the year, around a third of Zimbabwe's rainfall run-off flows through the Save and Runde River catchment areas. There was enough water; it just needed storing on its way to the Indian Ocean. Lake Mutirikwe was created from that need in 1961.

Triangle

TRIANGLE is, without doubt, the sugar capital of Zimbabwe, its surroundings full of memories of **Thomas Murray MacDougall** (see box p.203), an old-style pioneering Scotsman who wrestled with hostile conditions to green the lowveld with endless expanses of cane.

Now the archetypal company town, all Triangle's facilities – the schools, hospitals, housing and recreational facilities – are trimly laid on and out of the same packet. The Triangle corporate logo (the company is now owned by Anglo-American Corporation) is everywhere, on vehicles, buildings and signs. Local workers from Triangle speak very proudly about corporate excellence, and of the beautiful greenness of the place in times of plenty.

You can hang about a bit, but there's nowhere to stay and not really very much to do except time a visit to the **MacDougall Museum** in the pioneer's former house (daily 8.30–9.30am & 3.30–4.30pm. Small entrance fee). His whole heroic life story is told with excellent old photographs and school-projectish stuff on how sugar is grown and refined.

Murray MacDougall Drive – Chiredzi to Masvingo through the Manjirenji Park

Zimbabwean back routes are always interesting, and **Murray MacDougall Drive**, a good dirt route which provides a short cut between Chiredzi and Masvingo, is one of the best, burrowing through scenic communal lands. Transitional landscape, it has both highveld and lowveld features; as you approach **Manjirenji Recreational Park** you leave the last of the baobabs behind. Cattle and impala share this hilly country, while the seasonally dry river beds are lined with ilala palms.

Manjirenji Recreational Park

You'll find the turn-off to **MANJIRENJI RECREATION PARK** roughly 45km along the drive from Chiredzi, with the park itself starting a further 11km down the road. Another of those ubiquitous dams, Manjirenji forms part of the lowveld irrigation system. As at Lake Mutirikwe (which it resembles, although on a smaller scale) there aren't any large animals, but it's still a beautiful place set in hilly country, wooded and rocky with excellent views across the lake bed. The park is scattered with *braai* places and lakeshore thatched gazebos which are used by local kids for afternoon homework sessions.

A path runs around the dam in both directions across densely wooded hillsides. Local people use the dam for fishing; in the evenings you'll see them carrying their catch. Someone with a visitors book comes round sooner or later, but there are no charges to be paid and you can camp or spend the night in the shelters.

On towards Masvingo

Continuing on from the recreation area you make your way through granite outcrops and several picturesque villages with boldly patterned walls. At the administrative hamlet of **ZAKA**, there's a scattering of huts and a few trading stores and, nearby, a local **Heroes' Acre**. The series of graves with stencilled inscriptions – many already peeling and faded – are poignant reminders of the war in which everyone lost someone. Many locals are remembered for having died in fierce battles, but the majority perished, puzzlingly, of food poisoning. Smith's troops are rumoured to have contaminated food stocks, but "food poisoning" may have been a blanket term for inexplicable deaths.

Gonarezhou National Park

Remote and rough with few good roads and limited facilies, **GONAREZHOU NATIONAL PARK** shelters a profusion of rare species along its lush, riverine belts – oases in the unyielding dry lowveld. A myth-laden wilderness of 5000 square kilometres, this is the territory where tales of lost cities and Arab trading stations have always thrived and where less glamorous, modern accounts describe a ravaged battlefield of conflicting interests.

Gonarezhou (often *Gona-Re-Zhou*) is a Shona name meaning refuge of the elephants and has long been renowned for very marketable ivory, its tuskers being inordinately well hung. This was the stamping ground in the 1920s of the notorious poacher, Cecil Barnard, who felled the heavily toothed Dhlulamithi (Taller-than-the-trees). As his name suggests, Dhlulamithi was inordinately large, his tusks reckoned to be the largest taken south of the Zambezi, with a combined weight of 110kg.

Practicalities

Set aside as a national park in 1967, Gonarezhou is the second largest park in Zimbabwe. It has now re-opened after many years of closure, and although entry is currently restricted to Zimabweans and residents of other African countries, this may change. National Parks warn visitors to be extremely cautious when encountering elephants as they "bear a grudge against man due to persecution and harassment over the years".

Most of the park is accessible only by sturdy vehicles, but if you can get there, the scenic rewards are enormous, with every Zimbabwean terrain found within its borders. The park has one of only two **nyala antelope** concentrations in the country, the best population of the knee-high **suni antelope**, and the striped **king cheetah** is found nowhere else.

Gonarezhou has two developed regions: **Mabalauta** in the south, which has a small rest camp and camping site, and **Chipinda Pools** to the north with camping only. The park is normally open only during the dry season, May to October.

In the **Mabalauta** area, the rest camp at **Swimuwini** ("place of the baobabs") is 8km from the warden's office and overlooks the Mwenezi River. Seven chalets are available, and there is also a campsite, 600m from the warden's office at Mabalauta. The rest camp is 105km from Chiredzi, the turn-off indicated on the main Masvingo-Beitbridge Road. The road is very rocky and suitable only for high-clearance vehicles. Visitors are advised against using the main access road from Chipinda Pools via Twiza to Mabalauta, because of the security situation. Advance bookings can be made through Parks Central Booking Office in Bulawayo or Harare.

Chipinda Pools Area, situated on the park's northern side and taking in the Save and Runde rivers, is quite wild: 4WD transport is indispensible for exploring anywhere beyond the Pools or Massasanya Dam, though a normal car can get to the Chipinda Pools campsite itself. The campsite is 59km from Chiredzi; take the signposted dirt road twenty kilometres east of Chiredzi, fill up with petrol and take all your supplies as there are no shops or garages beyond Chiredzi. As well as the two camping areas at Chipinda Pools and Chinguli, there are seven undeveloped sites with minimal facilities. The best **game-viewing** is in the vicinity of the Runde River, near Gonarezhou's most photographed feature, the red sandstone **Chilojo Cliffs**.

If you don't have your own transport, **accommodation** is restricted to the luxurious *Cresta Sandstone Safari Lodges – Induna Lodge* and *Kwali Camp* (*Cresta Zimbabwe*, PO Box 2833, Harare; ☎703131). Prices start at an inclusive US$75 per person at *Kwali* and US$150 at *Induna*. Visitors are flown in on the daily twelve-seater *Air Zimbabwe* flight from Harare to Buffalo Range, then transferred to the lodge.

Riding safaris are available for the more adventurous from *Biza Saddle Safaris* (11 Rossal Rd, PO Box GD305, Greendale, Harare; ☎48548; Fax 48265). Guests stay in huge safari tents at a bush camp on the edge of Gonarezhou, and either do day rides from the camp or go out on three-day trips. Inclusive prices start at US$150 per day.

East to the Chimanimani and the Highlands

Masvingo is well connected by bus to the **Eastern Highlands**, with **Chimanimani** just half a day away via Birchenough Bridge. As you leave Masvingo, you gradually slide off the escarpment into the **lowveld**. Progress is marked by increasing numbers of baobab trees, donkeys and goats, and long views ahead of the silvery **Birchenough Bridge** arching across the wide **Save River**. In the brown water sand shows through and crocodiles lurk, though people wash their clothes undeterred. The ribbed steel structure of the bridge, incongruous in the flat, thorny landscape, provides a vital link.

The drab village of **BIRCHENOUGH BRIDGE**, hard by the southern tip of the Save Communal Lands, is another of those needy, out-of-the-way places designated by the government as Growth Points. Its single hotel, the *Birchenough Bridge Hotel* (Chipinge ☎225819; ③) close to the bus terminus, is used mostly as a call-in for drinks, though it has a few rooms with pleasant balconied prospects of the river and hills. From the *musika*, a couple of hundred metres across the road, you can get **buses** to Mutare, Chipinge and Chimanimani.

Some 7km east of Birchenough Bridge at Changadzi on the Chipinge Road, there's a group of **crafts stalls** – their goods of unusually high quality, particularly the rust-coloured baskets with plaited seamless bases joined onto decorated wooden rims. Other tempting buys are the woven vegetable-dyed, bark mats – available in other parts of the country but a lot cheaper here. In season, baskets of furry green baobab pods are also on sale; locals soak the cream of tartar seeds in milk to make a kind of yoghurt.

At **TANGANDA JUNCTION**, a stark red-earthed place on a bend, the road splits south down the Save Valley to Chisumbanje and Chiredzi and east to Chipinge and Chimanimani. The Junction consists of a bus stop and a collection of plastered and peeling stores. Women, relying on the passing traffic, sell small piles of fruit laid on plastic on the ground. An early morning **bus** from Chipinge goes via Chisumbanje to Chiredzi through the intensely cultivated and irrigated middle Save Valley. A good deal of the 200km on dirt roads though the Tanganda to Chiredzi section is now tarred.

travel details

Buses

Masvingo's historical role as a gateway to the hinterland has placed it in a pivotal transport position, from which you can get buses to almost any part of the country. There is now a handy coach service to and from Harare and Masvingo at weekends.

From Masvingo (Mucheke Terminus)
Beit Bridge 1 bus late morning (3–4hr).
Bulawayo 4 daily (3–4hr).
Chimanimani 1 daily 11am (4–5hr).
Harare 8 daily (3–4hr).
Morgenster Mission for **Great Zimbabwe** 3 daily at 8am, noon, 3.30pm (30min). Erratic.

Mutare 3 daily between 8am and 10am (4–5hr). There are also buses to **Chatsworth** for **Serima Mission**, **Chipinge**, **Chiredzi**, **Gweru**, **Hwange**, and **Shurugwi**.

Coaches
Harare weekend service 6am Sat, 2.30pm Sun. Pick-up at the *Chevron Hotel*. Book at *Express Motorways*, ☎720392 Harare.

Flights
From Masvingo to: **Harare** direct Mon, Thurs, 9.05am (45min); Harare via Gweru, Tues, Fri 8.20am (95min).

TELEPHONE AREA CODES

Telephone Codes: (Hyphen indicates second dialling tone)
Masvingo 139   **Chiredzi** 133–8   **Chatsworth** 130–8   **Chipinge** 127

CHAPTER SIX

THE EASTERN HIGHLANDS

Stretched along the Mozambique frontier, the **Eastern Highlands** of **Manicaland** rise from the plains in a natural barrier. Peaking at almost 2600m in the Nyanga belt, these Zimbabwean mountains reminded the original British settlers of the Scottish Highlands. They set about creating dams and lakes and planted pines in the mist, features that induce a sense of familiarity for Europeans raised within reach of hills and fir cones. But the climate is thoroughly Zimbabwean; there are some real expanses of jungle; and the earth is that unmistakeable African red.

What the Highlands lack is big game – which was shot out early here – or indeed any very specific tourist highlights. Their appeal lies more in exploring the superb **hiking trails** and **indigenous forest**, waterfall swimming pools and National Parks, each quite different in character. **Nyanga National Park**, closest to Harare, has long been a major holiday resort for Zimbabweans, with its forests and trout fishing, but hasn't yet been packaged for foreign visitors. Adjoining its southern edge, the less easily accessible **Mtarazi National Park** is a much wilder zone, with undisturbed indigenous forest, Africa's highest **waterfall**, and the luxuriant **Honde Valley**.

The southern reaches of these Highlands were among the worst affected areas in the bush war. Although tourism here has picked up, transport-wise it remains out on a limb – several hours from the capital and not on the road to anywhere else, but nevertheless connected by daily local buses and on no account to be missed. The **Chimanimani National Park**, accessible only on foot, has the best **hiking** in Zimbabwe, with spectacular mountains, and waterfalls and rivers to bathe in. Still further south, **Chipinge**, a workaday town in the centre of tea and coffee estates, serves as a base for **Chirinda Forest**, a primaeval woodland reserve with ancient red mahoganies.

As for more urban attractions, **Mutare**, Zimbabwe's third city and capital of Manicaland, is beautifully sited in a broad, mountain-rimmed valley on the Mozambique border, with the wonderful **Bvumba Botanical Gardens** and little-visited **Bunga Forest Reserve** within easy day trip reach.

The Road from Harare

Getting to the Eastern Highlands from Harare is easy enough, with regular trains and buses covering the 263km to **Mutare**. En route, you can linger at strategically placed tea gardens and craft shops, and there are a few hotels should you get stranded. **Rusape**, midway, offers the opportunity of heading straight to Nyanga National Park, as well as a highly recommended detour to the controversial rock paintings at **Diana's Vow**.

ACCOMMODATION PRICE CODES

Every hotel and accommodation option listed in this chapter has been given a **price code** in US$ to indicate the cost of a single night's lodging.
For a full explanation, see p.43.

① under US$8 ② US$8–14 ③ US$15–29 ④ US$30–59
⑤ US$60–89 ⑥ US$90–149 ⑦ US$150+

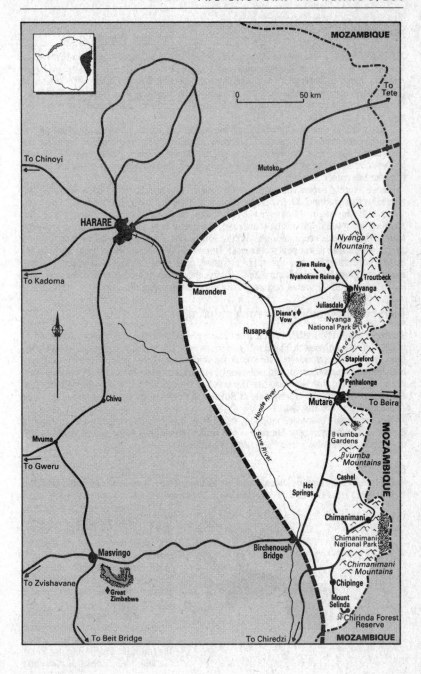

Marondera

MARONDERA, 74km east of Harare, was set up as a staging post between Mutare (or Umtali as it was then known) and the capital, and for travellers to the Eastern Highlands this remains its main, not to say only, interest. The town, the highest-sited in the country, stands at the centre of a prosperous farming region, dripping quietly, after the rains, amid a green and pleasant landscape of grazing sheep, orchards of pears and apples, and vineyards.

Marondera is one of Zimbabwe's **wine** regions, a product that's improving all the time and is now marketed abroad, albeit in the gift catalogues alongside Frontline tea bags rather than in supermarkets. In town, the **Monis winery** can be visited for a tasting session. Nearby is the Eton-ish private school, **Peterhouse** – presumably located here for the cooler climate.

These "sights" apart, the main reason for a stop would be to have lunch at the surreally British-titled *Ye Olde Tea Shoppe* in Fourth Street, the principal shopping street, off the main Mutare road. The one-star, recently refurbished hotel, the *Marondera* (☎4005; ③), on the main road, is a useful fall-back if you're taking it slowly. Much the nicest stop, though, is the *Malwatte Farmhouse Restaurant*, beyond Marondera at the 82km peg on the main Harare–Mutare road, where you can have tea in the garden or browse around their good craft shop. Before you reach Rusape, exactly halfway between Harare and Mutare, the Dutch-gabled *Halfway House* is similar, offering outdoor meals, takeaways, fresh produce and crafts.

Rusape and Diana's Vow rock painting

The next stop, **RUSAPE**, 170km from Harare, is where the road splits; northeast to NYANGA or southeast to Mutare. If you're here for the night, you could do a lot worse than the *Balfour Hotel* (☎2945; ③). Like other small-town colonial hotels it has a polished red wax verandah and, seemingly, scores of waiters in starched uniforms waiting to serve tea; this is where the Harare–Mutare coach makes its refreshment stop. Another option, on the Harare side of Rusape, is the recently reopened and good-value *Crocodile Motel* (☎2404; ③).

But the main reason for stopping off at this, now nondescript, town is to make a detour to the magnificent **Diana's Vow rock paintings** – some of the finest in the country and certainly amongst the most unusual.

Diana's Vow

You'll need a car to get to Diana's Vow. At Rusape, where the main road splits, take the fork towards Juliasdale. Before leaving town, just past the church on the left, you'll see a

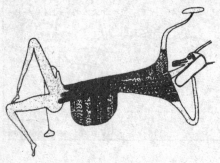

sign to **Diana's Vow Farm**. From here it's a 28-km drive on a good dirt road to the paintings, which are indicated by a very discreet sign at a farm gate on your right. Walk through the gate for half a kilometre until you reach the painted overhang in a dramatic circle of granite boulders.

A large recumbent figure, evidently in ceremonial dress and a sable antelope mask, dominates the tableau. According to Peter Garlake (see "Books" in *Contexts*) it depicts a **ceremonial dance**, in which the life force *n/um* is being activated. The stretched figure is shown in an advanced state of trance – elongation being a sensation commonly reported by modern-day San dancers, who achieve altered consciousness. The oval attached to the bodies is believed to represent *n/um* and hence the spiritual culmination of the dance. A now discredited interpretation had the central figure as a dead king wrapped in bandages, and about to be buried.

Mutare

MUTARE has a majestic-looking site and a distinctly provincial feel, with no hint of high-rise down the main street, and a neatly organised grid of flower-bedecked avenues. It is at its best in September and October when the hills around the town are a burnished red and yellow with spring msasa leaves. Local attractions within easy reach include **Murahwa's Hill** and **Penhalonga**, but a little further away the wonderful **Bvumba Botanical Gardens** are reason in themselves to visit the town.

Some history: Mutasa, Umtali, Mutare

Mutare's nineteenth-century history is bound up with **gold** and **railways**. The traditional head of the area was one **Chief Mutasa**, a man much courted by both Portuguese and British settlers wanting to prospect for gold in the **Penhalonga Valley**, north of modern Mutare. Two days after the British occupied Mashonaland in 1890, however, they took over the granting of prospecting rights and rapidly constructed a fort to "protect" the chief from the Portuguese.

A year later, as numbers began to swell, the fort was abandoned and a new township, **Old Umtali**, was established on the Mutare River. At the same time, the **railway** line begun in Beira was approaching the surrounding hills – which proved too big an obstacle. Everyone consequently packed up and moved 14km south into the wide valley of Mutare's present position. The **American Methodist Church** took over Old Umtali, with a mission and school which are still going (on the left on the way to Penhalonga). In 1982 the name of the city was revised from *Umtali* to the more accurate *Mutare*, though many older people still use the pre-Independence name.

Chief Mutasa's descendants remain in the area today. In beautiful, granite country on the Nyanga–Mutare road, where poverty looks picturesque, a hand-painted sign with an arrow points "To Chief Mutasa". The present chief's sphere of influence is said to be extensive, although rural areas are now under the official control of rural and district councils. As ex-officio members of the district councils, chiefs are still consulted and retain a certain amount of status and power, but the kingpins are government-appointed District Administrators, who have replaced the colonial Distict Commissioners. One of the main functions of chiefs is their right to settle out-of-court disputes.

Missions and chiefs aren't the only things to survive the last hundred years. **Traders** like the Meikles brothers set up shop and still have a department store in Mutare, where you can sit on the balcony for tea and scones from a silver service. Many lovely old verandahed houses remain too, while the elegant building taken over by the Mutare Club, in Main Street above the *Manica Hotel*, was the former Central Hotel built in 1898.

Orientation and accommodation

Arriving in Mutare **by road** from Harare or Nyanga is a real event: as you hit the top of Christmas Pass, the whole panorama of the town lies below you in a wide valley, the Bvumba Mountains rising to the southeast. Like all Zimbabwean towns, Mutare remains informally segregated, with **Sakubva**, the factory and sawmill side, and high-density suburb, set apart from the more salubrious areas of the city centre.

Points of arrival

Buses from the north come down Christmas Pass before pulling into the **town terminus**; hop off here, before the bus roars off to **Sakubva Musika** (4km out of the town – and with nowhere to stay). **From the south** most buses continue to the centre *after* stopping at Sakubva; if yours doesn't, take any **urban bus** from outside the *musika* bus station gates, or one of the **taxis** that are always lined up. **Luxury coaches** rendezvous at the conveniently central *Manica Hotel*.

The overnight **train** from Harare pulls in across town, an easy walk to lodgings.

Hotels

Most of the town's hotels are pretty classy places, catering for commercial travellers and business people, and sited some way from town. Besides two cheap hotels, there is at least one recommended backpackers' crashpad in the centre.

Anne Bruce's Guest House, 99 Fourth St/Sixth Ave (☎63569). Much the nicest – and the cheapest – of the budget options, this homely establishment has shared rooms and excellent food. It's part of the informal, countrywide backpackers' network of accommodation. The cheerful owner will put you in touch with the latest developments in other places, as well as current information on the route to Beira and places to stay once you're there. ①.

Balmoral Hotel, C Ave (☎61435). Near station and park, a slightly seedy rooming house with basic rooms, kept clean enough. The rooms leading onto the sunny verandah are best. It's used extensively by truck drivers, so you could be treated to the sounds of revving engines and prostitution. ②.

City Centre Hotel, Herbert Chitepo St/D Ave (☎62441). In the same vicinity as the *Balmoral*, more comfortable, a little pricier, and a major though rough nightlife venue, where pickpocketing is rife. The quietest rooms are those which face onto Third Avenue; all have private baths. ③.

Christmas Pass Hotel, (☎63818). On the brow of the hill at Christmas Pass, 5km from Mutare, with nice gardens and a swimming pool. ④.

Inn on the Bvumba, (☎60722). Recommended, with reasonable food. It's eight kilometres from Mutare on the Bvumba Road. ④.

Manica Hotel, Aerodrome Rd (☎64431). The only central upmarket hotel, usually full of business travellers. They offer a great weekend (Fri–Sun) deal, with rooms at half price. ⑥.

White Horse Inn, (☎60325 or ☎216612). Splendidly sited in mountains near Cloudlands, with the best food in the area, though smart-casual attire is a must. Cheaper and a lot nicer than *Manica*. ⑤.

Wise Owl Motel, near the campsite on Christmas Pass (☎84643). Friendly, with good food, a pool, and nice gardens. ④.

Camping

Mutare's **Caravan Park and Campsite** is halfway up Christmas Pass, 6km from the centre. If you're bussing from Harare, get off at the *Christmas Pass Garage* and walk

---

MUTARE STREET NAMES

As with most of Zimbabwe's towns, a series of **street names** in Mutare have recently seen their old colonial monikers replaced by more contemporary spirits, or place names rendered into more authentic spellings. Among the more important are:

Main St – Herbert Chitepo St

Churchill Rd/Milner Ave – Robert Mugabe Ave

Rhodes Drive – Jason Moyo Drive

Victory Ave – Aerodrome Rd

Allan Wilson Rd – Leopold Takawira Rd

Vumba Rd/Ave – Bvumba Rd/Ave

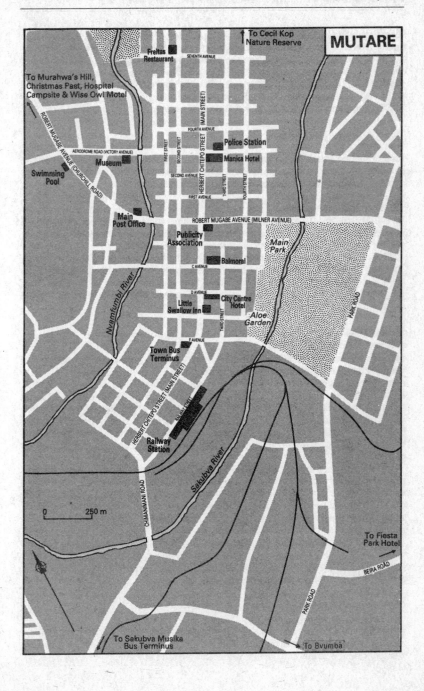

2km downhill to the site, just off the main road. Alternatively, take a taxi back up again once you reach the central bus station. Unless you've brought supplies, you'll have to go to town to stock up anyway. You can arrange to be picked up the next morning or walk a couple of kilometres downhill to a bus stop where you can flag down any passing bus. The site is clean and wooded, but be prepared for lorries rumbling past all night with their headlights shadowplaying on your tent.

The campsite is near **Murahwa's Hill nature reserve**, covered opposite.

The Town and around

Mutare has no grand sights, but, with its parks and surrounding natural landscape, plus a surprisingly good museum, it's a thoroughly pleasant place to pass a few hours or a day while waiting to move on into the Highlands proper.

The park and aloe gardens

To call Mutare the "Garden City" is a slight exaggeration, perhaps, but its **park** and **aloe gardens** are a great place to picnic and while away hot afternoons. They are popular, too, the park benches invariably taken up by students.

The park is shaded by numerous exotic trees and has a palm-lined stream running down its centre. The heart of the botanic collections are some 10,000 **aloes** – large tropical succulents at their best when they flower in fiery tones in June and July. Besides aloes you'll find ancient and protected **cycads**, one of the slowest-growing and most primitive plants on earth.

Mutare Museum

Daily 9am–5pm. Admission nominal.

Mutare's museum is worth a visit, if only to marvel at the goriness of its collection of stuffed animals. **Taxidermy** is quite an art and each practitioner is apparently able to recognise the work of others. If you look at enough stuffed animals you'll notice that some taxidermists are good at putting expressions on the faces, others better at sculpting the forms on which the skins are mounted, or at painting and reproducing the exact hide and hair tones. The taxidermist in Mutare was clearly fascinated by the hunt, and the more dramatic and fearful the better: in his tableaux, eagles sink talons into quivering hares, owls pounce on terrified rodents and red-eyed serpents prey on petrified rats.

Echoing violence in nature, the museum has an enormous collection of **weaponry** – from inlaid silver pistols to crude trading rifles. And there is a hall packed with **vintage vehicles** – some of which look like the 30-year-olds still going strong on Zimbabwean roads. The more serious **historical exhibits** are good, too, with explanations of the successive farming cultures in the region and examples of trade goods from the Arabs and Portuguese on the coast.

Lastly, don't leave without stepping into the **walk-in aviary**, a large and peaceful enclosure bursting with birdsong, where you'll certainly spot one of the most striking birds of the Highlands – the vermilion and jade **knysna lourie**, whose appearance is so at odds with its harsh, grating croak of a call.

Cecil Kop Nature Reserve

Open dawn to dusk. Small admission fee.

An easily walkable two and a half kilometres from the centre (up Herbert Chitepo Street past the *Manica*, then follow the "Tiger's Kloof" sign), this **wooded reserve** is a pleasant tea-time venue, and popular with locals over the weekend.

It's a contrived place, perhaps, but very pretty. In the late afternoon, you can sit overlooking a **dam** where elephant, buffalo, giraffe, wildebeest, zebra and antelope are drawn to food laid out for them at 4pm each day. Alternatively, go earlier on and have the place to yourself; you won't see the same number of animals, but with luck you may spot shy blue duiker, or samango monkeys, darker and with longer tails than the common vervet. These are species unique to the Eastern Highlands and you may well spot them in the wild.

Murahwa's Hill Reserve

If you've a few more hours to kill, and feel energetic, **Murahwa's Hill** – behind the most obvious kopje in the valley as you look from the town centre towards Christmas Pass – is a beautiful place to wander around. The drawback is the hour walk from town, though it's very convenient for the campsite.

To walk around the kopje will take you quite some time: the path initially snakes through the thick draping forest at the base, but then it tracks fairly steeply up to the rocky summit where you find the **remains of a village** protected on three sides by immense granite boulders. This abandoned settlement is thought to be of about the same vintage as Great Zimbabwe; its few remaining artefacts are now in the museum. In a nearby cave there's a collection of unexceptional paintings – evidence of a much earlier settlement.

One way **to get there** is to bus or walk to the *Wise Owl Motel*, where a road on the valley side climbs to one of the park entrances. There's also a gentler incline from the rear of the showgrounds in Jan Smuts Drive. A **map** of sorts at the reserve entrance shows the locations of these archaeological titbits but it's quite easy to get lost. Leave yourself plenty of time to get down while it's still light.

Markets and shopping

Mutare's **markets** are worth exploring, even though they're nothing on the Harare or Bulawayo scale.

The **Sakubva Musika**, by the long-distance bus terminus, is entertaining when you're killing time waiting for transport. Handicrafts on sale are generally utilitarian, but you can rummage around for something interesting and try to guess a use for some of the unidentifiable objects.

Elsewhere, due to the abundant forests of the region, good **wooden crafts** are easy to find: *Jairos Jiri* (41 First Street) and the Museum Shop (Victory Avenue) have ebony snuff boxes and vials, and the former wooden platters, bowls and spoons in ebony and other hard woods. Their stylish brown and white **woven hats** are also great – narrow brims, white zigzags and pleated crowns.

For more mundane requirements, the **Green Market** – just past the railway bridge on the right before the Bvumba turn-off – is a good place for stocking up on fruit and vegetables; macadamia nuts are a particularly nice regional speciality. Regular shops include the *TM Supermarket*, on the station side of town at Herbert Chitepo Street/B Avenue, and *Omar's Hyper*, near the *Manica Hotel* on Herbert Chitepo Street/Aerodrome Road. Mutare is also home to *Mitchells Bakery*, producers of the best **biscuits** in Zimbabwe.

Eating and drinking

Though not the most lively of cities, Mutare has plenty of snacks and cheap food during the day and a couple of good nightspots, where as well as drinking you can also pick up something to eat. The small centre makes access easy.

Restaurants

Breakfast options in Mutare range from basic eggs and toast on the terrace at *Meikles* to the expensive and overwhelming morning menu at the *Manica* and the similar *Wise Owl*, near the campsite. For a bottom line tea-and-bun breakfast, if you're waiting for a bus, try the *Povo Store* at the *Musika*, or hard-boiled eggs, mealies and fruit from vendors there and at the bus terminus.

Chick'n Lick'n, 46 Second St. Good solid food to take away.

Dairy Den, Manica Arcade, Second Ave. Cheap for hamburgers and sandwiches and open until 7.30pm during the week, later at weekends.

Jenny's Cottage, Eighth Ave/Herbert Chitepo St. Good for light lunches and tea on the verandah.

Meikles, Herbert Chitepo St. Old-established joint that really should be experienced at least once. Its terrace is the pleasantest place in town for a drink or light meal.

OK Bazaars, Herbert Chitepo St. Another substantial takeaway.

Station Kiosk, Railway Street. Useful for cheap traditional food if you're waiting for the 9pm Harare train.

Stax Steak House, Norwich Union Centre, Herbert Chitepo St. Apart from the hotels and *Freitas* (see below), the sole restaurant open in the evenings, around the corner from the *Manica Hotel*. The steaks hang over the edge of the plate.

Zvinoira Restaurant, E Ave, near the town bus terminus. Clean and less dingy than the other cheap eating houses.

Nightlife: music venues

Fiesta Park Hotel, out of town on the Beira road, (☎60755). Well worth a weekend visit if someone good is playing. Check the *Manica Post* and look out for posters up in town. The only way to get there is taxi.

Freitas, on the ground floor of Mountview Flats, Seventh Ave/Second St. Less hectic bar-restaurant which occasionally has live music.

Little Swallow Inn, next to the *City Centre Hotel*. Known locally as *Swallows*, this is the place to be if you feel like dancing and drinking heavily on weekends, when guest bands play. Beware pickpocketing and prostitution. Look out for Mutare's own Runn Family, a nationally known band of brothers.

Stirrup Cup. Through the car park behind the *Manica*, this smokey bar spins rock during the week, and a band performs transatlantic cover versions on Fridays and Saturdays.

Cinema and theatre

Both Mutare's **cinemas**, as well as its theatre, are to be found in Robert Mugabe Avenue. The two cinemas show a fairly meagre selection of action-packed popular stuff, but you might strike it lucky if there is a visiting (foreign) performance at the *Courtauld Theatre*. The *Drive-In Cinema*, on Mutare Road close to the campsite, is fun if you have a car.

Listings

American Express is handled by *Manica Travel Services*, Herbert Chitepo St/Second Ave (☎64112).

Automobile Association, Fanum House, Milner Ave (☎64422).

Banks Barclays, Zimbank, Grindlays all in Herbert Chitepo St. Mon, Tues, Thurs & Fri 8am–3pm, Wed 8am–1pm, Sat 8.30–11.30am.

Book exchange 94 Herbert Chitepo St next to *Manica Travel* will trade in your paperbacks.

Bookshop *Book Centre* Norwich Union Centre, Herbert Chitepo St/First Ave. Small but good selection of African and British novels.

Car rental *Hertz*, Tourist Information Centre, Market Square, (☎64711). They offer discounts at weekends, if cars are available, but only on a standby basis – you can't book ahead. *Hertz* do allow their vehicles to go on the dirt road to the Chimanimani National Park. Other firms include *Echo*, *Grant's Service Station*, 21 Robert Mugabe Ave (☎62367).

Chemists *Lancasters Pharmacy*, 95a Herbert Chitepo St (☎62579 after hours). *Central Pharmacy*, Cuthbert Building, Herbert Chitepo St (☎61211 after hours).

Doctors and dentists are listed at the front of Volume 1 of the phone directory.

Emergencies (fire, police, ambulance) ☎99.

Hospital Casualty, Robert Mugabe Ave. If you don't want to wait, it's better to go to the private *Seventh Avenue Surgical Unit*, 123 Herbert Chitepo St (☎64635 or ☎64681).

Immigration Department Milner Ave (☎62322).

Petrol (24 hours) *Grants Service Station*, Robert Mugabe Ave.

Police Aerodrome Rd, opposite *Manica Hotel* (☎64212).

Post office and public phones Robert Mugabe Ave (Mon–Fri 8.30am–4pm, Sat 8–11.30am).

Railway station Ticket office(☎62835) Mon–Fri 8am–12.50pm & 2–4pm. For 1st and 2nd class tickets on the day of travel, if the office has closed, queue up at the economy class ticket booth a couple of hours before departure.

Swimming pool off roundabout on Robert Mugabe Ave. Tues–Sun 6–7am & 10am–5pm. Closed May 15–Sept 1. Admission nominal.

Tourist information Market Square, Herbert Chitepo St/Robert Mugabe Ave(☎64711). Helpful and well-informed staff, who may let you leave your baggage here. Mon–Fri 8.30am–12.45pm & 2–4pm, Sat 8.30–11am.

Tours *Hertz* based at Mutare Tourist Information do minibus tours of the Eastern Highlands and *African Overland Expeditions*, 25 Selous Ave, Harare (☎790677)offer similar tours in their eight-seater Mercedes minibuses.

Taxis Ranks behind the Publicity Association, bus terminus and *Musika* (☎63344).

Travel agents *Manica Travel Services*, Herbert Chitepo St/Second Ave (☎64112) is the place to buy tickets for the coach to Harare.

Visas for Mozambique and South Africa can be obtained above the old cinema at Herbert Chitepo St/ C Avenue.

Around Mutare

Tourism to the **Bvumba Mountains**, which encircle Mutare to the south, wound down steadily during the war years. In more recent times, however, it has picked up considerably, and the **Bvumba Botanical Gardens** and nearby **Bunga Forest Reserve** in particular are worth any amount of hassle to get to. Accommodation is available to suit all pockets, with choices ranging from the famous *Leopard Rock Hotel* to camping at the most spectacularly sited of all Zimbabwean campsites. There are several self-catering cottages available for rent in the area as well as a backpackers' lodge. Moreover, a family-type hotel is rumoured to be opening soon on the Woodlands Road.

North side of Mutare, **Penhalonga** and the **La Rochelle Gardens** also make a good day trip. The Penhalonga gold mines are still in operation, alongside an attractive old village with run-down vintage buildings and trading stores. Accommodation possibilities here include the little-used Penhalonga campsite, or cottages on the La Rochelle estate, 5km away.

Bvumba Botanical Gardens

Open daily. Small entry fee.

An annual rainfall higher than London's has created lush cloud forest in the **Bvumba Mountains**, known in Manyika as the mountains of the mist. Such dream-like connotations have inspired the **Bvumba Botanical Gardens** themselves, which lie 32km south of Mutare, harmoniously landscaped in the best romantic tradition of English formal gardens.

Getting there

There's no public transport to the gardens but prospects for **hitching** are reasonable, especially over the weekends when the gardens are a popular tea-time trip; on weekdays, a number of people living on smallholdings and farms in the mountains also go into Mutare to work, so late afternoon would again be a good time. Wait at the *Bvumba Service Station* on the corner of Park and Bvumba roads, where you'll get cars from the centre bypassing the bottom end of town. Many of these lifts, however, don't go all the way to the gardens, so be prepared for a longish walk. A possible alternative is to use the weekend bus service to Bvumba which departs from E Street terminus, opposite Customs House, on Fridays, Saturdays and Sundays at approximately 8.30am and 2pm. The bus can take up to two hours to reach the gardens, along a circuitous route through the Zimunya communal lands.

At Cloudlands, the road forks, uphill to the gardens and down to the Essex and Burma valleys, where there are commercial farms and communal lands. The **walk** from here to the gardens is a rewarding hike through smooth green hills, flower-specked pastures and thick stands of forest and pine trees. Farmhouses with English country gardens look inviting as you slog on and every mile or so, as the road curves higher to reveal even more vistas, you'll find lay-bys – off-the-road concrete tables and seats created for family outings by a nation of picnickers. On the Bvumba road, before you reach the gardens, you'll pass through **Bunga Forest Reserve**, an extension of the rainforest preserved in the gardens and also waymarked.

Accommodation

The thick, shaded lawns of Bvumba's **campsite** are scented in the summer by magnolia blossom. The bathrooms are spotless and there's no shortage of water from the wood boiler outside. In the evening you have the whole estate to yourself and the views over Mozambique's Lake Chicamba Reial, a thousand metres below, are simply stupendous. Without a tent, those on a lean budget should head for *Cloud Castle Guest House* (②), which is intended specifically for backpackers, ten minutes from the entrance to the Botanical Gardens. There are four very small bunk rooms (2 per room) with facilities for cooking, as well as a couple of shared rooms in the owner's farm house. The atmosphere is relaxed and it's a good place to base youself for a day or two walking in the area. The owner does trips three times a week into Mutare and picks up people from *Anne Bruce's Guest House* (see p.212) or the Mutare Publicity Association – an ideal arrangement for a two-night stay in the Bvumba. Check out the current situation at the Association. To book for *Cloud Castle*, write to P. Hancock, Cloud Castle Estates (Pvt) Ltd, PO Box 957, Mutare (☎217620).

If you decide to make your own way to the guest house, you'll see a sign on your left just beyond the 28km peg on the main Bvumba Road, twenty metres before the dirt road which leads to the entrance of the Botanical Gardens. Bring fresh meat and vegetables from Mutare and get the rest at the *Naro Moru Store*. The store, a few hundred metres before the entrance to the gardens down a road to the right, sells bread and milk, tinned food and drinks. At weekends it doubles up as a bar, but the whole place is closed on Mondays.

The *Mutare Publicity Association* has a full list of **cottages** to let in the **Bvumba and Essex Valley**. They're usually fully booked during the school holiday season and are not places where you can just turn up hoping for the best, but ring ahead from town and you may strike lucky. Two, reasonably close to the gardens, are sited on an ornithological station (PO Box 812, Mutare; ☎215125). The station isn't open to the general public but the proprietor takes guests birdwatching. Another possibility is *Far Forest Cottage*, about 3km from the gardens near the summit of the Bvumba (PO Box 234, Mutare; ☎218524).

The gardens

Surrounded by indigenous forest, the **Bvumba Botanical Gardens** (now run by National Parks) were the creation of a former Mutare mayor and his wife, who lived here from the 1920s to the late 1950s and called them – in true homesick fashion – the Manchester Gardens. Remarkably, throughout the mayhem of the bush war, the gardens remained immaculately maintained.

Paths meander delightfully through flowering shrubs and trees gathered from all over the world. Waterlilies float on the central ornamental lake; scattered gazebos invite contemplative rests; and pristine lawns and flowerbeds give way on the fringes to a more African feel where giant tree ferns adorn streams – as they do all over the Eastern Highlands. The full range of Zimbabwe's upland flora is represented at Bvumba, including many varieties of orchid.

Summer downpours can flood everything in sight and it's a lot chillier up here than in Mutare. Weather permitting, a **teashop** is open every day except Monday from 10am until 4pm.

The rainforest

You can explore the **rainforest** which adjoins the gardens along a number of waymarked paths; maps are available at the main entrance. A **path** from the edge of the campsite takes you through the forest and back to the gardens – a two-hour circuit. It begins by leading down into jungly forest, where the indigenous trees rise about you – all darkness and silence until the monkeys catch sight of you and the birds screech in alarm. Further on you begin to hear the sound of chattering streams cascading over slippery rocks. For a shorter walk, several paths branch off the main trail.

Chinyakwaremba (Leopard's Rock)

Outside the gardens, it's possible to climb **Chinyakwaremba**, or Leopard's Rock hill. A path from a lay-by on the right of the main road, leads up one and a half kilometres from the turn-off to the botanical gardens. It's an easy twenty-minute walk up to the top where there are lovely views into Burma Valley, across to Mozambique, and down to the chateau-like hotels below.

Zimbabwe's most romantic hotel – *Leopard's Rock* – has recently been restored after closure during the bush war. It's a de luxe mountain resort with a casino, golf course and US dollar prices to match. Bookings to *Leopard's Rock Hotel*, P.O. Vumba (Harare ☎700711 or ☎708391; ⑨).

Nearby, further splendid accommodation is on offer at the Italian POW-built *Castle*. Its owners will only take one party at a time, cooking lavishly for them. It's reputedly wonderful but in ensuring the total privacy and seclusion of the place, we couldn't get a look in. The nights of bliss are reasonable (dinner, bed and breakfast) with a two-night minimum at weekends. If you're interested, write or phone well in advance (Private Bag V7401, Mutare; ☎210320).

Penhalonga and La Rochelle

A good day's excursion from Mutare easily combines **PENHALONGA** village and the somewhat overgrown La Rochelle Gardens, with the option of overnighting – or even spending a few days – at one of the charming cottages at La Rochelle.

Hidden in a valley on the old scenic route to Nyanga, 17km from Mutare, Penhalonga feels like a neglected outpost of the 1940s. It was the first of the settlers' **gold prospecting** sites – gold is still mined here – and retains the appearance of a trading post. All the shops have dark interiors, with tailors on the pillared verandahs sewing with old treddle Singers, and, inside, lengths of cotton-print hanging from the ceiling. Two of the town buildings are particularly handsome – the corrugated-iron **church** built on pillars and the red-roofed **school**. Dating from the beginning of the century, the church is in a Victorian Gothic style, a tin version of a medieval English country chapel.

Getting to Penhalonga is straightforward. Several **buses** a day pass on the way to Stapleford and Honde Valley from Mutare's *Musika*, while three buses (6am, 11am and 3pm) go to Penhalonga itself from the town terminus. Alternatively, and more easily, catch any of the numerous buses up Christmas Pass from Robert Mugabe Avenue, get off at the Christmas Pass Service Station – where the road to Penhalonga begins – and **hitch**, or catch another bus, from there. The **campsite** and caravan park is sadly under threat of closure – despite its backwater charm few visit Penhalonga these days.

La Rochelle

LA ROCHELLE, 4km south of Penhalonga in the Imbeza Valley, is a pleasant 3-km walk from the main Mutare road, past farms and smallholdings and some beautiful stands of *Acacia abyssinica* in the valley. In contrast to the exceedingly well-maintained Bvumba Gardens, this once magnificent estate is a bit run down – its name living on mainly through a brand of strawberry jam. However, the **teas** are good and there are some very nice cheap **cottages** in the garden (PO Box 34, Penhalonga; ☎250).

An infrequent **bus** goes to the Imbeza Valley from Mutare's **town terminus**; otherwise take any Penhalonga-bound bus and walk from the signposted turn-off.

Nyanga National Park

One and a half hours' drive north of Mutare (and just three hours from Harare) on good tarred roads, **NYANGA NATIONAL PARK** attracts largely Zimbabwean outdoor enthusiasts, who come for the mountains and forests, and for trout fishing. The park is devoid of big game, though most of the smaller animals and antelope are present in large numbers, and provides some rewarding walking country, criss-crossed by hundreds of well-defined footpaths and by current or abandoned fishing roads. There are less energetic pursuits on offer, too, such as lazing around the pools and waterfalls at one of the national parks' three camps.

In the southern sector of the park, there is more remote **wilderness territory**, where you could easily spend several days hiking, while, in the east, the looming mass of **Mount Nyangani** is a simple enough, though myth-bound, summit to scale. The Nyanga region is also scattered with intriguing **ruins and forts**, mostly unrestored and hidden beneath shrouds of ferns and undergrowth. On the grandest scale, Van Niekerk's ruins, now known as **Ziwa ruins**, straggle across at least fifty square kilometres of open country in a jumble of rubble-strewn stone terraces and levels. On the borders of the park itself are the mountain resorts at **Juliasdale** and **Troutbeck**.

Park practicalities

The best visiting **seasons** are either side of the school holidays (see p.47), in April–May and August–September. The scenery then is especially lovely and the weather as warm and dry as it ever gets. Be prepared, however, for cold nights all year round, and – if you come during the rainy season – for wet weather that can sometimes last for days on end. It never snows though.

Where you **base** yourself in the park is largely a matter of how pressed for time, and how well equipped, you are. The most convenient concentrations of overnight options are at **Rhodes Dam** and **Udu Dam** – at the western edge of the park, within a few kilometres of the main entrance and headquarters – and at **Mare Dam**, further afield to the east. Entry to the park is free, and lodges go for the normal low National Parks fees.

THE BEIRA CORRIDOR

Beira, on the Mozambique coast just 300km from Mutare, is the obvious outlet for land-locked Zimbabwe's export trade. This route, or corridor, to the sea has in the past been hazardous, but hopefully the 1992 ceasefire in Mozambique will change its status.

Until 1974, the port of Beira was used extensively and was also the place where many Rhodesians took their seaside holidays. Then the overthrow of the Portuguese and the establishment of the Marxist **Frelimo** government obliged Rhodesia to export its goods via the long, expensive rail link with Durban in South Africa.

In response, Smith's intelligence agency set up a 500-strong destabilisation force, the Mozambique National Resistance Movement (MNR) or **Renamo**. When majority rule emerged in Zimbabwe, Renamo was handed on to the South Africans, who built it into a monster of (according to some estimates) 20,000 fighters. During the 1980s South Africa used Renamo as an instrument of foreign policy, supplying it by means of parachute drops, its main function being to bring Mozambique to its knees. In this it was devastatingly successful; large parts of Mozambique were overrun by Renamo, whose grisly attacks helped to grind the country down into one of the world's poorest, and one easily manipulated by its neighbour.

After Independence Zimbabwe began, once again, exporting goods by rail to Beira. But Renamo attacks on the line brought traffic to a standstill in 1984. The crisis led to pragmatic co-operation between Zimbabwe's socialist leadership and predominantly white, capitalist interests, who formed the **Beira Corridor Group** to oversee the rehabilitation of the coastal link. Hundreds of millions of US dollars were being pumped into the programme in a concerted effort to break South Africa's stranglehold on the economies of both countries.

Up to seven thousand Zimbabwean troops were sent in to guard the route, costing around US$70 million annually. Renamo carried out its own atrocities against Zimbabwean border villages as well as continuing the civil war in Mozambique. Drought and famine in the 1990s has further crippled Mozambique.

A peace accord came into effect in October 1992 under the supervision of UN observers, which stipulated the withdrawal of Zimbabwean troops protecting the corridor, with elections late in 1993. President Mugabe said "we hope the Mozambican soldiers will be able to protect the routes". The ceasefire stipulated that Government soldiers and Renamo fighters be disarmed and formed into a unified army. At the time of writing, it's very unclear whether Renamo, like Unita in Angola, will give up the fight, and impossible to predict whether, or when, peace and stablitity will return.

Many more tourists though, are crossing safely into Mozambique, with minibus transport at the Machipanda border post, 10km from Mutare, available to take passengers to the palm trees and sands of Beira. Mozambicans also regularly cross into Mutare for shoppping. Check out the current situation at the Mutare Publicity Association and with other travellers. The association can also provide information on where to stay once you're there.

Apart from the single luxury hotel at Nyanga (situated in the north of the park), roofed accommodation around here consists of one- and two-bedroomed **lodges** (note that Udu has large lodges only). These lodges can sleep up to eight people; each of them is fully serviced, right down to there being loads of chopped wood and laid fires, although lighting it is left up to you. During school holidays or long weekends, it's virtually impossible to get lodge accommodation without having **booked** six months or more ahead (you can do this through the National Parks Booking Office in Harare, see p.43). In the off-season though, or during the week, you stand a fairly good chance of a place just turning up at the Parks' Office at Rhodes Camp. **Camping** however is cheap and space is never a problem. The river water throughout Nyanga is bilharzia-free and drinkable.

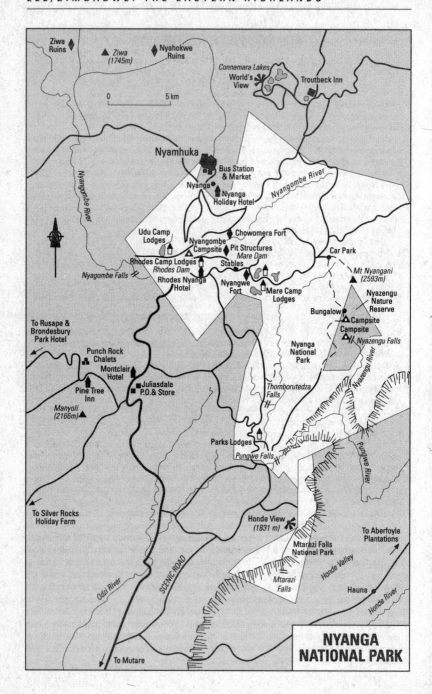

Ziwa Ruins

▲ Ziwa (1745m)

▲ Nyahokwe Ruins

Connemara Lakes

World's View

Troutbeck Inn

0   5 km

Nyamhuka

Bus Station & Market

Nyanga

Nyanga Holiday Hotel

Nyangombe River

Udu Camp Lodges

Nyangombe Campsite

Chowomera Fort

Pit Structures

Mare Dam

Car Park

Rhodes Camp Lodges

Rhodes Dam

Stables

Nyagombe Falls

Rhodes Nyanga Hotel

Nyangwe Fort

Mare Camp Lodges

Mt Nyangani (2593m)

Nyazengu Nature Reserve

Bungalow

Campsite

Campsite

Nyazengu Falls

To Rusape & Brondesbury Park Hotel

Nyanga National Park

Punch Rock Chalets

Montclair Hotel

Juliasdale P.O. & Store

Pine Tree Inn

Thomborutedza Falls

Nyazengu River

Manyoli (2166m)

Pungwe River

Parks Lodges

Pungwe Falls

To Silver Rocks Holiday Farm

Honde View (1831 m)

To Aberfoyle Plantations

Mtarazi Falls National Park

Honde Valley

Odzi River

SCENIC ROAD

Mtarazi Falls

Hauna

Honde River

To Mutare

NYANGA NATIONAL PARK

You will need to bring most provisions with you. There is just one park **shop** (on the south side of Rhodes Dam, open 9am–2pm) which sells essential food supplies, but nothing fresh. There are no **money-changing** facilities in the National Park, but a branch of *Standard Chartered* is open daily in Nyanga Village.

Juliasdale

Straggling along the main road to Nyanga, **JULIASDALE** is the last settlement before the park, a regional centre consisting of little more than a couple of shops, a petrol station and post office. The area around is a popular retirement location for white Zimbabweans, and Robert Mugabe, too, has a country retreat somewhere among the forests and fruit farms. Lower down, there are splendid granited valleys, msasa trees and tempting *gomos* to climb.

Accommodation in the district is restricted to three plush hotels and some **rented cottages** (for which advance booking is essential: see box above). Of the **hotels**, the *Montclair* (⑦) is seriously upmarket, with an evening dress code for the casino. However, you don't have to be a guest, or smartly dressed, to enjoy its valley-sided gardens for tea or drinks, or go one-armed banditting in its darkened gambling hall. The other hotels are the *Brondesbury Park*, on the Rusape side of Juliasdale, at the start of the Nyanga "vacationlands" (☎388-341 and ☎388-342; ⑤ all-in); and the *Pine Tree Inn* (☎388-25916; ⑥ all-in), which lies between it and the town, hard by some accessible granite tops. The *Pine Tree* has a top reputation for its food.

Rhodes Dam and around

Office open 7am–6pm; ☎Nyanga 274.

RHODES DAM is the most convenient, though the least exciting, of the camps, sited close to the main road and near the shop and hotel. The **lodges**, tucked between the pines, face onto a small lake – one of several recreational dams in the park. The area is tame, but pleasing, and it provides easy access to some historical sites as well as walks around the rest of the park.

Nyangombe Campsite and Brighton Beach

A couple of kilometres from the office, on the main Nyanga road, is **Nyangombe campsite**. From the office a shortcut over the Nyangombe River leads to the site.

Along the river you'll see a natural pool known in the ex-pat community as **Brighton Beach**, complete with changing rooms and gazebo. A small waterfall and rockslide culminate in a large pool of icy water surrounded by a riversand beach – good for sunbathing, and not as crowded as the name suggests.

Rhodes Nyanga Hotel and Museum

After visiting the Nyanga area in 1896, Cecil Rhodes wrote to his agent:

> *Dear McDonald*
>
> *Inyanga is much finer than you described. I find a good many farms are being occupied. Before it is all gone, buy me quickly up to 100,000 acres and be sure to take in the Pungwe Falls. I would like to try sheep and apple growing. Do not say you are buying for me.*
>
> *Yrs. C. J. Rhodes.*

The old colonialist was successful in acquiring a substantial slice of territory and, indeed, the park was known up until Independence as "Rhodes Inyanga".

Rhodes's former residence, a simple Georgian-style stone house set among English oaks and chestnuts, stands just across the lake from Rhodes Dam. It is now incorporated into the **Rhodes Nyanga Hotel** (☎377; ③–④), where the room-rate includes dinner and breakfast (it's cheaper to stay in a rondavel than an en-suite room). Non-residents are allowed to drift in to laze in the rose garden and look round its **museum** in the old stables (9am–1pm & 2.30–5.30pm, closed Mon). As well as a fair amount of Rhodes memorabilia, an interesting photo exhibition gives the history of colonisation in the area from the Portuguese and British up to recent resistance.

There's a comprehensive display in homage to **Chief Rekayi Tangwena**, one of Zimbabwe's nationalist stalwarts, buried at Heroes' Acre in Harare. Tangwena fought against the eviction of his people from their land in the Nyafara area beyond Troutbeck during the Smith era, gave considerable assistance to guerillas throughout the **bush war**, and provided a link with the spirit mediums who encouraged resistance. In 1975 he helped **Robert Mugabe** and **Edgar Tekere** escape into Mozambique. After Independence and his appointment as a senator, he participated in a programme here to resettle orphaned and homeless children.

The Pit Structure

A common sight throughout the Nyanga area are **pit structures**, or "slave pits" – roofless, two- to three-metre-deep enclosures that are something of a mystery. No archaeological evidence has been found to support the notion that they were used to detain slaves – certainly no one seems to know who kept the slaves, who the slaves were and why they didn't escape. Other interpretative stabs have included fortified refuges for women and children, grain stores, gold-washing tanks, and symbolic representations of the Phoenician fertility goddess Astarte's womb. The most widely accepted theory is that the pits were livestock pens, some say for miniature cattle that Portuguese travellers were supposed to have seen. But in view of the reputation of the Portuguese explorers for tall stories – and in the absence of any supporting material – it makes sense to retain some scepticism about that. It's more likely that ordinary goats, sheep and pigs were corralled in these sixteenth-century enclosures.

The restored pit structure which everyone visits is near Rhodes Dam on the road to Mare, but there are thousands more in Nyanga which you'll stumble across, sometimes literally, on walks. They occur singly or in groups of as many as twelve or more – look out for an isolated clump of trees or thick bush when you're walking in the region. If you're interested, it's as well to visit the developed site first so you know what you're looking for, and because the reconstruction spares you the difficulty of imagining what they might have been like in use.

At the Rhodes Dam Pit Structure, a **dry stone wall pit** on an earth platform is partially cut into the side of a hill and held back by a retaining wall on the lower slopes. This was the centre of the homestead, and from here you can creep into a pit, through a narrow, curved **tunnel**, roofed with flat stone slabs. You can't see the exit from the entrance, but halfway along, the sky penetrates through a gap that used to open into the largest hut on the platform above. A nifty floor-slot enabled the occupants to block and unblock the passage at will with a timber pole. According to one theory, the master of the house had his headrest at the top of the pole and no one could tamper with the security system without waking him. Evidence of a **drainage system** in the pits reinforces the idea that animals rather than grain were kept in them.

Chawomera Fort

The other ruins at Nyanga, equally mysterious, are of fort-like hilltop structures, always commanding superb views across the valleys and plains. From the pit structure exhibit, there's an agreeable one and a half hour walk to **Chawomera Fort** and pits, one of the easiest hilltop fort ruins to reach.

The function of these so-called forts, which are invariably sited next to a few pits, is uncertain, as all sorts of things indicate that they weren't actually built for defence. While all the walls have small, square **loop holes**, reminiscent of gun slits, when you look through them the views are restricted and no weapon could effectively have been fired from them. Assailants, moreover, would have quite easily been able to fire through the wide inside openings. And although the forts are in easily defensible positions, none has a nearby water supply, so inhabitants couldn't have withstood a siege for long. One theory suggests they were a series of beacons or signal points, from where a kudu horn sounded messages carried across the valleys. It is in fact possible to see several forts from one site, once you can recognise the hills on which they're constructed.

As you head for Chawomera from the Rhodes Dam Pit Structure, you'll see a dirt road leading to workers' houses attached to the Government Experimental Orchard. Follow it for a few metres and, just before a fence, take a well-defined path next to a pine plantation on your left. This path continues down to the **Nyangombe River**, hugging the river, with bathing spots along the way. Cross the river at the second bridge and continue uphill along the path until it hits the gravel road from Rhodes Dam, which leads east, in 6km, to the fort.

Mare Dam and Mount Nyangani

MARE (pronounced *mah-ree*) is the camp closest to Mount Nyangani and the isolated areas between the "back" of Nyangani and the Pungwe Falls in the south. Despite its proximity to these remote parts, though, pine-forested Mare Dam itself has no hint of the back-of-beyond. In a rare flight of fantasy, National Parks have built the well-sheltered **lodges** like Swiss chalets, complete with pitched roofs, wooden finishings and laid log fires (bring your own matches). If you're into riding, Mare is a convenient camp, just 3km from the stables.

FISHING, HORSE RIDING AND TENNIS

Boat hire is an option at any of the dams – for an afternoon drifting in the sun rather than any serious rowing (the lakes are pretty small). You need to claim a boat quickly though, as many are taken by trout fishermen. If you want to **fish**, rainbow, brook and brown trout can be hooked all year, though you need a licence from Rhodes Dam office. You'll need to bring your own rod.

Horse riding can be arranged at Rhodes, Udu or Mare camps; the stables are an hour's walk from Rhodes, on the Mare road. The horses are hired with a guide who'll take you on paths through the park for an hour and a half to the pit structures, Nyangwe Fort or the experimental orchard. Proficient riders can also book a horse for a full day's escorted ride. The terrain is ideal for brisk gallops and the Nyangombe river provides delightful picnic sites.

Tennis rackets can be hired at the rather underused courts at Rhodes Camp.

Nyangwe Fort

Nyangwe Fort, half an hour's uphill trudge (or a rather easier ride) above Mare Dam, would be worth visiting for the view alone. It is also, however, the most complex of the so-called forts, five enclosures surrounding the original one on the summit. Within the structure – possibly dating back to the sixteenth century – are the remains of nineteen circular stone bases for huts or granaries.

From Nyangwe you look straight across to **Chawomera Fort** (see P.225), a good two hours' walk away. To reach it, head down the hill just before the pony trails office and stables on the main road, from where a well-defined path on your right skirts pine planta-tions and heads straight across the grassy valley, over the Nyangombe River to the fort's twin hills.

Climbing Nyangani

Unlike Mount Ziwa in the north, which rises abruptly from the plain, **MOUNT NYANGANI**, long and flat-topped, seems scarcely higher than the mountains around it. Nevertheless at 2592m it's a substantial mountain, Zimbabwe's highest, and often mist-wrapped and shadowy. According to local legend it has frightening people-eating tendencies, and one or two walkers have disappeared without a trace over the years; mostly, it seems, teenagers. The mountain holds considerable religious significance for Shona people. Locals from the Honde Valley say the mountain should be approached very respectfully – one should never shout or make a noise on it – and that they wouldn't dream of climbing it themselves.

Despite the taboos, Nyangani is frequently climbed as a morning's hike. The two-hour **ascent** is clearly marked from the car-park, with white cairns along the way to guide you where the path becomes indistinct. The climb reveals spectacular panoramas into Mozambique, and around the summit you'll find lots of water; several rivers rise here. There are areas of quicksand up here too – it's certainly marshy towards the summit and trig point – and it's not difficult to see how the people-swallowing reputation might have arisen. Go up only in fine weather and take something warm in case the mist comes down. The very active **Mountain Club of Zimbabwe** does this climb regularly and has its own hut on Nyanga. If you're interested in joining, it's best to make contact in Harare: ring ☎36599, ☎792492, or ☎727703.

To **get to the trailhead** without a car you have to hitch the 10km from Mare. If you decide to walk, it means making camp at the base, which is ideal if you intend to hike for a few days beyond Nyangani to Mtarazi National Park and into the Honde Valley.

An ambitious and very beautiful three-day hike of 48km will take you from Nyangani to the Pungwe Falls, Mtarazi Falls and into the Honde Valley (see the section following), from where you can catch a bus to Mutare.

Nyazengu Nature Reserve

Perhaps the most rewarding way to explore the Nyangani area and beyond is to camp and hike through the privately owned, and very remote, **Nyazengu Nature Reserve** adjoining the National Park. The reserve, at the base of Nyangani, has exceptionally beautiful views of the mountain and across the grasslands towards the Pungwe Gorge. There's a choice of several well-marked trails, some of which take you to waterfalls and clear pools of amber rocks. The **Nyazengu Falls**, deep in forest, are easily as dramatic as the better-known Mtarazi Falls. One trail takes you right to their valley base, or you can soar upwards to the top of Nyangani.

While it's possible to go for a day's hike in the reserve, for a modest fee per vehicle and per person, it's an ideal base for a couple of days walking. The main campsite, near the office, is spectacularly situated and completely undeveloped, apart from a long-drop. Staff provide water for cooking – all the river water is safe to drink. It's also possible to camp at the Nyazengu Falls, in a sheltered forest site, though there are no facilities at all. If camping doesn't appeal, there is a lovely bungalow for rent, sleeping six people for a total rent of $US24 per night, perched on the side of the mountain. Book through Mr C. Trace, *Inyangani Farms*, 128 Upper East Road, Avondale, Harare (☎303518).

Unless you hike in on foot, which takes a full day from Mare Dam, you'll have to use a high-clearance vehicle – you have to ford a river, but the rough road is passable all year round. Take the road marked *NO ENTRY*, on the right just before the road climbs to the Nyangani car-park. From here it's eight kilometres to the office where you obtain a permit to walk. While there are no shops or supplies available in the reserve, you can buy fresh trout.

Udu Dam

Unlike Rhodes and Mare, **UDU CAMP** provides the opportunity to get out of the pines and into granite and indigenous vegetation. The **lodges**, with long sloping roofs, based on traditional Nyika thatching, face the dam and ruin-capped hills, and *Acacia abyssinicas* grow in a smooth V-shaped stand, up the facing hills. The **Udu River** flows through here, too – forming an exquisite, wide valley where waterbuck feed – before leading into the dam and out into a bathing pool, and eventually joining with the Nyangombe.

The **Udu Valley** preserves the gentle steps of ancient terracing, and remains dotted with pit structures, one outside the back door of the Park's Office. The chunky **Nyangombe Falls** with square-cut rocks are near Udu and make a nice walk. And orienting round about Udu is really easy: wandering in the encirling hills you can always spot the valley.

The two-kilometre **walk to the camp** from the main Nyanga road, opposite the Nyangombe campsite is pretty, heading first uphill, then opening out into a view of the camp in the valley; you'll invariably get a lift from a passing car, if you want it. Well-worn shortcuts between the loops in the road take you straight to the nearest **shop** – at Rhodes Hall.

Nyangombe Falls
The **Nyangombe Falls** are an impressive cubist plunge, half an hour's walk if you take the dirt road, or one and a half if you go over the saddle of the hills facing the lodges.

The Nyangombe tumbles dramatically over steep blocks before smoothing out into a densely wooded gorge below. Inviting as it looks, several people have been killed trying to climb down the walls of the gorge or edging too close to the waterfall, where the rocks are treacherously wet. You can see the waterfall quite clearly from dry rocks a short downhill walk from the car park.

To reach the falls over the hills, take the path which starts at the back door of Udu Camp reception and keep bearing right to cross the river, then cut up to the saddle between two hills through woodland with dwarf bonsai-like msasas, wild fruit trees and the odd antelope. Follow your nose down until you turn right onto the dirt road to the falls. Instead of descending, you could carry on to the top of the highest hill to inspect a collapsed **fort** marked by a single big tree, clearly visible from the Udu Camp office. A path from the ruins leads back down through trees, across the dam wall (next to the pool) and to the lodges.

Nyanga Village

NYANGA VILLAGE nestles in a valley surrounded by mountains and extensive grasslands, 23km north of Juliasdale on a good tarred road. A charming if unexciting place, it makes a good base, with fine walks nearby and easy hitching to the national park. It also services the nearby communal lands with shops and buses, and has the area's cheapest hotel.

The Three Sisters mountain, its slopes dotted with smart houses, dominates the village, with the huge rampart of the Troutbeck Massif beyond. The village itself straggles between two distinct characters: at the more upmarket end is the *Nyanga Holiday Hotel*, at the other the **Nyamhuka** township. **Buses** for Mutare, Harare and Troutbeck leave from Nyamhuka, which has a small **market**, street food and better stocked shops than in Nyanga centre.

Near Nyamhuka, your eyes will be drawn to a couple of brightly painted huts proclaiming a **craft village**. Quite a modest place, it sells mostly woven woollen mats and rugs made by local women in competition with the *Zuwa Weaving Co-op* in Nyanga centre. *Zuwa* has lovely handmade stuff in wool and cotton, subtly coloured with local plant dyes. You might consider posting home their chunky woollen rugs with bold and imaginative designs, or the handspun blankets.

The friendly and comfortable, if slightly barrack-like, *Nyanga Holiday Hotel* (☎336) does a reasonable full board deal. They also have a swimming pool, and you can pop in for tea and excellent home-made biscuits. If you're staying, a path leads up the Three Sisters mountain from the hotel. You could make a day of it from here to Nyangombe Falls or the stone forts, even on foot.

Troutbeck and World's View

Up in the mists beyond the northeast boundary of the national park, **TROUTBECK** was the fantasy creation of one Major McIlwaine, an Irishman who established the very swish **Troutbeck Inn**, planted acres of forest on the bare hills – in the early days of the inn he made each visitor plant a tree – and built several lakes. Almost in conspiracy with the artifice, the weather up here can be cool and drizzly when the rest of the country is sweltering.

They claim at *Troutbeck* that the log fire in the foyer has been kept burning since the place was built in 1950. It's very much a mountain resort, with all sorts of leisure-time activities from croquet to riding. The conspicuously rich take their holidays here with the nanny having been brought along to look after the kids. Still, the *Troutbeck* offers the best **cream teas** and meals in the area and non-residents are able to hire **horses** to ride up through the bracken and ferns to **World's View** – a thrilling scarp-edge panorama.

NYANGA'S FLORA AND WILDLIFE

The vast grassy areas of Nyanga hold a fantastic range of **wild flowers**. Look out for Zimbabwe's national bloom, the delicate **flame lily** (here more often yellow than red), **gladioli, ground orchids** and different kinds of **heather**. **Aloes** of all sizes grow in the various ruins, making beacons of them in June and July when they flower red and orange. After grass fires, the red **fire lily** springs up with extraordinary vigour in the blackened stubble. South Africa's floral emblem, the furry **protea**, grows well here too; eight species are native to Zimbabwe and three endemic to the Eastern Highlands. They are easily recognisable – small trees with white or pinkish-white flowers surrounded by rose, or deeper pink bracts covered with silvery hairs.

There's an amazing diversity of local **wildlife**, too. It's not as spectacular as in the big game parks, but kudu, reedbuck, klipspringer, leopard, hyena, and herds of wildebeest all inhabit the park, and Nyanga is well known for its populations of samango monkeys and blue duikers, which are found nowhere else in Zimbabwe. One of the former wardens compiled a checklist of mammals and birds – including rare sightings of buffalo, which occasionally penetrate into the Pungwe Gorge, and even lion passing secretively through. However, you're highly unlikely to meet any of these travellers.

World's View

World's View – not to be confused with the World's View where Cecil Rhodes is buried – is a seven-kilometre hike, or ride, from Troutbeck. At the summit of the steep neighbouring high ground, the remains of a **fort** are connected to the mountain by a narrow ridge. With precipices on three sides, this is definitely the wettest and windiest stonework site of all. In the wide-open treeless moorland of this lakes district, you can get an idea of what the country was like before the *Troutbeck* transformation. The lakes, disappointingly, aren't for public use.

Troutbeck settlement has only the general store selling basics, a garage and a very quaint post office.

Access

Getting to Troutbeck without your own car is not too difficult. Occasional **buses** run from Nyanga Village to Troutbeck and Nyamaropa Communal Lands, or it's a rather more reliable **hitch** from the Troutbeck turn-off, a couple of kilometres south of Nyanga on the main road. Buses back to Nyanga leave from outside the trading store opposite the hotel.

If you're just up for the day and get to **World's View** early enough, you can **walk** 10km directly back to Nyanga Village. Just below the World's View car park, a steep, narrow path leads down the mountain for 4km until it reaches a prominent dirt road, from where it's another 6km to Nyanga Village.

Ziwa and Nyahokwe: ancient farmlands

The remote (and tricky to reach) **ZIWA RUINS** spread for miles across the hillsides north of Nyanga. Their central reserve is 40 square kilometres in extent but this vast complex rambles very much further than that. They are also, confusingly, known by their old colonial name, **Van Niekerk's Ruins** – named after the Boer major of nearby Bideford Farm, who led the archaeologist Randall McIver around the site in 1905.

Exploring Ziwa

Exploring the ruins you meander on and on, drawn by yet another pathway or area of terracing to the next hill. Little restoration has taken place: stepping about the stone-littered bush you can feel what it must have been like for early archaeologists. At first it all seems somewhat puzzling, but after a time patterns do begin to emerge, with Ziwa Mountain a point of orientation back to the road. To help out, there's now a small museum on site, and guides to show you around.

The settlement's seventeenth- and eighteenth-century builders may have been influenced by Great Zimbabwe masonry techniques. But these are no monuments to a wealthy ruling class, rather the **homesteads and farms** of ordinary people. When the uplands over to the east lost fertility and crops began to fail, people shifted westwards into the valleys. They built **terraces** for crops and **enclosures** for huts and livestock; platforms for huts are less common than in the uplands as the abundance of stone meant that surrounding walls could be used for protection. Typically, entrances are lintelled and you may notice slots in the inner doorway for a wooden drawbar. **Grooves** are worn into some flat stones within enclosures where women ground grain.

You can walk down the networks of walled **lanes**, probably for driving livestock and still in good condition, but with candelabra trees and aloes growing out of the heavy stonework. And, if you've visited the Rhodes Dam reconstruction, you'll quickly be able to spot tree-spouting **pit structures**.

Standing back and trying to grasp the extent of it, it's tempting to imagine an enormous community peopling the hills and valleys. However it's more likely that these structures were the work of a relatively few agriculturalists, spread over two centuries, who had to move on every few years when the soil lost its fertility. Although scant excavations have been carried out, it is clear that the stonework was done by **Bantu people** and not by Portuguese or Arabs.

Getting to Ziwa

Visiting the ruins without your own car is pretty well impossible, as there is no public transport and apart from the odd visitor few vehicles, if any, pass this way. The ruins and museum are 29km from Rhodes Camp and signposted. The best route is to travel north out of Nyanga village for 14km, turning left to reach the Nyahokwe Village site (see below), 5km on; from here it's a further 8km to Ziwa.

Nyahokwe

The granite-built **NYAHOKWE VILLAGE SITE** lies crouched under the cliff face of the top of Nyahokwe Mountain and has similar features to the other Nyanga ruins. One really interesting feature is a **dare**, or meeting place for elders – a large circular area with upright stones around it. Also, about 100m below the ruins (on a bare granite plateau just off the path), there are some eighty or so **grinding hollows** in groups. Probably several people would have sat around each group grinding down iron-bearing rock for smelting. The remains of **furnaces** have been found in the area and trade was certainly pursued with border-crossing Portuguese.

Some of the nearby granite outcrops – as at Ziwa – are **sacred mountains**, probably centres of the old **Mwari Cult** and not a good idea to climb. Two North Korean officers who were training Zimbabwean brigades took a disdainful attitude to local prohibitions about Ziwa, climbed it and were never seen again.

Mtarazi National Park

Adjoining Nyanga Park's southern edge, **Mtarazi National Park** is essentially considered part of the Nyanga region. It is, however, a much wilder zone, with undisturbed indigenous forest, and is somewhat difficult to reach without a car. But, if you've time, you can hike there: two recently rebuilt national parks' cottages in the dramatic **Pungwe Gorge**, plus the unparalleled views into the luxuriant **Honde Valley** and Mozambique, provide strong incentive. It's magnificent country.

Most people tend to get only as far as the viewpoints along the **Scenic Road** which loops eastwards from the main Mutare–Nyanga Village road. These take in the much-photographed vistas of the **Pungwe Falls** and **Gorge**, the 762–metre drop of the **Mtarazi Falls** and the deep seat of the **Honde Valley**. If you're **hiking**, it's possible to penetrate these panoramas, either from the ridge of the Scenic Road itself or more adventurously walking the park from Rhodes Camp to Nyangani in the west, south to Pungwe and Mtarazi Falls, then dropping into the Honde Valley – approximately 60km in all.

The Scenic Road is lightly trafficked and you'll end up walking much of it if you're car-less. Hikers have got stranded along this route – not an experience to be recommended, as it's very wild, entirely without facilities, and patrolled by leopards and even the odd lion.

Accommodation in the area is thin on the ground. Apart from two national parks lodges at Pungwe, there are just a couple of private cottages for hire on the Scenic or Brackenbridge Road; there are no official campsites. For determined walkers, National Parks has developed a campsite – with shelters – at Mtarazi Falls. It's only possible to reach the falls by nightfall if you leave Rhodes camp first thing.

Pungwe Gorge and Falls

The first obvious stop on the Scenic Road is for the bird's-eye view of **PUNGWE GORGE** and the top of the falls before the Pungwe River, which rises at the foot of Mount Nyangani and flows southwards through the park before plummeting 240m into a wild and dramatic gorge. Coursing through the tree-gridded gorge the Pungwe eventually descends into the Honde Valley and Mozambique. Although you can't see the falls themselves, you'll certainly hear their roar.

Pungwe Drift and Lodges

Getting down to the river from the scenic drive isn't as daunting as it looks from the top, and the recently rebuilt National Park **lodges** (destroyed during the war), set idyllically next to the water at Pungwe Drift, must be the choicest places to stay anywhere in Nyanga. They make a wonderful base for hikes.

From the Scenic Road, follow the signposts to **Pungwe Drift** (40 minutes on foot) then walk another 20 minutes along a riverside path to the top of the falls. There's a great swimming spot in the river above the falls; the current here won't tow you over the edge and you can float downstream and safely duck out before the flow gathers speed. The bush comes right to the water's edge amid smooth rocks and clean river sand.

Basing yourself here, or hiking around the park, you can continue northeast along the **Drift Road** as it follows the valley and climbs onto the escarpment: high mountains rear up on your right and fantastic views open into the gorge all the way to the car park at the base of Mount Nyangani (24km). From this track you can drop into some very wild montane forest down in the gorge.

If you've less time, a couple of disused fishing roads leading off the Scenic Road make good shorter walks. Some 4km north of the turn-off to Pungwe Drift, a no-through-road leads a kilometre down to **Thomborutedza Falls**. Here, the fast-flowing river rushes over sink holes, which create an effervescent, natural Jacuzzi. Two kilometres beyond, a similar dead-end track passes various pit structures and trails the Pungwe nearer to its source on Nyangani.

Mtarazi Falls and Honde View

MTARAZI FALLS – the highest in Zimbabwe – are at the end of the line for Scenic Road view-spotters and a fair walk from their signposted car park. They spout from the cleaved edge of the vertical green cliff to disappear in virgin forest half a mile below.

The **best time** to be here is late afternoon, when the sun behind the water makes the slender falls gauzey and golden. To **swim** nearby, make your way to the river above the falls, marked by beautiful tree ferns. Here, brown rocks, sloping into the river pools, warm the water a few more sufferable degrees. On the road to Mtarazi, don't miss the turn to the **Honde View**; the aerial view of the **Honde Valley** where its contours relax to enter Mozambique, is stunning.

Into the forest

Several well-trodden **trails** lead down from the escarpment into the **Honde Valley**: two used by workers from the Valley connect the Pungwe and Honde viewpoints, but you'd really need a local person to show you. One of the overgrown paths is about half a kilometre from Mtarazi, heading east into the valley; without a guide, it's hard to know which fork to take when the path splits. The other, equally teasing, trail drops right into the Pungwe Gorge and hugs the river bank into the Honde Valley below. If you find someone to show you the way, though, either walk makes a good, day-long hike to the valley floor and back, through awesome **montane forest** which opens into clearings with views of the valley. From Honde you can catch a bus to Mutare if you're moving on.

The mountainous regions of Nyanga have over one hundred **ferns** (Britain has just 30), including four different kinds of the giant tree fern. Overhead, epiphytes – orchids of many varieties – dangle from the branches. This kind of forest, increasingly whittled away by tree clearance, once covered the whole of Nyanga. **Hardwoods species** include mlanje cedar and yellow wood. **Flowering trees** to look out for are cape chestnut, the forest fever tree with its giant leaves and sweet-scented flowers, the glossy-leaved wild holly and the tube-flowered notsung.

While you admire the canopy above, spare the odd glance for the forest floor, which has its own absorbing interest and occasional dangerous encounters. The **gaboon viper** spends its days half-buried in the leaves and litter of the forest floors of the Eastern Highlands. Although less aggressive than other vipers, it's the largest of the family and heavily built: up to a metre and a half long, gorgeous and deadly. Brightly patterned with white, buff, purple, pink and deep brown diamonds and triangles, it looks the epitome of the African carved wooden snake.

The Honde Valley

During the liberation struggle some of the bloodiest fighting and atrocities took place in the **HONDE VALLEY**. That's all, however, that most people know of it. Lying at the foot of the Nyanga range, adjoining Mozambique, it is effectively cut off from the rest of Zimbabwe. It remains important, before you take off, to ask around in Nyanga and Mutare to ascertain the **safety** of the Honde Valley – there are occasional MNR incursions.

The possible trails into the valley are detailed above. By bus, the easiest approach is to take any Mutare-bound bus from Nyanga to the Honde turn-off, then pick up one of the buses from Mutare into the valley; there are no direct buses from Nyanga. The turn-off for the valley is 25km along the main Juliasdale to Mutare road.

The other way of getting there is in a 4WD vehicle **from Troutbeck** on a rough, unsignposted road via **Nyafaro** – at least two and a half hours' drive.

Masimike and the Pungwe River

Dramatic landscape and temperature changes occur as you wind down the single tarred road from the main Mutare road into the valley's lush hothouse – a district of intensively worked communal lands and shiny green hills of tea. Dominating the centre of the valley are the **Masimike** – sentinel granite pinnacles up to 100m high, which make good orientation points. The **Pungwe River** flows through the valley, with rope footbridges crossing the clear water in a couple of places. The final section of the forested river gorge is well worth exploring if you're based in the valley.

Tea estates were established around Honde in the 1950s, when planters crossed Nyangani on foot into the roadless vale. In the populous **communal lands** people grow rice as well as maize, tea, and coffee; you can buy tropical produce from women who walk up the mountains to Juliasdale. While the land is very productive, villagers have a hard time deterring wild pigs and baboons which ravage their crops, while the absence of roads to some of the settlements, and thinly spread facilities, force people to trek up to 10km to the nearest shop or clinic. No strangers to foot-slogging, those who live closest to the mountains climb two to three hours to the top every day to work on commercial farms or private homesteads.

Mtarazi Falls – from below

To see the **Mtarazi Falls** again, but from below, take a path from Hauna, a village with a couple of main-road stores – to the base of the falls, camouflaged by cliff-base jungle. Lion-hearted hikers can push through to the secret **waterfall pool** which locals believe is inhabited by siren-like beings who'll lure you into its depths. If you decide to venture into the vegetable gloom, leave early: a night in the damp forest isn't recommended.

Accommodation

There's only one realistic place to stay in the valley – the gracious *Aberfoyle Country Club* on the Aberfoyle tea estate (Harare ☎708239; ④), 90km from Juliasdale, with a pool and lovely gardens. Book in advance. Staying at the cheap *Pungwe Hotel* (②)– a serious drinking venue in the heart of the communal lands – is a generally bad idea.

The Chimanimani Mountains

At the southern end of the Eastern Highlands the **Chimanimani Mountains** are completely different from the rest of the range and geologically unique in Zimbabwe. The apparently modest size of the peaks – Binga, the highest, is 2240m – gives no idea of their scale, the mountains rising in rugged ridges. Sheltering in this fortress, the **Chimanimani National Park** is an enthralling wilderness of rocks, caves, waterfalls and gentle valleys.

Chimanimani Village

CHIMANIMANI, 148km south of Mutare, comprises a small collection of shops, a hotel, a post office and a group of houses gathered around a red-earthed "village green". The 1899 administration building is a handsome example of an early colonial type that seems all roof – dominated by ruddy corrugated iron. Basically a centre serving the farms and forestry estates in the vicinity, the village is surrounded by mountains, with the **Chimanimani Rampart** in the blue distance; on some evenings the mountains appear to catch fire with a pink glow as the rays hit the rose quartz embedded in the rock face. It is a wonderful place to idle away a few hours, or even several mellow days: so pleasant, indeed, that visiting government officials reportedly ask to be put up here rather than in Chipinge, the region's real administrative centre.

White settlement in the region began after the pioneer **Dunbar Moodie** visited in 1890, and told his friend Marthinus Martin about the beauty and potential of the countryside south of Umtali. It sounded too good to pass up and, true to colonial form, Martin led a party from South Africa to take over the area in 1894. Sinking roots, they named the district **Melsetter**, after Moodie's family home in the Orkney Islands.

After Independence, Melsetter became **Chimanimani**, a name previously reserved for the nearby mountains. One version of the name's meaning has it that the main footpath between Zimbabwe and Mozambique runs in close parallel to the Msapa River and is so tight in places that you have to walk single file or even sideways: a *chimanimani*.

The Village – and practicalities

Buses arrive at the local market: the place for ridiculously cheap avocados, pineapples, bananas and vegetables. Over the road is the **hotel**, appropriately named *Chimanimani Hotel* (PO Box 5, Chimanimani; ☎511; ③ & ④), where you can collapse after the long bus journey in a 1950s lounge, complete with sleeping cats, polished floors, wicker chairs and log fires. The cheapest **rooms** are at the back, but consider spending a little extra for one with a glorious view of the mountains – and a bath. The hotel has also converted two back rooms into dorms for backpackers, at around US$3 per person.

For the same price though, you'd do a lot better at *Heaven*, Zimbabwe's best back-packer lodge, situated on the edge of the village over to the right, as you head out of town on the National Park Road. Most of the accommodation is in shared rooms, though there are a couple of single and double rooms, and it's always possible to camp in the garden. The views of the mountains are superb and the owners have put in a sauna and started horse trails. A chef, decked out in whites, is available to cook reasonably priced English breakfasts and an evening meal, or you can cook for yourself in a separate kitchen.

A new restaurant near the post office, the *Beta*, provides an alternative to eating at *Heaven* (the food at the *Chimanimani Hotel* not being recommended). Patronised by backpackers, it serves hamburgers and pies from early in the morning until 11pm. Change **money** before you come to Chimanimani: the bank is only open once a week, and the hotel will only change travellers' cheques for residents. Finally, although it never snows you should bring warm clothes, especially in July and August when the mountains can be very chilly. During the rainy season, a waterproof is recommended for hiking and evenings are cool enough for jumpers.

The local **craft shop** across from the post office has a small but excellent collection of **regional handiwork** – *gudza* dolls, bags and mats and, really fun, articulated wooden snakes. *Gudza* products are woven from bark that's been chewed and dyed in browns, ochres and oatmeal. No trip to Chimanimani is complete, either, without the delicious, homemade **cheese and jam** from the smallholding signposted as you leave town on the road to the National Park. Some self-catering and reasonably priced accommodation is also available here – dearer than *Heaven*, but more private. Another holiday cottage is available ten minutes' walk from the village, sleeping six to ten people. Contact Mrs MacCrimmon on Mutare ☎64721 (mornings) or ☎213915 (afternoons).

If you're interested in trees, the **arboretum** is worth a visit, if only to see the strangely named and stranger looking **cabbage tree**, which bears no resemblance to its namesake.

Nearby walks: the Eland Sanctuary and Bridal Veil Falls

There are a couple of good **walks** out of Chimanimani Village if you're not in a rush to move on to the National Park. For these and other possibilities, it's worth investing at the craft shop in the excellent local pamphlet-map produced by *Milkmaps* in aid of the rural hospital. Alternatively, *Heaven* provides its own local maps, which are slightly easier to follow.

The Eland Sanctuary

The **Eland Sanctuary**, just north of the village on the slopes of **Nyamzure** – or Pork Pie as it's also known – is a rugged terrain of cliffs, waterfalls and dense bush. It was created to provide a refuge for **eland**, Africa's largest antelope, which are indigenous to the area, and were coming into conflict with the timber-growing industry. The eland are now successfully kept away from the bark and buds of pine saplings behind a fence in an eighteen-square-kilometre tract. You'll also see zebra, waterbuck, bushbuck, klipspringer and noisy troops of baboons. Antelope can be spotted, too, roaming wild in the surrounding farmlands, though in considerably smaller numbers than the vast herds locals remember.

There are two **roads to the Sanctuary**, but you can explore it further on foot along the ridge. Alternatively, scale Nyamzure, either from the village or from the car park halfway up if you're driving. To get onto the Nyamzure road turn left at the end of the road past the Chimanimani post office, then first right and keep on up. The Sanctuary (free admission) is open all hours.

Bridal Veil Falls

Just as you enter the Sanctuary, the much-snapped **Bridal Veil Falls** cascade down a sheer rockface into an inviting pool of beautifully clear water that looks as if it ought to be inhabited by water sprites draping themselves across the mossy rocks. The falls are found lying at the bottom of a green, wooded valley where there is a neglected picnic site under the trees.

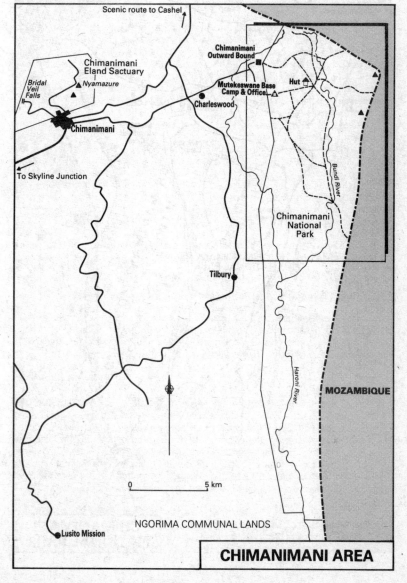

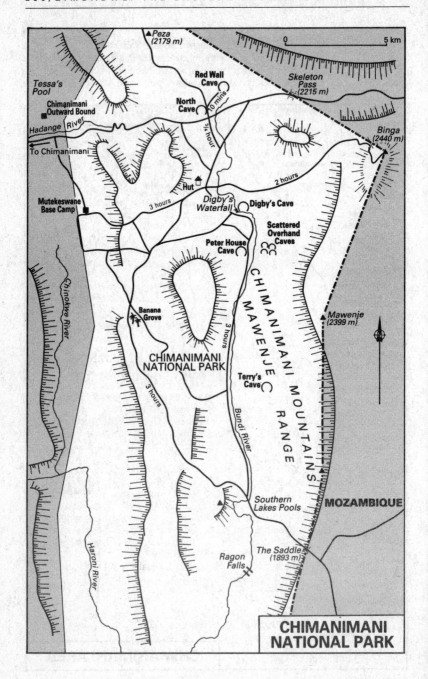

CHIMANIMANI NATIONAL PARK

It's a two-hour **walk** to the falls on a seldom used dirt road which meanders through msasa-clad valleys full of birds. You need to take the road leading out of town with the *Beverley Building Society* on your left, and then just keep going. If you want a challenging and longer walk back, take the ridge route, which runs to the south of the Eland Sanctuary.

Chimanimani National Park

The only way to penetrate the **CHIMANIMANI NATIONAL PARK** (which charges a nominal admission fee) is by scaling the blue rampart you see from Chimanimani village. It's possible to do a day's hike, if you have your own transport to get to the foothills and back to the village, but far more rewarding to spend some days exploring the mountains.

Between the park's mountain hut (at the centre of the park) and the soaring peaks shared with Mozambique, spreads the ample **Bundi Valley**. Spliced by the Bundi River, this is covered in grass which changes from wet-season green to maizey yellow and dried brown after the rains subside. Its downhill course is broken by a series of waterfalls splashing into icy cola-coloured pools, with smooth rocks to bask on. Giant **tree strelizias** (wild bananas), **tree ferns** and **cycads** fringe the banks, while the grass slopes are dotted with bright yellow helichrysm, grass-aloes, and small mauve gladioli.

But it's the **rocks** on the way up the valley which are most astonishing. Completely different from the granite formations peppering much of Zimbabwe, the folded and faulted silvery schist and quartz has been sculpted into fantastic stone forms. In the fine white soil, wild hibiscus, heather, aromatic tree shrubs and fiery pincushions grow.

Getting to the park

In the absence of any public transport, it's not easy to get to the National Park without a car, and prospective hitchers may end up walking the 19km on the Tilbury Road to **MUTEKESWANE** base camp from Chimanimani village; traffic is sparse on this rough road, though you may pick up the odd motorist heading for the Park or nearby Outward Bound School. They can tell you at *Heaven* or the *Chimanimani Hotel* if anyone in the village is organising pick-up truck transfers to and from the National Park – a handy service which depends entirely on the availability of vehicles in good order.

If you do have to **walk**, the route is some compensation, taking you through pine, eucalyptus and wattle plantations as the mountains loom closer. When the mountains seem almost on top of you, the road swings steeply up and along the **First Range**, thick with msasa trees. It then forks, heading left to *Chimanimani Outward Bound* and **Tessa's Pool** (see overleaf) and, continuing to the right another 3km uphill to the **base camp** where you report in. You will have to give details of your length of stay and agree to foot the bill if you get hopelessly lost and a search party comes looking for you. The **Ordnance Survey map** (1:50,000 Melsetter 1932 D4 and 1933 C1, C3, available from the Surveyor General's office in Harare) is invaluable, although *Heaven* also supplies hiking maps. The Parks people provide a much less detailed version.

Accommodation

Camping is permitted anywhere in the **National Park** or, as a base, you can use the mountain hut overlooking the Bundi Valley. If you arrive too late in the day to go into the mountains you can **camp** at Mutekeswane, with the usual facilities but no roofed accommodation.

Bring all your **food** with you – and a torch – as there's no shop in the Park. However, you don't have to lump a tent around. The **mountain hut** overlooking the Bundi Valley, two hours up from the base camp, has wooden beds and thin mattresses plus two gas cookers and washing facilities. You can choose one of the two dorms to sleep in (they are not segregated) or use the verandah. This is the place to meet other walkers and line up a lift back to Chimanimani Village.

An **attendant** lives nearby, down a discreetly camouflaged path (to give the feeling that he's not really there). Don't break in if you find the hut shut up – there's always someone around to unlock the door. If you plan to do day trips from the hut, it's safe to leave all your gear, but if you want to be extra cautious bring a padlock – the benches in the central area double as lockers.

For nights out in the park, there are several well-used **caves**, often near waterfalls. Each has its own informal name, and one or two are floored with dried grass.

The practical limits

Two thirds of the Chimanimani range is actually in Mozambique. On the Zimbabwean side, **hiking** is confined to a long thin stretch from the peaks in the north, scaleable on day trips from the hut, down the Bundi Valley to **Dragon's Tooth** and beyond, in the south. In the north, local mountaineers often ignore the border, which is drawn through Skeleton Pass, and head off to Martin's Falls, Valley of the Wizards and endless deserted peaks. There's no way up from Mozambique to this northern side of the park but Mozambicans do cross over at the **Saddle** in the far south, on a well-worn track to the store at Tilbury. We even saw two women, each with a bed on their heads, making their way back over the mountains to Mozambique – an incredible feat given the distance and steepness. As you'd expect, the army also uses this path.

It's not a good idea to go beyond the **Saddle and Ragon Falls**; besides army presence, the path fizzles out on the Zimbabwean side and you have to cross into Mozambique to get further south. The MNR is no threat in the park, but keep to the Zimbabwean side.

Routes to the peaks – and Tessa's Pool

Three routes head up to the mountain hut and peaks. **Bailey's Folly**, the most direct, leads straight up behind the Parks Office. It takes about three hours to the hut, with several false tops on the way – whenever you think you're nearly there, another ridge appears. The route is waymarked with cairns which should be diligently followed; when the path braids, keep going left.

Banana Grove – the "bananas" are actually tree strelizias – is a much gentler approach, good if you're heading for the **caves** along the Bundi River on the way to the Southern Lakes. From Mutekeswane follow the fire break until you meet the path going up from Dead Cow, the former base camp.

Hadange River, the third way up, is a route people more often take down because it leads to Tessa's Pool (see below). When it's **wet**, the Hadange route is not advised, as the path cuts through a very slippery forested ravine and criss-crosses the river, which is impassable after a storm. If you are caught out by the river – or any other in Chimanimani – simply wait a couple of hours and the water will subside. If you're descending, the path gives out about a third of the way down and seems to fork: keep to the left on higher ground rather than right which takes you into a tangled gully. Otherwise the path is good.

En route you'll pass a massive rock face – the aptly named **Temple of Doom** – where the Outward Bound people practice rock climbing and abseiling. **Tessa's Pool** is to be found down a clearly marked path off the main drive-way. Surrounded by luxuriant palm trees, lianas and ferns at the bottom of a waterfall, it is the perfect spot to cool your steaming heels after the descent. Either get permission at the Outward Bound before you swim, or check at the *Chimanimani Hotel* before you set out, to find out the latest position.

Peaks, caves and pools

Like all mountain climbs, once you've made it to the top there are still more tops. **Peza** and **Binga** (Kweza on some maps) are each a couple of strenuous hours' climb from the hut on good paths, with fantastic views. **Peza** is easier and you go along beautiful open stretches of the Bundi Valley to the waterfall at North and Red Wall caves before you start climbing. Both caves are big enough to sleep a troop of boy

scouts. **North Cave** is located right above the waterfall while **Red Cave** is a bit higher up on the other side of the river and is not quite as easy to find. A path leading straight down from the hut goes right across the valley and up formidable Binga. **Skeleton Pass** is an easy walk from here, but the views are not as exceptional as you might have expected.

If you want to **swim** and laze about, there's a waterfall, pool, and a small overhang – **Digby's Cave**, a good night shelter – a steep half-hour down from the hut on the main path to Southern Lakes. A little further on is yet another waterfall and **Peterhouse Cave**.

For a **full day trip**, you could continue on the path all the way to the **Southern Lakes**, where the swimming is exceptional. On your left, slate-blue **Mt Mawenje** (also called Turret Towers) dominates the horizon, while the river widens into a big oxbow creating reed-fringed, wine-dark pools – the "lakes".

Midway is **Terry's Cave**, set under a massive boulder, and with two compartments in the unlikely event of two parties arriving. No one seems to know who was responsible. One theory is that a priest spent some time here before leaving the country and this was his goodbye present. Terraces have been built to keep out the draughts, a fireplace made and the floor covered with masses of dried grass.

The snag is that the cave is difficult to find. If you want to spend the night here, locate it before going down to the lakes. It's in a very rocky area, quite a long way from the main north–south path; there's no direct route to get from it to the lakes, so you have to come back to the river. To get to the cave you must rock-jump the river. One path to it veers off opposite a small tributary, the other where a minor path back to Banana Grove joins the north–south one. Another, and possibly easier route is to take a path on the east side of Peterhouse Cave. From Southern Lakes it's a three hours-plus hike back to Base Camp.

There are no caves at the lakes themselves.

Corner

The only part of the National Park accessible by car is the northeast corner – known as **CORNER** – approached along an extremely rough, unsignposted road through commmunal lands. National Parks may build cottages here which would open up the area, but at present few venture in.

South to Chipinge and Chirinda

CHIPINGE, located 64km southeast of Chimanimani, is a working town which sees little tourism. Its small centre hides bottling plants, a brewery and storage depots down the backstreets, with the presence of two banks in the centre hinting at the wealth produced from this industry and from the surrounding commercial tea and coffee plantations. Chipinge is also the nearest town for the sugar plantations of the extreme eastern lowveld.

There are plenty of white farmers here, but while they still do business in the centre, they deserted it socially after Independence. The hotel is a boozer now and a pale face sitting in the former whites-only streetfront lounge elicits amused amazement from passing kids.

The Town: some practicalities

The *Chipinge Hotel* is clean, and gives surprisingly good value given its local monopoly. It's also the place for full-blown and reasonably priced **meals**, served with surprising panache. Half a kilometre from town, there's also a slightly derelict and little-used **campsite**.

There's **cheap food** in abundance from take-aways in town, down Seventh Avenue toward the market/bus station, and in the high-density suburbs. In the evening, try the **late-night** *Tasty Foods* in Joubert Street, open until 8pm. Otherwise, most of Chipinge shuts shop at 5.30pm. After dark, the best scene is the Joubert Street takeaway, or the hotel bar – you don't come here for the nightlife. An occasional **concert** brings the city beat to the high-density suburb's Gaza Hall or there may be **football** at the nearby Gaza Stadium.

Chirinda Forest Reserve

All that remains of a large primaeval woodland is preserved in the tiny enclave of **CHIRINDA FOREST RESERVE**, 30km south of Chipinge. It is almost a fantasy African jungle, with thick, dark undergrowth, lofty trees reaching skywards, science fiction plants with outsized leaves, and loud bird calls.

Getting to Chirinda – and camping

The forest surrounds a hill-top mission, known as **Mount Selinda**. Getting there, it feels, requires quite a commitment, especially as you're heading down the road towards the closed border with Mozambique, though as the mission provides education and basic health care to the local community there's usually a fair amount of traffic.

This traffic includes a number of **buses** from Mutare, Bulawayo and Masvingo, all of which pass through Chipinge en route to the mission. Chipinge's bus stop is just outside *Ron's Motors* on the corner of Main Street and Seventh Avenue. By far the best idea, though, is to travel up in one of the many fare-charging **pickups** that can be taken from the corner of the main drag and the Mount Selinda road. Many of these rides terminate at Chako Township, but try to make your way 2km further on to the mission hospital, which is close to the (signposted) **"Big Tree Path"** which heads into the forest. If your lift ends at Chako, get off at the T-junction and walk uphill to the signposted forest entrance.

There are no official **campsites** at Chirinda, but you can find a clearing for discreet pitching. The ones at the picnic site in the forest proper, or at Swynnerton's Memorial on the other side of the road are both possibilities. There's a small rural **store** at the T-junction, but it makes more sense to pick up supplies from the better-stocked shops in Chipinge.

Mount Selinda

There's no mountain as such at **MOUNT SELINDA**, just a big forested hill visible from some distance. It's a steep climb from Chipinge's farmlands; maize fields, grazing cattle and neat rows of coffee bushes fill the passing scene.

The mission was founded by Americans in 1889, but its main claim to fame is as the point of arrival in 1919 of Africa's first *agricultural* missionary. One of his big successes was the Nyanadzi irrigation scheme on the Birchenough Bridge to Mutare road – long before Triangle and Hippo Valley estates undertook their complex water diversions. Peasant agriculture thrives at Nyanadzi today: good grain and fruit yields are achieved in an otherwise dry and unpromising environment.

Across the tarred road and a little further toward the mission hospital, is the over-grown plinth of **Swynnerton's Memorial**, another evocation of good colonial works. Apparently forgotten, Swynnerton was an English entomologist who settled in Chimanimani in 1898. He researched tsetse flies and butterflies, and was appointed Tanzania's first game warden in 1919. His researches there led to an acclaimed paper on the reclamation of tsetse-afflicted districts. He's best known in Zimbabwe for his work as a naturalist, and gave his name to a number of plants and birds.

Into the forest

A web of paths weaves through the forest. From the picnic site, marked trails lead to the **Big Tree** and the **Valley of the Giants** – both routes worth taking.

The **Big Tree**, 70m high and 16m round, is probably the oldest living thing in the forest. The wildest estimates claim it as a contemporary of Christ – a nice myth for a tree near a mission. More realistic stabs reckon it's a thousand years old – and in decline, judging by the large sections of dead wood. Like many Valley of the Giants goliaths, it's a red mahogany, *Khaya nyasica*, used by Africans to produce massage oil from the seeds and an anti-colds infusion from the quinine-bitter bark.

Another remarkable lumber-type at Chirinda is the orange, yellow and black timbered **zebra wood**, found nowhere else. And, on the wildlife front, you may encounter the **forest elephant shrew**, which is unique to a small part of the southeast. This rat-like creature has kangarooish back legs and a mini-trunk, and beneath each lower eyelid a fluorescent spot acts as a recognition signal for other shrews in the forest's evening gloom. The more common **samango monkeys** emerge from the treetops at dawn and, after catching some sun, head off to breakfast on Chirinda's leaves, fruits and berries.

travel details

Buses
From Mutare to:
Beit Bridge 1 daily, 7am.
Bulawayo via **Masvingo** 3 daily, 6am–noon.
Chimanimani 4 daily, 6am–noon (4hr plus).
Chipinge 2 daily, 6–9am (4hr plus).
Harare 6 or more daily, most before noon (5hr).
Honde Valley via **Penhalonga** 3 daily, 6am–noon.
Nyanga 3 daily, 6am–noon (3hr 30min).

Mount Selinda 2 daily, 6–9am.
Stapleford via **Penhalonga** daily, noon.
Other bus routes
From Chimanimani to:
Mutare a bus leaves the market daily, 5.45am (4hr); check with locals.

From Chipinge to:
Bulawayo 2 daily, early (9hr).
Harare 2 daily, early (8hr or more).

Mount Selinda 5 daily, until 11.30am (1hr).
Mutare 5 daily, until 11.30am (4hr).

From Nyanga to:
Harare 3 or more daily, early (7hr).
Mutare 2 daily, early (3hr 30min).

Trains
From Mutare to:
Harare nightly, 9pm (9hr).

Coaches
The only service in Manicaland is run by *Express Motorways*, departing from the *Manica Hotel*. Book at *Manica Travel Services* (see Mutare *Listings*, p.217).

From Mutare to:
Harare stopping en route at Rusape and Marondera, daily except Tues & Thurs, 1pm (4hr 30min).

PART THREE

BOTSWANA

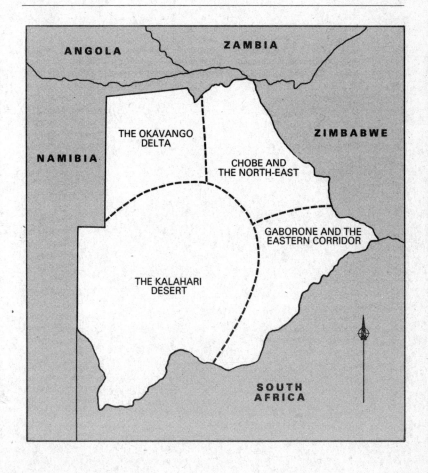

Introduction

Despite its natural bounty – magnificent landscapes trampled by some of Africa's finest wildlife herds – Botswana remains all but unvisited by independent travellers. Official policies designed to entice the well-heeled to luxury lodges while neglecting other tourist facilities are partly to blame. But away from the glamour zone, endless miles of untouched wilderness invite unparalleled – and safe – adventure.

As it sees out its third decade of independence, Botswana enjoys a rare distinction as a harmonious, peaceful and stable African country. While retaining a firm commitment to multi-party democracy, it has been transformed from one of the world's twenty poorest nations by the discovery of diamonds. It now boasts Africa's fastest-growing economy, and is at last able to develop health services and primary education, neglected under British colonial rule.

Nonetheless, Botswana has never fully slipped from the grasp of South Africa. Unlike Zimbabwe, it has no manufacturing sector of its own, and therefore imports almost all its manufactured goods from South Africa. Botswana walks a precarious tightrope, being simultaneously a leading member of SADCC – an economic union of front line states committed to reducing dependence on South Africa – and also a member of the Southern African Customs Union, which links it to a system of tariff-free trade with South Africa. The shops are full of South African goods. Though constrained by these pragmatic questions of survival, Botswana has consistently refused to have truck with apartheid, and has always offered asylum to political refugees from South Africa.

While existing cities such as the capital, **Gaborone**, have been re-planned and modernised, and whole towns have appeared in the new mining areas, **urban Botswana** is still no place for the traveller seeking excitement. However, the **wildlife tourist industry** is burgeoning, especially around the Okavango Delta in the north, with facilities available to suit every budget. But if Botswana looks undeveloped now as you travel through, imagine what it was like twenty years ago. President Quett Masire recently remarked:

The other day I saw the floodlights turned on at the new stadium in Gaborone. I remembered that in 1967 I flew to Kinshasa and saw street lights and wondered if ever such lights would be seen in some towns in Botswana. We have come a long way since then.

■ Botswana: Desert and Delta

Botswana, in contrast to varied Zimbabwe, is flat – basically a shallow sand-filled basin 800–1300m above sea level. A plateau broken with small hills runs along the eastern corridor – bordering South Africa and Zimbabwe – to form a **watershed**. Eighty percent of the population lives in a small area along the central watershed and the lands to the east up to the Limpopo River. There's just enough rain here for growing hardy crops, but also easily tapped underground water and ample grass ideal for rearing cattle.

Westwards, conditions are less favourable, giving way to the **Kalahari Desert**, which covers the central and southern two-thirds of the country and extends north, south and west – well into Angola, South Africa and Namibia. Although in essence the desert forms itself into huge dunefields, these are now largely stabilised by scrub, bush, forest and grasslands. Only in the extreme southwest do you find archetypal deserty dunes.

In stark relief, the northwest of the country is watered by the vast **Okavango Delta** – 15,000 sq km of channels, oxbow lakes, flood plains and islands. The entire north is splashed by periodically watered **lakes and salt pans**, which are more usually covered by a dried-out greyish salt-saturated clay hostile to any vegetation.

■ Where to go

Botswana's main appeal lies in its wild outdoors. For practical reasons most visitors concentrate on the accessible northern and eastern sections of the country. The top attractions, in the north, are the **Okavango Delta**, and its **Moremi Wildlife** and **Chobe Game reserves**. Also in the north, the **Makgadikgadi and Nxai pans** – each with a game reserve – are worth visiting for their plains and the vision of the endless salt pans.

Elsewhere, throughout the **Kalahari Desert**, are huge game reserves, more or less inaccessible without 4WD. **Ghanzi** in Botswana's wild west is an unlikely community where Batswana farmers, San hunter-gatherers and Afrikaner ranchers somehow work things out together.

Most of the **large towns** lie along the eastern corridor, with Mochudi, near Gaborone, worth a visit as a traditional village with vividly patterned hut walls. Sandwiched between the tar and the border with Zimbabwe is the farmland of **Tuli Block** – an obvious destination for the budget-minded – with fine private game reserves among red sandstone hills and the riverine forest of the Limpopo River.

Language and Peoples

The official language of Botswana is English. Newspapers are in English, which is used in parliament and in schools, from the fifth year upwards. However, many other languages are spoken, and Setswana is understood by ninety percent of the population. Setswana is a Bantu language, part of the western section of the great Sotho-speaking group that includes the people of Lesotho, and the South African Venda. It's useful to grasp the implications of its prefixes. The language is *Set*swana, one Tswana person is a *Mot*swana while several Tswana people are *Bat*swana. *Ba* is prefixed to all ethnic group names, for example *Ba*kgatla, *Ba*sarwa, *Ba*ngwato.

■ Peoples

Botswana is one of the most integrated countries in Africa. Although only around half of the country's people are Batswana, there's a tradition of incorporation in Tswana history, which meant that members of other groups were gradually absorbed (admittedly sometimes as second class citizens) to build up a Tswana community. In modern Botswana this custom has been adapted to forging a harmonious nation with scrupulous attempts by the government to promote equality.

One of the oddities resulting from the colonial carve-up of Africa is the existence of national borders that slice through ethnic and linguistic communities. Fewer than a quarter of **Setswana-speakers** live in Botswana, the vast majority being resident in South Africa. In Botswana there are several lineages, some of

which you'll come across periodically in this book. Broadly speaking you'll find the **Batawana** in the north centring on Maun, the **Bangwato** along the east with their capital at Serowe, and in the southeast the **Bakwena** around Molepolole, the **Batlokwa** around Gaborone and Lobatse, the **Bakgatla** just south of the Bangwato, and the **Bangwaketse** in the southwest. Despite these divisions, however, most people regard themselves first and foremost as Batswana* – citizens of Botswana – and only members of a subgroup as an afterthought.

Because of its forthright opposition to apartheid the Botswana government has declined to take a census of its people along tribal lines. Every citizen of the country regardless of origin or colour of skin is a Motswana. Nevertheless, here's a quick rundown of minorities mentioned in this book and elsewhere.

The oldest inhabitants of southern Africa are the **San-speakers** (often called "bushmen" – covered in some detail on p.338), whose traditional hunter-gatherer lifestyle has all but died out, but who still exist as a linguistically and ethnically distinct group. Botswana's earliest Bantu-speakers were the **Bakgalakgadi**, members of the Sotho-Tswana group. Migrants from South Africa who arrived well before the Batswana, they settled in the Kalahari Desert – which owes its name to them – and intermarried freely with the San.

---

* Batswana/Motswana has two subtly different meanings. In the first place it refers to the roughly three million Setswana-speaking people of Botswana and South Africa. But it also means any citizen of Botswana, irrespective of ethnic origin.

TRIBES

In southern Africa – probably more than almost anywhere in the world – the idea of a "tribe" is pregnant with political connotations. In South Africa the concept has been used to attempt to divide the country's black majority into "separate nations" and to sow ethnic division. The idea of "tribes" as concrete entities – with connotations of backwardness – is a controversial one. One fundamental problem is that cultures, linguistic groups and national boundaries frequently fail to coincide, making the absolute definition of a particular tribe hazardous. Secondly, the idea of "tribes" implies something fixed, whereas the history of the Batswana – who routinely oscillated between splitting up and incorporating other groups – shows that cultures are in a constant process of change.

Today the industrial and economic dominance of South Africa continues to change traditional patterns of life throughout the subcontinent. The large-scale flow of migrants across national boundaries to the great industrial magnet of South Africa means that, even where people continue to define their identity in ethnic terms, traditional ways fail to conform to banal stereotypes. Tribal definitions are at best rough categories denoting people from a particular region and linguistic group.

LANGUAGE

SETSWANA GREETINGS AND RESPONSES

People customarily **greet** each other, whether strangers or not, with the older people greeting the younger one first. Greet people courteously in all situations – at roadblocks, when asking directions, or meeting people at the roadside or when talking to the person servicing your room. The magic word is *dumela* with the stress in the middle, which means "hello" and can be said at any time. Onto *dumela* you tag *Mma* for women and *Rra* for men; thus *dumela Mma* and *dumela Rra*. Use *Mma* and *Rra* after questions (even when speaking English) like "Where is the station, Mma?", "How much is it, Rra?" The pronunciation of the "-a" is short, close to the "u" in "fun". The "Rr" is slightly rolled if you are up to that. To round off a conversation or to indicate everything's okay, say *Go siame*.

Hello (to one/many)	*Dumêla/dumêlang*	Goodbye (person leaving)	*sala sentlê*
Hello (in response)	*Dumêla/dumêlang*		
How are you?	*A o sa tsogile sentlê?*	Goodbye (person remaining)	*tsamaya sentlê*
Fine thanks	*Ee, ke sa tsogile*		

BASICS

Yes	*Ee*	What is your name?	*Leina la gago e mang?*
No	*Nnyaa*	My name is Peter	*Leina la me ke Peter.*
Thank you	*Kea itumêla*	Where do you come from?	*O tswa kae? (sing)*
Please	*Tsweetswee*		
Today	*Gompieno*	I come from England	*Ke kwa England*
Tomorrow	*Ka moso*	Do you speak English?	*A o bua Seenglish?*
Yesterday	*Maabane*	It is hot	*Go molelo*
Come in	*Tsena*	Rain	*Pula*

TRAVEL

What town is this?	*Motse o ke ofe?*	Is it far to town?	*A go kgakala kwa motseng?*
It is Molepolole	*Ke Molepolole*	Is there a hotel?	*A go ne le hotele?*
Where is the station?	*Seteisene se kae?*	Is the pan still far off?	*A mogobe o sa le kgakala?*
Where is the road to Maun?	*Tsela Maun e kae?*	Where are you going to?	*O ya kae?*

COMMONLY USED TERMS

vetkoek	from the Afrikaans - a fried dough ball best eaten hot	*bottle store*	off-licence
		combi	minibus
mielie pap	from the Afrikaans – stiff maize porridge, not formerly a staple food, but now becoming so	*San*	hunter-gatherers (also known as "bushmen" and "Basarwa" – see Chapter Ten)
pan	smooth salt-saturated clay depression, occasionally covered in water	*mokoro (pl. mekoro)*	dugout canoe
kgotla	traditional meeting place or court house	*camp*	lodge (often luxury). Distinct from campsite

PHRASEBOOK

The *Setswana–English Phrasebook* by A. J. Wookey, sold in bookshops in the country, is old-fashioned, inadequate, and difficult to use. Many phrases are inappropriate and often in the imperative. The first entry under general expressions is *my sister's child is dead* and the section on travel concentrates on inspanning the oxen for the wagon. Nevertheless it has a mini-dictionary and grammar worth looking at.

Around the Francistown area is a pocket of **Bakalanga**, descendants of Zimbabwe's Rozvi state, who speak a Shona dialect. After the collapse of the Rozvi state in the 1830s the Bakalanga became tributaries of the Bangwato, but have otherwise continued to live autonomously. The **Bayei**, who live in shallow river areas, and the **Mbukushu** (see Chapter Nine) living along deep waters of the Okavango Delta in the northwest both originated in Angola. The **Herero** (see p.323) were turn-of-the-century refugees from German brutality in neighbouring Namibia, and finally there are the **English- and Afrikaans**-speaking whites (see Chapter Ten), who came from South Africa in colonial times.

Christianity is now the official religion of Botswana, yet only one person in five can be regarded as a practising Christian – the remainder hold traditional beliefs. Most Christians belong to the United Congregational Church of Southern Africa.

Money and Costs

Although Botswana remained tied to the South African rand until well after independence – which shows just how close the economic links between the two countries were (and still are) – it now has its own currency, the pula (P). That "Pula" is the Setswana word for "rain" demonstrates the enormous value of water in a dry land. Pula come in notes of P1, 2, 5, 10 and 20, and there is a P1 coin. Each pula is divided into a hundred thebe (t), of which there are 1t, 2t, 5t, 10t, 25t and 50t coins. At the time of writing the exchange rate was £1=P3.4 and US$1=P2.

If you've come from a Western country, you'll find prices cheap but by no means negligible. In order to enjoy Botswana's major attractions to the fullest, especially in the Okavango Delta and the game reserves, you'll have to be prepared to spend a fair whack. We do give tips, however, on how to minimise the cost and how to get the most from your money.

■ Banks and Exchange

Upon entering and leaving Botswana, you have to complete currency declarations, which can be pedantic in the extreme. Customs officials have been known to make people account for their currency imports down to the last coin, so it's worth being as accurate as you can to avoid the hassle. You should hold on to your currency declaration form to hand in when you leave the country.

As the pula is effectively a hard currency, and residents are permitted to export considerable sums, there's no black market in Botswana. You can change travellers' cheques at banks or the larger hotels in big centres. But be warned, there are no banks in the vast tracts of the rural countryside. Change money when you're in towns and make sure you're carrying enough cash with you.

The following towns offer **full banking facilities**: Francistown, Gaborone, Ghanzi, Jwaneng, Kanye, Kasane (weekdays except Thurs), Lobatse, Mahalapye, Maun, Mochudi, Molepolole, Palapye, Selebi-Phikwe and Serowe. Banks which should change travellers' cheques but not foreign cash are also open for **limited morning hours**, on the following days at these villages: Bobonong (Tues), Moshupa (Mon, Thurs), Ramotswa (Tues–Fri), Sherwood (Tues), Thamaga (Tues, Thurs) and Tonota (Tues, Fri).

■ Costs

Unless you want simply to trek along the deserted backways of Botswana, it's going to be difficult to get around on a shoestring. The government's policy of low-density high-cost tourism, instituted in mid-1989 in an attempt to maximise revenue while minimising the harmful impact of too many visitors, has made things more difficult than they were before. In all the major game reserves it costs over P70 a day just to be there and to use an ill-equipped campsite. Outside the National Parks things are more affordable, and you can still have a good time. There is some good private game country in the

Tuli area in particular, where you can camp or stay in reasonably priced self-catering lodges.

Perhaps the best way to see Botswana is in a 4-wheel-drive vehicle. But neither 4WD nor saloon **car rental** comes cheap, at around P150 a day for an ordinary vehicle and twice that for 4WD.

Prices for **accommodation** vary wildly, depending more on the location than the quality of the room. Around the fringes of the sought-after Okavango Delta you'll pay upwards of P125 for a double room, whereas it could easily be four times as much once inside the reserve. **Camping** is a cheaper option, working out at P10–20 a head around Okavango. Elsewhere expect to pay around P70–120 for a modest double, and P200 or more for a posh one. Free camping, on the other hand, is allowed anywhere outside urban areas.

There's more scope to get by cheaply when it comes to **eating**, either buying takeaways or self-catering from shops or supermarkets. Even though most food is imported from South Africa, prices are considerably cheaper than in the West. A sit-down snack will set you back P5 and a takeaway about half that. For P20–30 you can eat well at a hotel or restaurant.

Getting Around

Distances in Botswana are huge and the roads can be surprisingly bad. Apart from the main highway and one or two short tarred stretches elsewhere, roads are dirt track of variable standard and in very sandy areas it can take hours to cover 40 or 50km in a 4WD vehicle. Neither is public transport plentiful in Botswana, except up and down the one main highway (and railway line) in the east. An alternative to formal public transport is to get a paid lift in a passenger-carrying truck; these may well stop for you when you're hitching. Generally hitching is safe enough, although there's a lot of drinking and driving.

◼ Buses, Combis and Minibuses

The few **buses** and **minibuses** that run in Botswana operate almost exclusively on the tarred Lobatse–Kasane highway; in fact the road network is so minimal that buses have little choice other than to go some distance up this main artery.

It's quite easy to travel between the principal towns; Gaborone is connected with them all, although in the absence of fixed timetables you have to ask around the bus station for specific times, and there's also a service from Francistown to Maun. In Gaborone and on short-haul trips from the capital you'll also find **combis** – small minibuses (see Chapter Seven for details). Elsewhere, however, services are meagre, if not non-existent. Public transport is simply not a viable option to get you around most of the country's vast west.

Perhaps the most useful of the buses are the **international express services** that run to neighbouring Zimbabwe and Zambia. Both routes begin at Francistown and are covered under its transport details (see p.300).

◼ Train

Rail travel in Botswana is totally straightforward. A single main line, with a branch line to Sua Spit, runs from Johannesburg to Bulawayo, passing through the major towns along the eastern corridor. It's extremely slow and in mid-summer can be desperately hot. On the other hand if you find doing nothing easy, and have plenty to read, it's superbly relaxing. There's more space than on a bus and for a couple a **coupe** is luxury – your own (admittedly small) private compartment, with washing facilities and bunks if you want to siesta away the afternoon through the scrublands.

Daily overnight trains link Lobatse and Gaborone with Bulawayo, with a once-weekly connecting service to Johannesburg. In addition, two trains run each way between Francistown and Gaborone with refreshments available. *Botswana Railways* boasts that these luxury daytime trains provide the only air-conditioned regular scheduled service in Africa. The first-class fare from Gaborone to Francistown on the day train is P55, and for a sleeper from Botswana's capital to the Zimbabwean border is P110.

◼ Flights

Air Botswana operates services between Gaborone and a handful of main towns: Francistown, Maun, Selebi-Phikwe and Ghanzi. **Charter companies** run flights to smaller destinations in the Okavango Delta, Tsodilo Hills and elsewhere in Botswana. The charter companies are based in Maun, Francistown and Gaborone. It's often worth enquiring at their offices whether

AIR DETAILS

Air Botswana offices

Francistown Thapama Lodge, Blue Jacket St (☎212393).

Gaborone IGI House, The Mall (☎351921).

Ghanzi Kalahari Arms Hotel (☎296311).

Lobatse Hillcrest Mansions, Main St (☎330512).

Maun Airport turn-off (☎260391).

Selebi Phikwe The Mall (☎810654).

Charter companies

Maun

Aer Kavango, Maun Airport, PO Box 169, Maun (☎260393).

Northern Air, Maun Airport, PO Box 40, Maun (☎260385 or ☎260211).

Merlin Services, Maun Airport, Private Bag 13, Maun (☎260351 or ☎260571).

Gaborone

Kalahari Air Services, Sir Seretse Khama Airport, PO Box 41278, Broadhurst (☎351804 or ☎353593).

Western Air, Sir Seretse Khama Airport, PO Box 40763, Broadhurst (☎373386 or ☎312453).

Kasane

Northern Air, PO Box 40, Kasane (☎250234).

---

they have unoccupied seats that they're prepared to sell on charters. If the flight is leaving imminently some operators may even discount the fare.

■ Driving Practicalities and Routes

While foreign driver's licences are valid for six months, driving is less a matter of a licence than of being able to cope with difficult road conditions and knowing how to mend punctures (of which you'll have many) and to effect minor repairs. Above all, **four-wheel driving** requires a fair amount of expertise, and you should familiarise yourself with what's involved before undertaking any major expedition into the wilderness. Many places are trackless and if you get stranded you may not see another human being for some time. If in doubt take along someone who knows the scene, and make sure that someone knows where you're going.

Botswana's main north–south artery is a very good, wide, tarred road. Several of the major dirt roads like the Maun to Nata route (now being tarred) and the Tuli Block roads are passable in an ordinary, though necessarily tough vehicle. Many of the roads, however, require 4WD or at the very least a high-clearance vehicle. Some roads are seasonally passable – ask locally for up-to-date information. Each chapter gives details on the road situation.

Car Rental

For **car rental** there are two national networks, Holiday Car Rentals with offices in Gaborone and

Kasane, and Avis with branches in Gaborone, Francistown and Maun. **Rates** for a saloon car are from P150 per day and for 4WD you'll pay from P200 per day; for both there's an extra collision damage waiver. In Maun you can also rent a vehicle with a driver from Island Safari Lodge, and in Shakawe from Shakawe Fishing Camp to get to Tsodilo Hills.

Further reading

A useful source of detailed information to help plan a 4WD expedition down the back routes is the Visitors' Guide to Botswana by Mike Main, John and Sandra Fowkes (Southern Book Publishers, Johannesburg 1987). It gives the lowdown on routes, preparations and driving technique, and should be available in Gaborone, Maun and other tourist centres in Botswana, as well as at specialist bookshops overseas (see p.22).

■ Hitching

Hitchers have succeeded in thumbing virtually everywhere in Botswana, and you'll certainly make it to any of the larger destinations. The amount of traffic in the more remote areas can be pretty limited, but that means drivers tend to be more sympathetic. The essence of hitching in Botswana is to be in no hurry and to carry enough supplies for roadside waits of a couple of days, depending on where you're waiting. Travel wellprepared; motorists have come across hitchers stranded in the middle of game areas, virtually starving after several days without food.

■ Dugout Canoe

Leisurely exploring the waterways by dugout canoe or **mokoro** (plural *mekoro*) is one of the most satisfying and adventurous modes of travel – for short stretches. Most visitors aim to go out for at least a few days on the Okavango Delta. This can best be arranged from Maun; see Chapter Nine for details, including practical tips on how to get the best out of a *mokoro* expedition.

■ Mobile Safaris

Mobile safaris are essentially mini-overland expeditions taking clients across Botswana in 4WD vehicles, and camping on the way. One typical route runs along a triangle from Maun through Chobe National Park and Moremi Wildlife Reserve and back to Maun. A longer one starts at the Victoria Falls in Zimbabwe and drives the full length of Chobe, through Moremi, to end at Maun.

South Africa looms large in the Botswana safari business; most operators have South African connections of some kind, and some South African-based companies start their safaris in Johannesburg (see p.10 for booking details).

Sleeping

Accommodation outside Botswana's tourist areas is limited. Even the capital Gaborone makes few concessions to the needs of visitors not there on business. In the tourist areas there's a fair scattering of lodge-style accommodation, which doesn't come cheap unless you really hunt around. There's always the rock-bottom option of camping.

■ Hotels

Gaborone has a number of hotels, mostly upmarket and usually fully booked. All the main centres outside the capital – Francistown, Ghanzi, Lobatse, Mahalapye, Maun, Molepolole, Palapye, Selebi-Phikwe, Serowe – have at least one hotel, where you'll generally find a room. They're rarely something to write home about, but you can count on getting clean linen and reasonable facilities.

Prices tend to reflect demand – based on the hotel's location – rather than the standard. Outside the capital the rates go from P70 upwards for a double room.

■ Lodges

As you approach big-game country, the workaday business hotels begin to give way to **tourist lodges**. These are found in the region around the Okavango Swamps, north and west of Nata, and in the private game reserves of the Tuli Block, clustered around the Motloutse River. They aren't always prohibitively expensive, although you can expect to pay a lot in the Okavango Delta and Chobe Game Reserve.

The more reasonably priced lodges are mostly on the fringes of these select areas. Prices range from P120 to P160 for a double room. Inside the boundaries of the Delta and Chobe National Park you'll pay upwards of P300 per person – the sky's the limit. But don't forget that the price includes all meals and game-viewing, activities drives, water safaris or guided walks.

■ Camping

Camping, as always, is the cheapest way to spend the night. But in Botswana it has the added dimension of being a really adventurous and exciting way to see the country. Once you get well away from urban areas you can camp anywhere. Near settlements, however, you should make an effort to contact the local chief for permission. Most National Parks charge P20 camping fee. Facilities are frequently limited to cold running water, showers and flush toilets, and even these can't always be relied upon to work.

Many areas adjoining the reserves are just as wild, and you're allowed to camp free of charge – but be cautious of game (see under Mana Pools, p.114). It goes without saying not to add to Botswana's litter problem, which is particularly severe – and notorious – in the Okavango Delta.

ACCOMMODATION PRICE CODES

Every hotel and accommodation option listed in our account of Botswana has been given a **price code** to indicate the cost of a single night's lodging. The prices we've given are **per person sharing**; there is usually a supplement for a single person in a room. Safari lodges are excluded from the system, a specific price being quoted.

① under P50 ② P50–100 ③ P100–175 ④ P175–250 ⑤ P250+

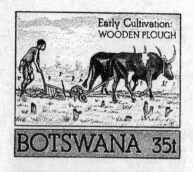

Early Cultivation:
WOODEN PLOUGH

BOTSWANA 35t

Communications – Post and Phone Services

Keeping in touch with home poses no problem in Botswana. The postal service isn't bad and the phone system is modern with up-to-date call boxes from which you can dial direct to the rest of the world. That's as long as you can find enough change – there are no phonecards, so you'll need a phenomenal number of thebe coins.

■ Mail

There are post offices in all towns and the larger villages, open weekdays 8.15am–12.45pm and 2–4pm, and Saturday 8–11am. Services tend to be slow but are reliable and cheap. Telegrams are the quickest form of mail.

■ Phone

All international calls to or from Botswana used to be routed through South Africa; the decision to develop its own phone system is another example of the country's determination to break out of that

---

INTERNATIONAL DIALLING CODES

To phone **to Botswana** from abroad, the country code is **267**. There are no area codes.

Phoning out **from Botswana**, the international access code is **00**. This is followed by the country and area codes and finally the destination number.

Country codes are the same as those dialled from Zimbabwe (see p.45). Unlike Zimbabwe, however, Botswana does not have a distinct regional code for neighbouring countries. Use the international access code.

---

degree of dependency. There's now direct dialling between most of the larger towns, which have their own automatic phone exchanges. Even the smaller towns have public call boxes – usually around the post office – and they work !

There are no area dialling codes; wherever you are in the country, you dial the same number.

The Media – Press, Radio and TV

In theory the media in Botswana remain uncensored, although custom and tradition act as curbs on what is considered acceptable in this still-conservative society.

■ The Press

The press consists of three independent weekly tabloid newspapers and the *Daily News*, a free-sheet published by the Department of Information and Broadcasting and available from their offices. Because it's gratis, the *Daily News* is very popular, but it consists of little more than official press releases and statements by ministers.

The most popular of the independent papers is *The Botswana Guardian*, published on Friday, which has a lot of hard local news. *The Gazette*, which comes out on Thursday, has a similar look and feel. Both tend toward unimaginative and safe coverage.

Of much greater interest is ***Mmegi – the Reporter***, published every Saturday, with its vociferously independent and campaigning stance. It goes in for investigative coverage rather than hard news and has high journalistic standards. Politically, it supports a more equitable wealth distribution in Botswana. Although it's undoubtedly the most exciting of Botswana's papers it has the lowest circulation and can be difficult to find in the smaller centres. *Mmegi*'s current editor takes a strong anti-apartheid line and is critical of Botswana's dealings with South Africa, which he acknowledges makes him a potential assassin's target. Campaigns have ranged across a catholic selection of issues including one supporting air-time for Botswana's bands rather than international pop. The paper's policy toward the government is one of constructive criticism.

Of the **South African newspapers**, the daily *Star* and *Business Day* are available in Gaborone on the day of publication. Both give reasonable news coverage. For more fiery opposition to the South African regime look out for the weeklies *New Nation* and the *Weekly Mail*. The former takes an uncompromising pro-ANC stance – as it did even when the organisation was banned and supporting it could mean a hefty prison sentence – while the *Weekly Mail* is more firmly ensconced in the South African liberal white community, though still a force to be reckoned with.

International magazines like *Time* and *Newsweek*, and ones with an African emphasis like *New African* and *Africa* are also available in the capital and Francistown.

■ Radio and TV

Radio Botswana has a single station broadcasting in both English and Setswana. Programmes are a mixed bag of religion, music, schools broadcasts and good news coverage. South African and Zimbabwean music are also played as well as western pop – but sadly little modern local music.

The frequencies and times of BBC World Service and Voice of America broadcasts are the same as for Zimbabwe; see the box on p.46.

There's one local TV station, broadcast by GBC (*Gaborone Broadcasting Corporation*) to the capital alone. Its diet consists mainly of British videos, with some US imports and the odd local documentary. Most watched, however, are the four channels filched from the South African airwaves and boosted for local consumption: the *South African Broadcasting Corporation*'s three ethnically segregated stations and the one beamed by Bop-TV, the Bophuthatswana *bantustan*'s broadcasting corporation. These stations can be picked up all along the southeastern border region, in most of the Eastern Corridor towns.

Opening Hours and Holidays

Shop opening hours in Botswana are generally 8am to 5pm, with some closing for lunch between 1 and 2pm. Bottle stores (off-licences) open and close two hours later. In larger centres you'll usually find a general store that stays open until 8 or 9pm. Many shops are closed on Saturday afternoon and all day Sunday. Botswana's handful of museums vary in their opening patterns, but more or less follow normal shop hours, and open at the weekend as well. The National Museum and Art Gallery in Gaborone is closed on Monday.

PUBLIC HOLIDAYS

January 1 *New Year's Day*

January 2 *Public Holiday*

Easter *Good Friday to Easter Monday*

Ascension Day

3rd Monday (+ day after) in July *President's Day*

September 30 (+ day after) *Botswana Day*

December 25/26 *Xmas/Boxing Day*

Music and Entertainment

Botswana has little in the way of public entertainment, and most of what there is centres on the capital. The country's only "place of culture" is the Maitisong Centre at Maru-a-Pula School in Gaborone. Although the centre is run by the school, it's open to the public and there are varied events every week, from Kalahari Conservation Society films to theatre festivals. Look for press and radio announcements.

Other entertainment tends to be of a more familiar and mundane variety. Each of the larger towns has one or two cinemas showing unexceptional programmes, and the most popular pastime of all is drinking in bars and at nightclubs, which are concentrated in Gaborone. On most evenings there'll be live music at at least one of the clubs in the capital, and lively disc-playing at the others. A few local bands have emerged, but the music scene has yet to develop the vibrancy of Zimbabwe's or the diversity of sounds offered by South Africa. The most popular bands, *Afro Sunshine* and the *Botswana Defence Force Bands* can usually be relied upon to provide a couple of hours of snappy listening.

Crafts

Botswana is known for its very beautiful basketry. The best-known style was brought to the country with Mbukushu refugees in the nineteenth century, followed more recently by a second wave in 1969, fleeing the Angolan war of independence. Most weaving therefore comes from those areas closest to the northern border, in Ngamiland. The baskets are woven from the mokolane palm (*Hyphaene ventricosa*) and the root of the mothakola tree is used to dye it in various brown shades. You'll find an incredible variety of baskets on sale in town shops, or you can go direct to the weavers in rural areas.

There's a **language** to the design motifs of the baskets, which plays with the contrasting chocolates and oatmeals. A dazzling variety of patterns signify events or important aspects of life. The *urine trail of the bull* – like those swirling hypnosis wheels you can get in novelty shops – celebrates the centrality of cattle in traditional life. Other spiralled and petalled forms have names like *ribs of the giraffe* and *back of the python*. Some have schematic animals and figures woven in.

The best range is in **Maun**, with a more expensive selection in **Gaborone**. If you travel up the **Panhandle**, you can buy them directly from the weavers. Tourist lodges usually keep a small collection and many in the Delta use the baskets for decorating the walls. Ngamiland baskets are not cheap, although in view of the fact that they're handmade and take many days of work, they can hardly be considered expensive. Cheaper baskets are also made in the **Shashe** area in the southeast, not as tightly or finely woven and using grass instead of palm. **Francistown** is the place to buy these.

Crafts created by the **San people** are unique and worth buying, not simply because Botswana is the only place you're likely to find them, but because they are traditional items which haven't yet moved into the realms of airport art or synthesised western bric-a-brac. The handmade **ostrich egg beads and bracelets** look no different from anything you'll see in a museum case. You may well come across really old stuff amongst the newly produced **leather beaded aprons and bags**. Among objects which are made solely for tourists (but still look like the real thing) are skilfully crafted bow and arrow **hunting sets**. Ghanzi has by far the best and cheapest array, but you'll find San jewellery, bags and hunting kits dotted around the craft shops in Maun and Gaborone.

Trouble

Violent crime is rare in Botswana, but petty theft is as endemic as in any area where poverty and wealth exist side by side. Avoid having your goods lifted in the first place, because once they're gone you're unlikely to see them again. Take common-sense precautions and keep an eye on your valuables.

If you're ripped off consider carefully whether it's worth the hassle of reporting the loss to the police and going through all the paperwork and bureaucracy. Of course, if you're insured you'll need to do so. Police are conscientious about taking down details and they'll give you the copy of the police report required for your insurance claim.

Your most likely encounter with uniformed authorities is going to be at one of the many **roadblocks** that pepper the roadways. There are roadblocks controlled by the Botswana Defence Force, ostensibly at any rate looking for weapons, outside Gaborone and Francistown (both on arriving and leaving). Travelling by road you're sure to pass through one or more.

The roadblocks are an attempt to counter South African mischief-making in Botswana, in the wake of numerous South African military incursions. The whole process does become tedious – one favourite technique of army personnel is to address you in Setswana, fully knowing that you won't understand – but it's important to remain cool and polite. You may be asked to unpack the entire contents of your vehicle and baggage, so bear this in mind when you pack, and divide all your stuff up into plastic bags which can easily be lifted out, examined and repacked with a minimum of trouble. Anything with a military look (billy cans for example, or khaki water-bottles) will draw attention, so leave them behind if possible.

■ Sexual Attitudes and Harassment

If you're a woman travelling on your own you are unlikely to be sexually harassed, although macho whites may well seriously chat you up in places like Maun. **Topless swimming** and sunbathing is not on, but otherwise there are no dress restrictions.

In general, **attitudes towards women** are conservative. There is no women's movement as such, but there is a group of intellectuals in Gaborone who are concerned with women's issues. Joyce Anderson at the *Women's Affairs Unit*, Ministry of Home Affairs, Private Bag 002, Gaborone, should be able to provide information about women's agricultural cooperatives and publications.

Directory

CONTRACEPTIVES Oral contraceptives, on prescription, and condoms are available from pharmacies in all the main towns. Do note, however, that the Maun pharmacy has no registered chemist and therefore can't make up prescriptions.

EMERGENCIES Ambulance (☎997). Fire (☎998). Police (☎999).

TAMPONS Available in all the main centres. But if you're doing any adventurous travelling, bear in mind that you may be far from shops, and so take your own supplies.

TIME Like Zimbabwe, Botswana is two hours ahead of GMT. Daylight is from 6am to 6pm, slightly extended either side in mid-summer. Unlike Europe, darkness falls quite quickly, so you shouldn't expect to count on lingering evening twilight.

TOILETS Hotel toilets are generally fine. There are toilets at National Park campsites but few public ones. On any journeys into the hinterland take a supply of toilet paper, particularly if you're camping rough. You'll have to get used to digging a hole in the ground. Remember to bury the paper securely.

WORK You shouldn't go to Botswana expecting to pick up casual work. Nonetheless, a skills shortage is developing as diamonds continue to fuel the fastest-growing economy in Africa, which means that there may be vacancies in some specialised sectors such as building design and construction. Your best bet is to write to private firms asking about work and including a CV – it's all a question of the right qualifications at the right time.

CHAPTER SEVEN

GABORONE AND THE EASTERN CORRIDOR

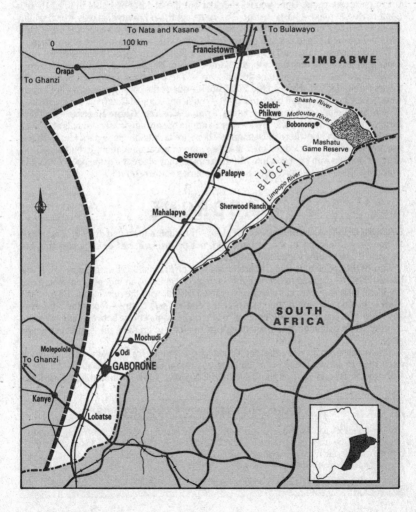

Most travellers see no more of Botswana's **Eastern Corridor**, where the bulk of the population lives, than a passing dusty landscape glimpsed through a train or car window. It's the **railway line**, with towns dotted along its length in a concentration found nowhere else in Botswana, that defines the eastern flank of the country; the road that runs parallel to it was only tarred after Independence. The railroad was always very much a through route, created by the British South Africa Company and used by Britain for the sole purpose of bringing raw materials such as copper and coal from its lucrative northern colonies to the South African ports. However, the riches carried by the train never spilt over into the vast undeveloped stretches of Bechuanaland, as it was then called.

Gaborone was just a dusty railway siding throughout the colonial years. Only after Independence did it take on its current status as national capital, and it feels as if it has yet to put down roots. Once you've checked out the handful of sights in town there's good reason to make a hasty escape. The route south, to **Lobatse**, is only worth taking if you're heading onwards to the Kalahari; otherwise, the nearby weavers' village, **Odi**, and the historic Bakgatla capital of **Mochudi**, just to the north, are more interesting.

The landscape to the east of Gaborone is flat and thorny. Apart from **Serowe**, royal seat of Sir Seretse Khama and adopted home of writer Bessie Head, there's nothing very much of interest until you come to that part of the country sandwiched between the tracks and Zimbabwe. Here, in the **Tuli Block** – one of the country's few freehold tracts (most of the country is still common land) – you'll find some of Botswana's most striking landscapes and fine private game country. Around **Mashatu Game Reserve** – southern Africa's largest private wildlife park – there's ample opportunity to see animals at a much smaller cost than elsewhere in Botswana. There are no add-on game park fees here and the several camps and lodges offer a wide range of accommodation. Even though the cheaper options won't get you into **Mashatu** itself, they share the same pool of animals, which wander back and forth across the boundaries of the reserve.

GABORONE

GABORONE is an amorphous sort of place – the kind of town you drive around trying to find only to escape as soon as you can, not precisely because it's unpleasant, but because it's incredibly vague and unsatisfying.

Part of the problem is that Gaborone is a new city and still growing. Although it was meticulously re-planned to become the showpiece capital of an independent Botswana, the life of its inhabitants has effectively refused to fit in with the new layout. Beyond the **Mall** – the cohesive main shopping precinct and *de facto* centre – footpaths crisscross any open space and, independently of roads, make connections between one area and another. New buildings sprout seemingly at random, to create a mess of construction sites.

While the town is new, the settlement site certainly isn't – Stone Age tools are unearthed in almost every major building operation. Colonialists set up the village of **Gaberones** around 1887 on the banks of the Ngotwane River where it functioned as a district headquarters. The name came from Gaborone, the king of the Batlokwa, whose capital perched on the opposite bank of the river. A couple of years later, when the railway arrived, another small colonial village was built 4km away at the station, known, reasonably enough, as **Gaberones Station**.

Gaborone's position on the **South African border** symbolises the ambivalent links between the two countries. The British government regarded it as such a foregone conclusion that Bechuanaland would become part of South Africa, that throughout the colonial years the Protectorate's capital was in **Mafeking** (now Mafikeng) inside South Africa. Despite increased pressure to take over the territory following South Africa's Act of Union in 1910, skilful manoeuvring by Batswana leaders avoided the cession of the country*. The city you see today, situated between the two earlier settlements, was built in the years immediately before Independence in 1966, when it became necessary to create a new capital in time to move the administration from Mafeking.

There's really very little reason to visit the functional and administrative city of Gaborone for any longer than a day, though it's nice enough to wander about the Mall, swim at the *Sun Hotel* pool and visit the excellent **museum** and art gallery. Most tourists pause only at the airport to change planes, and visitors are barely catered for in town. There's nowhere cheap to stay – the central hotels are frequently booked up by officials and business people, and there are no hostels open to travellers or public campsites. Even the budget hotel which once stood at the station has been pulled down.

The city's main interest lies in what it's becoming. In a country with vast areas of wilderness, bad communications and two tarred roads, Gaborone is as urban and sophisticated as Botswana gets. The most independent-minded **newspaper** has its offices here and the **university** and prestigious Maru-a-Pula School draw Botswana's middle class and intellectuals. **Television** broadcasts don't get further than the city outskirts, although in addition to local programming there's pirated South African TV as well (you can also pick it up in Francistown and Lobatse). A couple of South-African-influenced **pop groups** shuttle around at the sprinkling of nightclubs and discos, and there's a dawning sense of urban culture emerging. It is in Gaborone's expansion, too, that the country's diamond revenue is most clearly evident, not in the remote rural areas where, despite improvements, life mostly stays the same.

Arrival, orientation and public transport

If you arrive in Gaborone by **air**, the only transport from Seretse Khama Airport is **combis** run by the three main hotels, which will carry you the 14km into town even if you don't intend to stay at any of these places. You're by no means certain of being able to find a **taxi**, and neither is there an airport bus.

In the town itself, the principal transport hub is the **railway station** – despite the fact that there are only a couple of trains per day in either direction. At least the trains are reliable, if slow; the **long-distance buses** and **minibuses** which depart from outside the station to surrounding areas operate to no discernible schedules. The only way to get information is from waiting passengers – there are no bus offices or officials about. A **left luggage** service is available at the station (Mon–Fri only, 8am–1pm & 2–4pm).

Although Gaborone is dispersed and you'll end up doing a fair amount of walking, it's easy enough to find your way around. From the station it's a 15-minute walk to the bottom end of the **Mall**, the main focus of the city. Follow Station Road eastward and then north as it becomes Khama Crescent, or use the obvious footpaths as a short cut.

---

* Gaborone, of course, has a pivotal position on the front line. South African exiles have been going over the border since the 1960s – particularly nationalists who fled after the Sharpeville massacre in 1961 and the subsequent banning of the ANC and PAC. Several exiles became involved in Bechuanaland's Independence movement.

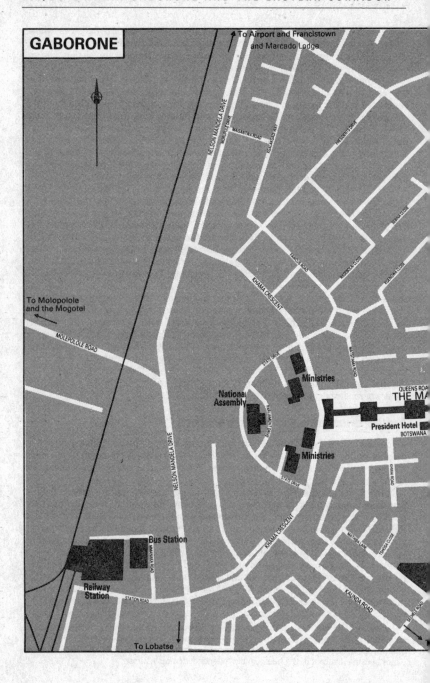

GABORONE

To Airport and Francistown
and Marcado Lodge

NELSON MANDELA DRIVE

MOKALE DRIVE

MAISANTWA ROAD

KGALAGADI WAY

PRESIDENTS DRIVE

SEBINA CLOSE

KSENGWA CLOSE

FAIROS ROAD

RADENCY CLOSE

KHAMA CRESCENT

To Molopolole
and the Mogotei

MOLEPOLOLE ROAD

STATE DRIVE

MUTO PARK ROAD

QUEENS ROAD
THE MA

Ministries

HAILE LANDER DRIVE

National
Assembly

President Hotel
BOTSWANA

NELSON MANDELA DRIVE

CHOI PARK

Ministries

STATE DRIVE

KHAMA CRESCENT

MACHELA PARK

TSWEKA CLOSE

Bus Station

Railway
Station

STATION ROAD

KAUNDA ROAD

SELANE ROAD

To Lobatse

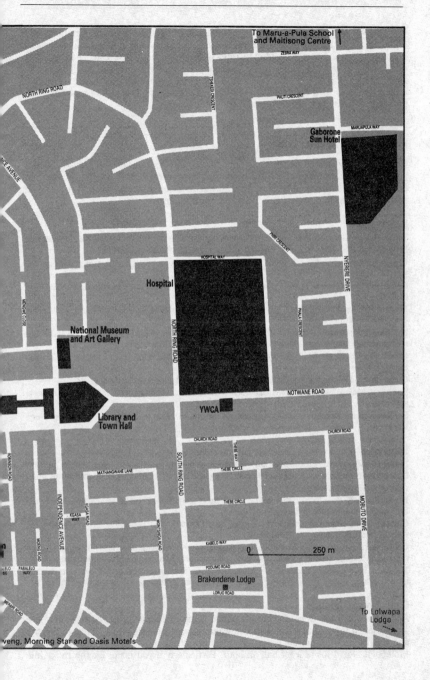

To travel to the suburbs, or one of the cheaper out-of-town hotels, flag down one of the tightly packed **combis** which ply the main arteries. They stop virtually anywhere for passengers and cost very little; the idea is that you should just squeeze in, whether or not there appears to be any room. **Taxis** are reasonably priced, and you'll find ranks at the station and outside the *President Hotel*. Once in the suburbs, you'll notice that unlike former British colonies with entrenched class-segregation, Gaborone has been planned deliberately to mix low- and high-cost housing.

Accommodation

Unless you have a wad of notes, accommodation in Gaborone is a nightmare. Even if you're prepared to fork out for one of the **luxury central hotels**, you'll probably find them all full of business travellers (though weekends are more promising). By ringing around, you may find a cheaper bed **away from the centre**.

Hotels

The most central hotels in Gaborone are of course also the most **expensive**, and there's little to choose between them, as they all cater for the business market.

Cresta Gaborone, Molepolole Rd, Private Bag 00127 (☎375200). Brand new, central and everything you'd expect for the price. ⑤.

Gaborone Sun, Nyerere Drive, Private Bag 0016, Gaborone (☎351111). Pleasant surroundings and pool. ⑤.

Mogotel, Molepolole Rd, Mogoditshane, PO Box 1352, Gaborone (☎372228). Cheapest of the lot, but hardly inspiring. ②.

Morning Star Motel, Tlokweng Village (☎352301). Six kilometres out on the Zeerust Road, this medium-range hotel is particularly convenient for the South African border. ②.

Cresta President, the Mall, Gaborone (☎353631). Smack in the centre, with a terrace overlooking the Mall. ④.

Oasis Motel, Tlokweng Rd (☎356396). Out of the centre and good if you're driving. ③.

Sheraton, Molepolole Rd, between Gaborone West and Mogoditshane (☎312999). Strictly expense accounts only. ④.

Sedibelo Motel, Pilane (see p.269). Less than 40km out, so within reach if you're driving and everywhere else is full. ②.

Lodges

Some of the lodges which normally cater for long-stay guests will take people passing through if there are vacancies. However, they are not particularly cheap and often full – ring before you turn up.

Brakendene Lodge, Ext 10, Plot 15113, Lerou Road (☎312888). Friendly establishment near the Princess Marina Hospital in the centre of town. ②.

Cresta Lodge, Samora Machel Drive, Private Bag 00126 (☎375375). Somewhat more expensive, but with the facilities to make it worthwhile. ④.

Lolwapa Lodge, Ext 12, Plot 3412, Maakakgang Close (☎359061 or ☎351646). Homely place reached by taking a second left after the circle just past the polytechnic going towards university. ②.

Marcado Lodge, 4863 Dinatla Close, Morupule Drive/Francistown Rd (☎373980). Conveniently located, price includes a good English breakfast and use of a swimming pool, kitchen and fridge. ③.

Camping and hostels

Although Gaborone does not have a public campsite, camping is allowed anywhere outside main towns and villages in Botswana. Thus it's possible to go outside the city and sleep somewhere in the bush – the most promising direction is to head out on the Molepolole Road for at least half an hour. Particularly if you make for the rocky hilltops, you should be able to find a fairly secluded spot. If your nerve fails, the *Mogotel* (see above) allows camping in an unappetising gravelly courtyard in the middle of the hotel. Minibuses to Molepolole leave from the station or you can wait on the Molepolole Road near the station off Nelson Mandela Drive, for a combi or lift.

Gaborone's only **hostel** is for women, at the *YWCA*, Notwane Road, opposite the hospital (☎353681). Dorm beds go for P40, but there's rarely bedspace as out of town locals stay here. Finally, if you're desperate, consider taking the overnight sleeper train to Francistown.

The City

Life in Gaborone centres very much on **The Mall**, a large, relaxed pedestrian precinct where you'll find everything from banks and embassies to chemists and bookshops. People stroll about the walkways, which are dotted with acacias and lined with bricked flowerbeds. Built on a ceremonial axis, the top end of the Mall leads to **government ministries**, the **National Assembly** and the President's Office. At the other end is the **library** and **Town Hall**, opposite the **National Museum** and **Art Gallery**. Behind the *President Hotel*, conspicuous and dominant at the centre of this precisely ordered show-piece, is the contrasting haphazard sprawl of downmarket shops and restaurants known as the **African Mall**. Everything north of Nyerere Drive is known as **Broadhurst**, where there are two other shopping centres, the **Kagiso Centre** and **Broadhurst Mall** with some upmarket shops.

Immediately around the station, you'll find the closest thing Gaborone has to a **market**. Botswana's desert climate means that little fresh produce is grown. What there is is sold in a desultory way, alongside the stalls selling fried bread, cooked meat and traditional sour milk.

The National Museum

Tues–Fri 9am–6pm; Sat, Sun, & public hols except Easter, Xmas and Boxing Day 9am–5pm. Free.

Botswana's **National Museum** provides a good opportunity to size up this vast country and get a grip on its different people, environments and fauna. Specialising in fauna and ethnographic material, the museum includes some fine examples of craftwork.

In the **wildlife** section there are stuffed cats aplenty. Besides the predictable lions, there are examples of two rare and beautiful desert cats: one, the **black-footed cat**, the size of a domestic cat, is an exquisite gingery brown feline about which little is known, beyond the fact that it is confined to the Kalahari. The other is the **caracal** or desert lynx, which leaps high into the air to catch birds. San-speakers call the female caracal *bride of the dawn*, the incarnation of the morning star with the same name. Less romantic, at the far end of the museum, is a dusty and battered reconstruction of the **biggest crocodile** ever shot in Botswana. Truly monstrous, it's the subject of innumerable tales surrounding its killing.

Although a permanent hunter-gatherer lifestyle has now largely come to an end in Botswana, the museum should satisfy your curiosity about how **desert dwellers** can survive – including what arrow poisons they use. Larvae of the beige-spotted *Poyclada flexuosa* beetles are the commonest raw material of the poison. These insignificant and deceptively innocuous-looking grubs are gathered from the marula tree.

The display of roots eaten by the Kalahari dwellers is intriguing. These vegetables are surprisingly large, around ten or twenty times as big as the average carrot or parsnip. Various gourds, such as the Tsama melon, supply the only source of moisture during the seven-month dry season, and continue to supplement the diet of San farm workers nowadays.

The best **regional craft collection** is in the display about the Hambukushu of the Okavango region. Notice particularly the beautiful oval grain storage basket – unmatched by any similar article you'll find for sale.

In the museum shop you'll find some good San crafts, baskets, books and postcards, and they also keep *Pelegano*'s ceramics (see "Crafts" below). You can't buy anything over the weekend or after 4.30pm.

The Art Gallery

Opening hours as for Museum. Free.

Although it has only two rooms, with a new gallery in progress, the **Art Gallery** is exceptionally interesting. The collection from sub-Saharan Africa ranges from painting and sculpture to crafts and textiles.

Batswana painters are represented in the first section of the gallery although the majority of works are by **South African artists**. Two eye-catching Batswana canvases emphasise the pervasiveness of rural influence in Botswana. Village life in **Keeme Mosinyi's** tapestry-like painting is depicted in neat rhythmic strands while **V. B. Moremi** goes for a gently naturalistic scene of cattle.

A small section is devoted to **foreigners' impressions** of Botswana: one Norwegian painter strikingly captures the exact orangey-red tones of the Kalahari sand. Most fascinating are the drawings and paintings by the **first European travellers** to Botswana. Wildebeest seem to have incited great fear – **Samuel Daniell's** nineteenth-century engraving *The Gnoo* shows a terrifying beast of almost mythical proportions while **Thomas Baines'** enormous wildebeest, from the same era, lunges towards a British soldier, who has his gun at the ready.

With a couple of notable exceptions, **cultural artefacts from Botswana** are represented in the main museum, leaving the art gallery to display works from West and East Africa. Of the Botswana offerings, look out for a prominent carved wooden buffalo. Thought to be of Yei origin the blockish buffalo, with another tiny buffalo on the tip of its tail, gives a sense of the solidity and implacability of the species. Before being drawn to the colourful **puppets from Mali** don't miss the case of **San artefacts.** Besides intricately beaded bags, the engraved ostrich eggs are of particular note. Some shells have only abstract designs while others are of animals. One shell has a group of four stylised giraffes with turtle-shaped backs, and a fifth curving its neck delicately round the shell to reach a plant.

Crafts

There's one **craft shop** to browse around in Gaborone – *Botswanacraft* in the Mall, where the representative collection of country-wide crafts includes some beautiful and well-displayed **baskets** (though the best selection of baskets, and slightly cheaper, is to be found in Maun). Expect to pay P60–80 for a fine one. Other worthwhile objects are

San pouches and **ostrich-egg shell jewellery** and some appealingly stylised **wooden animals** from around the Shashi area and Serowe. At first glance they all look alike, but some are more expressively carved than others, so it's worth choosing carefully. Favourite subjects are baboons, leopards and antelope.

Botswanacraft keeps a small selection of **woven items** from Mochudi, and various pottery from *Pelegano Crafts*. *Pelegano*'s hand-painted **animal ceramics** – which have every appearance of being wooden – are particularly nice. If you're in Gaborone for a while it's worth visiting their shop in GABANE village, 17km out of the city, off the Molepolole Road.

Another out-of-town craft excursion is to the *Mokolodi Co-operative*, signposted off the Lobatse Road, where women print brightly coloured cloth and make clay jewellery. While you can watch work in progress any time during the week, the shop is only open on Saturdays.

Eating, Drinking and Nightlife

Food is a lot cheaper and easier to find in Gaborone than a room, and **drinking** is the country's national pastime. You'll find several lively places, especially at the weekend when there's always **live music** and somewhere to dance. The end of the month, after payday, brings the most exuberant events. On the cultural front check out *Maitisong* at Maru-a-Pula School which hosts local drama as well as some exceptional performances from outside the country.

Daytime spots

Undoubtedly the most relaxed and enjoyable bar for visitors is the **terrace** of the *President Hotel* which faces onto the centre of the Mall, and provides unmatched opportunities for people-watching and contemplation of the passing scene. The grand steps and red, white and blue striped awning make it an obvious meeting place. The terrace is good for **iced drinks, tea and snacks** but is closed in the evening and on Sunday. Virtually opposite, the *King's Restaurant* does **takeaways**, stews, curry and mealie meal as well as pies and sandwiches (closed from 6pm, and all day Sunday). For chicken takeaways *Theo's Fried Chicken*, behind the Mall Post Office, is worth trying.

Away from the Mall, drinking and snacking at the *Gaborone Sun* pool on Nyerere Drive is a very pleasant way to idle away a few hours. In the absence of a public swimming pool, this is also your only chance for a dip; but it's a slim chance, as non-residents are unlikely to get past the vigilant doormen. With your own transport, *Pam's Place* in the Kagiso Centre at Broadhurst is recommended for coffee, snacks and lunches, as is the *Kgotla* in the Broadhurst North Mall near the BBS building, with great vegetarian options, as well as richer fare for meat-eaters (open 9am–9pm daily).

Look out for posters in town announcing occasional public **picnics**. These are delightful afternoon drinking and dancing affairs at out-of-town venues. There's usually a **live band**. For Sunday afternoon outdoor beer and bopping, try *Bodiba* on the road to Molepolole. **National holidays** bring forth a feast of activities in Gaborone which go on all weekend. If your visit coincides with **President's Day** or **Botswana Day** festivities (mid-July and end of September) be prepared for soccer matches, traditional dancing and singing, BDF (Botswana Defence Force) displays, exhibitions and church services on a grand scale.

Night-time

The choices for **eating out** – as opposed to the hotel dining rooms or grills, which are perfectly adequate – are confined to a sprinkling of restaurants. The *Park* in the African Mall is definitely the place to go. It's lively, fun and often crowded. The food is good and reasonably priced, and for once **vegetarians** can do well, with a good selection of savoury crepes and pancakes instead of the usual gigantic steaks and hamburgers. The *Taj*, also in the African Mall, is more expensive but serves reasonable **curries**. Near the railway station the *Crazy Bull* does excellent pizza. In Broadhurst, at the North Mall, *Mama's Kitchen* is recommended for Italian food.

For serious **drinking** the *Platform Bar* at the *Gaborone Sun Hotel* is a good choice. The strange railways decor doesn't diminish the exuberance of the place, and although it lacks a proper floor, people are always dancing to disco and African music. The *Cresta Gaborone* at the railway station is the most central of the nightspots with a rollicking bar and live music every weekend. For a British-style pub, try the *Bull and Bush* on the old Francistown Road.

Two clubs, both ten minutes' taxi-ride out of town, are good bets for **live music**, and especially so at the weekend. **Afro Sunshine**, Botswana's most popular band, frequently plays at the *Oasis Motel*'s *Cameo Club*. Look out also for the **Botswana Defence Force band** performances. Military bands may conjure up images of brass and marching, but the two BDF bands play slick African music, derivative of Soweto and Zimbabwean beats. Much of the live stuff you'll hear has South African influences. The other possibility for **live gigs** is *Night Shift* in the BBS Mall in Broadhurst – Gaborone's biggest suburb. The bar upstairs is preferable, away from the youthful invasion on the ground floor. It's popular with the town's rich kids, but not exclusively.

Nearer the centre, just ten minutes' walk from the *Sun Hotel*, *Club 585/Midas Touch* in the **Maru-a-Pula shopping centre** has a disco and occasional live bands at the weekend. Takeaways are on the go outside until 3 or 4am.

Botswana's only cultural centre is **Maitisong** (☎371809), the new hall at Maru-a-Pula School, around the corner from the *Sun Hotel*. While the school itself is private and highly exclusive, it does have an admirable policy of opening its facilities to the public. At weekends local kids can use the swimming pool, and Maitisong is not only the venue for **plays** from neighbouring states, overseas **performances**, **dance**, **concerts** or simply **films**, but also for functions such as conferences, and classes in dance and music. Performances are varied and average something like every third night throughout the year. Newspapers publish details of what's on.

The **theatre group** to watch out for is the newly formed *Baranodi* which specialises in drama by African playwrights, but you won't be missing much if you avoid the dull ex-pat *Capital Players*. Another interesting company is *Reetsanang*, a community-based theatre group, which occasionally performs at *Maitisong*. Funded by aid agencies they go into villages to research local social or political problems, which they then dramatise at the *kgotla*, the place where disputes are traditionally heard and settled.

For unchallenging escapism, the programme of **films** at the *Capitol Cinema* in the Mall is heavy on celluloid action and recent Hollywood releases.

Listings

Airline offices Lower Mall for: *BA*, Equity Building (☎372594); *Air Botswana*, IGI House (☎352812) and *Zambia Airways*, 1st Floor Zambia Hse (☎312027). *Kenya Airways* is opposite the Mall at Plot 764, Botswana Rd (☎374191 or ☎374192); *Air India*, Zambia Close (☎313880). *Air Botswana* also acts as the agent for *Air Malawi*, *Air Mauritius*, *Air Tanzania*, *Air Zimbabwe*, *KLM*, *Lesotho Airways*, *Lufthansa*, *Royal Swazi Airways*, *SAS* and *Swissair*.

American Express *Manica Travel Services* in the Mall, Botsalano House, Botswana Rd (☎352021).

Banks Mon–Fri 8.15am–12.45pm, Sat 8.15–10.45am. There are several branches of the three commercial banks around the Mall area. The smaller *Barclays* and *Standard Chartered* on the station side of the Mall won't change travellers' cheques. Try the bigger ones in the central section.

Books *Botswana Book Centre*, Upper Mall is the best bookshop in central Africa, with an excellent selection of African writing as well as paperback imports and books on Botswana. Imported reading matter is far cheaper here than in Zimbabwe, so this is definitely the place to stock up. *Botsalo Books* at Broadhurst Shopping Centre is also recommended, though not central.

Botswana Railways Information on ☎351401.

British Council Upper Mall. Reading room with British papers.

Camping equipment *Gaborones Hardware*, Lower Mall sells camping gas and tents.

Car rental *Holiday Car Rentals* at Sun Hotel, Nyerere Drive (☎353970). 4WD rental. *Avis* (☎375469) and *Hertz* (353970) both have offices at the airport for 4WD or sedan rental, with similar deals.

Car repairs and parts *AAA Motors*, Molepolole Road past the *Mogotel* is good for landrover spares. More centrally there are several places along Haile Selassie Road.

EMBASSIES, HIGH COMMISSIONS & FOREIGN REPRESENTATIVES

Denmark 142 Mengwe Close, PO Box 367 (☎353770).

France 761 Robinson Rd, PO Box 1424 (☎353683).

Germany 2nd Floor, IGI House, PO Box 315 (☎353143).

Netherlands Haile Selassie Rd, PO Box 10055 (☎351691 or ☎351692).

Nigeria Nigeria House, The Mall, PO Box 274 (☎313561).

Norway Development House, The Mall, PO Box 879 (☎351501).

Russia 4711 Tawana Close, PO Box 81 (☎353389 or ☎353739).

UK Queen's Rd, Private Bag 0023 (☎352841).

USA Badiredi House, The Mall, PO Box 90 (☎353982, ☎353983 or ☎353984).

Zambia Zambia House, The Mall, PO Box 362 (☎351951 or ☎351952).

Zimbabwe 1st Floor, IGI House, PO Box 1232 (☎314495, ☎314496 or ☎314497).

Chemists – emergency *Botschem*, Nyerere Drive (Mon–Sat 9am–7pm, Sun 9–10am; ☎353108, after hours ☎371385).

Contraceptives *Botschem* on the Mall sells condoms and prescription medicines (☎314603).

Doctors Dr D. B. Dickinson has a surgery on Independence Avenue (☎353424). Other doctors are listed in the first few pages of the pink section at the front of the phone directory.

Fabrics *Timber Trading* in the African Mall has a good selection of Zambian and Zimbabwean cottons.

Freight agents *DHL*, Red Cross Bdg, Independence Ave, PO Box 1077 (☎312000).

Groceries *Fairways* near the station and the *Gaborone Co-op* and *Corner Supermarket* in the centre of the Mall are well stocked. The *Spar* chain supermarkets in Nyerere Drive and at Broadhurst Shopping Centre are pretty good, as is *Pay Less* in the Kagiso Centre, Broadhurst.

Hospital Hospital Way off Notwane Road (☎353221).

Left luggage facilities at the station (Mon–Fri only, 8am–1pm & 2–4pm).

Library Gaborone Library, Independence Ave, below the Mall (Mon–Fri 9am–6pm, Sat 9am–noon) has a small range of international periodicals in the reference reading section. Next to the lending library in a separate building, the BNLS Headquarters is a room with publications just on Botswana. The University library's *Botswana Room* is open for reading and browsing only (off Mobutu Drive). The British Council has a good library, as does the US Embassy. The non-profit *Southern Africa Literature Society* (Plot 727, Khwai Rd; ☎373025) has a good selection of anti-apartheid and other progressive literature.

Maps The Department of Surveys and Lands, Private Bag 0037 (☎353251), has excellent OS maps at 1:50,000 – write off for their detailed catalogue. Aerial photographs are available if you're working in a small, featureless area of Botswana. There are also offices in Francistown and Selebi with 1:50,000 sheets of their immediate area.

Phones Efficient phones outside the post office – or try the quieter ones outside the Museum. Provided you have sufficient change, international calls are easy and the lines good.

Photocopying *Copy Girl* in the Mall next to the photography shop. This is also the place for quick passport photos, or try *Capital Studios* in the African Mall.

Photography *Photolab*, Upper Mall does one-hour developing and sells film.

Police Central Police Station, Gaborone Rd (☎351161) opposite the *Sun Hotel*.

Post office Mall centre (Mon–Fri 8.15am–1pm & 2–4pm, Sat 8.30–11.30am). Slow postal service but generally reliable.

Train tickets bookable at the station (Mon–Fri 7.30am–1pm & 2–7pm, Sat & Sun 4–7.30pm).

Travel agents In the Upper Mall: *Kudu Travel* (☎372224); *Manica Travel* (☎352021); *Pan African Travel*. All do air bookings and safaris and *Kudu* rents out cars. *Phuti Travel*, Nyerere Drive Shopping Centre (☎314166), sometimes does good deals on flights to London, Nairobi, Lilongwe and Dar-es-Salaam. Persistence pays off. It's worth enquiring about special rates at other travel agents.

Visa extensions Department of Immigration, State Drive, PO Box 942 (☎374545).

South from Gaborone

The only real reason for heading south **from Gaborone** along the main highway (unless you're going to South Africa) is in order to join the main route into the southwest Kalahari (see Chapter Ten), though it's worth taking time out to climb up **Kgali Hill** 8km out of Gaborone on the Lobatse Road. This easy climb which gives you great views over the city and the surrounding area, makes a good day trip in conjunction with a visit to **Gaborone Dam.** To get to the 10-kilometre long dam, take Mobutu Drive towards Lobatse, turn left at the *Sanitas* sign and continue for five kilometres to the dam wall. Permission to visit the dam wall itself must be obtained from the Water Utilities Corporation, Luthuli Road, near the railway station in Gaborone. *Sanitas* sells a wide range of fresh herbs, vegetables and plants from their garden nursery. The nearby, and signposted, **lion park** features a lot of lions in cages – not the most inspiring of places.

Lobatse

There's nothing at all to detain you in the road junction town of **LOBATSE**, 65km south of the capital. It was once Botswana's surrogate capital, because the territory's administrative centre was at Mafeking in South Africa and the **High Court** – the most important colonial institution inside the country – sat here, as it does today. But Lobatse never became important because of its lack of water. Its shining moment of glory came with the visit of King George VI in 1947, when 5km of road was tarred from Lobatse station to the High Court. At Independence, this remained the only piece of tarred road in the country. Now Lobatse is best known for having one of the largest abattoirs and meat-processing plants in Africa.

If you do find yourself stranded here *en route* to Ghanzi and the west, there are two business-oriented hotels on Khama I Avenue. The *Cumberland Hotel* (☎330278; ④) is expensive but comfortable, while the *Lobatse Hotel* (☎330157; ③) is less upmarket but not cheap. Also in Khama I Avenue, *Botswana Crafts* is worth a look for locally woven goods.

Outside Gaborone

If you're spending any time around Gaborone, make the effort to get out to two traditional villages – also worth the short detour if you're travelling the Gaborone–Francistown road. **Odi**, roughly 25km from Gaborone, is a boulder-strewn settlement with a weaving co-op producing outstanding tapestries depicting rural life and folktales. **Mochudi** is a picturesque traditional village about 40km north of the capital. It has the added attraction of a fine museum and craft centre in the old part of the village, where you'll find strikingly painted huts amongst rubbly hills.

Odi and the Lentswe-la-Odi Weavers

Getting to Odi by **car** is straightforward. Take the Francistown road out of Gaborone and turn right at the Odi sign, 17km further on, just beyond the roadblock. From here, follow the co-op signs assiduously as sandy tracks splay out through groups of huts and rocky outcrops.

Alternatively, any northbound **bus** from Gaborone will get you as far as the turn-off, from where it's a further 8km **on foot** or **hitching**. A couple of buses per day will actually get you all the way, if you can find out exactly when they're leaving. Otherwise, if you get off at the junction, there's a lively bar and bottle store, where you can refresh yourself before tackling the last stretch.

Lentswe-la-Odi Weavers

Lentswe-la-Odi Weavers is a Swedish-initiated co-operative, whose profits have been ploughed back into Odi village to start projects like a bakery, brickyard, general store and market garden.

The **tapestries** themselves are on informal display (no strict opening times) in a cool thatched building. One or two of the weavers have shifted from the formula of huts and livestock to bold animal subjects, like a massive lion reclining under a tree with a rabbit. Ask one of the women there to explain some of the mythological stories depicted in these bright wools. Besides the large hangings, they produce lovely woollen rugs and woven bedspreads, and browsing here is fun even if you can't afford anything. The tapestries, exhibited and sold abroad, aren't cheap, but they're realistically priced given the labour involved. To see what it takes, walk around and watch the weavers at work. Lemonade and *vetkoek* are on sale.

Mochudi

MOCHUDI is a short distance to the east of the main road to Francistown, about 40km north of Gaborone; **buses and combis** shuttle to and from the capital at a rate of at least one per hour.

At the junction of the main road and the Mochudi turn-off is one-street **PILANE**, where the *Sedibelo Motel* (②) is the only place to stay in the area (and easily reached if you want to avoid the Gaborone accommodation crush). You can get snacks, meals and teas, but expect a long wait. For something light try the *Lovers Rock* or *Arrow Restaurant*. There are also stores selling basics and a good sprinkling of bars.

From Pilane onwards, the approach to Mochudi is extremely unpromising, enough so to have you wondering just where this supposedly pretty and traditional place can be. For a couple of kilometres after the turn-off you proceed along a tarred road littered with the usual squashed cans and past a rash of general dealers and bottle stores. However, Mochudi does have an **historical core**, dominated by two impressive colonial-style buildings – the **Dutch Reformed Church** and the **Mochudi National School**. To get there, turn left at the T-junction, after the Pilane main-drag, and just before the hospital where the road forks, turn right and follow the road until it ends at the *kgotla*, set among the hills.

All activity in Mochudi centres around the *kgotla*, the traditional court, and it makes a fascinating area to explore. Meticulously maintained family compounds have their courtyard entrances and corners of walls decorated in grey and black abstract patterns. Thatched roofs extend beyond the walls to create circular verandahs where you may see big clay pots. Within the compounds you get remarkable double-walled granaries (*sefala*), but they aren't always easy to see from the outside. People aren't too bothered if you want to stroll around and take pictures, provided you ask politely.

Phuthadikobo Museum

Mon–Fri 8am–5pm, Sat & Sun 2–5pm. Entrance free.

Mochudi is the "capital" of the Bakgatla tribe, who settled here in 1871 when Boer harassment forced them off their lands in the Transvaal. Bakgatla chiefs have always been progressive, and the regent **Isang Pilane**, who was dissatisfied with missionary education, organised the building of the country's first secondary school.

Mochudi's one English-language school taught only up to standard 6 (12–13 years old). It was run by the Dutch Reformed Church, whose missionaries refused to teach such "worldly" subjects as arithmetic. However, useful subjects, not religious indoctrination, were exactly what the Bakgatla wanted and in 1920 they decided to build their own schoolhouse, at the top of the hill which overlooks Mochudi. Men and women worked side by side on the project, and it proved to be a real triumph of community

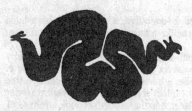

action, establishing a precedent that encouraged secondary education elsewhere in the country. Each man either contributed £5, made some of the school's 300,000 bricks or contributed other labour – and all the materials had to be painstakingly carried up the hill.

These days, it's a very pleasant walk to the top of the hill – one of the few places in Botswana to have an expansive view, out across the village and surrounding plains. Given the scarcity of high points in this flat land, it's perhaps not surprising that this one was sacred, and associated with rain-making and Kwanyape the **rain snake**.

The red-roofed former school, complete with wooden verandahs, now serves as the **Phuthadikobo Museum**, which deals simply with the small settlement of Mochudi. That might sound dull, but don't be put off. It's well displayed, with an excellent collection of early photographs. Among a wide range of weapons, tools, household objects and musical instruments is an impressive **drum** brought by the Bakgatla to Mochudi in 1871, of the kind traditionally used during the initiation of girls. A section on rain-making elucidates the hill's spiritual function.

In the hall of the museum (often used for meetings and training sessions of various kinds), two colourful Odi tapestries celebrate the achievements of the regent Isang Pilane, bringing alive the history of the Bakgatla migration. A couple of large papier-mâché **puppets** include a caricature of South African ex-President P. W. Botha reincarnated as a vampire.

A **silkscreen workshop** is housed in the same building, with fabrics sold at the **museum shop**. Everything is reasonably priced and it's a terrific place to buy gifts. The local hut designs are reproduced in calico; cotton hangings, cushion covers, table-cloths and fabrics which can be bought by the metre. Most imaginative of all are the T-shirts, which make fine souvenirs. If something takes your liking, you should buy it here as the stuff isn't distributed country-wide. Even the craft shop in nearby Gaborone carries only a meagre selection.

THE FRANCISTOWN ROAD AND THE TULI BLOCK

In a country with only two main tarred routes, the smooth ride from **Gaborone** to **Francistown** is not something to be taken for granted, even if you find the journey uninspiring. Botswana's single railway line runs virtually parallel to the north–south highway, with a station at each of the roadside towns, and there are corrugated-iron buildings and railway hotels at one or two of the bigger places like **Mahalapye** and **Palapye**.

The **railway line** was built by the British South Africa Company at the turn of the century as a vital link from land-locked colonies of Central Africa to the South African coast. In 1904, the British government transferred the land for the railway – as well as some blocks of land in Gaborone, Lobatse and Tuli – to the Company. These, together with the Tati District around Francistown, and the Ghanzi district, became the only white-populated areas in Bechuanaland.

In due course, the railway came under Rhodesian administration, with Rhodesia Railways' coaches and trucks doing the run. From 1974 Botswana began gradually to take it over, and prior to Namibian independence this was the only passenger-train link between the front line states and South Africa.

Branches from the road which fly off towards the mining towns of **Selebi-Phikwe** and **Orapa** are also tarred, as is the route to **Serowe**, 50km from the main road and worth a deviation. However, the only real attraction along the whole route is in the **Tuli Block** itself. This is a "block" in the simple sense that it is a grouping of private farmlands, and can be approached either from Selebi-Phikwe, or more divertingly through the back routes from Gaborone, hugging the South African border. Ironically, the easiest way to get to Tuli is via South Africa, where the roads are tarred up to the border posts.

North by Tar

The landscape changes little on the 433-km journey between Botswana's two largest towns, Gaborone and Francistown; there's just a relentless acacia-specked flatness waving with grass after the rains arrive. The sky is always enormous.

Local people never travel without a clutch of tins – either beer or coke – and you'll find **bars** in obscure places servicing the national thirst along this highway. One favourite is between Gaborone and Mahalapye, right on the **Tropic of Capricorn**. But the bar is no great tourist extravaganza, just a simple room in someone's back yard. There's no electricity here, so the deep freeze is powered by paraffin, but the drinks are always ice-cold. Outside, a dead bus, sunk in the sand to its wheel arches, has become a chicken coop. You'll know when the Tropic is imminent because a sign on either side announces: *Tropic of Capricon* (sic) *275m*.

Another notable bar is at the turn-off to Selebi-Phikwe, close to Serule. The *Kwena Bottle Store*'s murals painted on the verandah walls – the nicest has a crocodile about to gobble up a well-dressed woman who's dropped beer into its jaws – are almost worth a special halt.

Mahalapye

En route to Francistown, you pass through a succession of towns with nondescript garages, takeaways and bars straggled alongside the road – indeed the only attractive parts of these places tend to be the oldest areas, away from the main road and near the stations. One place in this mould is **MAHALAPYE**, 200km up the line (and eminently confusable with Palapye, the next town on). Cross the railway line opposite the Post Office, take the first left and round the bend 2km to the old and mellow *Mahalapye Hotel* (PO Box 526; ☎410200; ②), which overlooks a dry river bed with rocky banks and a village perched on the other side. The hotel is a good spot for a stop-over or a drink (the **bar** has a pin-up on the wall, really unusual in Botswana, where nudism is unheard of and attitudes towards women very conservative). **Camping** is possible in the grounds, though the washing facilities aren't too promising.

Between the hotel and the railway line, Mahalapye itself has a well-worn, established feel, pretty beneath its shady trees and rocky outcrops and quite different from the impression you get of it when you belt down the main road. Before you leave town, go to *Kaytees Restaurant*, at the southern end of town towards Gaborone for the best *vetkoek* in the country.

Palapye

The traditional mud huts of **PALAPYE** are surrounded by trimmed rubber bush hedges which thrive in the red sand. There's nothing to detain you here but there are **two hotels** if you get stuck. The *Palapye Hotel* (PO Box 1; ☎420277; ②) has more character, hidden behind masses of bougainvillea next to the station. The newish *Botsalo Hotel* (PO Box 35; ☎420245; ③) on the main road has the added attraction of a **swimming pool**.

SIR SERETSE AND RUTH KHAMA

Seretse Khama's marriage in 1948 to Ruth Williams, a white Englishwoman, carries echoes of Romeo and Juliet. Not only was the match opposed by the family of each, there was also the added dimension of murky political interests – both South African and British – cynically playing with individual lives. In this case, however, the couple emerged to become important figures in independent Botswana.

Seretse, the Bangwato heir, was sent to Oxford to read law shortly after World War II by his uncle, the regent Tshekedi Khama. While completing his legal education at the Inner Temple in London, he met Ruth Williams, originally through a mutual interest in jazz. The couple married in 1948 and returned to Bechuanaland.

Their personal affair turned into a constitutional crisis. Tshekedi Khama was furious; according to Bangwato custom the *mohumagadi* (great wife of the king) must be selected by the community and come from a Tswana royal family. Seretse apologised for not marrying according to custom, but insisted that if his people rejected his wife they would lose him too. Four thousand men supported Seretse against a mere forty for his uncle; but the defeated Tshekedi led his followers away to settle among the Bakwena. African leaders as far afield as Lesotho and Swaziland supported him, fearing the erosion of tradition. For entirely different reasons racist whites in southern Africa were horrified, describing the marriage as nauseating. South African prime minister DF Malan called on the British to put a stop to it.

The British Labour government bowed to prejudice and, without any legal basis, it rejected the marriage. It was particularly afraid that South Africa would withhold vital supplies of its recently discovered uranium. Seretse was called to London for talks in 1950, with an assurance that he would be allowed to return to Bechuanaland. He was offered £1100 to relinquish the kingship and live in England for the rest of his life; he refused, and also turned down a job in Jamaica. Breaking its word, the government banned him from returning home for five years. Sir Winston Churchill slammed Labour's dealings as "very disreputable," but when his Tories got their turn to govern in 1951 they made the exile indefinite.

A number of British MPs and organisations took up Seretse's cause in a campaign that continued for six years. In Bechuanaland the Bangwato resisted pressure to elect a new king and instead were subjected to a British-imposed "Native authority". Those who refused to obey him were flogged. Tshekedi Khama, seeing the ugly results of his traditionalist line, made a swift U-turn in 1952. He returned to his people, recognised Ruth as the *mohumagadi* and called for Seretse's immediate return. Tshekedi and the Tswana kings rounded on the British, who they believed were planning to use the Seretse affair to hand over Bechuanaland to South Africa.

The whole issue was finally resolved in July 1956, when Tshekedi travelled to London for a secret meeting with his nephew. They successfully mended their relationship and came to an agreement which they presented to the British authorities. Under its terms neither man would claim the kingship for himself or his children. Later that year Seretse and Ruth returned to Serowe, as private citizens.

Seretse's political involvement did not end there. He successfully led Botswana to Independence in 1966, when he was knighted, and he remained in the position of president until his death in 1980. The Bangwato for their part continued to insist on the restoration of their proper royal line. Though Seretse was never to take up his rightful role, in 1979 his eldest son Brigadier Ian Khama was installed as *kgosi* in Serowe. Lady Khama continues to live in Botswana, where she holds an almost regal status as *Mohumagadi Mma Kgosi* – mother of the *kgosi* – equivalent to the British queen mother.

A Marriage of Inconvenience, by Michael Dutman, published by Unwin Hyman in London in 1990 and linked to a BBC TV documentary, tells the whole story (see "Books" in *Contexts*).

Serowe

SEROWE is in theory a large traditional Batswana village, textured with rocky outcrops – though in fact the word "village" is rather misleading, as modern buildings have been grafted onto older, thatched areas to give it the appearance of a town rather than a rural hamlet. Electricity has been installed and a tarred road built since the town was immortalised in the writing of **Bessie Head**, Botswana's only internationally known writer, who made her home here after leaving South Africa (see "Books", in *Contexts*).

Serowe was also the birthplace of the late **Sir Seretse Khama**, the charismatic leader who took the country through Independence and was its first president until his death in 1980. He came from a strong line of chiefs of the Bangwato, a major Batswana grouping who were centred here. The Khama family graves, a revered site of pilgrimage, are on the rocky outcrop above the *kgotla* and District Council offices. On Khama III's grave (Seretse's grandfather) is a bronze duiker, totem of the Bangwato. It was sculpted, interestingly enough, not by a Motswana, but by the well-known South African artist, Anton van Wouw. If you're interested in the history of the Khamas, the fascinating **Khama III Memorial Museum** lies at the base of the hill in the middle of Serowe. For Bessie Head enthusiasts, this is the place to view all her papers. Viewing them is by appointment only; ring the Museum (☎430519) if you're keen.

There's yet a third reason for Serowe's prominence – the **Brigade Movement** begun in the 1960s by South African political refugee Patrick van Rensburg. Conceived as a revival of the kind of Tswana self-help groups so effectively organised at Mochudi earlier in the century, the Brigades were an attempt to solve the major, inter-related problems of unemployment and skills shortages, especially in the rural areas. Few primary school leavers were able to attend secondary school and their options were limited: to work as herders on cattle-posts, to find work in towns, or to go to South Africa and work on the mines. Schools offered no practical training and were elite-orientated.

Van Rensburg's first project was the **Swaneng Hill School**, near the Serowe airstrip, which emphasised manual work, and aimed to foster self-reliance and an awareness of development issues in the pupils. Growing out of these ideas, the Brigade Movement was aimed at equipping primary school leavers with **practical skills**. The first one was the Builders Brigade in 1965 in Serowe, followed by groups in metalwork, carpentry, weaving and leatherwork. The idea of self-help vocational training spread countrywide and students built their own classrooms and dormitories. From their manual work, they earned enough to pay for the running of the school.

The Tuli Block

The **TULI BLOCK** is the least visited of Botswana's main tourist areas, by-passed by most people as they roll on north. Much of it is privately owned but, despite the fences, there are accessible resorts which do not charge anything like the hefty National Parks entrance fees. Not just lodges either; on the banks of "the great grey green greasy Limpopo all set about with fever trees", (where Kipling's "elephant's child" got a good stretching of his trunk by the crocodile in the *Just-So Stories*), there's a lovely campsite, from which walking expeditions are operated.

Before the whites arrived, Tuli was Bangwato tribal land. Sites dating from the seventh and eighth century indicate an even earlier occupation. The Tuli Block now consists mostly of white-owned **game farms and private reserves**, many with Afrikaans names painted on their gate posts, dating from the time when the land was ceded to the BSAC for the building of the railway line. Rhodes' railway track didn't pass this way in the end, though, because there were too many rivers to cross.

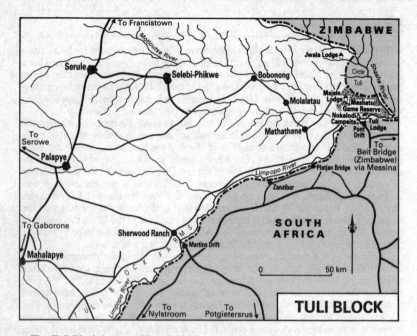

The Tuli Block is several hundred kilometres long, and a narrow 10km to 20km in width. Outside this strip you'll find traditional villages, some of them very beautiful and worth exploring. The roads are dusty and far from busy. Without a vehicle of some sort Tuli is difficult country to get around, although 4WD isn't essential.

Because Tuli hugs the **South African border**, and road connections there are easier than those within Botswana, many of the Block's white residents cross over to do their shopping and business. There are four border posts along Tuli's 350-km length. All have tarred roads on the South Africa side, making it only six hours to Johannesburg. Messina, in South Africa, (though near Zimbabwe's Beit Bridge border), is the nearest reasonably sized place with good shops.

The mining town of **SELEBI-PHIKWE** is Botswana's third largest, another purpose-built place, established in 1967, and complete with shopping malls and an expensive hotel. The *Bosele* (PO Box 177, Selebi-Phikwe; ☎810675; ③), is part of the upmarket *Marakanelo Group*. If you're **hitching** or going by **truck** through the Tuli Block, Selebi is the place for lifts, but it's not somewhere to visit otherwise.

Back routes through Tuli

The most interesting part of the region is in northern Tuli around the **Motloutse River**. But by car, if you're in no hurry, consider taking a longer, but more interesting route than following the mostly dull Francistown road. Turning off at Mosomane (Artesia on some maps), 53km north of Gaborone, this dusty route takes you through some attractive red-earthed villages – with a noticeable lack of the cans which litter most of Botswana's towns.

Twine, criss-crossed over the thatching, produces a braided look while neatly sculpted low adobe walls create wave patterns around courtyards. Villages in Botswana can look deserted. Many Batswana maintain three homes: a family house in the village,

Dear uncle Archie

just a quick postcard to say i am having a fanatastic holiday in Belveldere, Knsyna. Barbara invited me. I have just been water skiing, but not very successful. i only got up once and unfortinately the engine cut. Mom and Dad have just arrived home from the Pilansberg we visited the Pilansberg. we saw rinoceros twinking in the distance, and nearby the lights of Leisure island we saw yesterday.

LOTS of love

Zoe.

(have you received the report + letter yet).

MR A Sprott

51 Lothian St

Bonnyrigg

Lothian Region

Scotland

UK

22nd August 1994

75c

Suid-Afrika
South Africa
1993
DENNIS MURPHY
POECILOGALE ALBINUCHA

a building on cultivated land which women go
to from the beginning of the rains in
November until the harvest in May or June,
and a cattle post, often far away, where mainly
boys graze the cattle. Men are also often at the
cattle posts and you'll see them on long journeys riding donkeys or horses with a bedroll
behind.

Those with money employ others to do the
herding, often Bakgalakgadi and San. Despite
the fact that Botswana has three million cattle
and the population is only a million, the
national herd is concentrated in the hands of only five percent of the population. The
impression you may get of a large rural cattle-owning population is deceptive – nearly
half of the people own no cattle at all.

The more direct route through Tuli runs up the Francistown Road, as far as possible, then veers east just before Palapye. The road from Palapye to Martin's Drift then
hits **SHERWOOD RANCH**, a dilapidated staging post with a handful of shanties made
from *chibuku* cartons, one large house, a filling station, post office, general dealer, bar
and bottle store. Don't believe the *Shell* road map which indicates a hotel here, another
at Zanzibar and a couple of public campsites. They're all long gone. The *Zanzibar Hotel*
is a peeling film set of a place, deserted and no longer taking guests. Some miles on, a
sign for a hotel and bottle store leads to further derelict scenes. Wire tables and chairs
are still outside on the clay-baked terracotta earth. Someone lives in a silver caravan
propped up on bricks and the rubbed-out hotel sign now reads *general dealer*.

Mashatu Game Reserve and the Pont Drift area

Some of Botswana's most arresting topography is wedged in a triangular salient,
around **PONT DRIFT**, between Zimbabwe and South Africa. Strikingly eroded sandstone rock massifs rise out of flat, prickly plains in a landscape resembling the backdrop to a B-movie western.

The massifs follow the course of the rivers – principally the Motloutse and the
Limpopo – with riverine trees softening the landscape. Semi-precious stones such as
agates and crystal quartz litter the beds of the watercourses, which are often dry tracts
of sand.

This area has a lot to draw independent travellers, who nonetheless tend to bypass it
out of ignorance. A considerable **game** population drifts back and forth across the
border in the region adjacent to Zimbabwe's Tuli Circle. There are no national park
reserves, only the elephant-browsed Mashatu Game Reserve, privately owned land
made doubly attractive by the absence of park fees. But the stock of mammals and
avifauna is as good as in the Okavango Delta, and the fascinating landscapes attract
enough visitors, even out here, to support a number of **lodges** and a **campsite**, with
facilities and prices to suit all budgets.

Getting there and getting around

Pont Drift is the usual jumping-off point for the lodges of this area. There are no facilities here and it's little more than a border post, with South Africa clearly visible on the
other side of the Limpopo. In the rainy season the Motloutse and Limpopo rivers are
sometimes impossible to ford, cutting off Pont Drift, bar the **cable car link** across the
Limpopo to South Africa. (Few South Africans ford the Limpopo in their own vehicles,
preferring to park their vehicles and cross by cableway to the Botswana side, where
one of the lodges meets them.)

To get to Pont Drift without a car, **hitch** to Sherwood from Palapye and north up the main Tuli Block road. There isn't much traffic, so expect long waits. Pick-up trucks head that way, especially over the weekend. Another option is to go via Selebi-Phikwe – well connected to both Gaborone and Francistown – to Zanzibar and Pont Drift. Small trucks head, especially at weekends, from Bobonong (on the way from Selebi-Phikwe, and closest town to Pont Drift) for the pretty **villages near Talana Farm** along the Motloutse River. Talana, a huge commercial and irrigated farming concern is across the Motloutse River from Mashatu Game Reserve. A daily **bus** goes via Bobonong to one of these Talana vicinity villages, Molalatau. On Tuesday and Saturday it continues to Mathathane (about 30km further, to the southeast), returning to Selebi-Phikwe on Wednesday and Sunday. People also use donkey carts to get from one riverbank village to another.

The villages are very traditional and people are friendly, which is just as well as you can't be in any sort of hurry to get anywhere. There are **stores** for basic supplies and you'll have to camp. The villages, which always look freshly swept, are red-walled with boldly painted frescoes and abstract designs. The luxury lodges at Pont Drift are staffed with people from these surrounding villages.

Staying in Tuli

The budget option: Nokolodi campsite

Luxury lodges aside, there's only one way to see this area on the cheap. *Nokolodi campsite*, near Pont Drift (Private Bag X1040, Waterpoort 0905, South Africa; ☎Johannesburg 788 0740; ①–③) is set in the middle of Limpopo's riverine forest. It's dominated by a splendid mashatu tree, which is at least 1000 years old, with an immensely thick trunk. Behind the fringing forest alongside the river are sandstone cliffs and rocks which turn orange and red at dawn and dusk. From the top you look onto the forest canopy of slender pale-green fever trees and the giant deep-green mashatus and umbrella trees forming a dense covering. The Limpopo itself is a bright blur, with South Africa beyond. Looking the other way onto stony mopane hillsides, you may spot far-off **elephants**, moving methodically through the landscape. Old bones and bleached cat droppings suggest that leopards come here too. Among the riverside trees you're certain to see antelope coming to drink and shelter in the shade. There's seldom big game in the vicinity so you can walk and scramble around the rocks safely.

Walks are conducted by the trained guide and ecologist who runs the camp, and are included in the **camping fee**. He also does drives and has access to other areas of Tuli, which makes *Nokolodi* an excellent option if you want to explore this corner of Botswana. Besides camping, there are some two-person **huts** with self-catering facilities. Transfers from Pont Drift (see box below) are included in the fee. You can book ahead through their private bag or if you just turn up ask directions from *Tuli Lodge* (see below). If you're hitching and find yourself at *Tuli Lodge*, they may be prepared to put you in radiophone contact with *Nokolodi*.

Medium-priced: Jwala Lodge

Sharing the same game as the more expensive Mashatu Game Reserve, *Jwala Lodge* (Private Bag X1040, Waterpoort 0905, South Africa; ☎Johannesburg 788 0740; ②–③) kisses the border, where Zimbabwe's Tuli Circle bulges into Botswana. The landscape around *Jwala* is disturbingly harsh – mopane trees as far as you can see and dry riverbeds with coarse black sand. It has a gaunt beauty, nevertheless, and animals thrive here, especially elephants. You're certain to see some action; a couple of waterholes attract terrific concentrations of animals during the dry season.

The small unserviced **chalets** are a bargain while the more luxurious, serviced ones at a separate camp are more expensive. Both are self-catering. The price includes game drives and walks.

The owners of all the Tuli lodges named here are happy to come and collect from the cable car at Pont Drift.

Mashatu Game Reserve and the luxury lodges

The whole Pont Drift area is rich in game and must have been a wildlife paradise before colonial times. Elephant are prominent and you're likely to see the big cats, giraffe, eland and a wide variety of antelope. The only **game park**, *Mashatu*, is privately run and you're not allowed to camp or picnic on *Mashatu* property, however tempting. You can get a taste by **camping** on the opposite bank of the Motloutse River at the edge of Talana Farm. There are some beautiful spots under mashatu trees and in the early morning (when there's water) you can watch antelope and baboons coming to drink. Once you cross the river you're in the park, although the road itself is a public one leading to Pont Drift. The game reserve's *Majale Lodge* (PO Box 2575, Randburg 2125, South Africa; ⑤) is expensive, but does provide game drives and value-for-money luxury. They also have a bush-chic tented camp with a more remote feel.

Tuli Lodge (PO Box 335, Gaborone; ⑤) close to the Limpopo, is a garden oasis in dry country. Amidst the scorched surroundings *Tuli*'s clipped lawns, indigenous trees, cool bar and swimming pool, are made all the more delicious. It's thoroughly indulgent, with the big attraction of game drives in Mashatu Game Reserve. Scoring some publicity for the area, the owner of *Tuli* is sponsoring the work of Gareth Patterson, George Adamson's assistant. After Adamson's murder in Kenya in 1989, Patterson took the three young lion cubs he had been rearing from Kenya to Botswana, where he is teaching them to return to wild. Patterson intends to continue Adamson's *Born Free* work with lions in Botswana.

travel details

Buses

From Gaborone Daily buses and combis run north toward Francistown (Chapter 8) and south to Lobatse (Chapter 10). Some only go as far as intermediate towns and the closer the destination, the more frequent the service.

Trains

The single line running between Johannesburg and Bulawayo passes through virtually every town along Botswana's eastern corridor, south of Francistown. A 7-hour, twice daily service between Gaborone and Francistown, on brand new, air-conditioned trains has been proudly introduced by Botswana Railways. It's the best way to travel along the eastern corridor and is the only air-conditioned train in public timetabled service in Africa. The overnight service continues through to Bulawayo, arriving at 11.50am. The sleeper fare includes bedding.

The weekly train through Botswana between Johannesburg and Bulawayo, is the only overland public transport between the three countries. It leaves Bulawayo on Thursdays and Johannesburg

TRAIN TIMES
From Gaborone
Bulawayo daily 7pm
Francistown daily 6.10am & 2.10pm
Lobatse daily 6.50am
Johannesburg Fri 6.50am

on Tuesdays. It's a 24-hour journey but has the advantage of covering the ground and throwing in a night's accommodation too.

Crossing borders by train you'll have customs and immigration officials coming to your compartment instead of having to queue. Sometimes this makes things quicker, but at other times there are lengthy waits on the South African side of the border caused by officious Bophuthatswana immigration people (minions of South Africa in spite of the pretence otherwise – you fill in South African immigration forms when you cross from Botswana into the "independent" bantustan).

Flights

Air Botswana runs a limited internal service with barely a flight every day between main centres. The following routes **from Gaborone** are covered:

To Francistown daily.

To Maun daily.

To Selebi-Phikwe Wed & Fri.

To Ghanzi Mon & Wed.

To Kasane Thurs & Sat.

To Johannesburg daily.

CHAPTER EIGHT

CHOBE AND THE NORTHEAST

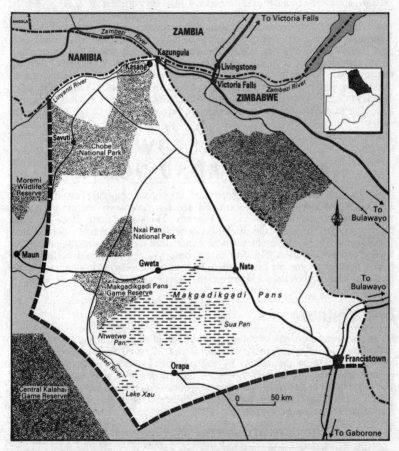

The pivotal position of **Francistown** led to its status in colonial times as the "capital of the north". At the end of the line on the Eastern Corridor, it's the last sizeable place you'll go through en route from Bulawayo or southern Botswana to the Makgadikgadi Pans and the teeming game reserves of the north – Chobe National Park and the Okavango Delta.

Making a special trip to traverse the spectacular **Makgadikgadi Pans** is strictly for experienced bush drivers. If you feel up to it, it's worth every penny to shell out and hire a vehicle and equipment for a self-sufficient camping expedition. An easier, and safer, option is to join one of the Maun-based **mobile safaris** operating in the area, or one of the overland companies which stop at the pans en route to the Okavango.

There's no big game on the salt flats themselves; their allure lies in the immense freedom of the vast skies and the lonely expanses of landscape. But there is game – huge herds of it – on the grassy plains which sweep away from them, at **Nxai Pan National Park** (best in the rainy season) and directly south, the **Makgadikgadi Game Reserve** (best in the dry). There are further beautiful places – **Baines' Baobabs** and **Kubu Island** – outside the boundaries of the parks, with no entrance fees.

Chobe National Park is renowned for its massive number of elephants, some of which you'll certainly see watering along the picturesque Chobe river running past **Kasane**, on the northern side of the park, close to the Zimbabwean border. You'll need your own 4WD and a tent to explore the park, or to stay in one of the luxury safari camps along the river, or to the south in the wonderful **Savuti**. If you don't have your own transport, it's worth considering one of the overland expeditions which travel through the park from Victoria Falls through **Kasane to Maun**. If you're hitching to Maun, you'll have to go the long way round via **Nata**, (it's on tar, at least) as there is no reliable tranport on the direct route through the park.

FRANCISTOWN
AND THE ROAD NORTH

Although it's Botswana's second-biggest town, there's no compelling reason to stay in **FRANCISTOWN** beyond its sheer convenience as a place where you can get a good night's sleep and stock up with all you'll need for adventuring north. Once you leave Francistown and the last of the roadblocks behind, the exhilaration of limitless space unrolls before you – there are no towns for hundreds of kilometres – and some thrilling wildlife experiences await. The first 195km bring you to the junction settlement of **NATA**, from where you can head north to **Kasane** and the elephant country of **Chobe National Park**, or west toward **Maun** and the **Okavango Delta** (see Chapter Nine).

Francistown

As well as being the centre of the region's official and commercial life, Francistown is at the hub of all Botswana's major transport routes. All tarred roads lead here, midway on the main north–south highway, it's well connected by rail and air to the rest of the country, and Bulawayo in Zimbabwe is just three hours' drive away on a direct road. The relationship to Zimbabwe is concretely visible – Francistown feels, and looks, like orderly, small-town Zimbabwe, with the main difference being that the shops are well stocked, and spare parts are available.

ACCOMMODATION PRICE CODES

Every hotel and accommodation option listed in this chapter has been given a **price code** to indicate the cost of a single night's lodging. Safari lodges are excluded from the system, a specific price being quoted.

For a full explanation, see p.251.

    ① under P50   ② P50–100   ③ P100–175   ④ P175–250   ⑤ P250+

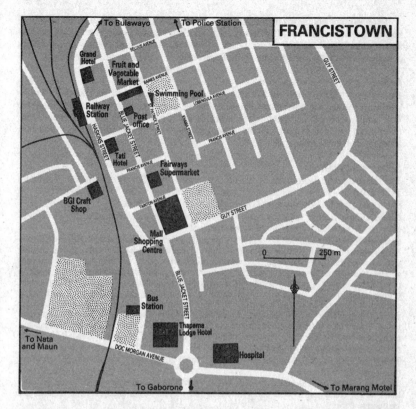

In fact Francistown's connection with Zimbabwe stretches back well before colonial times, when the present artificial boundaries were drawn. **Stone-wall villages** in the Francistown district are of the Khami type, and map the influence of the Rozvi state (see "History" in Zimbabwe *Contexts*), which by the fifteenth century had risen to power and extended into present Botswana. Unfortunately, the sites are almost all on private land and are difficult to visit.

The pre-colonial name of the settlement, **Nyangabgwe**, meant "approach the rock" in the Kalanga dialect of Shona (which is still spoken in parts of Botswana), referring to a hunter who mistook a rock for an antelope on a hill. Francistown's current name comes from **Daniel Francis**, one of the first white prospectors in the area in the 1860s. Francis was a co-founder of the *Northern Light Company*, set up to exploit the newly discovered goldfields, and Francistown developed primarily as a company town servicing the mineral extraction industry. Gold, copper and nickel are still mined round about, but are now eclipsed by other deposits in the vicinity – the diamond mine at **Orapa**, and the soda ash plant planned for **Sua Pan**.

Francistown today is a compact and neatly planned place, with jacaranda trees lining the streets, a couple of parks and a public swimming pool. The two main roads, **Haskins Street** and **Blue Jacket Street**, run parallel to the railway line, providing everything you're likely to need. However, there are no outstanding attractions to keep you here and most business can be done swiftly before pressing on.

If you do find yourself with the time, it's worth checking out the permanent collection at the **Supa-Ngwao Museum** in the old Francistown Court House. This is the new regional museum for the northeast, and also hosts cultural events. On land adjacent to the north, an open-air museum of traditional Botswana architecture is planned.

Arrival
Buses and trains arrive in Francistown right in the thick of things; the **railway station** is toward the north end of Haskins Street, and the **bus terminus** at the south. The small **airport** is just outside town, but as few if any independent travellers fly in, there's no public transport. If you've booked into one of the posh hotels, you can arrange in advance to be met.

Accommodation
The three **central hotels** are all within five minutes' walk of the station and terminus. Two of these establishments are run-down and **cheap** – rare in Botswana. There is only one campsite, slightly out of town, but highly recommended.

Grand Hotel, Haskins St/Selous Ave (☎212300). Definitely no longer deserves its name, with dingy, cockroach-ridden rooms and filthy washing facilities. ②.

Marang Motel, Old Gaborone Rd (☎213991). By far Francistown's nicest place to stay, on the tree-lined banks of the sandy Tati River, 4km out of town. It has a swimming pool below the terrace and self-contained thatched **chalets** perched on stilts, which are slightly more expensive than standard double rooms. The **campsite** beneath the shady trees along the river bank has washing facilities unparalleled in Botswana. A favourite of the overland expeditions, the campsite is full of people setting off for the wild north, or recently out of the bush having their first taste of such urban comforts as hot water, mirrors and electric lights. The self-service breakfast here is a great way to set yourself up for a long trek, with mounds of pancakes, corn-fritters as well as the customary eggs and bacon. Take a taxi, or by car follow Blue Jacket Street towards *Thapama Lodge*, take the Matsiloje exit off the big roundabout, keep going straight and the *Marang* is on the right, about a kilometre past the signposted turn-off to Matsiloje. ①–③–④.

Tati Hotel, Haskins St/Lobengula St (☎212321). Plumb in the centre and marginally better than the *Grand*. ②.

Thapama Lodge. Doc Morgan Ave/Blue Jacket St (☎213872). Francistown's upmarket business hotel, which could just as well be anywhere in the world with its anodyne bars, lounges and bedrooms. ⑤.

Eating and Shopping
Francistown is one of the very few towns in Botswana with a **fresh produce market** (corner of Baines and Blue Jacket streets). You can buy cooked maize and groundnuts here, and the bustling courtyard is one of the best places for **fast food**. There are several other fast-food joints and **takeaways**, around the bus station and in the Mall. A

good one with vegetarian possibilities is opposite *BGI Crafts* on the other side of the railway line.

Shopping in Francistown is easy and convenient, and if you've come straight from Zimbabwe, the selection of goods seems dazzling, with a wide range of foods in the *Mall Shopping Centre* on Blue Jacket Street/Tainton Avenue. Apart from meat for braaing, the *Mall Butchery* has a good range of imported foods, including dried noodles, soya chunks and dried curries – all ideal lightweight camping goods. Buy stuff here if you're on your way to Zimbabwe for some hiking, because such goods are unavailable there. For bread, and city luxuries like doughnuts and pastries, head straight for the excellent *Hot'n'Crusty*, also in the *Mall*. The biggest supermarket is *Fairways*, in Blue Jacket Street, near the *Mall*, open during lunch time. *Woolworths* does a tempting line in *Marks and Spencers* food for the homesick. The *Milky Bar* next door does a great waffles and ice cream breakfast.

Nightlife

Francistown's **nightlife** buzzes around hotel **bars**, but there are also a few actual **nightclubs**. In the centre, the *New Yorker* in Blue Jacket Street, where you can expect a predominance of disco with some African beat, is the easiest to find. You'll get up-to-date recommendations by asking in the record shop in Haskins Street; current favourites are the *Ghetto Blaster* and *The Cave*. You'll find the *Cine 2000*, the only **cinema** in town, down Blue Jacket Street – don't expect anything out of the ordinary.

Listings

Air Botswana *Thapama Lodge*, Blue Jacket St (☎212393).

Banks *Barclays* and *Standard Chartered* are both in Haskins Street.

Bookshop *Francistown Stationers and Bookshop* on Haskins Street has a motley collection of paperbacks and a couple of books about Botswana. There's also a good selection of stationery and magazines.

Car rental *Avis* at the airport (☎213901).

Crafts *BGI* across railway bridge in Francis Ave extension. The enormous elephant head outside leads you to a fine selection of Shashe area baskets, but nothing else is particularly riveting.

Doctor P. K. Sayana is in the Lobengula St Mall opposite the *Tati Hotel* (Mon–Fri 8.30am–noon & 3–6pm, Sat 8.30am–noon; ☎212400, res ☎213494). Other doctors are listed in the pink pages at the front of the phone directory.

Dentist Dr Bosman, Blue Jacket/Baines streets (☎212295).

Emergencies Ambulance ☎997, Police ☎999.

Hospital Jubilee Hospital (☎212333/4) off Haskins St across the railway line.

Left luggage facilities at the station (Mon–Fri 8am–4pm, Sat 7.30–11am).

Post office Blue Jacket St

Public telephones outside Barclays Bank, in the Mall, and at *Thapama Lodge*.

Pharmacy *Phodisong*, the *Mall*, Blue Jacket St (emergencies ☎213719).

Railway booking office Haskins St, opposite the *Tati* (Mon–Fri only, 8am–1pm & 2–4pm). *Botswana Railways* information on ☎213444.

Records *Meropa Music Salon* at the bottom of Haskins St has tapes and records of Botswana bands, as well as Zimbabwean and South African groups.

Swimming pool Baines Ave, opening hours vary between 9am and 6pm.

Taxis ☎212260, or hail cars with blue number plates.

Travel agents *Pan African Travel*, Lobengula Ave/Blue Jacket St.

Visa renewals at the Immigration Department in Blue Jacket St, opposite the cinema.

Francistown to Kasane

The tarred highway north from Francistown divides after 189km at NATA, with north-bound tar continuing to Kasane and westbound newly tarred road to Maun and the Okavango. One possible break in your journey before getting to Nata is the refugee camp at **DUKWE**, 103km from Francistown, just off the main road. Set up during the liberation struggle in Rhodesia, the camp now houses Namibian and Angolan refugees, and some Zimbabweans who have stayed on. Far nicer than it may sound, there's a tempting variety of craft work for sale and a photogenic thatched public bar. Keep your camera under wraps, however, as photography isn't allowed.

A new game sanctuary has been opened on the edge of Sua Pan, which offers the chance to see flamingoes, pelicans and many other water birds. The park currently holds springbok, hartebeest and wildebeest, and intends to introduce other species. This is the first successful project in Botswana where local tribespeople have taken their cattle off grazing land and converted it for the use of wildlife. Camping is available with hot showers and toilets. The signposted turn-off is about 10km south of Nata.

Nata

The small village of **NATA** – little more than a crossroads – is totally dependent on through traffic. It centres around the *Sua Pan Bottle Store* and **garage**, which offers the last petrol before Maun, 304km away. Everyone stops here, and it's very much the place to wait for **lifts** to Maun, just before the road swings off into the westbound dust. The **bottle store** has a wide range of drinks, and the fry-ups are very good at the hotel café, next door. If you just want a snack, there's first-class biltong to be had in season from the *Wild Beasts Butchery* (complete with paintings of very fierce wildebeest on the outside walls). For any **medical needs**, the newish clinic, signposted off the main road, is good. You should however fill your water containers in Francistown rather than relying on the supply at the garage, as Nata suffers from shortages.

The *Sua Pan Hotel* at the garage (no phone; ④) offers the only accommodation in town, conveniently situated on the main road, but it's a bit of a rip-off and not recommended. **Camping** is also available.

However, just 10km south of Nata on the Francistown–Kasane Road, the *Nata Lodge* stands in a far nicer setting, among ilala palms and marula and monkey thorn trees. You can **camp** or stay in comfortable self-contained three-bed **chalets**, or for a little less, sleep in large four-bed tents (①–③). Book through the *Marang Motel* in Francistown, or write to: Private Bag 10, Francistown (☎611210). As well as walking in the surrounding bush, it's possible to take an organised **drive** from the lodge to Sua Pan, for a minimum of four people, and mobile safaris throughout Botswana can be arranged. If you're only stopping off for a drink – and the bar is a good place to hear bush stories – you can use the swimming pool or have a shower for a couple of pula. If you do spend the night, splash out on a candle-lit dinner (set menu or *à la carte*) in the thatched dining room – especially good if you've been in the bush for a while. The lodge has a fine selection of **crafts**, which are no more expensive than anywhere else. The woven briefcases are particularly stylish.

Nata to Kasane

Between Kasane and Nata, a long straight stretch where the road borders on Zimbabwe's Hwange National Park, there's a good chance of seeing elephants, ostriches and the odd herd of impala. Along the second half of the 299 monotonous kilometres, the Sibuyu, Kazuma and Kasane forest reserves hug the Zimbabwe border in three separate enclaves of teak and *mukwa* **woodland** and offer some diversion from the endless tar strip. Hitching is difficult because there's little traffic, but there's a daily minibus (*combi*) service between Francistown and Kasane in both directions, via Nata. Enquire at the Nata garage for current times.

This northbound highway traverses the tracks of a nineteenth-century ivory route to the Zambezi. Known as the **Mpandamatenga trail** – the "pick-up-and-carry-road" – its name refers to the reliance of white hunters on black porters. Nowadays, **MPANDAMATENGA** (a former trading post) signals its existence with a series of grain silos, that rise like mirages from the surrounding maize and sorghum fields. A tamed island in the vast wilderness, it's one of the country's few farming areas, and home to a prosperous agricultural community. There's little more to tempt you to stop, though, than a café, general store and the recently opened *Shell* service station.

It's possible to drive into **Zimbabwe** from Mpandamatenga, although there's no official border post. If you decide to take this rarely used exit, you must report to the police at Mpandamatenga before leaving, and, once in Zimbabwe, clear yourself with immigration at Victoria Falls or Bulawayo. Inside Zimbabwe, the road branches north through Matetsi (a major hunting area) to the tarred Bulawayo–Victoria Falls road (65km), and south to Robins Camp in Hwangwe National Park (48km).

The Salt Pans

If you take the **road to Maun**, your long journey will carry you through some of Botswana's most remarkable landscapes, second only to the Okavango Delta itself. The road cuts between the enormous complex of the **Makgadikgadi Pans** to the south, and the relatively small – but no less interesting – **Nxai and Kudiakam Pans** to the north. If you're in your own vehicle, there's good reason to make a detour.

The choice of whether to visit Nxai or Makgadikgadi Pan depends on what time of year you're in Botswana, as game migrates from one area to another. In the dry season (April to October), Makgadikgadi is best, while during the rains (November to March) the animals are attracted northwards to Nxai Pan. It also depends on how bold you are. Nxai Pan has **camping facilities** and it's not too difficult to find your way around, while getting around Makgadikgadi is a matter of a good sense of direction. Neither compasses nor maps are much help here. Scores of unmapped tracks weave about the vast 4200 sq km of game-rich grasslands and bush country that make up the **Makgadikgadi Pans Game Reserve** – the northwest section of Ntwetwe Pan, which is the more westerly of the adjacent depressions of Makgadikgadi. The whole of the pans area demands self-sufficiency in food, water and fuel.

If you're not going to either Nxai or Makgadikgadi reserves, a smaller detour to the majestic Baines' Baobabs at Kudiakam Pan, south of Nxai Pan is highly recommended.

Gweta

GWETA, over halfway to Maun, is definitely worth a stop, whether you're heading off to the pans or not. It's a thatched village with towering palm trees, grey sand, and vagrant donkeys and horses. Its name is from San and means "where the big frogs meet". In the middle of the settlement *Gweta Rest Camp*'s modest thatched rondavels (②) blend with the stick- and bush-encircled village huts. A night spent here en route for Maun offers a rare opportunity to stay in a traditional village and experience life going on around you without feeling an intruder. The *Rest Camp* bar and darts' board draws both locals and travellers or, for variation, try the bar and restaurant down the road adjoining the shop and bakery – an obvious huddle of buildings on your left as you come into town. The fresh bread, baked in an outside oven, is a welcome surprise in such a small place. A new petrol station makes Gweta even more of a stopping-off place.

Makgadikgadi Pans

At 12,000 sq km, **MAKGADIKGADI PANS** make an impression through their sheer extent (and the fact that they're almost unpronounceable; the *kg* is pronounced like the *ch* in loch, and the *a* as the *u* in *cud*: *Muchudichudi*). On maps they look like massive lakes, giving a false impression of the landscape – but a strong clue to its origin. About two million years ago, the Okavango Delta and the pans were part of an enormous lake that flooded across northern Botswana. The deepest parts of the basin became today's Makgadikgadi Pans, comprising **SUA PAN** (sometimes spelled "Sowa") to the east, and **NTWETWE PAN** to the west, each roughly 100km long by more than 50km wide.

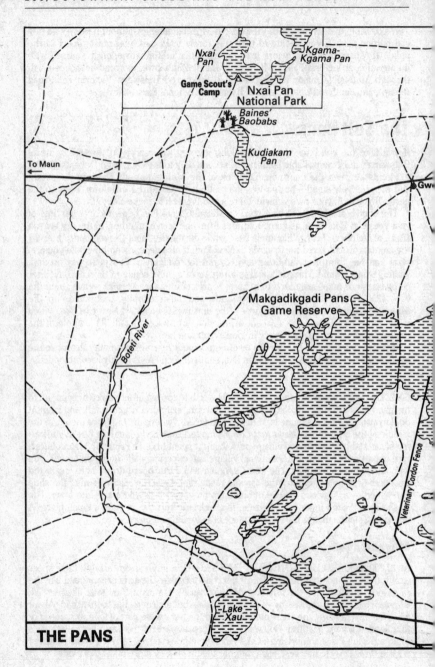

THE PANS

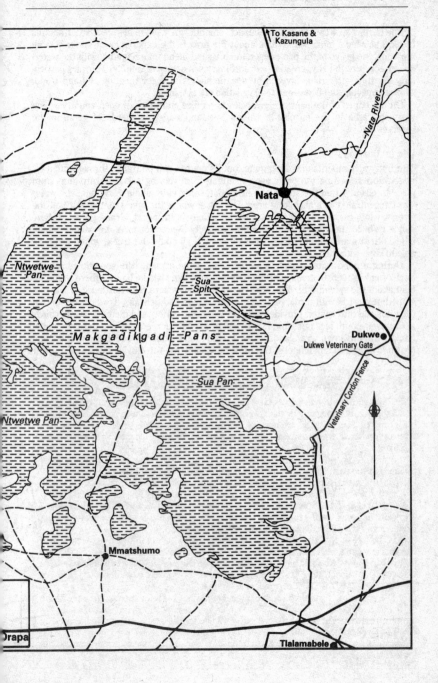

The surfaces of the pans are compact, smooth, grey, blemish-free clay. It sounds bleak, but what's most remarkable about the area is the experience of **space**. On all horizons, the greys of the pan deepen to blues and blend imperceptibly with the water-colour edges of the sky, creating extraordinary sensations of infinity. They are particularly beautiful after rain, covered by opaque sheets of water meeting sky and cloud. The expansiveness, silence and total isolation are awesome.

On the edges of the pans are **grasslands** – miles and miles of open country which supports cattle in the farmlands around Sua, and migrating herds of game in the reserves.

Life on the pans

The Botswana super-lake is long gone, but its demise can be traced through different **vegetation zones** on the pans, each resulting from varying salt concentrations from place to place. When the super-lake dried out, some two million years ago, the water was concentrated in a shrinking area. The place where the lake was deepest and the water lay longest is now barren because the salinity is strongest. **Grass** grows in abundance right to the edge of these featureless, salty depressions. As the salinity diminishes, **shrubs** are able to grow; furthest away of all come the **trees**, which are least able to cope with the salt.

During a good rainy season, a feeble echo of the ancient lake sometimes returns heel- or ankle-deep, in areas near the river mouths, like Nata Delta. But there's nothing faint about the splendid **birdlife** that comes to these waters. The northeast of Sua Pan sometimes swirls with birds, particularly flamingoes and pelicans. Towards the end of the rains and into winter, provided there *is* water, the variety and quantity of waterbirds at the river mouth is staggering. Ducks and geese nest in reedbeds and pelicans on the banks. On the open grasslands close to the water you can see both wattled and crowned cranes in small flocks. But most tantalising are the elusive **flocks of greater**

SODA ASH AND SOUTH AFRICA

The **Sua Pan soda ash project** is a mine on Sua Spit, a narrow promontory extending into the pan. Set up jointly by the government of Botswana (with a 48 percent share) and a group of South African companies, it's the most expensive project in Botswana's history, of great significance in the attempt to diversify the country's diamond-based economy.

It aims to provide both South Africa and neighbouring countries with thousands of tonnes of soda ash as well as 700,000 tonnes of salt for regional industrial consumption. (Soda ash, or sodium carbonate, is an alkaline chemical used in a wide variety of manufacturing processes including the making of steel, vanadium, paper, glass and detergents.) Wellheads will be dotted over a 200 sq km area and there'll be 20 sq km of evaporating ponds, with boiler plants. It's all a far cry from the days of San people mining salt, transporting it on donkeys and selling it to the Kalanga.

In the face of criticism of setting up a joint venture with South Africa in this fashion, a government minister argued that the relationship is one of interdependence. "For the first time South Africa will be relying on Botswana. Our exports there will help to redress the trade imbalance. And Sua Pan has enough resources to last more than 900 years. We don't expect the South African problem to last that long."

The major loss caused by the mining operation has been the feeding grounds of the greater and lesser **flamingoes.** To counter the dismay of environmentalists at the project, the mine has partly financed a new wildlife sanctuary at Sua Pan, administered by Nata council, rather than the Department of Wildlife which means more modest entrance fees. As most of the game was hunted out over the last century by white hunters, the area is being restocked.

and lesser flamingoes – here one day, gone the next – which come to feast on algae and the tiny shrimps that, remarkably, lie dormant in the dry sands until the rains return to bring them back to life. At times thousands of flamingoes descend on the pan and you can see them standing delicately in the shallows.

Kubu Island

One of the eeriest features of the Makgadikgadi Pans are the fossil-like extrusions of rock – "**islands**" in a sea of grey sand. Most notable, and magical, is **KUBU ISLAND**, a mound of lumpy rocks, pushing 10m above the Pan floor in the southwest corner of Sua Pan. It doesn't sound like much, but in a landscape as flat as a billiard table, it gives you a fantastic view of the surrounding brineland. On the outcrop are the grotesque red-tinged baobabs that inspired Michael Main to write, in his book *Kalahari: Life's Variety in Dune and Delta* :

> *Gnarled, usually leafless, their dwarfed and twisted forms suggest the agony of ages spent on salted waters beneath a remorseless sun. Some, seen in silhouette against the stark, grey pan, suggest a visit to another world, unutterably remote and lonely.*

Most remarkable is the fact that there have been **human settlements** here. On one corner of Kubu Island are the remains of a **dry-stone wall**. There are some stone cairns – not, as you'd expect, burial sites, but some other structure, still unidentified – and a scattering of **stone tools**. Artefacts are often found along the present shoreline – tiny arrowheads, scrapers, crescents and minutely hewn knife blades. Elsewhere on the island are the **ruins** of a village site, the earliest occupation dating as far back as 500 AD and the most recent 1400–1600 AD. Where the inhabitants drew their water remains the biggest mystery.

If all this doesn't suffice to fire your imagination, **mirages** are common. In the early morning, convincing mountains sometimes appear on the horizon. Or the Pan takes on an oceanic appearance.

Kubu Island can be reached from the track, between the Sua and Ntwetwe pans, beginning 16km west of Nata and heading south; or from the Francistown–Orapa road, setting out from the tiny village of Mmatshumo and climbing over a low escarpment. Kubu isn't terribly easy to find, as there are few landmarks and certainly no signposts. You need to be fully **self-sufficient** and should leave no trace of your stay behind, unlike recent visitors who marked their visit with piles of bottles and graffiti on the baobabs.

Exploring the pans

If you're adventurous and have your own 4WD transport, the *Visitors' Guide to Botswana* by Main and Fowkes (see "Books") is useful for its comprehensive directions for getting around Sua Pan. There's also a 1:1,000,000 map (obtainable from the Director, Department of Surveys and Lands, Private Bag 0037, Gaborone) of use only to familiarise yourself with the area and not for orientating on Sua. When it's dry and the surfaces firm, it's possible to drive across the pans, but you'll get covered in fine grey dust. If it's wet, creep cautiously around the edges, and wherever possible follow the tracks of any previous vehicle – if they made it, the route is probably safe. If there have been recent heavy rains avoid the pans altogether. And finally, if in any doubt about your driving competence in this unfamiliar territory, don't go.

It is however possible to make short **forays onto the edge of the pan** quite easily, without 4WD. A track that branches westwards off the main Francistown–Nata road will bring you to the fringes of Sua. The turn-off is 15km north of the Dukwe Veterinary Gate – one of the many gates in the network of fences set up across the country to fight foot and mouth disease – which itself is 145km north of Francistown. There's a sign (for once!) for "Sua", pointing west to the pan. The road it indicates will lead you to Sua Spit – a "peninsula" which jetties out into the sea of grey dust, and is the site of the soda ash mine (see box).

Failing that, another track, 20km south of Nata, leads a short way to the edge of the pan. It begins at an unlocked gate, by a big baobab to the left of the road. The management at *Nata Lodge* will be able to advise you on the current situation in the area: which areas are off limits and most importantly, whether **flamingoes** have been recently sighted and where to spot them.

Finally, a **longer excursion,** but a more rewarding one, is to take the good veterinary track at Thalamabele, 150km west Francistown on the Orapa road, and travel 97km up the eastern flank of the pan, to arrive at the Dukwe Veterinary Gate on the Francistown–Nata road.

Makgadikgadi Pans Game Reserve

Entrance fee P50 per person per day, payable at the Scout Camp, on the main Nata–Maun road, not far from Gweta. Maps are available here.

MAKGADIKGADI PANS GAME RESERVE is an unfenced area which takes in the northwestern edge of Ntwetwe Pan and reaches the Boteti river in the west, with the Nata–Maun road as its northern boundary. The best time to visit is between June and November.

To the north and west of Ntwetwe Pan lie extensive, and magnificently beautiful, grasslands with groves of tall **palm trees** in the north of the area. During the **dry season,** large herds of **zebras and wildebeest** roam between the Boteti River and the pan. The game migrates when there is surface water available, then returns to the Boteti from April onwards. **Gemsboks, springboks, ostriches** and a few **hartebeest**

are also found on the plains and there are many **lions,** a few **cheetahs** and occasional **brown hyenas.**

Several unmarked side tracks lead from the main Nata–Maun road to the Makgadikgadi grasslands. One quite major north–south route – unmarked but well worn – begins almost exactly halfway between the two, 150km from Nata. There are two campsites, one at **Khumaga** on the Boteti River with a shower, toilet and firewood, and a far more primitive one at **Njuca Hills** with pit latrines only.

Nxai Pan National Park

Open year round. Entrance fee P50 per person per day.

The turn-off to **NXAI PAN NATIONAL PARK** is 170km from Nata. You'll need 4WD, at least for the 35-kilometre sandy track which leads north from the main road to the park entrance. Unlike Sua, Nxai Pan is not grey clay, but a fourteen-kilometre stretch of grass with small islands of trees. It's best visited from December to April.

Whether or not you see the full array of wildlife depends on the rain and whether numbers have built up after years of drought. Outside the rainy season you may see next to nothing, as the game is migratory. Elephants and buffaloes are rare visitors, only coming if it's very wet.

If rains have fallen, the game-viewing on the pan can be spectacular, with huge herds of **wildebeest, zebras** and **gemsboks** up to a thousand strong and giraffes numbering up to fifty in a herd. **Cheetahs** and **lions** keep their watchful eyes on the bounty. There are small herds of **springboks** and **impalas** (the southernmost point of their range) and occasionally **eland** and **sable antelope**.

The most exciting small mammal to look for is the **bat-eared fox** – present here in large numbers. Scan the ant-heaps on which they like to sit and check near clumps of long grass. The size of the bat-eared's **ears** is an indication of their acute sensitivity to sound: they're able to hear insects moving about beneath the ground. Which is fortunate, as their staple diet consists of termites, beetles and locusts. As well as being perceptive, bat-eared foxes are incredibly nimble, and supplement their insect diggings by chasing rodents and reptiles at lightning speed, doubling back on their tracks and continuing the hunt in a single, fluid twist – a delight to watch.

There's a choice of two **campsites** in the park, the best of which is on the southern edge of the pan, 3km from the game scouts' camp and pleasantly situated in a grove of trees. The other site, on the northern edge of the pan, is less appetising, in a mopane tree clearing, where you may see impala, if nothing else. Both campsites have toilets and erratic cold showers.

Baines' Baobabs

South of the Nxai Pan boundary, the trees known as **BAINES' BAOBABS** are definitely worth taking. Overlooking **Kudiakam Pan**, the largest of a small salt pan complex, they are named after Thomas Baines, a nineteenth-century explorer. He was also an accomplished artist, particularly well known for his paintings of Victoria Falls. In May 1862, while travelling from Walvis Bay to the Falls with James Chapman, a hunter and trader, he immortalised these impressive baobabs. They look much the same today as when he painted them, 130 years ago – madly majestic in the flat emptiness. Here, outside the park boundaries, you may also see **game** during the rainy season, especially gemsbok and springbok. We found huge, and unnervingly fresh, **lion** prints in the wet clay.

The road to Baines' Baobabs is unmarked, but it's not too difficult to find. The easiest route takes the northbound Nxai Pan track, which branches off the Maun–Nata road, turning right at the crossroads 17km on. This takes you onto the **old Nata–Maun road**. One kilometre further on, where the road forks, take the right track for 11km until you reach the baobabs. During the rainy season this route can get flooded, in which case you should take the left fork and turn right 13km further on, to reach the trees.

KASANE AND
CHOBE NATIONAL PARK

The small town of **Kasane** is the obvious base if you don't have your own transport and want to get into **Chobe National Park**, Botswana's premier game reserve. It has ample accommodation and camping, and is the only place you'll catch Chobe **game drives** and **river cruises**. With your own transport, Kasane is a pleasant enough place to relax, as well as being the place to stock up with fuel and supplies before going into big game country.

Chobe National Park itself is a far cry from the soft paradise of the Okavango Delta or the watery edges of Moremi Wildlife Reserve (see Chapter Nine); instead, it's a raw and compelling wilderness packed with game. The Park was created in 1968, and

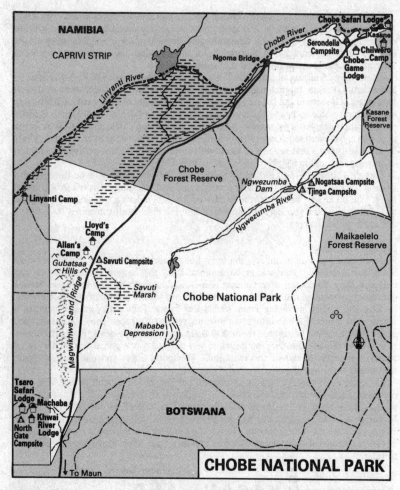

named after the river that defines its northern boundary. Confusingly, however, this river itself has a number of different names. Where it rises in Angola it's called the **Kuando**; where it first enters Botswana it's the **Linyanti**. It then becomes the **Itenge** and only when it reaches Ngoma back on the Caprivi Strip in Namibia, does it become the **Chobe**. Even its life as the Chobe is short-lived; it soon joins up with the **Zambezi** and together they hit the chasm at Victoria Falls.

Chobe National Park consists of three very distinct main areas – the **riverfront**, the **Ngwezumba region** and the **Mababe Depression** (usually known simply as **Savuti**) – each of which has its own ideal visiting time. The best time to visit the river is during the dry season from June to October, when animals come from the interior to the northern part of the park for water. Savuti and Ngwezumba are good from November to May, but if the Savuti Channel is flowing, you'll find animals there throughout the year.

Of the various **camps** (basic facilities only) scattered across the varying terrain of the park, the closest to Kasane, and the most popular, is **Serondella**, ribboning along the Chobe River. Although the whole park is called Chobe, you'll frequently hear it used to refer just to this river area. Four-wheel drive is recommended here, as sedan cars get bogged down in sand.

From Serondella two routes bow out southwards, before converging again on Savuti. The first runs west, parallel to the Chobe River, before bearing south into the heart of the national park. The second takes you through **Ngwezumba** with its mopane forests, pans and two less-used campsites, at **Nogatsaa Pan** and **Tjinga**. But the ultimate destination, in Chobe, is the **Mababe Depression**, a dead-lake area, comprising the **Savuti**

THROUGH CHOBE OVERLAND: KASANE TO MAUN TRAVEL OPTIONS

OVERLAND SAFARIS

The least expensive safaris through Chobe – and even they are certainly not cheap – are overland adventure trips of 7–16 days. Departures are normally from Maun or Victoria Falls, taking in the highlights of either or both countries. Without your own 4WD, these trips are the best way to get into remote game parks and have the experience of camping in the bush and sitting around camp fires. Trips are also available to Namibia, Malawi, Zaire and South Africa. Prices are US$150–240 per day and are mostly all-inclusive. On the cheapest safaris clients usually pitch their own tents and help with some of the chores like cooking, while at the top of the range you just sit pretty, with some of the accommodation in luxury camps or luxury hotels. This price ensures hot showers, sheets on your camp bed and iced drinks.

The companies listed below offer a wide range of departure dates throughout the year. It's best to write off for their brochures to find a trip which suits you. Children under 12 are normally not permitted on safaris.

Afro Ventures Safaris, PO Box 125, Victoria Falls, Zimbabwe (Victoria Falls ☎471/341; the dialling code from Kasane is 8, and from elsewhere in Botswana it's 0-0263-13). *Afro Ventures* takes groups no bigger than eight and overnights at the *A'Zambezi River Lodge* at Victoria Falls. They also fly into the Delta to stay at *Xaxaba Camp* on their Okavango package.

Karibu Safari, Central reservations PO Box 35196, Northway, Durban 4065, South Africa (☎031-8399774; Fax 031-83195). Camping safaris take groups of 8–13 people and are all participatory, with a food fund to cover all meals. One of the culinary delights is freshly baked bread every day. Seven days in the Okavango costs from US$800.

Okavango Overland Tours, Lot 6143, 6 Blue Jacket St, Francistown (☎213968).

Penstone Safaris, Private Bag 13, Maun (☎09267/660351). Exclusive upmarket mobile safaris under canvas, with all luxuries, starting in Maun, Kasane or Victoria Falls and spending between four and thirty days touring Botswana. Sixteen-day safaris for groups of 5–12 people cost US$2800 per person, in addition to the standard US$280 game park fees. Participation safaris are much cheaper.

Wilderness Safaris, Central reservations PO Box 651171, Benmore 2010, South Africa (☎011/884 1458; Fax 011/883 6255). "Participation" 12-day all-inclusive camping safaris to Chobe and the Okavango are thirty percent cheaper than the "first class" ones – from US$1800 for 12 days fully inclusive, departing from Victoria Falls or Maun. Groups are no bigger than eight.

Besides the larger overland companies, a plethora of small safari companies will take you around Botswana on exclusive, tailor-made trips. Prices are seriously high, but you can expect excellent photographic opportunities in the game parks, good guides and luxury camping. For information about them enquire at one of the travel agents in Maun (see p.308). Several are based in Johannesburg and have contact offices there, while at least fifteen start from Maun.

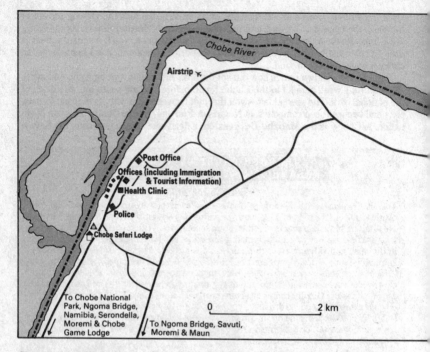

Channel and Marsh. It's renowned for the unusually gentle bull elephants roaming around the campsite, plus the prides of lions that prowl the marsh – a grassy plain formed during the years when this part of Botswana was under the big lake.

Chobe adjoins the Okavango's Moremi Wildlife Reserve in the south, and from here it's half a day's journey to Maun. The most direct route between Kasane and Maun is a 414-km 4WD trip straight through the Chobe National Park via Savuti. Together, Chobe and Moremi form a protected range 300km long, providing sanctuary for the great herds of game that follow the ebb and flow of water. There's no public transport through the wilds from Kasane to Maun and hitching is out.

The nicest way to see Chobe is in your own vehicle and at your own pace, stopping where you want. You can arrange **4WD hire** in Maun (p.303) or Kasane (below), but you definitely need 4WD experience to cope with the heavy sand, and strong nerves for being in the wild. There are no mechanics, breakdown services, petrol stations or shops, and only very primitive campsites. Without your own 4WD, and if you don't mind being in a group, the best option is to join one of the **mobile safari companies** who traverse the route as part of a Botswana/Victoria Falls trip (see box).

Kasane and Serondella

Graced by big trees and the beautiful Chobe River, **KASANE** provides a pleasant respite from the dust and dryness of the rest of the country. It was once the imperial centre of the Makololo – eighteenth-century invaders from what is now South Africa, who conquered the local Lozi people – although no evidence of that period now

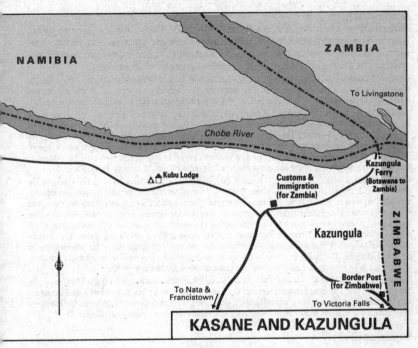

KASANE AND KAZUNGULA

remains. A bunch of newish administrative buildings, a supermarket, a couple of takeaways, a few basic shops, and some traditional huts are strung out desultorily along the main road. There's a centre of sorts at the western end of the village, the one closest to the park entrance. Here you'll find more shops, a garage, the bank and the *Chobe Safari Lodge*.

Arrival

Because Kasane is a border town, you're quite likely to hit it as you arrive from one of the neighbouring countries. **From Zimbabwe**, the daily *UTC* coach from Victoria Falls will let you off at any of the three Kasane lodges, or pick you up to go the other way. It's pricey (£20 one way) but thoroughly reliable. **From Zambia** you cross the Zambezi from Livingstone on the Kazungula Ferry to the Botswana border post. Try to line up a lift into town while you're on the ferry – it's too far to walk. If you arrive **from Namibia** over Ngoma Bridge, be sure to report immediately to the immigration authorities in Kasane. If their office is closed, make your presence known at the police station, then check in with immigration early the next day. They can get very sticky if they think you've been dallying. From Francistown or Nata **by bus** you'll get dropped near *Chobe Safari Lodge*.

The new Kasane **airport** has further opened up the northeast to international tourists, with direct passenger flights to Maun, Gaborone, Johannesburg and Victoria Falls. There's no public transport to and from the village, but if you're booked into one of the lodges you'll be met. Near the airport at the east end of town, *Holiday Car Rentals* (☎250226) hire 4WD and saloon cars, and *Northern Air* (☎250234) charter planes.

Accommodation

At present, the *Chobe Safari Lodge* is the best – and the only central – place to stay in Kasane. The brand new *Cresta Mowana Safari Lodge* got off to an inauspicious start when it was burnt down in 1992, but when it's rebuilt will be far bigger and more luxurious than the *Chobe Game Lodge*, with a wealth of game-viewing activities.

Chobe Chilwero, PO Box 22, Kasane (☎ 650234). A small, intimate camp with eight thatched bungalows and fantastic views over the river. The camp offers excellent river trips, on which you can see birds and monitor lizards at close quarters, as well as game drives as part of an all-inclusive price. ⑨.

Chobe Game Lodge, PO Box 32, Kasane (☎ 250340). On the riverbank inside the Park itself, Botswana's most famous and elegant hotel still trades off the fact that Elizabeth Taylor and Richard Burton had their honeymoon here (after marrying each other for the second time). Of course, the elephants that drink from the river, within sight of the rooms, are a more satisfying reason to spend time in these luxurious surroundings. Even if you can't afford to stay, you're welcome for a drink or meal: their lavish Sunday brunches are worth shelling out for if you're already in the Park. ⑨.

Chobe Safari Lodge, PO Box 10, Kasane (☎250336). The original Chobe hotel – not to be confused with the glamorous *Chobe Game Lodge*. It's a modest and comfortable establishment with a swimming pool on the river bank. There are camping sites and braaing places along the river, and reasonably priced accommodation in thatched chalets with shared washing facilities, or more expensive en-suite rooms or rondavels with baths. The food's not bad; you can get toasted sandwiches at any time on the terrace, breakfast or a set meal in the hotel dining room. The terrace overlooking the river is a splendid place to watch the sunsets, and listen to the hippos snorting in the dead of night. The lodge is conveniently close to shops and a few minutes drive from the Park gate. From here you can get river cruises and game drives into the Park. ②–③.

Kubu Lodge, PO Box 43, Kasane (☎650312). Some kilometres out of town on the river, near the Zimbabwean and Zambian borders, smarter than *Safari Lodge* with chalets, rondavels and camping. But the campsite here next to a crocodile farm, isn't nearly as nice as *Safari Lodge*'s and backpackers aren't made particularly welcome. *Kubu* offers game drives and river cruises into Chobe. ①–④.

Exploring Chobe

Open all year. P50 per person per day entry fee, reduced to P30 if you're doing a drive or cruise with a registered safari company.

Vehicle hire from *Holiday Car Rental* in Kasane is one way to get into Chobe on your own. But even without your own transport, **getting into the Park** is easy enough. **Game drives** leave morning and evening from *Safari Lodge* and *Kubu Lodge*; book at either. The drives aren't cheap (P35 per person, plus P30 park entry fee) but you're likely to see a lot of animals in the dry season. The rainy season can be disappointing, especially for elephants – you may not see even one!

Afternoons are usually the favoured time for **elephant herds** to make their way to the river, and consequently a wonderful time to see them, *en masse*, in really lovely surroundings. Chobe's 50,000-strong population is legendary. At water they provide excellent slapstick entertainment, as their playfulness comes to the fore in the elephantine equivalent of a booze-up. The best way to see something of the Chobe is to take the **afternoon cruise** from *Chobe Safari Lodge* which goes slowly upriver past the *Chobe Game Lodge*. As you skirt the flood plains you'll see a wealth of animals and birds from the deck of the launch, and you can have a drink at the same time. The "Chobe Fish Eagle" leaves the lodge every day at 2.30pm for the 3-hour cruise and should be booked in advance (P25 per person, plus P30 park entry fee).

The flood plains, with their different vegetation types – thickets of bush, open grassland and riverine forest – are ideal for game-viewing. Besides herds of elephant and buffalo, look out for **tsessebe, waterbuck, roan and sable antelopes, eland, sable, rhinoceros, giraffe, hyena, kudu** and **Chobe bushbuck**.

Common **waterbirds** you'll spy on the margins include herons, storks, geese, ducks, jacanas and skimmers. One of the greatest delights is a huge colony of **carmine bee-eaters** that nests in holes in the bank, although not always in the same place each year.

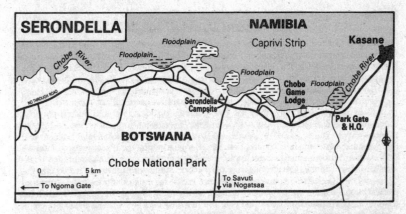

Close to the water, you may spot one of the rarest Botswanan antelope, the **puku**, which bears a passing resemblance to the impala but lacks the latter's distinctive black and white markings. **Red lechwe** are far more commonly sighted antelope in northern Botswana's wetlands – their southernmost range. Although still one of Chobe's common sights, the species faces extinction due to competition with humans for its specialised waterside habitat. Hippos loll in the water and you may spot water monitor lizards or crocodiles basking on the sandy edges of the flood plains.

Serondella

SERONDELLA used to be a village and trading station, before the Park was created. Forests of teak and mukwa were felled and sent on barges downriver to the Livingstone railway line, and across to Zambia on the Kazungula Ferry. The patch of rubble you see on the way to the campsite is a reminder of the villagers who were shifted from here when it was declared parkland, to be resettled at Kasane.

Renting a car at Kasane (see p.295) for a night or two at Serondella is more rewarding – if you have the cash – than staying in town and doing pricey game drives into the park. Serondella is on the old road from Kasane to Ngoma, the crossing point into Namibia. From this road there are several loops, through varied landscapes – down to the **flood plains**, into areas of **thicket**, or inland into **mopane forest**.

At the western end of Serondella, you can sit on the river bank and watch **elephants** drinking and frolicking a hundred metres away, but be on your guard and never get too close. If you're very lucky and patient, you could see some of the river's beautiful **otters**. For some curious reason, the airstrip near *Chobe Game Lodge* is a preferred spot for **lions** (perhaps because it provides them with a cleared area from which to watch game) and you can usually hear their chilling roars at night. **Baboons**, on the other hand, are the menacing louts of the animal world. They sometimes destroy tents and you should pack everything securely – take it in the car with you, if possible – and leave your tent open, and empty if you don't want to return to find it ripped to shreds by these sharp-nailed rogues.

THE CHOBE ELEPHANTS

The big issue at Chobe is **elephants**. The Botswana government prohibited hunting of them and rejected a culling policy for some years until the decision was sadly reversed with effect from 1991. The original hunting ban was motivated by the notion that if the elephants have nothing to fear outside reserves, they'll migrate freely beyond the national park boundaries, and thus ease the pressure on park land itself.

The reason for the policy change is that the land available cannot support the 1990 count of 67,000 elephants, although this number includes migrating elephants from neighbouring Zimbabwe, Zambia and Namibia. The elephant population is said to have risen from 40,000 to 67,000 in nine years, causing serious environmental damage and threatening other species. Around Serondella, true enough, you'll see wrecked mopane trees, ravaged by elephants, which are turning woodland savannah into degraded bush-veld. When elephants are disappearing off the face of the earth, it seems ironic that the only solution both in Botswana and Zimbabwe is culling. Both countries voted against an international ban on the ivory trade in 1989, arguing that their well-managed herds have become so big that regulated trade is in the best interests of the species and the countries' economies. The Southern Africa Centre for Ivory Marketing has agreed a system for marking legally culled tusks: a self-adhesive strip with a hologram, plus a bar code and number. The hope is that illegal traders and poachers will be unable to copy the official hologram on poached ivory.

The Serondella **campsite** (cold showers, taps and toilets) is Chobe's most accessible and popular site. It's a nice place to spend a couple of days, but you won't experience any great solitude (even if it is quiet by the standards of game parks elsewhere in Africa).

Savuti via the Ngwezumba Pans route

Most people take the riverside route from Kasane to Savuti, because it's shorter. But the pans route through Nogatsaa has several advantages; the road is better, it's quicker, there are two campsites and you'll see more game at certain times of year. You can expect the whole Kasane–Savuti journey, which traverses the Mababe depression, to take at least four hours. Crossing the depression during the rains, however, when the "black-cotton" soil is wet, is heavy going, if not impossible.

NOGATSAA and **TJINGA** camping sites in the Ngwezumba area, about 70km south of the Chobe River, are part of an extensive complex of pans set in forest which attracts herds of buffalo and elephant, particularly during the rainy season. **Nogatsaa campsite** has the usual rudimentary facilities and the bonus of a hide overlooking a big dam, where you can safely spend a couple of hours. Twenty-two kilometres further on, **Tjinga campsite** has no facilities other than a water tank, and you can't even rely on that working. Bring your own water or draw it from the Ngwezumba Dam in an emergency. But don't be put off, it's a great place.

The Nogatsaa-Tjinga region isn't as spectacular as the riverfront area, but you'll see antelope on the wide-open plains and, in clearings in the mopane woodlands near the pans, you may glimpse **oribi**. This is the only place these compact, dun-coloured antelope occur in Botswana. They live in small parties of two to five, in distinct territories, which the male marks out by rubbing glandular secretions on twigs and grass stems. You're most likely to see them in the early morning, when they're feeding. During the day, and when danger threatens, they lie quietly in tall grass or by a bush or rock.

After Nogatsaa Pan, the route runs parallel to the Ngwezumba River, which flows when rains are good. The Ngwezumba Dam near Tjinga is a fine place to watch elephant and buffalo, while rhino, too, make a frequent appearance.

Savuti and the Mababe Depression

Savuti is on the route of every four-wheel drive expedition to Botswana, and deservedly so. The game, particularly in years when the Savuti Channel is flowing, gathers in the area in staggering quantities. Besides **camping and driving** around the **Mababe area**, you can fly in and stay at one of three **luxury bush camps**, usually as part of a package to Moremi and the Okavango Delta. And overland trips from Maun to the Chobe River and Victoria Falls invariably spend a night or two at Savuti.

Savuti lies within the **MABABE DEPRESSION**, a plain covered with grass and scattered bush, that was once the bed of the primaeval lake that covered large parts of the Kalahari. If you drive south to Savuti, on the more westerly river route, you'll cross the **MAGWIKHWE SAND RIDGE**, which curves across the track and then runs southward, parallel to it. You'll see the low sandy bank on your right as you head toward Maun. The Ridge is believed to have formed the western shoreline of the former lake. Progress through the deep, soft sand around here is slow and bumpy.

The **SAVUTI CHANNEL**, part of which runs through the campsite, periodically carries water over 100km from the Linyanti River through a gap in the Magwikhwe Sand Ridge, and spills it onto the floor of the depression, creating the small Savuti Marsh. Sometimes it's deep in water, other times cracked dry.

The ebb and flow of the Savuti Channel is something of a mystery. It doesn't flow as a matter of course and has been dry for many years, including all of the 1980s and early 1990s. Connected as it is to the Linyanti (Chobe) River, it would seem to stand to reason that when the river's in flood its waters would push through and fill the Channel. But as with other waterways in Botswana, nature conspires to confound logic. In some years of exceptional flood the Channel has remained dry, and it seems that the flow has more to do with shifts beneath the earth's surface than the state of the waterways themselves. The caprice of the Channel leaves its own scarring mark on the landscape. Trees that eagerly took root in the dry bed of the Savuti Channel, now stand gnarled and dead – drowned when the waters unexpectedly came flooding down.

The **GUBATSAA HILLS** are Savuti's other notable geographical feature, just as intriguing as the Channel. These dispersed, rocky outcrops have almost sheer northeastern faces formed by powerful waves crashing into them during the lake days. Sea-smoothed pebbles, rounded by the long-gone tides, can still be found on the lee side. On some of the hills there are rock paintings – not easy to find unless someone who knows directs you. Ask one of the game scouts at Savuti camp to point you in the right direction.

The drama of the ancient lake is now replaced by a dazzling display of wildlife. Once the first rains have greened the yellow grass, and allayed the dust, magnificent stretches of grassland fringed with mopane woodland attract thousands of animals. And when the Channel spills over, the game pours in too, frequently in herds of epic proportions.

From June to December, if the Channel has had water, huge herds of **buffalo** feed at the Marsh in the surrounding mopane scrub. On the surrounding plains you'll see **elephant, wildebeest, impala, giraffe, tsessebe, hartebeest, kudu, warthog, jackal** and **zebra**. When the water disappears on the Marsh there is adequate grazing for some time, and when that has gone, many animals move off to the riverfront.

You can spot **prides of lions** on the plain until the grass grows long during the rains, hiding them. A lion research team, and an intrepid Englishwoman who crept around at night studying **hyenas**, are among the scientific groups to have spent time here.

Savuti campsite and luxury camps

The name Savuti casts an almost mythical spell in the minds of seasoned Botswana veterans. Every one of them has a tale of a close shave with one animal or another and you're assured of some sort of wildlife action at the campsite. It really has the flavour of big game country, not a place where you'd contemplate stumbling to the loo after dark.

Elephants stroll about the campsite, which is no more than a large unfenced area of bush along the Savuti Channel. There are rudimentary toilets and taps, which have had to be elephant-proofed – recessed in large concrete cubes to prevent prehensile trunks opening the taps. Fresh fruit, particularly oranges, also bring out the mischievous element in elephant populations, so don't carry them with you and don't feed the elephants, no matter how appealing. A number have had to be shot because their appetite for citrus had them tusking open car boots.

Hyenas also do the rounds at the campsite every night. It's unnerving to hear them sniffing around the tent, inches from where you lie, but they won't bite through tents and they go away if you shout at them. **Baboons** are a more serious menace; they will lay into tents in search of booty (for precautions see Serondella p.297). You'll almost certainly be treated to the roars of lions in the distance.

Two **luxury bush camps** are located close to the public campsite, overlooking the Savuti Channel, but neither is open to campers or casual visitors. They're run by bush veterans and and you'll be treated to excellent game-viewing. The highly recommended *Lloyd's Camp*, PO Box 37, Maun (⑤) is run by Lloyd Wilmot, one of the sons of Robert Wilmot, a legendary crocodile-hunter. It's the nicer of the two with a good hide from which you can watch animals coming to drink at very close quarters. Spotlights make for exciting nocturnal viewing as well. *Allan's Camp* is bookable through *Gametrackers* at PO Box 100, Maun (☎260302; ⑤). The tame hornbills hopping around the breakfast table emphasise a chirpy atmosphere.

travel details

Buses
Francistown to:

Gaborone daily 9am and lunchtime (5hr).

Kasane daily (once it's full, 6hr) via **Nata**. This combi service goes in both directions.

Maun supposedly twice a week, but the service is erratic, and information hard to track down. If you plan on trying your luck with it, be at the bus station early. The trip takes anything between 8 and 18 hours.

Harare Tues/Sat 11.30am (10hr or more, depending on duration of border formalities) via Bulawayo.

Lusaka Fri 6am (16hr). This bus stops at the following en route: Nata, Kasane, Kazungula (ferry crossing into Zambia), Livingstone, Kalomo, Choma, Monze and Mazabubuka.

Express minibus from Kasane to Victoria Falls *UTC* runs a fast, reliable daily service in either direction. As the buses begin their trip in Victoria Falls and then turn round at Kasane to go back, Kasane departure times depend on what happens along the way, and how long the border crossing has taken. But you can expect the return to Zimbabwe to set off around mid-morning. It is at least £20 one-way.

At Kasane it pulls in at the three lodges: *Kubu Lodge*, *Chobe Safari Lodge* and culminates at *Chobe Game Lodge* before turning round. You can also use it as shuttle between these places. *UTC* has a desk at *Chobe Game Lodge* (☎250340) to reserve a seat.

Flights
All the scheduled flights listed below are on *Air Botswana*.

Francistown to:
Gaborone at least one daily (70min).
Maun twice a week (1hr 15min).
Johannesburg twice a week (2hr).
Selebi-Phikwe Wed & Fri 8.30am (25min).
Bulawayo twice a week (40min).

Kasane to:
Maun Tues & Thurs.
Johannesburg twice weekly direct.

CHAPTER NINE

THE OKAVANGO DELTA

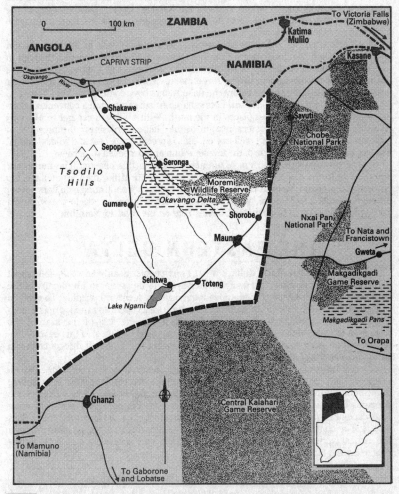

The Okavango River, which rises in Angola, flows inland across 1300km of sands and never makes it to the sea. Instead it forms one of the largest inland deltas in the world, trapped between deep fault-lines and imperceptibly dammed by rising land in the east. Most of the river's water evaporates on its way downstream, and on the fringes it seeps into the desert. The mighty river dies in a sandy trickle in the Kalahari.

As the explorer Aurel Schultz put it in 1897:

The country was one intricate labyrinth of swamp, with many small streams moving outward from the river into the sandy wastes of the southwest. Where all this water goes to is a mystery.

The **Okavango Delta** is a luxuriant oasis in the desert – a place of lagoons, palm islands and secret waterways weaving through papyrus and water lilies. At the bottom of the clear waters are the white sands of the Kalahari Desert. On the edges of the Delta, once riverine trees give over to desert thorn and grass, it's hard to imagine you're so close to so much natural bounty.

The Delta alters its character seasonally – most people visit in the **dry season** (April–Oct) when the flood waters from the Okavango River have pushed through to the southernmost fingers. Up at the Panhandle (between the Caprivi Strip and the main delta) the water arrives two or three months earlier. The channels are at their lowest during the rainy season before the flood waters have come down from Angola.

On the southern edge lies **Maun**, Botswana's tourism capital and a convenient starting point for journeys to most places in the north. With 4WD you can get to **Moremi Wildlife Reserve** on the eastern margin of the Delta, increasingly the preserve of princes, film stars and the very well-heeled. This is probably the best and wildest animal reserve in southern Africa, one of the few set within untrammelled wilderness.

Several **onward options** from Maun are covered in this chapter. The northward route leads to the Delta's **Panhandle** and the **Tsodilo Hills**, then around the top through the **Caprivi Strip** to **Chobe**. Returning to Maun from Chobe, you come down through **Savuti** and Moremi, while travelling westwards takes you to the wild-west cattle ranching town of Ghanzi (see Chapter Ten) on the **road to Namibia**.

THE EASTERN DELTA

The papyrus-matted **eastern delta** is what most people mean when they talk about "Okavango". This is where most of the lodges are to be found, in the depths of the exciting island and waterway landscapes that positively teem with wildlife. The way in is through Maun – a dusty frontier town of hunters, safari operators and tourists, superimposed on a sprawling traditional village which was the seat of the king of the Batawana (an offshoot of the main Tswana tribal grouping) for most of this century. It's simply not possible to go it alone in the swamps, but you'll find all the contacts you need for Delta travel in Maun.

The real heart of the Delta is **Moremi Wildlife Reserve**, an exclusive zone (which charges a daily fee of P50 per head) with one foot in the water and the other in savannah. It includes the two high-ground land masses of **Chief's Island** to its west and the **Moremi Tongue** jutting out of the mainland to the east. Between the two is a changing landscape of both permanent and seasonal wetland that ebbs and flows with the delta's waters. The contact of extreme drylands with the quenching Okavango gives Moremi the richest variety of habitats in southern Africa, and access to it is both tightly controlled and bitterly fought over.

ACCOMMODATION PRICE CODES

Every hotel and accommodation option listed in this chapter has been given a **price code** to indicate the cost of a single night's lodging. Safari lodges are excluded from the system, a specific price being quoted.

For a full explanation, see p.251.

① under P50　② P50–100　③ P100–175　④ P175–250　⑤ P250+

The Road from Nata to Maun

Short of taking the cross-Chobe route (see Chapter Eight), most trips to Maun by road from Kasane in the north or from Francistown in the south, pass through **NATA** (see Chapter Eight). From there, the once notoriously rough Nata–Maun road, now tarred, hauls you through 300km of desert plains and scrubland.

The main **landscape** interest on the Nata–Maun road is the gentle transition from dense bush and stunted trees to vast, open **grasslands** with tall, stately palms. Gweta (see p.285) is an access point for the **Makgadikgadi Pans** and the grasslands. Keep your eyes peeled for game as you make your way from Gweta to Maun – the road goes right through the gap between the boundaries of the Makgadikgadi Pans Game Reserve and Nxai Pan National Park (see Chapter Eight) and you can regularly spot **giraffes**, **zebras**, **ostriches** and various **antelope** species. You also cross part of the Pans complex – a hostile white and grey skin of salty clay stretching to the horizon, where nothing grows.

Near Maun, a detour worth considering is to visit **MATOPI**, a tiny village a couple of kilometres off the main road. The diversion takes you across the lily-padded Boteti River, the first intimation of what the Delta holds in store. But the big attraction of the village is **Mr Vos' butchery**, which sells the best **biltong** in Botswana – not to mention ice-cold drinks. Some taxidermy buff tried out a goat's head, which rather bizarrely adorns the store.

Maun

MAUN (pronounce to rhyme with "town"), raw and remote, is the sort of place you reach with a real sense of achievement. However, although you're finally at the edge of the Okavango Delta, don't be fooled by the maps – you're not in the swamps yet, and access can be expensive. Nevertheless, you'll find everything you need here for the final push into the Okavango.

The town is small but sprawling. Straddling the Thamalakane River, it's grown around the traditional capital of the Batawana (a branch of the Batswana) that was first established here in 1915 (see box overleaf). The traditional village is still there and you're bound to see Herero women (relative newcomers from Namibia, who sought refuge among the Batawana) sweep the dust with their colourful bustled Victorian dresses. Superimposed on the original village, unfortunately without any apparent plan, and ever growing, is the main town. A collection of concrete boxes is optimistically known as "the mall" – the centre of sorts, where you'll find most of the shops.

You can't really speak of Maun having a "centre", though. Basically everything is stretched out along a five-kilometre strip, with the area around the busy airport, which lies a couple of kilometres east of the mall, also laying some claim to being the heart of town. Most of the travel agents are out here, as well as the best drinking hole in the area (the *Duck Inn*). Four-wheel-drive vehicles roar back and forth, stocking up on supplies for long journeys, collecting tourists from the airport or going about government business. Continuing east along the strip, you jolt off the tar and onto corrugated earth. Fourteen kilometres further, you reach Matlapaneng on the **Thamalakane River**, effectively a suburb of Maun with the area's only affordable **accommodation** for travellers.

Maun's white residents value the town's **frontier image** – rough, tough, hard to reach and hard-drinking. There was a time when you needed 4WD to drive through the town centre; these days you still won't see many saloon cars about, because once you're off the tar, you're on desert roads.

MAUN – TRADITIONAL CAPITAL OF THE BATAWANA

Since 1915, Maun has been the capital of the Batawana people. The Batawana are now one of the main Batswana groupings, having emerged through strife at the end of the eighteenth century, when they broke away from the Bangwato over a succession dispute.

The disagreement among the Bangwato arose when their king married out of the clan. The bride, who was merely a minor wife, had a son called Tawana. Trouble came when the king declared that Tawana was to be his successor, rather than Khama, the son of his principal wife. The clan split and, following an attack on Tawana by Khama, the king took Tawana away on a migration. After wandering for some years the king took his leave to return home, leaving the breakaway band under his son's leadership and the tribe became known as the Batawana.

During their migrations the Batawana intermarried with other tribes and so managed to swell their numbers. Around 1824 they settled on the banks of Lake Ngami gathering strength and building a powerful state and military force, which dominated the other people of the region: the Bangologa, Bayei and San. In 1830, now under Moremi I, they moved on to escape the marauding Bakololo, who were sweeping north from South Africa. The Bakololo pursued and eventually caught up with the fleeing Batawana on the Linyanti River, surrounding them and taking them as captives to the Chobe River. After a few years the dispossessed Batawana escaped, and eventually managed to re-establish themselves and to rebuild their cattle herds.

Their recovery was impressive. By the mid-nineteenth century the Batawana had forged an effective state that stretched across northern Botswana and extended as far south as Ghanzi. They established their capital at Maun in 1915. The settlement developed along traditional Tswana lines – it became enormous by absorbing foreigners, who were incorporated in geographically distinct wards. You can still pick out the customary organisation. In its clearest form, the adobe huts were arranged around courtyards, at the centre of which was the ruling family. Further out were the wards of the Batswana who had split off from other groups and people from other tribes like the Herero and Mbukushu were on the very outskirts. The San were outcasts, not allowed to live in the village unless as servants. Those who chose the settled life had their own separate villages within the orbit of the main settlement.

Patterns are gradually changing. The government is attempting to raise the status of the San and there are some concessions to modern building methods. On mud hut walls in Maun, you can see a kind of "appropriate technology", though, with the shiny ends of beer cans decoratively poking through, where they've been put to good use as infilling.

In-town practicalities

Although Maun's **airport** is the busiest in Botswana, it's small enough to bring you instantly into the heart of things. People park right next to the airstrip and walk across the tar to the plane. Everything to do with **tourism**, bar a few exceptions, clusters around the airport: **car rental**, **travel agents**, **air charter outfits**, **curio shops** and **tourist information** (see "Listings").

The elusive twice-weekly **bus** from Francistown, which can take anything from 8 to 24 hours, drops you off in Maun's other hub – the mall area. On its return journey **to Francistown** it leaves from there at about 8am. If you're making that trip, it makes sense to start **hitching** an hour before at the bridge going out of town – if you haven't got a lift by 8, catch the bus as it comes past.

The most popular place for **food and drinks**, and deservedly so, is the *Duck Inn*, opposite the airport. Set under a cool pergola, the ultra laid-back *Duck* is a place you can sit for hours, and probably will – service is slow, but it doesn't seem to matter at the time. They serve toasted sandwiches, pies and chips and the like, as well as tea, lager and other cold drinks. The only place for really substantial meals is *Riley's Hotel* opposite the mall (PO Box 1, Maun; ☎260204; ⑤), which has gone through innumerable changes since its original makeshift construction on the banks of the Thamalakane by the hunter Harry Riley. There's also a great outdoor bar, in the garden alongside the swimming pool – an escape from Maun's omnipresent tar and sand. It's the one **central hotel** in town, but is way too luxurious for the ordinary backpacker and is used mainly by expense-account business travellers.

For **bottom-line food** there are a couple of **cheap eating places** and takeaways around the mall area, *Meet and Eat* next to *Barclays* and *Roots*. All the shops selling basic **supplies** are in the mall area. **Food** is easy to come by, although fresh fruit and vegetables are thin on the ground as nothing is grown locally. *Maun Fresh Produce* down the main road is the only place you can get fresh goods, and is the best place for other edibles, with a surprisingly varied selection – from rye bread and tinned chocolate pudding to Cape melons. As you might expect from a cattle-ranching nation, **meat** is plentiful and cheap, and in several of the butchers around the mall you can buy biltong in season. The Post Office is here too, and newspapers, batteries, toiletries and clothes are all available.

Matlapaneng and the Maun lodges

All the **affordable accommodation** within reach of Maun is downstream on the Thamalakane River at **MATLAPANENG** – an area which was teeming with game twenty years ago, now long vanished. There's no public transport; the lodges will collect you from the airport for around P35, reasonable considering the distance. Otherwise hitching isn't too difficult.

Whichever eastward track you launch out on from Maun you'll end up at the narrow and very pretty **Matlapaneng Bridge**. The water of the river below looks tempting, but a big crocodile often suns itself on the banks. Ignoring it, local kids swim anyway. The bridge is notoriously difficult to cross late at night after heavy drinking (there's a Maun Bridge Club with a dozen members – you join once you've taken the corner badly and landed in the water).

Some kilometres beyond this bridge are the affordable Matlapaneng lodges and camping sites, all with bars and food available. Upstream of Matlapaneng, three lodges cluster along the waterway, paradoxically dry in the rainy season before the flood waters come down. But with plans for "Lake Maun" – the damming of the river – there may well be a permanent pool in the near future.

There's little choice pricewise between the lodges; you can expect to pay around P125 for a single room, P150 for a double. Camping costs from P10 per person. The lodges, although thoroughly pleasant, are only points of passage, the real destination being the Delta. One advantage is that one way or another, some provide the cheapest means to penetrate into the exclusive waters, by running their own packages (see p.312).

Crocodile Camp, PO Box 46, Maun (☎660265; Fax 660793). The camping sites, which must be booked in advanced, are away from the river and inside a fence – safe, but unappealing. The chalets are pleasant and if you share washing facilites are cheaper. Rates do not include meals, though all meals can be catered for. Motorboats or canoes with a poler can be hired. The Camp organises de luxe mobile safaris into the Delta, using its own tented camp, as well as safaris into other parts of Botswana, Namibia, Zimbabwe and Malawi. They can accommodate groups of up to seven, with rates depending on the size of the party. For 3–4 people expect to pay upwards of P300 per day per person.

Island Safari Lodge, PO Box 116, Maun (☎260300; Fax 660300). Most popular of the lodges with the nicest setting and chalets. Prices are the same as *Crocodile*, though *Island*'s rate includes an excellent breakfast. Children under 16 stay for free if they're sharing. There's a swimming pool and boat hire. The lodge hires safari vehicles with a driver, does trips into the Delta and also country-wide tours.

Okavango River Lodge, PO Box 32, Maun (☎260298). Next door to *Crocodile Camp*. Pleasantest camping site right on the river front, the best Sunday lunch braai and wildest bar. The modest thatched chalets are comfortable enough and slightly cheaper than the two above. There is a pool and self-paddle canoes can be hired for very little to explore the river.

Kubu Camp (☎260307). Currently the cheapest of the places around for camping, which despite the hot showers is sparse on both facilities and shade. *Kubu* will also hire out tents if you don't have your own, and has some new chalets. It's the least appealing of the lodges, but the lower rates may compensate.

Koro Safari Lodge, PO Box 22, Maun (☎260205). 20km from Maun, and beyond the other lodges at Matlapaneng, but with cheaper accommodation in rondavels taking up to four people. It's only a convenient option if you've got transport at your disposal or are heading out overland to Moremi or Chobe. Nevertheless the proprietors go into Maun daily and getting a lift shouldn't be a problem.

Sitatunga Camping Safaris, Private Bag 47, Maun (☎260307). 14km from Maun as you head out on the Toteng Road, adjacent to the well-signposted crocodile farm. You can camp, or there's tented accommodation and chalets with a restaurant and a store selling basic provisions. The owners have been in Maun for a good while and are knowledgeable about the region.

Entertainment

Entertainment comes down to **films** at *Island Safari Lodge* four times weekly (look for posters near *Maun Fresh Produce* in town or ask at the lodge) or boozing. **Drinking** goes on not only in town but at the Matlapaneng lodges, and at some is pursued as an acrobatic fine art: *Okavango River Lodge* has guests climbing a pole in the middle of the bar and drinking beers whilst doing handstands. Their unmissable speciality is the *upside-down marguerita* (shaken not stirred). The volunteer leans back on the bar, face up, mouth open, while an assortment of hooch, including tequila, is funnelled in at the same time as the barman vibrates the victim's head. They also have relatively normal darts evenings.

During the day – when there's water – you can hire canoes or pedalos at *Island* or *River Lodge* to take a leisurely trip down the still, clear and lily-padded river. Lazing beside the swimming pool is a less energetic option. If you want to cross from one lodge to the other there's a ferry operated by *Island Safari Lodge*. To get to the pick-up point from *River Lodge* leave the main gate, turn left and follow the path toward the river bank.

Transport: hiring landrovers and chartering planes

Remote as it is, Maun is nevertheless the focus for most travel in Botswana. One consequence of its isolation is that modes of transport are strictly limited: four-wheel drive, boat or air.

Self-drive vehicles can be rented at *Avis* for adventurous travel into the northern game parks and pans, up to Shakawe or westwards to Ghanzi – all of which are conceivably hitchable but will require some lengthy roadside waits. *Island Safari Lodge*, in Matlapaneng also hires vehicles. Expect to pay P300 per day for a vehicle and driver to negotiate the desert roads.

Plane charter isn't as expensive as you'd expect, but can be difficult to arrange in the high season without prior booking. In low season the charter companies are more flexible about taking you to places like Tsodilo and waiting while you look round, as long as they haven't got queues of clients gathering back in Maun. Five-seater planes can be chartered, which is a real option if there's a group of you, for a trip to the Tsodilo Hills. Enquire from *Northern Air*, *Aer Kavango* and *Merlin Services*, who have offices around

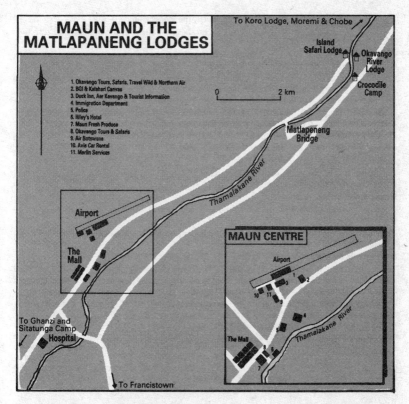

MAUN AND THE MATLAPANENG LODGES

To Koro Lodge, Moremi & Chobe

Island Safari Lodge

Okavango River Lodge

Crocodile Camp

1. Okavango Tours, Safaris, Travel Wild & Northern Air
2. BGI & Kalahari Canvas
3. Duck Inn, Aer Kavango & Tourist Information
4. Immigration Department
5. Police
6. Riley's Hotel
7. Maun Fresh Produce
8. Okavango Tours & Safaris
9. Air Botswana
10. Avis Car Rental
11. Merlin Services

0   2 km

Matlapaneng Bridge

Thamalakane River

Airport

The Mall

To Ghanzi and Sitatunga Camp

Hospital

To Francistown

MAUN CENTRE

Airport

Thamalakane River

The Mall

the airport. These companies also run charter flights to Gaborone, Kasane, Victoria Falls and Johannesburg – much cheaper than the regular services but not as frequent.

The air charter companies arrange **game flights**, offering the chance to see the Delta from above – a memorable vision, but one you'll be rewarded with anyway if you're flying into one of the Delta's camps. From the air, you see the rich patchwork of green and brown inkblot islands. Spiked with upright palms, their dense green centres bleach out to sandy rings which seep into the water. From the air too, you may see large herds of game scattering away. For **lifts or sharers for a plane charter**, leave messages on the notice board at *Maun Fresh Produce*, or even better at the *Duck Inn* where all paths ultimately cross.

Listings

Air Botswana (☎260391) is on the airport turn-off, in a stand-alone thatched building on your left.
Air charters *Northern Air* (Box 40, Maun; ☎260385) is in the shopping block within the airport enclosure. *Aer Kavango* (Box 169, Maun; ☎260393) shares the same block as the *Duck Inn*, just outside the fence.
Banks *Standard Chartered* and *Barclays* are both in the mall and are potluck as far as queues go (both open Mon–Fri 8.15am–12.45pm, Sat 8.15–10.45am). There are no foreign exchange dealings at banks on Saturday, but most travel agents will oblige.

Books Curio shops have books on Botswana, mostly the glossy kind.

Camping equipment rental *Kalahari Canvas* on the main street in the Matlapaneng direction. *Island Safari Lodge* at Matlapaneng rents gear, as does *Oddballs* within the Delta.

Car rental from *Avis* at the end of the left branch just before the airport (Box 130, Maun; ☎260258), or *Island Safari Lodge* in Matlapaneng.

Chemist There is no qualified pharmacist and prescription medicines must be issued by the town's doctor (see below). *Mantsoro's Cosmetique* supply patent medicines and suntan lotions, vitamins, travellers' first-aid kits, mosquito repellent and even condoms.

Curios Best places are *Maun Gallery* and *Okavango Tours and Safaris*, opposite the airstrip. Excellent baskets from Ngamiland. Also some San crafts.

Doctor Dr Jourdan (☎260482) is the only qualified private medic in town.

Garage *Riley's Garage and Service Station* near the hotel.

Hospital 2km along the main Ghanzi road.

Immigration is in one of the lone buildings on your right as you head toward Matlapaneng, 1km before the airport turn-off.

Newspapers Stationers at the mall.

Police in one of the buildings near Immigration, heading for Matlapaneng on the right just before the airport turn-off.

Post office Along the main road in front of the mall slightly toward Francistown (Mon–Fri 8.15am–1pm & 2.15–4pm, Sat 8.30–11.30am).

Photographic Curio shops opposite the airport. Film is generally available.

Tourist information Next to the *Duck Inn* (Mon–Fri only, 7.30am–12.30pm & 1.45–4.30pm). They can't provide much of real help, although you can usually pick up some stuff about National Parks and maps of Botswana, Moremi, Nxai Pan and Chobe.

Travel agents for bookings into the Delta: *Travel Wild* at the airport (PO Box 236, Maun; ☎260493) are probably the most helpful, but *Okavango Tours and Safaris* (PO Box 39, Maun; ☎260220 or ☎260339) opposite the mall or at the airport are part of the same company as *Oddballs Camp. Merlin Services* (PO Box 13, Maun; ☎260351) over the road from the *Duck Inn*, deputises for *Gunn's Camp* as well as several others including the recommended *Gametrackers* lodges. In the mall, *Bonaventures* (PO Box 201, Maun; ☎260502) deals with ultra-expensive pre-booked packages and you're liable to come out feeling like a worm if you don't have an *American Express* Platinum Card in your wallet. For serious and expensive photographic safaris contact *Ker, Downey and Selby Safaris* (PO Box 40, Maun; ☎260211) or *Crocodile Camp* at Matlapaneng (PO Box 46, Maun; ☎260265).

The Delta – Geography and Geology

Although the **OKAVANGO DELTA** looks like a large lake on the map it is the most complex of mazes – channels twisting and turning in on themselves through the thick wetland vegetation, some rejoining main river channels, others coming to a dead end of matted papyrus as far as the eye can tell.

The archetypal Okavango of islands, lagoons and secret waterways is the eastern Delta, incorporating the eastern sanctuary of Moremi Wildlife Reserve which straddles both wet and dry terrain. Due to sizeable **park entrance fees**, budget travellers are being forced to satisfy themselves with the region outside Moremi's boundaries. The cheapest deals can get you to the borders of Moremi, north of Maun, which have a very similar geography and vegetation to the reserve itself.

Up in the far north, where the Okavango River enters Botswana as a wide, strong river is the area known as the Panhandle. Here, close to the border with Namibia, are a number of **fishing camps** – mostly in the luxury class, but at least two (both of which offer camping) are moderately priced (see p.324). Along the remote west bank of the Okavango River, you'll still find traditional villages, in an exotic region of palm trees and thick riverine vegetation, reachable only along the raw dirt road that leads to SHAKAWE and Namibia's Caprivi Strip.

Shifting sands: Delta geology

The stillness of the slow-flowing Okavango Delta (a one-in-several-thousand gradient) masks a turbulent character beneath the deep sands over which it drifts. Not only does the Delta change with the seasons, its level varying as the flood waters come down from Angola, but it's also **geologically unstable**, its base shifting, twisting and turning constantly but imperceptibly.

The region suffers **earthquakes** – 38 minor ones in one ten-year period – which have brought frequent dramatic changes to the Delta's shape. Channels open and close, one suddenly becoming dry as another bursts forth. One large tremor in Maun in 1952 restored the flow of the bone-dry Boro River. Over the last century these movements have caused the Delta's boundaries to shift over 100km. You can tell this from the distribution of **papyrus** and **palms**. Papyrus is fast-growing and quickly establishes itself where conditions are suitable, whereas the phoenix palm grows much more slowly. Whenever the swamp extends, papyrus marks the new map until the palm catches up. The limits of the two plants are 150km further south than the current perennial swamp on the Thaoge River, while on the Ng-gokha River, the papyrus growth far outstrips that of the palm indicating that the eastern extent of the swamp is recent.

Behind these mysterious shifts and changes lies a deep and ancient past. Long ago, some experts believe, when the Kalahari was wetter and the rocky plate at its base was tilted differently, the Okavango River drained into the Limpopo, which flowed into the Indian Ocean. At this time, much of northern Botswana was flooded by a **super-lake**. As the lake silted up, sedimentation led to the current drainage patterns, and the Delta was left behind as a remnant.

"Wasted waters"

Okavango is now regarded as one of the world's great wildernesses, but it wasn't always so. As recently as 1955 it was described as a useless swamp by one J H Wellington, who proposed its wasted waters be turned to transforming it "into one of the richest gardens in Africa". He planned to throw up a mud dyke, the considerable distance from Sepopa to Chief's Island, in order to drain about 12,000 square kilometres to the southeast, which would be farmed.

Before that, **Cecil Rhodes** too had his eye on the swamps as a block in his great empire-building schemes. Convinced that Ngamiland was rich in diamonds and minerals – a belief that proved correct after Independence, when diamonds were found at Orapa – Rhodes planned to settle the swamp area with Boer families who would farm it using the plentiful supply of water. But the British government was reluctant to get involved with Okavango, which they saw as a watery wasteland that would just be an administrative liability. Placing people in Ghanzi, on the border of Namibia, to nip any German expansion in the bud, seemed a far better investment.

The Delta has remained a contentious issue ever since, with some outlandish proposals to utilise its seemingly **wasted waters**. In a country that suffers badly from low rainfall, the water promises to be a wonderful resource for farming and mining. There are clamouring demands for water from nearby Maun, which has no permanent supply – the water runs out in the taps occasionally – and the Orapa diamond mine, a big currency-earner, is looking for more water. Irrigable land in the west could be utilised to provide great self-sufficiency in crops. The Eastern Corridor, too, needs far more water.

But tapping off the waters is liable to create major **ecological changes** in the region and international conservation agencies are lobbying for protection of the wetland habitat. If it goes, so will some endangered species and thousands of wild animals and birds. Already cattle are encroaching and tsetse fly-spraying has undesirable effects on the ecology. The veterinary **cordon fence**, passing across the southern edge of the Delta, just north of Maun, marks the present boundary between domestic and wild animals.

Getting into the Delta: the lowdown

It's easy to get lost in the Okavango Delta. Not just in the mazes of islands and papyrus; negotiating the tour operators, and trying to get what you want without facing bankruptcy can be equally confusing. There's virtually no way of getting onto the waters on your own, so, to set out into the Delta, you'll have to go on some kind of **package**. Although booking well ahead ensures a reservation, you can usually organise something from Maun. Maun and Matlapaneng are the hopping-off points for most of Okavango's camps and *mokoro* packages. Beware though of local operators making a quick buck out of this. There are reports of unsuspecting or ill-informed travellers being taken into areas outside of Moremi by ill-equipped and largely ignorant guides, where not only are there no controls over littering and general environmental degradation but where there's little or no game.

The fees to enter Moremi were raised sharply a few years ago in an attempt to cut down the number of visitors and minimise destruction of the environment. In practice, however, the effect seems to have been that the ecological danger has been shifted out of the parks and into areas where there is no jurisdiction at all. Since this situation is very fluid, information needs to be re-checked on the spot when you arrive.

There are no **bargain deals** into Okavango – you won't get away spending much under P200 for two or three days in a *mokoro*, but even this won't get you deep into the

---

PEOPLE OF THE WATERS

The first people of the waters were the **Banoka** – sometimes called the River Bushmen – of whose origins little is known. The **Mbukushu** and **Bayei**, who arrived in the area in the eighteenth century, appear to be fairly closely related, both being adept wetland farmers and fishermen with the unusual matrilineal system of a chief's succession passing on to his eldest sister's son.

From oral traditions it's reckoned they were living in close proximity around the seventeenth century. Both made similar **migrations** from central Africa and in recent times fled southwards to escape the tyranny of Lozi conquest on the Zambian side of the Zambezi Valley. By 1800 the Bayei appear to have moved into Okavango and to have surrounded the delta. The Mbukushu, too, fled from the expanding borders of the Lozi first to the Kuando River, dividing Botswana from Caprivi, then westwards to Andara on the Okavango River, just south of Angola.

Things in Andara were no better and possibly worse. **Mambari traders** (sons of Portuguese men and African women) arrived on the quest for ivory and Mbukushu leaders began selling their own people as slaves. The subjects got fed up and left their leaders, paddling down the Okavango River until they arrived around the panhandle area of the Delta, where most still live today. **Mekoro** remain the means of getting around on water, poling (like punting) in the shallows, and paddling where the water is deep, in the panhandle area.

The Mbukushu were more reliant on **farming** than the predominantly fishing Bayei, their methods better suited to the deep waters, where they could plant on river banks without the floods rising to spread over the plains. They continue to till the alluvial soils deposited in flood zones, planting, as the waters recede, sorghum, millet, maize and cane in the wet earth. Mbukushu **architecture** is unusual in the use of rectangular rather than round buildings surrounded by high reed fences. The women are justly renowned for their fine **basketry**.

In the past Mbukushu chiefs were great **rainmakers**. So widespread was their reputation that distant rulers paid handsome tributes for the benefit of their services. Their use of child-sacrifice in rain ceremonies and the involvement of the Mbukushu kings in slaving are said – understandably – to have been major factors in precipitating the departure of their subjects. When the migrating Mbukushu arrived in Botswana they brought their

really desirable regions. For your money, you'll be transferred from the lodges in Matlapaneng to the Delta's edge in a 4WD vehicle or a powerboat, and from there you'll be poled around the Delta north of Maun. This gives a good feel of Okavango, although it's hardly the ideal way to get the most out of your visit; the game-viewing is a far cry from the sights inside **Moremi Wildlife Reserve**, nearer to the eastern Delta shore.

Moremi – the ultimate destination – is geared mainly towards the well-off. It incorporates the large **Chief's Island** and **Moremi Tongue**, which has the advantage of both wetland and dryland habitats, and hence attracts a large variety of game.

There are two **low-budget options**: the popular *Oddballs Camp* and *Gunn's Camp*, self-catering outfits geared mainly for campers, exceptions inside Moremi. The usual scheme of things is to base yourself at the camp (in a tent at either, or in a more expensive roofed shelter at *Gunn's*), whence you hire a *mokoro* to spend several days on the water, camping on islands. *Oddballs* operate an "honour system" which means that when you return from a *mokoro* trip, they ask whether you've entered the reserve or not and for how many nights.

All the other places in Moremi are **luxury camps**, with tariffs that include all meals, all *mokoro* trips and at the dryland camps all game drives. The least expensive of these camps starts at P350 (per person per day), and that's in the low season and excludes game park entry fees (for details about the Okavango camps, see below).

---

fame for opening the skies with them. The custom of sending tribute for rainmaking was taken up by the Bayei and continued by the Batawana in the early nineteenth century, once they had penetrated the northern delta.

The **Bayei** are flood-plain farmers who excel at **fishing and hunting** – far more important to their subsistence than for the Mbukushu. Bayei hunters developed elaborate methods for catching fish and game, particularly hippo, the meat of which was a great delicacy. Two methods were used for **hippo hunting**. The more dangerous involved floating down the river into a herd and harpooning the animals, a rope attached to the weapon then being tied to a tree. Once the struggling animal had exhausted itself the hunters would move in for the kill. The second appealed to the Victorian sense of invention; this engraving shows a spear weighted with rocks and triggered by a trip-wire. At the critical moment, the spear (D) held in position by the rope (E) was released and plunged into the beast (A).

When the **Batawana** arrived in the delta, toward the middle of the last century, they conquered the Bayei and forced them into servitude. The vanquished Bayei, who'd previously lived only in small groups, began to adopt the lifestyle of their masters and are now found in large villages, where many raise cattle. The Mbukushu were less affected by contact with the Batawana, but colonialism brought changes to the whole region, probably the most significant being migration to the great economic magnet of southern Africa: the Johannesburg gold **mines**. The mines had recruitment agencies deep in the bush, flying out new workers. Many men still work on the mines while a number of people are employed in tourism – as polers, bush-guides, cooks, cleaners and hunting safari attendants.

OKAVANGO HORSE SAFARIS

If you ride, one of the most thrilling ways to explore the Delta is on horseback. Safaris run between March and September for an average of six days, though it's possible to do a four-day trip in April, May, August and September. Between October and December you can do a safari by request, though it's pretty hot and not recommended. Children are welcome as long as they have passed a pony club riding test. The longest trip is ten days and you move to a different camp every three nights. Trips cost P440 per person per day. Book through *Okavango Horse Safaris*, P/Bag 23, Maun (☎660822).

The cheapest options: skirting the fringes

The very cheapest packages on offer cannot be wholeheartedly recommended; they all run unlicensed operations and aren't supposed to be on the Delta at all. They may be cheap, but this can mean a less reliable service. There have also been some complaints that lack of control over their clients and polers means litter being left on islands.

Island Safari Lodge, PO Box 116, Maun (☎260300; Fax 660300). Based just outside Moremi. You are taken by powerboat to the edge of Moremi, where you set off on a canoe with a poler for a few days' camping. Kit can be hired.

Okavango River Lodge, PO Box 32, Maun (☎260298). First you are driven to Ditshipi, a village just beyond the veterinary fence. Here they provide you with polers and *mekoro*, and you float among the reeds, spending nights on islands. The poler will also guide you on island walks. They will supply rations and equipment (including tents) if you ask.

Kubu Camp (☎260307). Virtually the same as *Okavango*, comparable prices, and welcoming to backpackers.

The Swamp Thing, PO Box 319, Maun (Fax/☎668206). A new outfit, running daily self-catering trips into the Delta. Trips last 2–14 days, and cost from P50 per person per day. Transfer fee of P80.

Into Moremi: medium-priced options

Oddballs, on Noga Island. One of the two "budget" camps in the Moremi area, and only accessible by air. It has developed a reputation as the trendy young place in the Delta – easy-going, sociable and friendly. It's principally a camping place, though there are some dearer tree houses if you don't fancy camping. A P700 camping package will give you three nights in the Delta, with at least one out of camp in the bush with a guide, plus a return flight from Maun to the Delta, *mokoro* and guide hire, two nights Park fees, and hire of all equipment. Food and alcohol is not included. Facilities at the camp include an expensive bar, a small store selling tins and hiring out camping equipment (you will probably have to hire stuff unless everything you have is ultra-lightweight, as there's a 10-kg baggage allowance for the flight). Book through *Okavango Tours and Safaris* in Maun or London.

Gunn's Camp, on Ntswi Island. The other cheapish Moremi camp, with prices comparable to *Oddballs*. Transfers are either by air or by boat, and besides camping there are basic shelters with four beds, gas lamps and cooking equipment. Other facilities include a bar, store and the hire of camping equipment. It's much quieter and smaller without the social scene of *Oddballs*, and just as pretty. Book through *Merlin Services*; see Maun Listings.

Crocodile Camp Expeditions, one of the Matlapaneng lodges (see Maun Listings). Hires out *mekoro*, but goes more upmarket with overland or motorboat mobile safaris in Moremi that provide meals and accommodation. Rates are on a sliding scale depending on number of people – the more clients the cheaper the rate per head.

The luxury camps

If you're after something more luxurious and exclusive, prepare to empty your wallet with minimum inclusive prices upwards of P350 per person per day in the low season (Jan–June), P450 in the high (July–Dec).The lodges are comfortable, bush-camp style with a limited number of guests. For the price, you can expect food and **activities** (game drives, *mokoro* outings or walks) to be included and you'll be hosted **and taken** good care of. Transfers from Maun (usually flights), park entrance fees and **booze** are typical add-ons. All have single supplements.

You're unlikely to be disappointed though, if you do decide to go for one of these. This list below, while fairly comprehensive, isn't complete – camps do come and go. Some are definitely plusher than others, but all are beautifully set in the Delta. Depending on whether they're land or wetland camps, the emphasis is on game drives or getting onto the water. They offer similar basics: game-viewing, birdwatching, boating of some kind and usually fishing. There are several safari operators, usually offering a combination of land or wetland camps, some offering packages that take in several camps with a variety of terrain. A typical minimum stay in the Delta would be three nights, P1900 per person, including flights from Maun into the Delta, flights between camps, game park fees, food and accommodation. All are bookable through travel agents in Europe or North America, but you could save yourself a lot by booking directly. None of the camps caters for casual drop-ins and all must be booked in advance. Many are closed during January and February.

Camp Okavango (*Desert and Delta Safaris*). Silver tea service caps the luxury style, with *mekoro* trips and plenty of bird life.

Camp Moremi (*Desert and Delta Safaris*). Mozart and waiters in black ties, crystal glasses and stilted conversation. Gorgeous tree-top dining room and big game.

Delta Camp (*Okavango Tours and Safaris*). One of the oldest of the luxury camps, in the permanent swamp waters, with access by air only. Days centre around guided walks and *mokoro* outings.

Jedibe Island Camp (*Okavango Explorations*). Tented camp, just east of the Panhandle, in the best fishing area in the Delta. Sitatunga and red lechwe country. There are no motor vehicles on the island which means getting around on foot or *mekoro*.

Khwai River Lodge (*Gametrackers*). Near North Gate in Moremi, with self-contained brick and thatch chalets. Game – especially elephants and (resident) hippos – can be viewed from the grounds. Accessible by road, maximum 24 guests.

Machaba Camp (*Ker Downey Selby*). A maximum of 12 guests in excellent game-viewing country sited on a 3200 sq km concession adjacent to Moremi.

Mombo Camp (*Wilderness Safaris*). On the border of Moremi in the heart of the Delta in an area of wide expansive plains with all the big game you could wish for. It's primarily a land camp with 4WD game drives. Maximum 16 guests.

Pom Pom Safari Camp (*Ker Downey Selby*). A tented camp in one of the remotest spots in Okavango, with both game drives and water trips.

San-ta-wani (*Gametrackers*). Moremi, South Gate area. More of a land camp with excellent game-viewing on flood plains, palm-covered islands, riparian bush and mopane veld. It takes its name from a Khoi mythical animal. Brick-built African-style huts house a maximum of 16 guests.

Shinde (*Ker Downey Selby*). An island with fine bird-watching and fishing.

Tsaro Lodge (*Tsaro Safari Lodge*, PO Box 78304, Sandton 2146, South Africa; ☎011-7933957). On the banks of the Khwai River, 160km by road from Maun (or a short flight), just outside the North Gate entrance to Moremi. Game walks and drives are on offer and there's a swimming pool. Thatched bungalows accommodate a maximum of 16 people.

Xaxaba Camp (*Gametrackers*). Reed chalets amongst trees on Chief's Island, with walking, boating, fishing and a swimming pool. Maximum 24 guests.

Xakanaxa Camp (*Okavango Tours & Safaris*). Tented camp accommodating a maximum of twelve in a large grove of old trees at the beautiful Xakanaxa Lagoon. The Xobega and Godikwe lagoons are a couple of hours by motorboat, with large heronries en route. There are also game drives through Moremi's ancient forests.

Xugana (*Okavango Explorations*). On one of the largest lagoons and loveliest settings in Okavango. Angling for tiger fish is one of the attractions and tackle is available. A good bet for photographic tours with chances to see some rare birds and the sitatunga antelope. This was Prince Charles' choice during his 1984 stay in Okavango.

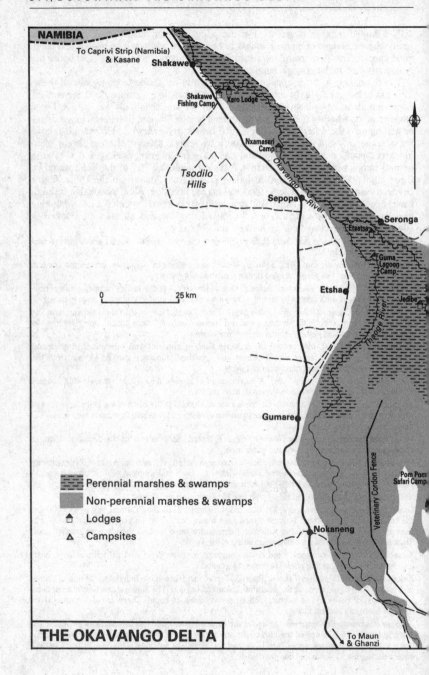

NAMIBIA

To Caprivi Strip (Namibia)
& Kasane

Shakawe

Shakawe
Fishing Camp   Xaro Lodge

Nxamaseri
Camp

Tsodilo
Hills

Okavango River

Sepopa

Seronga

Etsatsa

Guma
Lagoon
Camp

0   25 km

Etsha

Jedibe

Thaoge River

Gumare

Perennial marshes & swamps
Non-perennial marshes & swamps
Lodges
Campsites

Veterinary Cordon Fence

Pom Pom
Safari Camp

Nokaneng

THE OKAVANGO DELTA

To Maun
& Ghanzi

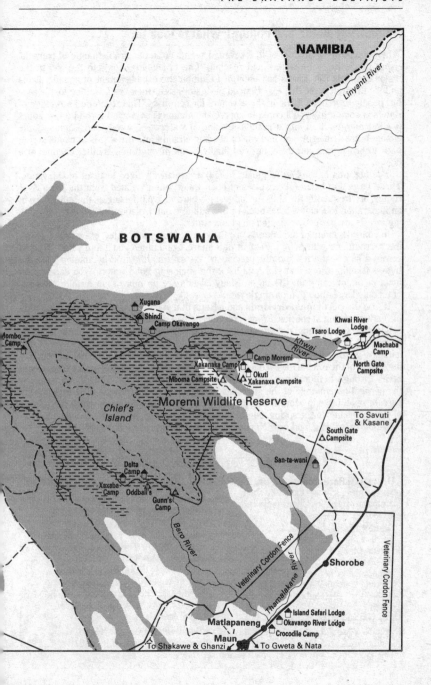

Animal, vegetable and mineral: what to look for

When you're in the middle of it, Okavango seems an impenetrable jungle of papyrus, rising dense from the waters and reaching fine brush-like ends into the air. In the major channels the flow is fast enough to inhibit the establishment of aquatic plants and it's through these that experienced navigators steer their craft. Getting lost is easy but people have been living in these waters for centuries. Their esoteric knowledge of routes is something you'll come to appreciate: channels come and go and a few hours floating merges it all into a seamless vision of waterways, weeds and islands. Some channels are so narrow you feel you're heading straight into the weeds as plants spring back to brush past your face, but you finally break through into another channel or a lagoon.

The **lagoons** or *madiba* (singular: *lediba*) are relatively fixed features of Okavango. These large and beautiful expanses of open water, often isolated from the main river routes, are frequently the sites for lodges. It's hard to avoid feeling as though you're in an illustration in a coffee-table book in this stillness and isolation, where the surrounding forests are perfectly reflected on glassy water.

In contrast, many of the **islands** are there only during low water, often raised above the surrounding waters by a fraction of a metre. Sometimes you'll find yourself poled across a lake that a few months previously was savannah grazed by antelope. On the higher islands (those that still hold back the enclosing flood waters) you can hop off for a picnic or camp for the night. Many islands are no more than termite mounds, often only large enough for a single tree.

It's on the **permanent drylands** and islands that you get huge **trees** and an incredible variety of animal species. From your low angle of vision in the *mokoro*, the only indications of the islands dotted about are the towering boughs. **Hyphaene palm savannah** is one of the common land features in the Delta's depths. Often you'll find antelope grazing in open grasslands surrounded by thick forest – the palms dominating. Some of the forests have a deepest-Africa feel and can be slightly unnerving till you break through to more open, sunnier country. A common sight in the damp woods is the serpentine embrace of the strangler fig webbing itself around a host tree. Ninety percent of all trees in Moremi are mopane. You'll also see rain trees which are a mass of pink blossoms in the spring, combretum bush willows (lead wood), African ebony or jackal berry, wild fig, and near North Gate, camel thorn.

DELTA SAFARI OPERATORS

Desert and Delta Safaris, P/Bag 10, Maun (☎564 or ☎585; Fax 569). Their camps are top of the range luxury and price-wise.

Gametrackers, 1st Floor, 137b Sandton Terraces, 11th St, Parkmore, Johannesburg 2196, South Africa (☎011/884 2504; Fax 011/884 3159). London office: c/o *Orient Express*, 20 Upper Ground, London SE1, UK (☎071/620 0003). Good all-rounders with several camps.

Ker Downey Selby, PO Box 40, Maun (☎260211). London office: 14 Old Bond St, London W1X 3DB, UK (☎071/629 2044). The only company offering elephant safaris

in the Delta. Five days on an elephant will cost US$3300 per person.

Okavango Explorations, P/Bag 48, Maun (☎260528).

Okavango Tours & Safaris, PO Box 39, Maun (☎260220). London office: 28 Bisham Gardens, London N6 6DD, UK (☎081/341 9442; Fax 081/348 9983). An excellent choice if you are planning a trip from the UK. They sell their own, recommended camps, as well as being a more general agent.

Wilderness Safaris, PO Box 651171, Benmore 2010, South Africa (☎011/8841458; Fax 011/883 6255).

Mekoro are hewn from ancient trees in these forests. Large trunked wild ebony is a favourite, specimens between one and five centuries old being used. These craft have been used by the Bayei on the Delta since the middle of the eighteenth century. With their rounded hulls they require quite some skill to balance and manoeuvre. Sitting low in the water the dugouts sway wildly every time you move and it's not a little hair-raising at first. But with experience, you get the hang of being a passenger and take cheer from the rhythmic confidence of the skilled **polers** who have not only to pole, but to balance standing up as well. Be warned though, that all *mekoro* leak – you will end up sitting in a puddle unless a seat has been provided (standard practice at the luxury lodges).

Although the mirror-still surface is deceptively tranquil, this is still wild Africa. Beneath the delicate waxy **lilies** in all their pale pinks, mauves, blues and whites, are **crocs and hippos**. At one time the swamps were a crocodile hunters' free-for-all and it's reckoned that as many as 20,000 may have been shot in a fifteen-year period. The big two crocodile killers are said to have divided the Delta between them in the late 1950s and 1960s and to have taken every one of the reptiles they came across. One of them, Bobby Wilmot, died from a black mamba bite in the swamps.

Crocodiles notwithstanding, local children wade through the water collecting the rhizome, stems and flowers of **water lilies**. The rhizome and lower stem are roasted (six make a good meal for an adult), while the flower is eaten raw and is used to flavour porridge. During drought, people crack open dry stems of papyrus reeds to chew the sweet pith; it tastes rather like sugar cane.

Keep your eyes open along the water's edge and you may see the leguaans or **water monitors** – large dragon-like lizards whose terrifying looks are all show. They skirt between wet and dry, scavenging for birds' eggs, chicks and anything they can catch.

Delta species

The variety of habitats thrown together produces a wide spectrum of game – 114 species of large mammal. The actual numbers that can be supported by the delicate ecosystem, however, are relatively few. In fact if you're simply after game your visit to Okavango could prove a disappointment – especially if you don't move far from Maun.

As elsewhere, the **dry season** is best for game-viewing and the variations in game from season to season are enormous. Some species like sable antelope increase their numbers nearly thirtyfold from their nucleus of only 100 in the wet season. Nomadic elephants, too, converge here in increased numbers in the dry season. Elephants are mainly seen in the Moremi Tongue between Third Bridge, Xakanaxa and Hippo Pool on the Khwai River. Other species are here more or less permanently – not only water-dwellers like hippos, but also warthog and antelope such as lechwe and sitatunga.

Red lechwe are an endangered water antelope occurring in pockets of Zaire, Zambia and Botswana, with Okavango now being the furthest south they're found. Like sita-tunga, they have become highly specialised to wetland living, following the ebb and flow of the flood waters, sometimes going belly-deep to graze on submerged grasses. Dusk and dawn feeders, they retreat to reed-hidden termite mounds to rest up during the day. Their hooves are long and spread sideways, an adaptation that facilitates rapid passage through mud and enables them to venture onto mats of floating papyrus. **Lions, leop-ards** and **hunting dogs** will pursue lechwe into the wetlands for food. But their real danger has been of slaughter by humans, not for their unappetising meat, but for their lovely skins which are greatly prized as sleeping mats, aprons and cloaks. In Botswana the Bayei and Basubiya developed their own technique for hunting lechwe using *mekoro*. A team on land would herd the animals into a lake where an awaiting party in dugouts would pole at speed into the animals stabbing in all directions. Nowadays only licensed hunters are allowed to kill lechwe, and a much greater threat is the one to the wetland habitat itself.

GETTING THE MOST FROM THE DELTA

Although the luxury lodges are highly recommended if you can afford them, the best way fully to experience Okavango remains the traditional one. That is, to get into the depths of the wilderness by going out on a *mokoro* for several days. You should take the Okavango as slowly as you possibly can. People who fly in for a night and out the next day are usually disappointed – and are wasting their money. We suggest an absolute minimum of two nights **camping** in the Delta. It is a unique and special place and it takes a while to synchronise with its rhythms.

What you get out of your *mokoro* expedition depends firstly on yourself, and secondly on your poler. *Your* effort and enthusiasm are vital. If you know what you want, are enthusiastic and are prepared to make an effort you stand a good chance of having a wonderful time – and one that begins to touch the essence of the Delta.

Do not regard your poler as simply a taxi driver. His familiarity with the waterways, his abilities at manoeuvring the craft and his knowledge of fauna and flora make you completely dependent on him. The greater the rapport you develop the more you'll see and learn. As far as **tasks** go, polers are expected to **pole**, to take you on game-viewing **walks** and to find an island to **camp** on at night. They may well do more, such as cooking, fishing or making coffee in the morning. These are extras and you should reciprocate by sharing your food, or in some such way as tipping.

Aficionados suggest throwing yourself headlong into the experience by taking the minimum of food – a little maize meal – and relying on the fruits of the Delta. You eat the fish you catch, and gather wild foods with your poler – delicacies like palm nuts, water lilies and honey. But this is strictly for the hardy, must be arranged beforehand and you should offer your poler a decent tip.

SOME PRACTICAL TIPS

• **Don't rush off into the Delta**. Spending a couple of days in Maun, just relaxing and talking to people who have come back from the Delta, is an investment that will pay dividends. Get an idea of what is available, what people did there and what's going to suit you. This will give you an idea of which operator to go for.

• **Find out which polers gave people a good service**, and which camp they work from. Seek them out and ask to go out with them.

• **Fly to your Delta camp**. It's not much more expensive than boating in, and you get a superb overview of Okavango; and you'll have plenty of time on the water once you go out in a *mokoro*. There's a 10-kg baggage allowance; leave tents and heavy items in Maun (booking agents will look after it) to make space for food supplies.

• **Buy supplies in Maun**. Prices are inflated inside the Delta. Maize meal, packet soups, rice and tinned foods are convenient. Don't forget matches and a torch.

• **Find out whether your poler is provided with rations** before you leave Maun. Don't get caught in a sticky situation in the wilderness, eating while your poler starves; or cutting your trip short after you ran out of food because you shared yours. If in doubt assume that you'll be feeding him and take enough food.

• **Spend at least a night at the camp** before launching out into the waters, to give yourself a chance to adjust to the environment.

• **Don't swim without asking**; most places are too risky for swimming. If you want a dip say so, and you can be taken to safe shallow waters.

• **Be prepared to walk to see game**. Most animals are likely to be on the islands and dry areas. It requires some effort to see them, but you'll probably welcome a chance to stretch your legs.

• **Sleep under a mosquito net**. Leave your tent behind, it's bulky and unnecessary out of the rainy season.

Rarest and most fascinating of all is the **sitatunga**, a medium-sized antelope completely adapted to the world of water and papyrus. Shy and rarely seen, this denizen of the reeds has unusually widely splayed hooves that perform well on mud, and when frightened it completely submerges itself leaving only its nostrils protruding for air. One repulsive technique used to hunt them is to set fire to their reedland habitat to flush them out.

If the variety of mammals is broad, the range of **birds** is overwhelming – something around 400 species. With wetland, forest, savannah and desert in such close proximity, the assortment of ecological niches makes this possibly the most concentrated cross-section of birds in the world. Every season in Moremi is unique. Depending on the water level, different waves of animals and birds move through to feed and to breed. Most spectacular of all are the **breeding colonies** in the Xakanaxa and Godikwe lagoons where marabou, open-bill, yellow-bill and saddle-bill **storks**, purple, goliath, grey, black-headed and squacco **herons** as well as egrets and pelicans breed in August and September. Intra-African migrants like **carmine bee-eaters** and various **kingfishers** arrive in the summer when they fill the skies. At *mokoro*-level, African jacanas with stretched-out toes trot over the lily pads as if they're on ballroom floors. The usual waterside **birds of prey** occupy the trees – the fish eagles and the Pel's fishing owl, large and specially adapted with featherless legs for dips in the water and extra-long claws for gripping fish of up to two kilograms.

The best chance you'll get of seeing a **fish eagle** doing its famous downward swoop and lift-off is at the camps, where they toss a fish on the water and whistle for an obliging bird. The **lilac breasted roller** is here too, one of the sub-continent's most beautiful birds and familiar to visitors to drier areas like Hwange National Park in Zimbabwe. It was held in high regard by the Ndebele, whose king Mzilikazi reserved the use of its vivid lilac, blue and green feathers for himself.

After dark, once the people have retired, the wilderness matches urban energy. Night sounds pierce the darkness: distant hyenas whooping or lions roaring far off (sounding far more like wind blowing over an open bottle than the MGM snarl you might expect). But one of the most surprising sounds of all is the quadrophonic chorus of tiny reed **frogs** piping their message into the night – not froggy croaking but like melodic, amplified wind chimes.

Moremi Wildlife Reserve

Vehicle entrance P10 (foreign reg). P50 per person daily.

MOREMI WILDLIFE RESERVE is the centrepiece of the Okavango Delta, the most desirable destination for travellers in Botswana – if not all of southern Africa. In 1963, after extensive depletion of game populations in Botswana, due to hunting and habitat destruction, the **Batawana** declared a reserve on 1800 sq km of their tribal land. It was named in honour of their leader, Moremi, as was Chief's Island.

In Moremi, you'll find all the major Okavango **ecotypes**: savannah woodland, mopane forest, riverine woodland, flood plain, reed beds and permanent swamp. The reserve breaks down into **three main areas**, roughly corresponding to broad terrain types: the **dryland peninsula** bounded by the Khwai River to the north, the **seasonal swamp** dominated by Chief's Island, and the **permanent flood lands**, which comprise everything else.

This impressive range of habitats means a prodigious variety of **animals**. Large herds of elephant, buffalo, giraffe, zebra, kudu and impala are regularly seen as well as lions, hyenas and hippos; less frequent, but by no means scarce, are magnificent sable antelope, leopard, wild dogs and large crocodiles.

As far as **birds** go, Moremi has no equal. Bee-eaters, darters and kingfishers flock among the reeds and dead wood in the channels. Fish eagles are commonly positioned on their "sentry posts" around lagoons and oxbows, and you'll see some very fine heronries at Xakanaxa. The Moremi pans are a sure bet for birdwatchers, always jostling with ducks, waders, storks and as wide a range of waterfowl as you could hope for.

Prime visiting time is April to November, out of the rainy season. Many camps close after Christmas until March, though some of them do stay open all year. November and February can sometimes produce soaring temperatures, up to 40°C, and from December to March during the rains, flooding can occur. The roads traced over thick sand may be submerged and the only practical route by car is to go straight from South to North Gate. Midwinter (June & July) can be very chilly in the mornings, although the days are generally bright and sunny. **Mosquitos** are always a problem in the rainy season. And don't let the beauty of the place lull you into a false sense of security. Tourists have been killed here; for example, one who swam in the river and met a large crocodile, and another who slept in the open and was taken by lions.

Moremi by private vehicle

The only independent way into Moremi is to **four-wheel drive** on dry land masses and **camp**, although the substantial entrance and camping fees make this far from cheap. Moremi is quite beautiful and one of the few places in the region where you can camp out, on your own, and follow small tracks into thick bush, in an open vehicle if you wish.

Although driving is an effective way to see animals, it doesn't help you get onto the waters – there's no DIY alternative there. While many parts of Moremi are accessible by 4WD, you do need to be fully self-sufficient.

A popular route is **northwards from Maun** through Moremi to Savuti and then on to Serondella in northern Chobe (see Chapter Eight), camping all the way. While you're in Moremi, it's worth spending at least four days and doing a circuit around the four **public campsites** – from South Gate to Mboma, Third Bridge, Xakanaxa and round to North Gate. If you're not going to fly into the Delta, visiting Third Bridge and Xakanaxa at its edge will give you magnificent views of flood plains, open lagoons and reed banks.

You won't find anywhere to hire *mekoro*, but there's the less ambitious option of hiring boats, when not being used by clients from *Moremi Safaris*. There are no facilities in Moremi; the private camps will help in emergencies, like minor repairs to broken vehicles, but they're otherwise out of bounds.

At the **campsites** drinking water is available, but facilities are rudimentary (drop toilets). You'll have to get used to the idea of drinking the "swamp" water. It's cool, pure and absolutely free of bugs because it's filtered by extensive areas of reed beds which out-perform any artificial filtering system. Driving after dark is prohibited and camping restricted to official sites.

THIRD BRIDGE can get fairly full, especially in July. But it has earned its reputation as the best of the campsites with some wonderfully secluded shady spots to dream away a couple of days. It's a lovely place to swim, if you must: but be on the lookout for crocs – a visitor was attacked there in 1989. **Baboons** at the campsite are a real menace – they'll do anything to get at food, including ripping tents apart, opening trunks, turning over trailers, and even confronting humans. The **bridge** at Third Bridge consists of rough-hewn poles sitting on heavy logs tied together which shudder as you trundle over. **Lions** cross here as well as vehicles – in fact Third Bridge is a regular hang-out for them, especially at the end of their hunting season after September. At this time there is no more food in the hunting grounds and more lions return to Moremi, especially males which are too lazy to hunt most of the time. Moremi lions are buffalo-killers which makes for exciting game-viewing, but the buffalo themselves, not surprisingly, tend to be skittish.

DELTA NAMES

Many of the **names** in the Delta date back to earlier San-speaking inhabitants and are characterised by the large number of "x"s and "c"s, that represent the click sounds released by air escaping when the tongue pulls away from the palate or teeth. Most Europeans find the sounds impossible, and you'll hear places like Xakanaxa pronounced as Ka-cun-icka or Xugana as coo-gunner.

The **routes** between the campsites are all game drives in themselves. Coming from Maun it's three hours to Third Bridge from the South Gate entrance, and an hour or so from Third Bridge to **Xakanaxa**, making a total of 130km from Maun. At the crescent-shaped lagoon there's a public campsite as well as an exclusive one. Look out for elephants and hippos at night and baboons during the day. At the western extremity of the Moremi peninsula is **Mboma**, about 30km from South Gate and 7km from Third Bridge. Mboma Road from Third Bridge is quite different from Third Bridge/Xakanaxa area, the former more open grass and trees, the latter dense trees and mopane forest.

North Gate, the nicer of the park entrance camps, is 50km from Xakanaxa, taking three or four hours along the Khwai flood plain past large hippo pools. The North Gate camp is well wooded and, on the edge, looks onto a large plain where impala often graze. Another clattery log bridge crosses the River Khwai with clear, Delta-brown water and water lilies. There are toilets and cold showers. Watch out for the monkeys that help themselves to anything left unattended, and the troops of baboons that breeze through.

Maun to Savuti

There are two routes to Savuti from Maun; the longer runs through Moremi (245km), while the other bypasses the park (197km) and is an hour shorter. Both are a good half day, if not more, on sandy roads. It's been done without 4WD, but definitely isn't recommended. Digging yourself out of sand with a herd of elephants nearby is no joke. From Maun take the road past the airport to **Matlapaneng Bridge** and on past Okavango River Lodge to **Shorobe**, 1hr 30min away. The road to Shorobe is slow going. A third of the way there, it forks and there are no signposts. The right-hand track is in far better condition. At Shorobe you can often buy baskets – there are always a few good ones among the clusters hung at the roadside. Past the tsetse-fly barrier, ignore the next fork in the road and continue 20km to the next junction where you turn left for South Gate. There is a sign – a tiny hand-painted one resting on the road. If you miss this turning, where the two routes divide, you'll find yourself at Savuti, having bypassed Moremi.

WEST: UP THE PANHANDLE OR WESTWARD TO GHANZI

Heading west by road from Maun, you can either go northwest up the Panhandle, skirting the Delta to the border with Namibia at Shakawe and taking in Tsodilo Hills, or southwest to Ghanzi and beyond (see Chapter Ten). There's no big game up the Panhandle, but the rewards are magnificent bird life and fishing alongside the Okavango River. If you're based at Shakawe, it's a couple of hours drive through thick sand to the awe-inspiring Tsodilo Hills, with their 3000 rock paintings. From Shakawe you can turn east, scoot through the Caprivi Strip and end up at Chobe National Park. If you want to complete the circle, drive through Chobe to Savuti and take in Moremi before arriving back in Maun. It's a highly recommended 4WD circuit.

Maun to Shakawe

The 370-kilometre Maun to Shakawe road is currently in the process of being tarred; until it's all done, the journey will remain a full day's **drive**. Where the tar hasn't reached, the heavy sand requires 4WD. There's no **fuel** along the route, and nor is there any public transport, but you may well get a **lift** in vehicles taking supplies up to the fishing camps and stores. Be prepared for very lengthy waits and take plenty of water and some food out on the road. By contrast, *Air Botswana* has recently introduced scheduled flights twice a week from Maun to Shakawe which would neatly zip you up the Panhandle and give you enough time to visit Tsodilo Hills.

The first stop by road is **TOTENG**, where the track branches north to the Panhandle and south to Ghanzi (route details for Ghanzi continue on p.333). The fork is marked by a simple box-like general store stocked with cold cans and lemon creams.

Although the road from Maun looks alluringly close to the Delta on the map, you don't see the swamp at all until after 345km, when you reach Sepopa, a watery settlement with lots of riverine trees. The new tar between Sepopa and Shakawe means that the Delta's permanent water is now far more accessible and vehicles sporting canoes have been seen on this road. Mostly though, you'll be treated to less sophisticated scenes – expanses of thorntrees and white sand broken by the occasional village. You'll often pass people going about their business; lone cattle-herders on horseback coming or going to distant cattle posts with provisions and a bedroll tied behind saddle; Herero women going shopping or visiting on donkeys; *mekoro* being dragged like sledges by oxen through the sand, with goods or perhaps a passenger inside.

Lake Ngami

Toteng (see above) is also where you head off to **LAKE NGAMI**, which, if there's water in it, is recommended for its fabulous bird life. In fact, before visiting Ngami, you should first establish at Maun whether there's water – if there isn't, don't bother going.

Less than two hours' driving from Maun (accessible without 4WD since the road is now tarred to Sehitwa) brings you to the lake, whose fabled reputation was fed largely by the accounts of nineteenth-century **explorers**. The area was inundated with hunters, traders and missionaries after David Livingstone and his party arrived in 1849. At that time it spread out as far as he could see, thousands of people lived on its shore and the reed beds were full of hippos and crocodiles. Buffaloes gathered in enormous herds and elephants drank at the water's edge.

The once fine sheet of water is now ephemeral, shrunken this century by the gradual drying up of the Thaoge River. In 1962 it flooded again but was a dry grassy pan 20 years later. During drought years tremendous numbers of animals die, and their emaciated carcasses lie all over the grass-tussocked lake flats. With reasonable rain, even if there's little or no water in the lake, the floor gets covered by nutritious grasses which support many herds of Batawana and Herero cattle.

When it's wet, the lake is spectacularly rich in **bird life**. Aquatic plants and algae spring to life in the shallow, warm water overlying decomposing reeds and grass, and providing food for millions of birds. Waterfowl – ducks, teal and geese are there by the million, as well as flamingoes, storks, pelicans and ibis. The best place to view them is from the lake promontory where a fishing camp operated in wetter times and may have made a comeback.

There are no signposted roads to the lake but plenty of tracks. Take either the Ghanzi or Shakawe road from Toteng for 15–20km; any track heading into the bush will get you to the shore. For the promontory area, head 25km towards Sehitwa; about 4km before you reach the village, take a prominent track to the left, south to the shore. There are no lodges or official campsites, but nothing to stop you finding your own spot.

Gumare

If you don't deviate to Lake Ngami, **SEHITWA** is the next settlement you'll hit – a small traditional place with many Herero inhabitants. From here it's 46km to Tsao. The former capital of this northern district (before Maun), Tsao isn't worth a stop.

There's nowhere to stay in the unpretentious village of **GUMARE**, but you'll find stores and fresh bread. This is one of the basket-making centres of the northwestern delta, and one recommended stop is the new basketry shop – Gumare's first – next to the bakery, just 700 metres from the main road. You'll pay less for baskets here than in Maun. A sign indicating *Barclays Bank* points optimistically towards some huts, but don't count on changing money here. It's open on the government monthly payday only, for one and a half hours.

It's worth strolling around Gumare to appreciate the considerable beauty of the simple textures of thatched roofs, mud walls, reed screens and wooden gates that provide privacy to individual **homesteads**. Usually a central courtyard area contains a thatched unwalled shelter – just poles – where the women thresh or stamp grain. Some days you can witness the gory **butcher's tree**, under which a carcass is hacked into marketable pieces. Dripping bloody slabs of meat are hung up to attract an eager crowd, and the flesh is sold by a vague estimate of size – graphic gestures show how much you'll get for a pula.

Baskets are also woven in the **ETSHAS**, on a right branch off the main track about 10km outside Gumare. There are thirteen numbered villages all called Etsha along this minor route, inhabited by **Mbukushu refugees** who came into Botswana in the late

---

THE HEREROS

One of the striking sights of northern Botswana are Herero women in Victorian-inspired dress: floor-length bustled skirts, cloaks and elaborate headgear in intense reds, blues and greens. The costume was inherited from nineteenth-century German missionaries in Namibia.

The Herero had originally migrated from east and central Africa to Namibia, where they settled in the sixteenth century. Traditionally they were **nomadic pastoralists**, herding cattle which were at that time absolutely central to their culture; their staple diet was sour milk, and the sale of cattle was taboo in their ancestor-worshipping religion. So important were the **ancestors** that even the supreme being Ndjambi was of little significance next to the first ancestor Mukuru who descended from an omumborombonga tree in Namibia's Etosha Pan. Often as many as two hundred of a man's cattle were killed after his death to please the ancestors.

In 1894 Namibia became a German territory and the colonialists followed the procedures of their European imperialist colleagues elsewhere: the disarming of the Herero, the setting-up of reserves and the imposition of fines and taxes. The Hereros resisted and in 1904 there was an **uprising** in which a large number of German settlers were killed. The whites retaliated with a campaign of extermination that concluded in a crushing Herero defeat. Some Herero managed to flee across the border into Botswana, an event that was to have a profound effect on their culture.

During their wanderings in the desert they lost all their cattle and were forced to throw themselves on the mercy of the Batawana, whose vassals they became. Over time they rebuilt their herds and regained independence, but in the process the cattle lost their religious importance and became financial assets simply to be traded and cashed in. Today the Herero are among northern Botswana's major cattle-owners. Christianity has displaced the old religion, although some Herero still insist on burial in Namibia with the ancestors. It used to be taboo to photograph Herero women, but that has changed as well. Now you will be asked to pay a fee, for what's become a stereotypical posed snap.

1960s. A second wave which followed the route of their nineteenth-century forebears fleeing from the Lozi, these new émigrés were escaping from war-ravaged Angola. While waiting to be resettled, they formed themselves into thirteen parties representing the groups they belonged to in Angola. For an outsider, it's hard to distinguish between, for example, Etsha 2, Etsha 7, and Etsha 12.

The Panhandle fishing camps

Shakawe Fishing Camp, (*Travel Wild*; Maun ☎660822). 14km before Shakawe as you drive up the Panhandle, and the most conveniently situated base for the crowning destination of the northwest, Tsodilo Hills. It's also the only place where you can get **fuel** between Maun and Shakawe. The **campsite** here provides the only affordable **accommodation** in the area – in addition being the only such place where you can turn up without a reservation. Their daily all-inclusive rate is P350 per person.

The fishing camp is attractively set on the banks of the Okavango River, where the river is smooth, fast-flowing and wide, edged by huge papyrus beds stretching to a horizon of riverine trees. After the lengthy journey you'll need a break and it's not a bad idea to take a couple of days here.

The game has been largely shot out in this area, so the emphasis is on **fishing** and **bird life**. The best time for fishing is between April and November, though if you're after that aggressive freshwater fighter, the **tiger fish**, try August to October. *Mekoro* trips close to the camp can be arranged, though the deeper waters are not ideal: the *Fishing Camp*'s proprietors report hippo attacks and tell of a Japanese tourist who insisted on going it alone and ended up capsized and clinging to papyrus for days. The camp's **bird-watching boat trips** are worth considering, as the proprietors are knowledgeable ornithologists. Just south of Shakawe a daily ferry crosses the river to the **eastern side** of the Panhandle, where the biggest settlement is **Seronga** – enquire at the *Fishing Camp* for details.

Nxamaseri Camp, Private Bag 23, Maun (☎260205). An intimate camp, catering for a maximum of eight people, halfway up the Panhandle. Mostly for anglers but good bird-watching too. It's possible to get there by 4WD, but most clients fly in.

Qhaaxwa Camp, (*Gametrackers*; address on p.316). At the base of the Panhandle with the most Delta-like feeling of camps in this area, Qhaaxwa offers the opportunity of seeing red lechwe, sitatunga and water birds. Reed chalets, *mekoro* and motorboat trips, bird-watching, fishing. Max 16 guests.

Xaro Lodge, (*Okavango Explorations*; address on p.316). Right up the Panhandle, this luxury fishing camp with boating excursions is accessible by 4WD in the dry season.Open March to September. Trips to Tsodilo Hills are also offered.

Shakawe – and into Namibia

SHAKAWE is a one-track town, with several shops all called *Wright's*. You can buy the most basic of basics at *Wright's Trading Store*; over the road in an unpromising looking hut is a home-industry bakery, selling warm bread and buns. However, Shakawe is not simply the dusty roadside village it looks. It's also a great transport nexus for local people crossing the river by *mekoro*. Although you don't realise it at first, the river runs just behind the bakery and on a gentle beach you'll come across a *mokoro* terminal, with *mekoro* parked on the bank or in the water, women laden with goods on their heads going to and fro and piles of things waiting to be loaded for the journey back across the water.

Until the border post with Namibia is completed, you must report to the police in Shakawe to clear customs and immigration before crossing into Namibia; and if you need to **change money**, ask for Mrs Wright at *Wright's Trading Store*. The **border** itself is 17km to the north. The boom where you exit Botswana is manned by languid, but armed, troops hiding beneath camouflage netting. In fact, there's nothing to worry about; they check your papers, make a cursory search and wave you on . . .

Doing the Caprivi Strip

For practical and overland entry information on Namibia, see the "Onwards" section in *Contexts*, p.394.

The **CAPRIVI STRIP**, named after a certain Count Caprivi, is a wedge between Botswana and Angola, stretching out from Namibia to touch fingers with Zambia and Zimbabwe. It should properly belong to its northern or southern neighbour; it's one of those arbitrary chunks decided in the negotiating chambers of Europe. The German equivalent to the north–south British Cape to Cairo railway was a projected east–west route, across the Caprivi to the coast. The railway was never built because the Germans never had enough colonies to join the route together. It came to a dead end where it hit the Zambezi, opposite Kasane.

The Caprivi Strip used to be the major flashpoint for battles between SWAPO guerillas and occupying South African troops. Since the South African withdrawal and Namibian independence, it is calm and can be visited easily. A couple of resorts and rest camps on the river punctuate the way to the main town of **Katima Mulilo**. You may still see elephants, although many of those which once walked the roads have been exterminated.

Poppa Falls

The *Namibian Department of National Parks* has provided excellent timber chalets along the Zambezi at **POPPA FALLS** – nothing on the scale of Victoria Falls, but very pretty nevertheless and a recommended stop-over. Camping is cheap, and the sites manicured. The place is mainly a retreat for Namibian Afrikaners whose radios cut through the stillness with the fearsome strains of *sakkiesakkie* music – a southern African equivalent of proto-C&W on piano accordions. *Suclabo Lodge* (☎067/372 6222) is a posher place on the hill overlooking the river, and it offers boat trips and game drives into Khaudum Game Reserve. It's also possible to camp here or hire self-catering bungalows.

From Poppa Falls you could get a ride west and head onto Etosha Pan or the dramatic Atlantic coast. Or do the strip eastwards to Katima Mulilo and have the choice of going to Botswana, Zambia or Zimbabwe.

Katima Mulilo

KATIMA MULILO has an old history, but as a white settlement it's young and raw. Stretched out along the Zambezi, like suburbia in the bush, it's the largest town in Caprivi, (nevertheless still pretty small). A virile vein of morbid humour throbs here. The sign on one gate asks *IS THERE LIFE AFTER DEATH?* and answers in the next breath: *TRESPASS AND YOU'LL FIND OUT*.

Katima Mulilo was one of the first big South African bases set up in Namibia after SWAPO began sending fighters in. Apart from the beautiful Zambezi, Katima has only one tourist attraction – which anywhere else in the world would be firmly ensconced in a modern art gallery – the **lavatree**, a hollow old baobab fitted with a public flushing toilet. It's quite surreal, down one of the town's quiet suburban streets, near the *Guinea Fowl Inn*.

The **hotels** and the **campsite** are situated along the river, on the Kasane road. The rather smart *Zambezi Lodge* (☎067/352203) offers cheap camping with excellent showers and fairly expensive rooms. Breakfast (or drinks) is a treat outside on the hotel terrace overlooking the Zambezi. The homelier, prefabricated *Guinea Fowl Inn* is cheaper and does reasonably priced snacks. The **commercial centre** is set back about a kilometre away in the opposite direction – a small shopping mall with basics, a bank and a reasonable crafts outlet.

Tsodilo Hills

Eulogised by Laurens van der Post in his *Lost World of the Kalahari*, the **TSODILO HILLS** have an undeniably magical, compelling quality. Although most visitors fly in for a quick visit, the spell of the hills isn't quickly absorbed, and it's well worth spending a few days here exploring the rocks and the three thousand paintings at two hundred different sites. The four hills in the surrounding flatness are a kind of shrine, described by Van der Post as "a great fortress of once living Bushman culture, a Louvre of the desert filled with treasure". Few experiences in Africa can match the excitement of a first glimpse of them – the sand-covered bedrock erupting in four monumental humps which lure you ever closer on the excruciatingly slow journey over gentle sand dunes.

The local !Kung* people call the hills "Male", "Female" and "Child", in descending order of size. The smallest one remains nameless like an infant. In the !Kung tongue they're also known lyrically as the "copper bracelet of the evening" from the way they light up in the dying sun. As hills – offering rocky scrambles over chunky rock levels with crevasses, caves, chimneys and castles – they're fascinating in themselves. It's possible to camp out here, in which case on a windy night you can expect unnerving whisperings as the wind fingers the great boulders and eroded masses. From the hill tops you get an incredible panorama over the desert – tree-dotted grassland stretching to all four horizons. An island world, Tsodilo is also home to a variety of gecko lizard found nowhere else on earth.

Tsodilo practicalities: getting there and finding a guide

Getting to Tsodilo isn't easy and 4WD is essential. The 40km from Shakawe are likely to be the longest and bumpiest you ever do; it takes between two and four hours. During the rainy season the sand is firmer and the journey easier. The road is extremely narrow with bushes scraping the sides of the vehicle. There are two routes to the hills: the first turn-off is 13km before Sepopa on the left, with a Botswana museum zebra logo marking the track; the other is close to the *Shakawe Fishing Camp*, 8km before Shakawe. From Maun, it's longer to go via Shakawe but the road is marginally better and Shakawe worth a visit anyway. Astonishingly enough people have done it **on foot**, but if you follow, take plenty of water and don't go alone. The thick sand will make the journey (two days) hard going. Inform the management at Shakawe Fishing Camp. They have a cautionary tale about an intrepid hiker who laughed off their advice to take more than the litre of water he was carrying. The way they tell it, he returned peeling, swollen tongued and in a state of near collapse. Luckily he did return.

Shakawe Fishing Camp has **4WD vehicles** (5 seats) for hire at P2.50/km to get you to Tsodilo. Find out if any of their guests intend going to the hills – you may be inordinately lucky and find a lift. Air Botswana has a scheduled flight twice a week to Shakawe, which would speed up the journey from Maun. *Shakawe Fishing Camp* charges P50 for transfers to and from the airport. Another option, besides a group of you hiring a five-seater plane in Maun, is to ask around at the air charter offices in Maun to see whether anyone has booked a **plane** to Tsodilo, who may be willing to sell off one of the seats (see Maun, "Transport").

On arrival at the hills you have to report to the Mbukushu village to fill in the visitors book. You can **camp** anywhere around the hills (no charge) and there are some useful caves for the tentless, including a large, convenient one at the Tsodilo Hills sign. Be sure to take your rubbish and empty bottles away with you – there's no garbage

---

* The exclamation mark "!" is used in writing a number of African languages to represent one of the several click sounds. See the box on p.340 for more about San clicks.

collection. Take sufficient **food**, water and petrol. Although there is a well near the village, it is not to be relied on and villagers can only spare water in the direst of emergencies. During the rainy season you may well find a spring in the hills; there are a couple on the Female. Ask the guides – but don't count on it.

To see the **paintings** you'll need **a guide**, which can be arranged either at the Mbukushu village or the nearer San village. The !Kung-speaking guides are extremely knowledgeable about painting locations and can show you plants used for medicines and poison. They're also exhaustingly energetic and will take you to some of the more inaccessible sites. Assuming you speak no !Kung it can be difficult that the guides speak little or no English. On the other hand, Benjamin, at the Mbukushu village, does speak English but is now quite old and insists on being driven as close as possible to the paintings, rarely climbing up himself. Charges for a day out are very reasonable and the fee agreed on before you go. The San also have a few curios for sale, such as bows and quivers of arrows and ostrich-shell beads, but if you go to Tsodilo brimming with visionary Van der Post romanticism about the "bushmen", their desultory village near the Male Hill, with its rude shelters and people sitting around in the dust, is bound to disappoint.

Paintings and Legends

Most of the **paintings** are on exposed rock faces, some high above the ground. They're displayed on all the hills, but the Female has the majority. While on the whole they were painted by San people, here and there you'll come across some by the Bantu-speakers who also lived here. These latter, mostly done in white, differ in style and colour from the reddish San outlines. The pastel colours of the rocks – mauve, pink, honey and ochre – blend strikingly with animals drawn finger thickness in a deep russet. Tiny, spine-tingling hand-prints accompany many of the friezes.

Although thousands of years old, the colours are still ardent. The paintings on the other hand are variable: some animals are breathtaking while others merely indifferent sketches. Besides recognisable animals there are mythological ones, many abstract symbols such as gridded circles and shields containing ladders and depictions of people dancing. Some of the paintings may be as recent as 100 years, while others could easily be 20,000 years old. Authoritative dates have not been established for the Tsodilo paintings, but similar ones in a cave in Namibia have been verified as 26,000 years old. Nobody knows for sure what was used to paint the pictures and there's no evidence to support the popular idea that blood or eggs were used. It seems most likely that the colouring agents were predominantly earth pigments, plant juices, ash and burnt bone, water and possibly animal or plant oils.

Besides the San who have many legends about these hills, the Mbukushu have a myth that the omniscient being lowered their first ancestors by rope to the summit of the Male Hill. If you ask Mbukushu, they'll confirm that their origin was on the Zambezi but say spirits live in the hills. These spirits are the ones Van der Post and his party inadvertently angered, which jammed the cameras and prevented all filming, stopped the tape recorders from working and sent bees to attack them at dawn three days in a row. Their party couldn't leave fast enough, but not before they had made a symbolic gesture of contrition – a note buried in a bottle at the base of the paintings now called Van der Post's panel.

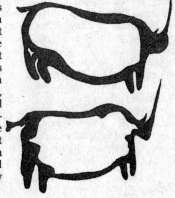

travel details

Bus
Maun to Francistown supposedly twice a week, but days and times are indeterminate and it's not to be relied on at all.

Flights
From Maun to:
Gaborone daily (1hr 30min).
Kasane twice weekly (50min).
Francistown twice weekly (1hr 15min).

Ghanzi twice weekly (50min).
Johannesburg Wed & Sun (1hr 30min) direct. Maun to Johannesburg via Gaborone daily.
Shakawe Mon & Wed (50min).
Windhoek Wed, Fri & Sun (2hr).
Victoria Falls Fri & Sun (50min).
Apart from scheduled flights, you can also often get a seat on one of the many **chartered flights** that leave Maun. For these ask around the travel agents, and the air charter companies.

CHAPTER TEN

THE KALAHARI DESERT

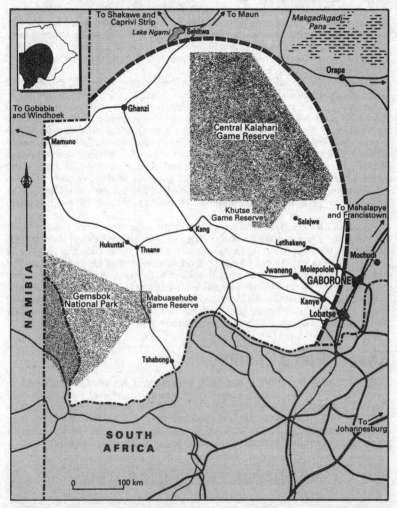

T he Okavango Delta aside, the **Kalahari Desert** is for most visitors the defining feature of Botswana. Over two-thirds of the country is covered by the desert and its influence on the life of Botswana is paramount. What distinguishes it as desert is the lack of surface water and scant rain, disguising the underground wells which nourish a cover of grass and acacias, not to say supporting a wide variety of animals and birds. Only in the far southwest will you see archetypal sand dunes.

The Kalahari (also spelt Kgalakgadi) is the remaining territory of one of Africa's oldest peoples, the **San** – the "Bushmen" about whom Laurens van der Post wrote with such passion. Over the centuries, they have been pushed by migrating farmers and herders from the easier lands of their ancestors into this harsh environment, where they now barely survive.

Many practical difficulties confront travellers who come in the hope of **seeing the Kalahari**, but it is feasible. As potential targets, four little-visited **game reserves** lie isolated in the vastness, west and northwest of Gaborone. The closest and most accessible from the capital is **Khutse**, 220km to the north. Khutse is an annexe of the **Central Kalahari Game Reserve**, itself off limits to the public, and one of the last preserves of the hunter-gatherer lifestyle.

Mabuasehube Game Reserve, in the southwest corner of the country, abuts the **Gemsbok National Park** which spills over into South Africa. These reserves are far better than Khutse for game-viewing. And the landscape of the southwest is archetypal Kalahari – pans, red dunes and scrubby vegetation. But getting to the region takes time and effort (not to mention money) and it's a trip recommended only for experienced desert drivers and campers. There is, in any case, no way in to the Gemsbok National Park from Botswana. Access to it is either from South Africa's northern Cape Province, or from Namibia, and all the roads and camping facilities are inside South Africa, beyond the seasonal Nossob River which forms the border. For hardy adventurers, however, the far southwest circuit outlined in this chapter runs southwest of Gaborone through Mabuasehube Reserve and back again along the rough Kalahari cattle trail.

Despite its booming diamond mine, **Jwaneng** on the route from Gaborone and Lobatse is not a recommended stopover. The most compelling Kalahari town, and the de facto capital of the desert is **Ghanzi**, out in the remote west. Ghanzi is about as far out and cut off as you can get. It rests on a vast limestone ridge (despite the deceptive flatness), 300km from its nearest neighbour Maun to the north, and Lobatse more than twice that to the southeast. Both routes follow punishing roads that impact your spine and coat you with dust, though the trans-Kalahari Lobatse-Ghanzi route is now being tarred. From Ghanzi, with your own transport, it's possible to explore the extremely remote southwest corner of Botswana, with its numerous San settlements.

Khutse Game Reserve

KHUTSE GAME RESERVE is something of a misnomer. It's less a place to see game – you may see very few animals indeed – than a park to experience the unspoilt isolation and immensity of the Kalahari. The night skies are recommendation enough on their own; no light within hundreds of miles interferes with the brilliance of the thick clusters of stars. Yet, in Botswanan terms, the reserve isn't far from Gaborone, and it's a good place to get away from the drabness of the capital for a long weekend.

ACCOMMODATION PRICE CODES

Every hotel and accommodation option listed in this chapter has been given a **price code** to indicate the cost of a single night's lodging. Safari lodges are excluded from the system, a specific price being quoted.

For a full explanation, see p.251.

① under P50   ② P50–100   ③ P100–175   ④ P175–250   ⑤ P250+

Khutse doesn't have dunes, but a low cover of herbage and acacias, nourished by underground water and **pans**. The pans are the reserve's dominant feature, remnants of a wetter period some ten to fifteen thousand years ago.

Some are wide and grassy, others bare and open, and they offer the best of the park's limited **game-viewing**. The severe drought of the 1980s decimated animal populations as well as food sources but you stand a chance of seeing small herds of **springbok** and **gemsbok**, **hartebeest** and **wildebeest**, and families of **ostriches**. Wildlife is seasonal, passing through in the perpetual search for grazing and water. You can come here at any time, however, and chance on animals licking minerals from the salty pan surfaces.

The **smaller mammals** which you may spot on the pans (often at night) are perhaps the most interesting. Take a good mammal book and sharpen up your eyes to identify **mongooses**, **black-backed jackals**, **genets**, **caracals**, **ratels**, **porcupines**, **hedgehogs**, **ground squirrels**, **bat-eared foxes**, **African** and beautiful **black-footed cats**, **spring-hares**, **pangolins**, **aardvarks** and **aardwolves**. If herds of **antelope** are around, there will also be **predators**, including lions.

The number of **bird species** (150 plus) doesn't match what you'd see at Chobe or Okavango, but it's still impressive. One big bird in evidence here and in many parts of Botswana is the **kori bustard**, the world's heaviest flying bird. It weighs an astonishing 40kg and has an immense wingspan. You're more likely to see one on the ground than in the air and you can get quite close before they reluctantly take off. During the mating season, the male makes himself even bigger, puffing out his throat to two or three times its normal size.

Khutse practicalities

Getting to Khutse is a 4WD journey of around five hours from Gaborone. Bring fuel sufficient for at least 600km, and everything you need. You can arrange both **vehicle and camping equipment hire** from *Holiday Safaris* (P/Bag 0016, Gaborone; ☎53970).

When to go depends on what you're after, but, as a rule of thumb, August to November is best avoided – it's desperately dry and unbelievably hot and much of the wildlife disappears. The ideal time is in April and May, when the nights, which can get icy in the Kalahari, aren't too bad. Nevertheless, the park is open throughout the year, and other times have their own attractions. After the first rains, at the end of November, the pans are covered with **wild flowers**. December to March has the disadvantage of long grass, with seeds that block the radiator, creating a fire hazard and entailing frequent stops to unclog it. The thick grass also hides many of the animals.

From Gaborone, take the road through Molepolole (last petrol) to Letlhakeng, where the tar ends 65km from the capital. The road deteriorates rapidly thereafter, with deep sandy stretches, making for a bumpy ride with little signposting. Salajwe, 39km from Letlhakeng, is the last village before the Khutse gate, 44km further on.

At the gate you can get borehole **water**, but consider bringing your own as it's a bit salty. You can also get a Kgalakgadi or San **guide**, who will camp with you, if you want to be shown around the park and to be initiated into some of the ways plants are used by desert-dwellers. You'll be expected to provide their food and to pay a reasonable daily rate. They also know where best to find animals. Their powers of observation and eyesight are formidable. If you decide to go it alone, though, you're unlikely to lose your way, as there's only one road in the Reserve.

The nicest place to **camp** is at **MORESWE PAN**, two and a half hours beyond the Park gate, which you'll almost certainly have to yourself. At Khutse II Pan, 13km from the gate, the road forks. Take the left-hand fork to Moreswe Pan, which is 53km further on. The expansive pan stretches out, in inconceivable vastness, all but filling your field of vision. Where the road peters out, two trees mark the lonely campsite.

Central Kalahari Game Reserve

Adjacent to Khutse's northern border and dominating the centre of the country is the mysterious, boxed-off **CENTRAL KALAHARI GAME RESERVE** which has no facilities of any kind, no water and no public access. It's the second largest game reserve in the world: though only a patch in the middle of the Kalahari, whose sands cover about eighty percent of the country.

Until recently, small bands of **San** people, pursuing a traditional hunter-gatherer lifestyle, shared the reserve with a wide variety of game. The droughts of the 1980s have effectively ended this traditional life. The drought hasn't stopped **mineral exploration**, though, and geologists are among the few people given permission to traverse the endless grassy scrub.

Mabuasehube Game Reserve and Around

Entrance free.

In the sand dune country of the southwest is **MABUASEHUBE GAME RESERVE**, Botswana's most remote and least-visited park. Its name, spelt *Mabuashegube* in the Kgalakgadi language, means "red soil", and applies specifically to its bare, northernmost pan, contrasting it with the others, which are grassy.

Terrible roads serve as a considerable disincentive to casual visitors. This is a destination only for the intrepid. You may not see another vehicle for a week in these parts, so a trip here is not to be undertaken without adequate preparations – lots of water, spares and experience. Naturally enough, it's not a good idea to stray off the main road. At the park itself there are no facilities of any kind, although borehole water is usually available from the game ranger.

Poaching has long been a problem in the southern Kalahari and this reserve, although unfenced, is a real animal sanctuary. Among the many pans and sand dunes, the rainy season attracts abundant antelope and predators – including lions, rare brown hyenas and caracals.

The **usual approach** is from the south through **TSHABONG**, the administrative capital of the Kgalakgadi District. There's precious little here and the road to the Mabuasehube crosses 120 kilometres of gentle sand dunes. Plans for a motel at Tshabong, and to tarmac the road to Gaborone, are likely to increase traffic to the Reserve. You may well come across camels wandering around the village. These were originally imported by the police, who used them extensively for patrols in this sandy terrain, but now Tshabong is the last place dromedaries can be seen in Botswana.

Tshabong to Kang through the reserve

The track from Tshabong to Mabuasehube passes northwards through the reserve to **TSHANE**, a tough eight-hour drive, with no settlements or facilities en route. Tshane is one of a cluster of four villages in the Kalahari's heart, along with Lokgwabe, Lehututu and Hukuntsi. Together they're of interest as repositories of Botswana's early history.

Tshane has a notable colonial police station built on high ground overlooking the magnificent **TSHANE PAN**, where animals are still watered from hand-dug wells on the pan's edge – a practice unchanged for over 150 years. **LEHUTUTU**, about 10km north of Tshane, features in the accounts of early Kalahari explorers as a thriving commercial centre. Although the place is now all but deserted, the original store is still there and operating. At **LOKGWABE**, 11km southwest of Tshane, you'll find descendants of Simon Cooper who in 1904 led a Khoi Khoi anti-colonial rebellion in South West Africa, and was given protection and land here by the British administration. **HUKUNTSI**, 10km west of Tshane, is the administrative centre of the area and here you can get **diesel and petrol**, and **supplies** from the well-stocked store.

The main interest of the final stretch, from Tshane to Kang is the sprinkling of **San settlements**. But you should only go here if you're doing some serious and informed exploration of the southern Kalahari and are aware that you may not encounter any traffic for a long time. Once you reach KANG you're back on the relatively important Lobatse–Ghanzi road, which does at least see a reasonable number of vehicles each day.

The route from Gaborone

To reach Mabuasehube **from Gaborone**, you should first head 65km south of the capital to **LOBATSE**, in order to pick up the northwest road. **JWANENG**, 127km further on, is the last major place for petrol and supplies and supports one fairly expensive hotel, the *Mokala* (☎380614; ③) with a restaurant and bar. It's modern and takes *Visa*, for those stranded in the Kalahari. For snacks, ice creams and cokes, there are a couple of places in the Mall. Indicative of its move from cattle post to an urban settlement, one of Botswana's best pop groups, *Kwanyape*, comes from here.

Jwaneng would have remained just another tiny cattle post in the desert, were it not for the discovery of **diamonds**. All Botswana's mining towns are new and Jwaneng is the newest. Opened in 1982, the **Jwaneng mine** is the largest gem mine in the world, producing a staggering 8.9 million carats in 1988. Australia and Zaire produce greater caratage, but most of their output is industrial grade; Botswana is the world's leading diamond producer in terms of value.

Maun to Ghanzi

It takes five hours, at least, to cover the 280km **from Maun to Ghanzi**, on potholed roads, with very little on the way. While 4WD isn't necessary, you need a high-clearance vehicle.

The Ghanzi district starts at the Kuke Gate – little more than a post in the scrub with huts and a primary school. From its location on a rise you get a rare overview of the Kalahari, stretching endlessly into the blue, and of the infamous **veterinary cordon fence** – an inexorable straight line through the bush.

The gate is attended round the clock, and you'll be asked some routine questions, such as whether you're carrying any animal products; a cursory search may be made, after which you'll be waved on.

THE VETERINARY CORDON FENCE

An extensive system of barriers has been erected around Botswana in an attempt to keep the dreaded **foot-and-mouth disease** under control – an absolutely vital priority in a nation so locked into cattle farming. The fences are an emotive issue; some people, like Mark and Delia Owens, authors of *Cry the Kalahari*, claim that they have been responsible for decimating game populations.

The Owens lived in the Kalahari for seven years between 1974 and 1981, studying predators. Their book contains harrowing accounts of thousands of wildebeest and other animals following their old migration routes across the Central Kalahari Reserve, in search of fresh grazing and water, and dying at the fences, like the one at Kuke, that blocked their way. The Owens assert that no one knows for certain that the wild ungulates are a reservoir of infection, or that foot-and-mouth disease can be held in check by fences. But other scientists question the Owens' allegations, holding up the old theory that disease is transmitted from wild animals to domestic stock. Whoever is right, the Owens' vociferous campaign got them thrown out of the country, and they continue their crusade with lecture tours, mainly in the US.

D'KAR too is a small place, though bigger than Kuke, and not devoid of interest. A very active **mission** runs projects to lessen the traumatic transition of a number of San people, settled permanently here, from their ancient self-sufficient way of life into the shock of a global economy. The mission is run by an Afrikaans minister of the traditionally segregated and conservative South African Dutch Reformed Church. The people here, he says, are the same outcasts as those who have always come to missions: the dispossessed, the sick, the old and thieves. The missionary talks of his guilt at being a privileged white in an unequal South Africa, and now he's channelling those feelings in concrete action.

The original mission was set up to bring Christianity to the San living on the Ghanzi farms, but now international aid money is being used to assist **income-generation projects**. Mission residents can raise livestock and participate in arable farming on their own behalf. Many produce leather goods, notably saddlery, for sale, as well as traditional crafts. There is a **store** in town and the possibility of renting a **room** if you get stranded – ask at the **craft shop** on your left as you head towards Ghanzi.

Ghanzi and the Western Kalahari

GHANZI is an historical quirk. Now the centre of an Afrikaner farming district in southern Africa's oldest independent black republic, it was for millennia the centre of the hunter-gatherers' range. Despite its unpromising appearance, Ghanzi's very remoteness from all other major settlements makes it one of Botswana's most interesting towns for the traveller who manages to penetrate it and gets to meet local inhabitants. The name probably derives from the San word meaning a one-stringed instrument – an unintentional metaphor for its one horse, dead-end feel. The Batswana imposed their own gloss on the place respelling it *Ghantsi*, which in Setswana means *place of the flies* – an equally apt description.

A fitful history

It's something of a miracle that Ghanzi exists at all. It progressed fitfully out of the dusty wastes that were the traditional hunting grounds of three San-speaking groups, and, later, cattle-owning Khoi. The first white settler – in the 1870s – was a larger-than-life Afrikaner, **Hendrik van Zyl**, an ex-member of parliament and cabinet minister from the Boer South African Republic (now the Transvaal), who must have had good reasons to leave a prestigious life to gather an existence out of the dust. In fact he seems to have lived well: legend relates he had a two-storey mansion with imported stained-glass windows, and a hundred servants. A notorious hunter and killer, he's said to have shot 400 elephants in his first year at Ghanzi and was responsible for the death of many San. One story relates how he invited a number of San to a party, accommodating them in a specially built stockade. In retaliation for the murder of a fellow Boer, he shot 33 of them in cold blood. There are several accounts of how he was killed – enough people had good reason. One version claims a revenge killing by San, another that he was murdered by Khoi herders and a third says he was killed by Damara tribesmen for interfering in local affairs. Other Boer trekkers followed in his footsteps, most of them either passing through or staying only briefly.

The real establishment of Ghanzi probably began in the late nineteenth century around one of the largest pans in the district. And at this juncture the even larger figure of **Cecil Rhodes** makes another appearance. Hungry for land Rhodes had his eye on the western edge of Bechuanaland where it bordered on German territory. Generous historians have said that he recruited settlers to Ghanzi to act as a buffer against German expansionism. Others question how a small group of farmers could do

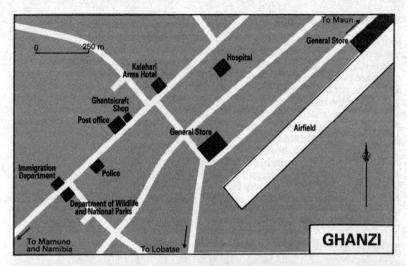

this, contending that Rhodes was more interested in annexing the land in the name of his British South Africa Company, to pave the way for its commercial activities in the hinterland. Rhodes' aim was to occupy the area with bodies, and to do this, a less generous version of history tells how he hijacked a Boer trek that was gathering to go north. Farms and provision of equipment were offered, and the word was put about describing the wonderful climate of Ghanzi. As he had done with such success in Matabeleland, Rhodes sent a delegate to obtain signatures to give him access to lands he had his eye on. A fraudulent title deed was produced in Dutch – a language Sekgoma (the Batawana chief) could not speak, let alone read or write. When the Batawana complained to the British Government, they ordered Rhodes to get a new concession. Sekgoma then refused him access. Rhodes tried to force the government's hand by encouraging the trek to go ahead regardless.

Meanwhile Rhodes finally went too far with the abortive **Jameson Raid** (led by his associate Dr L S Jameson), aimed at overthrowing the South African Republic. When the world heard that Botswana had been used as a base for launching the raid, an embarrassed Britain abruptly terminated Rhodes' territorial ambitions. Jameson was tried and imprisoned, while Rhodes was forced to resign as Prime Minister of the Cape Colony. However the forces set in motion by Rhodes were released in 1898. The area is unquestionably fine cattle country and the British High Commission was keen on settling the Ghanzi district. It made an ultimatum to Sekgoma: either give up Ghanzi or Britain would take all Ngamiland.

White settlers headed north to Ghanzi, and the Ghanzi farms joined the Tuli Block and Tati District as the only European areas of Bechuanaland. The trekkers were not the salt of the earth that the government had imagined, but fortune-hunters, most of whom deserted their farms within ten years. Things spluttered on for the next half century, until the road was built from Ghanzi to Lobatse, providing more convenient access to the country's big abattoirs. On the new dirt road, landrovers replaced the camels of the early colonial police force. The farming community is now extremely prosperous, producing large quantities of Botswana's finest beef. To overcome the isolation, several farmers have their own planes, and landing strips outside their Beverly Hills-style mansions.

Ghanzi practicalities

The main street of Ghanzi – a wide, pink, dusty swathe – heads like a ceremonial axis straight up to the bougainvillea-enclosed **hotel**, around which all activity in Ghanzi seems to revolve. The *Kalahari Arms Hotel* (PO Box 29, Ghanzi; ☎ 296311; ③) is the sole place to stay, but don't count on a room – it's often full and not cheap. The **campsite** at the back is pleasant enough, with ablutions, and a place to braai. Get on the right side of the manager who is extremely genial and great fun. In addition Ghanzi has a couple of bottle stores, a general dealer, butcher, shoe shop and a bunch of government offices, all basic concrete sheds. There is no electricity and no fresh fruit or vegetables. Although there are a few phones, most people communicate by radio.

Ghantsicraft, between the hotel and Post Office, shouldn't be missed. It has one of the best collections of San crafts in the country and, as a non-profit organisation, costs are kept really low, with ninety percent of the price going to the producer. At the moment **San crafts** must be among the very few, in southern Africa at least, that are still made to high standards the traditional way and it's a rare opportunity to get an authentic if not actually used artefact. It won't be possible for long. As the hunter-gathering culture comes to an end (bows and arrows are more or less out of use), the old skills of making

---

KALAHARI FLORA AND DESERT FOODS

There are about 250 **edible plants** throughout Botswana. Some of the San, such as the Dau/oa-speaking people in the Kalahari, use as many as 180 of them, although only three or four as staples. Knowledge and use of edible plants is on the decrease with the introduction of new crops, imported foods and a cash economy. Coca-cola, canned beer, peanuts and chewing gum are ousting their traditional counterparts and there's a social stigma attached to eating tubers and roots – considered food only for the poorest. During the severe droughts of the 1980s when many plants and animals died, the government provided drought relief in the form of maize meal. For many people, this has now become their staple diet.

Collecting vegetables from the bush is the job of women and girls, a major responsibility given that for traditional hunter-gatherers, this accounts for more than eighty percent of their diet. San working on farms still supplement their diet with wild food, although domestic livestock inevitably tramples and destroys edible plants so they're not so easy to find. From November to May people collect berries, nuts, fruits, roots, tubers, bulbs, shoots, succulents, wild honey and even a species of delicious truffle. Besides plants they also forage for less appealing mopane worms (there are 20 species of edible insect), small mammals, bullfrogs, reptiles, birds and their eggs, and ant eggs. Before the rains break, from August to November, food is at its scarcest. The sun burns everything up and it becomes very difficult to detect the moisture-bearing plants which are necessary for survival away from any other water sources. Before the advent of boreholes, people obtained all their liquid for eight months of the year from plants. The most remarkable of these, the *morama*, develops a massive, moisture-bearing underground tuber which contains as much as sixty litres of liquid. It betrays its presence by runners above the surface. The runners bear bean-like pods, each containing a couple of *morama nuts* – a great delicacy roasted in the hot sand. Young tubers are chewed for moisture, or roasted and eaten. Also widely eaten are *tsama* melons and wild cucumbers, eaten raw or roasted. Their seeds can be dried and pounded into flour. In the northwest, the !Kung-speaking people rely on the *mongongo* nut. The kernel is highly nutritious while the sweet flesh and skin are eaten raw or boiled.

Botswana has its own intoxicating **palm wine** made from the sap of the palm tree which is left to ferment. Unfortunately, many of the palm trees along the Shashi and Limpopo rivers have died from being over-tapped – the palm juice used to be distilled into a highly toxic and illegal beverage, apparently causing great pain behind the eyes.

hunting sets, beads and bags are disappearing too. It takes a woman weeks of concentrated bouts of work to make one ostrich-egg shell necklace. Besides what *Ghantsicraft* has for sale, it's like a mini-museum, with cases of beautiful artefacts.

Nightlife in Ghanzi all happens at the hotel, with discos at weekends that have to be seen to be believed. Unintelligible music blares out at a phenomenal wattage from rumbling old speakers. All you hear is a thumping beat but the pace is frantic and people friendly. Outside in the gardens things are sometimes quieter, but no less drunken and in a wild west town the brawling comes as no surprise – it's unlikely to be directed at you if you maintain a bit of discretion. Inside you can get a good **meal** (steak naturally) at the dining room-cum-bar. It's the only place to eat in town. Order before you feel hungry as it takes a while. Meantime, in an outside bar with pack-'em-in pews you can catch an action video of some description.

The Kalahari San

Ghanzi is an area of convergence of all the **San** linguistic groupings – the **!Ko, G/wi, Gana, Tsau, /Dau** and **Nharo** (see box on p.342). The Nharo are one of the largest San groups in Southern Africa and over half live in the Ghanzi district, in the white farm block where they constitute the ethnic majority.

Most San are employed on farms or are simply squatters; a few are petty entrepreneurs or settled food producers, while many go between life on farms and life in the bush. According to a 1976 government report, the biggest problem facing the San is outright oppression and discrimination by other Ghanzi residents. On numerous occasions they've been asked to leave public meetings or even village Independence celebrations. Tension between Nharo and blacks often leads to fights and brawls, especially at drinking sessions.

The San face a list of chronic **problems** including poverty, massive unemployment, dependency, landlessness, powerlessness and despair, with a standard of living well below that of the average Motswana. Their existential distress has increased so sharply that the healing trance dance, which used to be performed only sporadically, is nowadays conducted very regularly. The word *sheeta* is used to describe the concept of life as a toll of misfortune, sickness and death. The kind of labour they've developed a tradition in – tracking, trekking, riding and unskilled work – has become obsolete on modern ranches where many San have been replaced by black labour. Pay is very low and they're dependent on the farmer for water, food, tobacco and a place to stay.

Poverty and hunger is a certain recipe for stock theft. As the poorest people in Botswana, San have a disproportionate involvement in cattle-rustling and other poverty-related misdemeanours such as hunting without a licence, tax evasion and squatting. At least a third of stock theft is committed by other groups.

What San people want most is a place to be, to combine an agricultural existence with some hunting and gathering. To its credit the government has taken all this on board, approaching the problem by providing water and land as a fundamental means for the San to move into the mainstream of Botswana's development, combined with literacy campaigns and better health facilities to help combat common illnesses like tuberculosis and sexually transmitted diseases.

The San have never had a sense of belonging to a common heritage and consequently there are few San, if any, campaigning for their rights. However outsiders from a variety of perspectives do **campaign** on their behalf, some wishing to maintain what they believe is the ancient lifestyle of these people. The question is a fraught one, with the Botswana government assiduously avoiding any racial recognition – it wants to steer clear of any policy that even vaguely smacks of apartheid. It doesn't want to regard the San as a distinct group with separate rights, but rather as citizens of Botswana in the process of integration.

THE SAN

The San should not be regarded as backward people who failed to progress from hunting and gathering to a "higher" and more sedentary way of life, but as people whose adaptation to the environment was well-nigh total.

David Stephen – *The San of the Kalahari*

The social system of the San embodied everything a searcher for Utopia could want: there were no chiefs, people possessed only one or two items of personal property, a high premium was placed on relationships set up through sharing, decisions were made communally (women participated equally in decision-making) and there was a rich spiritual life which stressed the unity of existence. This "ecological" way of life enabled them to survive continuously for longer than any other society. Sadly, though, that's all over – in the 1980s the traditional San way of life finally fizzled to an end.

Terminology

The sensitivity of the so-called *bushman problem* is reflected in the linguistic agonising over what to call them. The most widely used term, with racist and sexist connotations, is **bushmen**, deriving from the early settler *bosmanneken* (men of the bush). It grew out of the belief that they were animals and not people. In the eighteenth and nineteenth centuries, *bushmen* was used for all social outcasts in conflict with the laws of the Cape. The stridently racist "bushies" is also used. Many people, including liberal writers still use *bushmen*, waiting for an acceptable, non-pejorative term to be found.

Several historians have plumped for **San**, but the term refers to a language group and not a culture, and is a word used derisively by the Khoi Khoi (cattle-herding contemporaries of the San) to mean hunter-gatherer. It is currently the respectable term in most academic circles. It's not a term used by the hunter-gatherers themselves, and is rarely used in Botswana outside books.

The Setswana word **Basarwa**, meaning people from the uninhabited country, is apparently disliked by San themselves because it connotes negative sentiments. The Botswana government, too, has made its own contribution to the debate. In its vigorous attempts to avoid any racial categories associated with apartheid, it has adopted a socially rather than ethnically defined term: **Remote Area Dwellers**. This gets abbreviated to RADs, an unfortunate choice as in Setswana "t" and "d" aren't clearly differentiated, and RADs become *RATs*.

The original South Africans

As southern Africa's earliest inhabitants, the San are also the most direct descendants of the late Stone Age. They have hunted and gathered on the subcontinent for a considerable period – paintings in Namibia by their ancestors date back 25,000 years. At one time San-speakers probably spread throughout sub-Saharan Africa, living for most of that period a fairly unaltered existence. But in the last 2000 years, the southward migration of Bantu-speaking farmers forced change upon the San, and the pace has been ever more rapid over the last 400 years, since the arrival of Europeans.

Archaeological evidence suggests that as **Bantu-speaking farmers** progressed south from west Africa they moved into the moister areas avoided by the San and that for a millennium the two groups lived more or less harmoniously side by side. In fact, far from the newcomers simply dominating the incumbents, the modern phonetics of Bantu languages like Xhosa in the Eastern Cape, Zulu in Natal and Swazi in Swaziland show that the blacks from the north were influenced by the people they found. With the arrival of the whites at the Cape in the seventeenth century, a twofold threat eventually brought the San to blows with both Bantu-speakers and Boers.

Over the centuries whites began to annex lands for hunting and farming, hence restricting the hunting grounds of the San and depleting the stocks of huntable game.

San began turning to taking cattle from both Bantu and Boer farmers. The whites in particular came to regard the San as vermin, and early Dutch settlers in the **Cape** felt free to ride out in extermination parties. In the eighteenth century, a full-scale genocidal campaign was under way which resulted in the slaughter of thousands of San and their extinction in the Cape. They were eventually wiped off the South African map and now survive only around the Kalahari Desert – sixty percent in Botswana and the remainder in eastern Namibia and southern Angola.

By the 1850s most of **Botswana** was either claimed by Batswana or other farmers. In these areas the San became absorbed into farming communities and in the more heavily populated areas completely disappeared as a distinct group. They came – and still come – rock bottom of the social order. It was only in remote areas like the Central Kalahari that their traditional way of life continued. By the turn of this century most San had made contact with pastoral people. Many lived semi-traditional lifestyles close to cattle posts – the men became cattle-herders and the women continued to gather wild food. But the fencing of farmland made hunting and gathering more difficult – game became scarce and wild food difficult to find until eventually the San were left with little option but to learn Afrikaans and to work for white farmers.

In 1964, prior to Independence, the British administration became concerned about the plight of the San, who they feared – not without justification – would be badly treated in the new country. In the past San who became attached to Tswana villages were little more than slaves of Batswana families, with no rights under Tswana law. But contrary to British fears, the Botswana government took the problem on board and now regards the San as equal under law, although social prejudice persists.

Traditional ways

Traditional San **bands** consisted of between fifteen and eighty members and had no chief, decisions being made communally. Individuals were free to come and go and those who failed to get on in one group would simply take themselves elsewhere. Bands were flexible and would vary in size depending on the amount of food locally available – small dispersed groups were better suited to scarce food resources.

San **beliefs** centred around the notion that everything was part of the great web of nature with an equal right to existence. They believed that humans, as mere parts of the cosmos, have no special rights over the animals and birds.

At first sight, **hunting** seems to contradict this idea, but the San were not excessive hunters, rather getting most of their nutrition, often up to ninety percent, from plants collected by women. Hunting was an important social activity stressing the custom of sharing – all the meat from the hunt ended up shared through complex rules. Killing an animal was simultaneously sad (because a fellow creature had died) and joyous (because a spiritual unification had taken place). Wanton killing was totally taboo with the danger of great disaster for overstepping the bounds. In keeping with their cosmology, the San were sensitive to the suffering of other beings and would often go out of their way to spare pain. One researcher reported an incident in which a dung beetle heading for a camp fire was turned around to prevent its injury. And among some groups, even scorpions are spared, unless about to sting.

In San **religion** there was a good god, the giver of life who was also a distant being not much concerned with the mundane dealings of mortals. The evil god on the other hand was a meddlesome trickster, who spent his time stirring trouble. He could change his form, but usually took that of a human. The night-long **trance dance** was the San means to deal with evil and to communicate with the spirit world. It was a healing dance in which a powerful healing force called *n/um* was activated. The men danced while the women sat around the fire, rhythmically clapping and singing. It remains one of the most persistent aspects of their culture, continuing even where San have deserted the traditional ways and lived for generations on white farms.

SAN LANGUAGE

With the end of their traditional culture, language has become the most fundamental factor defining the San. One of the distinctive characteristics of all San languages is the **click sounds**, made by air escaping when the tongue is pulled away from the palate or teeth. All San languages have some common clicks:

/ (dental, tongue pulling from two front top teeth)

// (lateral, tongue pulling from upper right teeth)

! (palatal, tongue pulling from roof of mouth)

Additional clicks are found in some dialects. The above three clicks have been absorbed into the Nguni (southeastern Bantu languages), where they're written as: c, x and q respectively.

San languages are extremely difficult for outsiders to pick up, because of their click consonants and the use of high, middle and low tones to distinguish meanings. Most words are monosyllables ending in a vowel or nasal sound. In some languages there's no gender such as "he" and "she", sex being denoted by distinct words like "hen" and "cock". The languages are poor in words referring to abstract concepts but very rich in ones describing everyday actions. There are few terms to distinguish colours, which in the San world-view have no separate existence – colours are simply attributes of plants or objects which already have detailed descriptions.

Romantics, some of them doubtless influenced by the work of Laurens van der Post, say they want the traditional hunter-gatherer lifestyle of the San to be retained. But it's too late for that. A Ghanzi District Council report which came out in 1980 found that something would have to be done fairly urgently about the poverty and the acute hardship of people living in the Central Kalahari Game Reserve, and that their most consistently expressed wish was to be able to live like other Batswana. The report concluded that any development should take place within their home ground, where they had been resident as a group for generations. An important element in the development plans was to be the provision of **water holes** and self-help agricultural projects.

Many of the San have been attracted out of their traditional lifestyle by permanent water sources of this nature which obviate the need for eternal wandering. Hunting is severely restricted and the old knowledge is disappearing. Alcohol abuse is becoming a growing problem and the transition to life at these borehole villages is a painful one. Packaged government maize meal provides the San with far less nutrition than the array of wild foods that was formerly available to them. Some of the boreholes started off as watering places for game, like the one built in 1963 at Chade, but now there are at least 1300 people living there in very demoralised conditions, dependent on food hand-outs.

On the other hand, the powerful US-backed **wildlife conservation lobby** is keen to see any remaining San out of the Central Kalahari Reserve (it's for animals and tourists only) while mineral exploration goes on unabated. Recent government policy seems to have shifted toward bringing Remote Area Dwellers (as the government now calls the San, see p.338) into the mainstream of Botswana's development – removing them from the Central Kalahari to a life of more dependable water sources and food. This is certainly not what all San want. In a 1988 Swedish documentary *When Manna Falls from Heaven*, which looks at Botswana after the diamond revenue, an articulate inhabitant of the Central Kalahari Reserve says his people want to stay exactly where they are. He says he doesn't understand why the government claims it can help them elsewhere and not where they already are.

Onwards from Ghanzi: south, east or Namibia?

Ghanzi is a staging post in the Kalahari, dull unless you meet local people and get under the skin of it. Getting there is quite a feat, only matched by the journey away again.

It is possible to **hitch** out of Ghanzi, but be prepared to wait a couple of days. Aid workers, researchers and teachers are a noticeable presence in town and you're bound to bump into them at the hotel. They're a mine of information about local gossip and politics and a grapevine for arranging **lifts**. Locals drive to Maun or Gaborone; ask at the hotel and around for lifts. Monday and Tuesday when cattle trucks go off to Lobatse are said to be good days to try your luck getting to Gaborone. A much more comfortable alternative if you can afford it is to take one of the twice-weekly flights to Gaborone or Maun. Book through the *Kalahari Arms*.

If you're overlanding, the obvious route out of Ghanzi is west to Windhoek in Namibia, a journey of 575km which takes around 10 hours. Roads are rough but you don't need 4WD. The distance from Ghanzi to the border at Mamuno is 210km; not many vehicles use this route so hitching can be difficult. Note that the Namibian border post closes at 4pm, while Botswana shuts at 5pm. Once at Windhoek, right in the centre of Namibia, there is a camping site, but it's unappealingly floodlit and next to a main road. Nevertheless you're in the heart of one of the most beautiful countries in Africa with the lure of an undeveloped coastline and superb game parks and wilderness areas.

Back to base: the cattle route to Lobatse

Ghanzi is closely associated with Lobatse. Down those deep sandy roads, Ghanzi's big cattlemen send their stock on the near-legendary cattle run to the **abattoirs** – apparently the longest in the world and one that confirms your impression that Ghanzi is the capital of Botswana's wild west.

Although most farmers now truck their animals, the practice persists of droving the cattle across the Kalahari plains. Herds many hundred strong kick up dust for the month-long journey, which by all accounts can turn into quite a festive event. Treks leave throughout the cooler dry season. The **cowboys** are invariably skilled San on horseback. Nowadays back-up vehicles take tents and supplies and bring back the horses. The treks move at cattle-pace and night stops are determined by watering points, kraals and boreholes along the route, about every thirty kilometres. Where there are **lions** (there aren't so many these days) fires are built all around the kraals to ward them off. The cattle can smell predators and without being corralled would stampede, leaving the drovers with days of work to recover them.

Ghanzi to Lobatse by car (4WD only) is an arduous twelve-hour journey and a route used, among others, by serious desert rally drivers, though the **Trans Kalahari Highway** has got the green light and the route is slowly being tarred. The settlements en route are all watering points with boreholes established for trekking cattle. Most have a bottle store, a bar and a general dealer. You'll need to carry petrol, water and food, although you can usually get petrol (exorbitantly priced) at KANG, the biggest village en route which has shops and a school. There's very little sign of habitation on the 280km stretch between Ghanzi and Kang, although there are some small unsignposted settlements and boreholes set back from the road. One of these, Takatshwaane, 125km from Ghanzi, is a large San settlement. The only evidence that you are there is when you cross a dry river bed and see a Roads Department Camp on the right. There's deep sand up to Kang, with the kind of ruts you pray you're not going to have to swerve out of for an oncoming vehicle. At Kang, the road forks, left takes you ultimately to Lobatse, mostly along tar, while the one on the right heads off to Tshane and Tshabong in the southern Kalahari. Southeast of Kang en route to Lobatse, is a small, cheap hotel at Mabutsane – one of the few places to stay in this part of the desert.

PART FOUR

THE

CONTEXTS

ZIMBABWE: AN HISTORICAL FRAMEWORK

Pre-colonial Zimbabwe enjoyed a political continuity unique in sub-Saharan Africa, being dominated, from the tenth century on, by a succession of Shona states. In successive centuries, the influence of these states stretched east to the coast of Mozambique and west into Botswana's desert lands. It was only in the 1890s, with the arrival of white colonists and the creation of "Rhodesia", that the country's modern boundaries were drawn.

ROCK ARCHIVES

Zimbabwe's **Stone Age** leaps the millennia through the vivid records of its **rock art**. These paintings, often finely realised, most commonly represent religion and ritual – suggesting a long-gone spiritual world that respected all living things as equal in creation. But they also give firm clues about their **hunter-gatherer** artists, depicting the bows and stone-tipped arrows of the male hunter and the digging sticks and bags of the female gatherers. Who exactly were the successors of these, the plateau's first people, remains in some dispute: some theories suggest they were San, like the remaining handful of the region's hunter-gatherers in Botswana; while others favour a people more akin to today's Bantu-speakers.

Farming was the plateau-dwellers' first social revolution – a quantum leap into a vastly different existence that was firmly established by around 200 BC. Although hunter-gatherers had mastered subsistence existence – needing no more than twenty hours a week to forage – farming provided more security and a stable lifestyle, which enabled people to accumulate produce against barren years. It was, though, the slowest of transitions. Hunter-gatherers already possessed the elements of farming, burning grass to bring new shoots to attract animals, and protecting useful plants.

Following the establishment of farming, occasional pictures of sheep appear on cave walls. People still moved about with their herds, but agriculture meant a slower, more static way of life – tilling, seeding and reaping is a lengthy process. Some discovered that ore from certain rocks could be used to make labour-saving tools, and weapons; the first **miners and ironworkers** were farmers. And then came trade, with people who had access to iron (and later gold) bartering their minerals for other goods.

LINEAGES

Hunter-gathering supported only small nomadic bands, but farming culture gradually created more complex societies as people began to map relationships within communities, and to trace back family trees to their first ancestors – the spiritual guardians of each piece of land.

Late **Iron Age** people lived in collections of homesteads, which belonged to **lineages.** Each lineage had its own ancestor, but there was a single major figure – the big daddy of them all. The more direct the relationship to him the more senior the lineage, so daughters from senior lineages began to command a high bride price, as they brought a large number of cattle into the lineage.

In questions of marriage, therefore, the balance of trade favoured the senior lineage every time, and these groups, in consequence, could become quite rich. Around the **tenth century**, the first **towns** emerged in the cattle-lands of Zimbabwe's southwest and in eastern Botswana. The lands here were too dry for horticulture, but great for cattle with plenty of grass and mopane trees – juicy leaves perfect for the dry season when grass died back.

THE SHONA STATES

It was from the senior lineages that the large herd-owning **ruling classes** came. Their wealth and power catapulted traditional society from subsistence to a patronage system that could muster large armies to build the great public works of the plateau – the **stone-walled towns**. Few other sub-Saharan countries have such imposing evidence left by powerful states over the last millennium.

THE ZIMBABWE STATE

Toward the end of the eleventh century Iron Age Shona-speakers settled at the hilltop site of **Great Zimbabwe**, building a village of pole and dagha huts. Despite large cattle herds, they weren't inordinately wealthy, but by the fourteenth century this had changed. The lineage **herds** had grown to unprecedented numbers and so the power of the rulers had increased. They began to organise their subjects into armies of builders, herders and soldiers.

Although the wealth of Zimbabwe's rulers rested on cattle, the state also developed a **gold trade**, trading on the Mozambique coast. Zimbabwe armies policed the trade and the rulers charged a toll, supplementing their growing riches, which they used to build the famous walls – today's national symbol.

Great Zimbabwe itself became the largest regional centre, with over ten thousand inhabitants. The reason for its eventual **decline** is another disputed issue, but current evidence favours the theory that the area suffered from overpopulation – too many people, too much farming and too many cattle. The land lost its fertility and by the sixteenth century the site of Great Zimbabwe was deserted.

THE MUTAPA STATE – AND THE FIRST PORTUGUESE ENCOUNTERS

The **Mutapa State**, a looser confederation of ruling families, rose as the Zimbabwe State was sliding, to span the fifteenth to twentieth centuries. Better placed for the gold trade, near the northern gold-fields and the coast, they surrounded their homesteads with stone walls.

Written accounts of the state come from **Portuguese** sailors, who first heard of central African empires, gold and untold riches, from Arab traders. The Portuguese had a tendency to exaggerate, perhaps to encourage backers to give financial support to expeditions – one very apocryphal story had the adventurer Vasco da Gama, dubbing the Zambezi "the river of good omens" in 1497, after encountering gold-dust-laden Arab dhows in its Indian Ocean delta.

By 1505 the Portuguese were in control of Sofala on the Mozambique coast, and soon their attention turned to the hinterland, heralding a history of **colonial interference** that was to last over the next four centuries.

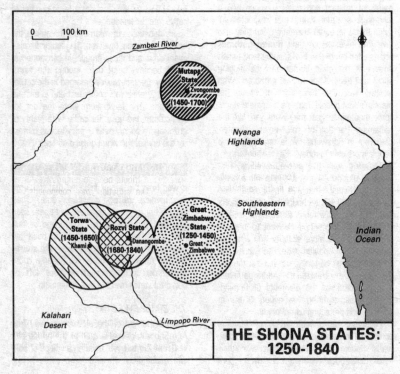

THE SHONA STATES: 1250-1840

In Zimbabwe the Mutapas were the first to taste contact with Europeans; sweet at first, it was soon to sour. The whites were enthralled by tales of Mutapa wealth, the elite garbed in gold and silver embroidered cloths and so over-laden with precious bangles that they could hardly move their arms. Their wealth was in fact quite great, stemming from their ability to impose taxes on gold-seekers, ivory-hunters and traders.

Mutually beneficial **barter** between the two powers took place until the Portuguese decided they could no longer brook Swahili competition. In 1569 an army of one thousand led by **Francisco Barreto** set out from Portugal to invade the Mutapa State. Defeated by disease and starvation, the expedition flopped before it arrived, but toward the end of the sixteenth century the Portuguese seized a new opportunity to gain a foothold when they took advantage of successive ruling-class splits in Mutapa. In exchange for military help they eventually gained a free hand in the territory.

In 1629 the Mutapa (or king) became a **vassal of the Portuguese** monarchy, and the Portuguese occupied several towns along the Zambezi, notably Tete and Sena. At its height, their influence extended along the river beyond Kariba and south of Harare to the Kadoma gold-fields. Territory was divided into *prazos* – mini-fiefdoms controlled by ruling families. Each of these formed private armies and raided the countryside, taking slaves and land, and build-ing markets all over the north.

This first colonial nightmare ended, however, in 1663, when the Mutapa was assassinated and the new ruler rejected Portuguese domination. Forming an alliance with the Rozvi Changamire in the southwest, he drove the Portuguese from Zimbabwe, and they never returned as a credible political force. When they did, it was to Manyika on sufferance of the Manyika rulers, and they had to content themselves with trading through African go-betweens.

For the next 250 years Portuguese influence in the region was very tenuous, with small stretches of coast and a handful of islands coming under their control. It was only after the Berlin Congress of 1884 that they succeeded in getting recognition for the colony of Mozambique and set up an administration to control the entire territory.

TORWA AND THE ROZVI

In its declining years, Great Zimbabwe was eclipsed by a new state – the **Torwa** – in the southwest around present Bulawayo.

As an off-shoot of Great Zimbabwe, the Torwa State carried the tradition of **stone construction** to new heights. The ruling dynasty kept apart from the peasantry, inter-marrying only within the ruling classes and setting up centres throughout the country. Its *mambos* or rulers wore spun cotton garments and gold, copper and ivory jewellery. They taxed peasants, traders and farmers, and controlled most of the state's cattle. By the seventeenth century, though, the economy was crumbling – mainly through a slowdown in gold exports – and the rulers began to lose their grip. The building of stone walls stagnated, coming to a complete standstill by the end of the century.

There is uncertainty about the origins of the next dynasty, the **Rozvi**. They may have been invaders from the north who conquered the Torwa, or perhaps just a new Torwa dynasty under a different name. Their capital was at **Danangombe** – the walls are still standing – and although the size of the state was rela-tively small, the extent of their influence was considerable. The state's wealth was based on its powerful army and its capacity to exact trib-ute even beyond its own borders. This differed from the Mutapa State which was far more dependent on trade.

Rozvi **military power** took it into Mutapa territory where it attacked the ruling dynasty in the 1680s. In the nineteenth century Rozvi might began to weaken from within, and the exaction of tribute became progressively more difficult. The situation was compounded by waves of invading Nguni, and culminated in **Zwangendaba**'s hordes sweeping through on their way north.

THE MFECANE

Through the preceding millennium, Zimbabwe's affairs had been determined largely by the Shona-speakers, who dominated the plateau. At the onset of the nineteenth century, however, an explosion of external events rever-berated into the region, bringing the first seri-ous threat from **non-Shona elements**. Over the Drakensberg Mountains, in what is now

South Africa's Natal Province, a storm was brewing among the small **Nguni** groups who, as a result of land hunger — aggravated by the encroachment of white settlers — had entered into a virtually constant state of feud with each other.

In 1818, **Shaka**, the illegitimate son of a minor Nguni chief, turned his father's small **Zulu** clan into the most powerful fighting machine in southern Africa. A shrewd commander and ruthless absolute ruler, he tolerated no opposition and during the 1820s his army swept through the subcontinent, conquering and expanding his power base. Many clans fled, hence the term *mfecane*, meaning "forced migration".

Some of these were the marauding hordes that passed through Shona territory, pillaging but enforcing few lasting changes on the communities they encountered. But two of these raiding armies stayed, exerting very much longer-term effects. In the east, Shoshangane set up the iron-handed **Gaza State**, but it was the **Ndebele State** that made the most lasting impression.

THE NDEBELE STATE

In 1822 an army of the **Khumalo** clan, under their ruler, Mzilikazi, left Natal to escape Shaka's conquests. Wherever they went, however, they were pursued by the unrelenting Zulu *impi*, which moved throughout the region, raiding well into Zimbabwe. Unable to settle and farm, these refugees, who became the Ndebele, were forced to rely on seizing cattle and food as they marched. After years of wandering, which took them to Botswana and brought them into conflict with the advancing Boers in the Transvaal, they eventually established a capital at **Bulawayo** in the 1840s.

Mzilikazi, who was succeeded by his son, Lobengula, in 1870, had forged a united state from disparate elements. Although at core Zulu, his **Ndebele State** comprised Nguni, Sotho, Tswana and Shona people, picked up on the Khumalo's northward migration. Far from resenting cultural eclipse, Shona youth was eager to be identified with this go-ahead society, to the extent that in 1888 a missionary, Reverend Knothe, commented that:

They have completely taken over the language, costume and customs of the Ndebele and do not want to know that they are descendants of the Karanga [Shona speakers].

Although Ndebele status was affected by ethnic origins, Mzilikazi wisely ensured that all captives were fully incorporated into the state. Women and children went to live with Ndebele families to learn their language and customs and had the same rights and duties as everyone else. When the boys were ready to marry the king provided them with the necessary bridewealth cattle.

Most Ndebele were cattle-farmers living in homesteads, others were in the powerful army, which ensured Ndebele control well beyond the farms of its own people. A **tribute system** operated, whereby small states on the periphery signified their dependence on the Ndebele by offering food and cattle. The intention was not to cripple the subject states, which retained most of their wealth, but rather to symbolise their client status. The relationship was symbiotic. The Ndebele wanted peaceful states on their doorstep in which they could graze their cattle, but at the same time their army offered protection against hostile raiders to the smaller states.

THE GAZA INVASIONS

Also in the 1820s, **Shoshangane** fled north with one of the sections of the Zulu-shattered Ndwandwe (Nguni) State, eventually settling amid the **Ndau** (Shona dialect speakers) and completely disrupting their culture. Gaza words passed into the Ndau language, while Ndau men were conscripted into the army and women became Gaza wives.

Unlike the Ndebele, who successfully incorporated their conquered subjects into their state, the **Gaza** were themselves eventually absorbed. They treated the people they conquered as second and third class citizens. Subjects such as the Ndau from the southern Eastern Highlands, who accepted Gaza domination, were simply exploited, while others such as Mozambique's Tsonga and Chopi were often sold as slaves to the Portuguese.

A huge area of eastern Zimbabwe and parts of Mozambique were harassed and controlled by the small, permanent **Gaza army**. As in society, the forces were separated according to class. The elite were all born Nguni, while conquered people formed cannon-fodder regiments. In the end the Gaza State was brought down by internal divisions and finally succumbed to **Portuguese** forces in 1895, becoming part of their Mozambique colony.

The Gazas' main mark on the area was the title *Shangaan*, a corruption of Shoshangane's name, which became prized by people of the east. Gaza identity was very attractive to many subjects, especially the youth, some of whom adopted Nguni clan names – which continue today. In military matters Gaza influence was total; the Ndau completely changed their uniform, and adopted the methods of their conquerors.

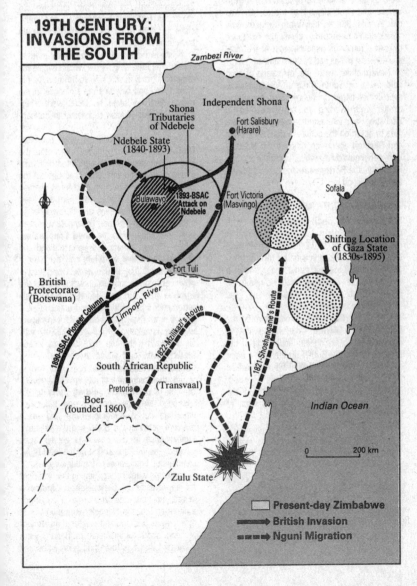

19TH CENTURY: INVASIONS FROM THE SOUTH

Zambezi River

Independent Shona

Shona Tributaries of Ndebele

Fort Salisbury (Harare)

Ndebele State (1840-1893)

Bulawayo

1893-BSAC Attack on Ndebele

Fort Victoria (Masvingo)

Sofala

Shifting Location of Gaza State (1830s-1895)

Fort Tuli

British Protectorate (Botswana)

1890-BSAC Pioneer Column

Limpopo River

1822-Mzilikazi's Route

1821-Shoshangane's Route

South African Republic

Pretoria (Transvaal)

Boer (founded 1860)

Indian Ocean

0   200 km

Zulu State

☐ Present-day Zimbabwe
➡ British Invasion
⬛⬛➡ Nguni Migration

BRITAIN'S PRIVATISED INVASIONS

A pair of British hunter-adventurers, Henry Hartley and Frederick Courteney Selous, arrived in Zimbabwe in the 1870s, possibly on the trail of Portuguese stories of gold wealth. They were to find the remains of hundreds of **gold mines**, and wrote home that the country was rich in gold. But, as they were to learn, gold mines didn't necessarily signify the existence of gold – rather its removal; most of the local shallow-cast mines had been exhausted.

Nevertheless, with the discovery of vast gold reefs on South Africa's Witwatersrand, speculators began to believe that something similar was waiting to be discovered in Zimbabwe, and interested parties gathered like flies to get in on the action. In the 1880s **Boer** and **German** agents approached the Ndebele king, Lobengula. Meanwhile, along the Eastern Highlands, the **Portuguese**, too, were surreptitiously muscling in.

THE BRITISH SOUTH AFRICA COMPANY

In the end it was **Cecil John Rhodes** – with the backing of Britain – who gained control of the area north of the Limpopo. Britain was eager to block any expansion by rival powers, while Rhodes, for his part, having made a fortune in the Kimberley diamond mines in South Africa, but losing out on the Witwatersrand, saw rich pickings.

With powerful friends, Rhodes formed the **British South Africa Company**, with the express brief to exploit the lands north of the Limpopo. From the British government's point of view this was a convenient bit of privatised foreign policy, which they naturally endorsed. The BSAC was granted a Royal Charter for the territory north of South Africa and west of Mozambique, to

make treaties, promulgate laws, maintain a police force, acquire new concessions, make land grants and carry on any lawful trade, commerce or business.

Rhodes's long-term plan was to occupy Zimbabwe, Zambia and Malawi – but his approach was gradual and intent on avoiding immediate confrontation with Lobengula's powerful Ndebele State. In 1890, his private army, the **"Pioneer Column"**, marched north to the site of Harare, skirting lands under Lobengula's control. Immediately the settlers set about looking for gold, which never materialised; many turned to farming instead, taking over traditional Shona lands.

LOBENGULA – AND WAR

Ndebele influence over large parts of Zimbabwe was, at this time, immense. So strong, in fact, that businessmen and politicians in South Africa concluded that it would have to be removed, and by means of war.

A shrewd statesman, **Lobengula** tried to concede as little as possible while keeping his regiments firmly in check. War, he knew, would bring to an end Ndebele pre-eminence in the region. But the forces he faced were insurmountable and Rhodes succeeded in outmanoeuvring him.

Several times Lobengula was deceived. **Moffat**, an agent of Rhodes, presented the king with a treaty which prohibited him from making further agreements with anyone but the British. He refused to sign, but Moffat claimed otherwise and the phoney document was used to keep out the Germans and Portuguese. To tighten the noose further, Lobengula was then lured into agreeing to the **Rudd Concession**, which allowed miners into Matebeleland and provided the means for white entrenchment in Mashonaland. The British made empty verbal promises that the concession would protect the Ndebele from further colonial pressure: only ten miners would prospect and notices would be put in all English and South African papers warning Europeans off. But the BSAC was simply waiting for the right time to invade Matabeleland – an action that began, with a fairly routine event, in 1893.

The first act in the drama was Lobengula's sending of a **Ndebele raiding party** to the Masvingo area, to punish Shona tributaries who had cut a telegraph wire and made mischief between the BSAC and the Ndebele. Similar raids in the past had always been ignored – as was this at first by the local BSAC commander, one Leander Starr Jameson.

But some weeks after, judging the time right for an invasion of Matabeleland, **Jameson** seized on the incident, told the British authorities that the Ndebele were planning to attack white settlers, and mustered an army of pioneers and black mercenaries. Reports were fabricated that this force had been ambushed by Ndebele troops, and the British sent in a powerful battalion from neighbouring Botswana. Jameson, eager to see the destruction of Lobengula's kingdom and concerned that his hands would be tied by less partial forces, hastened to pre-empt their arrival.

Aware of the impending disaster, Lobengula desperately tried to avoid war. Delegates were sent to Cape Town, stressing his **desire for peace** – but they were intercepted and shot. Furious at this, Lobengula, according to one account, appeared before his war-ready troops repeatedly shouting the salute, *Bayete*, before thrusting his assegai to the ground. Its shaft broke – a bad omen.

The **battle**, when it came, was swift. As Ndebele troops approached to meet the advancing enemy they were mercilessly mowed down by machine guns. Their capital, **Bulawayo**, was subsequently razed, and Lobengula fled into the wilderness, where he died the following year.

THE FIRST CHIMURENGA

The Shona had not been conquered by the British in the way that the Ndebele were, and at first welcomed the settlers. **Trade** took place and successful Shona farmers generated sufficient surplus to feed the whites and earn themselves a tidy profit. Only after the gold dream turned to dust did the newcomers start farming seriously, nabbing any fertile land they fancied. For the Shona too, the daydream was short-lived – the happy days of trade and neighbourliness turned into a reality of domination and eviction.

COMPANY LAW

Within years, both Ndebele and Shona found themselves trespassers in their own land, evicted by whites, and subject to British South Africa Company decrees.

Both peoples saw their rights whittled away as they were relegated to dry, infertile and tsetse-infested reserves. The Company, meanwhile, seized the majority of **Ndebele cattle** as spoils of war, claiming it had belonged to Lobengula. In fact the herd had been held in trust by the king on behalf of the whole community. Cattle were more than a treasury, resting at the very core of social relations, and

this seizure was an attack on Ndebele culture and society itself. What cattle remained to them were wiped out in the 1895 Rinderpest epidemic, many of them shot by white ranchers eager to stem the spreading disease. The sight of whites randomly potting the dwindling Ndebele herds rankled.

And if that wasn't enough, the colonials sought ways to bring the blacks into the cash economy. Only the payment of pittance wages made it possible for the whites to make the worn-out mines profitable, so a **hut tax** was devised to flush out the "idle natives" from their subsistence existence and into the job market. Blacks saw their traditions under fire and their way of life crumbling.

"LET THEM EAT DOGS"

Speech by Chief Somabulana, rebel leader and spokesman at the 1896 Matopos *indaba* with Rhodes:

We, the Amandabili, the sons of Kumalo, the Izulu, Children of the Stars; we are no dogs! You came, you conquered. The strongest takes the land. We accepted your rule. We lived under you. But not as dogs! If we are to be dogs it is better to be dead.

I myself once visited Bulawayo. I came to pay my respects to the Chief Magistrate. I brought my indunas with me, and my servants. I am a chief. I am expected to travel with attendants and advisers. I came to Bulawayo early in the morning, before the sun had dried the dew, and I sat down before the Court House, sending messages to the Chief Magistrate that I waited to pay my respects to him. And so I sat until the evening shadows were long.

I sent again to the Chief Magistrate and told him that I did not wish to hurry him in an unmannerly way; I would wait his pleasure; but my people were hungry; and when the white men visited me it was my custom to kill that they might eat. The answer from the Chief Magistrate was that the town was full of dogs; dog to dog; we might kill those and eat them if we could catch them. So I left Bulawayo that night; and when next I tried to visit the Chief Magistrate it was with my impis behind me; no soft words in their mouths; but the assegai in their hands. Who blames me?

(Quoted in Terence Ranger: *The Nineteenth Century in Southern Rhodesia*)

UPRISING

In 1896, when Rhodes's hatchet man Jameson staged an **abortive coup** against the Boer-controlled South African Republic, a large number of the British South Africa Police (the Company's army) were captured. Spotting their chance, the Ndebele initiated the **First Chimurenga** (liberation war), attacking and killing white farmers and traders.

Much to the surprise of whites, many **Shona** joined forces with the Ndebele, having developed a greater resentment towards the settlers than to their former overlords. The Shona **spirit mediums** of Kaguvi and Nehanda moved around the country inspiring the battle to regain ancestral lands. Whites fled to the forts in the main settlements.

For a while chiefs again controlled their traditional domains, but British reinforcements were sent to crush the Ndebele – a war that proved costly for both sides. Villages and crops were destroyed, while at the same time the conflict was a drain on BSAC coffers. Eventually, both parties came together in the infamous **Matopos *indabas*** – an agreement made between Rhodes and Ndebele *indunas* (captains). Rhodes made all sorts of promises, including the return of all occupied land; none was kept.

With the Ndebele subdued, the BSAC set about putting down the **Shona rebels**. Unlike the Ndebele, the Shona lacked political unity, and their chiefdoms sometimes sided out of opportunism with the British, happy to see rivals cut down to size by the settlers. Clinically, systematically and with total ruthlessness the colonial forces moved through Mashonaland, picking off the disunited groups one by one. By 1897 it was all over, though on the scaffold the defiant **medium of Nehanda** prophesied that "my bones will rise". For her, final victory was certain.

RHODESIA – LIMITED COMPANY

Until 1923 the **British South Africa Company** (BSAC) ran **Rhodesia** – as the colonists had dubbed the territories of Mashonaland and Matabeleland – and virtually everything in it.

The Company, and its associated white settlers and immigrants, had hopes that these territories would become a "white country" along the lines of Australia or New Zealand, or even South Africa. Blacks were regarded as somewhat incidental. But in the eighty years following the British takeover Rhodesia's white population reached only 270,000, alongside a black majority that grew from 700,000 in the 1920s to nearly eight million at Independence.

SELL-OFF: THE 1923 CONSTITUTION

The BSAC had anticipated huge profits from their African fiefdom, but by the 1920s these had signally failed to materialise, and they began looking for a way to rid themselves of the albatross. The solution was a referendum offering whites a new constitution. The recommendation of the British High Commission and the Company was to incorporate the territory into the more profitable Union of South Africa, which in 1910 had brought together the two British colonies of the Cape and Natal with the defeated pair of Boer republics.

The idea of being dominated by Afrikaners, however, horrified the Rhodesians, who voted instead for an option of so-called responsible government in a new state that became known as **Southern Rhodesia**. In effect, "responsible government" meant that they were responsible to no one but themselves. Although the British authorities technically reserved the right to veto any legislation that affected African rights, this was never invoked – despite decades of hut taxes, segregation, and land-filching legislation.

The new constitution maintained power in the hands of whites while paying lip service to the idea of a non-racial democracy – a **qualified franchise** based on British citizenship and a minimum annual income that worked to keep most Africans out of the polling booths. With insufficient numbers to maintain control simply through white administrators, the government set about creating a network of sympathetic chiefs by installing puppets and unseating those who didn't go along with official policies.

WEALTH AND INEQUALITY: THE LAND ISSUE

Rhodesia's mineral wealth proved a disappointment to early settlers, and soon after the turn of the century white immigrants looked instead to rewards from **large-scale farming**. The country, in their wake, became one of the most unequal in the world.

A BLACK WORKING CLASS: THE MINES

The Rhodesians' great white myth – developed at the turn of the century and maintained to the present – was that blacks were better off under them because of their modernising influence. Yet, while it's true that colonialism brought benefits like modern medicine and technology, at the same time it robbed Africans of a way of life that had worked successfully. Poverty was not the natural condition of Africa that the colonials fondly imagined they were improving, and was in fact created by the destruction of the traditional economy.

At the root of these problems lay the land question and the deliberate, forcible creation of a black working class. Cheap black labour was the backbone of white commercial activity, and, through taxes and the restriction of African access to farmlands, blacks were forced out of communal farming into selling their labour as workers. When even that policy failed in the first decade of this century, blacks were simply rounded up and press-ganged into the mines – a system known as *chibaro*.

The **Rhodesian mines** were more notorious than even those in South Africa. Because they were extensively mined-out, only very low wages could make them profitable – and working in them was to be avoided at all costs. Workers gave the mines their own coded names, warning of what could be expected. Celtic Mine was known as Sigebengu (*thugs are in charge*), Old Chum Mine was called Makombera (*you're closed in*) and other names included Maplanki (*planks for punishment*), and Mtshalwana (*you will fight one another*).

THE LAND APPORTIONMENT ACT

The **1930 Land Apportionment Act** set aside half of the country for whites – territory that invariably included the good fertile lands. Enclaves of poor land, meanwhile, became the so-called **"Native Reserves"** (later called the Tribal Trust Lands – many still refer to them as *TTLs*). Land pressure combined with infertile soils gradually forced many more people off the land and into the white economy.

It was from observing the destruction of the reserves through overcultivation that many whites later drew the conclusion that Africans were bad farmers, forgetting that blacks had farmed these lands effectively for millennia, some accumulating tidy profits by selling off

their surplus to white settlers at the turn of the century. For settler farmers, things were pretty rosy, with huge farms and help from the Land Bank to assist commercial agriculture – plus revenue from taxes extracted from Africans.

FEDERATION

Following the 1923 constitution, the influence of the BSAC gradually waned. The mines were bought by the government in 1933 and the railways taken over by South Africa shortly after World War II. Also, despite black opposition, the **Central African Federation** of Southern Rhodesia, Northern Rhodesia (Zambia) and Nyasaland (Malawi) was forged, providing the means for Southern Rhodesia to cream off the mineral riches to the north. The copper wealth of Northern Rhodesia did a lot for Southern Rhodesia, accounting for much of modern Zimbabwe's infrastructure – roads, hospitals and public works such as Lake Kariba.

Through its brief life, the Federation was dogged by black opposition, especially from nationalist movements in Northern Rhodesia and Nyasaland, which brought its collapse in 1963, followed by the independence of the two northernmost members the following year.

NO LEFT TURN

In 1951, in an attempt to counter the overcrowding caused by the Land Apportionment Act, the **Land Husbandry Act** was passed, causing further resentment. To make space for thousands evicted from white-designated lands, the common grazing areas in the "Native Reserves" were divided into smallholdings of private land. Households were forced to reduce their herds to six head of cattle – most small-scale African farmers ended up worse off than before.

During the 1950s, however, there seemed the possibility of liberalisation, as **Garfield Todd**'s ruling United Rhodesia Party discussed the idea of black suffrage. Although Todd saw liberalisation essentially as a way to secure a peaceful place for whites, the electorate perceived him as a traitor and booted him out in the 1958 election. While the rest of the country drifted to the right, his sympathies for the nationalists grew and he ended up house-arrested by Ian Smith in the 1960s.

Each government after 1958 was more reactionary than its predecessor, not only putting

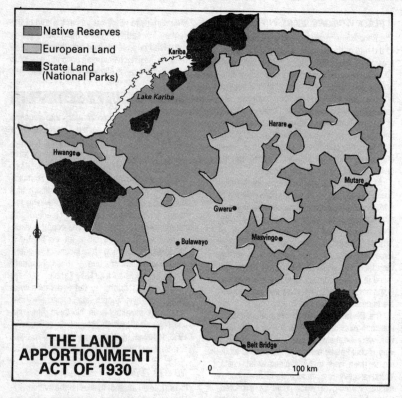

Native Reserves
European Land
State Land
(National Parks)

**THE LAND
APPORTIONMENT
ACT OF 1930**

0   100 km

the brakes on African advancement, but shifting into reverse gear. The crown prince of white domination was **Ian Smith**, whose Rhodesia Front Party led the country down the dead-end road to UDI in 1965. His "thousand year republic" barely hobbled its way to mid-adolescence.

NATIONALISM: THE GATHERING STORM

In the early years of colonisation, black campaigners hoped to use **persuasion** to get the British authorities to give them rights. Before 1923 there was little activity apart from unsuccessful demands by Lobengula's son, Nyamanda, for the return of his father's cattle. In the 1920s, though, a proliferation of pressure groups were set up to represent middle-class black professionals. The government simply ignored what they had to say. But during the 1940s Benjamin Burombo's **African Voice Association** heralded a more militant phase,

spreading resistance among workers and peasants, demanding improved working conditions, higher wages, parliamentary representation and better education.

CONSTITUTIONALISM: THE FIFTIES

It was under the Central African Federation that a **mass nationalist movement** was born, bent on action. The first major challenge was presented by the City Youth League, formed in Harare in 1955 and later expanded into the **African National Youth League**. Its newspaper *Chapupu* was used to galvanise support – which focused on the land question. In 1956 the League organised a bus boycott in Harare against fare increases. The following year it merged with another organisation to form the **African National Congress (ANC)** under **Joshua Nkomo**.

Nkomo's ANC attempted a **broad-based approach** covering worker and peasant issues.

In the rural areas it organised resistance to unpopular measures like the Land Husbandry Act, while in the urban areas meetings and demonstrations were held. 1959 was a year of expansion and protest against the Federation, prompting Sir Edgar Whitehead's governing United Rhodesia Party to ban the organisation, declare a state of emergency, slap nearly 500 members behind bars and introduce a range of legislation to put an end to African demands. Nkomo narrowly escaped arrest because he was in Britain at the time canvassing support.

1960: ZHII, THE NDP AND ZAPU

Far from ending black political activities, this course of repression caused black frustrations to erupt in the resounding explosion of *Zhii*. The term has no direct English translation: it is basically a drastic act against an arch-enemy and signifies total annihilation, complete destruction or reduction to rubble.

A result of the largest uprising since the First Chimurenga, *Zhii* swept the cities when three leaders of the newly formed **National Democratic Party** (NDP) were arrested, and the party responded with the **Salisbury March**. The government banned all meetings, and popular outrage, involving almost 50,000 protesters, spread to Bulawayo, where workers went on strike and symbols of government were attacked. After a week, government bullets put a temporary end to *Zhii*, taking eighteen lives and leaving hundreds injured.

The Federation consequently swung into the Sixties cracking visibly at the edges. Northern Rhodesia and Nyasaland were on target for independence, but the settler government of Southern Rhodesia was intransigent on majority rule. At a conference in Britain a **constitution** was proposed giving blacks 15 seats in a 65-seat parliament. The four NDP representatives accepted the proposal, but on their return were fiercely rebuked by the domestic leadership and party rank and file. The NDP continued to organise against the government until it was banned and its assets seized in 1961.

A week later it re-emerged as the **Zimbabwe African People's Union (ZAPU)**, led by Joshua Nkomo. Sabotage replaced demonstrations, though Nkomo was still convinced that diplomatic pressure could be put on Britain to grant independence to Southern Rhodesia under a majority government. Inside the country, rural dwellers were organised in campaigns of burning the fields of unpopular farmers and destroying equipment, and others squatted white-designated unoccupied lands. In 1962 ZAPU was banned and the leadership exiled to remote rural areas for three months.

SPLITS IN THE RANKS : ZAPU AND ZANU

There was some doubt about where to go from the banning of ZAPU. Nkomo favoured the idea of setting up a government-in-exile to lobby international support, while others urged remaining inside the country and organising local action.

Under Nkomo's instructions the government-in-exile headed for Dar es Salaam only to receive a lukewarm reception from President Nyerere; they returned home. There were rumblings about Nkomo's leadership on questions of both judgement and the principle of operating from exile. After some arguments Nkomo suspended four members of the ZAPU executive: Robert Mugabe, Ndabaningi Sithole, Moton Malianga and Leopold Takawira. In 1963 this "dissident" group formed the **Zimbabwe African National Union** (ZANU), with Sithole as president and Mugabe as secretary-general.

An outbreak of fighting between the two organisations provided a convenient excuse for the government to ban them both in 1964 and to declare a state of emergency once again in some urban centres. Various top leaders were arrested, while the organisations set up headquarters in exile in Zambia and Tanzania, and began looking at broadening the struggle to all classes – and to the use of guns.

TALKING TOUGH: UDI

To pacify an increasingly alarmed white electorate, Prime Minister Ian Smith moved swiftly to demonstrate that he was made of stern stuff. Raising two fingers to the nationalists and an increasingly hostile world he issued the **Unilateral Declaration of Independence** (UDI) in 1965, promising White Rhodesians:

We have struck a blow for the preservation of justice, civilisation and Christianity and in the spirit of this belief we have this day assumed our sovereign independence. God bless you all.

Alongside this defiance of Britain, Smith refused to speak to the nationalist leaders. Instead, he installed a council of chiefs, paid by his government but which he insisted represented the people.

CHIMURENGA PHASE ONE

UDI was the signal to the nationalist organisations to begin armed action. The **Second Chimurenga** began on April 28, 1966, when seven ZANU guerillas engaged Rhodesian forces at Chinoyi – and were killed. This episode set the pattern for the next four years of commando hit-and-run actions. The guerillas were no match for the Rhodesian army and enjoyed virtually no support organisation within the country.

The following year, fighters from South Africa's ANC joined forces with ZAPU and operated for some months in Hwange National Park. A number of **ZAPU-ANC camps** were also established inside the country, but once discovered they were fairly easily destroyed by Rhodesian forces – themselves now assisted by South African units. Overall, this first phase of the war remained low-key, and continual setbacks for the nationalists served to encourage the white belief in their own invincibility.

Britain, meanwhile, despite Rhodesian intransigence, was still eager for some kind of negotiated settlement and Ian Smith and British Prime Minister Harold Wilson met on two occasions on the British warships *HMS Fearless* and *Tiger*. Wilson wanted a few more rights for blacks and moves to majority rule in some far-flung future, but Smith always maintained there would never be a black government in Rhodesia in his lifetime – or those of his children. Both meetings achieved little except to add Wilson to the Rhodesian demonology of degenerate socialist sell-outs.

THE 1969 CONSTITUTION

As the 1960s came to a close, Smith still had everything to play for. The guerillas were looking pretty impotent and British-imposed **sanctions** were a distinctly half-hearted affair – white Rhodesians could boast the boycott was actually stimulating Rhodesia's internal economy, while the flow of trade remained more or less unchanged in the five years after UDI. South Africa was openly defying sanctions and several multinational companies continued trading: with the knowledge of the British government, Shell and BP were both supplying Rhodesia with oil.

Smith tried to pre-empt any further negotiations by taking matters into his own hands. Yet another constitution was put forward, giving blacks a derisory eight elected seats in a 66-seat parliament. This was Smith's starting point for further discussions with the mother country. But Britain insisted on testing black opinion on the new dispensation prior to any further talks. **Lord Pearce** was despatched to the rebel colony to probe opinion in the cities and the remote rural areas.

Organising a response was a problem for the nationalist movement, most of whose leaders were either in jail or in exile – but it was also a golden opportunity. ZANU and ZAPU united to form an internal campaigning body under the leadership of **Bishop Muzorewa**. While Rhodesia's government pumped massive resources into cajoling a positive response from blacks, they banned ANC views from the national media. However this small chance to campaign openly was exploited by the nationalists to set up internal networks – the lifeline in the final stage of the liberation struggle.

This was, in fact, the first time in Rhodesia's history that whites heard an authentic voice of black opinion. Having always assumed that they "knew their Africans", they refused to believe the resounding "NO!" that echoed across the country. The Rhodesian Broadcasting Corporation reflected the white prejudice that they alone were in touch with reality:

> The British Government's report revealed very clearly the extreme naivety of the British approach to the test of acceptability, and of the basic assumption that uneducated tribesmen could comprehend a complicated constitutional arrangement.

THE EARLY 1970S: LEARNING THE LESSONS

The early 1970s were a time of rethinking and consolidation. The Pearce Commission findings had shown that contrary to the regime's beliefs, blacks fully comprehended the constitutional arrangement. The bush war of the Sixties had vividly demonstrated the futility of a struggle fought without popular support.

FIGHTING FISH

Early in the 1970s, **Josiah Tongogara**, the commander of ZANU's military wing, **ZANLA**, went to China for training. He came back with

Maoist doctrines and strategies, remarkably well suited to Rhodesia. As in China, the Rhodesian revolution was primarily rural, playing on decades-old resentments – the eviction from ancestral lands – and it was in these areas that the liberation movement needed support.

ZANLA adopted the Maoist principle of "guerillas swimming like fish in the water of the people" – without water they would flounder. Mutual trust and co-operation between farmers and fighters was vital to military success, while at the same time helping to spread political ideas. Young boys were recruited as *mujibas* to spy for the guerillas and carry messages; girls became *zvimbwidos*, who carried weapons and cooked for them. In the end, so effective were the networks that guerilla intelligence far outstripped the information the Rhodesian forces were gathering.

ZIPRA – ZAPU's military wing – followed a different strategy that relied less on villagers and more on infiltrated reception committees. Internal divisions hampered their implementation and their battle plan wasn't fully operational until the war was well advanced in 1977. Some observers put down ZANU's subsequent electoral success to their better wartime organisation and integration with the people.

PLAYING FOR TIME

The 1974 **Portuguese coup** and consequent liberation of Mozambique and Angola were catalysts that changed the geopolitics of southern Africa almost overnight. Suddenly the minority regimes in South Africa and Rhodesia found themselves flanked by independent black governments. The South Africans became concerned about the prospects of radical nationalists coming to power in Rhodesia and began tightening the screws on Smith to force him to the negotiating table.

In a most unlikely bout of co-operation, Kenneth Kaunda of Zambia united with South African Prime Minister John Vorster in persuading Smith to release nationalist leaders like Nkomo and Sithole. **Talks** were held in 1975 on the Victoria Falls railway bridge in the no-man's land between Rhodesia and Zambia. Smith refused to include majority rule on the agenda, and observing that there was a temporary let-up in fighting he saw little reason to pursue the talks, which collapsed like all the previous ones.

THE FINAL PHASE OF WAR

The collapse of the Victoria Falls talks heralded an intensified, no-holds-barred, armed struggle. The Smith regime's complacency about controlling the situation was soon translated into increasingly bitter repression and resistance. In 1975 the ZANU chairman, **Herbert Chitepo**, was blown up in Lusaka by the Rhodesian Central Intelligence Organisation. Amid this and other assassinations and disappearances, continued government claims to be fighting for civilisation rang extremely hollow.

PEOPLE'S WAR

In white farming areas, **guerilla attacks on farmers** increased, and a siege existence became the norm, with a whole industry developing around the supply of security equipment, fences, communications networks and an array of "counter-insurgency" devices – tripwire-triggered grenades, mine-proofed vehicles and cars bristling with elaborate "anti-terrorist" weaponry for use on the road. Throughout many areas of the country, whites could travel along main roads only in armed convoys, and even these were frequently ambushed. Guerillas also hit hotels and tourist centres, while missions and schools could be arbitrarily closed or opened by armed nationalists, who would often demand tithes from teachers in the rural areas.

In the shadowy world of attack and retribution, countless sickening **massacres** occurred – frequently at schools or mission stations – with each side blaming the other. The people who invariably suffered most were ordinary villagers trapped in a nightmare of guerilla appearances under cover of darkness and armed visits by day from the Rhodesian forces who would brutally beat and torture suspected nationalist sympathisers. The law laid down heavy sentences for people who failed to report the presence of guerillas – by the end of the war, death was routine punishment for helping armed nationalists. On the other hand the guerillas were frequently ruthless with informers and government collaborators.

TOTAL WAR

The **Rhodesian army** solution was to hold whole villages responsible for the presence of guerillas, and army units would storm settlements when nationalists were suspected of

Zimbabwe must be free!

being present. In the first half of 1977, Combined Operations HQ reported the killing of 58 "curfew breakers", 53 "running with or assisting terrorists", 13 "failing to halt" and 54 "caught in crossfire".

Official policy, as espoused by the suave right-wing Minister for Information P K van der Byl, was:

If villagers harbour terrorists, and terrorists are found running about in villages, naturally they will be bombed and destroyed in any manner which the commander on the spot considers desirable in the suitable prosecution of a successful campaign.

A different approach was the introduction of the dubiously named **protected villages** – intended to isolate the guerillas from their life-blood, the peasantry. These "PVs", supposedly to protect villagers from the nationalists, were known by their inhabitants as "the cage" – little more than concentration camps, with guards, curfews, poor sanitation and walks of up to 10km to their livestock and land. Such measures only served to increase their hatred of the government.

By 1976 things were already looking dire for the Smith regime. The war was by now costing over a million dollars a day and the close of 1978 saw over half the country under **Patriotic Front control**. White males were being called up for increasingly lengthy stints, a "Dad's Army" of everyone up to 60-year-olds found themselves involved in the war, while conscription for blacks drove many over the border to

join the nationalists. Only by employing a force of 10,000 **mercenaries** – mainly British and South Africans – was Smith able to keep things afloat.

CONTEMPLATING THE IMPOSSIBLE – ELECTIONS

Smith by now admitted that majority rule was inevitable and hoped for a negotiated settlement on his own terms, which would simultaneously bring international recognition. His favoured "moderate" candidate, **Bishop Muzorewa**, seemed a sharp choice at the time – malleable in a way which Nkomo and Mugabe were not, but also with some apparent street credibility through his part in trouncing Smith over the 1969 constitution.

Smith negotiated an internal settlement with Muzorewa and other tame black "leaders". In a 1979 ballot, which excluded ZANU and ZAPU, Muzorewa's **UANC** swept the board. In fact the bishop's campaign was financed by Smith's government, and most of the cleric's speeches and statements were written by an advertising company. Muzorewa, however, became Prime Minister, while Smith continued to control all the instruments of power: the army, police, judiciary and civil service. The now supposedly liberated country was called **Zimbabwe-Rhodesia** – jokingly called Rhobabwe by some.

No one was fooled. The accolades of international recognition failed to materialise, and nor did the expected hordes of demoralised ZANLA and ZIPRA personnel. Instead the **war** rose to an unprecedented ferocity. In May 1979 a relieved and grateful white Rhodesian public joyfully welcomed the election of Margaret Thatcher in Britain, but their elation was short-lived when she proved as unsympathetic as her "socialist" predecessors – the Iron Lady had no intention of recognising the "Internal Settlement".

LANCASTER HOUSE AGREEMENT

Under siege, the Smith-Muzorewa team found themselves in Britain, and by the end of the year were discussing a new constitution with the Nkomo-Mugabe Patriotic Front at the **Lancaster House conference**. Eager for a rapid settlement in the wake of some Conservative opposition at home, Britain's foreign secretary, Lord Carrington, succeeded in bulldozing through an agreement in just fourteen weeks.

Patriotic Front demands were toned down in the agreement. One man one vote was diluted by allowing the whites, a mere three percent of the population, to hang on to twenty of the one hundred parliamentary seats. The Rhodesian army would form the core of the new defence force and pensions would continue to be paid to civil servants, even if they left the country. Perhaps the biggest concession the PF made was to agree that unoccupied **white farmlands** could not be expropriated without compensation. As the central issue of the liberation struggle, this was – and indeed remains today – a potential post-Independence time bomb.

THE ELECTION

Following the Lancaster House Agreement, the **Patriotic Front split**, and **ZANU** and **ZAPU** launched separate campaigns. The election that followed was crammed with drama, edgy nationalist troops corralled at assembly points, while Rhodesian troops were freely deployed by the interim Governor-General. Neatly collected in one place the guerillas were sitting ducks, but a post-election **coup plan** to massacre them was jettisoned once the extent of the ZANU victory emerged. Several attempts were made on Mugabe's life, while the government and South Africa pumped enormous quantities of cash into Muzorewa's campaign – the slickest razzmatazz ever in central Africa.

Despite a four-day pro-Muzorewa rally, with bands, free food, films, prizes and all, attracting over a million people, the cool cleric failed to win more than three of the eighty seats. ZAPU took twenty, and whites, for decades accustomed to believing their own propaganda, woke on **March 4, 1980** to the nightmare of a 57-seat **ZANU landslide**.

INDEPENDENCE: THE FIRST DECADE

Independence failed to mark the beginning of the great decline that whites had predicted, as it soon became apparent that **Robert Mugabe** wasn't going to turn the protected villages into re-education camps. In stark contradiction to Bishop Muzorewa's shock-horror predictions,

churches were not turned into barracks, concentration camps and dance halls. In fact, for those whites who remained, standards of living remained at much their previous level.

A CAUTIOUS ADVANCE

The government's hands were tied by the Lancaster House Agreement, the fact that 70 percent of investment came from outside the country and by a hostile South Africa breathing over its shoulder. Mozambique's President Samora Machel had advised Mugabe to avoid alienating whites, as had happened in his country, where most of the colonists followed a vindictive scorched-earth tactic of sabotaging infrastructure before leaving for Rhodesia, South Africa or Portugal.

Acknowledging the economic importance of white farmers, reassuring noises were made. Appearing on TV on March 4, Robert Mugabe declared that

there is a place for everyone in this country. We want to ensure a sense of security for both the winners and the losers.

A year later, once things had settled and it was apparent that no hasty radical reforms were under way, Mugabe, on a visit to Britain, was asked whether he was heading toward a "new Kenya" or a "new Mozambique", to which he replied "a new Zimbabwe", indicating that no rigid ideological moulds would guide the way.

Minority representatives, from ZAPU and the white community, were brought into the cabinet and the minimum wage for farm workers was rapidly raised by 50 percent, but industrial workers made fewer gains. While moves were made to reassure white farmers and foreign investors, other efforts were made to Africanise Zimbabwe. Segregation was ended, education was enormously extended and free health care was provided to low earners – most of the population.

Zimbabwe raved into the 1980s, with Bob Marley offering his final performance at the **Independence celebrations** on April 17, 1980. The first years were euphoric and the London *Times* reported that the economy had taken off "like a rocket", with GDP advancing at eight percent for two successive years following the nil growth of the final Smith years. But by 1982 growth fell to zero and the precarious national unity began to fracture.

DISSIDENTS

In the ZAPU stronghold of **Matabeleland** there were rumblings of discontent and fighting broke out between ZANU and ZAPU supporters. ZIPRA guerillas loyal to ZAPU began drifting back to the bush, insisting that they were continuing the struggle for socialism against capitalism and white economic power. When an arms cache was found on Joshua Nkomo's farm, relations between the nationalist parties were severely soured and Nkomo was dropped from the cabinet.

There were renewed attacks on white farmers and, for a couple of years, it looked like the country would again be torn apart by civil war. In sinister moves that looked like a carbon copy of Smith tactics, the government insisted that the dissidents were simply armed gangsters, and refused any negotiations. The ruthless Korean-trained **Fifth Brigade** was sent in to put down the rebels, and thousands of civilians were killed in brutal attempts to flush out the dissidents. Some estimates put the Matabeleland death toll as high as 20,000.

The repression only served to strengthen ZAPU support in Matabeleland, and the government realised the dangers of a tactic that played into the hands of a South Africa eager to export destabilising wars to its neighbours. Mugabe admitted the error and began talks with Nkomo.

In 1987 the two **parties merged**, although some felt that it was more a case of ZANU swallowing the opposition. Nkomo was given a senior position and Mugabe was upgraded to executive president. By May 1988 the dissidents had given themselves up under an **amnesty**, and all attacks have ceased since then. Emerging from years in the bush, Mhkwananzi, a dissident spokesman declared:

Disunity does not pay. We have gone on operations twice, first against the white colonisers and then against the party. We have liberated everybody and now we must forge ahead with our lives.

THE LATE 1980S: UNITY

Any fears that the effective **one-party state** brought about by the merger of the two main parties would close the door on healthy criticism were rapidly dispelled in the late 1980s. There was uproar in parliament over accusations of **corruption** at *Air Zimbabwe*, with some MPs maintaining that money ought to be spent on buses for the people rather than planes. The usually tame press published articles attacking the government for professing socialism while pursuing capitalism for the elite. There were frustrations, too, over the pace of reform with the pre-colonial inequities still remaining firmly in place.

In 1988, the Bulawayo-based *Chronicle* newspaper itself became the centre of the news by breaking a corruption scandal linking senior cabinet ministers with distribution malpractices at the Willowvale car assembly plant. The so-called **Willowgate scandal** created popular outrage, in spite of threats against the *Chronicle* from the Minister of Defence, Enos Nkala. It was in fact Nkala who eventually ended up getting the boot, along with four other ministers.

On the University of Zimbabwe campus, students joined in the protests over government corruption, but were quelled, first by police and then by the removal of grants from student leaders. Believing that the president was on their side, with his "leadership code" aimed at keeping the government clean, they watched him return from a foreign trip to rebuke them for childish behaviour. Only after apologising for embarrassing him were the grants restored. Meanwhile, support gathered for the rabble-rousing freelance parliamentary opposition led by **Edgar Tekere** – who was expelled from ZANU in 1988.

But the biggest obstacle of all remained **South Africa**, which was constantly making veiled threats against Zimbabwe, and occasionally sending in agents to bomb alleged ANC personnel. Most of Zimbabwe's trade went through its southern neighbour's ports, and South Africa was able to use this fact to apply pressure. At the same time, moves were made to shift trade to the Mozambique port of Beira, Zimbabwe deploying 10,000 troops in Mozambique to defend the **Beira corridor** railroad. As a result, South African-backed **Renamo** (MNR) rebels declared war on Zimbabwe. Although there have been tentative peace moves in Mozambique, at the end of the 1980s MNR activity inside Zimbabwe continued with raids for supplies on peasants in the Eastern Highlands.

PROSPECTS FOR THE 1990s

If Zimbabwe kicked off the 1980s in a mood of euphoria and wild optimism, the 1990s began as the decade of disillusion and discontent. In the first ten years of independence the government made remarkable headway in improving conditions for ordinary people. Health care was made more accessible, average life expectancy rose and infant mortality fell; free primary school education was provided and for many people wages increased.

By the end of the 1980s, however, the country faced a series of economic problems. Dissatisfaction with the government found expression in **strikes** and demonstrations by nurses, students and trade unionists. When a "student" anti-corruption meeting was banned in October 1989, **Morgan Tsvangirai**, leader of the Zimbabwe Congress of Trade Unions, spoke out against the "naked use of force to suppress the growing disenchantment of the masses over the rising cost of living, transport problems, unemployment, destitution and other negative socio-economic developments". Tsvangirai was later arrested for unspecified reasons.

The hottest issue, however, is the **land question**, which remains unresolved more than a decade after liberation. The Lancaster House Agreement failed to make funds available to buy out white farms for redistribution to small-scale farmers and there have already been rumblings of dissatisfaction among some landless ex-combatants, who feel betrayed by the revolution. In its first decade in power, Mugabe's government only managed to **resettle** 52,000 families, less than a third of the 162,000 targeted for the first three years following Independence. In March 1990 Mugabe announced that the government was drafting a plan to provide for the landless, but at the same time he assured nervous white property-owners that the process would be fair. Under the Lancaster House Agreement, Zimbabwe's constitution ensured that for a decade after Independence the government could buy only land that was offered for sale.

Mugabe announced, as a prelude to the March 1990 elections, that the government was planning to amend this restriction to coincide with the tenth anniversary of Independence on April 19, 1990. For Mugabe the heart of the election campaign was to gain a mandate for his cherished ideal of establishing a one-party state, and, aware of the importance of the land issue, he hoped to capture vital rural support.

THE 1990 ELECTION

In the event, the 1990 election campaign was an ugly affair. As Edgar Tekere had promised, his fledgling **ZUM** (Zimbabwe Unity Movement) fought the election, standing on a capitalist and multi-party ticket. Small and poorly funded, it was never a serious threat to ZANU, though, surprisingly, Mugabe seemed to take the opposition threat very seriously. One of the grimmest series of events centred on the Gweru North constituency, where vice-president Simon Muzenda was locked in a tight campaign against ZUM's Patrick Kombayi. On the Saturday before the ballot Kombayi suffered a sharp setback when Mugabe issued a presidential proclamation altering the electoral boundaries to exclude his stronghold. Later that week Kombayi was shot and seriously wounded. Several other ZUM candidates withdrew from contests in other constituencies.

The voting failed to live up to the excitement promised by the campaigning. As was widely expected, ZANU won a massive victory, taking 116 of the 119 contested seats to ZUM's mere two. In the presidential race against Tekere, Mugabe took 78 percent of the votes cast. But the most powerful statement of the poll was apathy – with around half the electorate failing to vote.

Mugabe described his victory as a mandate for the establishment of a **one-party state**. But across Africa the trend was in the opposite direction. In Eastern Europe the domino theory was working in reverse and one-party regimes were successively collapsing. When Mugabe put the idea to the ZANU Central Committee it was roundly defeated.

The real issue for Zimbabwe was the problem of **growth** and **job creation**. In conjunction with the IMF and World Bank, the government unveiled the five-year **Economic Structural Adjustment Programme** in October 1991. The plan, known in Zimbabwe by its acronym *Esap*, sought to liberalise the economy and make imports easier, hence rebuilding the country's aging infrastructure. It marked the Mugabe government's final retreat from socialism.

The most visible effect of the plan has been the appearance of previously unavailable imported goods. The plan appears to be working for business and particularly the tourist industry, which is now able to modernise itself. Less visible is the really serious hardship caused to ordinary people, for whom maize meal and bread, not *Kodacolor Gold*, is the big issue.

Esap was inspired by a monetarist penchant for slashing government spending. This meant a major reversal of ZANU policies for improving living conditions through public services. Free education ended and the public health care system ceased to deliver affordable care. For example, fees for maternity wards rose by 300 percent in two years. The lifting of price controls saw the cost of staple foods rocket. According to some analysts, living standards fell below those under the Smith regime of the mid-1970s.

The government argued that *Esap* was short-term pain in the interests of long-term gain. But its timing could not have been worse. The launching of the plan coincided with the most severe **drought** for a century. Dams became puddles and the "great, grey, green, greasy Limpopo" was reduced to a dirty, desperate, dry dustbowl. Zimbabwe, once the grain basket of the region, struggled in the grip of a **famine** in which two million lives were at risk.

The seriousness of the situation was as much due to failures of government policy as natural disaster. With the approval of the IMF, Zimbabwe had sold off its contingency maize supplies to pay off the interest on its debt. Maize had to be re-imported to feed the starving – at a considerably higher price.

In 1992 after a visit to her homeland, Doris Lessing wrote that "this year may make or break Zimbabwe: bring down a successful country . . . Meanwhile it is only June, with five months to go until the rains." In the dry lowveld wildlife began to die off and farmers were forced to shoot starving cattle. The country's tobacco crop (a major forex earner) was devasated, maize (the staple food) withered, and the entire national sugar plantation was wiped out.

At the end of the year relief did come. 1993 brought normal rains – and respite. But the thirsty dams could well need a decade to fill up. To restore the country's planatations and herds will take about three to four years. Which, according to Ministers, is about when *Esap* will begin to bite. The mid-1990s could be crucial for Zimbabwe, and the nail-biting question remains: can the government deliver the promises of improved living conditions through *Esap* or is the country going down a path of gradual decay ?

BOTSWANA: AN HISTORICAL FRAMEWORK

The looming presence of South Africa is a recurrent theme in Botswana's history. By the eleventh century, Transvaal province in what is now South Africa was firmly in the hands of Sotho people – of whom the Tswana are the western group. Here they lived unchallenged until the eighteenth century. Meanwhile the territory that is today the Republic of Botswana was the undisputed range of San hunter-gatherers and the Kgalakgadi people, descendants of very early Batswana immigrants who had mixed freely with them.

The major pre-colonial events in the history of **Tswana-speaking people** – which is very much the same thing as the history of Botswana – were enacted offstage in South Africa. Three hundred years before gold drew whites to establish trade, industry and mines in what became Johannesburg, Tswana people were farming sheep and cattle and cultivating crops in the area. Where skyscrapers now stand, Batswana established the first orderly trading centres, exchanging the livestock of these southern grasslands for iron spears, hoes, tools and ornaments made by the African iron-smelters living in the northern wooded districts – which are today the most luxurious of Johannesburg's whites-only suburbs.

For further details on the San, see pp.338–39, and for an idea of the prehistory of the Botswana area, see the opening sections of the Zimbabwe Historical Framework, preceding.

THE FORCED MIGRATIONS

The other main theme of Tswana history has been the constant cycle of fractures and amalgamations within and between **political groups**. When disputes arose, people would split off from the main tribe and migrate under a rival leader.

The most important splits, which formed the modern **Tswana divisions**, again happened in South Africa. Around the mid-eighteenth century some Batswana began to drift **across the Malopo River** into the territory of modern

Botswana. Their northwest advance would probably have gone quite slowly had shattering events not disrupted the sedate progress of history.

LAND HUNGER

The fission and fusion that typified Tswana political life in the centuries leading up to the 1800s were small change compared to what was about to follow. As populations grew throughout southern Africa, **land hunger** arose, caused by movements of people from all directions into the sub-continent.

In the southeast, **Nguni** people occupied the area between the Drakensberg Mountains and the Indian Ocean. The **Sotho-Tswana** group was firmly settled to their north, while from Zimbabwe **Shona** people extended well into Botswana's east. North of Botswana, the **Lozi** empire was extending its grasp south and westwards, while from the west **Hereros** were being forced into northern Botswana. From the Cape Colony, the **British** were relentlessly extending their control northwards and eastwards, and **Boers**, resentful of their constant interference, were trekking north to escape.

POPULATIONS IN 1800

It was **Zulu amalgamation**, though, that had most dramatic effect. In a very short time during the 1820s the powerful Zulu nation coalesced and sent the shock waves of the *mfecane* – "forced migrations" caused by conquest – throughout southern Africa. Although the Zulus themselves did not move through the Tswana country, **refugee bands**, fleeing from Zulu terror, did. These groups had in their turn adopted Zulu tactics, and to crushing effect. Two of the fiercest invaders were the band who swept northwards under **Sebitoane** in the mid-1820s, attacking various Batswana groups on their way, and the **Ndebele** who confronted and defeated them, while on their own terrifying campaign of conquest.

The victorious Ndebele, under Mzilikazi, remained in Tswana country, which they planned to settle and make their base. By 1830, they had conquered and absorbed or driven off large numbers of Batswana who were living north of the Vaal River. A network of military *kraals* was set up and the surrounding districts were cleared of any potential enemies.

In the mid-1830s yet another wave of invaders arrived in the Transvaal: **Boers** trekking beyond British control in the Cape. The Boers' advance party had found the land unoccupied and, either unaware of Mzilikazi's *cordon sanitaire* or else simply ignoring it, they began to settle territory that the Batswana still claimed as their traditional lands. A series of battles followed in which Mzilikazi's forces were routed by superior Boer weaponry. The Ndebele retreated into Botswana, where they wandered for a decade before finally coming to rest at Bulawayo in Zimbabwe in the 1840s.

With the Ndebele out of the picture many Tswana returned to the Transvaal, but the apparent respite from conquest was the beginning of the bitter relationship that has marked Tswana relations with the whites to the south ever since.

POLITICAL CHANGES

The forced migrations – *mfecane* – led to major changes in **Tswana political organisation**. The harsh realities of conquest meant they had to adapt or die – the old rules ceased to apply. It was no longer feasible for dissenting groups to split off and go it alone, as there was no longer anywhere to go. In such war-ravaged times, small groups were very vulnerable. One vivid lesson of the 1820s and 1830s was to show just how effective centralised states could be against the less organised.

The Batswana probably came out of the chaos better equipped to deal with the colonial onslaught to come. In the aftermath of the forced migrations bigger communities emerged from the wandering fragments. In the 1840s

the **Bangwato** heralded the future shape of things, when **King Kgari** reorganised his state, shifting the balance of power away from competing royals and consolidating his own power in a more tightly unified system.

Absorbing the painful lessons brought by the Ndebele, Kgari drove potential competitor tribes out of the surrounding lands and subdued all the weaker local groups, forcing them to pay him tribute. Finally he drew his conquered subjects into an unprecedentedly close political association. He appointed a deputy, to provide a direct link between the centre of power and the subjects on the fringes and to keep an eye on the surrounding districts.

THE BOERS AND THE PROTECTORATE

The peace brought by the **Boer** defeat of Mzilikazi was short-lived, and soon the **Batswana** found themselves under different pressure. Those who streamed back to their traditional lands found they were there on Boer sufferance and many were pressed into forced labour. **Britain** was quite happy to allow this, and in 1852 signed papers acknowledging Boer independence across the Vaal River. Indeed, it went so far as to promise the Boers free access to the gunpowder and weapon markets of the Cape, while agreeing to prevent Africans getting hold of arms and ammunition.

After signing the **agreement with the British**, the Boers called together those Batswana who were still independent and informed them they were now under Boer control. One Tswana ruler who rejected Boer overlordship was **Sechele I** of the **Bakwena**, against whom the whites launched a punitive campaign. Those groups who refused to co-operate against Sechele, like the **Bangwaketse** and **Barolong**, were also punished. Hundreds of women and children were captured by the Boers, crops were destroyed and houses razed. Sechele appealed to Britain for protection but was turned down – Britain had no need for Tswana territory in the 1850s. Right up to the 1870s repeated appeals to the British government for protection were refused. The British attitude only changed in 1884–85, when their own interests became threatened.

In 1885, with unannounced suddenness, Britain told Germany, which occupied neighbouring German South West Africa (now Namibia), that it had declared a **protectorate** over **Bechuanaland**. Almost as an after-thought, the Batswana states were informed. The annexation was prompted by an attack of British panic that the Germans to the west and the Boers to the east were conspiring to close the gap between them and shut off Britain's route to expansion – the "**Suez Canal to the north**" as arch-colonialist Cecil Rhodes called Tswana country.

COUNTDOWN TO PROTECTORATE

During the three years prior to the declaration of the protectorate, British fears took form when Boer mavericks from the Transvaal set up the two small **Republics of Goshen and Stellaland**, just south of the Molopo River in Tswana country and right across the "road to the north". In 1884 British public opinion was aroused by the killing of Christopher Bethell, son of "an important British family" and married to a Morolong. The death had come during a Boer raid on the Barolong capital at Sehuba (just south of modern Botswana). John Mackenzie, a missionary, who had been push-ing for British protection of the Batswana for some time, used this incident to demonstrate why Britain should take control of Tswana terri-tory – to put a stop to Boer bullying.

The British government declared a protecto-rate over Barolong lands with John Mackenzie as Deputy Commissioner. His role, however, was short-lived. The British High Commissioner to South Africa, **Sir Hercules Robinson**, was disturbed by Mackenzie's oversympathetic atti-tude to the Africans and his failure to deal with the Boers, and he quickly replaced him with **Cecil John Rhodes**.

Rhodes was no more effective at persuading the Boers to jettison their petty republics, which continued to wage war against the Batswana. In 1885 **General Charles Warren** was sent in with a force of 4000 to sort out the troublesome Boers. The Boers took fright at the size of Warren's force and fled back to the Transvaal without firing a shot. Warren extended the Protectorate to 22 degrees south – well into modern Botswana. The territory, designated as the **Bechuanaland Protectorate**, incorporated the lands of three major Tswana kingdoms: Ngwato, Ngkwaketse and Kwena.

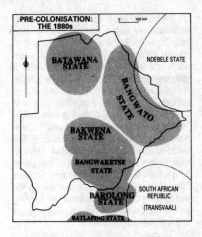

PRE-COLONISATION: THE 1880s

Following this agreement, though, Sir Hercules Robinson again became unhappy with what he saw as an oversympathetic attitude to the Africans – this time from Warren, whom he duly dismissed. Suddenly horrified by the new territory on their hands, the British tried to transfer it to the Cape Colony, but the politi-cians there were no more keen to bear the responsibilities of administering a huge chunk of land that offered them no benefit.

In desperation, later in 1885, Britain subse-quently divided Bechuanaland in two. The part south of the Molopo River became a Crown Colony – **British Bechuanaland** – which was annexed to the Cape in 1895 and now forms part of South Africa. The northern section was given the title of **Bechuanaland Protectorate**, and until Independence had its administrative centre inside South Africa at Mafeking (now Mafikeng).

To many **Batswana**, the declaration of a protectorate came as a surprise. The British justified the move as protection against the Ndebele, the Boers and the Germans. For several decades, pleas for just such protection had been totally ignored, but the British had arrived now that King Khama of the Bangwato had seen off Mzilikazi, and the threat from the Boers had fallen off. As for the Germans, there had never been any trouble from them anyway. Of all the kings, only Khama welcomed British protection. The others spoke out, but eventually resigned themselves to it. All stressed the fact that they wanted no interference in the way they ran their own territories.

The whole issue of protectorate status remained very vague, no one quite knowing what it meant. The British authorities had no interest in wasting any money trying to govern the territory. They simply wanted to maintain a **military presence** there to secure the road to the north and to protect their regional interests. Even when the Tswana offered men to serve in a territorial police force this was turned down.

Within a few years, discontent became manifest as Tswana leaders complained that British control had failed to stop Boer raids into their territory. In 1889 a conference was called by Rhodes's friend Sydney Shippard, Resident Commissioner for the territory, to discuss the setting-up of an administration. At the meeting all the kings expressed their misgivings about undue British interference.

RHODES SHOWS HIS FACE

During the 1890s the colonial administration encouraged **concession-seekers** to swarm into Bechuanaland – the government stood to collect considerable revenue in taxes if minerals were discovered. However, in 1893 they had a rethink when they realised that a single large company – Rhodes's British South Africa Company (BSAC) – could administer the whole territory to the benefit of British interests, and set up a **Concessions Commission** to cancel as many as possible of the concessions granted by the Tswana rulers.

This was a complete breach of the agreement not to interfere in Tswana domestic affairs, and the kings were outraged, not least at their loss of revenue. The BSAC agreed to pay them an annual allowance.

By 1894 Rhodes and the BSAC were ready to take control of Bechuanaland, having crushed the Ndebele in neighbouring Rhodesia and secured a formal assurance that Britain would transfer the Bechuanaland territory to the Company. To smooth the way, Sir Henry Loch, who opposed the deal, was replaced as High Commissioner by Rhodes's friend Sir Hercules Robinson, who also happened to have shares in the BSAC.

Kings Khama, **Bathoen**, **Sebele and Linchwe**, meanwhile, heard of the secret negotiations and petitioned Colonial Secretary Joseph Chamberlain to prevent the proposed transfer. The Tswana leaders had seen the Company's tactics in Rhodesia, and had no intention of following Lobengula's path to disaster (see p.352-3).

Three of the kings decided to take their campaign to England, with Rhodes trying to waylay the men before they could set sail. First he sent his trusty accomplice Leander Starr Jameson to negotiate a deal with Khama in exchange for all sorts of promises. The shrewd king wasn't taken in. Rhodes himself proved no more successful when he collared the rulers in the Cape, en route to London, and tried to persuade them to cancel the visit. High Commissioner Robinson also tried to abort the trip, but was equally ineffective. The kings finally set sail with their interpreter, the missionary W C Willoughby.

In a meeting with Chamberlain they attacked BSAC mismanagement in Rhodesia and insisted on remaining under the Queen's protection. Chamberlain weakly responded that the territory had been promised to the BSAC and he couldn't break his word. He refused to have any further dealings on the matter and, before heading off on a planned holiday, told the kings to deal with Rhodes.

Chamberlain returned from his break to a clutch of letters from church groups and industry, opposing the handover. The kings had wasted no time while Chamberlain was away, campaigning vigorously throughout England and addressing well-attended meetings with the backing of the **London Missionary Society**, which was fully behind Khama – a strong Christian ruler who banned liquor. The **temperance movement**, influential in Britain at the time, gave a lot of support, too, fearing that the BSAC would allow alcohol in Bechuanaland. **Humanitarian** and **anti-slavery groups** lent support as well, outraged by BSAC activity in Rhodesia, and believing that the Crown, not commercial enterprises, should rule the Empire.

Chamberlain backed down. Each king was granted a reserve in which he retained autonomy and the Tswana territories remained a Protectorate under the Queen. Meanwhile, small concessions were made by the Tswana rulers. Land was to be given up for the construction of the BSAC railroad and taxes would be introduced to pay for administration. Rhodes was furious at being outwitted but, despite an array of threats against King Khama, was forced to accept the situation.

During 1895, Rhodes's friend Jameson trained British South Africa Police from Rhodesia, in preparation for an **attack on the Boer republic** from inside Bechuanaland. Later that year he led his armed band into the Transvaal, expecting the support of British residents. The attack was a fiasco and Jameson's party was rounded up by Transvaal forces.

Britain became the object of international condemnation, both for using Bechuanaland as a base and for attacking an independent republic. Had the raid succeeded, the British government would probably have been more sanguine, but instead Rhodes was forced to resign as Prime Minister of the Cape, Jameson was imprisoned, and any chances of a Bechuanaland under BSAC control were ended.

Just four years on, however, in 1899, Britain followed in Jameson's tracks and declared war on the Transvaal to further British imperial interests, which leaders like Chamberlain and Milner believed could only be achieved by a unification of southern Africa. The **Boers** were defeated, but lived to win the peace. In the subsequent union of the two Boer republics and the two British colonies, self-government was granted to the white inhabitants.

The **Afrikaner leadership** of **South Africa** posed a renewed threat to the High Commission territories of Basotholand, Swaziland and Bechuanaland, now with the clout of a large and powerful state. The **South Africa Act** that established the Union of South Africa in 1910 made provision for these territories and Southern Rhodesia to be added to the Union at a later date.

When the issue of **unification** was raised in 1910, Tswana leaders again put up unanimous opposition. But the pressure was on and in 1924 the South African Prime Minister **General Herzog** began to insist that moves be made for the transfer of the territories. He was eager to extend South Africa's "native policy" throughout southern Africa, and had considerable support from the white farmers in Bechuanaland. Fearing an uprising in the High Commission territories, Britain refused.

Herzog used **economic pressure** – a tactic that has remained one of South Africa's major levers in its relations with neighbouring states. First he banned the import of cattle from Bechuanaland that fell below a certain weight: an act with potentially devastating effects on a

DEALING WITH THE BOERS

Rhodes and the BSAC didn't give up hope of laying hands on Bechuanaland. While the three kings were in England, BSAC agents had approached some of the minor rulers, such as Ikaneng of the Balete and Montshiwa of the Barolong. Both ceded lands in the east, which the Colonial Office agreed to hand over to the BSAC; but it refused to transfer other territory on the Transvaal border.

Rhodes also despatched his agent, **John Bosman**, to northern Bechuanaland, where he extracted a fraudulent land concession from **Sekgoma**, king of the **Batswana** (the texts of the English and Setswana documents were different). Rhodes planned to settle a group of Boers there, who were preparing to leave for the Ghanzi area. The British government rejected the Bosman Concession at the end of 1894, but Rhodes decided that he would go ahead and encourage the Ghanzi trek with or without permission.

Apart from settling the country, Rhodes had other reasons for wanting territory north of the Transvaal. British miners in the **Transvaal** were annoyed by the way the Boer bureaucracy was treating them. Rhodes, himself a mine-owner in the republic, wanted, for economic and political reasons, to see the Transvaal brought into a federation of southern African states under Britain.

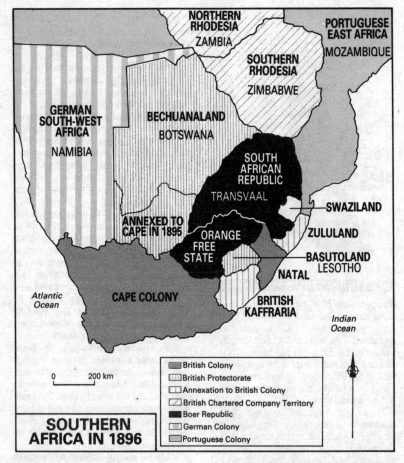

GERMAN
SOUTH-WEST
AFRICA

NAMIBIA

NORTHERN
RHODESIA
ZAMBIA

BECHUANALAND

BOTSWANA

SOUTHERN
RHODESIA

ZIMBABWE

PORTUGUESE
EAST AFRICA

MOZAMBIQUE

SOUTH
AFRICAN
REPUBLIC

TRANSVAAL

SWAZILAND

ZULULAND

ANNEXED TO
CAPE IN 1895

ORANGE
FREE
STATE

BASUTOLAND
LESOTHO

NATAL

*Atlantic
Ocean*

CAPE COLONY

BRITISH
KAFFRARIA

*Indian
Ocean*

0   200 km

British Colony
British Protectorate
Annexation to British Colony
British Chartered Company Territory
Boer Republic
German Colony
Portuguese Colony

**SOUTHERN
AFRICA IN 1896**

country whose sole export then was beef –
though new markets were found in Northern
Rhodesia and elsewhere. Further pressure
came with the prevention of Tswana migrant
labourers from seeking work in South Africa –
the main source of wages for Botswana, which
had no industry of its own.

The Tswana leadership and British government stood firm against this blackmail. But the
question continued to be raised by successive
South African governments and General Smuts
again threatened to stop beef exports in the
1930s. The question was only laid to rest in
1961, when South Africa became a republic
and was expelled from the British
Commonwealth.

COLONIAL DEVELOPMENTS – AND UNDERDEVELOPMENT

Once Britain had secured control of
Bechuanaland and the road to the north, it
more or less forgot about the territory. Already
stretched by a huge empire, the government
was very reluctant to put any money into the
new protectorate. An indication of the half-
hearted attitude was the establishment of a
tiny **administration** – which was maintained
outside the country.

Bechuanaland was different from most
other British colonies, where the usual pattern
was white occupation to exploit the natural
resources of the territory. In such cases there

would be mining or farming, and the imposition of taxes to force peasants off the land to seek wages from white employers. Although some areas of the country were set aside for white settlement and did become occupied by white ranchers, Bechuanaland had the rare distinction that the vast majority of its land stayed in the hands of traditional communities.

All this meant that when the colonial administration imposed **taxes**, there weren't sufficient jobs inside the country to support all the employment-seekers. Vast numbers of Bechuanaland's men were forced to seek work in South Africa, cementing in time a long, complex and none-too-happy economic relationship between the Protectorate and its powerful southern neighbour. One of the tragedies of the colonial years is the waste of migrant labour that went into developing South Africa and impoverishing Bechuanaland.

Although Britain ostensibly aimed at minimal intervention in the long-established way of life of the Protectorate, taxation led the way to a breakdown of traditional patterns of life. The kings were responsible for tax collection, from which they received ten percent. Some used the money to develop the community, but others accumulated personal wealth, driving a wedge between themselves and an increasingly impoverished people. With many men away on the South African mines the responsibilities of farming, like ploughing and reaping, increasingly fell to women. Many Tswana rulers were appalled by the damage caused by the migrant labour system – high death rates on the mines, maltreatment, poor wages and the disruption caused to the community – and banned it altogether for a while.

In 1927 the energetic **Sir Charles Rey**, a colourful but somewhat snobbish figure, replaced a succession of time-servers as Resident Commissioner. From then until 1937 he took a very active interest in the territory, attempting to develop the country despite the lack of monetary support. He also tried to reduce the power of the local kings, whom he saw as obstacles to progress.

An incident that sparked action was the trial of a young white called **Phineas McIntosh** by a traditional court in Serowe in 1933. McIntosh had got some Bangwato women pregnant and, tried by traditional court, was found guilty and sentenced by the Bangwato Regent, Tshekedi

Khama, to be flogged (a traditional punishment still meted out). There was outrage from racist whites in South Africa and in the Protectorate itself, and the Regent was deposed by the administration, only to be reinstated two weeks later after protests from whites in Serowe and England.

However, the following year a proclamation was passed to cut the power of the kings. Its most offensive element was that no king could rule without the approval of the British government. This went against traditional law, which held that a leader was born and could only be removed by his own community. **Kings Tshekedi** and **Bathoen II**, with the backing of other leaders, challenged the proclamation on the grounds that it contravened all the agreements made between Britain and the Tswana. They pointed out that Britain had agreed not to interfere with domestic politics, fearing that the erosion of their power was leading toward incorporation into South Africa. They took the administration to court and lost – though the hostility caused thereafter hampered government activity. Eventually the administration softened its stance, in the face of a possible uprising. Rey was sacked and many of the traditional powers restored to the kings.

NATIONALISM AND THE ROAD TO INDEPENDENCE

Throughout the colonial years Bechuanaland remained a rural country, underdeveloped in terms of infrastructure, education and health care. There was hardly any industry to speak of and consequently no urban working class ready to strike for nationalist ideals. **Nationalism** developed almost sedately from the ranks of the African Civil Service Association.

The **African Civil Service Association** had been formed in 1949, mainly to protest the discrimination against black civil servants. It was not until the 1960s that Africans began to be promoted to higher posts than previously. More important perhaps was pressure for a **Legislative Council** along the lines of those which by then existed in other African countries, and which were seen as the first step to independence. In 1961 the first Legislative Council met, with an equal number of blacks and whites. Africans used the body as a forum for criticising the administration for its neglect of the Protectorate, and to demand independence.

In 1959 came the formation of Botswana's first political party, the **Bechuanaland Protectorate Federal Party**, which opposed the discriminatory racial balance of the Legislative Council. The party, however, never got a real foothold and it folded in 1962.

A more vigorous form of nationalism came via South Africa, following the Sharpeville Massacre in 1960, in which police fired on a crowd of peaceful protesters, killing sixty-nine. In the ensuing repression, 1500 people fled across the border to Bechuanaland, bringing ideas from the developing South African struggle. Many were **ANC** (African National Congress) or **PAC** (Pan-Africanist Congress) members and many were Batswana. Two of these Batswana activists, Motsamai Mpho of the ANC and Philip Matante of the PAC, formed the **Bechuanaland People's Party (BPP)**. The Party demanded immediate independence and organised demonstrations, but failed to get crucial rural support.

It was only with the formation of the **Bechuanaland Democratic Party (BDP)** in 1962 that a truly broad-based force came into existence, under the leadership of the popular **Seretse Khama**. (Seretse had been prevented by Britain from taking over the kingship of the Bangwato, because of his marriage to a white woman – see p.272.) The BDP was an authentically local party, with no links to external political organisations, and a base in the conservative rural areas, where it played on the popular support enjoyed by traditional leaders like Khama.

The BDP's policies were also far milder than those of its predecessors, which made it more acceptable to many whites and to the colonial government. In 1965, in line with the new British policy of decolonisation and the formation of a Commonwealth of the former colonies, supervised **elections** were held prior to the granting of full independence. The BDP won 28 out of 31 seats, with the other three seats going to the BPP.

INDEPENDENCE – AND DIAMONDS

On September 30, 1966 the territory became independent as the **Republic of Botswana** – one of Africa's poorest nations, with just 11km of tarred road and little visible means of support. There was one consolation – at least the traditional capital at Gaborone was now within the nation's own borders.

In the face of dire forecasts, Botswana saw out its first year unremarkably, though continuing to be little more than a labour pool for the South African mines. However, 1967 saw the beginning of a miraculous transformation, heralded by the discovery of **diamonds** at Orapa.

By the early Seventies the mine was on line and it turned out to be the second largest pipe in the world. This was a real Cinderella story, Botswana turning out to be one of the big three gem diamond producers in the world, alongside South Africa and Russia. Not that this prevented South Africa maintaining its age-old policy of harassment towards the new state, demanding a heavy price for its provision of employment, transport and the supply of raw materials, food and consumer goods.

Botswana's government nonetheless made skilful use of its diamond wealth to negotiate a favourable deal with the huge South African diamond monopoly, **De Beers**, to exploit the new-found mineral wealth. Because the international price of diamonds is maintained by a cartel that finds South Africa and Russia in an unlikely collusion, it would have been easy enough for Botswana to flood the market and ruin this cosy arrangement. Consequently the government managed to secure an agreement that gave it a 50–50 share in diamond mining with De Beers, along with 75 percent of the profits.

OPPOSITION TO APARTHEID

At Independence Botswana found itself hemmed in by Rhodesia to the northeast, South Africa to the south and illegally occupied Namibia wrapping round its west and north, leaving only a tiny gateway of just 100 metres connecting it with sympathetic Zambia.

Sir Seretse Khama, however, was not deterred from expressing his opposition to his neighbours' racist policies. He consistently **condemned apartheid**, criticising both Rhodesia and South Africa for their racial policies – a bold move considering Botswana's precarious position.

Botswana's anti-apartheid stance wasn't limited to words, either, with Seretse Khama offering asylum to **refugees** from the white minority-run countries. In 1974 – following the coup in Portugal that brought independence to its colonies – Botswana, along with Angola, Mozambique and Tanzania formed a grouping known as the **Front Line States** with the aim of providing diplomatic support to the Rhodesian and Namibian liberation struggles.

Beyond this moral support, Botswana assiduously avoided taking any active part in the southern African liberation wars and it has never allowed any external organisation to have military bases on its territory. This has failed, however, to prevent **attacks** by its white-ruled neighbours. In 1977 the Rhodesians began a campaign of terror against Botswana, launching several raids across the border on the pretext of pre-emptive strikes

against non-existent guerilla training camps. As a result, unarmed Botswana formed its small professional army, the Botswana Defence Force.

Economically, the Front Line States fought back against South Africa's stranglehold over the region by uniting in 1979 in the **Southern African Development Coordination Conference** (SADCC). Since the preparatory talks in 1977, Botswana has played a leading role in the organisation, Botswana's president chairing SADCC since 1980. The other members of the conference are Zimbabwe, Mozambique, Lesotho, Swaziland, Angola, Zambia, Malawi and Tanzania. Independent Namibia is likely to join. Aside from edging out of South Africa's economic orbit, SADCC aims to develop the combined infrastructure of its members through joint projects, the promotion of trade between them and coordination in attracting foreign aid.

THE 1980S: PROBLEMS

Sir Seretse Khama, Botswana's president from Independence, lived just long enough to see Zimbabwe achieve independence. After his death in 1980, the Vice-President **Dr Quett Masire** took over leadership of the BDP and the country. The new president had a narrower support base than his predecessor. Sir Seretse was both a member of the Ngwato royal family – the largest of the Tswana groups – and a genuine populist, who had led his country to independence. Masire lacked the benefit of tribal authority and drew far narrower support from his own small Ngwaketse group, among which he faced considerable opposition from conservative elements.

There were fears that Masire's administration might signal a break with Sir Seretse's social concerns. While Khama was bothered by the prospect of growing inequality in his country, Masire favoured an unapologetically rampant form of capitalism, despite its attendant problems. Questioned on the issue he commented:

I don't think it's a feature we can hope to prevent altogether. Men are born equal, but they are not equal in their intellectual capacities, in their willingness to put their shoulder to the wheel, and their desire to acquire knowledge.

In the **1984 general elections**, Masire's BDP party again won a decisive victory, taking 29 of the 34 elected seats. But local elections, held on the same day, indicated different trends. Disquiet about **growing unemployment** emerged when the BDP lost control of every town council apart from Selebi-Phikwe.

Throughout the 1980s, Botswana's internal problems were compounded by **harassment from outside the country**. Although the collapse of the Smith regime in Rhodesia brought incursions from the northeast to an end, a more frightening onslaught began from the south. **South Africa's strategy** was altogether more coordinated, more comprehensive and more sinister than anything Rhodesia had dreamed up. While using the same pretexts as its Rhodesian allies – attacks on non-existent guerilla camps – the real reason behind South Africa's web of military, economic and diplomatic pressure was to bring Botswana to heel: to put an end to its anti-apartheid statements, gain formal recognition for the bogus "independent" bantustans, get South African refugees

expelled and to sign a phoney non-aggression pact – like the Nkomati Accord forced on a desperate Mozambique.

In 1981 South Africa was annoyed when Botswana received Soviet arms supplies for the BDF. The incident was blown up and the Afrikaans pro-apartheid newspaper *Beeld* accused Botswana of being "a Cuba" in South Africa's backyard. President Masire explained that the weapons would enable Botswana to police its own borders more effectively to prevent guerillas from crossing into South Africa – exactly what South Africa was demanding. The stepping up of border security failed to stem South African destabilisation.

Despite South African incursions, bombings and commando raids into Gaborone and unsuccessful political interference aimed at creating a Mozambique-style MNR movement to destabilise from within, Botswana stood its ground and has refused to give in on any of these issues. In the face of this, Botswana remains the most democratic country in southern Africa. It is one of the rare African **multi-**

SOUTH AFRICAN INTERVENTION IN THE 1980S

1981–82 Almost-monthly incidents take place, involving South African troops in Namibia firing on the Botswana army, fishermen and game rangers, and the kidnap and murder of civilians.

February 1982 Peter Lengene, Soweto student leader and refugee for six years, kidnapped in Gaborone and hustled over the border.

August 1982 Bomb explodes in alleged SWAPO house in Gaborone.

1983 Border clashes and problems with South African agents persist through the year.

November 1983 Botswana army patrol intercepts two South African vehicles near Dukwe apparently intent on taking dissidents to the border to infiltrate Zimbabwe.

1984 Three meetings are held between South Africa and Botswana. South Africa uses threats, including economic blackmail, to pressurise its neighbour into signing a "peace accord". Botswana refuses to give in.

February 1985 Nat Serache, former journalist in South Africa and BBC correspondent, escapes an explosion at his Gaborone house.

May 1985 Car bomb in Gaborone kills Vernon Nkadimeng, son of the general secretary of the South African Congress of Trade Unions.

June 1985 South African commandos launch mortar and machine gun attack on houses of refugees in Gaborone killing twelve, including several people with no South African links.

May 1986 South African units launch a combined series of attacks on Zambia, Zimbabwe and Botswana. One person in Mogaditsane, near Gaborone, dies.

April 1987 The South African government plays to its domestic audience in the face of an approaching May general election with renewed warnings of attacks on the front line states. A Gaborone bomb blast kills four, just hours after one such threat.

March 1988 South Africa admits involvement in killing four alleged ANC members in a raid on a Gaborone house.

June 1988 Two South African soldiers are arrested south of Gaborone after opening fire on the BDF during an abortive commando raid. A car bomb goes off in Gaborone soon after.

September 1988 An attempt to spring the South Africans from prison in Botswana fails, and they receive ten-year sentences.

December 1988 South African commandos kill two people in a border village. One person dies when a bomb goes off in Gaborone.

party states with the distinction of having no political prisoners. And in 1985, even the Johannesburg *Financial Mail* described Botswana's as "the best managed economy in Africa".

Remarkable as Botswana's economic and political success has been since Independence, with its status shifting from one of the world's twenty poorest countries to Africa's fastest-growing economy, it is still dogged by **dependency**. Most of its imports continue to come from South Africa and it's easy, with all the South African products around, to feel that you're simply in a province of that country. In certain vital sectors, however, Botswana has made a determined effort to detach itself from South Africa, opting for independent electricity supplies and satellite telecommunications and its own currency and international airport.

But Botswana faces **internal problems** of its own for the future – most seriously, a rapid **population explosion** that threatens to far outstrip job creation. Urbanisation, too, with its attendant problems of housing shortage, high rents and growing inequality, has taken place at a phenomenal rate that far overtakes all planning predictions.

While the traditional and rural-based BDP has maintained control of the country, winning every election since Independence, there are signs that the large urban population may stray

towards the new **Botswana National Front**, which calls for far greater state intervention in the economy and accuses the government of allowing an excessive capital outflow.

But **BDP rural support** continues, despite large disparities in wealth distribution in the countryside, with much of the fertile lands in the hands of cattle barons and wealthy farmers while elsewhere there's poverty. The BNF has criticised the government's policies for dealing with these issues as short-sighted tinkering, and has attacked the government for making little attempt to restructure wealth distribution. "All the BDP can do is give away hand-outs as if the people are chickens", BNF representative Paul Rantao said in 1989, referring to food aid provided during droughts.

However, with 80 percent of the population still in the rural areas – traditional BDP country – there's unlikely to be any change in government this century. And the BDP does seem to be taking criticisms on board, initiating **rural projects** to transfer some resources to the poor rural areas. But social changes continue apace and the increasingly young population has rising expectations and declining allegiance to the old guard of tribally based political leaders. A wave of strikes in the late 1980s pointed to new problems for the government, whose future is going to depend on its ability to satisfy the demands of the growing urban populations – and particularly so given whatever changes take place across the border in South Africa.

WRITING FROM ZIMBABWE

Zimbabwe has long possessed a rich oral literature but until the 1890s Shona and Ndebele were not written, and although before Independence there may have been blacks ready to bare their souls about the experience of being colonised, the printing presses were in white hands. Black writers, therefore, had limited possibilities for publication. All manuscripts were vetted by the Rhodesia Literature Bureau, which allowed for more than direct government censorship: through its workshops, pamphlets and advice to authors, it forced the creative production of several decades through particular, restricted channels. Anything political was, naturally, quite out of the question.

During the **liberation struggle**, some fiction and its authors found their way to Britain and acclaim. Writers such as **Dambudzo Marechera** appeared in print outside the country. But at home, throughout the war, non-fiction and music proved more effective voices than literature, for the story that had, with increasing urgency, to be told.

With **Independence** in 1980, however, poets came home from foreign universities and from the guerilla camps. From the offices, factories and classrooms people came together in workshops and a writers' union was formed. The liberation struggle was naturally enough a major concern for most writers, combined with an optimism for the new order. Creative opportunities seemed unlimited.

A decade on, despite the occasional reappearance of government censorship, the result is a stimulating mixture: fine, crafted works from masters such as **Charles Mungoshi** are published alongside fast, bad, township **gangster stories**; **war novels** alongside **love poems**; **love novels** alongside **war poems**; the first stabs at **satire** in a new black state. Perhaps most fascinating are the **autobiographies** out of the silenced past – prison life, existence on farms, on the frontline, behind guns, or simply picking veld flowers – from a society that was divided and remains so. These are still early days in Zimbabwe's search for its voice. Expect everything, especially surprises.

> *I scratched around in the rubbish dump with other kids, looking for comics, magazines, books, broken toys, anything that could help us kids pass the time in the ghetto ... You could say my very first books were the books which the rabidly racist Rusape whites were reading at the time.*
>
> *I took to the English language like a duck takes to water. I was therefore a keen accomplice and student in my own mental colonisation ... For a black writer, the language is very racist: you have to have harrowing fights and hair-raising panga duels with it before you can make it do all you want it to do.*
>
> Dambudzo Marechera: quoted on the cover of *Dambudzo Marechera 1952–1987* (Baobab Books, Harare, 1988).

CHARLES MUNGOSHI

Charles Mungoshi is arguably the finest voice of pre-Independence black despair. His characters face each other across a desolate silence that language cannot bridge – an historical or human condition depending on your reading. "Words are handles made to the smith's fancy and are liable to break under stress," he wrote, "They are too much fat on the hard unbreaking sinews of life."

The story below is from the *Coming of the Dry Season* – not overtly political, but nevertheless banned by the Smith regime.

THE LIFT

When they were tired of going round the factories and shops in search of jobs, the boys went to the tall buildings at the heart of the city for their daily ride in the lifts. It was the only fun they had and it made them forget a little their burning bellies and tired feet.

There were lots of clouds flung about the sky like cotton balls in a field. It was rather chilly and the boys felt sharply the pleasant warmth of the sun when it came out of the clouds, and both of them unconsciously looked up irritably when it darted behind another cloud.

At present, their minds, usually the colour of the changing streets and just as desolate, were fixed on the ride in the lifts.

Pearl Assurance Building, one of the tallest buildings in the city, had a guard at the wide entrance.

'Can I help you?' the guard asked.

'We would like to go up'

'Floor?'

'Tenth'

'What for?'

The boys looked at each other and hazarded an answer.

'We are doing correspondence courses.'

The guard looked at them suspiciously and then dismissed them with a flick of the hand.

'You are not allowed up there.'

The boys looked at the guard as if they had not heard him. Then their eyes turned to gaze at the wall above the lift where numbers went on and off in amber to show the lift coming down.

'There has been much stealing up there lately,' the guard said.

'We are not thieves.'

The guard's eyes swept over their heads and he dismissed them from his attention.

'Go away, boys.'

The boys turned to go. They passed two European boys of their own age. Looking back, the boys saw the guard take off his cap to the Europeans who did not answer him and quickly entered the lift and disappeared.

'Why did you allow those two to go up?'

'*You* are not allowed up there.'

The boys went out onto the street. It was not yet noon and they had nowhere to go and nothing to do to kill the time until night when they would go home to sleep.

'Wish I had kept that shilling after all,' one of them, thinner than the other, said.

'We had to have something to eat.'

'All the same, we could have used it now. It's so much nicer to have something to eat when you don't have anything to do.'

They were moving toward Salisbury Park. They had not talked of the park yet both of them knew that that was the only place left to go and rest.

'I was a fool to use that shilling,' the thin one said again.

His friend didn't answer because he always felt irritated by his companion's mourning for

things that could have been. He felt like shouting at him to stop it but he controlled himself. He didn't care for words when he was tired. They made him even more tired than he really was.

'This is unbearable,' the thin one said once more.

But his friend kept quiet. He was hungry and there was nowhere to get money from. The thin one looked at him, knew that he would be asked why he was looking at him, and kept quiet, knowing that this would only lead to a quarrel. But all the same, it could have been so much better if his friend would talk, then he wouldn't have to think and feel that he was not wanted, so lonely and so hopeless. The park was almost deserted except for two or three people lying on the forbidden grass, asleep or pretending to be asleep.

The thin one said, 'They are going to start trouble with the authorities.'

His friend answered him this time. 'It's silly to forbid people from lying on the grass. What is it there for?'

'It's the rules.'

'To hell with the rules.'

They found a bench under some bamboos and sat down. Immediately they had sat down, the talkative one said, 'They are not allowed to lie on the grass.'

'You have said that already.'

The thin boy looked at his friend and said nothing more. His friend leaned back on the bench and closed his eyes, pretending to go to sleep but the other one knew that this was the cue for him to keep quiet. Both of them were under a strain. They wanted to be somewhere else; the swimming pool, the beer hall — anywhere where there were people and fun and a chance to forget themselves. But there was only the wide empty park and themselves.

The sleepless one looked around the park. He tried to steady his thoughts on the flowers and the trees and the light in the leaves of the trees on the grass and the tall buildings of the city beyond the trees and the immense space of sky above the city, but there was nowhere his thoughts could rest and he was forced to come back to himself.

But he was tired of looking into himself, of asking himself why he was like this and not like that, tired of examining himself, of finding faults with himself, tired of judging and condemning himself. He was tired of the whole circling process of his thoughts, so tired that he wanted movement – any movement, to feel that he was going somewhere and not just stationary. The feeling of doing nothing, of being nothing, oppressed and frightened him. He must talk at least: that gave him a sense of direction, a feeling of really moving towards something. But his friend would not talk.

'That guard was just a nuisance. We wanted nothing except a ride. Only one ride in the lift.'

His friend stirred impatiently and said, 'Perhaps he was right. Lift rides are so short anyway.'

'But sometimes you get off a lift and find the sun has set.'

'Why don't you try to get some sleep? The sun would set faster.'

'I can't sleep during the day.'

'Then shut up please and let me sleep.'

The thin boy watched his friend as he moved towards the further end of the bench after these words. He moved towards the other end and closed his eyes. But he opened them again, worried about the space between them and the empty space that had opened up in him on closing his eyes.

'Can't we do something?' he asked.

Without a word, his friend rose and walked away to another bench and sat down, staring through the trees across the park toward the city. The thin one stayed in his place and struggled to keep himself seated, afraid to stand up and follow his friend, afraid to make even the smallest movement with his body that he knew before he had made it would fall into the pattern of yesterday, today and tomorrow.

So he tried to hurry the night when the darkness would hold his thoughts together and he wouldn't be worried by the distance between their two benches, the space that isolated them; so that looking at the two of them from afar, he saw that they were not friends. Not quite friends.

*Reproduced, with permission, from **Coming of the Dry Season** (Zimbabwe Publishing House, 1981).*

FREEDOM T.V. NYAMUBAYA

Writers published after Independence are invariably involved in the debate as to whether a writer should be primarily concerned with burning political issues, or with "art". The poet Freedom T. V. Nyamubaya fought with ZANLA in the Second Chimurenga. Military comparisons in her work are irresistible: the poems are forceful, direct and bullet-like. Despite her political objectives, her poems remain funny, perceptive and tender.

The poem below is the opening piece of her first collection of poems, *On the Road Again*, which establishes Comrade Freedom's position in the argument for a literature of commitment:

Now that I have put my gun down
For almost obvious reasons
The enemy still is here invisible
My barrel has no definite target
now
Let my hands work –
My mouth sing –
My pencil write –
About the same things my bullet
aimed at.

*Reproduced, with permission, from **On the Road Again** (Zimbabwe Publishing House, Harare, 1986).*

CHENJERAI HOVE

Chenjerai Hove, too, calls for engaged, progressive writing; authors who identify with the lives and struggles of the people. The following extract from his Noma Award-winning novel *Bones*, (interestingly narrated by a woman), addresses, as do his poems, the issues and experiences of the Independence War.

FROM "BONES"

'Do you know Chisaga? He is a good man, but his greed for women is a bit too much. He came to me and pleaded that he will do anything if he can sleep with me. I said that was also my idea for a long time. But since he was the first to mention it, I want him to do something before he can sleep with me. I said he should steal some money for me from Manyepo's safe in the house where he cooks for him every day. Since Manyepo trusts him so much, he will not think it is him. Manyepo will think of other people who have been caught stealing mangoes, but not Chisaga. So Chisaga has stolen the money for me. He expects to sleep with me when he is not working, one of these days. But he will have nobody to sleep with because I knew what I was doing. Do not open your mouth so much, child. The things men will do to satisfy the desire of their things are very surprising. Men will kill their own mothers if they stop them from satisfying the desire of their things. They can dig a hole through a mountain if you tell them you will be waiting the other side of the hill to give them your thing. Men are like children, my mother used to say. They rule everything, like children. Do they not say children are like kings? You let them play with fire, but you always keep looking. You always keep looking at them so that they do not burn their fingers. This is what we do all the time. Look and watch over them. If it were not for men, do you think your grandfather would have died in places where they could not return his body for burial? Did your mother not say that your grandfather died fighting a war started by a man called Hikila who wanted to rule the whole earth? Think of that, a man who does not even know how to cook for himself wants to rule the whole earth. That is what men are like. They look after their things erect in front of them and think they are kings. They do not know that it is just desire shooting out of them, nothing else. So child, you do what you can with the weaknesses of men, but do not let them play with your body. It is your last property, you will die with it. So do not let people waste it like any rubbish they pick up in the village rubbish heap. I know this because my mouth has eaten medicines which even a dog would vomit. My ear has heard things even a witch would faint to hear . . .

* * * * *

The fighters leave him to go home without making any promises. Then after a few days of walking and seeing with their own eyes the poverty of the people, they decide they cannot wait much longer. The people did not have much to give them. If the fighters do not feed,

Marita says, they will stop fighting and go working in the fields. But they had seen so much poverty that it became harsh to their eyes. Let us leave, they said to each other. Let us look for better areas where there are fields that can give something to the farmers. Our hopes will die if we continue to see children dying every day and the cattle licking the soil as if it contains salt. We have learnt that we must free our people from poverty. Poverty is worse than war, they say. You can stop war through talking. You can't stop poverty through talking. So we must fight with all we have so that our people cannot continue to be buried in this ant-hill of poverty.

*Reproduced with permission, from **Bones** (Baobab Books, Harare, 1988).*

DAMBUDZO MARECHERA

Not all Zimbabwe's literary figures share Hove's and Nyamubaya's view of the artist's role. Most flamboyant and controversial among the dissenting was Dambudzo Marechera, well known outside Zimbabwe since his novella and short stories, *House of Hunger*, won the Guardian Fiction Prize.

Before his death in 1987 at the age of 35, Marechera was the *enfant terrible* of Zimbabwean letters. Genius or madman — public opinion remains undecided, although he had become a minor cult figure by the time of his death. Some refuse to label him an "African writer" — and they include Marechera himself: "I would question anyone calling me an African writer. Either you are a writer or you are not. If you are a writer for a specific nation or a specific race, then fuck you."

IDENTIFY THE IDENTITY PARADE

I am the luggage no one will claim;
The out-of-place turd all deny
Responsibility;
The incredulous sneer all tuck away
beneath bland smiles;
The loud fart all silently agree never
happened;

The sheer bad breath you politely confront
with mouthwashed platitudes: 'After all, it's
POETRY.'
I am the rat every cat secretly admires;
The cat every dog secretly fears;
The pervert every honest citizen surprises
in his own mirror: POET.

THE FEAR AND LOATHING OUT OF HARARE

What is it about Harare . . .?
Is it the nightlife, the hotels,
the nightclubs? Or the melancholy
solitary walk back to the flat
when a tawny, almost rubescent dawn
is signalling from within the dark
confines of another pent-up night? For four
years I had not ventured out of the City –
the rest of the country only existed in
news reports about dissidents, co-operatives,
and Blair toilets, not to mention Binga
where it was reported that the main meal
of each drought-stricken day was a
tray of fried grass.

THE TREES OF THE DAY

Trees too tired to carry the burden
Of leaf and bud, of bird and bough
Too harassed by the rigours of unemployment
The drought-glare of high rents
And the spiralling cost of water and mealie-
meal
Trees shrivelled into abortion by the forest fires
Of dumped political policies
Trees whose Kachasu-veined twig-fingers
Can no longer clench into the people's fist
But wearily wipe dripping noses, wearily wave
away
The fly-ridden promises issuing out of the
public Lavatory
Trees under which, hungry and homeless
I emerge from seed to drill a single root into
the
Salt stone soils
The effort a scream of despair.

*Reproduced, with permission, from **Dambudzo
Marechera 1952–1987** (Baobab Books,
Harare, 1988).*

TSITSI DANGAREMBGA

**Tsitsi Dangarembga is a formidable new
talent from the same generation as
Marechera: her first novel, *Nervous
Conditions*, excerpted below, won the
1989 Commonwealth Literature Prize. The
book is a triumph for women's writing as
well as for Zimbabwean literature. Its
opening sentence, "I was not sorry when
my brother died", signals its defiance of
what is acceptable in a dutiful daughter in
its tale of a young black woman growing
up in Rhodesia. This extract is about the
return of the young narrator's uncle,
Babamukuru, from university in Britain.**

FROM "NERVOUS CONDITIONS"

Babamukuru came home in cavalcade of motor
vehicles, sighted four miles away on the main
road by three jubilant pairs of eyes. Netsai and
I and little Shupikai, whose mother was one of
the relatives gathered to celebrate the occasion of Babamukuru's return, watched as the
cavalcade progressed, distressingly slowly,
now disappearing behind clumps of trees, now
reappearing hours later, or so it seemed, no
more than a few hundred yards nearer. The
vigil lasted twenty minutes. We watched from
a rock on the hill behind the homestead until
the carts disappeared for the last time into the
home-stretch. Then we went wild. We slid off
our rock, skinning elbows and knees on the
way, scrambled oblivious through bushes that
scratched our legs, dashed out on to the road
and ran on. 'Ba-ba-mu-ku-ru! Ba-ba-mu-ku-ru!'
we chanted, running and jumping and waving
our skinny arms about all at the same time,
skirts swirling, bottoms jutting as we capered.
Shupikai, several yards behind, started to cry,
still tottering along and chanting through her
sobs, because we had left her behind and
because she was excited. Her crisis was so
inconvenient. I considered ignoring her, which
could not be done. Dashing back, I snatched
her up to continue the mad welcome with her
perched on my hip.

My aunt Gladys, the one who is my father's
womb-sister, older than him but younger than
Babamukuru, came first, her husband behind
the wheel of a gallant if rickety old Austin.
They hooted long and loud. We waved and

shouted and danced. Then came Babamukuru, his car large and impressive, all sparkling metal and polished dark green. It was too much for me. I could have clambered on to the bonnet but, with Shupi in my arms, had to be content with a song: '*Mauya, mauya. Mauya, Babamukuru!*' Netsai picked up the melody. Our vocal cords vibrating through wide arcs, we made an unbelievable racket. Singing and advancing we ushered Babamukuru on to the homestead, hardly noticing Babamunini Thomas, who brought up the rear, not noticing Maini Patience, who was with him, at all.

Slowly the cavalcade progressed towards the yard, which by now was full of rejoicing relatives. My father jumped out of Babamukuru's car, and brandishing a staff like a victory spear, bounded over the bumpy road, leaping into the air and landing on one knee, to get up and leap again and pose like a warrior inflicting a death wound. '*Hezvo!*' he cried 'Do you see him? Our returning prince. Do you see him? Observe him well. He has returned. Our father and benefactor has returned appeased, having devoured English letters with a ferocious appetite! Did you think degrees were indigestible? If so, look at my brother. He has digested them! If you want to see an educated man, look at my brother, big brother to us all!' The spear aimed high and low, thrust to the right, to the left. All was conquered.

The cars rolled to a stop beneath the mango trees. Tete Gladys disembarked with difficulty, with false starts and strenuous breathing; because she was so large, it was not altogether clear how she had managed to insert herself into the car in the first place. But her mass was not frivolous. It had a ponderous presence which rendered any situation, even her attempts to remove herself from her car, weighty and serious. We did not giggle, did not think of it.

On her feet at last, Tete straightened herself, planted herself firmly, feet astride, in the dust. Clenched fists settling on hips, elbows jutting aggressively, she defied any contradiction of my father's eulogy. 'Do you hear?' she demanded, 'what Jeremiah is saying? If you have not heard, listen well. It is the truth he is speaking! Truly our prince has returned today! Full of knowledge. Knowledge that will benefit us all! Purururu!' she ululated, shuffling with small gracious jumps to embrace my mother. 'Purururu!' They ululated. 'He has returned. Our prince has returned!'

Babamukuru stepped out of his car, paused behind its open door, removed his hat to smile graciously, joyfully, at us all. Indeed, my Babamukuru had returned. I saw him only for a moment. The next minute he was drowned in a sea of bodies belonging to uncles, aunts and nephews; grandmothers, grandfathers and nieces; brothers and sisters of the womb and not of the womb. The clan had gathered to welcome its returning hero. His hand was shaken, his head was rubbed, his legs were embraced. I was there too, wanting to touch Babamukuru, to talk, to tell him I was glad that he had returned. Babamukuru made his fair-sized form as expansive as possible, holding his arms out and bending low so that we all could be embraced, could embrace him. He was happy. He was smiling. 'Yes, yes,' he kept saying. 'It is good, it is good.' We moved, dancing and ululating and kicking up a fine dust-storm from our stamping feet, to the house.

Babamukuru stepped inside, followed by a retinue of grandfathers, uncles and brothers. Various paternal aunts, who could join them by virtue of their patriarchal status and were not too shy to do so, mingled with men. Behind them danced female relatives of the lower strata. Maiguru entered last and alone, except for her two children, smiling quietly and inconspicuously. Dressed in flat brown shoes and a pleated polyester dress very much like the one Babamukuru bought for my mother the Christmas before he left, she did not look as though she had been to England. My cousin Nyasha, pretty bright Nyasha, on the other hand, obviously had. There was no other explanation for the tiny little dress she wore, hardly enough of it to cover her thighs. She was self-conscious though, constantly clasping her hands behind her buttocks to prevent her dress from riding up, and observing everybody through veiled vigilant eyes to see what we were thinking. Catching me examining her, she smiled slightly and shrugged, 'I shouldn't have worn it,' her eyes seemed to say. Unfortunately, she had worn it. I could not condone her lack of decorum. I would not give my approval. I turned away.

Reproduced, with permission, from **Nervous Conditions** *(The Women's Press, London; and Zimbabwe Publishing House, Harare, 1988).*

BRUCE MOORE-KING

The work of a new white writer, Bruce Moore-King, *White Man Black War* has had a considerable impact within Zimbabwe and abroad. A former soldier in one of Rhodesia's crack regiments, Moore-King questions the society and the interests he fought for and for which so many died, interspersing military experiences of terrible brutality, recounted in unflinching dead-pan style, with philosophical deliberations.

FROM "WHITE MAN BLACK WAR"

A man hangs spreadeagled, handcuffed to a steel bed-frame. Outside the small, prefabricated rondavel, the land is wet and soaked, a quagmire of mud, farm roads turned into river beds. Half a mile from the rondavel an army truck stands buried to the axles in clay. Twenty yards from the rondavel stands the main ranch house. Over the gate leading into the garden a sign reads "Makorski River Ranch – Manager". In the garden around the rondavel, bedraggled rose bushes, thick clumps of bougainvillea, a group of tattered banana trees.

The bed-frame is standing propped against the interior of the rondavel, almost vertical. The man is naked, handcuffs tight at each hand and each ankle, stretching him. His head is lolling, face gazing blindly down at his feet, but shortly the frame will be rotated and he will hang upside down.

Around the ranch house a maze of trenches and barbed wire meanders, dotted with green canvas tents and heavily covered ammunition pits. There are numerous mortar craters, the freshest having arrived the night before. The ranch manager and his wife have elected to stay, a show of deliberate defiance, and the man on the bed-frame is their boss boy, they've known him for nine years.

There are three elements of the security forces present on the ranch, a company of territorials on call up, a platoon of special police constabulary – black men in blue overalls – under the command of an eighteen-year-old white policeman, and the troop of Grey's Scouts that have been helicoptered in because of the deteriorating situation on the ranch.

There are two men in the rondavel with the prisoner, an SB officer, and the commander of the Grey's troop. The latter is a short, very powerfully built man in his early forties, a professional soldier, ex-British SAS, ex-Foreign Legion, former Warrant Officer in the Rhodesian SAS. The two are sitting on camp stools, drinking Cokes.

The special police constables are equipped with old .303s, but their commander has taken their magazines away from them, as they have developed a tendency to fire somewhat erratically when the base comes under mortar attack. The night before the Grey's commander had found himself under fire from two directions, as the enemy fired into the base, and the constables fired out from the centre, with the troops in the middle.

The man on the bed-frame groans, and the troop commander speaks: "Give us a hand". Together they rotate the bed-frame until the man is hanging upside-down. The troop commander, Kelly, picks up a length of thick, high-pressure compressor hose and hits the prisoner across the thighs and testicles with it. The prisoner screams.

"I thought that would wake you up, you sonofabitch!".

A corporal enters, muddy and wet. He glances at the two men, nods to the SB officer, then sits down, propping his rifle beside him. He opens a Coke, picks up a *Playboy*, and begins reading it.

*   *   *   *   *

I do not think my memories of the reality of the society we held before the war are incorrect.

I can understand, now, why our countrymen took up arms against us. And if these actions and attitudes and forms of selective ignorance displayed by my tribe once caused blood and fire to spread across the land called Rhodesia, what will these same actions and attitudes and forms of selective ignorance produce in this land called Zimbabwe?

Must my tribe reinforce their Creed of racial superiority by denying these, the victors of the war, the basic humanness of the ability to Anger?

*Reproduced, with permission, from **White Man Black War** (Baobab Books, Harare, 1988).*

• *article by Annie Holmes*

WRITING FROM BOTSWANA

While there is no written literary tradition in Botswana, oral literature has always thrived, as throughout southern Africa, and has inspired collections from numerous outsiders – most notably Sir Laurens van der Post, who retells various San myths in *The Heart of the Hunter*, the sequel to the *Lost World of the Kalahari*. Extracts that follow include both San tales and the less well-known (at least outside Africa) form of praise poetry.

That there is, as yet, little written literature is perhaps inevitable, given a rural country with such a tiny population. Furthermore, Botswana did not experience a liberation struggle – the impetus or inspiration for so much modern African writing. However, the country's literature has a towering figure in the South African exile Bessie Head, who made her home in Serowe; her novels explore inner states and universal concerns through the particular of rural Botswanan life.

PRAISE POETRY

Poetry praising a chief was traditionally one of the most important forms of literary expression in southern Africa. Here's a translation of a Tswana praise poem with a difference. In a twentieth-century adaptation of the form, it eulogises the Bulawayo–Johannesburg train that passes through Botswana.

THE TRAIN

I am the black centipede, with my shining nose, rushing through the peoples' hills, minding none of these.
I drink water from the fountains of the powerful magicians
yet no one could e'er bewitch me, neither sorcerers or witches.
Searing sunshine does not stop me, nor does darkness halt my journey.
I have conquered hills and valleys where the leopard is a-lurking,
where the lions crunch the thighbones of their victims, warm and bloody.

When I race along the sand dunes whirling sandclouds fill the skyline.
People ask me where I come from, but they never heard those place names,
ask what journey-food I carry, but I shall arrive tomorrow!
I am not delayed by hunger, nor do blistering feet delay me.
Distant hamlets hear my warning when I overtake the springbok.
I am like a moving village, full of people, never tiring.

SAN TALES

The innumerable **San myths** vary from region to region, and from clan to clan. The G/wi San of central Botswana, for instance, attribute the fierce rainstorms of the Kalahari to the anger of a mythical giant leopard. Lightning is the light of rage flashing in its eyes and at the same time its thunderous roar rolls round the land. Other stories seek to explain features of the night sky, such as the waxing and waning of the moon and why the stars are in particular formations. The !Kung San reckon the stars of the belt of Orion are three zebra, shot at by the Great God while out hunting.

The piece below is a typical cosmological San myth, translated into poetic form.

THE REBIRTH OF THE OSTRICH

He is an ostrich. He is male.
A hungry man goes out to hunt.
He kills the ostrich at his eggs.
The man's wife plucks the ostrich while
the ostrich's feathers are with blood.
She throws the feathers in the bush.
She and her husband eat the flesh.

A whirlwind comes. He blows up high
a little feather dipped in blood.
The whirlwind leaves, the feather falls
into a pool where it gets wet.
The little feather that gets wet
becomes alive because it soaks.
While it drinks water it becomes
a living thing of ostrich flesh.
The living thing gets legs and wings.
It puts on feathers, grows a head.
It lies and grows inside the pool.

It leaves the water. It is soft,
with little feathers that are black,
for he, who from the water comes,
he in an ostrich. He is male.

The little ostrich wants to grow.
He lies upon the water's edge.
He dries his feathers in the sun.
He, stretching, lifts his neck. He moves
his legs. He stands upon his feet.

His feet are weak. He walks. He goes
to make them stronger. He lies down
upon his breast to make it hard;
he makes his breastbone hard.
His bones are strong, his heavy flesh
is full of feathers that are black.
His legs are big, his knees are large.
He roars. He has grown up. He is
a grown-up ostrich. He is male.

The ostrich wants to scratch. His claws
scratch out a place that is a nest.
He roars because his ribs are strong.
His voice is loud. His voice is sweet.

He, strutting, goes to look for wives
on plains where she-ostriches feed.
He calls to them. His voice is sweet.
They come to him. He takes them home,
they lie upon the ground. They make
it soft. They sleep. They flap their wings.
Flapping their wings, they make their eggs.
He lets them go that they may eat,
while he remains to tend the eggs.
They are his children. Therefore he
takes care of them when the jackals howl.
He kicks the jackal with his feet.
The jackals fear him. He is strong.

He is the one the wind blew up,
the feather that was dipped in blood,
the feather that fell in the pool.
He is the feather that became
once more an ostrich who is male.

THE DAY WE DIE

The day we die
the wind comes down
to take away
our footprints.

The wind makes dust
to cover up
the marks we left
while walking.

For otherwise
the thing would seem
as if we were still living.

Therefore the wind
is he who comes
to blow away
our footprints.

Translated by Arthur Markowitz.

Reprinted with permission from **The Rebirth of the Ostrich** *(National Museum and Art Gallery, Gaborone, 1971).*

BESSIE HEAD

Bessie Head's portrayals of village life are unparalleled, and throughout her work she imbues Botswana's flat dry landscape with a lasting beauty. The novels are pretty heavyweight offerings; in her short stories, by contrast, she shows a warm, humorous touch. Until her death in 1988, she was undeniably the country's leading literary figure.

THE SPECIAL ONE

I was a newcomer to the village at that time and teaching at one of the primary schools. Mrs Maleboge was one of my colleagues, a short, stout woman, with a very sad face, who always wore a shawl and a white cotton kerchief wound rather unbecomingly around her head; the kerchief obscured a quarter part of her face so that her sad black eyes stared out from under it. She moved very slowly like the olden-day sailing ships blown by a steady breeze and her speech was as slow and steady as her walk. As soon as one became acquainted with her, she'd start to talk about the great tragedy in her life. Apparently, her husband had left her a small inheritance of cattle at his death, enough to have made her life comfortable in old age. The inheritance had been stolen from her by his brothers and so she was forced to seek employment in her old age when she should have been resting (she was sixty years old). She could stand for about an hour and outline details of the court case she had had with her brothers-in-law, and then stare quietly into the distance and comment: "I lost it because women are just dogs in this society." She did it to me twice, pinned me down and made me listen to this story, so that I developed an anxiety to avoid her. It was impossible to say: "Excuse me, I have to hurry somewhere" – she was too regal and commanded attention once she had started talking.

One day, without any change of expression, she said to me: "You must come to the baptismal party for my grandchild. It's on Sunday." Perhaps she didn't mean it, she was just self-absorbed, but her expression implied that the baptismal party was sad too like everything else. She also gave me directions to her home: "I live near the church. Just get near the church, then ask anyone in the surroundings where I live. They will show you my yard..."

So that was what I did, used the church as a guide mark and then stood looking around, confused. Thousands of little footpaths spread out all round it towards thousands of yards, all with the same look. Where did I go from here? Suddenly along the footpath on which I was standing, a woman came walking towards me. She was walking rather rapidly and in a peculiar way with the wide, swaying footsteps of a drunk. She only cared about herself because she was looking at nothing and she would have walked right past me had I not said, with some desperation: "Please, do you know the yard of Mrs Maleboge?"

She stopped abruptly in the midst of her wide, swaying walk, turned around and looked directly at me.

"Why do you want to know where Mrs Maleboge lives?" she asked.

"She invited me to the baptism party of her grandchild," I replied, uneasily. There was something wrong with the woman and she frightened me a little. To my surprise, she gasped and broke into a very friendly smile.

"How can Mrs Maleboge do this!" she exclaimed. "I am her best friend and she never told me that she was having a party! I am going to the party too! Come, I'll take you to her home. It's just around the corner."

That settled me a little and I was enchanted by the way she had had her mind entirely set on going somewhere else, and now had her mind entirely set on going to Mrs Maleboge's party. She had a light chiffon scarf wound around her head and she suddenly wrenched it off and began swinging it to and fro with the rhythm of her walk, like a young girl. I thought she might be in her late thirties and her mat of closely-cropped brown hair clung neatly to her head. She told me later that her name was Gaenametse, which literally translated means there-is-no-water but translated in a figurative way meant that at the time she was born, the marriage between her parents had been very unsatisfactory.

When we entered the yard of Mrs Maleboge, there were quite a number of guests assembled already. The old woman walked straight towards us, looking brighter and brisker than usual and taking me by the arm she said: "Special guests must enter the hut and be served separately. That is our custom."

Gaenametse and I entered the hut and as soon as the door was closed, my companion flung herself at Mrs Maleboge and began teasing and joking about the fact that her best friend had not invited her to the party but she was here all the same. They were really old friends, with a dialogue, and as soon as we were seated, Gaenametse picked up the dialogue at the exact point at which it had been left off when they last met.

"He's gone to her again!" she burst out. "I am at my wit's end, Mma Maleboge. My love for my husband has reached the over-limit stage. I cannot part from him."

So acute was her misery that her whole body was shaken by sobs. And I thought: "That clears up the mystery of her frightening way of walking. She's at the point of breakdown."

I gathered from what they did next, that they had been through this ritual a number of times. Mrs Maleboge sank to her knees, closed her eyes and began earnestly to implore Jesus to come to the aid of her friend. They formed a touching and complete circle of concentration. Gaenametse did not close her eyes. She stared intently at Mrs Maleboge's face as though expecting her at any moment to make contact with Jesus, and she did not want to miss that moment when it arrived. This effort of concentration so sharpened and heightened every feature in her face that I remember wondering why the unknown husband did not love such a beautiful woman. I had the impression of someone glowing with life, charm, and vitality.

Mrs Maleboge's prayer went one for well over fifteen minutes. Then she stood up and calmly carried on with her duties as hostess of a baptismal party. Neither woman was put out that a stranger had been witness to their private affairs. Gaenametse sat back, relaxed and calm, prepared to enjoy the party. She made some friendly conversation asking who I was and where I had come from. We were both handed plates of rice and chicken and salad by Mrs Maleboge. She had gone up in my estimation. I was deeply moved by the kindness she displayed towards her distressed friend and the touching and almost futile way in which the two women tried to cope with this eternal problem. Towards evening, Mrs Maleboge walked me a little way home and her final comment on the event was:

"Gaenametse has a very bad husband. He is off from woman to woman, but we are praying about the matter," and she stared quietly and sadly into the distance. She did not have to add that women are just dogs in this society. I believed her by then.

Six months later Gaenametse walked slowly down the road past my home; at least I saw someone I vaguely recognised. She had exchanged the lovely light chiffon scarf for the white cotton kerchief worn by Mrs Maleboge and wound it unbecomingly around her head so that only her eyes peeped out beneath it. A shawl was about her shoulders and her dress reached to the ankles. She had a piece of white crochet work in her hand and worked the crochet needle up and down as she walked. She looked very old and she recognised me more readily than I recognised her. She turned around with that sudden, impulsive movement and friendly smile.

"Oh," she said. "So this is where you live," and she turned in her path and walked straight up to my door.

I made tea, puzzled all the while. I just could not see the wild and beautiful woman of that Sunday. She soon informed me about this chameleon-like change of personality.

"I am divorced from my husband," she said, with a complacent smile.

"I'm sorry to hear that," I said, thinking that

that was expected of me. I could see that she did not care a damn.

"Oh everything is going to be alright," she said airily. "I have need of nothing. My father left me a lot of cattle when he died."

She put her head to one side, still with that complacent smile, and stroked the dead body of her marriage: "No one could have loved my husband as much as I did. I loved him too much."

"It's very sad when such things happen," I said.

"Oh, life isn't so bad," she said. "I can tell you a secret. Even old women like Mrs Maleboge are quite happy. They still make love."

I was so startled by this that I burst out: "You don't say!"

She put on the sweet and secret smile of a woman who knows much about this side of life.

"When you are old," she said, "that's the time you make love, more than when you are young. You make love because you are no longer afraid of making babies. You make love with young boys. They all do it but it is done very secretly. No one suspects, that is why they look so respectable in the day time."

It was a bit beyond my imagination – Mrs Maleboge and a young boy! I shrugged my shoulders, lost. It never occurred to me either that this might also be Gaenametse's preoccupation. After we had drunk tea I walked her a little way down the road, and as I was returning to my own home I was accosted by a woman neighbour.

"What are you doing with that one?" she demanded.

I looked back at her, discomforted. It was the height of insult to refer to someone as that one but I was a bit appalled by that story of old women and young boys getting together.

"Don't you ever know what's going on in the village?" the gossipy neighbour persisted. "No one will talk to her. She's a wash-out! She had a terrible divorce case. She was driving the husband mad. She pestered him day and night for the blankets, and even wanted him to do it during the time when she was having her monthly bleeding. Many women have killed men by sleeping with them during that time. It's a dangerous thing and against our custom.

The woman will remain alive and the man will die. She was trying to kill the husband, so the court ruled that he'd better be parted from such a terrible woman."

I stared back at her in petrified horror. She must have thought I understood and approved of some of the insane beliefs of a primitive society, and the society was primitive in certain respects — all primitive societies have their holy fear of a woman's menstrual cycle; during that time she is dirty, and a source of death and danger to the surroundings in general. No, what horrified me was the memory of that Sunday; the wide, drunken swaying walk of extreme emotional distress; the tender appeal two women had made to Jesus for help and a sudden insight into the depth of wickedness of the unknown man. He must have anticipated this social reaction to his wife and deliberately invoked the old tribal taboo to boost his image. How she must have cringed and squirmed, and after the divorce tried to build up an image of respect by dressing up like old Mrs Maleboge! It was quite impossible to convey all this to the snickering village gossip, so I simply told her quite seriously, without knowing anything definite about it, that where I came from the men usually slept with the women when they were menstruating so it was all right for me to talk to Gaenametse.

Shortly afterwards, I saw Gaenametse in the central shopping area of the village. She was dressed like Mrs Maleboge but she was off her beam again. Her walk was her own, wide, drunken, and swaying. Soon I noticed that she was following a young man and a young girl who were strolling casually down the dusty dirt road, hand in hand. She caught up with the couple and with a swift movement planted herself firmly in their path. She looked at the young man with a terrible ugly expression. Since I could read it, he must have read it too. It said plainly: "So, I am only good enough to visit at night. I'd like to stroll casually through the village with you, hand in hand." But no word was exchanged. She turned abruptly and swayed her way off into the distance. She was like that, a wild and wayward learner. She must have decided there

and then that Mrs Maleboge's tricks were beyond her. She could not keep her emotions within bounds.

Her last image was the final one I saw. A business matter forced me to take a walk to a remote and far-flung part of the village. While on my way back a voice called out gaily: "Hey, what are you doing here?" I turned around and there was Gaenametse briskly sweeping a yard with a broom. She was still dressed like Mrs Maleboge but she looked happy in a complacent kind of way, like the day she had walked down the road with her crochet work.

"Won't you come in for some tea?" she asked. "I watched you walking right to the end of the village and you must be thirsty."

As we walked towards the single mud hut in the yard, she lowered her voice to a whisper: "I have a husband. We are not quite married yet, but he is the priest of our church. He started the church himself because he can heal people. I went to him when my heart was troubled and so we found love. He is a very good man. He's inside now studying the Bible."

The man was seated on a low wooden stool. He was quite elderly, with greying hair. He stood up as we entered and politely clasped his hands together, exchanged greetings, and quietly went back to his Bible study. We drank tea, talked, and then she walked with me a little of the way home.

"You seem happy now," I said. "I cannot forget how unhappy you were that day at Mrs Maleboge's party."

She smiled, that sweetly secret smile of a woman who knows how to sort out her love life.

"I have all I need now," she said. "I have a good man. I am his mosadi-raa."

"What does that mean?" I asked.

"It means I am the special one," she said.

As I walked on alone I thought that the old days of polygamy are gone and done with, but the men haven't yet accepted that the women want them to be monogamists.

*Reprinted with permission from **The Collector of Treasures** (Heinemann African Writers Series, 1977).*

TAKE COVER! ZIMBABWE'S POP MUSIC

Zimbabwe resounds to music — traditional, reggae, soul, funk, rock. Loudspeakers bounce on the pavements outside the downtown record bars; nighttime city streets echo with the discos of the central hotels; and transistor radios crackle with ZBC's *Radio Two* — even out at Nyaminyami on the remote banks of Kariba.

The music is varied but dominated by one style today, **local jive**. After years of flirtation with Europe and the Americas, pop music has returned to its roots. Zimbabweans have discovered that their traditional rhythms are as danceable as any in the world — and as marketable! That makes life very exciting for musicians and music lovers alike. Many hotels in Harare, Bulawayo and other major centres have a band of sorts performing live six nights a week, while numerous restaurants, bars, beer halls, community halls and stadiums provide venues for nights and days of good live music. There is no shortage of talent. Equipment, however, is not so plentiful.

And that's where the fairy-tale of music falls apart in Zimbabwe. Not many bands can afford to maintain, let alone purchase, the sparse musical equipment that's available. So people with the money buy the gear, then overwork musicians and underpay them. The record companies play it pretty much the same way, paying some of the lowest royalties in the world. Inevitably some enterprising groups and individuals do manage to escape this web of exploitation, but for the majority it's a hard way to earn a living. But it's also an age-old way of having a good time, telling a story, and quite romantic into the bargain; so the bands plug away, the joints are jumping, records are selling, music videos are being made . . .

TRADITIONAL MUSIC

Zimbabwe's most popular form of **traditional music** is based on the rhythms and melodies of the **mbira** or thumb piano — basically a small sound box, held between the hands, with a row of metal strips of different lengths plucked by the thumbs. *Mbiras* are used in traditional rituals and players are often spirit mediums, communicating with ancestral spirits through music. The music tends therefore to be hypnotic and repetitive, encouraging simple responses from the audience and inviting participation. Its melody lines run through trilling treble patterns while the bass bounces about in spongy steps reminiscent of a reggae bass line. Because *mbiras* are played with the thumbs only, single notes rather than chords carry the songs. Traditional accompaniment consists of voices (lead and response), *hosho* (shakers and gourds filled with dried seeds etc), drums, and other forms of percussion — such as wooden blocks clapped together, or stamping feet.

MBIRA GROUPS

There are hundreds, if not thousands of **mbira groups** in the country, and if you're lucky you may wander into some village and find one jamming at the local meeting place. Traditional music and dance groups take part in all the festivals and celebrations, from Independence Day to the annual agricultural shows.

Few of these musicians make the transition into the world of mass electronic media unadulterated, but some, such as **Ephat Mjuru**, still play and record within a strictly traditional cultural format. Traditionally a man's instrument, there are now many women *mbira* players in Zimbabwe. One of them, **Amai Muchena**, who performs with Muri ko Muchena (the Muchena family) has been playing since she was five years old. She views the instrument as a sacred thing "I don't play in beerhalls, because the spirit is like a God to go to if there are problems, but I can play in the Sheraton – there are no drunks there."

In contrast, **Beulah Diago**, a quiet but serene woman who believes strongly in the message of her music, plays in beer halls in Chitungwiza: "Some people don't know *mbira*, like youths in bars, so I take *mbira* to them."

Stella Chiweshe is perhaps the best-known *mbira* player outside Zimbabwe – she's based half the time in Germany, and performs more often overseas than at home. She bends the boundaries by occasionally combining pure *mbira* or *marimba* (a wooden xylophone) with electric bass and western drum kit, underpinning her truly regal voice and presence with dreader-than-dread rhythms. She has provoked some criticism for her avant-garde mixture of sacred and commercial music – controversial in a country where music is so close to the spiritual centre of life. She certainly uses the mystique of the instrument in her shows to good effect, sometimes going into a trance on stage.

Electric guitars slot easily into *mbira* music: turn up the treble, cuff the strings lightly, pluck sequences with a plectrum and a reasonable facsimile of the *mbira* sound is created. A lot of local jive revolves around this technique, the best respected exponent of which is **Thomas Mapfumo**.

Probably the finest *mbira*-style guitarist is **Jonah Moyo** – a veteran of Mapfumo's band, who sometimes plays with his own. His over-tracked lead sequences on Mapfumo's *Shumba* album bear repeated listening.

MARIMBA

The ***marimba*** is another widely used traditional instrument. Visitors to the Victoria Falls are served up endless renditions of *Auld Lang Syne* and *When the Saints Go Marching In* played on *marimbas*, while trying to enjoy a quiet hotel lunch. *Marimbas* are not meant for such martial music – and it shows (painfully). For the real thing, check out Stella Chiweshe's *Ambuya* album, which uses *marimba* extensively and to brilliant effect.

Authentic ***marimba*** **groups** are also found throughout the country, often in schools and community centres. The best-known of these is the **St Peter's Kubatana** school band in Harare.

DANCE, DRUM AND CHORAL GROUPS

Dance, drum and choral groups exist all over Zimbabwe, too. The **National Dance Troupe**, based in Harare, performs at festivals and special venues. Many songs and dances were created by guerillas in the 1970s in order to politicise the masses, and can be heard on the ***Chimurenga Songs*** series of LPs.

Interestingly, one of the former ZANLA choir-masters became the contemporary pop singer **Comrade Chinx**, who combines political lyrics with *mbira* and drum machines (see below).

BEST JIVE ALIVE

Most foreigners think *Jit Jive* is a generic name for contemporary Zimbabwean music – it's not. *Jit Jive* was coined by the internationally successful Bhundu Boys to identify their brand of upbeat jive. Local bands play music influenced by *mbira*, rhumba, zouk, reggae, salsa, kwela, rock, jazz and soul. What emerges is a complex but coherent mix, shot through with occasional pure strains of Hendrix or Charlie Parker. Styles that defy pigeonholing in established categories are collectively labelled ***smanjemanje*** which translates as *something new*. And there's something new every day.

THOMAS MAPFUMO AND THE BLACKS UNLIMITED

Thomas Mapfumo is a musical and political veteran, having been jailed some time before Independence for his protest songs and populist stance. A hypnotic-eyed, dreadlocked vocalist, he is backed by some of the finest musicians around – and was one of the first African musicians to achieve star status overseas. Some of his chimurenga songs were directly political, while others used the Shona tradition of "deep proverbs" to conceal messages of resistance. Mapfumo's earlier LPs are classics: *Hokoyo*, *Gwindingwi Rine Shumba*, and *Ndangariro* stand out, as do 12" singles like *Kariba* and the recent *Corruption* (which as a consequence of its subject received little airplay). Thomas's reggae outings can, by comparison, be a little tedious, but, if you enjoy dread beat, listen to *Mugara Ndega* (12") and the *Chimurenga for Justice* LP. Don't miss a chance to see him live, at the *Queens Garden* or any of the venues advertised along Harare's Robert Mugabe Road.

OLIVER M'TUKUDZI

Sometimes to be seen with the Zigzag Band (good in their own right), or the Black Spirits, **Oliver M'tukudzi** (*Tuku*) is the other major contender for the title of giant of Zimbabwean music, with a deep soul voice and a high energy well-choreographed stage act. Though heavily influenced by Thomas Mapfumo's chimurenga, he easily outsells Thomas in Zimbabwe and has produced dozens of LPs. Other influences include mbaqanga and rhumba beats, and M'tukudzi is a strong traditionalist who remains commited to his roots.

As with all Zimbabwean musicians, M'tukudzi is very conscious of the importance of his lyrics. He is a deeply moral man – he sang the first AIDS song in a (subsequently banned) Zimbabwean film. His lyrics deal with tradition, and place an emphasis on discipline.

THE BHUNDU BOYS

Jive kings who in the Eighties seemed on the verge of conquering half the western world (starting with London), and catapulted Zimbabwean jive into the big league, the **Bhundu Boys** were for some years great heroes at home (when they *were* home), playing the very biggest venues. The music which brought them their fame was hard, fast and always melodic, rippling guitars on solid bass and drums beneath multiple vocal harmonies. Their full five-piece sound, regrettably overproduced and overdubbed on their British-recorded *Jit Jive* LP, was at its best on their first two LPs, *Bhundu Boys* and *Hupenyu Hwepasi* (the best!), as well as singles like *Simbimbimbo*, *Chemedzevana*, *Chimaninmani* – and stacks more.

They have however in the last few years suffered a series of staggering blows, including the deaths of three successive bass guitarists, and an acrimonious break-up with charismatic front man Biggie Tembo, which involved great scandals in the Zimbabwe papers. While the Bhundu Boys struggle on, Biggie himself, now studying video and sound engineering in Bristol with the hope of setting up his own studio in his hometown Chinoyi, has teamed up with the Ocean City Band.

THE JAIROS JIRI BAND

The **Jairos Jiri Band** (or JJB) have been around for many years, having originated in a welfare organisation founded by Jairos Jiri to assist disabled Zimbabweans in their full integration into the local culture and economy. They too are no longer the force they used to be, following the imprisonment for rape of their former leader, the blind singer-songwriter Paul Matavaire. However, their back catalogue is extensive, and their songs are renowned for their acute social observations: "Our music differs from overseas music. It has moral lessons telling you how to behave. Songs from overseas are only for entertainment". Look out for their 1980 single *Take Cover*, the story of a guerilla group's journey through the war zone, *JJB Style* from the 1987 LP *Amatshakada*, their 12" versions of *Taurai Zvenyu* (remix), *Handirambi*, and 7" singles such as *Muphurisa*.

SOLOMON SKUZA AND THE KWENJANI BAND

In the same vein as Oliver M'tukudzi, both physically and musically, **Solomon Skuza** has a classic blues/soul crooner's quality. He and his band come from Bulawayo, which is where

---

MUSIC AND FILM

Queens Garden – at the time the epicentre of Harare music – features, albeit emptied of its unrulier elements, in the Zimbabwean music film, *Jit*, directed by Michael Raeburn in 1990. The film, a light-hearted look at Shona tradition and how some people abuse it in their greed, was released in the UK in 1992. It includes a long string of performances by the top Zimbabwean bands, unfortunately all playback music rather than real performance, with Oliver M'tukudzi in a leading role. M'tukudzi also wrote the sound track of *The Winds of Change*, 1992.

Simon Bright's film, *The Spirit of the People* (Zimmedia, 1990), named after Ephat Mjuru and his band, examines the links between traditional *mbira* music and modern electric jit. It demonstrates the transition from Ephat Mjuru playing traditional *mbira* music, with singing and dancing at the fireside in the rural areas, to the electrified stage sound of Thomas Mapfumo in an urban commercial show with lights, electronic instruments, and microphones, but still featuring unmistakable *mbira* strains. The sound quality is poor but the film gives a good overview of different music styles in Zimbabwe.

you'll find them most of the time. Their LP *Zihlangene* is varied and accomplished, and they've issued wonderful singles such as *Iquino Aliso*, *Jennifer* and *Sobukhu*. He's definitely a rising star and a favourite local musician.

COMRADE CHINX

The ex-ZANLA choirmaster with the foghorn voice, **Comrade Chinx** is a great entertainer, strutting the stage in combat fatigues, beret and sunshades, as well as an incisive social commentator. His early singles *Zvikomborera*, *Nerudo*, *Magamba Ose* and others, experimented with sequencers and drum machines mixed into traditional *mbira*/chant.

Chinx also broke into synthesiser pop; his biggest-selling record *Roger Confirm*, about love through a shortwave radio, was made with the help of the group Ilanga. Even with six singles and an excellent LP behind him, however, he can't make music pay and works five days a week for the Zimbabwe Broadcasting Corporation. **Ilanga** themselves were a talented bunch of session musicians, responsible in their own right for a number of LPs, of which the first, entitled simply *Ilanga*, is the best. Shortly after a rather sour split from Chinx, they went their separate ways.

> For love with love only I walked in my father's
> land, in my mother's land, in my grand-
> mother's land
> You can see for yourself love is enough
> Mugabe said this and so did the comrades
> Only love love is enough
> Comrade Chinx and Mazana Movement

ZEXIE MANATSA AND THE GREEN ARROWS

The **Green Arrows** have been playing roots jive for about twenty years now, but their upbeat mix of groaning lead vocals (**Zexie**), shrill vocal chorus, and solid rhythm unit is still entertaining and danceable. In 1988 a car accident killed two band members and injured others, including Zexie. Fortunately Zexie and the band are back, and they're stirring it up with their savage satire, infuriating many sections of Zimbabwean society. They're not resident at any venue but tour a lot and make the best music videos around. Best LPs are *Mudzimu Ndiringe*, *Antonyo* and *Chipo Chiroorwa*. There are lots of singles.

THE RUNN FAMILY

The only Mutare-based band to make it big in the pop charts in recent years, the **Runn Family**'s peak was a single released

WOMEN MUSICIANS

I have been going around looking for girls but when I find one she can't come to the stage and perform because she's scared of what people will say about her.

Oliver M'tukudzi

The conservatism and chauvinism of Zimbabwe society has meant that women musicians have had a difficult time, and some brilliant musicians are unable to make their way. Thandeka Ngono, formerly singer with Southern Freeway, explains that "it's a lot to do with the attitude that women in show business are whores – that they're cheap and loose. Zimbabwe really does not want to cater for women musicians, but since we are there, there's nothing they can do about it."

Thandeka says that in her experience this is a problem unique to Zimbabwe: "I performed a lot in South Africa, and there were no problems about being a woman musician. The stigma is not there that is here. When I tried to inflitrate here, I had problems. In order to get into a group I would first jam with them so that they could hear that I could sing, but that made it worse! Maybe they thought I was going to take their jobs!"

Her comments are frequently echoed by other women musicians – many of whom feel frustrated by their lack of freedom. Few women make decisions within their band, often finding that the band will not release them to perform alone, and they tend to get a poor deal with money and recording rights. Sexual harassment by band managers and even the audience is also a problem.

In 1990 however a Women Musicians' Advisory Group was set up. Amongst its members are the top female Zimbabwean musicians: Stella Chiweshe, Busi Ncube (Ilanga), Doreen Ncube (Mudzimu), Virginia Jangano (Harare Mambos), Amai Muchena, and Beulah Diago. The group aims to educate women about their rights and advise on discrimination. As Stella Chiweshe puts it: "we are slow but we are coming up – you will see us."

immediately after the suspicious air crash death of Mozambicquan president, Samora Machel. *Hatchina Wekutamba Naye* encapsulated a nation's grief over the death of a proven ally and friend. Honey-sweet vocals keen over a rippling rhumba-ish backtrack, the beat picks up and the sound swells to a remarkably sweet pop crescendo.

The group play a broad spectrum of pop and jive, numerous cover versions included. You'll find them live in the clubs and hotels around Mutare and, occasionally, Harare. *Hatchina* is one of *the* classic songs of Zimbabwe, and singles such as *Moyo Muti* are worth listening out for. They have released two albums, *Ndoita Wekudinko* and a compilation of old songs.

THE FOUR BROTHERS

The Four Brothers are a straightforward fast Shona band, lyrics above rippling guitar riffs, and strongly influenced by Mapfumo (one of them, Marshall Muhumwe, is Thomas' uncle, and learnt the drums and singing from him). Their first hit, *Makoro* (Congratulations), was dedicated to the freedom fighters at Independence, and they continued to become one of the top Zimbabwean bands during the 1980s.

They call themselves the Four Brothers so that they remain equal and no one brother becomes "big" – a fate that has split too many Zimbabwean bands apart in the past. And despite their prolonged exposure in the West, they stick firmly to their traditional roots, claiming to have "learnt from the lesson of the Bhundu Boys". They deliberately choose to record in Harare rather than the technically superior studios of the UK.

OTHER PROPONENTS OF ELECTRIC MBIRA

Ephat Mjuru and the Spirit of The People are

> She's the girl I was telling you about
> Vimbai is a beautiful girl
> a heart snatcher – God's masterpiece
> it's not only my idea; many praise her
> Her eyes reflect real tenderness
> Vimbai has a warm heart, warm as a winter
>   blanket
> Her neck is as smooth as the King's horse
> She is a nice girl
>
>   The Four Brothers

one of the best electric *mbira* groups around. Their music borders on the chimurenga beat, as well as a variety of other influences: afro-jazz, soca and reggae. **Pengaudozoke**, a very dancey new band with a fast rhythm borrowing from rhumba as well as chanting traditions, is Oliver M'tukudzi's favourite group – "people thought they wouldn't go far but I could sense they had a unique touch in their music. They are different from the others".

Vadzimba adopt a similar approach to Thomas Mapfumo – drawing from traditional songs and treating them with a *mbira*-guitar translated beat – though with less success. At one time Thomas threatened to sue them for infringement of copyright, but as Vadzimba member Farai put it "Our music is not Thomas' music – just as reggae is not only Bob Marley. The traditional tunes belong to everyone."

The powerfully voiced **Robson Banda**, who plays instantly infectious music with **The New Black Eagles**, has also been influenced by Mapfumo's electric *mbira* music, as well as strains of South African mbaqanga and rhumba beats.

RHUMBA

The Zairean-born **Real Sounds** claim to be "the rhumba kings of Zimbabwe" and they certainly have the brass to prove it, bopping till they drop in fine rhumba style, *Ray-Bans* and all. Now resident in Zimbabwe (at the whim of the Ministry of Home Affairs), they blast away with heart-warming good vibes. At the *Children on the Frontline* music festival they backed Manu Dibango with finesse, and that's a fine credit for any group in the world. Their record releases don't always match the live magic, but go to one of their regular weekend sessions with visiting artists at the *7 Miles Motel*, outside Harare, and judge for yourself if they deserve their self-proclaimed crowns.

Among their rivals on the rhumba scene are the up-and-coming **Khiama Boys**.

JOHN CHIBADURA

John Chibadura, backed by the Tembo Brothers, has been one of the biggest-selling artists in recent years. Shy, private, and introverted, and posing as an "anti-star", he has had amazing success, winning the following of young Zimbabweans with the result that all records routinely turn gold. His music combines fast-moving Zimbabwean dance music and rhumba. His lyrics are a grim reflection of social conditions, but, with typical Zimbabwean stoicism, are sung over a defiantly happy beat.

DEVERA NGWENA JAZZ BAND

Long-standing local top-sellers, **Devera Ngwena** play under contract to one of Zimbabwe's big mines. Their music is mainly *rhumba* with occasional *smanjemanje* infusions. Since they're based outside the cities it's difficult to catch them live. Like the Bhundus they tend to play larger venues: Their records (all just called *Devera Ngwena Jazz Band*) are numerous but it's easy to find their latest LP: they're numbered – somewhere around twelve by now . . .

JAZZ AND THE SOUTH AFRICAN INFLUENCE

Jazz groups are coming up fast in Zimbabwe, particularly in Bulawayo where the close proximity of South Africa can be clearly heard in the music. **Dorothy Masuka** ("Auntie"), the "mama" of jazz from Bulawayo, with a musical career that spans over forty years, sang with Miriam Makeba and Hugh Masekela in South Africa in her early days, later fleeing to London to escape Ian Smith's Rhodesia, and then campaigning for Zimbabwe all over in Southern Africa.

Like many Bulawayan musicians, she draws a lot on South African influences, playing a mixture of jazz swing and local melodies in a style known as *marabi*. A glamorous and dominating personality, she is one of Zimbabwe's strongest female performers – "to tour with me is a serious thing." A great performer, she dresses in vibrant colours and sweeps up Southern African jazz with her amazingly powerful voice linking it to more traditional beats.

Until their recent split, **Mudzimu** were perhaps the best experimental jazz band in Zimbabwe. Now former members, including drummer Jethro Shasha, are achieving notable success in South Africa.

BROADWAY QUARTET/JAZZ SURVIVORS

Broadway started out in the 1960s and made it big all over central Africa. They split up in 1983 to form two groups – **Broadway Quartet** and the **Jazz Survivors**. They all play regularly

at the *Hunyani Hills Hotel* outside Harare, the *Rose and Crown* in Hatfield, Harare, and around the clubs and hotels. Who's playing with whom changes frequently, but you can depend on superb drummers, very hot guitarists, and fine brass players combining to produce all imaginable styles of jazz.

If you're a jazz fan you may be pleasantly surprised by the excellence of these groups' repertoires. Unfortunately, no recordings are available.

SOUTHERN FREEWAY

Southern Freeway is a new group with members from Bulawayo, South Africa and Harare – including the talented session guitarist, Louis Mhlanga. They have backed the South African Steve Dyer, a versatile musician who has spent much time in Botswana, and Bulawayan singer Thandeka Ngono. Their music ranges from mbaqanga, jazz to more Shona-influenced guitar playing and a mixture of all kinds of music. They sing in six languages – Zulu, Xhosa, Ndebele, Shona, Tswana and English. Their first album concentrates on the South African penny whistle, but more recent music has acquired a Shona sound.

LOVEMORE MAJAIVANA AND THE ZULUS

Lovemore Majaivana's music has been shaped by so many influences that he sounds either brilliant or vacant. He's been Zimbabwe's Elvis, its Tom Jones, its Little Richard, and even its Engelbert Humperdinck. His music is based on Zulu/Ndebele rhythms fused with Shona/*mbira* melodies.

His current band, **The Zulus**, originate in Bulawayo, and crank out a powerful beat behind Lovemore's rich, strong voice . . . but there are still those mindless moments. In live performances it's always dance time, but the records don't capture energy. His best LP is an old one – *Isitimela* (with Job's Combination) – but even that had a producer with cardboard ears.

BLACK UMFOLOSI

This a cappella group of singers and dancers from Bulawayo are an amazing sight live with their precise and acrobatic singing and dancing to a strong Zulu beat. They even perform the rarely seen South African miners' gumboot dance.

LOCAL IDIOMS AND WESTERN POP

There is a wealth of choice of good Zimbabwean music, each band exploring its own ways of linking local idioms with western pop.

The late **James Chimombe** was a very talented musician, vocalist and songwriter with the Ocean City Band, with a touch of country in his music, and a great influence on younger Zimbabwean groups.

Tobias Areketa, who also died in 1990, initially worked with Mapfumo. The music he made with the Shazi Band is remarkable for its haunting mournful melodies with words packed in over a relentlessly poignant beat. Unfortunately he only recorded two albums before his death.

The Frontline Kids, a fast young teenage band, whip the crowd up into frenzies with their energetic and aerobic dancing with at times catastrophic results — when they were performing at the Chico and Chinamora concert in Harare in 1991 the crowd twice broke down the gates.

Also known as *Mukadota*, a comic with his own TV series, **Safirio Madzikatire** sings and clowns with a large group of musicians/comedians — collectively known as **The Sea Cottage Sisters with the Brave Sun Band**. He's regarded as the most accurate satirist of local culture and is much beloved across all age groups. Though now into his fifties, his act remains tirelessly energetic, entertaining and slick. He's Zimbabwe's *Mr Showbiz* in the nicest way and his songs are consistently good, even if they do tend to repeat themselves over the decades. Good LPs include *Ndatenga Motor*, while singles like *Katarina* and *KwaHunyani* stand out. Watch TV for the *KwaHunyani* video and the *Mukadota* series.

AND THE OTHERS . . .

Other bands to watch out for in Zimbabwe include the prolific **Pied Pipers**, **Simon Chimbetu and the Dendera Kings**, **Harare Mambos**, **The Marxist Brothers**, **Leonard Dembo**, **Nyami Nymai Sounds**, the **Rusike Brothers**, **OK Success**, **Sabuku**, **Talking Drum** and **Fanyana Dube** (responsible for the *Nhamo Inerushambwa* single and video).

If you're hooked on **Hendrix** there's even **Doctor Footswitch**, featuring Manu *the superstar*, who plays his Fender with his teeth while upside down over an amp . . . and all that. **Seven Seals** from Harare play steady **reggae**. **Murupha** popped up in 1987 with a lovely single (*Zimbabwe Ndeyenyu*/*Mai Rugare*) then vanished; and anonymous **guitarists** appear with patched boxwood instruments and nasal voices. There's lots more to find out . . .

• *Michael Philips and Judy Kendall*

ESSENTIAL LISTENING: A DISCOGRAPHY

BANDS

The Frontline Kids
Hupenyu ZINLP005

Stella Chiweshe
* *Ambuya* ZMC / ORBO29

Thomas Mapfumo
Hokoyo (Thomas Mapfumo and the Acid Band),
  Gramma
Gwindingwi Rine Shumba Gramma
Shumba EWV22 (compilation of early work)
* *Chimurenga Singles (1976–1980)* ELP 2004
Greatest Hits ASLP5001
* *Zimbabwe-Mozambique* TML100
Corruption MLP51059
Chamunorwa M1075

Ephat Mjuru
Ndiani waunoda baba namai – hit single in
  Zimbabwe
The Spirit of the People ZML1003

Oliver M'tukudzi
1980 Afrika ZMC
* *Sugar Pie* CSLP5001
Psss Psss Hallo CSLP5005
Africa TEL2015

Comrade Chinx
Ngorimba (with Ilanga) ZMC

**Paul Matavire and the Jairos Jiri Sunshine
  Band**
Amatshakda Gramma
Take cover! Various Artists AFRILP01

Bhundu Boys
* *Shabini* AFRILP02 – at their best
* *Hupenyu Hwepasi* Gramma
True Jit WX 129 (1987) – a dreadful warning (with-
  out Biggie):
Absolute Jit AFRILP09 (1990)
Live at King Tut's Wah Wah Hut 09 (1991)

Ilanga
Ilanga ILGLP2

The Four Brothers
Bros COOK023
* *Makorokoto* COOKC014
Rudo Chete KSLP124
Rugare KSLP111

The Runn Family
Hachina Wekutamba Naye and * *Moyo Muti* – hit
  singles in Zimbabwe
Ndoita Wekudiniko Gramma (a compilation of old
  songs, Zimbabwe 1991)

John Chibadura and the Tembo Brothers
The Essential CSLP5002
More of the Essential CSLP5004

Pengaudozoke
Kwatakabva Nenhamo RTP

The Real Sounds
Harare ZML 1015
Seven Miles High BIG1
* *Vende Zako* COOK004 (includes songs for foot-
  ball fans!)

Devera Ngwena
(In Zimbabwe they have produced a series of
  numbered LPs, all titled *Devera Ngwena Jazz
  Band*)
* *Taxi Driver* KK01

The Nyami Nyami Sounds
Kwira Mudenga ZML 1030

James Chimombe and the Ocean City Band
Munakandafa ZIL218

Tobias Areketa
Mavambo

Southern Freeway
Southern Freeway RTP (2nd album includes
  compositions from other members)

The Pied Pipers
People of the World Unite WIZ 5000

Lovemore Majaivana
* *Istimela*
Amandla! ZIM003

Black Umfolosi
* *Unity* WCB020
featured on *Boiling Point – musicians from hot
  countries* WCB022

Dorothy Masuka
Pata Pata Mango Island Records

COMPILATIONS

* *Virgin Records Zimbabwe Frontline 88* EWV9.
  Includes Thomas Mapfumo, Four Brothers,
  Jonah Moyo and Devera Ngwena, Zexie
  Manatsa, Oliver M'tukudzi, Susan Mapfumo
  and Robson Banda.

Spirit of the Eagle Zimbabwe Frontline Vol 2
  EWV 18. Includes Robson Banda, Thomas
  Mapfumo, Four Brothers, Nyami Nyami
  Sounds.

Under African Skies REQ 745 (BBC). Includes
  Bhundu Boys, Comrade Chinx, Ilanga and
  Lovemore Majaivana.

TRAVELLING ONWARDS IN THE REGION

Zimbabwe and Botswana are two of the easiest countries in the continent for new visitors, and good places to tune into Africa before setting off on wider, or wilder, adventures. From Botswana, it's a straightforward trip to the newly independent and consistently astonishing nation of Namibia. From Zimbabwe, Harare makes an ideal launch pad for African travel, with good transport links to Zambia, which holds plenty of surprises if you forget about the capital Lusaka, and to Malawi, where the magnificent Lake Malawi is perfect for lazing about or admiring the tropical freshwater fish in its clear depths. Finally, if you can afford to get to them, the Indian Ocean islands make sublime escapes; Madagascar, in particular, is an extraordinary cultural gem.

NAMIBIA

Namibia is an arid country. The **Namib Desert**, a virtually uninhabitable band, stretches for 1600km along its entire length – punctuated by distantly separated **seaside towns**. Inland, the **Great Escarpment** rises from the coast up to a plateau which gently descends into the less fierce lands of the Kalahari sands before they merge with Botswana.

It sounds a harsh and forbidding world – and many people leave overwhelmed by the implacable dryness. But those who take time over Namibia are increasingly fascinated by its extraterrestrial vistas of incredible **rock formations** and **unfamiliar foliage**. The dryness might seem a disincentive to wildlife, but Namibia is excellent **game-viewing** country because animals are invariably drawn to the relatively few predictable water sources.

Although the transfer of **colonial** control from Germany to South Africa in 1914, at the outbreak of the First World War, made little difference to South West Africa's oppressed indigenous population, it has left an infrastruc-ture with an incongruously cosmopolitan feel. Among the heat-shimmering sand dunes of the Atlantic seaboard, where even drizzle is an event, the main **towns** wear steeply pitched Bavarian roofs – perfect for shedding Alpine snow. In the vast rural areas the Ovambo, Herero, Kavango, Damara, Himba, Nama, San and people of European descent farm dryland crops such as maize and pumpkin, and herd cattle and sheep, while in the towns bakers beat out fine strudel pastry and you'll find delis selling traditional German food and Namibian lager – the best brew in southern Africa.

As **Africa's newest independent state**, Namibia has all the makings of an exciting destination. If Zimbabwe is anything to go by, the early post-Independence years are likely to prove a stimulating period of transition. A decisive SWAPO victory in the 1989 pre-Independence elections meant the country was not rent by internal divisions, while the fact that it fell short of taking a two-thirds majority prevented SWAPO from writing the new nation's constitution single-handedly. The new political framework, therefore, is the product of dialogue between all Namibia's parties – a promising democratic start. Together with hopes for reform in neighbouring South Africa, Namibia's own well-developed infrastructure and mineral wealth, there are reasons for considerable optimism.

THE ESSENTIALS

• **Getting there by air**. You can fly to **Windhoek**, Namibia's capital, from **Maun** (Botswana), **Gaborone** or **Harare**. There are also regular flights from Johannesburg and Cape Town, and _Air Namibia_ flies twice a week to Windhoek from London, with very reasonable fares.

• **Getting there overland**. The two principal overland routes from Botswana, along gravel roads of variable quality, are feasible by **car**. Without your own vehicle, you have to hitch across the border and continue into Namibia via a combination of **buses and hitching**.

The **southern route** crosses the border at Mamuno, normally reached from the Kalahari outpost of Ghanzi. The road heads directly for Windhoek via Gobabis, where the tar begins and from which a bus service may now be operating to the capital.

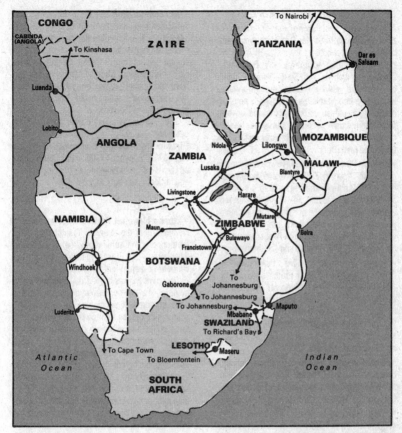

The northern route begins at Ngoma Bridge – reached through the Chobe Game Reserve at Kasane in Botswana – and traverses the Caprivi Strip, going via Katima Mulilo, Kongola, Bagani to Rundu, where the tar begins.

An alternative, if you're in a **4WD vehicle** in Botswana, is to enter Caprivi from Mohembo, just north of Shakawe.

• **Entry Requirements**. Citizens of the following countries do not need visas to enter Namibia: Botswana, Britain, Canada, France, Germany, Norway, Sweden, South Africa, Switzerland, the US, Zambia and Zimbabwe.

• **Money**. Post-Independence, Namibia's official currency remains the South African **rand** (R), divided into 100 cents (c). The exchange rate at the time of writing is £1=R4.3. Namibia's economy is so closely linked to that of South Africa that it seems unlikely that a new currency will be issued for some time. It took Botswana ten years following Independence to leave the rand currency zone, and even in Lesotho and Swaziland, which have their own currency, exchange rates are directly linked to the rand after 25 years of independence.

Because of the troubled rand, Namibia is at present a moderately cheap country to visit. But with reform in South Africa designed to improve economic prospects, the financial situation is unpredictable and we can only suggest you make enquiries when you're about to travel.

GETTING ABOUT AND ACCOMMODATION

A **road and rail spine** runs north–south through the centre of Namibia, with westward branches to the coast and eastward roads to the neighbouring countries of Botswana, Zambia, Zimbabwe and South Africa. Travel between the main towns is straightforward, but getting into Namibia's hinterland is another matter and, unless you're an intrepid adventurer, the national parks and marvellous desert lands are accessible only by **car** or on an organised **tour**.

• **Trains**. *Namibian Railways* operates trains much like those in Zimbabwe and Botswana, and from Windhoek the tracks head out north, south and west to all main centres, passing within striking distance of many of the national parks. From Windhoek there are connections with Walvis Bay (still a South African enclave), Swakopmund, Otjiwarongo and Keetmanshoop.

• **Buses**. At present Namibia's bus network is restricted to a handful of routes operated by *Mainliner* and the *National Transport Corporation*. This could well change in the coming years. The basic routes are from Windhoek to Gobabis, Tsumeb, Oshakati, Keetmanshoop, Karasburg, Mariental, Johannesburg and Cape Town.

• **Flights**. *Namib Airline*, the national service, operates scheduled **flights** from Swakopmund to Walvis Bay. *Air Cape* flies from Walvis Bay to Luderitz.

• **Cars**. Driving is easy along Namibia's 4000km of tarred roads, which connect all the main towns, and a further 40,000km of gravel. Many of the latter are good-quality, high-speed tracks that make travel at the national speed limit of 100km per hour possible. Most of the national parks and hiking trails can be reached in a normal saloon car and 4WD is only necessary for remoter areas. **Car rental** can be arranged in Windhoek (where you can also rent camper vans), Swakopmund, Keetmanshoop and Katima Mulilo.

• **Hitching**. Lifts, inevitably, are constrained by the infrequency of traffic, particularly along minor routes. On the plus side, most vehicles, when they do come, will pick you up. On the major tarred roads there should be little problem getting a ride, as long as you're in no hurry, but take food and water for long waits, especially off the tarred roads.

• **Accommodation**. All the main towns and settlements – and many small ones off the beaten track – have **hotels**, generally in the mid- to high-price range. For something cheaper, you'll frequently find **caravan parks** with **campsites**. Many national parks also have reasonably priced "bungalows" – much like Zimbabwe's national park **lodges** – with generally good facilities.

The *Accommodation Guide for Tourists*, published annually and available from the **Directorate of Nature Conservation** (Private Bag 13267, Windhoek 9000; ☎061-36975), lists all types of accommodation, from campsites and national park huts to hotels.

WHERE TO GO

• **Etosha National Park**. Located in northern Namibia, near the towns of Tsumeb and Outjo (detours off the Caprivi route from Botswana to Windhoek), the Etosha matches any of the continent's major wildlife reserves.

The park centres around the **Etosha Pan**, a gigantic, shallow depression similar to the salt pans of northern Botswana. The surrounding countryside ranges from dense bush to endless open plains and, although the pan is only full during exceptionally rainy periods, large concentrations of **big game** and **birds** are attracted by perennial springs on its verges. Lions are common, as are elephants, giraffe, springbok and zebra. Eland, the largest of all antelope, and the Damara dik-dik, the smallest, both occur here alongside a very rich variety of other wildlife, including leopards and cheetahs.

There are three **camps**; Namutoni is open throughout the year, while Okaukuejo and Halali are open from mid-March to the end of October. All have restaurants, swimming pools, reasonably priced "bungalows" and campsites.

• **Waterberg Plateau**. Some 53km east of Otjiwarongo (south of Tsumeb), Waterberg is a table-top mountain, adorned with well-watered woods. Most of its huge roof has been declared a **national park**, where rare species such as roan and sable antelope, and white rhinos, can breed unhindered. Guided hiking trails lead from the **campsite** at the foot of the mountain to the top. Book well ahead through the Directorate of Nature Conservation.

• **Skeleton Coast National Park**. The remotest of Namibia's big northern reserves, Skeleton's 15,000-square-kilometre coastal strip is an endless stretch of dunes, gravel plains and fog-beset coastline that has drawn many ships to their graves over the centuries. But it's nevertheless a place of exceptional beauty with mountains, canyons and water holes that attract desert wildlife.

Only the **southernmost section** is accessible and even that is neither cheap nor easy. To enter the park a **permit** is required from the Directorate of Nature Conservation (see "Accommodation") and you must also book accommodation at one of the fishing resorts – **Torra Bay** (open Dec & Jan only) which has campsites and tents, or **Terrace Bay** (open throughout the year) which has full board only. You can fly in to Terrace Bay from Windhoek, but a more exciting option is by 4WD up the coastal track from Swakopmund.

• **Namib-Naukluft Park**. Abutting the south of Skeleton Coast park, and due west of Windhoek, Namib-Naukluft is Namibia's biggest national park, covering an enormous coastal area of over 23,000 square kilometres. It's no cliché to say that its combination of terrains and ecosystems is unique: granite mountains, grasslands, gargantuan dunes, an estuarine lagoon, and a monumental canyon, abundant with game.

There are **campsites** around the park with limited facilities – often bookable from nearby towns like Luderitz. Prior booking is essential for campsites in the northern Naukluft section of the park. And, unfortunately, you'll certainly need your own vehicle – preferably 4WD – to get around the reserve.

• **Fish River Canyon**. In the extreme south of Namibia – just beyond the grasp of South Africa – Fish River Canyon is a fine conclusion to any voyage through the frontline states. Second in the world only to the Grand Canyon, the Fish is over half a kilometre deep and 161km long – and eminently hikeable.

A popular 90km trail along the ravine takes up to four days, and must be booked a year in advance through the Reservations Office at the Directorate of Nature Conservation and Recreation Resorts (see "Accommodation"). Minimum group size is three, and because it's quite strenuous you need a medical certificate issued within the forty days prior to departure. The trail is open between May and August.

• **Mukurub**. Finally, don't head for Mukurub, **"The Finger of God"**, an enormous eroded rock formation supported on a slender stalk, near Asab. Having stood for aeons, this geological icon of the Namibian tourist industry collapsed in 1989, when some sightseers slammed a car door. The Afrikaner neo-fascist leader Eugene Terreblanche portentously saw it as God's disapproval for Independence and commented that the Lord had symbolically closed his hand. He left open the question of why God had been sticking a finger in the air throughout the South African occupation.

ZAMBIA

Zambia isn't geared up for self-directed tourism, but for the intrepid and patient traveller it holds great potential. Situated in a high plateau and criss-crossed by river valleys, its predominant savannah landscape gives an impression of endless, empty space and untrammelled wilderness. The country is thinly populated – just seven million people in an area similar in size to France and England combined – but villages are scattered everywhere, blending invisibly into the landscape. On its peripheries, there are also forests and hilly areas.

Zambians are very kind and helpful – hospitality is dictated by tradition. English is widely spoken in the urban areas, less so in the countryside. Travelling about the less developed parts of the country, you can camp rough anywhere, or for a bit of extra comfort try at one of the mission stations. Missionaries are usually delighted to have someone new to talk to, and are also mines of information. Secondary schools are another possibility for the odd night, where camping proves impossible.

The limited circuit of tourist Zambia, by contrast, is far removed from people's everyday life, if no less alluring for that. Most visitors take in the handful of well-known attractions comprising the **Victoria Falls** and four of the nineteen **game parks**: **South Luangwa**, **Kafue**, **Sumbu** and **Nyika**. You'll find hotels and lodges at these places, with organised game drives and tour guides, all of which you pay for in hard currency.

Lusaka boasts a Ministry of Tourism and many travel agencies, which leave little to brag about – expect to find little joy here. Staff are unlikely to know about the less visited game parks, the many exquisite waterfalls, aside from Victoria Falls, and the great number of **prehistoric**, **colonial** and **scenic national monuments**. According to the National Monuments Commission about 1500 of these are waiting to be explored.

THE ESSENTIALS

• **Getting there by air.** There are direct flights from **Harare to Lusaka** on *Air Zimbabwe* or *Zambia Airways* every day except Saturday. *Air Botswana* and *Zambia Airways* each have a flight from **Gaborone to Lusaka** once a week.

• **Getting there overland.** You can approach Zambia by bus from northern Botswana or from the Victoria Falls area of northwest Zimbabwe.

From Botswana, a Friday bus service operates from **Francistown to Lusaka**. Starting midway along this route at **Kasane** you can cross into Zambia via the nearby **Kazungula ferry**; there are no buses from there but if you hitch to the Shesheke road you may be lucky enough to catch one of the infrequent buses heading for Livingstone.

A more circuitous, but ultimately more reliable route from Kasane is **via Zimbabwe**. You can hitch or catch the daily *UTC* minibus which runs between Kasane and Victoria Falls, and from there simply walk across into Zambia. Buses and taxis ply the approximately 10km from the border to Livingstone.

The **Victoria Falls/Livingstone border** is the busiest of all crossings and, because of the tourist traffic, also the easiest. Trains **from Livingstone** connect to Lusaka and further north right up to Dar es Salaam. Aside from the normal services, a weekend tourist bus which leaves from Lusaka to Livingstone on Fridays and returns on Sundays will take one-way passengers if it has seats available. The direct **Harare to Lusaka** buses all go via Chirundu.

• **Entry Requirements.** Most Commonwealth citizens can enter Zambia without a visa, though you'll still need one if you're a *UK and colonies passport holder of Asian descent* and have at any time been resident in Kenya, Tanzania or Uganda. Everyone else requires a **visa**, which can usually be issued at the border post, though it probably pays to get it in advance if you know you're going to be passing through. **Citizens of "communist" countries** (fast becoming an indeterminate category) and **South Africans** must apply for visas in advance.

If you've passed through a **yellow fever** or **cholera** zone, inoculation certificates are required.

• **Money**. Zambia uses the **kwacha**, divided into 100 **ngwee**. Recent years have seen the value of this much-troubled currency fluctuate wildly and collapse.

In an attempt to control widespread currency black-marketeering, the government has imposed a **dual pricing system**, which means that Zambians pay for certain goods and services in kwacha, but visitors must pay in hard currency. This applies to many hotels, air fares, and game park tours. Zambia's top safari camps are, however, superb, with excellent guides, service, facilities and food and a safari here is equal to, if not more rewarding than, one in East Africa where there are more tourists and no facilities for walking in the national parks. The undisputed UK travel specialists for Zambia are at *World Wide Journeys* (8 Comeragh Rd, London W14 9HP; ☎071/381 8638), who can arrange a safari or give advice about camps.

• **Maps and guides**. Maps of Zambia are available in Lusaka from the **Government Map Office**, Independence/Nationalist Road (opposite the US Embassy and tucked behind the Ministry of Lands, Mulungushi House – not to be confused with Mulungushi Hall). For **town maps** and **guide books** try *Zintu Shop*, Ridgeway or the bigger hotel bookshops.

• **Telephones**. All phones are problem-ridden, particularly in Lusaka, but be patient and keep dialling if you get strange noises instead of a ringing tone. If nothing happens, the dialled number is either out of order or has changed (phone Directory Enquiries ☎103 or the Operator ☎100 to find out). **Long-distance calls** are easier, but **public phones** are virtually non-existent, except at the Main Post Office, where you'll have to endure long queues. One of the hotels, travel agents or your embassy may let you use their phone if you're sufficiently persuasive.

GETTING ABOUT AND ACCOMMODATION

Travel by bus or train in Zambia has a few problems. Be particularly vigilant around bus and railway stations, all of which (and Lusaka above all) are plagued by thieves and bus company touts.

• **Trains**. Two **railway systems** operate in Zambia. The Lusaka–Livingstone and Lusaka–Kitwe **domestic services**, run by *Zambia Railways*, are pretty unreliable timewise. The **international service** between Dar es Salaam and Kapiri Mposhi, administered by the joint Tanzanian-Zambian corporation, *TAZARA*, is contrastingly punctual. *TAZARA* trains have a dining car, but it's still as well to take food and water, as they tend to run out of meals.

• **Buses**. The *United Bus Company of Zambia* (*UBZ*) runs a comprehensive, if unpunctual, bus service radiating **from Lusaka, Kitwe, Mpika and Ndola**, and connecting the main centres. A number of smaller private companies also operate routes such as Lusaka to the Copperbelt, which isn't covered by *UBZ*. Reliable *UBZ* **coaches** travel a number of routes as do the **postbuses**, operated by the *Posts and Telecommunications Company*, infrequently serving the major provincial towns. Although more expensive than *UBZ* coaches, the service is reliable and punctual. Enquire and book through Lusaka Main Post Office.

Luggage is usually loaded on top of buses – where it promptly gets stolen, right there at the station or otherwise en route. Travel lightly enough to take your baggage inside with you. If in doubt avoid *UBZ* ordinary buses altogether. Also be prepared for **breakdowns** – to which all Zambian buses are prone – and you may have to wait by the roadside for some time. Travel well-equipped and always take extra food and water for the journey.

• **Cars**. Car **rental** is expensive, and can only be arranged from Lusaka.

• **Hitching**. Getting rides is very easy in Zambia, particularly now the main thorough-fares have been mended. Only the Mongu road between Mumbwa and Kaoma remains to have its potholes filled.

• **Sleeping**. Zambia's graded **hotels** are expensive and must be paid for in hard currency. Even small ungraded hotels are seldom cheap, and are frequently terrible dumps. Government and District Council **resthouses**, scattered throughout the country, are the only genuinely cheap places available; the bad news, however, is that they're usually full of workers, who are victims of Zambia's dire housing shortage.

If you find yourself stranded, you can always try the nearest **mission station** or **secondary school**, or simply sleep outdoors – **camping** is permitted anywhere in the countryside.

THE ZIMBABWE–MALAWI ROUTE

Most overlanders hurry through Zambia, often without stopping a night. However, there are undeniably beautiful parts to the country and it seems a pity not to make your through-trip as relaxed and pleasant as possible.

• **Kafue National Park**. About 125km east of Livingstone you'll hit the poor road that veers north from the main highway for a further 75km to **Kafue National Park**'s Dundumwezi Gate. For budget accommodation, Kafue, in southern Zambia, is a good bet, but has smaller game concentrations than the impressive South Luangwa National Park. Because it's so close to populated areas, it's suffered badly from poaching.

In the **southern part of the park**, there are **self-catering rondavels** at *Ngoma Lodge* and *Kalala Camp*, both of which also offer full board. **Camping** is possible next to *David*

ZAMBIAN RAILWAY AND COACH SERVICES

Zambia Railways services:
Livingstone–Kapiri Mposhi daily 8.30pm (16hr) **via Lusaka** (12hr).
Lusaka–Kitwe daily 1.30pm (12hr) via Kapiri (6hr).

TAZARA services:
Kapiri Mposhi–Dar es Salaam
Ordinary trains depart Mon 5pm, arrive Wed 5.30pm, and depart Fri 11.15am and arrive Sun 9am; express trains depart Tues 8.45pm and arrive Thurs 11.53am.

UBZ coaches

From Lusaka (Freedom Way station) to:
Kitwe daily 8am, 10am, 3.30pm (6hr); £22 via **Kapiri Mposhi** (3hr).

Chipata daily 8am (9hr).
Mongu Sat 8am (9hr).
Mansa Mon/Sat 10am (12hr), via **Serenje**.

BUDGET HOTELS IN ZAMBIA

The following towns have 2-star-or-less hotels, some of which permit camping:

Chingola *Nchanga Hotel.*
Chipata *Crystal Springs Hotel* (camping).
Choma *Choma Hotel, Kalundu Motel.*
Kabwe *Mulungushi Motel, Horizon Hotel.*
Kafue *River Motel* (camping).
Kalomo *Kalomo Motel.*
Kapiri Mposhi *Unity Motel, Kapiri Motel.*
Kasama *Kwacha Relax Hotel, Kasama Hotel.*
Kitwe *Nkana Hotel, Buchi Hotel.*
Livingstone *North-Western Hotel, Zambezi Motel.*
Lusaka *Barn Motel* (out of town past airport), *Masiye Motel, Zani Muone Hotel, New Londe Motel, Garden Hotel, Blue Boar Hotel* and *Makeni Caravan Park* for camping.

Mansa *Mansa Inn.*
Mazabuka *Mazabuka Motel.*
Mbala *Arms Hotel, Grasshopper Inn.*
Mongu *Ngulu Hotel* (camping), *Lyambai Hotel, Mwanawina Resthouse* (camping).
Monze *Monze Hotel.*
Mufulira *Mufulira Hotel, Kamuchanga Hotel.*
Mumbwa *La Hacienda.*
Ndola *Hotel Continental Cuisine, Welcome Hotel, Copper Smith Arms Hotel, Falcon Hotel.*
Nyimba *Kacholola Hotel* (camping).
Petauke *Nyika Motel.*
Simba *Simba Motel.*
Zambezi *Zambezi Motel.*

Shephard Camp, which, like *Kalala*, is beautifully situated on the edge of Lake Itezhitezhi, and also at the otherwise defunct *Chungu*. Since the flooding of Itezhitezhi the road that connects the north and south of Kafue has been cut, so that it's now necessary to leave the park to get from one part to the other.

In **northern Kafue** *Lufupa Camp* has **self-catering** and **camping** facilities, and *Kafwala Camp* self-catering only. Both must be booked through *Busanga Trails*, Cairo Rd, in Lusaka.

• **Gwembe Valley**. Further east along the Livingstone to Lusaka road there are some potentially interesting detours. Between Pemba and Monze is the 72-km road down to part of the **Gwembe Valley** that survived the flooding of Lake Kariba.

• **Lochinvar National Park**. Just before Monze, not far from Lusaka, a northward turn-off leads to **Lochinvar National Park** (48km from the main road). For bird-watchers this small reserve should not be missed. The flood plain area, fringed by woodland and termite mounds, has the greatest variety of bird life imaginable. It's open throughout the year, but during the rains 4WD transport is essential. The **campsite** near *Lochinvar Lodge*, and close to some hot springs and the **Sebanzi Hill** archaeological site, is extremely cheap.

• **Lusaka**. 130km east of Monze the main road meets the major artery from Chirundu to

Lusaka, the Zambian capital, approximately 50km to the north.

Lusaka is the most difficult of all Zambian towns to spend time in, not simply due to lack of accommodation but also because of thieves and pickpockets (be especially vigilant around Cairo Road). Travellers stick out and make easy pickings. If you want to use **taxis** ask someone the going rate and be prepared to negotiate vigorously with the taxi driver – otherwise you're bound to be ripped off.

For somewhere to **stay**, consider sleeping outside town and hitching in. The **Kafue River**, south of town, is set in lovely surroundings with a wealth of water-bird life to watch and some snorting hippos to serenade you. Try the *RIMO* – *River Motel* – or the *Fishing and Angling Club* (unsignposted, but the turn-off is just south of the *RIMO*). A new place, just south of town, boasting "self-catering chalets", may also be worth a try.

There's a fair amount of choice for **food**. In the centre, the *Longhorn* (Lusaka Showgrounds, Great East Road), is cheap; further up the Great East Road, the *Oasis* offers excellent (though pricier) buffets; and the upmarket *Polo Grill*, across the Showgrounds, serves basic European cuisine (along the same lines as the hotel menus). In Northmead, *Pete's Steak House* does evening discos as well as food. Close to the caravan park in Makeni, there's an Italian and a Greek restaurant, both good but expensive. For something on the budget side, street food is offered by roadside sellers, around lunch time.

• **Luangwa River escarpment**. West of Lusaka on the Great East Road to Malawi, there's a halfway stop at the *Kachalola Hotel*, in the town sharing the same name, which allows **camping**. The route is very pretty, passing through the **Luangwa River escarpment** hills, but there's little of exceptional interest to detain you before the Chipata border post.

OTHER NATIONAL PARKS

Zambia's tourism drive aims to raise hard currency and consequently, like Botswana, facilities tend to be directed toward big-spending visitors. If you're on a budget, most of the **game reserves** will prove difficult to get around and prohibitively expensive, although there are a few cheap options – camping or

---

AIRLINE OFFICES

Airline offices in Lusaka are found on Cairo Rd: *Air Malawi*, Farmers' House (☎217690); *Air Tanzania*, Chester House (☎213717); *Air Zimbabwe*, Anchor House (☎215431); *Air Zaire*, Design House (☎218466); *British Airways*, Findeco House (☎214037); *Kenya Airways*, Findeco House (☎214569); *KLM*, Chester House (☎217629); *Royal Swazi*, Chester House (☎214222); *UTA*, Central Arcade (☎212046); *Zambia Airways* (☎213678).

EMBASSIES

Australia, Ulendo House, Cairo Rd (☎219002/3).
Botswana, 2647 Haile Selassie Rd (☎250804/253883).
Canada, Cairo Rd, Barclays Bank North End (☎216161).
Kenya, 5207 United Nations Ave (☎212531).
Malawi, Woodgate House, Cairo (☎213750).
Netherlands, 5028 United Nations Ave (☎250468/945).
Sweden, Kulima Tower, Katungila Rd (☎216018).
Tanzania, 5200 United Nations Ave (☎211422).
United Kingdom, 5201 Independence Ave (☎216770).
United States, Independence/United Nations Ave (☎214911).
Zimbabwe, Ulendo House, Cairo Rd (☎219025/6).

---

self-catering *rondavels*. For the self-catering camps, you need only take your own food as cooking facilities and linen are all provided.

• **South Luangwa National Park**, in the southernmost part of the country's northern bulge, is one of Africa's finest game reserves. Alas, poaching has reached such levels that the black rhino population, rare from the start, has been reduced to non-breeding levels. The remaining individuals are so scattered that they can no longer find a mate. On the plus side, though, other mammals, especially elephant, are still plentiful and Thornicroft's giraffes, unique to the valley, are found in the southern sector of the park in considerable numbers.

Travellers can, and do, go to Luangwa without their own **transport**. You can sometimes get lifts from *LIRP*, the *Luangwa Integrated Resource Development Project*, in Chipata, or with any of the government or aid agency offices that make frequent trips into the valley. There is no bus service. Once in the park you're reliant on hitching lifts or else on the reasonably priced game drives from the tourist lodges.

The one **self-catering camp** in South Luangwa, the privately run *James Schultz Camp* near **Mfuwe Bridge**, allows camping. The Wildlife Society of Zambia, Chipata branch, runs a **campsite** next to **Chinzombo**, and *Chibembe Safari Camp* in the north of the park has camping for a small charge and also allows travellers to join their game drives.

• **Sumbu National Park**. One of the least-accessible of Zambia's developed game reserves, **Sumbu**, lies on the southern shore of Lake Tanganyika. A weekly **flight** goes to Kasaba Bay, but by car it's hard work and there are no self-catering facilities, so it's only a destination for the most determined independent traveller.

• *Ilse Mwanza*

MOZAMBIQUE

Under Portuguese colonial rule **Mozambique** was the exotic-Mediterranean resort of white Rhodesians and South Africans. Not only did it have palmed beaches along the closest coastline to Rhodesia, but Lorenzo Marques (as Maputo was then), with its Portuguese feel, gave whites isolated on the tip of Africa a taste of Europe. In 1972 tourism brought considerable revenue to Mozambique, with its 282 hotels hosting almost 300,000 visitors. By 1978, just three years after Independence, all organised tourism to Mozambique had stopped.

After Mozambique's independence, the main export of South Africa and Rhodesia (before its own liberation) there was war, as the apartheid states became concerned that Mozambique was harbouring nationalist guerillas who were infiltrating into their countries. South Africa helped to set up and back the *Renamo* rebel movement, initially as a small band that would harass Rhodesia's liberation fighters, then, after Zimbabwe's independence, as a monstrous destabilisation machine that by the middle of the 1980s had brought war, famine and starvation to the rural areas of all ten provinces of Mozambique.

Happily, October 1992 saw the signing of a peace declaration between the Frelimo government and Renamo. The UN is overseeing the peace-keeping process and substantially reducing the number of weapons within the country. The infrastructure is slowly being rebuilt and the country painfully getting back on its feet, crippled by foreign debt, the appalling aftermath of sixteen years of war, drought and acute poverty. In the face of all this, the people remain hearteningly friendly, and full of goodwill to outsiders.

THE ESSENTIALS

• **Getting there by air**. Far and away the easiest way to get to Mozambique is to **fly** on the national airline *LAM* or on *Air Zimbabwe*, from Harare to Maputo, or from Johannesburg on *SAA* or *LAM*. *LAM* also flies between Harare and Beira. Be warned though: *LAM* can be disorganised and there have been reports of flights leaving before schedule, despite tickets having been confirmed. Be prepared to spend hours in the *LAM* office confirming the return leg.

• **Getting there overland**. It is possible to travel safely by daily minibus from Machipanda, on the border with Zimbabwe, three kilometres from Mutare, to Beira 300km away on the coast . The other route is to take a truck from Harare to Blantyre via Tete – a route formerly known as the *Tete Hell Run,* owing to the large number of ambushes en route, and still not recommended. Trucks also leave daily from Johannesburg to Maputo via Swaziland, often used by migrant workers.

• **Entry requirements**. All visitors require visas; they are issued at point of entry, but advance approval must be obtained from a Mozambique diplomatic mission abroad, or through the Ministerio dos Negocios Estrangeiros, CP 290, Maputo. See under Harare listings for the embassy in Zimbabwe. Visas may take up to five days to be issued and you'll need two photos. Offices issue visas in Johannesburg (3rd Floor, Noswall Hall, 3 Stiemens Street, Braamfontein), Mbabane, Lusaka, Dar es Salaam, Lilongwe and Blantyre.

• **Money**. Mozambique's currency is the *metical*, or *metacais* (MTS) when there are two or more of them, divided into 100 *centavos* (which have only infinitesimal value and are rarely used).

You're obliged to change US$30 into local currency on arrival at the airport. US dollars are very useful for the Maputo hard currency shop and for the black market. There's an airport departure tax of US$10 for international flights. Banks are slow – hand in the paperwork and return in an hour.

• **Shopping and food**. You can buy fresh fish and vegetables in the market, and pricey goods imported from Zimbabwe and South Africa in the shops. On the coast you'll find wonderful seafood such as huge prawns and squid; a local speciality is the delicious *matapa*, a mix of cassava, dried shrimps and cashew nuts.

GETTING ABOUT

All the major cities are safe to visit but overland travel between them is not very advisable, with a number of police barricades as well as many armed teenage soldiers. Occasionally it is necessary to travel with a convoy. Transport is normally on the back of overloaded trucks. **Air travel** is the only secure way to get from one town to another, with fares cheap by European standards. **Coastal steamers** are a safe option, but limited to once or twice a week and subject to cancellation at short notice. **Trains** still appear to be "temporarily suspended", but occasionally deliver cargo. **Car rental** is available in Maputo and Beira, but be aware that rules of the road are often not observed. **Taxis** also operate in these cities, though you should be sure to negotiate the price beforehand.

People everywhere are highly **security**-conscious, and suspicions can easily be aroused. Always ask permission before taking photographs and if in doubt, don't; and carry all **documents** at all times – including vehicle registration forms if you're in your own car.

WHERE TO GO

• **Maputo**. The **beach** is not recommended due to pollution, and the jellyfish and bluebottles which get washed ashore – both can give nasty (but non-lethal) stings. If it all sounds too hazardous, keep your feet dry and just watch the fishermen and clam collectors.There are cleaner beaches at Catembe, a short and cheap ferry ride away. Although run-down, Catembe boasts a reasonable restaurant.

In town, the **Natural History Museum** exhibits are on the faded and dusty side but entertaining nevertheless (closed Mon). There's also a coin museum and a museum of the revolution. Two buildings in town worth visiting are the 1924 railway station and the French Club – Cassa de Ferro. The French architect Eiffel desiged the dome of the station and the Club itself. The market at Avenue 25 de Setembro shouldn't be missed for its large selection of fresh fish, fruit, vegetables and local handicraft. A smaller market at Xipamanine, out of town, doubles as the main transport hub.

Surprisingly perhaps, **eating out** is an enticing possibility. The most upmarket restaurant is the South-African-run *Restaurant Lulas Pequim* near the *Polana Hotel*. The *Costa Do Sol* is great for seafood and very popular – booking is advisable on Sundays. *Zambi*, on the seafront near the Catembe ferry has deteriorated, while the *Continental*, opposite the main post office, with its pavement terrace, remains popular, though there are large numbers of beggars outside. The *Impala* on Karl Marx Avenue does tasty, good-value steaks and fish, while the *Peri Peri* does excellent *prego* and prawns. **Nightlife** is restricted to beer halls.

The *Polana Hotel*, Avenida Julius Nyerere, has a reputation as one of southern Africa's grandest hotels and is very expensive. Better value is the *Cordosa* on Avenida Patrice Lumumba, which has a swimming pool, seaside terrace and restaurant; it isn't cheap but has been recommended. *Hotel Escola Andalucia* is the training school for hotel staff and retains a real Portuguese character. Away from the seafront, the *Rovuma Hotel* next to the cathedral is good value, with the business-oriented *Turismo* and *Tivoli* hotels in the same vicinity,

but neither cheap nor remarkable. There is also a selection of cheap *pensaos*, often doubling as brothels. Negotiate the price and be sure to check the availability of water and electricity.

• **Inhaca Island**. A broken-off section of the peninsula which projects south of Maputo Bay, Inhaca is a perfect tropical island with a good reef and swimming.

The island is a two-hour **charter boat ride** away or a 20-min **flight** from the capital. Locals use boats which are much cheaper, take three hours and go two or three times per week. The boats normally return to Maputo after a couple of hours at Inhaca; enquire at the quay for times. The *Hotel Inhaca*, on Inhaca, has fairly expensive doubles and there is a campsite.

Take all your supplies. Inhaca has no shop– nor rubbish collection, so be sure not to add to the growing piles of litter. Several paradise islands off the coast between Maputo and Beira which were never affected during the war, primarily remain exclusive havens.

• *John Bradshaw*

MALAWI

With its mountains, game reserves and lake vistas, **Malawi** is an almost ideal country for independent travellers. A regular and inexpensive transport network covers the length of the country, there's cheap accommodation all over and very few tourists to share it with. Along with Chichewa, English is the national language – and widely spoken. Malawians are extremely friendly and courteous, making it an easy and pleasant place to travel in. The country's shortcoming is its political reputation for authoritarian rule, internment or assassination of trade unionists, opposition leaders and writers, and for maintaining full diplomatic relations with South Africa over the years. In June 1993 change was on the way with the first ever countrywide referendum overwhelmingly voting for the end of a one-party state, and Parliament repealing legislation entrenching single-party government.

THE ESSENTIALS

• **Getting there by air**. *Air Malawi* and *Air Zimbabwe*, between them, provide daily direct flights from Harare to Lilongwe. *Air Ethiopia* also flies to Lilongwe en route to Addis Ababa. *Air Botswana* flies between Gaborone and

Lilongwe once weekly. There's an airport **departure tax**.

• **Getting there overland**. Overland routes through Zambia leave Zimbabwe at Livingstone or Chirundu, with a minor crossing at Kariba. The rebel-beleaguered route that leaves Zimbabwe at Nyamapanda to go through Mozambique isn't currently recommended, although travellers do occasionally use it.

• **Entry requirements**. Visas are not required by EC passport holders, North Americans, and nationals of Australia, New Zealand and Southern African countries except Mozambique and Angola. All visitors are required to show a return/onward ticket, and **passports** must be valid at least six months beyond the duration of your intended stay.

• **A note on dress and appearance**. Under Hastings Banda's autocratic rule, Malawi has a host of bizarre, conservative regulations. It's illegal, for example, for women to appear in public in above-the-knee cuts or in trousers – a rule exempted only at the resorts. For men, long hair (below the collar) and flares are prohibited. This may well change soon, but take a skirt!

• **Money**. The basic unit of currency is the Malawian *kwacha* (K), divided into 100 *tambala* (t). Travellers' cheques are accepted by banks, and credit cards are usable at some places in the main centres of Blantyre, Lilongwe, Mzuzu and Zomba.

GETTING ABOUT AND ACCOMMODATION

Although Malawi runs a slow and cursory **rail** service, the best way to get about overland is on the comprehensive **bus** network, which includes speedy coaches on major routes. Undoubtedly the most desirable form of transport is the **ferry** that steams up and down the lake, calling in at the ports and islands.

• **Accommodation**. Towns and resorts alike have a whole range of accommodation, from expensive **hotels** to cheap **rest houses**. The rest houses vary from good in some places to pretty seedy in others; the following places have inexpensive ones: Dedza, Karonga, Likoma Island, Monkey Bay, Mount Mulanje, Mzimba, Mzuzu, Nkhata Bay, Nkhotakota, Ntcheu, Nyika National Park (Chilinda Rest Camp), Zomba.

WHERE TO GO

• **Lake Malawi**. The country's overwhelming attraction, Lake Malawi's 24,000-square-kilometre body of water floods the local section of the Great Rift Valley. The lakeside beaches, with mountain views, provide the perfect settings for a series of resorts, while its clear waters and 350 or so species of freshwater tropical fish – the world's greatest variety – provide a wonderland for snorkelling.

Most **accommodation**, varying from simple chalets to luxury hotels, is concentrated along the southern shores of the lake at Salima and Mangoche.

• **Cape Maclear**. At Cape Maclear in the **Lake Malawi National Park**, also in the south, you'll find the most talked-about budget camp in Malawi: the popular and very sociable *Mr Steven's Camp*.

• **The lake steamer route**. The steamer that meanders up and down the length of the lake starts its three-day-long northward haul at nearby **Monkey Bay**. It pulls in at **Nkhotakhota**, one of Africa's oldest market towns (with plenty of cheap accommodation) and at **Likoma Island** – site of an historic mission and an imposing church – which has two budget rest houses. Before the final haul to Chilumba, the boat harbours at **Chitimba**, nearest port to Malawi's loveliest settlement at **Livingstonia**, set 800m above the lake, with superb views, in spectacular countryside.

• **Blantyre and Zomba**. South of the lake, Malawi's nicest large towns are sited amid impressive mountain country. **Blantyre** is the commercial centre of Malawi and has the feel of a bustling living organism in contrast to the straightjacketed appearance of the planned capital at Lilongwe. But the most charming centre of the south is the university town and former capital of **Zomba**. Set at the foot of **Mount Zomba**, with a rest house and lively market, it makes a good base before setting off for the heights. The mountain itself is very pretty with sparkling streams and tiny waterfalls. Up here you'll find a pleasant campsite and the breathtakingly set *Ku-Chawe Inn*. You can sip tea sitting on its jettying balcony 2000m above the scooped-out valley.

• The **Mulanje Massif**, rising 3000m above sea level, in the southeast, is magnificent. This huge mountain range offers challenging rock climbing and excellent walking and trout fishing. Further attractions include impressive bird and wildlife, marvellous wild flowers and, growing among the ravines and along streams, the unique Mulanje cedars and aloes. Trails weave through the rugged and rolling terrain and on the mountain top is a series of seven shelters.

• **Lengwe National Park**. Away from the hills and the lake, Malawi's main attractions are the game reserves. In the south, on the Mozambique border, the **Lengwe National Park** is set in a pocket of the riverine forest that once extended down the Shire River to Chiromo. This is the northernmost range of nyala antelope and you'll also see a wide variety of other ungulates. Cats are rarer although lions make occasional visits and leopards and caracals are both present. Among the perks of Lengwe are the hides built over water holes, which provide excellent vantages for seeing animals. Self-catering accommodation is provided by the Department of Tourism.

• **Kasungu National Park**. Abutting Zambia, 112km north of Lilongwe, **Kasungu** is the largest of Malawi's game reserves and also has the country's richest variety of wildlife. Its biggest attractions – both in size and appeal – are the elephants that drink in the region's characteristic *dambos*, or river channels, at dawn and dusk. There are also some sizeable buffalo herds and all the herbivores and hunters you could hope for: lions, leopards, cheetahs, servals, jackals and hunting dogs. Lodge accommodation is available and camping is also permitted.

• **Nyika National Park**, in the far north, is remote and beautiful, covering most of the Nyika Plateau, at an altitude of 2000–3000m. The climb through the rugged hills and valleys breaks into a world of rolling downs, dense stands of trees, peaty streams and cloud-masked hilltops. The area's wildlife populations are on the increase. Large herds of eland – 100 or more – make frequent appearances along with zebras, lions and leopards; equally enchanting are the wondrous butterflies and many rare bird varieties. There's reasonably priced accommodation at *Chilinda Camp* run by the Department of National Parks and Wildlife.

• **Other game reserves** include **Majete Game Reserve**, 40km north of Lengwe, **Mwabvi Game Reserve**, southeast of Lengwe, which boasts a small black rhino population, **Nkhotakhota Game Reserve** near the lakeside town of the same name, **Lilongwe Nature Reserve** in the capital, and **Michiru Mountain Park**, near Blantyre, offering excellent bird-watching.

MAURITIUS AND THE COMORO ISLANDS

Southern Africa has an exceptionally tempting array of tropical islands: Mauritius, the Comoros and Réunion, and Madagascar.

Curiously, **MAURITIUS**, the most distant of the islands off the Mozambique coast, is the easiest to reach, with a **direct flight from Harare** on *Air Zimbabwe* every Saturday . Its direct local air links make it the obvious springboard for exploring the region's other islands, while other flights from Mauritius link it to Kenya, several European capitals, India, Hong Kong and Malaysia.

Mauritius itself is generally sold to package tourists as the archetypal "tropical island paradise". But away from the world of smart hotels, stylish swimsuits and posers is the undoubtedly beautiful island that moved Mark Twain to write: "God saw Mauritius and designed Heaven in its image." For independent travellers, there are cheap beach huts, delicious seafood, hikes and miles of gorgeous beaches.

THE COMORO ISLANDS

After Mozambique's offshore islands, the closest to the continent are the seldom-visited **COMORO ISLANDS**. The three northernmost Comoros – **Ngazidia** (or Grande Comore), **Masamoudou** and **Mohéli** – have strong South African links, but the fourth island of the group, **Mayotte**, meanwhile, remains connected to France.

Despite the Comoros' obvious attractions, there are a number of disincentives to visits, not least of which is the exceedingly high **cost** of being there. This is partly due to everything being imported from South Africa and partly to the fact that visitors are more or less captive to local monopolies. As far as **accommodation** goes, there's little besides expensive luxury **hotels**; there are no **campsites**.

The local **language** is Comoran, a mixture of Arabic and Swahili, but you'll get by with Swahili or French.

• **Getting there**. Air travel, the principal way of getting to the Comoros, is pricey but relatively easy, with a surprising number of flights between the archipelago and the African mainland. Apart from services from France and South Africa, there are regional connections on *Air Madagascar* with Nairobi, Antananarivo (Madagascar) and Mauritius; *Air Tanzania* with Dar es Salaam; and *South African Airways* with Lilongwe (Malawi). For a taste of the Comoros you can get good-value excursions from Dar es Salaam and Nairobi to Madagascar, stopping off for a day or two at Moroni – all most people can afford. *Réunion Air Services* flies from Réunion to the French island of Mayotte.

You can **travel between the four islands**, including Mayotte, by boat or on *Air Comores*.

• **Ngazidia**. The main island, **Ngazidia**, boasts the world's largest volcanic crater and the 2362m-high **Mount Kartala**, an active volcano surrounded by fields of sweet-smelling ylang-ylang, jasmine, cloves, cinnamon and vanilla. Its winding medieval streets and the mosques of the compact capital, **Moroni**, have a strong Arabic feel, reflecting centuries of Islamic influence overlaid on African and Malagache culture. Near town a beach of fine sands slides into an aquamarine bay; in the evenings flying foxes sweep through the skies.

Arriving at Moroni, there's nowhere to change **money** at the airport, so make sure you have some hard currency in cash. **Taxis** are the only way to get into Moroni. There's a **bank** in town, where you can change money, or try one of the hotels.

MADAGASCAR

For the adventurous traveller, **MADAGASCAR** unquestionably deserves to be the ultimate destination. The island, the globe's fourth largest, houses wide diversities of both **culture and geography**, and though its infrastructure is legendarily run-down, there is plenty of good, cheap accommodation and excellent food.

Madagascar's **people**, too, belong to some eighteen different cultures, though they are united by a common **language**, *Malagache*, of which there are a number of dialects. Many people also speak French, especially in towns; unless you learn Malagache it's absolutely indispensable for getting around, as English is virtually unknown.

THE ESSENTIALS

• **Getting there**. Madagascar can be reached **by air** from the neighbouring islands of Mauritius and the Comoros on *Air Madagascar* or *Air Mauritius*. South African Airways also has flights to the island. Reasonably priced excursions from East Africa depart from Dar es Salaam and Nairobi. From Europe there are flights from Paris, Zürich and most cheaply from London on *Aeroflot* via Moscow.

• **Entry requirements**. All visitors require visas, which are quite expensive, and must be obtained in advance from a Malagasy representative. There are **diplomatic representatives** in the Comoro Islands, Mauritius, Tanzania and Kenya, plus, outside Africa, Australia, the US, UK, and elsewhere.

An initial **entry permit** of up to a month is given with no problem. For longer you must reapply, which can take a while but because of the incredible friendliness of Malagasy people, is less hassle than usual.

Customs is a lengthy business, with officials counting all money and travellers' cheques note by note. On no account lose your currency declaration form – it's taken very seriously indeed – and make sure figures tally.

• **Money and costs**. The currency used is the *Malagache Franc*. Madagascar is one of the cheapest African countries for travellers. On the small offshore island of Nosy Boraha, you can eat three excellent meals a day and have a bed in a traditional-style hut for next to nothing. Elsewhere **hotel rooms** are similarly good value outside the capital, which is only slightly more expensive. Cheap **food** – fruit, fish and vegetables – are easy to buy at markets, and you can eat extremely well on the hybrid French-Malagache cuisine. The downside of the good value offered to Western visitors is the poverty. Begging is rife, especially in the towns.

• **Guidebooks**. Hilary Bradt's *Guide to Madagascar* (Bradt) is the only reliable and useful guide.

GETTING ABOUT AND ACCOMMODATION

Madagascar is a huge country and **getting around** can be an adventure in itself.

• **By air**. The easiest and most reliable way to travel to all corners of the country is on *Air Madagascar's* internal network. It's cheap and heavily booked.

• **By rail**. Unless you're short of time, far and away the most interesting way to travel is overland. The **rail** service is limited to a few stretches of track which can't really be considered a network but there are two memorable journeys to the coast. One goes from the capital to Taomasina, stopping on the way at **Perinet**, where there's a fantastic rickety old station hotel. Within walking distance is the forest reserve inhabited by indri, the largest of all the lemurs. The second coastward track tumbles down from the regional centre of **Fianarantsoa** to the coastal town of **Manakara**.

• **By road**. Road travel presents its own uniquely Madagascan problems due to total lack of maintenance of roads and a shortage of spare parts. There are no buses, only *taxi-brousses* – small Peugeot pickups into which up to 25 passengers are crammed – or larger trucks, which ply the routes between all the centres. Neither are there timetables; vehicles leave only once they're full, which can be days after the first passengers arrive. The dilapidated state of the roads means that the vans veer wildly on and off the road depending on where the best surface is, and will often make detours through the bush to avoid the terrible ruts. But local people routinely travel this way and it is a great way to make contact. **Car rental** is possible, but only with a Malagasy driver. Vehicles are precious imports not entrusted to foreigners unfamiliar with the road.

WHERE TO GO

• **The Central Plateau – and wildlife**. After Madagascar broke off and drifted from the mainland, many of its animals and plants developed along their own lines. The island's **central plateau** is covered in parts with wonderful **rainforests**, inhabited by forty varieties of **lemur** – gentle primates found in their natural state nowhere else – which are as exciting to track as gorillas. The forests – ideal for hiking – also host other unique denizens such as the two-foot-long **horned chameleons**. And there's nothing dangerous – no fierce animals and not a single poisonous snake.

Around the forests people live in **villages** of pitch-roofed traditional timber huts, cultivate rice in flooded paddies, and herd cattle. On all sides the plateau falls away to beautiful **tropical beaches** edged with coconut palms – so plentiful that fruits remain unpicked.

• **Coral islands**. Off the east and west coasts are the two small **coral islands** of **Nosy Be**, which has a *Holiday Inn* – the only international hotel apart from the capital's *Hilton* – and **Nosy Boraha** (Isle Ste Marie), a less pretentious place and perfect for cheap beach holidays with snorkelling and scuba diving.

• **The South**. The semi-desert of the **south** is foliated by the thorn-succulents of the **spiny forest**, among which locally adapted lemurs live. Berenty Reserve near Fort Dauphin, where sightings of ring-tailed lemurs are guaranteed, is recommended.

BOOKS

Reading up on Zimbabwe before you go poses few problems, and there's no need to take everything with you, either – the country has a flourishing high-quality domestic publishing industry producing both fiction and non-fiction. The best covered topics, not unexpectedly, are colonisation and the two *chimurengas* (liberation struggles), but you'll find material on most subjects. Zimbabwe-produced books aren't always easy to get hold of outside the country, but specialist African/Third World bookshops sometimes stock them, and will certainly be able to order them. The biggest publishing concerns are Zimbabwe Publishing House (ZPH), Baobab and Mambo.

Botswana is another story, with no real indigenous book-publishing apart from branches of big British companies involved in educational books. Several glossy tomes are, however, published outside the country, covering natural history and landscape.

ZIMBABWE'S HISTORY

*A number of good school texts give a quick and easy **overview** of Zimbabwe's history. They include:*

David Beach, *Zimbabwe: A New History for Primary Schools* (College Press, Harare 1982). Account by one of the country's leading historians, giving reliable, readable and condensed coverage of 15,000 years of history.

Peter Garlake and Andre Procter, *People Making History* (2 volumes; ZPH, Harare 1985). The first volume covers pre-colonial history, and the second the twentieth century.

In **Britain**, the ***Africa Book Centre*** (38 King St, London WC2E 8JT; ☎071/240 6649) stocks many books on Zimbabwe, and also offers a mail-order service. Particular titles published in Zimbabwe may also be ordered via *Leishman and Taussig* (2B Westgate, Southwell, Notts NG25 0JH).

Aimed at secondary schools, they go into more depth than Beach, with considerable emphasis on class analysis.

S I G Mudenege, *A Political History of Munhumutapa* (James Currey, London 1988). A picture of life in a stable African state, inter-reacting with the Portuguese on the coast of Mozambique.

PRE-CHIMURENGA

David Beach, *The Shona and Zimbabwe 900–1850: An Outline of Shona History* (Mambo Press, 1980). *The* history of the Shona groupings in their heyday and of events on the Zimbabwean plateau before the arrival of the Ndebele and their conquests in the southwest.

David Beach, *War and Politics in Zimbabwe 1840–1900* (Mambo, 1986). A kind of sequel to the above, covering the crumbling at the edges of Shona domination of the region with the arrival of Nguni raiders and finally the *coup de grâce* of British colonial conquest.

Stanlake Samkange, *On Trial For My Country* (Heinemann African Writers Series, Oxford 1967). Set up as two trials, this classic dramatised account has Rhodes and Lobengula called in the afterlife to account for their conduct in the events leading up to the BSAC's colonisation of Matabeleland.

Elizabeth Schmidt, *Peasants, Traders and Wives: Shona Women in the History of Zimbabwe, 1870–1939* (James Currey, London 1992). Fascinating documentation of the lives of women in Southern Rhodesia.

Charles van Onselen, *Chibaro: African Mine Labour in Southern Rhodesia 1900–1933* (Pluto, London 1976). Don't be put off by the dry, academic-sounding title. *Chibaro* means "forced or slave labour" and in van Onselen's inimitable way this lively book reveals exactly how the colonial system's tentacles reached into workers' everyday lives, and their response.

THE SECOND CHIMURENGA

The Second Chimurenga was a significant formative phase in the birth of Independent Zimbabwe, so it's no surprise that there's a lot of material on the war, the nationalist movement and the decade leading up to liberation.

During this period white Rhodesians published a lot from their point of view, with no shortage of bizarre coffee-table books with dramatic pictures of Fireforce units swooping down on "terrs" – always a simplified vision of good versus evil, in which right (white) was winning. Only since Independence has the other side of the story been told, and although sometimes the picture is again reduced to goodies and baddies, the reader now at least has the freedom to choose which view to take.

Julie Frederikse, *None But Ourselves: Masses vs Media in the Making of Zimbabwe* (James Currey, London; Ravan Press, Joburg; ZPH, Harare; Viking Penguin, New York: 1982). An amazing quantity of material, collected and collaged into a complex tapestry of interviews, photographs, quotes from contemporary media and commentary. Very highly recommended.

David Lan, *Guns & Rain: Guerillas & Spirit Mediums in Zimbabwe* (James Currey, London/ University of California Press, Berkeley & L.A. 1985). A fascinating excursion into the world view of the people of Zimbabwe's remote Dande region along the eastern Zambezi River, and the role of spirit mediums in fostering the liberation struggle among the peasantry.

Terence Ranger, *Peasant Consciousness and Guerilla War in Zimbabwe* (James Currey, London; University of California Press: 1985). Anything by Ranger (and he's prolific) is worth reading for the entertaining, rolling narrative argument and gripping insights. *Peasant Consciousness* draws comparisons between the anti-colonial struggle in Zimbabwe and those in Kenya and Mozambique.

Irene Staunton (ed), *Mother of the Revolution* (James Currey, London 1990). A vivid portrait of the war experiences of thirty Zimbabwean women, telling their story in their own words.

POST-INDEPENDENCE ZIMBABWE

John Hatchard, *Individual Freedoms and State Security* (James Currey, London 1993). An interesting look at the strength of the Zimbabwean state, and its hold over society.

Ibbo Mandaza and Lloyd Sachikonye (eds), *The One Party State and Democracy* (SAPES, 1991). Outlines the debate that ensued upon the suggestion by ZANU that Zimbabwe should adopt the one-party system so prevalent in the rest of Africa in the 1980s.

Robin Palmer and Isobel Birch, *Zimbabwe, A Land Divided* (Oxfam, 1992). A brief, lively and well-illustrated introduction to the country, which looks at culture as well as providing social information.

Colin Stoneman and Lionel Cliffe, *Zimbabwe* (Pinter Publishers 1989). Part of the Marxist Regime Series and aimed mainly at students, this somewhat dry account still provides a solid and up-to-date summary of available material on the country's politics, economics and society.

Colin Stoneman (ed), *Zimbabwe's Prospects* (Macmillan 1988). An essay collection looking at possible and probable directions for Zimbabwe into the 1990s – not all of it optimistic, although not all gloom and doom either.

BOTSWANA'S HISTORY

There are few up-to-date histories of Botswana. The only easily available general history is the school text: **T Tlou and A Campbell, *History of Botswana*** (Macmillan Botswana, Gaborone 1984). It gives solid coverage from prehistoric times through to developments in the early 1980s.

Bessie Head, *Serowe: Village of the Rain Wind* (Heinemann African Writers Series 1981). The story of Serowe over the last 100 years, largely collections of testaments by residents. There are also sound pieces on the Swaneng Project and the Brigades Movement.

Fred Morton and Jeff Ramsay (eds), *The Birth of Botswana* (Longman Botswana 1987). A useful collection of essays on parties, rulers and regions up to 1966.

THE KALAHARI

Michael Main, *Kalahari: Life's Variety in Dune and Delta* (Southern Books, Johannesburg 1987). Fascinating and lively mêlée of personalised history, natural history, geology, sociology and anthropology, with great anecdotes, well-chosen photographs and a lightness of touch that belies its intelligence.

Mark and Delia Owens, *Cry of the Kalahari* (Fontana 1986). A thoroughly readable Botswana version of *Born Free* by two young US naturalists who spent seven years in the Kalahari studying lions and brown hyenas. Much more of a good yarn than straight natural history, the book has become something of a cult, with tours organised to Deception Valley where the authors worked. They tackle the thorny issue of fences in Botswana which protect cattle, but which they believe cause the deaths of countless wild animals.

Karen Ross, *Jewel of the Kalahari: Okavango* (BBC Books, London 1987). Similar in scope to Main's text, this book of the BBC television series isn't quite as well written. On the other hand, coverage is very sound and it provides excellent and interesting background.

Marjorie Shostak, *Nisa* (Earthscan 1990). A fascinating book – both bawdy and romantic – based on the life of a !Kung woman living in a hostile Kalahari environment.

Laurens van der Post, *The Lost World of the Kalahari* (Penguin, Harmondsworth 1962). The author's almost spiritual quest to find, and film, San people still existing as pure hunter-gatherers. *The Heart of the Hunter* (Penguin, Harmondsworth) is the sequel, although it can be read on its own, dwelling on the San he met and their mythology.

Joseph Hanlon, *Beggar Your Neighbours: Apartheid Power in Southern Africa* (CIIR/ James Currey, London; Indiana University Press, Bloomington: 1986). A comprehensive examination of South Africa's role in the region, its manoeuvres to maintain pre-eminence through military and economic pressures. There's detailed background on its dealings with each of the frontline states.

Carol B Thompson, *Challenge to Imperialism: The Frontline States in the Liberation of Zimbabwe* (ZPH, Harare 1985). A look at the role of the frontline states in supporting Zimbabwe through its liberation birth-trauma, and strategies for aiding attempts for all the countries to disengage from South African neo-imperialist control.

William Plomer, *Cecil Rhodes* (David Philip, Cape Town 1984). There are countless books on Rhodes. Most feed the legend, although the distance of time has made some historians readier to regard him as a flawed colossus – but a giant nonetheless. This is a re-publication of one of the most interesting critical accounts, written several decades ago, against the prevailing grain, by a South African poet-novelist, when colonialism was still regarded as a good thing. It pulls no punches in presenting Rhodes as an immature person driven by his weaknesses.

D N Beach, *Mapondera 1840–1904* (Mambo 1989). More than simply biography, this account of one of Zimbabwe's last independent rulers, who resisted European conquest, also looks at life in the region just south of the eastern Zambezi River at the eve of colonisation. Equally absorbing is the way the book is put together – a fascinating example of the art and craft of writing history. The author eschews "established facts", a notion which he says "involves no original thinking", and instead lays bare the contradictory accounts, which are his raw material.

Frederick Courtenay Selous, *Travel and Adventure in South East Africa* (Century 1984). Reprint of an account by one of Africa's notorious Victorian hunters and adventurers, who spent time in Zimbabwe just prior to colonisation and in the early colonial years.

Sir Charles Rey, *Monarch of All I Survey: Bechuanaland Diaries 1929–1937* (Botswana Society, Gaborone/Lilian Barber, NY/James Currey, London 1988). These dashingly colloquial diaries by the energetic parvenu who was governor of Bechuanaland for eight years, reveal as much about his attitudes to his colleagues and associates as about colonial neglect of the territory. And all brought alive by his humour and personal detail.

Peter Garlake, *The Painted Caves* (Modus Publications, Harare 1987). A well-illustrated account of San rock art in Zimbabwe – essential reading for anyone with even the slightest interest in the topic, and the first attempt at a coherent analysis with both interpretation and detailed instructions on where to find 38 of the finest painting sites.

Peter Garlake, *Great Zimbabwe Described and Explained* (ZPH 1982). A useful little booklet by the leading authority on the topic, condensing his research into a guide for visitors and seemingly discussing every bit of stonework. It includes a useful bibliography for enthusiasts.

Garlake has also produced another brief booklet called ***Life at Great Zimbabwe***, which is in many ways the most accessible publication about the place, with pen and ink illustrations providing an impression of how it might have been, and discussion that succeeds in bringing the ruins alive.

And if you're very interested in the whole topic of unravelling the meanings of rock art, look at the large body of work by **J D Lewis-Williams**, a pioneer in the field and the starting point for Garlake. Although Lewis-Williams' research is based on rock art in South Africa, it's sufficiently related to be enlightening. Two of his books worth reading are ***Believing and Seeing*** (Academic Press, London 1981) and ***The Rock Art of Southern Africa*** (University Press, Cambridge 1983).

H Ellert, *The Material Culture of Zimbabwe* (Longman Zimbabwe/Sam Gozo, Harare 1984). Authoritative coverage of all aspects of Zimbabwe's traditional arts and crafts, including jewellery, vernacular architecture, carving, ceramics, tools and games.

F Mor, *Shona Sculpture* (Jongwe, Harare 1987). Written in idiosyncratic and at times impenetrable English, by an Italian sculptor, this book is nevertheless good value for the copious outstanding colour photographs of sculptures.

M Arnold, *Zimbabwean Stone Sculpture* (Books of Zimbabwe, Bulawayo). Altogether the most solid account of the subject, if less lavishly illustrated than Mor's.

A B Plangger, *Serima* (Mambo). Subtitled *Towards an African Expression of Christian Belief*, a well-illustrated account of the sculpture movement nurtured at Serima Mission.

Peter Jackson, *Historic Buildings of Harare* (Quest, Harare 1986). The only coherent assessment of colonial architecture in Zimbabwe by one of the country's top architects. Apart from a catalogue of some of the finest examples of historic buildings, there's also a run-through of the development of Zimbabwe's distinct architectural styles.

COFFEE-TABLE BOOKS

One of the cheapest and most interesting coffee-table books on **Zimbabwe** *is the paperback picture book* ***The Nature of Zimbabwe***, *published in 1988 by the International Union for the Conservation of Nature and Natural Resources, which covers the ecology, the environment and development. Similar volumes have also been published on Botswana and Zambia.*

De luxe, glossy books about **Botswana** *abound, especially of the Okavango Delta, the Kalahari Desert and its hunter-gatherers. None can be recommended above the others. Spend your £20 or so and marvel.*

Herman Potgieter and Clive Walker, *Above Africa: Aerial Photography from the Okavango Swamplands* (New Holland, London 1989).

Jacques Gillieron, *Kalahari* (New Holland, London).

MUSIC

Fred Zindi, *Roots Rocking in Zimbabwe* (Mambo, Gweru 1985). A quick run-through of Zimbabwe's musicians by one of the country's major promoters.

Chris Stapleton and Chris May, *Africa All-Stars – the Pop Music of a Continent* (Paladin, London 1989). The best book on popular African music with country-by-country coverage . . . even though the section on Zimbabwean music is disappointingly brief.

FIELD GUIDES

BIRDS

Gordon Lindsay Maclean *Robert's Birds of Southern Africa* (New Holland, London 1988). The standard reference work on the subcontinent's entire avifauna population: if it's not in Robert's it doesn't exist. Alas, the weight of this tome makes it more a book to consult in a library than to take along.

Michael P Stuart Irwin, *The Birds of Zimbabwe* (Quest, Harare 1981). Targetted on Zimbabwe, this is smaller than *Robert's* (although still quite heavy), but it nevertheless gives outstanding coverage for the area.

Ian Sinclair, *Field Guide to the Birds of Southern Africa* (Collins, London 1985). A reliable and thankfully, portable guide with good illustrations. Probably the most convenient to take along.

MAMMALS

Chris and Tilde Stuart, *Field Guide to the Mammals of Southern Africa* (New Holland, London 1989). Unless you're visiting countries further north, this is the best book – with its local focus – to take along. It gives excellent background and has clear illustrations to help you recognise a species.

Theodor Haltenorth and Helmut Diller, *Field Guide to the Mammals of Africa* (Collins, London 1989); **Jean Dorst and Pierre Dandelot, *Larger Mammals of Africa*** (Collins). Less handy, but solidly researched, detailed and well-illustrated volumes.

TREES AND PLANTS

Keith Coates Palgrave, *Trees of Southern Africa* (Struik, Cape Town 1977). The authoritative book on the subject, but a hefty tome.

Eve Palmer, *A Field Guide to the Trees of Southern Africa* (Collins, London 1977). Covers South Africa, Botswana and Namibia, but not specifically the trees of Zimbabwe. On the other hand it's smaller and easier to carry than Coates Palgrave.

THE BUNDU SERIES

White Rhodesians, keen outdoor enthusiasts, produced a series of compact, easily portable field guides on all topics to do with the country's natural history, archaeology and geology. Many of these original, illlustrated, pocket-size Rhodesian **Bundu Guides** are still on sale in Zimbabwe – often discounted because of the outmoded word "Rhodesia" in their titles.

Since Independence a **new and even better series** has begun publication, but only a couple of titles are presently in print. The one covering mammals, with sound information and clear colour photographs, is outstanding value and easily available throughout the country at bookshops and larger hotels at a fraction of the price of any British equivalent. Both series are published by Longmans Zimbabwe.

MAPS AND TRAVEL GUIDES

Maps have become easier to find in Zimbabwe. The small ***Minimap of Zimbabwe*** *(Struik, 1992) is useful, as is the Automobile Association's Zimbabwe map, available from shops or the Association's offices in Harare.*

Alec Campbell, *The Guide to Botswana* (Winchester, Johannesburg and Gaborone 1980). The classic guide to Botswana as far as background information goes. From archaeology and system of government to traditional foods and tourist attractions, it's all there, but the guide is short on practical information for travellers and is now rather dated.

Michael Main and John and Sandra Fowkes, *Visitors' Guide to Botswana* (Southern Books, Johannesburg 1987). Excellent for off-road driving and camping in Botswana – detailed route directions and information on road conditions, journey lengths, and bush driving, as well as camping tips.

FICTION: ZIMBABWE

Only a fraction of the writing produced in Zimbabwe finds its way abroad, but if you've a taste for fiction prepare to splurge when you get there. For extracts from some of the best writers, see p.376.

Charles Mungoshi, *Waiting for the Rain* (Heinemann African Writers Series, Oxford 1977); ***Setting Sun and The Rolling World*** (Heinemann African Writers Series); ***Coming of the Dry Season*** (Oxford University Press, 1972/ZPH 1981). In spare, aching prose, informed by traditional oral forms, Mungoshi explores the dusty, overworked "native reserves", the urban townships and the terrible bond of abandonment and empty hope between them. Masterly.

Dambudzo Marechera, *House of Hunger* (Heinemann African Writers Series 1978); ***Black Sunlight*** (Heinemann African Writers Series 1980). Zimbabwe's internationally best-known writer shocks and amazes with his vigorous and often abrasive prose. His exploits and lifestyle attracted as much notoriety as his writing won acclaim. ***Dambudzo Marechera 1952–1987*** (Baobab, Harare 1988) is a posthumous collection of writing, quotations and tributes.

Chenjerai Hove, *Bones* (Heinemann African Writers Series 1991). Award-winning experiences of the war, from a politically engaged writer. His ***Shadows*** (Heinemann African Writers Series 1991) is a tragic story of lovers who opt for death.

Wilson Katiyo, *A Son of the Soil* (Longman African Classics). A compelling story of a young Zimbabwean's struggle against oppression and hardship, remarkable for its lack of bitterness.

Nevanji Madanhire, *Goatsmell* (Anvil 1992). A lively love story focusing on the conflicts dividing modern Zimbabwe – between the sexes, between the Shona and the Ndebele, and between the powerful and the powerless.

Tsitsi Dangarembga, *Nervous Conditions* (Women's Press, London/ZPH 1988). A riveting story of race, class, gender and growing up in colonial Rhodesia, told with wit and great psychological depth. The best novel yet to emerge from Zimbabwe.

Doris Lessing, *The Grass is Singing* (Heinemann African Writers Series 1973). A portrayal of white Rhodesia unmatched by any writer – as are her physical descriptions of the country. Equally powerful, and emotionally intense, are the novels in the later *Children of Violence Masterwork Series*: ***Landlocked***, ***Martha Quest***, ***Proper Marriage*** and ***Ripple from the Storm*** (Plume 1970). In the same vein, her ***Collected African Stories***, published in two volumes, ***This was the Old Chief's Country*** and ***Sun Between their Feet*** (Panther 1979), are not to be missed. ***Going Home*** (Panther 1968), which chronicles her return to witness the supposed transformation of the colony during the Federation in the 1950s, still rings unnervingly true to the hardcore sections of the white community today. Her latest book, ***African Laughter*** (Harper Collins 1992) tells of the changes she observed on four visits between 1982 and 1992.

Bruce Moore-King, *White Man Black War* (Baobab Books, Harare 1988). A courageous, semi-autobiographical work by an ex-soldier who, out of hindsight or guilt, switches sides and exposes the brutality of the liberation struggle and the underpinning ideology of white supremacy.

Among other books worth looking out for in Heinemann's African Writers Series are *The Setting Sun* and *The Rolling World* by Charles Mungoshi, *Stories from Central and Southern Africa* by Paul Scanlon, *Smouldering Charcoal* by Tiyambe Zeleza, and *Harvest of Thorns* by Shimmer Chinodya.

POETRY

It's worth looking out for the following editions.

Chenjerai Hove, *Up in Arms* (ZPH 1982).

Freedom T.V. Nyamubaya, *On the Road Again* (ZPH 1986).

Kadhani and Zimunya (eds), *And Now the Poets Speak*.

Colin and O'Lan Style (eds), *The Mambo Book of Zimbabwean Verses in English*.

SOME OTHER NAMES TO WATCH FOR . . .

Poetry: Samuel Chimsoro; Kristina Rungano; Musa Zimunya; Eddison Zvobgo.

Fiction: Barbara Makhalisa; Tim Mcloughlin; Cont Mhlanga; Habbakuk Musengezi; Stanley Nyamfukudza.

CHILDREN'S LITERATURE

Tim Matthews, *Tales of the Secret Valley* (Baobab Books, Harare 1988). A collection of Batonga tales, colourfully illustrated by Colleen Cousins, and interesting for coming out in Ndebele, Shona, Tonga and English, covering the mother tongues of most Zimbabweans.

Hugh Lewin's *Jafta* series (Baobab) are all beautifully illustrated and written with the poetic simplicity of a child that feels universal.

Meshack Asare, *Chipo and the Bird on the Hill*. Life at Great Zimbabwe through a child's eyes. Recommended by the authoritative Peter Garlake as a "convincing work of the imagination".

Jayne Pilossof, *The Mana Pools Colouring Book*.

Anne Edwards-Tack, *Ngoni's Dream and Other Stories*.

FICTION: BOTSWANA

There's little indigenous fiction in English from Botswana. The paradox is that a number of outsiders have been inspired by Botswana to write novels, while Setswana-speakers in South Africa have made their contribution in English to South African literature.

Bessie Head, *When Rain Clouds Gather* (Heinemann, London 1989). Set in the heart of rural Botswana, this outstanding writer's first novel deals with a South African exile who becomes involved in an agricultural project. The book deals with love, friendship, drought and the fierce forces of tradition. Among her other books, ***Maru*** (Heinemann African Writers Series, London 1987) is on one level about racial prejudice and loneliness, but a beautifully told love story that is also firmly in the mystical realm. ***A Question of Power*** (Heinemann African Writers Series, London 1986) goes much further into subjective states and suffering, sliding in and out of sanity. By comparison, the short stories in ***The Collector of Treasures*** (Heinemann African Writers Series, London 1977) are mostly light and amusing, and alongside her first novel are the best introduction to her work and village life.

Norman Rush, *Whites* (Paladin, London 1987). Entertaining and well worth reading, these short stories by a US Peace Corps worker give vivid glimpses into the white sections of Botswana society.

SOL T PLAATJE

"Having access to the writings of Sol T Plaatje", wrote Bessie Head, "has been one of the richest experiences of my life. Never was there a man richer in spirit than he. *Native Life* is an astonishing book, crowded with information about all aspects of a black man's life."

Native Life in South Africa (Longman African Classics) is one of the finest pieces of campaigning political journalism to emerge from southern Africa. It was a response to the South African Natives' Land Act of 1913 – the legal foundation stone for the subsequent formalisation of apartheid some 35 years later. The Land Act provided for the division of South Africa into distinct African and white areas, with blacks confined to less than ten percent of the country. It was this policy that led the Batswana kings to fight so hard and ultimately successfully to avoid the realisation of white objectives to incorporate Bechuanaland into South Africa.

Plaatje's book begins chillingly: "Awaking on Friday morning, June 20, 1913, the South African native found himself, not actually a slave, but a pariah in the land of his birth." *Native Life* is his eloquent account of his travels through South Africa and the misery, tragic dispossession, poverty and homelessness caused by the shattering law.

Despite his Dutch-sounding name, Sol T Plaatje's Tswana origins are given away by his rarely mentioned middle name – Tshekisho. And although he was born in 1876 in South Africa he was a full member of the Rolong branch of the Tswana. Largely self-educated – he spoke six African languages as well as English, Dutch and German – he transcended tribal boundaries to become one of the pioneering figures of South African writing and politics, co-founding the African National Congress in 1912.

His later novel ***Mhudi*** examines the significance of tribal custom and the importance of an African historical perspective.

INDEX

Aberfoyle 233
Accommodation price codes, Botswana 251
Accommodation price codes, Zimbabwe 43
Accommodation, Botswana 251
Accommodation, Zimbabwe 42–44
Adventure pursuits 12; *in Zimbabwe* 48; *at Victoria Falls* 166, 169
Africa Overland operators: British 5; *North America* 7; *Australasia* 9
African Art, Zimbabwe 65
AIDS 18
Airlines, in London 4; *in the US* 6; *in Australasia* 8
Airport tax, Zimbabwe 50
Alcohol 24
Alfa Trail 90
Allan Wilson Memorial 152
Aloes 214
Antelope 28
Archaeology (see also *Rock Art*)
  Chawomera Fort 224
  Great Zimbabwe 192–200
  Nyahokwe Village Site (Nyanga) 230
  Nyanga pit structures 224
  Nyangwe Fort 226
  The language of Rozwi Planning 196
  Torwa ruins 139–42
  Ziwa Ruins (Nyanga) 229

Baines' Baobabs 291
Bangwato 364
Banks, Botswana 248
Banks, Zimbabwe 37, 47
Barbecue see *Braaivleis*
Batawana 304
Batonga people 115, 116, 119; see also *Tonga*
Bayei 310
BBC World Service 46
Bechuanaland 365
Beer 24
Beira Corridor 221, 361
Beit Bridge 143
Bicycles see *Cycling*
Bilharzia 18
Biltong 24
BINGA 118–121
Birchenough Bridge 206
Bird safaris 13

Birds 28
  at Kazuma Pan National Park 185
  at Khutse Game Reserve 331
  on Makgadikgadi Pans 288
  at Mana Pools 115
  at Moremi 320
  at Okavango 319
  on the Upper Zambezi 171
Bobonong 276
Book publishing, Zimbabwe 46
Books 408–414
Books Specialist suppliers UK & North America 22
Border posts, opening times 14
Botswana Democratic Party 371–373
Braaivleis 23
Bridal Veil Falls 235
British South Africa Company 350–352
Bulawayo 351
BULAWAYO 125–138
  Accommodation 130
  Arrival 129
  Art Gallery 132
  Beer gardens 136
  Centenary Park 133
  Central Park 133
  Chipangali Wildlife Orphanage 133
  Crafts 134
  Entertainment 137
  Eating, restaurants 135; *self-catering* 134
  Gardens 133
  Hillside Dams 133
  History 126
  Home Industries Centre 135
  Kwanangoma College 137
  Markets 134
  Museums 131
  Music 136, 137
  Mzilikazi Art and craft centre 134
  Natural History museum 132
  Parks 133
  Railway museum 132
  Record shops 134
  Shops 134
  Street name changes 130
  Swimming Pool 133
  Tashabalala Sanctuary 133
  Transport 129
Bumi Hills 118
Bundi Valley 237
Buses and coaches, Zimbabwe 39
Buses, Botswana 249
Bush Camps 12
  Hwange 180
  Kariba 107
  Savuti 300
  Upper Zambezi 171
  Victoria Falls & Upper Zambezi 161

Bush camps and Safari lodges, Zimbabwe 43
BVUMBA BOTANICAL GARDENS 217–219

Campfire Project 119
Camping
  food 25
  in Botswana 251
  in the bush 27
  in National Parks 28, 29
  in Zimbabwe 44
Canoeing 13, 48; Kariba 109; Matusadona 109;
  Zambezi 99, 109
Caprivi Strip 325
Car rental, Botswana 250
Car rental, Zimbabwe 41
Carving, Zimbabwe 49
Centenary 90
Central Kalahari Game Reserve 332
Charara Safari Area 99
Cheetah at Gonarezhou 205
Chegutu 85
Chewore Safari Area 99
Chibuku 24
Chilapalapa 34
Chilojo Cliffs 205
Chiluba, Frederick 172
Chimanimani Eland Sanctuary 234
Chimanimani Mountains 233–239
Chimanimani Village 233
Chimurenga, First 99, 351–352
Chimurenga, Second 99, 356–358
Chinoyi 95
Chinoyi Caves 95
Chinyakwaremba 219
Chipinda Pools 205
Chipinge 240
Chiredzi 203
Chirinda Forest Reserve 240–241
Chirundu 98
Chivu 88
CHIZARIRA NATIONAL PARK 121–123
CHOBE NATIONAL PARK 291–300
Climate ix, x
Clothes; what to take 15
Comoro Islands 405
Contact lenses 19
Contraceptives, Botswana 255
Contraceptives, Zimbabwe 50
Corner 239
Costs, Zimbabwe 37
Costs, Botswana 248
Crafts
  Batonga 120
  Botswana 253
  Bulawayo 134

Gaborone 264
Ghanzi 336
Nyanga 228
San 264
  Zimbabwe 49, 69
Crash pads, Zimbabwe 44
Credit cards 37
Cricket, Zimbabwe 48
Crime, Zimbabwe 49
Crocodiles, at Victoria Falls 166
Currency declarations 14
Currency, Botswana 248
Cycling, Zimbabwe 42
Cyrene Mission 143

D'kar 334
Dagga 49
Danangombe 141, 142, 347
Dande Safari Area 99
De Beers 370
Deka 121
Deka Camp 185
Dental care 19
Dhlo Dhlo see Danangombe
Diamonds 370
Diana's Vow 210
Diplomatic missions abroad 14
Discounted flights see Flights
Doma Safari Area 99
Drama, Zimbabwe 47
Driving, Botswana 250
Driving, Zimbabwe 41
Drought 362
Drugs, Zimbabwe 49
Dugout canoe 251
Dukwe 283
Durban connections 9

Economic Structural Adjustment Programme
  362
Electricity, Zimbabwe 50
Elephant-back safaris 13
Elephants 28, 106
  Chobe 298
  Gonarezhou 205
  Hwange 184
  Tuli Circle 144
Emergencies, Botswana 255
Emergencies, Zimbabwe 50
Emergency taxis see taxis
Entertainment, Botswana 253
ESAP 362
ETs see taxis
Etsha 323

Exchange control regulations, Zimbabwe 37
Exchange rates, Botswana 248
Express coach routes 39

Farms, safari 12
Field Guides 411
Fish 24
Fish eagles 107
Fishing
  Kariba 107
  Nyanga 225
  Shakawe 324
  Zimbabwe 48
Flights
  discount agents in Britain and Ireland 4
  discount agents in US 6
  discounted via central Europe and Africa 3
  discounted via western Europe 3
  from Australasia 8
  from Britain 3
  from North America 6
  from Zimbabwe & Botswana to
    African destinations 11
  in Botswana 249
  in Zimbabwe 40
Flora, Kalahari 336
Flora, Mtarazi 232
Food and Drink 23
Fort Victoria 189
Fothergill Island 108
Fothergill, Rupert 106
FRANCISTOWN 280–283
Front Line States 371
Fruit and vegetables 24

GABORONE 258–267
  Accommodation 262
  African Mall 263
  Arrival 259
  Art Gallery 264
  Broadhurst Mall 263
  Crafts 264
  Eating 265
  History 258
  Kagiso Centre 261
  Listings 266
  Mall, The 263
  National Assembly 263
  National Museum 263
  Nightlife 265
  Orientation 259
  Transport 259
Game reserves see *National Parks*
Game viewing at Mana Pools 114
Game viewing at Okavango 318
Game viewing tips 175
Gay life, Zimbabwe 50

Gaza state 348
Geography, Zimbabwe 33
Ghanzi 334–337
Glasses 19
Goldmining museum, Kwekwe 85
Golf, Zimbabwe 48
GONAREZHOU NATIONAL PARK 205–206
GREAT ZIMBABWE 192–200, 345
Great Dyke 95
Gubatsaa Hills 299
Gumare 323
Guruve 89, 90
Gwayi River 176
Gweru 86
Gweta 285

Hadange River 238
HARARE 55–80
  Accommodation 58
  African Art 65
  African Unity Square 64
  Architecture 63
  Archives, National 67
  Arrival 56
  Bars 74
  Borrowdale Park 71
  Botanic Gardens 64
  Bushman's Point 82
  Chapungu Village 71
  Chinamora Rock Paintings 83
  Chivero, Lake 80
  Clubs 74
  Crafts 66, 69, 76
  Crocodile Rock 82
  Dombashawa 83
  Drinking 72
  Eating 72
  Embassies 78
  Epworth Balancing Rocks 71
  Ewanrigg Botanical Gardens 82
  Fabrics 76
  Farm stays 62
  Films 74, 75
  Food, self-catering 76
  Foot safaris 71
  Galleries, commercial 66
  Gardens, Harare 64
  Greenwood Park 64
  Heroes' Acre 70
  High Commissions 78
  History 55
  Horse racing, Borrowdale Park 71
  Lake Chivero 80
  Larvon Bird Gardens 80
  Lion and Cheetah Park 81
  Listings 79
  Market, Mbare 69
  Mbare 69

HARARE continued
  Mukuvisi Woodlands 70
  Museum shop 66
  Music 74
  Musical instruments 77
  National Gallery 65
  Ngomakurira 83
  Nightlife 74
  Orientation 56
  Parks 64
  Restaurants 72
  Sculpture 65, 66, 71
  Security 58
  Shopping 76
  Snake Park 81
  Souvenirs 77
  Street name changes 57
  Suburbs, The 70
  Swimming pool 64
  Theatre 74, 76
  Transport 57
  Victoria Museum 67
Health Advice, Britain & US 17
Health and insurance 16–20
Health Publications 20
Herero people 323
Hiking safaris see *walking safaris*
Hippo Pools 91
Hippos 165
Hitching, Botswana 250
Hitching, Zimbabwe 41
HIV 18
Holidays, Botswana 253
Holidays, Zimbabwe 46
Honde Valley 231
Horse racing, Zimbabwe 48
Horse riding 48
  Gonarezhou 206
  Matopos 150
  Nyanga 225
  Victoria Falls 168
Horse safaris 13
Hospitals 19
Hotel bills, Zimbabwe 37
Hotels, Botswana 251; *price codes* 251
Hotels, Zimbabwe 42; *price codes* 43
Hukuntsi 332
HWANGE NATIONAL PARK 174–185
  Accommodation 178
  Deka Camp 185
  Game drives 182
  Game viewing 175
  History 175
  Main Camp 181
  Mobile safaris 182
  Nantwich Camp 185
  Orientation 175

  Robins Camp 185
  Sinamatella 183
  Transport 176
  Walking 182
  Wildlife 182
  Hyenas 182

Independence 360
Inoculations 16
Insurance 19
Insurance Medical Air Rescue Service 17
International dialling codes, Zimbabwe 45
International dialling codes, Botswana 252

Jameson Raid 335
Johannesburg connections 9
Juliasdale 223
Jwaneng 333

Kadoma 85
Kaguvi 352
Kalahari Desert 330–341
Kalahari Flora and Desert Foods 336
Kame see Khami
Kang 333, 341
Kanyemba 109
Kapenta 24, 107
KARIBA 100–104
  Accommodation 101
  Cruises 104
  Dam 101
  Drink 104
  Ferry 116
  Food 104
  Kariba Heights 100
  Lake 101
  Mahombekombe 100
  Music 104
  Nyamhunga 100
  Observation point 103
  Orientation 100
  Santa Barbara church 103
  Town 100
Kariba ecology 106
Karoi 98
Kasane 295
Katima Mulilo 325
Kaunda, Kenneth 172
KAZUMA PAN NATIONAL PARK 185
Khama, Ruth 272
Khama, Sir Seretse 272, 273, 370–371
Khami 139
Khutse Game Reserve 330–332
Kubu Island 289
Kung people 326

Kwekwe 85
Kyle Game Park 202
Kyle see Lake Kyle

La Rochelle 220
LAKE KYLE 200–202
Languages and Religions, Zimbabwe 34
Languages, Botswana 246–249
Lehututu 332
Lentswe-la-Odi Weavers 269
Leopard's Kopje 139
Leopard's Rock 219
Limpopo River 275
Linyanti River 299
Lions at Hwange 183
Livingstone 173
Livingstone, David 163
Lizards 28
Lobatse 268, 333
Lobengula, King 126, 350–351
Lodges, Kariba 108
Lokgwabe 332

Mababe Depression 299
Mabalautu 205
Mabele 24
Mabuasehube Game Reserve 332
MacDougall 203, 204
Madagascar 406–407
Madila 24
Magwikhwe Sand ridge 299
Mahalapye 271
Mail, Botswana 252
Mail, Zimbabwe 44
Main Camp, Hwange 181
Makgadikgadi Pans 285–290, 303
Makgadikgadi Pans Game Reserve 290
Makuti 95
Malaria 20
Malawi 403–404
MANA POOLS NATIONAL PARK 111–115
Mana Pools 95, 99
Manjirenji Recreation Park 204
Mapondera 91
Maps 21, 414
Marondera 210
Mashatu Game Reserve 275, 277
Masimike 232
Masire, Dr Quett 371
MASVINGO 187–192
Matlapaneng 305
Matlapaneng Bridge 321
Matobo National Park (see also Matopos)
144–154

MATOPOS, THE 144–154
Accommodation 145
Camps 145
Crafts 152
Horse riding 150
Inanke Cave 153
Lodges 145
Maleme Dam 144, 150
Matopos Game Park 153
Mtsheleli Dam 145, 153
Mwari Cult 146
Nswatugi Cave 151
Pomongwe Cave 150
Rhodes' Grave 152
Rock art 150
Shangani Patrol memorial 152
Silozwane Cave 153
Toghwana Dam 145, 153
Toghwe Wilderness Area 145, 153
Tours 146
White Rhino Shelter 152
Whovi Wilderness Area 145, 153
Wildlife 150
World's View 144, 151
Matopi 303
Matusadona Mountains 104
Matusadona National Park 104–109
MAUN 303–308
Mauritius 405–406
Mavuradonna Mountains 90
Mavuradonna Wilderness Area 90
Mawenji, Mt 239
Mazowe 89
Mbanje 49
Mbare 69
Mbare, Chief 69
Mbukushu People 326
Media, Botswana 252
Media, Zimbabwe 45
Medical Air Rescue Service (Zimbabwe) 17
Medical Kit 19
Mfecane 347, 363
Midlands, The 84–92
Minibuses, Botswana 249
Mlibizi 116, 121
Mobile safaris 12
Mochudi 269
Mokoro 251
Molopolole 331
Money and costs, Zimbabwe 37
Money and costs, Botswana 248
Moremi Wildlife Reserve 302, 319–321
Moreswe Pan 331
Mosquitos 20
Motloutse River 274
Mount Selinda 241

Mozambique 221, 401–403
Mpandamatenga 284
Mpata Gorge 110
MTARAZI NATIONAL PARK 230–233
Mtarazi Falls 231
Mugabe, Robert 355, 359
Murray MacDougall Drive 204
Music, Botswana 253
Music, Smanje Manje 125
Music, Zimbabwe 47, 386–392
Musika 39
Mutapa state 98, 346
MUTARE 211–217
  Accommodation 212
  Aloe gardens 212
  Arrival 212
  Cecil Kop Nature Reserve 214
  Food 215
  History 211
  Listings 216
  Markets 215
  Murahwa's Hill Reserve 212
  Museum 212
  Music 216
  Nightlife 216
  Orientation 211
  Sakubva 211, 212
  Shops 215
  Taxis 212
Mutekeswane 237
Mutirikwe, Lake see Lake Kyle
Muzorewa, Bishop Abel 356, 358
Mvuma 88
Mvurwi 89, 90

Mwari Cult at Nyanga 230
Mzilikazi 34, 35, 348
Naletale 141
Namibia 341, 394–397
Nantwich Camp 185
Nata 284
National Parks accommodation, Zimbabwe 43
National Parks, Botswana 29
  Chobe 291
  Central Kalahari 332
  Makgadkgadi Pans 290
  Nxai Pan 290–291
National Parks, Zimbabwe 28
  Chimanimani 237–239
  Chizarira 121–123
  Gonarezhou 205–206
  Hwange 174–185
  Kazuma Pan 185
  Mana Pools 111–115
  Matobo 144–154
  Matusadona 104–109
  Mtarazi 230–233

Nyanga 220–230
  Victoria Falls 163
  Zambezi 170–171
Ndebele 34, 35, 119, 350–352
Ndebele state 348
Nehanda 99, 352
Neharawa, Chief 55
Ngami, Lake 322
Nicolle Hostes Highway 95
Njelele 147
Nkomo, Joshua 354–355
Nogatsaa 298
Ntwetwe Pan 285
Nxai Pan National Park 290–291
Nyama 23
Nyaminyami 102
Nyaminyami Wildlife Trust 119
Nyamzure 234
NYANGA NATIONAL PARK 220–230
  Accommodation: National Parks 221
  Accommodation: Private cottages 223
  Brighton Beach 223
  Buses 228
  Camping 221
  Chawomera Fort 225
  Craft village 228
  Fishing 225
  Flora 228
  Horse riding 225
  Juliasdale 223
  Mare Dam 220, 225
  Mount Nyangani 226
  Nyahokwe Village Site 230
  Nyanga Village 227
  Nyangombe Campsite 223
  Nyangombe Falls 227
  Nyangombe River 225
  Nyangwe Fort 226
  Nyazengu Falls 226
  Nyazengu Nature Reserve 226
  Pit Structures 224
  Practicalities 220
  Rhodes Dam 220, 223
  Tennis 225
  Troutbeck 228
  Udu Dam 220, 227
  Wildlife 228
  World's View, Nyanga 228
  Ziwa Ruins 229
Nyazengu Nature Reserve 226

Odi 268
OKAVANGO DELTA 301–328
  environment 316
  flora 317
  geography 308
  geology 309
  wildlife 317

Opening hours, Botswana 253
Opening hours, Zimbabwe 46
Operation Noah 106
Operation Windfall 119
Orapa 370
Outdoor pursuits, Zimbabwe 48
Overland arrival 14
Overland travel
 from North Africa 5, 7
 in Southern Africa 9
 trans-Africa 10

Package tours
 British 4–5
 North America 6
 Australasia 8
Palapye 271
Pandamatenga see Mpandamatenga
Pangolins 182
Panhandle, The 324
Patriotic Front 358
Penhalonga 219
Peoples, Botswana 246–249
Phone, Botswana 252
Phone, Zimbabwe 45
Photography 25
Phrases, Setswana 247
Phrases, Shona and Ndebele 35
Phuthadikobo Museum 269
Pilane 269
Pioneer Column 350
Place name changes, Zimbabwe 36
Poaching, rhinos at Chizarira 123
Police, Zimbabwe 50
Pont Drift 275, 276
Poppa Falls 325
Post office opening hours, Zimbabwe 47
Post, Botswana 252
Post, Zimbabwe 44
Press, Botswana 252
Press, Zimbabwe 45
Price Codes, Botswana 251
Price codes, Zimbabwe 43
Prices in Zimbabwe 37
Public Holidays, Botswana 253
Public holidays, Zimbabwe 46
Pungwe Drift 231
Pungwe Gorge 230
Pungwe River 232

Rabies 19
Radio and TV, Botswana 253
Radio and TV, Zimbabwe 46
Raffingora 89

Railway museum, Livingstone 174
Rain shrines 147
Records, Zimbabwe 47
Religion 34, 37
Renamo 221, 361
Renkini 39
Rhinos at Chizarira 123
Rhinos, relocation to Lake Kyle 202
Rhodes' Grave 144, 146, 152
Rhodes, Cecil John 55, 129, 334, 350, 365, 366
Robins Camp 185
Rock art 345
 Diana's Vow 210
 Dombashawa 83
 Lake Kyle 202
 Matopos 150
 Ngomakurira 83
 Tsodilo Hills 327
Rozvi 196
Rozvi state 347
Rural areas, Travelling in 26
Rusape 210

SADCC 371
Sadza 23
Safari bookings 169
Safari farms 12, 44
Safari Lodges 12
 in Botswana 251
 in Zimbabwe 43
 Chobe 296
 Hwange 180
 Okavango 311
 Savuti 300
 Tuli 276
 Upper Zambezi 171
 Victoria Falls & Upper Zambezi 161
Safaris 11
 canoeing on Zambezi 109
 horse safaris at Gonarezhou 206
 horse safaris in Okavango 312
 horse safaris at Victoria Falls 168
 mobile safaris in Botswana 251
 mobile safaris at Hwange 182
 mobile safaris through Chobe National
 Park 293
 Mokoro 310
 Okavango operators 316
 steam 13
 walking at Chizarira 122
 walking at Kariba 109
 walking in Kazuma Pan National Park 185
 walking at Mana Pools 113
 walking at Victoria Falls 168
Sales tax, Zimbabwe 38
Salisbury 55
SALT PANS, THE 285–291

San languages 340
San people 327, 337–340, 345
San tales 381
Sanyati Gorge 107
Sapi Safari Area 99
Save River 206
Savuti 298–300
Savuti Channel 299
Schistosomiasis see *bilharzia*
School holidays, Zimbabwe 46
Scorpions 19, 28
Sculpture, Zimbabwe 49, 65, 66, 71
Sehitwa 323
Selebi-Phikwe 274
Self-catering accommodation, Zimbabwe 43
Selous, Frederick Courteney 175, 350
Serima Mission 192
Serondella 297–298
Seronga 324
Serowe 273
Sexual attitudes, Botswana 254
Sexual attitudes, Zimbabwe 49
Shaka 348
Shakawe 324
Sherwood Ranch 275
Shona 34, 35
Shorobe 321
Shoshangane 348
Shurugwi 88
Siabuwa 118
Siacobvu 118
Sinamatella 183
Sleeping see *Accommodation*
Smith, Ian 354
Snakes 19
Soccer, Zimbabwe 48
South Africa 143
South Africa, connections 9
South Africa, travel sanctions 9
Southern African Development Coordination
  Conference 371
Southern Lakes, Chimanimani 239
Souvenirs, Zimbabwe 49
Sowa Pan see Sua Pan
Spiders 19, 28
Spirit mediums 352
Sports, Zimbabwe 47
Steam safaris 13
Steam trains, Zimbabwe 40
Sua Pan 285
Swimming, Zimbabwe 48
Swimuwini 205

Talana Farm 276
Tanganda Junction 206
Tanning 18
Taxis and emergency taxis, Zimbabwe 41
Telephone, Botswana 252
Telephone, Zimbabwe 45
Tengenenge 49, 89
Tennis, Zimbabwe 48
Tessa's Pool 238
Thamalakane River 303
Thaoge River 322
Third Bridge 320
Tick-bite fever 19
Time zone 50
Tingwa Palm Reserve 91
Tipping, Zimbabwe 51
Tjinga 298
Toilets, Botswana 255
Toilets, Zimbabwe 51
Torwa state 139, 347
Toteng 322
Tourist offices abroad, Zimbabwean 21
Trains 13
Trains, Botswana 249
Trains, Zimbabwe 40
Transport, Botswana 249
Transport, Zimbabwe 39
Travel agents Europe, North America,
  Australasia (see *package tours*)
Travel from Australasia 8
Travel from Britain and Europe 3–5
Travel from North America 6–7
Travel in Southern Africa 9–10
Travel overland through Chobe 293
Triangle 204
Tribes 246
Trouble, Botswana 254
Trouble, Zimbabwe 49
Tshabong 332
Tshane 332
Tshane Pan 332
Tswana 363
Tuli 143
Tuli Block 273–277
Tuli Circle 144

UDI 355
Umtali see Mutare
Upper Zambezi 170

Vaccinations 16
Vegetarian food 23
Victoria Falls National Park 163–166

VICTORIA FALLS 156–170
Accommodation 160
Adventure bookings 169
Arrival 157
Crocodile Ranch 166
Cruises 166
Eating 162
Flights over falls 166
Game drives 166
History 156
Horse safaris 168
Listings 169
Nightlife 162
Orientation 157
Snake Park 165
Steam train 157
Town 156
Victoria Falls Hotel 162
Walking safaris 168
White-water kayaking 167
White-water rafting 166
Victoria Falls, Zambian side 172
Village visits near Binga 120
Visas 13
Voice of America 46
Vumba see Bvumba

Walking safaris 12, 48
Water, drinking 18
White-water canoeing at Victoria Falls 167
White-water kayaking 13; *at Victoria Falls* 167
White-water rafting 13, 48; *at Victoria Falls* 166
Wild dogs at Hwange 183
Wildlife 28
Chirinda Forest 241
Chobe 296–298

Gonarezhou 205
Hwange 182, 183, 184
Kazuma Pan National Park 185
Khutse Game Reserve 331
Lake Kyle 202
Makgadikgadi Game Reserve 290
Mana Pools 114
Matopos 150
Moremi 319
Nyanga 228
Nxai Pan National Park 290
Okavango 317–319
safety considerations 114
Savuti 299–300
Upper Zambezi 171
Victoria Falls rainforest 164
Wildlife and National Parks 27
Wine, Zimbabwean 25, 210
Work, Botswana 255
Work, Zimbabwe 51

Xakanaxa 321

Youth hostels, Zimbabwe 44

Zaka 204
Zambezi National Park 170–171
Zambezi River 94, 99
Zambezi, Upper 170
Zambia 172, 397–401
ZANU 355–362
Zanzibar 276
ZAPU 355–362
Zimbabwe tourist offices 21
Zulu state 348, 363–64
Zwangendaba 347

HELP US UPDATE

We've gone to a lot of effort to ensure that this edition of *The Rough Guide to Zimbabwe and Botswana* is completely up-to-date and accurate. However, things do change – places get "discovered", opening hours are notoriously fickle – and any suggestions, comments or corrections would be much appreciated.

We'll credit all contributions, and send a copy of the next edition (or any other *Rough Guide* if you prefer) for the best letters. Please mark letters "Rough Guide Zimbabwe & Botswana update", and send to:

Rough Guides, 1 Mercer Street, London WC2H 9QJ
or Rough Guides, 375 Hudson Street, 4th Floor, New York NY10014

DIRECT ORDERS IN THE UK

Title	ISBN	Price
Amsterdam	1858280869	£7.99
Andalucia	185828094X	£8.99
Australia	1858281415	£12.99
Barcelona & Catalunya	1858281067	£8.99
Berlin	1858281296	£8.99
Big Island of Hawaii	185828158X	£8.99
Brazil	1858281024	£9.99
Brittany & Normandy	1858281261	£8.99
Bulgaria	1858280478	£8.99
California	1858280907	£9.99
Canada	185828130X	£10.99
Classical Music on CD	185828113X	£12.99
Corsica	1858280893	£8.99
Crete	1858281326	£8.99
Cyprus	185828032X	£8.99
Czech & Slovak Republics	185828029X	£8.99
Egypt	1858280753	£10.99
England	1858280788	£9.99
Europe	185828077X	£14.99
Florida	1858280109	£8.99
France	1858281245	£10.99
Germany	1858281288	£11.99
Goa	1858281563	£8.99
Greece	1858281318	£9.99
Greek Islands	1858281636	£8.99
Guatemala & Belize	1858280451	£9.99
Holland, Belgium & Luxembourg	1858280877	£9.99
Hong Kong & Macau	1858280664	£8.99
Hungary	1858281237	£8.99
India	1858281040	£13.99
Ireland	1858280958	£9.99
Italy	1858280311	£12.99
Jazz	1858281377	£16.99
Kenya	1858280435	£9.99
London	1858291172	£8.99
Mediterranean Wildlife	0747100993	£7.95
Malaysia, Singapore & Brunei	1858281032	£9.99
Mexico	1858280443	£10.99
Morocco	1858280400	£9.99
Moscow	1858281180	£8.99
Nepal	185828046X	£8.99
New York	1858280583	£8.99
Nothing Ventured	0747102082	£7.99
Pacific Northwest	1858280923	£9.99
Paris	1858281253	£7.99
Poland	1858280346	£9.99
Portugal	1858280842	£9.99
Prague	185828015X	£7.99
Provence & the Côte d'Azur	1858280230	£8.99
Pyrenees	1858280931	£8.99
Romania	1858280974	£9.99
St Petersburg	1858281334	£8.99
San Francisco	1858280826	£8.99
Scandinavia	1858280397	£10.99
Scotland	1858280834	£8.99
Sicily	1858280370	£8.99
Singapore	1858281350	£8.99
Spain	1858280818	£9.99
Thailand	1858281407	£10.99
Tunisia	1858280656	£8.99
Turkey	1858280885	£9.99
Tuscany & Umbria	1858280915	£8.99
USA	185828080X	£12.99
Venice	1858281709	£8.99
Wales	1858280966	£8.99
West Africa	1858280141	£12.99
More Women Travel	1858280982	£9.99
World Music	1858280176	£14.99
Zimbabwe & Botswana	1858280419	£10.99

Rough Guide Phrasebooks

Title	ISBN	Price
Czech	1858281482	£3.50
French	185828144X	£3.50
German	1858281466	£3.50
Greek	1858281458	£3.50
Italian	1858281431	£3.50
Spanish	1858281474	£3.50

Rough Guides can be obtained directly in the UK* from Penguin by contacting: Penguin Direct, Penguin Books Ltd, Bath Road, Harmondsworth, West Drayton, Middlesex UB7 0DA; or telephone our credit line on 0181-899 4036 (9am–5pm) and ask for Penguin Direct. Visa, Access and Amex accepted. Delivery will normally be within 14 working days. Penguin Direct ordering facilities are only available in the UK.

The availability and published prices quoted are correct at the time of going to press but are subject to alteration without prior notice.

DIRECT ORDERS IN THE USA

Title	ISBN	Price
Amsterdam	1858280869	$13.59
Andalucia	185828094X	$14.95
Australia	1858281415	$19.95
Barcelona & Catalunya	1858281067	$17.99
Berlin	1858281296	$14.95
Big Island of Hawaii	185828158X	$12.95
Brazil	1858281024	$15.95
Brittany & Normandy	1858281261	$14.95
Bulgaria	1858280478	$14.99
California	1858280907	$14.95
Canada	185828130X	$14.95
Classical Music on CD	185828113X	$19.95
Corsica	1858280893	$14.95
Crete	1858281326	$14.95
Cyprus	185828032X	$13.99
Czech & Slovak Republics	185828029X	$14.95
Egypt	1858280753	$17.95
England	1858280788	$16.95
Europe	185828077X	$18.95
Florida	1858280109	$14.95
France	1858281245	$16.95
Germany	1858281288	$17.95
Goa	1858281563	$14.95
Greece	1858281318	$16.95
Greek Islands	1858281636	$14.95
Guatemala & Belize	1858280451	$14.95
Holland, Belgium & Luxembourg	1858280877	$15.95
Hong Kong & Macau	1858280664	$13.95
Hungary	1858281237	$14.95
India	1858281040	$22.95
Ireland	1858280958	$16.95
Italy	1858280311	$17.95
Jazz	1858281377	$24.95
Kenya	1858280435	$15.95
London	1858291172	$12.95
Mediterranean Wildlife	0747100993	$15.95
Malaysia, Singapore & Brunei	1858281032	$16.95
Mexico	1858280443	$16.95
Morocco	1858280400	$16.95
Moscow	1858281180	$14.95
Nepal	185828046X	$13.95
New York	1858280583	$13.95
Nothing Ventured	0747102082	$19.95
Pacific Northwest	1858280923	$14.95
Paris	1858281253	$12.95
Poland	1858280346	$16.95
Portugal	1858280842	$15.95
Prague	1858281229	$14.95
Provence & the Côte d'Azur	1858280230	$14.95
Pyrenees	1858280931	$15.95
Romania	1858280974	$15.95
St Petersburg	1858281334	$14.95
San Francisco	1858280826	$13.95
Scandinavia	1858280397	$16.99
Scotland	1858280834	$14.95
Sicily	1858280370	$14.99
Singapore	1858281350	$14.95
Spain	1858280818	$16.95
Thailand	1858281407	$17.95
Tunisia	1858280656	$15.95
Turkey	1858280885	$16.95
Tuscany & Umbria	1858280915	$15.95
USA	185828080X	$18.95
Venice	1858281709	$14.95
Wales	1858280966	$14.95
West Africa	1858280141	$24.95
More Women Travel	1858280982	$14.95
World Music	1858280176	$19.95
Zimbabwe & Botswana	1858280419	$16.95

Rough Guide Phrasebooks

Czech	1858281482	$5.00
French	185828144X	$5.00
German	1858281466	$5.00
Greek	1858281458	$5.00
Italian	1858281431	$5.00
Spanish	1858281474	$5.00

ART·OF·TRAVEL

**INDIVIDUAL TAILOR-MADE SAFARIS TO
ZIMBABWE
BOTSWANA, MALAWI, ZAMBIA, NAMIBIA**

Staying in small, personal camps and lodges with excellent safari guides.
Or joining adventurous, overland safaris to remote wilderness areas.
Canoeing, horse-riding, walking and other activities can all be included in
your safari.
Wherever you want to go, whatever you want to see and do, Art of Travel
has the knowledge and enthusiasm to make it work!

For more information and a chance to discuss your holiday plans further,
telephone 071 738 2038

**268 LAVENDER HILL, LONDON SW11 1LJ
FAX 071 738 1893 TELEX 917265 ARTTVL**

ABTA

AFRICA
BOOK
CENTRE LTD

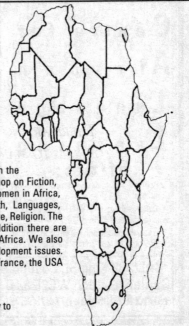

38 King Street
Covent Garden
LONDON WC2E 8JT
☎071-240 6649
Fax 071-836 5691

We provide a comprehensive range of books on the
continent of Africa. There are sections in the shop on Fiction,
Poetry, Drama, Criticism, Fiction by Women, Women in Africa,
Art, Music, Children, Education, Travel, Health, Languages,
History, Politics, Economics, Food and Agriculture, Religion. The
above sections cover Africa as a whole. In addition there are
sections on regions and individual countries in Africa. We also
have some general books on Third World Development issues.
The books we stock come from Britain, Africa, France, the USA
and elsewhere.

Our opening hours are 9.30am to 5.30pm Monday to
Friday, and on Saturday 11am to 5pm.

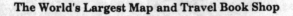

You are A STUDENT

You travel THE WORLD

You want TO SAVE MONEY

Here's how

The International Student Identity Card

International Student Identity Card

ISIC

9 2185982

Family Name/Nom de famille
Sian
First Name/Prénom
Sharoush
Born/Né le
20/8/1975
Nationality/Nationalité
French
Student at/Établissement
University of Paris
STUDENT

Available at Student Travel Offices Worldwide.

Entitles you to discounts and special services worldwide.